Resources for Writers with Readings

Resources for Writers with Readings

From Paragraph to Essay

SECOND EDITION

Annotated Instructor's Edition

Elizabeth Cloninger Long
Sacramento City College

PEARSON

Longman

New York San Francisco Boston
London Toronto Sydney Tokyo Singapore Madrid
Mexico City Munich Paris Cape Town Hong Kong Montreal

Editor-in-Chief: Joe Terry
Acquisitions Editor: Melanie Craig
Director of Development: Mary Ellen Curley
Development Editor: Katharine Glynn
Marketing Manager: Tom deMarco
Senior Supplements Editor: Donna Campion
Media Supplements Editor: Jenna Egan
Production Manager: Ellen MacElree
Project Coordination, Text Design, and Electronic Page Makeup: Electronic Publishing
    Services Inc., NYC
Cover Design Manager: Wendy Ann Fredericks
Cover Designer: Nancy Sabato
Photo Researcher: Vivette Porges
Senior Manufacturing Buyer: Alfred C. Dorsey
Printer and Binder: Quebecor World–Taunton
Cover Printer: Coral Graphic Services

For permission to use copyrighted material, grateful acknowledgment is made to the copyright hold-
ers on pp. C-1–C-2, which are hereby made part of this copyright page.

Library of Congress Cataloging-in-Publication Data
Long, Elizabeth Cloninger.
    Resources for writers with readings: from paragraph to essay/
     Elizabeth Cloninger Long.—2nd ed.
       p. cm.
    Includes bibliographical references and index.
    ISBN 0-321-41481-0 (pbk.)
  1. English language—Rhetoric—Problems, exercises, etc. 2. Report writing—Problems,
exercises, etc. 3. Readers I. Title.
PE1413.L66 2007
808′.0427—dc22   2005035398

Copyright © 2007 by Pearson Education, Inc.

Please visit us at http://www.ablongman.com/long

ISBN 0-321-41481-0 (Student Edition)

ISBN 0-321-42084-5 (Annotated Instructor's Edition)

1 2 3 4 5 6 7 8 9 10—QWT—09 08 07 06

Contents

v

PART FIVE
Writing Essays   373

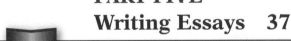

PART SIX
Writing for Different Purposes   431

PART SEVEN
Writing Correct Sentences   469

PART EIGHT
Punctuation and Mechanics　619

PART NINE
Readings for Informed Writing   713

Lab Manual   LM–1

Preface

Students must learn to write clearly. Even if their writing never takes them beyond composing a simple cover letter for a new job, students must understand how to craft logical, clear sentences and paragraphs if they are to be taken seriously.

Resources for Writers with Readings, 2nd edition, the second book in a three-book series, is designed to take students from simple sentence construction through short essay writing and offers students an opportunity to practice their paragraph-writing skills as they learn to eliminate the sentence-level errors that mar their writing.

The **second edition of *Resources for Writers with Readings*** has been reorganized to provide chapters in a more logical sequence. We've added new readings, new exercises, and new cultural literacy themes all with improved student appeal. In addition, a model student paper in MLA format has been added to Chapter 32.

Content Overview

Part One, "Your Strengths as a Writer," shows students that they already practice key thinking skills on a daily basis. Demonstrating those skills in writing is simply one more step in a process they've already begun. Part One also introduces the four cornerstones for good writing, which also serve as four bases for evaluation. The Four Cs—concise, credible, clear, and correct—provide students with the foundation to understand and practice the elements of good writing.

Part Two, "The Writing Process," introduces the concepts of prewriting, drafting, revising, and editing, offering students multiple opportunities for practicing each step in the writing process.

Part Three, "The Elements of Good Writing," links key writing skills to the Four Cs showing students how practicing each skill also leads to the mastery of the Four Cs. In addition, chapters devoted to topics including sensitive language, choosing the best words, and help with spelling give students specific guidance in improving their writing.

Part Four, "Strategies for Paragraph Development," gives students explanations of, examples of, and practice in writing paragraphs in nine traditional modes of paragraph development.

Part Five, "Writing Essays," introduces students to those skills necessary to writing an essay, all the while linking skills to the Four Cs.

Part Six, "Writing for Different Purposes," gives students explanations, examples, and practice in writing for specific real-life purposes. A chapter on proper format is also included.

Part Seven, "Writing Correct Sentences," provides logical, common-sense explanations of grammar with a rich array of practice and exercises.

Part Eight, "Punctuation and Mechanics," gives helpful explanations and practice, with line-by-line exercises and editing practices for each skill being studied.

Part Nine, "Readings for Informed Writing," includes 18 high-interest readings clustered around three themes which illustrate a range of writing styles, patterns of development, and subject matter. The readings are accompanied by supportive pre- and post- reading questions.

Chapter Features

Every feature of *Resources for Writers with Readings* is specifically designed to support the goal of helping students improve their sentence-level writing as they develop their writing skills through the writing process—that is, to learn how to write clearly and write correctly at the same time.

Modular Text Format

The modular text format provides opportunities for lessons and assignments within a single chapter but allows for connections between chapters as well. Students can read new information, receive tips to help them integrate that new information into what they've already learned, and find cross-references to other chapters for easy reference to past and future lessons. Instructors can tailor chapter assignments to the needs of a specific class—or an individual student.

Lab Manual and Lab Manual Online

The Lab Manual is a collection of 56 in-text lab activities designed to provide additional practice for every topic in *Resources for Writers with Readings*. The *Lab Manual Online*, consisting of corresponding online activities for each chapter, gives instructors a highly effective way to use computer lab time. Instructors can assign the lab activities as part of weekly lessons or as individual supplements for students on a case-by-case basis. Further, the Lab Manual Online is interactive, so students needing additional feedback on their drafting and grammar exercises receive online guidance even as they complete practice activities or skills quizzes.

Cultural Literacy Theme

The cultural literacy component offers students easily digestible information beneficial to them in college and in contemporary society. For a variety of reasons, many beginning writing students lack basic cultural literacy. For this reason, in classes that presume a certain knowledge foundation—such as history, political science, or literature—students find themselves behind. In *Resources for Writers with Readings*, each chapter begins with a note that introduces a cultural theme; some notes are whimsical and some are serious, but all are designed to illuminate a part of the cultural heritage of the United States. Sample paragraphs and exercises in the chapter revolve around these themes, so students can see concepts illustrated with real subject matter, not just with fictionalized or overly personalized material. In addition, these themes offer students from diverse backgrounds insight into the historical bases of materials they read in their classes, and they also offer a broad range of topics students can write about.

Cultural Literacy Photos

Resources for Writers with Readings contains more than 35 full-color photos that reinforce the cultural literacy themes in the chapters. The photos give students additional insight into our complex cultural heritage, and photo captions provide writing prompts to stimulate students' ideas.

Four Cs of Writing

Resources for Writers with Readings uses a simple mnemonic device to help students remember that their writing must be *concise, credible, clear,* and *correct*. This formula is completely integrated into text, examples, and exercises so that students learn how to check their work for the elements of good writing at every stage of development. Graphics and checklists reinforce the four Cs and provide ready reference for students.

Writing Process

Resources for Writers with Readings uses a clear, step-by-step writing process approach to guide students through the how-tos of writing a paragraph—*prewriting, drafting, revising,* and *editing*. Examples, exercises, graphics, and checklists consistently support and reinforce this paradigm.

Writing Skills

Four basic writing skills—*writing an effective topic sentence, using specific details for support and illustration, organizing and linking ideas,* and *writing correct sentences*—are integrated into the writing process steps. The skills are also keyed to the four Cs so that students experience a coherent approach to paragraph writing. For example, students learn that writing an effective topic sentence will make their writing concise and that using specific details will make their writing credible.

Rhetorical Modes

Resources for Writers with Readings guides students through an understanding of nine patterns of paragraph development. Each pattern is thoroughly defined through explanation, examples, and model paragraphs. Culminating exercises integrate specific writing process steps for each pattern with writing skills and the Four Cs. Checklists provide handy reference for students.

Readings

Eighteen readings illustrate a range of writing styles, patterns of development, and subject matter of interest to students. Each reading is prefaced by a biographical note, prereading questions, and a vocabulary-building activity. Readings are followed by additional activities and writing exercises. Instructors can use readings in conjunction with teaching the modes they illustrate or as independent assignments.

Grammar and Language

Each chapter addressing grammar, punctuation, mechanics, word use, and other language issues is developed with the same care and creativity featured in the writing chapters. Cultural literacy themes are used so that students can see sentence-level edits in the context of real subject matter. One significant chapter, Chapter 12, "Sensitive Language," addresses the issue of writing for and about diverse groups in nonbiased ways—a subject hardly touched on in other writing texts for students at this level.

Additional Features

Resources for Writers includes a wide range of features that provide alternatives for practice and instruction.

- **Guided writing assignments** lead students through every step in the writing process for both paragraph and essay assignments.
- **Chapter exercises** throughout a chapter give immediate reinforcement of content.
- A **wide range of writing topics** gives students relevant writing assignments to choose from.

- A **real-life writing** section in each of the modes chapters shows students how particular patterns of development are used in educational, personal, and professional situations.
- **"What You Know Now"** at the end of each writing chapter summarizes the key points of the chapter.
- An **individual goal sheet** template on page 102 allows students to evaluate completed writing assignments and set goals for improvement in future writing assignments.
- A **peer editing worksheet** template on page 97 helps students organize their responses to their peers' writing, emphasizing the Four Cs and sensitivity to others' feelings.
- **Perforated pages** allow students to tear out and hand in assignments.
- **Diagnostic exercises/quizzes** for grammar and punctuation sections help students see their sentence-level strengths as well as identify their areas of opportunity.
- **Editing exercises** in grammar and punctuation chapters give students line-by-line and whole-paragraph practice in identifying and correcting grammar errors.
- **Prereading critical thinking and writing exercises** allow students to consider a topic without the pressure of a formal assignment.
- **Vocabulary activities** as both pre- and post-reading activities enhance students' comprehension and sentence-variation skills.
- **Reading comprehension** quizzes give instructors opportunities to quickly check students' reading comprehension for each essay in the text.
- **Content and structure questions** for every reading give students tools for greater comprehension and analysis.

Supplements Package

For Instructors

Annotated Instructor's Edition (0-321-42084-5): An Annotated Instructor's Edition is an exact replica of the student text, with the answers and teaching notes provided.

Instructor's Manual to accompany _Resources for Writers with Readings_ (0-321-41952-9): The Instructor's Manual, written by Melissa Rowland at Rock Valley College, will assist the instructor by offering Learning Objectives, Teaching Tips, and Transparency Masters for each chapter. Also featured to enhance the instructor's resources are Activities, as well as cultural notes.

Test Bank (0-321-41953-7) and TestGen (0-321-41954-5) to accompany *Resources for Writers with Readings:* The Test Bank, written by Phillip Sbaratta at North Shore Community College, contains two tests for each writing chapter and three tests for grammar chapters.

The Longman Instructor's Planner (Instructor/0-321-09247-3): This planner includes weekly and monthly calendars, student attendance and grading rosters, space for contact information, Web references, an almanac, and blank pages for notes.

Printed Test Bank for Developmental Writing (Instructor/0-321-08486-1): This test bank features more than 5,000 questions in all areas of writing, from grammar to paragraphing through essay writing, research, and documentation.

Electronic Test Bank for Developmental Writing (Instructor/CD 0-321-08117-X): The electronic TB features more than 5,000 questions in all areas of writing, from grammar to paragraphing through essay writing, research, and documentation. Instructors simply choose questions from the electronic test bank, then print out the completed test for distribution OR offer the test online.

Diagnostic and Editing Tests and Exercises, 9/e (Instructor/Print ISBN 0-321-41524-8/CD ISBN 0-321-43323-8): This collection of diagnostic tests helps instructors assess students' competence in standard written English to determine placement or to gauge progress.

The Longman Guide to Classroom Management (Instructor/0-321-09246-5): This guide is designed as a helpful resource for instructors who have classroom management problems. It includes helpful strategies for dealing with disruptive students in the classroom and the "do's and don'ts" of discipline.

The Longman Guide to Community Service-Learning in the English Classroom and Beyond (Instructor/0-321-12749-8): Written by Elizabeth Rodriguez Kessler of California State University—Northridge, this monograph provides a definition and history of service-learning, as well as an overview of how service-learning can be integrated effectively into the college classroom.

For Students

My Writing Lab (www.mywritinglab.com): This complete online learning system is the first that will truly help students become successful writers and, therefore, successful in college and beyond. It includes the following features:

- **A Comprehensive Writing Program:** MyWritingLab includes over 9,000 exercises in grammar, writing process, paragraph development, essay development, and research.

- **A Customized Learning Path:** Based on their text in use, students are automatically provided with a customized learning path that complements their textbook table of contents and extends textbook learning.

- **Diagnostic Testing:** MyWritingLab includes a comprehensive diagnostic test that thoroughly assesses students' skills in grammar. Based on the diagnostic test results, the students' learning path will reflect the areas where they need help the most and those areas that they have mastered.

- *Recall, Apply,* **and** *Write* **Exercises:** The heart of MyWritingLab is this progression of exercises within each module of the learning path. In completing the *Recall, Apply,* and *Write* exercises, students move from literal *(Recall)* to critical comprehension *(Apply)* to demonstrating concepts to their own writing *(Write).* This progressive learning process, not available in any other online resource, enables students to truly master the skills and concepts they need to be successful writers.

- **Progress Tracker:** All student work in MyWritingLab is captured in the site's Progress Tracker. Students can track their own progress, and instructors can track the progress of their entire class in this flexible and easy-to-use tool.

- Other resources for students in MyWritingLab: access to an interactive **Study Skills website,** access to **Research Navigator,** and a complimentary subscription to our **English Tutor Center,** which is staffed by live, college instructors.

For more information and to view a demo, go to **www.mywritinglab.com!**

Penguin Discount Novel Program: In cooperation with Penguin Putnam, Inc., Longman is proud to offer a variety of Penguin paperbacks at a significant discount when packaged with any Longman title. Excellent additions to any Developmental Reading or English course, Penguin titles give students the opportunity to explore contemporary and classical fiction and drama. The available titles include works by authors as diverse as Toni Morrison, Julia Alvarez, Mary Shelley, and Shakespeare. To review the complete list of titles available, visit the Longman-Penguin-Putnam Web site: http://www.ablongman.com/penguin.

The New American Webster Handy College Dictionary (Student/ 0-451-18166-2): This handy paperback reference text comes with more than 100,000 entries.

The Longman Writer's Portfolio (Student/0-321-16365-6): This unique supplement provides students with a space to plan, think about, and present their work. The portfolio includes an assessing/organizing area, a before and during writing area, and an after-writing area. This package also includes 10 Practices of Highly Effective Students.

Acknowledgments

I wish to acknowledge the contributions of my colleagues and reviewers who provided valuable advice and suggestions:

Sarah Juno Allen, Phoenix College; Mark Altschuler, Bergen Community College; Jackie Atkins, Pennsylvania State University, DuBois; Irene Anders, Indiana University–Purdue University; Linda A. Austin, Glendale Community College; Liz Ann Baez Aguilar, San Antonio College; Holly Bailey-Hofmann, West Los Angeles College; Linda Barro, East Central College; Emily Blesi, Virginia Highlands Community College; Candace Boeck, San Diego State University; Vicky Broadus, Lexington Community College; Tim Brown, Riverside Community College; Dr. Dottie Burkhart, Davidson County Community College; Eileen Call, Wake Technical Community College; Patricia H. Colella, Bunker Hill Community College; Judy D. Covington, Trident Technical College; Joyce L. Crawford-Martinez, DeVry University; Dana Crotwell, El Camino College; Lillian J. Dailey, Cuyahoga Community College; Catherine Decker, Chaffey College; Ann D. Ecoff, Lambuth University; Jeannine Edwards, University of Memphis; Susan Lynne Ertel, Dixie State College of Utah; Debra Farve, Mt. San Antonio College; Laraine Fergenson, Bronx Community College, CUNY; Clarinda Flannery, Eastern Michigan University; Jane Focht-Hansen, San Antonio College; Yvonne Frye, Community College of Denver; Kathleen Furlong, Glendale Community College; Nadine Gandia, Miami–Dade College, InterAmerican Campus; Dr. Richard F. Gaspar, Hillsborough Community College; Nicole E. Glick, Long Beach City College; Sherrie E. Godbey, University of Kentucky, Lexington Community College; Kay Grosso, Glendale Community College; Adam C. Hartmann, California State University, San Bernardino; Lauri Humberson, St. Philip's College; Dr. Laura Jeffries, Florida Community College at Jacksonville; George Z. Jiang, Riverside City College; Suzanne Joelson, Macomb Community College; Barbara Ann Kashi, Cypress College; Trudy Kirsher, Sinclair Community College; Julie Kozempel, Camden County College; Patsy Krech, University of Memphis; Sarah R. Lahm, Normandale Community College; Elizabeth Langenfeld, California State University, San Bernardino; Michael J. Lee, Columbia Basin College; Keming Liu, Medgar Evans College CUNY; John R. Lutzyk, DeVry University; Sharon Mabin, Portland Community College; Mimi Markus, Broward Community College; Elizabeth M. Marsh, Bergen Community College; Ann Marie McCarte, Lexington Community College; William S. McCarter, Eastern Shore Community College; Jason McFaul, Mt. San Antonio College;

Kathy McWilliams, Cuyamaca College; Jack Miller, Normandale Community College; Emily H. Moorer, Hinds Community College; Suzanne Morales, Central Texas College; Sandra Nekola, Normandale Community College; Virginia Nugent, Miami–Dade College, Kendall Campus; Tanya Olson, Vance-Granville Community College; Sam Pierstorff, Modesto Junior College; Esther Sapell Rachelson, DeVry University; Meredith Melissa Rayborn, Valencia Community College; Jeanette E. Redding, Oxnard College; Susan Reiger, Porterville College; David Robinson, DeVry University; Lori J. Roth, Chicago State University; Melissa Rowland, Rock Valley College; Shannon Runningbear, Long Beach City College; William L. Ryder, West Los Angeles College, College of the Canyons, and Los Angeles Trade Technical College; Justina Sapna, Delaware Technical and Community College; David Schwankle, Riverside Community College; Laurie Sherman, Community College of Rhode Island; Maria Sortino, Sortino International Training; Debbie Stallings, Hinds Community College; Frances Stewart, Bessemer State Technical College; Drema Stringer, Marshall Community and Technical College; Terri L. Symonds, Normandale Community College; Michele Taylor, Ogeechee Technical College; Jennifer Berlinda Thompson, Richard J. Daley College; Barbara L. Tosi, Community College of Allegheny County, Boyce Campus; Arlene Turkel, Lamar State College, Orange; Sinead Waters Turner, Wake Technical Community College; Joseph Patrick Wall, Modesto Junior College; Thurmond Whatley, Aiken Technical College; Beverly J. Wickersham, Temple Community College; Kirstin Wiley, Lexington Community College; and Ellen Willard, Community College of Rhode Island.

The editorial staff of Longman Publishers deserve a special recognition and thanks for the guidance, support, and direction they have provided. Melanie Craig, editor, did a masterful job of plunging into this project midway through and guiding *Resources* to its completion. Katharine Glynn's apt, thoughtful editing shaped this text into a coherent whole. Susan Messer's careful eye was invaluable in the final stages of editing. Outside of Longman, I also wish to thank Steven Rigolosi for his painstaking reading of the manuscript through its first draft and early revisions and, primarily, for giving me the opportunity to write this book. Further, I wish to thank Paul N. Cloninger, M.D., for his expert information on all sports, health, and garden-related topics. Charlotte Cloninger deserves great thanks for her expedient research work and Chicago-oriented information, and Andy, Dave, and Rob Cloninger provided special knowledge in the areas of investing, geography, and history. Deborah Cloninger provided information for the quilting chapter, and Mike Long provided information and suggestions for nearly every chapter. Robin Ikegami deserves tremendous thanks for writing the *Lab Manual Online*. Nancy Garcia's expertise was invaluable in bringing the Lab Manual Online to life. Kristin Ramsdell, librarian at

California State University, Hayward, was invaluable in her help with the research chapter. The following people contributed their knowledge or materials to other chapters: John Borovica, Grace Cloninger, Phil Cloninger, David Guy, Clyde Malone, Phil McCarthy, Matt Pera, and Kathy Sorensen. And finally, I would like to dedicate this book to the English faculty and students at Sacramento City College; Steve Rigolosi; Linda Stern; and my family, Mike, Annabelle, Annelise, and Susannah.

ELIZABETH CLONINGER LONG
SACRAMENTO, CALIFORNIA

PART ONE
Getting Started

CHAPTER 1

CHAPTER 2

CHAPTER 3

1 Your Strengths as a Writer

CULTURE NOTE *Roller coasters*

Originating as rough ice slides in Russia in the 1600s, roller coasters have undergone many changes and transformed into multiple types of thrill rides: scenic coasters, where riders view lovely real-life or fantasy scenes; suspended rides, where riders' legs hang from the coaster car; and stand-up coasters, where riders assume a standing position for the ride. The oldest roller coaster in the world—the "Leap the Dips" coaster at the Lakemont Park in Altoona, Pennsylvania—is a wooden structure built in 1902.

You Already Have the Tools to Write Well

Chances are, you're a better writer than you think you are. Without even realizing it, you use many essential writing and thinking skills on a daily basis. For example, you may have described what happened to make a day at work or school particularly bad, using examples to illustrate your point. You might have told your friends what you did at the mall, or you might have told them what someone or something looked like. You've probably organized your closet, drawers, or school supplies, grouping items in ways that make sense.

All these everyday tasks require skills you already possess. You'll use these same strategies, listed below and on the next page, to communicate in writing.

- Illustration and example
- Narration
- Comparison and contrast
- Cause and effect

The Powder Keg

FOOD FOR THOUGHT

The Powder Keg roller coaster in Branson, Missouri, offers thrills as well as the theme of being blasted from a powder shed. What aspects of roller coasters—heights, twists, or themes, for instance—are most important for a good roller coaster ride? Write a few sentences explaining why certain aspects are especially important for a good coaster ride.

- Description
- Classification and division
- Process analysis
- Definition
- Argument

These are strategies we employ on a daily basis to make our ideas clear to other people.

We All Have Different Experiences and Perspectives

Even if our ideas are clear to us, they may not always be clear to others. For example, write down the first thoughts that flash into your mind when you read the next two words shown at the top of the following page.

Car: _____

_____

Music: _____

_____

Now, ask two friends or classmates to write down their ideas. Compare their ideas with yours. Have any of you written exactly the same responses? Even if your ideas are similar, they very likely differ in some ways. We all most likely agree that *car* and *music* are not difficult words to define, we all bring our own experiences and interpretations to those words. If we want people to understand and agree with our point of view, we have to learn to communicate convincingly. Since we can't assume that people automatically understand and agree with us, we must anticipate others' ideas and explain ourselves clearly.

Every Point Needs Proof

Most of the examples and assignments in this textbook focus on writing a clear **paragraph.** A typical paragraph is a group of five to twelve sentences related to one idea. Paragraphs are usually around one hundred and fifty words long.

The subject matter of a paragraph is called its **topic.** The topic of your paragraphs will sometimes come from your teacher and sometimes from your own ideas. Often, your teacher will give you a general topic. Then, you can use your own experiences to narrow that topic into one that you feel familiar with and comfortable writing about.

The main idea expressed in a paragraph is called a **topic sentence.** The topic sentence is often the first sentence of the paragraph, and every other sentence in the paragraph should help support the topic sentence. A clear topic sentence helps readers understand what we're trying to communicate.

However, a clear topic sentence doesn't guarantee that we will win people to our point of view. Because no two humans think alike, we need to explain our points of view through clear examples. In other words, we need to offer proof. In writing paragraphs and essays, proof is called **support.** Your support points are the reasons you feel the way you do and thus the reasons people should believe you. Read the following paragraph to see how the support points make the topic sentence clear.

Ups and Downs

Riding the Powder Keg roller coaster at Silver Dollar City in Branson, Missouri, is a thrilling experience. First, the sounds around me build excitement. I hear a low rumbling broken up by loud squeaks and clacks which I hope are normal. I think people are screaming, but I can hardly hear anything because my heart is pounding so loudly. Next, the coaster's track makes me think twice about riding. Its huge hills and deep plunges seem unsafe, and the track seems too skinny to hold up the cars. Then comes the scare of getting on the ride. My mouth goes dry and my hands sweat as I sit down and the lap bar locks me in. As the ride begins, an entire track section lifts up, and my stomach drops. The ride itself is a blur: we "explode" from a powder mill, climb a giant hill and then drop, race through beautiful scenery, and finish with a crazy "dragonfly" turn. As soon as I stop shaking, I step off of the waiting platform and get in line again.

The topic of "Ups and Downs" is roller coasters, specifically, the Powder Keg coaster. The topic sentence, "Riding the Powder Keg roller coaster at Silver Dollar City in Branson, Missouri, is thrilling," gives the main idea of the paragraph. The writer supports the topic sentence by using words that allow the reader to experience the ride. For example, the first support point is "First, the sounds around me build excitement." To strengthen this support point, the writer gives three specific details.

Support Point	Specific Details
Sounds of the ride build excitement.	a low rumbling broken up by loud squeaks and clacks
	I think people are screaming
	My heart is pounding so loudly.

The writer also uses **transition words,** terms that give us clues about what's coming next. In the paragraph, the transition words *first, next,* and *then* keep the support points in order.

EXERCISE 1 IDENTIFYING SUPPORT POINTS

Reread the "Powder Keg" paragraph. Write down the points offered to support the topic sentence. Then list the specific details that illustrate each reason.

Topic: _____ Powder Keg roller coaster _____

Topic sentence: _____ Riding the Powder Keg roller coaster at Silver Dollar City in Branson, Missouri, is a thrilling experience. _____

Support point 1: _Sounds of the ride build excitement._

    Specific details: **a.** _Low rumbling broken up by loud squeaks and clacks_

                        b. _I think people are screaming_

                        c. _My heart is pounding so loudly._

Support point 2: _Seeing the track_

    Specific details: **a.** _Huge hills and deep plunges seem unsafe._

                        b. _The track seems too skinny to hold up the cars._

Support point 3: _The scare of getting on the ride_

    Specific details: **a.** _Dry mouth_

                        b. _Sweaty hands_

Support point 4: _The ride itself_

    Specific details: **a.** _explode from a powder mill_

                        b. _Climb a giant hill and then drop_

                        c. _Race through beautiful scenery_

                        d. _Finish with a crazy "dragonfly" turn_

EXERCISE 2 CONNECTING TOPICS WITH SPECIFIC DETAILS

To write clearly, you must be able to distinguish between support points and specific details. First, read the lists of specific details, and then circle the topic that ties them all together. An example is done for you.

Specific details: Telephones, pagers, answering machines, pad of paper

Topic: **a.**   Helpful tools

              b.   Electronic communications devices

              (c.)   Communications devices

Answer c is the best choice because it includes all four details without being too broad. Answer a—"helpful tools"—could refer to many other devices. Answer b is too narrow, because it does not include the pad of paper.

1. Specific details: Jelly-filled, glazed, covered with chocolate sprinkles

Topic:

    a. Sweets

    (b.) Doughnuts

    c. Doughnuts with topping

2. Specific details: Broken windshield, missing stereo

Topic:

    a. Old car

    b. Unfortunate events

    (c.) Car burglary

3. Specific details: Grand Canyon, Golden Gate Bridge, Empire State Building

Topic:

    a. Impressive natural sights

    b. Man-made structures

    (c.) Impressive sights

4. Specific details: Television, movies, CDs, comic books

Topic:

    (a.) Forms of entertainment

    b. Forms of electronic entertainment

    c. Electronic devices

5. Specific details: Put on sport shoes, put on comfortable clothing, go to gym, do stretching exercises

Topic:

    a. Ways to relax

    b. Strenuous exercise

    (c.) Ways to prepare for exercise

6. Specific details: Smiles at Rasheed, blushes when Rasheed speaks, sneaks peeks at Rasheed during class

Topic:

    (a.) Someone with a crush on Rasheed

    b. Someone who's not interested in Rasheed

    c. Someone Rasheed has embarrassed

7. Specific details: Suit and tie, briefcase, hand-held organizer

     Topic: **a.**   Recreation items

                b.   Academic items

                (**c.**)   Business items

8. Specific details: Candlelight, roses, chocolate hearts

     Topic: **a.**   Expensive gestures

                b.   Birthday gestures

                (**c.**)   Romantic gestures

9. Specific details: Drinking coffee, walking in cold night air, holding eyes open with clothespins

     Topic: **a.**   Studying for final exams

                (**b.**)   Ways to stay awake

                c.   Bad habits

10. Specific details: Thick pads, hard helmet, long stick, big jersey

     Topic: (**a.**)   Hockey equipment

                b.   Ways to cover up flab

                c.   Protective gear

EXERCISE 3 IDENTIFYING TOPICS

First, read the lists of specific details, and then choose a topic that ties them all together. An example is done for you.

Topic: _Visit to the beach_

    Specific details: **a.**   Sunburn

                    b.   Seashells and jellyfish

                    c.   Sand in everything

1. Topic: _Subjects in school_

    Specific details: **a.**   Math

                    b.   English

                    c.   Science

2. Topic: Rush-hour traffic

Specific details: **a.** Blaring horns

b. Frustrated drivers

c. Cars moving very slowly

3. Topic: Facial expressions

Specific details: **a.** Smile

b. Frown

c. Wink

4. Topic: Breakfast foods

Specific details: **a.** Coffee

b. Cold cereal

c. Oatmeal

5. Topic: Family vehicles

Specific details: **a.** Minivan

b. Station wagon

c. Large SUV

6. Topic: Signs of the desert

Specific details: **a.** Cactus

b. Rattlesnake

c. Tumbleweeds

7. Topic: Cold-weather clothing

Specific details: **a.** Mittens

b. Wool hats

c. Heavy coats

8. Topic: Tools

Specific details: **a.** Hammer

b. Drill

c. Screwdriver

9. Topic: Circus acts

    Specific details: **a.**   Clowns

                     b.   Trapeze artists

                     c.   Performing animals

10. Topic: Types of music

    Specific details: **a.**   Classical

                     b.   Rhythm and blues

                     c.   Rock and roll

Learning While You Write

You probably noticed the Culture Note at the beginning of this chapter. Every chapter of this text has a similar note. Each note focuses on a key topic in American and world culture. You'll be learning about many of these topics in your college career. Additionally, this book will give you a taste not only of your college studies but also of the world's rich social, historical, and intellectual achievements.

What You Know Now

You already know the most important skills you need to write a paragraph.

1. Make a point.

2. Offer reasons to support that point.

3. Illustrate your reasons with specific details.

WRITING PRACTICE   Write Your Own Paragraph

Your assignment is this: On a separate piece of paper, *write a paragraph about the best or worst food you have ever eaten.* Use the sample paragraph "Ups and Downs" on pages 5–6 to guide you.

- Write your main idea in your topic sentence.
- Give three reasons that support your topic sentence.
- Offer specific details as proof.

Introduction to the Lab Manual Online (LMO)

If you've thumbed through this text, you may have noticed many opportunities to improve your writing, through both exercises and readings. One more way *Resources for Writers* helps you improve your reading and writing skills is through the Lab Manual, found at the end of the book and online. These provide two additional sets of exercises and assignments for you to complete on your own, with or without help from your instructor. Many of these activities can also be done collaboratively (with your peers in a group).

HOW THE LMO WORKS

After you've finished a particular chapter, you can access additional activities through the Internet.

1. Turn to the Lab Manual at the back of this book (pages LM-1–LM-114). Find the activity that corresponds to the chapter you've just completed.

2. Complete the printed portion of the Lab Activity. For example, turn to page LM-3 to complete the printed portion of Lab Activity 1.

3. To complete the online portion of the Lab Activity, log on to **http://www.ablongman.com/long.** Click on *Resources for Writers*. Then click on the Lab Activity that corresponds to the chapter you've just completed.

4. Work through the online Lab Activity, checking your work through the Online Tutor.

At the end of each chapter of this book, you'll see a reminder to complete that chapter's Lab Activity (see below).

Lab Activity 1

For additional practice with main points, support points, and specific details, complete Lab Activity 1 in the Lab Manual at the back of the book.

2. The Bases of Good Writing: The Four Cs

CULTURE NOTE *World Geography*

At a time when technology has allowed us to connect to many other people and countries of the world, knowing where places are is important. Geography—the study of the earth's surface and how it is divided into continents, countries, and cities—lets us look at how our world is organized. Geography also lets us understand our connection to other cultures and appreciate our place in the world.

Good Writing Is . . .

If you've ever eaten a well-prepared meal, you know that different parts of the meal serve different functions. A light appetizer can get you ready for the main course, while a spicy sauce can tickle your tongue, and crusty bread can mellow the effects of the sauce. Finally, the perfect dessert can leave your taste buds—and your stomach—feeling just right. Even though all the parts serve different purposes, they are all necessary to create the complete effect of a satisfying meal.

Your writing is similar to such a meal. Several different elements combine to make your writing effective. Understanding what these elements are and how they work together is important. Effective writing has four characteristics. Good writing is concise, credible, clear, and correct.

Concise. When your writing is *concise,* you have a clear point (your topic sentence) and you include only the information absolutely necessary to communicate that point. Concise writing gets to the point quickly and does not introduce unnecessary information.

Credible. When your writing is *credible,* it is believable. For your reader to believe what you say, you must offer proof—in the form of specific details—to illustrate your topic sentence.

Clear. When your writing is *clear,* it signals to your reader what points are important and how those points fit together under the umbrella of your topic sentence. **Transitional words** are essential to clear writing.

Correct. When your writing is *correct,* it is free of errors in spelling, grammar, and punctuation.

Recognizing Concise Writing

Concise writing simply makes a point as directly as possible, without giving any information that does not support the topic sentence.

Read the following paragraphs. Then decide which one is more concise. Why?

One Continent's Contributions

Africa, the second-largest continent, has contributed much to the world. Recently, African countries such as Kenya have produced the world's best distance runners. Dominating races longer than fifteen hundred meters for twenty years, African men runners have won the Olympic gold medal in the ten thousand meter run since 1988. In addition to runners, Africa has contributed diamonds. Even though diamonds were valued long before their discovery in South Africa in 1867, no diamond deposits in other countries, such as Canada, Brazil, Russia, and Australia, were as large as those in South Africa. Even today, most of the world's diamonds come from Africa. Finally, Africa has contributed links to our past. Known as the cradle of humanity, Africa is home to Lucy, a human skeleton that is estimated to be between 3 and 3.8 million years old, the oldest human remains yet discovered. These are just some of the vast resources the African continent has given the world.

A Large Land

The African continent has made many contributions to the world. It is also the second-largest continent, big enough to contain the United States, India, Europe, Argentina, and China. One of Africa's contributions comes in the form of distance runners, particularly male distance runners. African runners have been dominant in races longer than fifteen hundred meters for many years, and they have been undefeated in the ten thousand meter Olympic race since 1988. The marathon, however, poses a greater challenge for African runners. Another African contribution comes in the form of diamonds. Diamonds are still considered an appropriate gift when two people become engaged. Since their discovery in South Africa in 1867, diamonds have been an important African product. Most importantly, Africa has provided information about human history. Lucy, the name given to the oldest human remains, was found in Ethiopia. Thus, Africa is responsible for significant human discoveries. The name *Lucy* supposedly comes from the Beatles song "Lucy in the Sky with Diamonds," which Lucy's finders sang in the evening after they made their discovery. Though Africa has made other important contributions to the world, these are a few.

The first paragraph, "One Continent's Contributions," is more *concise* and therefore more effective. It offers no information other than those details that support the topic sentence, "Africa, the second-largest continent, has contributed much to the world." Even the title "One Continent's Contributions" offers a clue as to what the paragraph will contain. In contrast, "A Large Land" contains many details that do not directly support the topic sentence, which is "The African continent has made many contributions to the world." For instance, one unnecessary detail is this:

> It is also the second-largest continent, big enough to contain the United States, India, Europe, Argentina, and China.

This detail explains how big Africa is but says nothing about the continent's contributions.

EXERCISE 1 CONCISE WRITING

Use a pen or pencil to cross out any sentences of "A Large Land" that do not support the topic sentence.

How many sentences did you cross out? ___3___

You should have crossed out the following sentences:

> The marathon, however, poses a greater challenge for African runners.

> Diamonds are still considered an appropriate gift when two people become engaged.

The name *Lucy* supposedly comes from the Beatles song "Lucy in the Sky with Diamonds," which Lucy's finders sang in the evening after they made their discovery.

These details, while they might be interesting, do not help to develop the idea that "the African continent has made many contributions to the world." Thus, they need to be removed from the paragraph.

Concise Writing Leads to Unity

One important aspect of good writing is *unity*. In unified writing, all elements of a paragraph work together to communicate a single idea. By making your writing concise—and, thus, free from ideas that do not contribute to the overall message of your paragraph—you are ensuring that your writing will also be unified.

In Your Own Writing

To write concisely, you must do the following:

1. Have a clear topic sentence that states exactly what your paragraph is about.
2. Make sure every detail you use supports your topic sentence.

As you add details to your paragraph, ask yourself if they help to explain or clarify your topic sentence. If not, take them out. For instance, suppose you are writing a paragraph on your favorite food; describing places *to find* such food would lead your reader away from your main point.

Making Sure Your Writing Is Concise

Ask yourself the following questions in order to determine whether your paragraphs are concise.

1. Do I have a clear topic sentence?
2. Does *every* specific detail support my topic sentence?

Identifying Concise Writing

Remember that everything in concise writing must connect to and support the topic sentence. For instance, in the list below, most of the items support the topic sentence, but a few do not. The items that do not support the topic sentence are crossed out.

Topic sentence: I want to visit England.

Many music groups from England

I like fish and chips and tea.

Want to see double-decker bus

~~Friend, Sam, got lost in London~~

I like rainy weather.

~~Museums are boring.~~

EXERCISE 2 CONNECTING SUPPORT POINTS WITH TOPIC SENTENCES

Each numbered item gives a topic sentence and list of support points. Cross out any items that do not support the topic sentence.

1. Topic sentence: Costa Rica sounds like a good place for vacation.

a. Cool rain forests

b. Most civilized Central American country

c. ~~High literacy rate in Costa Ricans~~

d. Great beaches

e. Good food

2. Topic sentence: Traveling can be uncomfortable.

a. Stiff bus and train seats

b. ~~Maps are essential.~~

c. Lumpy beds

d. No ice in some restaurants

e. ~~Great scenery~~

3. Topic sentence: There are many great sights all over the world.

a. Grand Canyon in Arizona

b. Pyramids in Egypt

c. Eiffel Tower in Paris

d. ~~Great photo opportunities~~

e. ~~Lots of exercise exploring~~

EXERCISE 3 FINDING SENTENCES THAT ARE OFF-TOPIC

Read the following paragraphs. Then, underline the topic sentence, and cross out any sentences that do not relate to the topic sentence. The hint at the end of each paragraph will tell you how many sentences are off-topic.

A.   **Geography Is a Waste of Time**

   [1]<u>Studying geography is a waste of time for many reasons.</u> [2]First, I'm perfectly happy here in the same neighborhood, the same city, even the same house that I grew up in. [3]My grandfather built this house with his own hands. [4]I don't need to know where Africa or China is because I will never go there. [5]Second, geography is confusing. [6]So many cities and countries sound alike that I can't keep them straight. [7]I don't know if Austria is the same place as Australia, or if the Berlin Wall was anything like the Great Wall of China. [8]Even if I wanted to know these things, I don't think I could get them right. [9]Spelling has never been my best subject. [10]Finally, it's scary to learn geography. [11]Any time some foreign country or city makes the headlines, the news is always bad. [12]Someone's been killed or trapped or bombed. [13]I don't see why I need to learn about other people's bad news when there's plenty of it right here at home. [14]I got mugged last week, and the mugger stole my watch. [15]Geography is one place I don't want to go.

Three sentences are off-topic: _____3_____, _____9_____, and _____14_____.

B.   **The Benefits of Studying Geography**

   [1]<u>Studying geography has many important benefits.</u> [2]First of all, it helps me understand people better. [3]In my English class alone, there are people from Russia, Vietnam, and Ukraine. [4]Knowing that some of my classmates have had great struggles in their lives makes me admire their courage. [5]They had to leave family, friends, and home to make better lives in the United States. [6]My own family has been in the United States for more than one hundred fifty years. [7]I also like knowing where things are so that I can see why people make the choices they make. [8]For instance, a few years ago, a basketball player named Steve Francis refused to play for a team in Vancouver, Canada. [9]He said that he was from Maryland and that Vancouver was too far away from his family. [10]It is pretty far away! [11]Vancouver doesn't even have a team now; the Grizzlies moved to

Memphis, Tennessee. [12]Finally, knowing geography helps me understand how much our world is changing. [13]In just the last few years, some countries such as Yugoslavia and Czechoslovakia have split up and no longer exist. [14]In fact, on the African continent, many countries have changed borders or names recently. [15]Sometimes even the newest maps don't show all the changes. [16]It's interesting to see how some places become independent and make progress while others seem to stay pretty much the same.

Two sentences are off-topic: _____6_____ and _____11_____.

C.

Changing Geography

[1]<u>Over the last few decades, many changes in geography have taken place.</u> [2]One of the biggest changes involves the breaking up of the USSR, or former Soviet Union. [3]The USSR used to have fourteen republics in it, ranging from Latvia to Kazakhstan. [4]Now the former Soviet Union republics run themselves as independent countries. [5]The breaking up of the USSR caused more individual countries to win medals at the Olympics. [6]Second, the borders of African nations have changed a lot in recent years. [7]A few years ago there was a country called Zaire. [8]Now there's no such place! [9]Instead, it has become the Democratic Republic of Congo. [10]This is confusing because there's also a country called the Republic of Congo. [11]Many countries throughout the world have names that are hard to spell. [12]Rhodesia has changed its name to Zimbabwe. [13]It's amazing that whole countries can just change their names like that. [14]Third, Southeast Asia has also changed a lot. [15]Cambodia is now called Kampuchea. [16]Thailand, too, had another name—Siam—and Myanmar used to be called Burma. [17]It's hard to keep up with all the changes!

Three sentences are off-topic: _____5_____, _____11_____, and _____13_____.

D.

Why Geography Changes

[1]Political decisions can have long-lasting effects. [2]<u>Borders of countries can change for a number of political reasons.</u> [3]One reason borders change is that big nations break up into smaller ones. [4]The former Soviet Union, or USSR, is a good example of this. [5]At one point, the USSR was an extremely powerful communist nation, consisting of many different republics. [6]However, after the Berlin Wall came down in 1989, many of the former Soviet republics wanted to

govern themselves. [7]Their governments took different forms. [8]The borders of what was once the USSR are now borders between smaller countries. [9]Borders can also change when one country buys land from another. [10]In the United States, the land from the Mississippi River to the Rocky Mountains was once owned by France. [11]In 1803, the United States bought this parcel of land in what is called the Louisiana Purchase, so the borders of the United States expanded. [12]Napoleon, the leader of France at that time, was eventually banished. [13]Another reason borders change is that sometimes smaller countries are swallowed up by bigger ones. [14]The former Soviet Union is a good example of this type of change also. [15]Estonia, Latvia, and Lithuania—all Baltic countries—were originally part of the Russian empire. [16]After the Great War (World War I), they became independent nations, but during World War II they became part of the USSR. [17]Eventually, they became independent again when the USSR broke apart.

Three sentences are off-topic: ____1____, ____7____, and ____12____.

Recognizing Credible Writing

Credible writing gives your readers reason to believe you. Credible paragraphs include specific details that help convince your readers that they should believe you.

Read the paragraphs below. Then decide which is more credible. Why?

Over the River

Though the world has many rivers, three in particular—the Nile, the Amazon, and the Mississippi—are important. Located in Egypt, the Nile River is the world's longest and was important in early agriculture. Its people used its resources to master farming techniques. Not found in Egypt, another significant river is the Amazon, which carries a lot of water and has an interesting history to its name. Finally, the mighty Mississippi River is located in North America and is important for many states and two Canadian provinces.

A River Runs Through It

The world's rivers play important roles on every continent. Three rivers—the Nile, the Amazon, and the Mississippi—are worth studying. More than four thousand miles long, the Nile River flows northward through Africa to the Mediterranean Sea. Aside from being the world's longest river, the ancient Nile was significant to agriculture. Egypt's water and fertile soil presented perfect conditions for farming, and ancient people living along the Nile were some of the first to use a plow. In South America, the Amazon River is extremely powerful. It flows across northern Brazil to the Atlantic Ocean, carrying more water—184,000 cubic meters per second—than any other river. Named for legendary female warriors, the Amazon River has a mouth measuring more than two hundred fifty miles wide. Last, the mighty Mississippi River is important to many regions in North America. It acts as a watershed for—draining water from—thirty-one U.S. states and two Canadian provinces. Flowing from Lake Itasca to the Gulf of Mexico, the Mississippi River carved its upper path with the water of melting glaciers from the last Ice Age, but it is actually considered a very young river. Regardless of the continent you're on, there's probably an important river that runs through it.

The second paragraph, "A River Runs Through It," is more *credible* and therefore more effective. Both of these two paragraphs are concise and relatively easy to follow. They both have topic sentences and clear support points. The second paragraph, however, includes specific examples as proof of the writer's points. For instance, in "A River Runs Through It," the writer makes the point that the Nile is significant to agriculture and then offers a specific detail—the example of how early Nile residents were the first to use a plow—to show that the Nile is, indeed, important.

EXERCISE 4 CREDIBLE WRITING

Listed below are the other support points in "A River Runs Through It." Read through the paragraph. Then underline the sentences containing specific details for these support points.

Support point 2:	In South America, the Amazon River is extremely powerful.
Support point 3:	Last, the mighty Mississippi River is important to many regions of North America.

Here are the specific details you should have found.

Specific details for support point 2:	It flows across northern Brazil to the Atlantic Ocean carrying more water—184,000 cubic meters per second—than any other river. Named for legendary female warriors, the Amazon River has a mouth measuring more than two hundred fifty miles wide.

Specific details for support point 3: It acts as a watershed for—draining water from—thirty-one U.S. states and two Canadian provinces. Flowing from Lake Itasca to the Gulf of Mexico, the Mississippi River carved its upper path with the water of melting glaciers from the last Ice Age, but it is actually considered a very young river.

In "Over the River," the writer makes these points: the Nile is "the world's longest river and was important in early agriculture," and "its people used its resources to master farming techniques." However, these points are unsupported by any detail. How long is the Nile? From where does it flow? In what ways was the Nile important in early agriculture? What were its resources? How did people use them? What early farming techniques did people use? The writer answers none of these questions through examples. Thus, we are left doubting whether the writer knows much about the topic.

In Your Own Writing

To write credibly, offer specific details to show that you have reasons to back up your topic sentence. Specific examples can be the following:

1. Actual examples from your life.
2. Incidents that you've seen happen to someone else.
3. Facts that you've heard about or read, as long as you can give the source, such as a newspaper or magazine.

For instance, suppose you are writing a paragraph on your least favorite food. You could include comments describing liver as being so slimy that it kept skidding away when you tried to spear it with your fork or tell about an artichoke that stuck your hand as you tried to eat it.

Making Sure Your Writing Is Credible

Ask yourself the following questions to determine whether your paragraphs are credible.

1. Do I provide enough information so that my reader will believe me?
2. Have I made sure my reader knows what I mean?

Practicing Credible Writing

Credible writing offers enough proof for your readers to believe that you know something about your subject. Remember that in credible writing, support points are illustrated by specific details.

EXERCISE 5 FINDING SUPPORT POINTS THAT NEED MORE DETAIL

Read the following paragraphs. For each one, underline the topic sentence. Then write down the number of any sentence in which you think the writer needs to be more specific or provide more information. The hint at the end of the paragraph will tell you how many sentences need more detail.

A.   **Effects of Changing Geography**

[1]Changes in geography bring about many different effects. [2]One effect of changing geography comes in the form of new names for old places. [3]Another effect is that borders change, such as in the former Soviet Union. [4]Finally, people can die. [5]In what used to be Yugoslavia, many ethnic Albanian people moved into the area called Kosovo. [6]That region was traditionally inhabited by Serbian people. [7]When the Albanians moved in, the Serbian people felt threatened. [8]Plus, the Albanians decided that they wanted the Kosovo region for themselves, and they tried to take it over. [9]This led to a huge civil war between the Albanians and the Serbs, during which thousands of people died. [10]Eventually, Kosovo became an area run mostly by the Albanians but with some input from the Serbs.

Two support points need more detail in sentences ___2___ and ___3___.

B.   **Reasons to Visit Paris**

[1]People should visit Paris for a number of reasons. [2]First, it's beautiful. [3]All you need to do is look around. [4]Second, the food is fantastic. [5]Everywhere you go people are eating the most wonderful-looking pastries and drinking heavenly coffee. [6]The croissants and sauces alone are worth visiting Paris for. [7]Next, there's the history. [8]So many important events occurred in Paris! [9]Finally, Paris is romantic. [10]There are so many places with wonderful views, perfect

The Eiffel Tower

SURF THE NET Rising 324 meters above Paris, the Eiffel Tower has become a symbol of that city. However, the tower has not always been loved by its people. What is the tower's history? Why was it built? How did people initially react to it? Surf the Internet and write a few sentences summarizing what you learn.

for lovers. [11]If you happen to be awake late at night, so many night sights can make you fall in love all by themselves. [12]It's a great city!

Three support points need more detail in sentences ___2___, ___7___, and ___10___.

C.   **Reasons Not to Visit Paris**

[1]Why anyone would want to go to Paris is a mystery to me. [2]For starters, it's so boring. [3]People say that there's a lot to do, but who wants to spend all day looking at museums or old buildings? [4]I heard that I should visit the Louvre museum, so I did. [5]But it was crowded

and full of paintings I'd never even seen before. ⁶For the whole time I was in Paris, I tried to find a good baseball game to watch, or even football highlights from last season. ⁷I never did have any luck. ⁸Next, I can't understand what the big deal is with the food. ⁹I kept hearing that French food was great, but did I ever find one good French fry? ¹⁰I never did. ¹¹In fact, in Paris French fries aren't even called French fries. ¹²They're called *pommes frites,* and if you ask for them using any other name, people look at you as if you're from another planet. ¹³That brings me to another reason Paris is no great vacation for me: the language. ¹⁴Last but not least, Paris isn't very pretty. ¹⁵Sure, you can look at the view from the Eiffel Tower or take a cruise down the Seine River, but there are towers and rivers everywhere. ¹⁶I just don't understand why Paris is supposed to be so special.

One support point needs more detail beginning in sentence ____13____.

D.   **Climbing Mount Everest**

¹Climbing Mount Everest is an extraordinarily difficult task. ²One challenge climbers face is being physically fit. ³Since Mount Everest is the world's highest peak (over twenty-nine thousand feet), teams of climbers must be in top physical condition before they can even start their trips. ⁴Climbers must eat well and exercise to ensure that their hearts, lungs, and legs are in good shape. ⁵Next, they must get acclimated to (used to) the thin air. ⁶Usually, groups stay at what's called a base camp (located above seventeen thousand feet) for about four weeks in order to train their bodies to operate on less oxygen. ⁷Another step involves dealing with physical discomfort. ⁸It's so cold on Everest that toothpaste freezes, as does people's hair right after being washed. ⁹Also, since the air is so thin, horrible headaches pound in people's heads, and people get terrible aches in their joints from the cold. ¹⁰Finally, fear presents a huge challenge for the climbers. ¹¹No matter what, though, climbing to the summit of Mount Everest is a huge accomplishment!

One support point needs more detail beginning in sentence ____10____.

Recognizing Clear Writing

Clear writing lets your readers easily follow and understand your ideas. In clear writing, information is placed in a logical order. Two common ways in which information can be ordered are chronologically and emphatically.

Transitions That Signal Chronological (Time Sequence) Order

finally	last of all
first (second, third)	next
in the first place	then
last	

In **chronological order,** also called **time sequence order,** events or steps are given in the order or sequence in which they occur. For example, suppose you are telling some friends about a terrible day that you just had. If you were following chronological order, your description of your day might go like this:

First, my alarm didn't go off, so I overslept and didn't have time to take a shower. **Then,** I found out that the reason my alarm didn't go off was that the power had gone out. So, of course, I couldn't make coffee. **Next,** my boss chewed me out for being late to work and told me I needed to work on my appearance because I looked as if I had just rolled out of bed. **Finally,** my boyfriend canceled our date so he could watch the basketball game, completely forgetting that it's our anniversary.

Paragraph in Chronological Order

Topic sentence...
....

↓

First event or step...
...........................Specific details............................
Second event or step...
...........................Specific details............................
Third event or step...
...........................Specific details............................
Last event or step..
...........................Specific details............................

In this example, you're telling your friends the events that happened *in the order in which they happened.* The transition words, in bold type, signal this order of events. The illustration "Paragraph in Chronological Order," on the previous page, shows this way of organizing a paragraph.

In **emphatic order,** support points are given in order of importance. You as the writer decide which points are least interesting or important and which are the most important ones. Using emphatic order, you place the points that *you think* are less important first, and you end with the points that *you think* are most important. Placing examples at the end of a paragraph often sends the message that those points are the most important, so you need to decide which points should come last. For instance, if you are telling someone why it's important to clean out a refrigerator, you might want to use emphatic order to emphasize the idea that eating spoiled food could make you sick.

Cleaning out the refrigerator is important for many reasons. **First,** a messy fridge—one that has rotten food or spills everywhere—just doesn't help anyone's appetite. **Second,** a messy fridge makes finding things difficult. If you know you have milk but can't find it because there are so many other old containers in front of it, you can end up frustrated. **Most important,** a messy fridge can be dangerous. If you eat something that's been in the fridge awhile because it *looks* all right, you could get sick.

In this example, you're placing your reasons for cleaning a refrigerator *in order of least to most important.* The transition words in bold type signal the emphatic order used. The illustration "Paragraph in Emphatic Order," on the following page, shows the form of a paragraph organized in emphatic order.

Clear writing also includes transition words that reinforce the order of the points. In chronological order, words like *first, then, next,* and *finally* tell your

Transitions That Signal Emphatic Order

above all	most of all
best of all	most important
finally	most significantly
first (second, third)	worst of all

Paragraph in Emphatic Order
Topic sentence... ....
↓
Least important support point................................... ....Specific details........................... Important support point.. ....Specific details........................... Important support point.. ....Specific details........................... Most important support point.................................. ....Specific details...........................

reader what comes next in the sequence. In emphatic order, transitions like *above all* and *most important* tell your reader that your points are becoming more important as you go on. See Chapter 11 for more lists of transition words.

Read the paragraphs that follow. Then decide which one communicates more clearly. Why?

Sights in China

If you visit China, there is much to see. However, to hit the highlights, three sights should be on your tour route. First, you should see the Great Wall of China. Spanning more than fifteen hundred miles, the Great Wall is actually a series of walls designed over the centuries to keep enemies out. You'd think that its huge walls—some as high as twenty-five feet and fifteen to thirty feet wide at the base—would be enough to deter enemies. Another great sight is the Forbidden City, right in the center of Beijing. This enormous complex, with some eight hundred buildings and ten thousand rooms, was once the imperial headquarters. Finally, one last grand sight is Tiananmen Square, a huge plaza also in Beijing. Its gates to the north and south are impressive, as are the Monument to the People's Heroes and the mausoleum of Mao Zedong, which stand in the center of the square. This sight is significant to Americans because Tiananmen Square was the site of violent protests inspired by American democracy in 1989.

Tiananmen Square

CRITICAL THINKING Named for the Tiananmen (literally, *Gate of Heavenly Peace*) which sits to its north, Tiananmen Square is seen by many as the symbolic heart of China. Indeed, when Chinese students organized a pro-democracy demonstration in 1989, it was held in Tiananmen Square. What place or monument could be considered the "symbolic heart" of the United States? Write a few sentences explaining your thoughts.

Seeing China

Of all the sights to see in China, three are most important. Tiananmen Square was the site of violent pro-democracy protests in 1989, so put that on your list. It also has huge monuments in the center and ancient gates to the north and south. The Great Wall of China—actually a series of shorter walls—was built to prevent enemies in Mongolia from entering China. The Forbidden City sits in the center of Beijing, and it covers an enormous area. It also has approximately eight hundred buildings and ten thousand rooms. The Great Wall has walls twenty-five feet high and fifteen to thirty feet wide at the base. Tiananmen means "Gate of Heavenly Peace." The Forbidden City was once the imperial headquarters.

The first paragraph, "Sights in China," is clearer than the second one and therefore more effective. The examples are organized in emphatic order—from least to most important. The writer also clearly signals the order of the points through the use of transitional words such as *first*.

EXERCISE 6 CLEAR WRITING

Underline the transitional expressions in "Sights in China."

How many expressions did you find? ___4___

You should have underlined the following terms: __first__ , __another__ , __finally__ and __last__ .

The second paragraph, "Seeing China," is both concise and credible, but it lacks any directions for the reader to follow. The writer does not include transitional expressions. Consequently, the reader can't easily distinguish the support points or understand the reason for the order in which they are given.

In Your Own Writing

To write clearly, you must do the following:

1. Organize your ideas effectively and logically. For instance, if your topic is "The Worst Course Schedule I Ever Had," you should probably use chronological order rather than emphatic order to make your case.
2. Use transitional expressions to let your reader know when important points are coming and how important those points are.

Making Sure Your Writing Is Clear

Ask yourself the following questions to determine whether your paragraphs are clear.

1. Do I have a logical organizational format that my reader can easily follow? What is it?
2. Do I use transitional expressions to communicate what my points are and which ones are most important?

Identifying Clear Writing

Clear writing gives your reader clear signals to your support points and how important those points are.

Remember that paragraphs can be organized chronologically (according to the order in which events happened), or they can be organized using emphatic order (where points appear in order from least to most important).

EXERCISE 7 USING EMPHATIC ORDER

Read the following paragraph. Underline the topic sentence, and then answer the questions that follow.

Packing for Afghanistan

Although traveling to Afghanistan is a difficult journey, some simple tips can make the trip safer. Make sure you have the proper travel documents. Even if you have a passport, this will not be enough all by itself. Different parts of Afghanistan require different permits to enter, so you should consult a travel guide to make sure that you have the right papers. Otherwise, you might travel all that way and not be allowed into the country. Prepare yourself by dressing as the Afghans dress. Keep your arms and legs covered with long-sleeved, loose garments, and don't walk around with lots of money or valuable jewelry showing. Looking like the native people will help you move easily in crowds and stay safe. If you are a woman, make sure you are well covered as a sign of respect for the Muslim religion of the country. A little of your ankle can show, but not much else. Be respectful to the people around you. Since the terrorist attacks in the United States on September 11, 2001, the Afghan people have been sensitive about Osama Bin Laden, the man who is believed to have organized the attacks. Bringing his name up in conversation might make people angry or unhappy, so it's best not to mention him. Most importantly, you should obey the laws of the country. If you are not supposed to bring a car into the country, for instance, then find another way to travel. When the Taliban—an extreme Islamic group—was in power, its rulers did not want tourists taking pictures of the Afghan people. Travelers at that time showed respect by keeping their cameras put away. Have a good trip!

1. This paragraph should use emphatic order. Write 1, 2, 3, or 4 before each of the support points. The number 1 should represent your least important point, and the number 4 should represent your most important point.

_____1_____ Get proper travel documents.

_____2_____ Wear native dress.

_____3_____ Be sensitive to people around you.

_____4_____ Obey laws.

2. Choose an expression from the following list that could introduce the first reason given: *First, Next, In addition.*

_____ First _____

3. Choose an expression from the following list that could introduce reason 2: *Second, For Starters, Last.*

_____ second _____

4. What reason is the most important? Obey the laws of the country. _____

_____

5. What signal words tell you that this reason is the most important?

Most importantly
_____

EXERCISE 8 USING CHRONOLOGICAL ORDER

Our Changing Nation

Different European nations have controlled large tracts of United States territory. Originally, the Spanish settled parts of what is now the United States. Spain sent explorers into what is now New Mexico as early as 1542, while in 1565 Spain established the fort of Saint Augustine in Florida. From the mid-1500s through the mid-1800s, the Spanish held vast sections of American land. In the 1600s, the English made their mark in the New World. After trying to establish a colony unsuccessfully on Roanoke Island, the English finally established thirteen colonies on the east coast of North America. The English held this large section of land until the Revolutionary War, which ended in 1783. France was another European nation that once held large areas of land in what eventually became the United States. French holdings spanned what are now the states of Louisiana, Arkansas, Missouri, Nebraska, Iowa, South Dakota, and North Dakota, as well as part of Minnesota, Montana, Colorado, Kansas, Wyoming, and Oklahoma. In 1803, Emperor Napoleon Bonaparte of France sold this tract of land to the United States for $15 million. This transaction is known as the Louisiana Purchase. Russia held different sections of American soil. Russia held Alaska and parts of northern California until 1867, when the United States bought Alaska from Russia for $7.2 million. The United States may be one nation now, but it took a lot of change to get to that point.

1. This paragraph should be organized using chronological order. Use the dates in the paragraph to guide you, numbering the support points 1, 2, 3, and 4 according to which comes first, second, third, and fourth.

   _____4_____ Russia held parts of American land.

   _____2_____ England held parts of American land.

   _____1_____ Spain explored different parts of the United States.

   _____3_____ France held land that became the Louisiana Purchase.

2. Which support point is signaled by the word *originally?* The Spanish
   settled parts of what is now the United States.

3. Should this point come first, second, third, or fourth? _____
   First

4. What other signal words the writer can use to introduce points 2, 3,
   and 4? Next, also, later; answers may vary.

EXERCISE 9 PUTTING SUPPORT POINTS IN ORDER

Read the following paragraph. (It is a slightly different version of a paragraph you read earlier in this chapter.) Locate the four support points. Then find the specific details for each point.

Reasons Not to Visit Paris

[1]Why anyone would want to go to Paris is a mystery to me. [2]For starters, it's so boring. [3]People say that there's a lot to do, but who wants to spend all day looking at museums or old buildings? [4]I heard that I should visit the Louvre museum, so I did. [5]But it was crowded and full of paintings I'd never even seen before. [6]For the whole time I was in Paris, I tried to find a good baseball game to watch, or even football highlights from last season. [7]I never did have any luck. [8]Next, I can't understand what the big deal is with the food. [9]I kept hearing that French food was great, but did I ever find one good French fry? [10]I never did. [11]In fact, even though I looked everywhere, I couldn't find one "Denny's." [12]I looked high and low for some plain old American food, but all I found was stuff with fancy French names. [13]That brings me to another reason Paris is no great vacation for me: the language. [14]Hardly anyone speaks English at all! [15]When I asked a lady for directions, she pretended she didn't understand me. [16]Last but not least, Paris isn't very pretty. [17]Sure, you can look at the view from the Eiffel Tower or take a cruise down the Seine River, but there are towers and rivers everywhere. [18]I just don't understand why Paris is supposed to be so special.

Topic sentence: Why anyone would want to go to Paris is a mystery to me.

Support point 1:   Paris is boring.

Specific details that make support point 1 clear:

Only museums and old buildings to see

No baseball or football to watch

Support point 2:   The food is not good.

Specific details that make support point 2 clear:

No french fries

No Denny's. No plain old American food

Support point 3:   The language is a problem.

Specific details that make support point 3 clear:

People don't speak English.

A woman didn't understand when the writer asked for directions.

Support point 4:   Paris isn't very pretty.

Specific details that make support point 4 clear:

Views from the Eiffel Tower and Seine River are just like views anywhere.

Recognizing Correct Writing

Correct writing tells your readers that you take yourself seriously and that you care about your work. In correct writing, sentences are free of errors in grammar, punctuation, and spelling.

Read the paragraphs below. Then decide which one communicates correctly. Why?

Mapping It All Out: Draft

[1]While the first map was etched on a clay tablet in the third millennium B.C.E. [2]Maps today they are drawn on paper. [3]In drawing the maps, mapmakers—called cartographers—have alot to consider. [4]First, since the earth is round and paper is flat, cartographers cant make a map that looks exactly like the earth. [5]Instead, they must think about what's called projection, or the ways there maps will differ from the earth's real shape. [6]Maybe the continents will be the right shape but the wrong size, or maybe they'll be the right size but the wrong shape, for instance these are some kinds of differences that mapmakers must show. [7]Second, cartographers deciding what kind of map to make. [8]For instance, they can make political maps which show cultural details such as the outlines of countries states and cities. [9]Showing natural features such as mountains, rivers, and oceans, cartographers can also make physical maps. [10]A road map show highways and intersections as well as tourist attractions, while

a thematic map shows information according to a theme such as population, economy, or religion. [11]Many maps are combinations of themes. [12]Who would have thought that a bunch of colored lines could be so meaningful?

Mapping It All Out: Final Version

[1]While the first map was etched on a clay tablet in the third millennium B.C.E., maps today are drawn on paper. [2]In drawing the maps, mapmakers—called cartographers—have a lot to consider. [3]First, since the earth is round and paper is flat, cartographers can't make a map that looks exactly like the earth. [4]Instead, they must think about what's called projection, or the ways their maps will differ from the earth's real shape. [5]Maybe the continents will be the right shape but the wrong size, or maybe they'll be the right size but the wrong shape, for instance; these are some kinds of differences that mapmakers must show. [6]Second, cartographers must decide what kind of map to make. [7]For instance, they can make political maps, which show cultural details such as the outlines of countries, states, and cities. [8]Cartographers can also make physical maps, which show natural features such as mountains, rivers, and oceans. [9]A road map shows highways and intersections as well as tourist attractions, while a thematic map shows information according to a theme such as population, economy, or religion. [10]Many maps are combinations of themes. [11]Who would have thought that a bunch of colored lines could be so meaningful?

The final version of "Mapping It All Out" is *correct*. It has no grammatical errors. Therefore, it is more convincing. Even if you're not sure what errors are in the final version of "Mapping It All Out," do the following: Read over both paragraphs. Put a check mark next to or underline the sections where the draft of the paragraph differs from the final version. Then do the following exercise.

EXERCISE 10 CORRECT WRITING

Identify the types of errors in the numbered word groups in the draft paragraph of "Mapping It All Out." Circle the letter next to the type of error you see in each group of words. *Note:* Don't worry if you're unable to answer these questions. By the end of the term, you'll be answering these questions will ease.

1. In item 1, the type of error is

   a. Run-on sentence

   b. Spelling error

   c. Sentence fragment

   d. Pronoun error

2. In item 2, the type of error is

   a. Run-on sentence

   b. Nonstandard English

   c. Sentence fragment

   d. Verb tense error

3. In item 3, the type of error is

   a. Run-on sentence

   b. Pronoun error

   c. Sentence fragment

   d. Spelling error

4. In item 4, the type of error is

   a. No error. This section is correct.

   b. Apostrophe error

   c. Misplaced modifier

   d. Pronoun error

5. In item 5, the type of error is

   a. Run-on sentence

   b. Verb form error

   c. Word choice error

   d. Dangling modifier

6. In item 6, the type of error is

   a. Verb form error

b. Apostrophe error

c. Sentence fragment

d. Run-on sentence

7. In item 7, the type of error is

   a. Missing comma

   b. Sentence fragment

   c. Verb form error

   d. Subject-verb agreement error

8. In item 8, the type of error is

   a. Missing comma

   b. Sentence fragment

   c. Misplaced modifier

   d. Run-on sentence

9. In item 9, the type of error is

   a. Misplaced modifier

   b. Pronoun error

   c. Run-on sentence

   d. Apostrophe error

10. In item 10, the type of error is

   a. Sentence fragment

   b. Spelling error

   c. Pronoun error

   d. Subject-verb agreement error

You should have chosen the following answers.

1. c	**6.** d
2. b	**7.** c
3. d	**8.** a
4. b	**9.** a
5. c	**10.** d

In Your Own Writing

To write correctly, you must do the following:

1. Review sentence skills to avoid making errors.

2. Proofread (Chapter 7) to find and correct mistakes.

For a review of sentence-level writing, refer to Part 7, "Writing Correct Sentences" (Chapters 33–53).

Making Sure Your Writing Is Correct

Ask yourself the following questions to determine whether your paragraphs are correct.

1. Have I reviewed guidelines for grammar, punctuation, and spelling (Chapters 33–53)?

2. Have I proofread to find and correct errors (Chapter 7)?

Identifying the Four Cs Together

Understanding how each of the four Cs works by itself is important, and you have already had a lot of practice doing this. The next step is for you to practice identifying each of the four Cs as they appear together. The best writing integrates all four key elements into a unified paragraph.

EXERCISE 11 IDENTIFYING EACH ELEMENT OF GOOD WRITING

Read the following paragraphs. Underline the topic sentences, and then circle the answers that best describe each paragraph.

A.   **Preparing for the Sahara**

^{1}If you ever need to go to the Sahara—a huge desert located in northern Africa—you had better take steps to make sure you're prepared. ^{2}Most importantly, bring water. ^{3}It doesn't matter if you carry water in plastic or metal bottles; just be sure the bottles are tough. ^{4}You should also bring water purification tablets in case the water you drink hasn't been chemically treated. ^{5}One tip for desert survival is having the right clothing. ^{6}Though the Sahara can get extremely hot, you'll want to stay covered up. ^{7}Bring loose-fitting, long-sleeved shirts and long pants. [8]If too much skin is exposed, you'll get a brutal sunburn, and you might even get sun poisoning. [9]In addition, windblown sand can become stuck to your body if you're not covered well (and probably even if you are). [10]Finally, care for your face, especially your eyes. [11]You should bring at least two pairs of sunglasses with ultraviolet protection, along with sunscreen for your face and lips. [12]Another solid piece of advice is to have good maps and guides. [13]The Sahara covers approximately 3.5 million square miles, so even if you're familiar with desert terrain, it's best to take along someone who knows the area.

1. The topic sentence is sentence ____1____.

2. Circle the letters of all the answers that apply to the paragraph above. This paragraph is

(a.) Concise

(b.) Credible

c. Clear

(d.) Correct

3. Choose Answer a or b below. If you choose Answer b, write one of the four Cs in the blank below.

a. This paragraph is fine.

(b.) This paragraph would be more effective if it were more _clear._

B.

A Meal of Geography

[1]Geography has had a major impact on the names of food. [2]First of all, Germany has contributed the Berliner doughnut, a jelly-filled yeast doughnut named for the city of Berlin, and the Bismarck doughnut, an elongated doughnut filled with custard. [3]Sometimes a Berliner is called a Bismarck, too, which is the name of a famous German leader. [4]Two names for the same doughnut is pretty confusing! [5]My uncle Jerry often went by Jed, and that was very confusing. [6]Frankfurters, commonly called hot dogs, get their name from the German city of Frankfurt. [7]I love hot dogs with lots of mustard and pickle relish. [8]France has played a role in naming food, too. [9]Vichyssoise, a fancy name for cold potato soup, gets its name from the French city of Vichy. [10]Supposedly, cooks should use Vichy water, which comes from springs around the city of Vichy, when making the soup. [11]I can't understand how water that comes in bot-

tles is supposed to be better than tap water. [12]Champagne, the sparkling wine, gets its name from the French province of Champagne, where the wine is made. [13]Cities in the United States have contributed names to food as well. [14]Boston brown bread (a sweet, moist bread that comes in a can) gets its name from a geographical source. [15]Philadelphia gave us the Philly cheese steak, and New York provided the name for the New York–style cheesecake. [16]All in all, I think I eat much better thanks to geography.

1. The topic sentence is sentence _____1____

2. Circle all the answers that apply to the paragraph above. This paragraph is

   a. Concise

   b. Credible

   c. Clear

   d. Correct

3. Choose Answer a or b below. If you choose Answer b, write one of the four Cs in the blank.

a. This paragraph is fine.

b. This paragraph would be more effective if it were more __concise__

C.   **Floating in the Dead Sea**

    [1]Floating in the Dead Sea, the salt lake on the border between Israel and Jordan, is an unusual experience. [2]First, the Dead Sea doesn't look like a typical sea. [3]Next, the areas around the sea look different from usual vacation resorts. [4]Third, regular swimming in the Dead Sea is impossible. [5]The buoyancy of the salt water makes diving under water almost impossible; you just pop back up to the surface like a cork. [6]Also, the water of the Dead Sea can make you very sick. [7]Finally, the name Dead Sea makes the place seem like a punishment rather than a vacation spot.

1. The topic sentence is sentence _____1____.

2. Circle all the answers that apply to the paragraph above. This paragraph is

   a. Concise

b. Credible

c. Clear

d. Correct

3. Choose Answer a or b below. If you choose Answer b, write one of the four Cs in the blank.

a. This paragraph is fine.

b. This paragraph would be more effective if it were more <u>credible</u>.

D.   **On the Road Again**

^{1}Streets, roads, and highways are extremely important, no matter where you are in the world. ^{2}For example, in Germany, taking the autobahn is crucial if you want make good time getting around, people zip by with their horns blaring and their lights flashing if you going too slowly, you'd better get out of the way! ^{3}On the other hand, in paris, France, the most famous street has a slower pace. ^{5}The Champs Elysées, which means "Elysian Fields," or paradise, is known for its elegant shops and cafés and is a key tourist spot. ^{6}In addition, Khao San Road in Bangkok, Thailand, is not very pretty or very long. ^{7}However, it important because it gives backpackers an affordable place to stay and get used to Asia before they travel further. ^{8}Last but not least, Wenceslas Square in Prague, Czechoslovakia, is long and thin. ^{9}Even though its' name says it's square. ^{10}It slopes gently uphill from the streets that form the boundary of the old town and is a main road in the Czech Republic.

1. The topic sentence is sentence ___1___.

2. Circle the letters of all the answers that apply to the paragraph above. This paragraph is

a. Concise

b. Credible

c. Clear

d. Correct

3. Choose Answer a or b below. If you choose Answer b, write one of the four Cs in the blank.

a. This paragraph is fine.

b. This paragraph would be more effective if it were more <u>correct</u>.

What You Know Now

You've learned that good writing is concise, credible, clear, and correct. You also know that support points can be given in chronological (time sequence) order or in emphatic order (from least to most important). Transition words introduce support points and make their order clear. Now you get the chance to put this knowledge to work in your own writing.

WRITING PRACTICE   Write Your Own Paragraph

In this chapter you were introduced to different places around the world and to some ideas about world geography. Your assignment is this: *Using the information on world geography that you learned in this chapter, write a paragraph on a place you would like to visit.* The place you choose can be somewhere you've heard about on the news or from a friend, or it can be a place you've read about in this chapter. Just be sure to explain why this place is somewhere you'd like to go.

Remember to do the following:

- Write your main idea in your topic sentence.
- Give support points for your topic sentence.
- Put your support points in chronological or emphatic order.
- Introduce your support points with transition words or terms.
- Offer specific examples for your support points.

Write your paragraph on a separate piece of paper.

Lab Activity 2

For additional practice with concise, credible, and clear writing, complete Lab Activity 2 in the Lab Manual at the back of this book.

3 Writing for a Reader and a Reason

Songs that lull us to sleep, lullabies have long been important pieces of music for parents. Though they are generally soothing and slow in tempo, some lullabies have a wider range of expression.

Writing for a Reader

Every time you write something, you're writing for *somebody*. Recognizing the person you're writing for, or your **audience,** is essential to making sure you get your point across.

Think about the situations described below. Then, write down the type of music you think would be most appropriate in each situation.

You're trying to fall asleep. _____

_____

You're celebrating the end of finals week with your friends. _____

_____

You're preparing a romantic dinner for two. _____

_____

Probably you chose different music for each situation. If you played the romantic music for the celebrating friends or if you played the celebration music while trying to fall asleep, would you get the results you wanted? What did you consider when you chose the music for each situation? In writing, as in music, your message needs to match your audience, or you won't have much success getting your point across.

✔CHECKLIST Identifying Your Audience

Ask yourself the following questions to identify your audience.

- Who will read the document I am writing? My instructor? My friend? My supervisor at work?
- How can I best appeal to my audience?
- What does my audience need to know?

EXERCISE 1 IDENTIFYING THE AUDIENCE

Read the following paragraphs. Then, choose the response that you think best describes the probable audience.

A.   **Songs for Sanity**

Lullabies have many benefits. First, they calm children. One famous saying goes "Music hath charms to soothe a savage breast," which means that music can calm wild people or beasts. Lullabies, thank goodness, get kids to stop their howling. Second, lullabies calm the people singing them. Parents of the selfish little beasts often have been robbed of their precious sleep by the children's constant noise. Understandably, these parents have frayed nerves. Lullabies are easy to listen to and repetitive, so the parents have a chance to calm down, too. Lullabies give the adults in kids' lives a little hope of staying in control.

This paragraph would be most convincing to someone who

    a. Likes children.

    b. Dislikes children.

    c. Fears children.

B.   **Worthless Lullabies**

Lullabies are a complete waste of time. First, they're good only if you want to fall asleep, and with so many things to do, who has time for sleep? If you're out on the town trying to have a little fun, you're not going to be listening to lullabies. Another reason lullabies are a waste is that they're so boring. The same melody is played over and over; there's nothing new and exciting about listening to a lullaby. Last of all, lullabies are uncool. I mean, who would be caught listening to a lullaby, especially on a Friday night? Only people who want to waste time and miss the real action listen to lullabies.

This paragraph would be most convincing to someone who

    a. Likes to go out.

    b. Goes to bed early.

    c. Never goes out.

The paragraphs in Exercise 1 are based on the same subject matter, lullabies, but the messages are very different. Your own writing changes, too, depending on who your audience is. When you write for your instructor, your most common audience, you will probably pay more attention to writing with a topic sentence, specific details, and a clear organizational plan. When you write for your friends, however, you can get away with being more casual. You don't worry about getting a grade for your notes or e-mail messages to friends. Knowing your audience when you write helps you choose the best way to make your point.

Johannes Brahms

SURF THE NET

Known for his often forbidding personality as well as his gifted composing, Brahms made his lullaby familiar to many. What else can you learn about Brahms? Visit biography.com or perform a search on google.com to learn more about Johannes Brahms or lullabies.

Writing for a Reason

In choosing music for the situations earlier in the chapter, you considered two things. First, you thought about your audience. Second, you thought about your goal, what you wanted to accomplish. Your goal might have been to put the baby to sleep, have fun with your friends, get to know someone better.

In your writing class, your **purpose,** why you are writing, will usually be to convince your reader that what you say is worthwhile. Your purpose will often fall under one of three headings:

- To inform
- To entertain
- To persuade

CHECKLIST Identifying Your Purpose

Ask yourself the following questions to identify your purpose.

- Do I want to inform, entertain, or persuade?
- Do I want to present information or explain a situation (inform)?
- Do I want to get a certain reaction (entertain)?
- Do I want to give an opinion or suggest a course of action (persuade)?

Writing to Inform

When you write to **inform,** your purpose is to present information clearly and accurately. You will list causes and effects, define unfamiliar terms, and provide facts that make your point clear. For instance, if you are writing to your new doctor to tell her about your current health, you would emphasize details that describe your health. You could make jokes or use slang in your letter, but these would not help your new doctor understand your overall level of health. Thus, it would be more effective simply to inform her of the facts.

EXERCISE 2 WRITING TO INFORM

Imagine that you are writing a letter to a person who is older than you and whom you respect. The subject of your letter is your home. Make a list of the details that would best inform that person of what your home is like.

> Answers will vary. Possible responses: Small rooms, cozy
>
> kitchen with calico curtains, lots of windows, big bathtub,
>
> chipped sink.

Writing to Entertain

When you write to **entertain,** you want to elicit a certain reaction from your reader: laughter, anger, surprise, or fascination, for example. Your job, then, is to include details that lead your reader to *want* to read on. While writing to inform requires that you include just the facts, writing to entertain demands that you focus on the unusual, the trivial, and the unexpected elements of a situation.

For instance, suppose you are writing to your old roommate about how terrible your day was. You might emphasize the little details that all added up to make your day bad. If you were writing to inform, you might simply write that you spilled food on your clothes, but to entertain, you would exaggerate the ridiculousness of your day. Being specific and personal is more likely to be entertaining than giving a dry list of the events of your day.

EXERCISE 3 WRITING TO ENTERTAIN

Write a letter to someone you know very well. The subject of your letter is an unusual person or place you know. Keeping in mind that you want to entertain your reader, make a list of the details describing that person or place.

> Answers will vary. Possible responses: Baggy pants, messy hair, glasses keep
>
> falling off, crooked smile, socks never match, always wears "Hello Kitty"
>
> backpack.

Writing to Persuade

When you write to **persuade,** you write to convince someone to accept your point of view. Writing to persuade, then, requires that you include details that appeal to emotion, reason, or both.

For instance, if you are trying to convince your parents to lend you money, you can use emotion to appeal to their sense of being good, caring parents who can help their troubled, loving child. You can also use reason to convince your parents that you are a trustworthy, hardworking person who looks upon their loan only as a temporary means of gaining money. Either way, you want to include details that will most likely convince your reader to think as you do.

EXERCISE 4 WRITING TO PERSUADE

Write a letter to an instructor. The subject of your letter is your current grade. Include details that will best convince your teacher to give you a higher grade.

<u>Answers will vary. Possible responses: Excellent attendance, hard work on</u>

<u>homework assignments, out-of-class visits to instructor for extra help,</u>

<u>improvement in many areas of the class.</u>

In your academic writing, your purpose will usually be to persuade your audience of your main idea. For that reason, most of the sample writing in this book is persuasive writing. An effective topic sentence tells your reader whether your purpose is to inform, entertain, or persuade.

What You Know Now

Before you write, decide on your audience and your purpose. Your audience consists of the people who will read your writing. Your purpose will be to inform, to entertain, or to persuade. Most academic writing is persuasive.

WRITING PRACTICE   Write a Letter for Change

You and your roommate live in a basement apartment. Your upstairs neighbor left the faucet on too long and flooded the apartment above yours.

Unfortunately, water leaked through the floor and ruined your ceiling, wall-paper, and linoleum. Your lease says that in situations like this, all tenants must share the repair costs with the landlord. Thus, you and your roommate, your neighbor, and the landlord are equally responsible for fixing the damage.

Your assignment is this: On a separate piece of paper, *write a letter about your apartment situation.*

1. Choose your *audience* from the following list.

   Your upstairs neighbor

   Your landlord

   Your roommate

2. Decide your *purpose*, what you want your letter to accomplish: *inform* the reader of the cost and extent of the damage, or *persuade* the reader to pay his or her share of the costs.

3. If you want to *inform* your reader of the damage, begin with a topic sentence like this: "The water damage in my apartment is extensive and costly." Then include support points and specific details that show your reader the extent of the water damage and the costliness of repairs. Some possible details are puddles in the kitchen, ruined wallpaper, and sagging ceiling.

   If you want to *persuade* your reader to share the costs, begin with a topic sentence like this: "As part of a residential community, we all should share the costs of damage caused by the recent flooding." Then include support points and specific details that show your reader why sharing costs is important. Here are some possible support points: you and your neighbors are like a family; all of your homes are affected by the damage; next time, the water damage could be in someone else's apartment.

4. When you finish, share your paragraph with your classmates and discuss the types of details you included in order to make your point.

   Remember to do the following:

   ■ Identify your audience through the greeting in your letter (Dear _____,).

   ■ Write your main idea in your topic sentence.

   ■ Make sure your purpose is clear in your topic sentence.

   ■ Give support points for your topic sentence.

   ■ Offer specific details for your support points.

Lab Activity 3

For additional practice with audience and purpose, complete Lab Activity 3 in the Lab Manual at the back of the book.

PART TWO
The Writing Process

4 Prewriting: Coming Up With Ideas

  The Roaring Twenties

Fueled with enthusiasm after helping to win World War I, Americans wanted to have fun. They experimented with new forms of music, danced new dances, and wore new fashions. Business boomed as well-employed Americans spent their money in search of entertainment and comfortable lives. Finally, major political change occurred. Women gained the right to vote, and the right to drink alcohol became a constitutional issue.

Getting Started

Writer's block can happen when writers feel pressured to produce a "perfect" first draft or feel that they have nothing to say. As you follow the writing process, you will learn many techniques to help you come up with good ideas to write about. Here are some strategies to help you with **prewriting,** the first step in the writing process.

- Freewriting
- Listing
- Questioning

- Keeping a journal
- Clustering
- Outlining

Look at the diagram on page 54 to see how prewriting strategies fit into the writing process. As you read about these techniques, think about how well they might work for you. Then, as you complete the exercises in this chapter, pay attention to what prewriting strategies actually do work best for you.

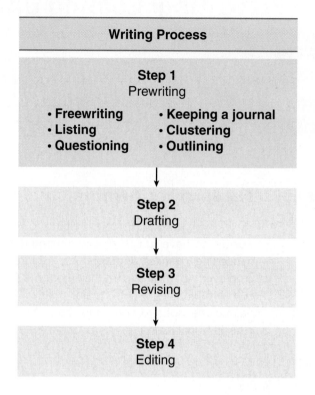

Freewriting

The easiest way to get started is simply to start writing, even if you feel you have nothing to say. This technique of "dumping" anything in your brain onto the paper is called **freewriting.** In freewriting you write as much as you can, as fast as you can, without stopping. Essentially, freewriting removes the factors that cause stress while you're writing. When you freewrite, you don't worry about organization, correctness, or connections between the ideas.

TIPS for Freewriting

1. Using a computer or a pen and paper, write the first word that comes into your head, and keep going.
2. If you get stuck, just keep writing the same word or group of words until something else comes to mind.
3. Don't go back to fix mistakes. Not everything you write will end up in your draft.

1920s Flapper

CRITICAL THINKING Women became active in religion and politics during the 1920s. Write a few sentences explaining how a group you know about has taken action. (Your group may be local, such as a neighborhood association, or it may be national, such as the Susan G. Komen Breast Cancer Foundation.)

Below is some freewriting by a student writer, Frida, on the topic "The Roaring Twenties." Notice that Frida's freewriting contains some grammar and spelling errors. Also, Frida writes that she is not sure about a lot of the details.

Why do we have to write on this topic? I don't no anything about the roaring twenties except that women were called flapers. Don't even know what that means, and I'm not even sure if all women were called that or just the ones who wore those funny dresses with fringe on them. I think that the roaring twenties had a lot of gangsters, too, but not the kind we have today. More like the Al Capone mobster type, and they blew things up and made people pay them for protection even though the protection was from them, I think. Man, what else? What else? What else? My mind's blank. I think my grandpa said that the twenties was a time of prohibition, but I'm not even sure what was prohibited.

Freewriting serves to give you a starting place. The point is just to get everything onto paper. Freewriting helps you generate ideas that you can redefine or develop later in your writing process. Additionally, you can note any interesting details that come to mind without forcing them to fit into a larger idea somewhere.

EXERCISE 1 FREEWRITING

On your own paper, freewrite for five minutes about a time in your life when a lot of changes occurred. Remember: Write as fast as you can without stopping, and don't worry about making mistakes.

Listing

Sometimes freewriting can leave you with what seems like a mass of words that don't make sense. If freewriting doesn't work for a particular paragraph, another type of prewriting can help. **Listing** allows you the freedom of freewriting without the sense of disorganization. Simply write down everything you know about a topic, but do this in list form rather than paragraph form.

TIPS for Listing

1. On paper or on a computer, write the first word that comes into your head, and keep writing.
2. Include everything that comes to mind, even if you have no idea how it will fit with any other ideas on your list.
3. Don't go back to correct mistakes.

Below is a list that another writer, George, developed on the topic "The Roaring Twenties."

The Roaring Twenties	Major crime
Flappers	Al Capone
Women's changes	Gambling
Getting the vote	Prostitution

Prohibition   Jazz Age

Bootlegging

In this list, George has concentrated on gathering as many ideas and details as possible on his topic. Later he will sort through his list to start developing his paragraph.

EXERCISE 2 LISTING

On a separate piece of paper, make a list about a time when you had to make a big decision.

Questioning

Sometimes the best place to start is with the information you *don't* have. Many times writers are unable to organize their ideas because they don't have enough specific details to use in their writing. A helpful strategy here is a technique called **questioning.** Asking and answering questions using a **T-chart** can help you identify areas where you need more information. Questioning can also help you organize the information you do have.

TIPS for Questioning

1. Divide the page vertically, with a line down the center, or use the Columns or Table feature on your computer.

2. In the left-hand column, write every question that comes to mind about your topic.

3. In the right-hand column, write any answers you have to the questions you've written on the left.

4. When you can't think of any more questions or answers, look at your chart to see what areas you have details for and what areas are lacking details.

Soua was not sure how much information she had for her paragraph on the Roaring Twenties. She did some questioning to examine her ideas.

The Roaring Twenties

Questions	Answers
What was Prohibition?	Made alcohol production and drinking illegal.
How did Prohibition start?	Religious movement, then political.
What effects did Prohibition have?	18th Amendment passed to prohibit alcohol; 21st Amendment repealed 18th Amendment.
Why did crime increase?	Al Capone and other mobsters sold illegal alcohol, ran gambling and prostitution rings.
What changes did women experience?	Gained vote through suffrage movement (Susan B. Anthony). Dressed against convention (short hair and skirts, no corsets). Acted against convention (smoked and drank in public, ran for office).
Why were the 1920s "roaring"?	Business boomed. People had jobs in factories. People invested in stock market.

In this T-chart, Soua has asked key questions that she needs to answer to write a detailed paragraph on the Roaring Twenties. At first, she had little information under the "Answers" heading. Through reading and research, she was able to find the answers to the questions she asked.

EXERCISE 3 QUESTIONING

On your own paper, make a T-chart, writing questions in the left-hand column about the best or worst birthday you ever had. Put your answers in the right-hand column.

Keeping a Journal

The best way to improve your writing skills is to write as often as possible. Keeping a **journal**—an informal record of thoughts or ideas—is like freewriting a little bit every day. Although keeping a journal may not seem like a formal prewriting strategy, it can help you work through your ideas.

Your journal should be what *you* want it to be. Some writers use a special notebook that serves as their journal. Others use a computer to record their thoughts. The main point is to do some writing every day.

In your journal you can write ideas when they come to you. You can also ask yourself questions about topics you want to research. That way, you'll also be practicing your questioning strategy. In your journal you can even practice writing different versions of the same sentence. The more you write, the more confident you'll become.

TIPS for Keeping a Journal

1. Keep a specific notebook, folder, or computer file as your journal, and write all your entries there.
2. Write in your journal at the same time, for the same amount of time, every day.
3. Keep your journal with you if possible so you can also write ideas as they come to you.
4. Write everything that comes to mind and don't worry about making mistakes.
5. Keep all your journal entries so that you can see your progress.

Here are entries from the journal of a writer named Adam.

Monday. My instructor says I still have to write on a time called the roaring twenties even though I don't know much about it. I guess I can look it up at the library or on the Internet. In the meantime, I did learn that Prohibition made drinking alcohol illegal, but that many people still drank anyway. I also learned that only some women were flappers, but I still don't know why they were called that. I can't figure out why I have to write about something that happened eighty years ago. Maybe learning about the twenties will help me in history.

Wednesday. I still need help on this twenties paragraph, but Brad showed me how to do some searching on the Internet. Back to Prohibition, it started in the late 1800s. This preacher, William (Billy) Sunday, who used to be a pro baseball player (cool!), preached in favor of Prohibition, and the antidrinking idea caught on. In fact, there was even a constitutional amendment (the 18th) that made Prohibition legal, but it didn't last long. It became an amendment in 1919 but was repealed in 1933. That's all I've learned so far, but at least I've done something!

Friday. I've written a draft of my roaring twenties paragraph, but I don't like it. And I'm stuck again. I want to learn more about Al Capone, but all I can find is how bad he was. Not only was he a bootlegger (he made and sold alcohol illegally), but he also ran prostitution rings. He also ran gambling operations and made a name for himself by being really violent. I'll work on women's rights on Monday. Nothing else to write now.

These entries show how Adam used his journal to write about both his concerns and his progress. We learn that he is worried about not having enough information for his assignment, but these worries motivate him to gain more information.

EXERCISE 4 KEEPING A JOURNAL

Set up a journal. For one full week, write for five minutes a day about whatever comes to mind. Here are some sample topics.

- Your experiences at school, at work, or at home
- Your view of current events in the world
- Your view of what's happening in your personal relationships
- Your ideas on a subject you're studying

Clustering

Another prewriting technique is **clustering,** also called **diagramming** or **mapping.** Clustering helps you organize your ideas visually and offers more structure than freewriting. It also helps you see what ideas might be off-topic when you are ready to write your draft.

TIPS for Clustering

1. Write your main idea in the center of a piece of paper.

2. Write supporting ideas around your main idea. You may want to circle your main and supporting ideas.

3. Use arrows to make connections between ideas. If all the arrows point from the same idea, that idea should probably be in your topic sentence. If no arrows point to an idea, you will probably want to omit it.

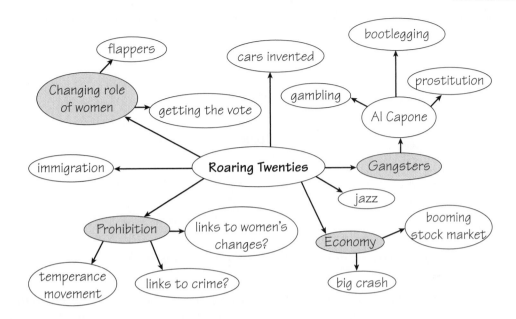

Martina made a cluster diagram around the topic "The Roaring Twenties." From her diagram, Martina can see that she knows a lot about some aspects of the Roaring Twenties. However, she has also written down ideas—cars, jazz, and immigration—about which she doesn't seem to have much information. She'd do better focusing on the topics she does have information about: Prohibition, gangsters, the economy, and the changing role of women.

EXERCISE 5 CLUSTERING

Make a cluster diagram on the topic "How Students Disrupt Classes." Use the space provided on page 62. Concentrate on clarifying connections between your ideas by using arrows and circles.

Outlining

Possibly the most helpful prewriting tool is outlining. **Outlining** is an effective means of organizing your ideas without actually writing sentences. Outlining also helps you see any gaps in your support because an outline is a

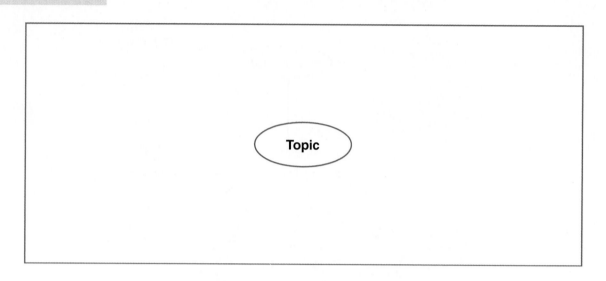

list that organizes your whole paragraph on paper before you begin to write. In general, to outline, begin with your main idea and then add supporting points and specific details.

TIPS for Outlining

1. Write your main idea, even your topic sentence, at the top of the page.

2. Write the letter *A* beneath your main idea, and write your first support point next to the letter *A*.

3. Write the number *1* under your first support point, and add a specific detail—if you have one—to support your first point.

4. Add more support points and details.

5. When you have added all the information you know, read your outline to see which points lack specific details. These are the points that you will need to either research or omit when you write your draft.

Note: Your instructor may want you to use Roman numerals (I, II, III, etc.) for your support points and letters for your details, which follows the traditional outline format.

Minh did an outline for the topic "The Roaring Twenties" before she began her paragraph.

I The Roaring Twenties

  A. Prohibition

    1. Temperance movement

       2. Religious revival

       3. Passage of 18th and 21st Amendments

    B. Gangsters

       1. Bootlegging

       2. Gambling

       3. Prostitution

       4. Violence

       5. Al Capone

    C. Women's changing roles

       1. Getting the vote

       2. Flappers

       3. Running for office

Minh's outline is based on information she knew and material she researched. An effective outline presents all your information in a clear, organized pattern, one that you can easily turn into a paragraph.

EXERCISE 6 OUTLINING

Write an outline of all the prewriting techniques covered in this chapter. Let the headings in the chapter—such as "Freewriting" and "Outlining"— serve as the headings for your outline. Refer to the tips boxes for each technique in this chapter to gather specific details for your outline. Some of the outline has already been filled in for you. *Hint*: There may be more than two details for each prewriting technique. Your job is to decide how many to include in your outline and in what order to place them.

Prewriting Techniques

A. Freewriting

   1. Write without stopping. _____

   2. Don't worry about mistakes. _____

B. Listing

   1. Writing ideas in a list. _____

   2. More structure than freewriting. _____

C. Questioning

   1. Lets you see what information you don't have.

   2. T-chart works well.

D. Keeping a journal

   1. Like freewriting: do a little every day.

   2. Helps you remember ideas. Helps you practice writing ideas on paper.

E. Clustering

   1. Visual way to organize ideas.

   2. More structure than freewriting.

   3. Helps you see off-topic ideas.

F. Outlining

   1. Organize ideas without writing sentences.

   2. Lets you see gaps in support.

   3. Usually start with main point, move on to support points.

EXERCISE 7 OUTLINING FOR A PARAGRAPH

On your own paper, make an outline of the steps you follow to get ready for work or school. Work on your outline for five to ten minutes. Focus on adding specific details and on organizing your ideas.

Using a Computer for Prewriting

If you're a fast typist, a computer is great for prewriting. Just follow these guidelines. For general information on writing with a computer, see "Tips for Using a Computer" on page 77 in Chapter 5.

- Type as fast as you can to record every idea that enters your head.
- Don't stop to correct sentence-level errors.
- Try **invisible writing:** turn off the computer monitor (screen) and just type. Once you're off to a good start, turn the monitor back on.
- Turn your freewriting into a list, a question-and-answer chart, or an outline by pressing Enter to start a new line.
- Use your prewriting file when you're ready for drafting (Step 2 in the writing process).

A computer can also help you keep a journal.

- Create a file for each month. When you write in your journal, date each entry.
- Name your files so that they appear in chronological order in the directory menu: Journal 0206 (for February 2006) or Journal 1006 (for October 2006). That way, it will be easy to find specific files.

EXERCISE 8 USING PREWRITING TECHNIQUES

Use these prewriting techniques to develop and organize ideas on one of the following topics. On a separate piece of paper, start by *freewriting* for a few minutes. Then do *listing, questioning,* and *clustering.* Finally, make an *outline* of your ideas. At the end of this exercise, you should have an idea of what techniques work well for you.

Topics

Tips for car maintenance

Reasons to stay in school

Tips for going backpacking

Different ways to meet members of the opposite sex

Ways to save money

Factors to consider in choosing college classes

Reasons to learn a musical instrument

Answers will vary.

EXERCISE 9 **CLUSTERING AND OUTLINING**

Now you can use the clustering and outlining techniques to organize ideas and details that support a topic. Use your own paper to make a cluster diagram and outline for Topics A and B.

> **A.** Topic: Different ways to insult someone
>
> **B.** Topic: How easy it is to show affection for someone you like

EXERCISE 10 **COMBINING STRATEGIES**

Below is a topic followed by a list of ideas to support it. In the outline that follows, the major ideas (A, B, C) have been filled in. Choose the minor ideas from the rest of the list to complete the outline. *Hint:* Check off each item on the list as you write it in the outline. Answers will vary.

Topic: Women's changing roles in the 1920s

A.   Gained political power.

    1. Gained right to vote.

    2. Ran for office.

B.   Broke from convention in fashion.

    1. Wore short skirts.

    2. Refused to wear corsets.

    3. Cut hair short.

C.   Acted more independent.

    1. Smoked in public.

    2. Drank in public.

    3. Acted bolder, less shy.

Ideas

Gained right to vote.	Cut hair short.
Smoked in public.	Acted bolder, less shy.
Wore short skirts.	Refused to wear corsets.
Ran for office.	✓ Acted more independent.
✓ Broke from convention in fashion.	✓ Gained political power.
Drank in public.	

EXERCISE 11 OUTLINING A PARAGRAPH

1. Read the paragraph below.

2. Identify the topic sentence and write it in the space provided.

3. Reread the paragraph and underline each support point. Check the outline that follows to see if you have correctly identified the support points (A, B, C).

4. Write the sentences containing the specific details for each support point in the spaces provided.

Hint: The purpose of this exercise is to show you how effective paragraphs are developed from good outlines.

The Many Faces of Jazz

Early jazz music (before 1960) has many different forms. The first form of jazz, called Dixieland jazz, is named for its origins in the South. Dixieland jazz often has no written music, but it does have a clear melody played on a horn and a strong beat played on the drums. One of the most famous Dixieland jazz bands was King Oliver's Creole Jazz Band, which included the famous Louis Armstrong, who played cornet. Another form of jazz music is known as swing music. Swing featured call-and-response playing, a lot of improvisation, and no written music. Duke Ellington, though, was an exception to the no-written-music rule because he wrote down the swing music he composed. A third type of jazz is bebop, or bop. This kind of jazz is a reaction to swing music. While swing music

Louis Armstrong (1901–1971)

FOOD FOR THOUGHT The Roaring Twenties were known for their jazz music, as played by Louis Armstrong. How do you think the early 2000s will be remembered? Write a few sentences explaining how you think the early 2000s will be characterized. Use examples from politics, sports, and entertainment.

was simple, bop was complicated. While swing used big bands, bop focused on smaller groups. Where swing emphasized the melody, bop stressed the beat. The most famous bop musicians were Dizzy Gillespie and Charlie Parker.

Outlining

Topic sentence: Early jazz music (before 1960) has many different forms.

A. The first form of jazz, called Dixieland jazz, is named for its origins in the South.

1. Dixieland jazz often has no written music, but it does have a clear melody played on a horn and a strong beat played on the drums.

2. One of the most famous Dixieland jazz bands was King Oliver's Creole Jazz Band, which included the famous Louis Armstrong, who played cornet.

B. Another form of jazz music is known as swing music.

    1. Swing featured call-and-response playing, a lot of improvisation, and no written music.

    2. Duke Ellington, though, was an exception to the no-written-music rule because he wrote down the swing music he composed.

C. A third type of jazz is bebop or bop.

    1. This kind of jazz is a reaction to swing music.

    2. While swing music was simple, bop was complicated.

    3. While swing used big bands, bop focused on smaller groups.

    4. Where swing emphasized the melody, bop stressed the beat.

    5. The most famous bop musicians were Dizzy Gillespie and Charlie Parker.

What You Know Now

Prewriting, the first step in the writing process, helps you come up with ideas and specific details for your writing. Prewriting techniques are *freewriting, listing, questioning, keeping a journal, clustering,* and *outlining.* You can use just one technique or several together. Practicing prewriting techniques is a good way to find out which techniques work best for you. After you have done some prewriting for a paragraph, you're ready to go on to Step 2 in the writing process, drafting.

WRITING PRACTICE 1 Start Your Own Journal

Your assignment is this: With the details of keeping a journal fresh in your mind, *start your own journal.* Set aside at least five minutes today and write. You may write about academic subjects, or you may write about anything that's on your mind. The point is to begin your habit of keeping a journal today.

WRITING PRACTICE 2 **Write Your Own Paragraph**

You spent the last few pages reading about the 1920s. Now it's your turn to write. Use the information from this chapter or from your own life to help you find specifics. Your assignment is this: *Write a paragraph on either Topic A or Topic B below.*

Topic A: *The 1920s sound like a time in which I would (or would not) have wanted to live.*

The following steps will help you get started.

1. Use one or more of the prewriting techniques to organize your ideas.
2. Write a topic sentence like "I would have liked living in the 1920s for many reasons" or "I would not have liked living in the 1920s for many reasons."
3. Use specific details from this chapter as proof for your support points.

Topic B: *Tell about a time in your life that was particularly good or bad.*

The following steps will help you get started.

1. Use one or more of the prewriting techniques to organize your ideas.
2. Write a topic sentence like "Seventh grade was one of the best (or worst) years of my life."
3. Use specific details from your own life as proof for your support points.

Lab Activity 4

For additional practice with prewriting, complete Lab Activity 4 in the Lab Manual at the back of the book.

5 Drafting: Writing a Rough Draft

CULTURE NOTE *Quilting*

Brought to America in different styles by people from different countries, quilting has found its place among American pastimes. The skill and art of choosing, arranging, and connecting fabric combines creativity with a sense of history. Quilting is celebrated at county and state fairs around the country.

Ready to Put Pen to Paper

Now that you've spent some time prewriting, you're ready to move on to the next step in the writing process—drafting. **Drafting** is no more than writing a rough version of your paragraph. In drafting, you use the information you discovered during prewriting to write sentences that flow together to convey your ideas.

Rough Drafts Are Not Perfect

Some people think that they should be able to crank out a perfect paragraph on the first try, but very few writers work this way. Sometimes writing does come easily, but often it takes time and practice. All that work has a benefit, though: the more you write, the better a writer you will become.

Professional writers agree that writing is important. In his essay "Free-writing," Peter Elbow writes that the way you express yourself on paper is your *voice*.

Maybe you don't like your voice; maybe people have made fun of it. But it's the only voice you've got. It's your only source of power. . . . If

71

you keep writing in it, it may change into something you like better. But if you abandon it, you'll likely never have a voice and never be heard.

In her book *Bird by Bird*, the author Anne Lamott claims that writing just requires getting ideas on paper.

The first draft is the child's draft, where you let it all pour out and then let it romp all over the place, knowing that no one is going to see it and that you can shape it later.

It's important to remember that the rough version, or **rough draft,** of your paragraph will not be perfect or finished.

- *A rough draft is not usually concise.* It may contain too many irrelevant details.
- *A rough draft is not usually credible.* It may not have enough specific details to support its topic sentence.
- *A rough draft is not usually clear*. Its support points may not be organized logically, and it may have few or no transitional words.
- *A rough draft is not usually correct.* It may contain many errors in grammar, punctuation, and spelling.

As you work through the writing process, you'll get the chance to correct the flaws in your draft and make your paragraph more concise, credible, clear, and correct. When writing a rough draft, your goal should simply be to *get your ideas out*. Once they're on paper, you can change them, but you can't revise something you haven't written.

Writing a Rough Draft

When you're ready to start drafting, allow plenty of time. Gather your prewriting materials and notes, and have your writing assignment handy. Then clear your mind of outside worries as best you can, and start writing.

Your Topic Sentence

The key to writing an effective paragraph is having a clear topic sentence. The topic sentence controls the direction of your entire paragraph and represents the most important idea that you want to communicate. If your readers remember nothing else about your paragraph, they should remember your topic sentence.

Keep in mind, though, that your topic sentence may change as you discover more details and find more points that you want to explore. Don't feel locked into a certain idea just because you've already written it down. You can always change your topic sentence if you think of another idea that works better. For more help with writing a topic sentence, see Chapter 9.

After doing some prewriting on the topic of favorite pastimes, Toya decided on the following topic sentence: "Quilting is an enjoyable activity." She then started writing a rough draft. (Notice that Toya's draft contains several sentence-level errors.)

Tip: Students should see errors in all of the sentences except the first.

Quilting is an enjoyable activity. Finding a pattern can be frustrating because their are so many to chose from, and then you need to find fabrics that coordinate with each other. Finding fabric is harder then it seems because the material have to fit in with the concept of the pattern. Cutting out the pieces of fabric for the quilt top isn't hard, but its tedious. Since the fabric can be expensive, you have to be carful not to make mistakes that could require extra material. Sewing the quilt top is exciting, but it can be hard, too, because you have to follow the pattern and sew in strait lines.

After writing these sentences, Toya realized that a number of her ideas didn't directly support the idea that quilting is an enjoyable activity. She decided to change her topic sentence to reflect the challenges of quilting—since many of her ideas focus on them—as well as the enjoyment. Her new topic sentence was "Quilting is a challenging but rewarding activity." The new topic sentence more accurately states the main idea that grew from Toya's writing.

Your Support Points and Specific Details

Your prewriting is the source for support points and details for your paragraph. Once you have a topic sentence, you can identify the most convincing support points and decide on the right order for your paragraph. Using a pencil, underline support points in your prewriting and then number them in chronological or emphatic order. See Chapter 10 for more on choosing support points and specific details, and see Chapter 11 for help with organizing your support points.

Your Rough Draft

Using the work you have done in your prewriting activities, start writing. If you are using a pen, skip every other line to leave space for Step 3 (revising) and Step 4 (editing) in the writing process. If you are using a computer, refer to "Tips for Using a Computer" on page 77.

After changing her topic sentence, Toya wrote another rough draft. This draft uses more specific detail from Toya's prewriting, but it still has sentence-level errors.

Tip: Students should see errors in the second and last three sentences.

Quilting is a challenging but rewarding activity. Finding a pattern can be frustrating because their are so many to chose from, and then you need to find fabrics that coordinate with each other. My first quilt had an easy pattern, called a double Irish chain pattern, and I had seen my mom make this kind of quilt many times before, so I was confident I could do it. However, when I started choosing fabric for my quilt, I could tell that the saleswoman at the fabric store thought my choices were horrible. She kept coming out with others, saying, "Here,

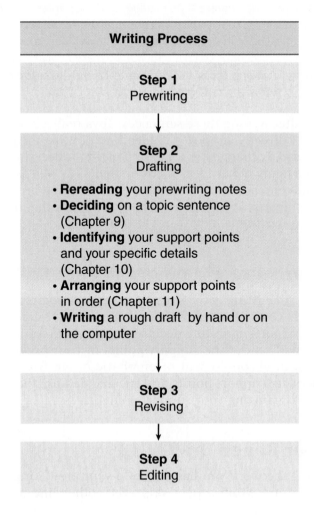

Writing Process

Step 1
Prewriting

↓

Step 2
Drafting

• **Rereading** your prewriting notes
• **Deciding** on a topic sentence
  (Chapter 9)
• **Identifying** your support points
  and your specific details
  (Chapter 10)
• **Arranging** your support points
  in order (Chapter 11)
• **Writing** a rough draft by hand or on
  the computer

↓

Step 3
Revising

↓

Step 4
Editing

dear, wouldn't <u>this</u> look lovely in your quilt?" It was very frustrating, but I eventually chose the materials that <u>I</u> wanted: dark green, black, navy, charcoal, and deep brown. Cutting out the pieces of fabric for the quilt top isn't hard, but its tedious. Since the fabric can be expensive, you have to be carful not to make mistakes that could require extra material. Sewing the quilt top can be hard, too, because you have to follow the pattern and sew in strait lines.

The "Writing Process" diagram shown at the bottom of the preceding page shows how drafting fits into the writing process steps.

EXERCISE 1 REVIEW

Fill in the blanks in the sentences below.

1. Some people believe that writing should be _____ easy _____.

2. The key to writing an effective paragraph is having a

clear _topic sentence_.

3. Staying flexible allows you to change your _topic sentence_ even after you've begun writing your paragraph.

4. *Drafting* means writing more than one _____ version _____ of your paragraph.

5. Be sure to keep all your _____ notes _____ from prewriting to refer to as you write a rough draft.

Using a Computer for Drafting

While you can follow the same steps for any kind of drafting, some specific guidelines for using a computer can make drafting easier.

Computers can help you greatly by letting you see your whole work, typed out, on the screen. Probably the greatest benefit of using a computer is *flexibility*. You can type, move, save, and generally manipulate your information before you ever print out your document.

1. Use your prewriting to try different versions of your topic sentence.

2. If you are using emphatic order, try out your support points in different places in your draft by using the Cut and Paste functions.

Quilters at Work

PLAN AN INTERVIEW Quilting is a form of sewing that has become distinctly American. What kind of art, craft, or skill comes from your heritage? Interview someone in your family about the special skills that have been handed down, or remembered, from earlier generations in your family.

3. Include examples as you write your paragraph. If ideas come to you when you're working on something else, type those examples in a separate file (or even at the end of your draft) and insert them into your paragraph later.

4. Don't delete anything at this point. If you're not sure about a support point or specific detail, move it to the end of your document. Later, when you finish your draft, you can delete it. Until then, you have information that may come in handy at other points in your work.

"Tips for Using a Computer" on the following page has more information on writing with a computer.

What You Know Now

Drafting is the process of writing a rough version of your paragraph. Rough drafts are not perfect, but you have many chances throughout the writing process to correct their flaws. It's a good idea to be flexible as you write a draft and to try to be relaxed. Once you have a rough draft, you can go on to the next step in the writing process—revising.

Tips for Using a Computer

- **Save your work often.** Word processing programs have a Save function that allows you to update your work every time you make changes.
- **Back up your work.** Be sure to save your work to a backup drive. You can also e-mail a copy to yourself.
- **Save different versions of your work.** Sometimes a certain sentence or piece of information doesn't seem to fit into your paragraph at first, but later it seems perfect. Saving your various drafts allows you to refer to earlier versions and use whatever information you need. Rename the version of your assignment that has your most recent changes.
- **Single-space to work; double-space to print.** Single spacing on the computer lets you see more of your draft at a time. See Chapter 7 for tips on preparing your work for printing.
- **Print out your drafts.** Printing enables you to see your work in terms of length and detail.
- **Plan for your computer time.** If you work on your school's computers, make sure you allow enough time to use computers or printers during peak hours and around midterms.

WRITING PRACTICE 1 Compare Writing by Hand and Writing on the Computer

Your assignment is this: *Spend five minutes writing by hand, and then (at a later time) spend five minutes writing on the computer.* Here are some possible topics.

- Health benefits of a food you've eaten
- A skill you are good at or would like to be good at (such as quilting or auto repair)
- Strategies for making friends in college
- Reasons to live with roommates

Then answer these questions. Use another sheet of paper, if necessary.

1. Which writing method is easier for you—using a pen and paper or using a computer? Why? _____

_____

_____

_____

2. What are some ways that using a computer can help your writing? _____

_____

_____

_____

WRITING PRACTICE 2 Write a Paragraph

Now that you've read about and practiced the first two steps in the writing process, it's time to put them together. Your assignment is this: *Write a paragraph on one of the following topics.*

Topics

- Reasons why a specific television program or movie is (or is not) entertaining
- Reasons to eat at (or not eat at) a specific restaurant
- Benefits (or drawbacks) of staying friends with people you knew in high school
- Benefits (or drawbacks) of using public transportation

Follow these steps to write your paragraph.

1. Use at least two prewriting techniques to come up with ideas for your paragraph.

2. Use your notes from prewriting to write a rough draft of your paragraph. Don't worry about making your rough draft perfect; just do your best to write down your ideas.

When you're finished, your paragraph should include the following:

- A clear topic sentence
- Support points that relate to the topic sentence
- Specific details that give proof of your support points
- Transitions that connect your support points and specific details

Lab Activity 5

For additional practice with drafting, complete Lab Activity 5 in the Lab Manual at the back of the book.

6 Revising: Making Changes in Your Draft

Think You're Done? Take Another Look.

If you're like many people, you'd prefer writing to be more like a short-answer test: you respond with your first instincts, answer the questions, and you're done. However, good writing most often results from rewriting your paragraph until the finished product is polished. Once you've finished Step 2 of the writing process (drafting), you get many chances to improve your writing in Step 3, revising.

Revising is the process of "re-seeing" or "re–looking at" what you've already written. When you revise, you step back and try to look objectively at what you've written. The best revision is the result of many read-throughs on your part. Each time you read your paragraph, you focus on one of the first three of the four Cs—*concise, credible,* and *clear*—until each one is present. (You address the fourth C, *correct,* during the editing stage, explained in Chapter 7.)

The "Writing Process" diagram that follows illustrates how revising fits into the writing process steps. As the diagram shows, sometimes you need to go back to Steps 1 and 2 to do more prewriting and drafting before you can finish your revision.

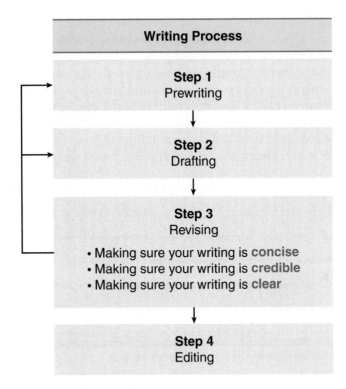

Writing Process

Step 1
Prewriting

Step 2
Drafting

Step 3
Revising

- Making sure your writing is **concise**
- Making sure your writing is **credible**
- Making sure your writing is **clear**

Step 4
Editing

Doing Step-by-Step Revision

Read your paragraph at least one time for each characteristic of good writing listed below. As you read your paragraph, concentrate on only one area at a time. Take breaks between readings to clear your mind and help you refocus your attention. *Hint:* After making changes by hand, you can insert the changes into your computer file. Save this second draft and print it out for further revising.

Making Sure Your Writing Is Concise

Check the length requirement for your assignment (if there is one) to make sure that you're not trying to do too much in your paragraph. Identify any support points that you think will need extra time and effort, and check to make sure that you have room to develop each point well. If the topic is so broad that you can't cover it thoroughly, refer to your prewriting to

determine what parts of the subject interest you the most. Then focus your paragraph accordingly. Very often, after you've made changes to your draft after the first reading, the new version of your paragraph will be *shorter* than your original. Don't be alarmed. The shorter length comes from eliminating unnecessary details and repetitive sections. When you read your draft to check that it's credible and clear, you may add new information.

For instance, Jonathan wrote the following paragraph for the topic "My Favorite Flavor." Then he read through the draft to make sure his writing was concise. He crossed out every detail that did not support his topic sentence.

Chocolate is my favorite flavor for many reasons. It's my dad's favorite flavor. Ever since I can remember, I've wanted to be like my dad, and loving chocolate was an easy way. ~~One time, my dad and I went on a wilderness camping trip, just the two of us. He's a really cool dad.~~ I like chocolate because it offers a variety in flavors. ~~My sister loves vanilla, but that's no surprise since she is the most boring person on the face of the planet.~~ Chocolate is distinctive. ~~One time I ordered this huge strawberry smoothie and drank the entire thing. I had a stomachache that you wouldn't believe!~~

The details that Jonathan crossed out do not help support the idea in the topic sentence, "Chocolate is my favorite flavor for many reasons."

✔**CHECKLIST Is Your Paragraph Concise?**

Ask yourself the following questions to determine whether your paragraph is concise.

_____   **Do I have a clear topic sentence?**

_____   **Does *every detail* support my topic sentence?**

_____   **Are there any points that do not support my topic sentence?**

_____   **Are there any details that are irrelevant to my topic sentence?**

EXERCISE 1   REVISING TO MAKE A PARAGRAPH CONCISE

The following draft of a paragraph on chocolate needs improvement. Underline the topic sentence. Cross out any sentences that don't directly support the topic sentence. You may be tempted to make other changes in the paragraph, but *change the paragraph only to make it support the topic sentence.*

Nutritious Chocolate (Draft 1)

¹Many myths surround chocolate. ²The most significant myth is that chocolate makes you fat. ³~~My aunt once ate too much chocolate for a whole year, and she couldn't fit into her best suit for my sister's wedding~~. ⁴A myth surrounding chocolate is that it's unhealthy. ⁵This isn't true. ⁶~~Osteoporosis, the bone-weakening disease, runs in my family, so I make sure to get a lot of calcium in my diet.~~ ⁷~~I hope to keep good posture as long as I can by having strong bones~~. ⁸One myth is that chocolate is made up only of fat. ⁹Really, chocolate provides different types of calories. ¹⁰In one ounce of milk chocolate, people get one gram of protein and fifteen grams of carbohydrates. ¹¹Of course, they also get nine grams of fat, but regular exercise will take care of that. ¹²Overall, chocolate is healthier than people realize.

1. The topic sentence is sentence _____1_____ .

2. Three sentences are off-topic: ___3___ , ___6___ , and ___7___ .

Making Sure Your Writing Is Credible

On your second pass through your paragraph, look for gaps in your support. Check your support points, and make sure that you have specific details to illustrate all your points. If necessary, look back at your prewriting exercises to find additional examples.

During his second reading of his draft, Jonathan noticed that he needed specific details to illustrate his support points. The specific details that Jonathan added are underlined.

Chocolate is my favorite flavor for many reasons. It's my dad's favorite flavor. Ever since I can remember, I've wanted to be like my dad, and loving chocolate was an easy way. <u>I have great memories of the two of us licking dripping chocolate ice cream cones in summer and eating sticky chocolate candies right after Halloween.</u> I like chocolate because it offers variety in flavors. <u>Depending on my</u>

mood, I can choose dark chocolate, milk chocolate, white chocolate, or even a combination. I love knowing that when I walk into an ice cream parlor, I can choose from at least five different ice cream flavors that have some kind of chocolate in them. Other flavors, like vanilla, come in only one boring flavor. Chocolate is distinctive. No one could ever confuse it with another flavor like banana or strawberry, but some fruit flavors all blend together and taste the same. My mother loves to bake different kinds of fruit pies. Her pies taste great; they all taste the same, no matter what kind of fruit she uses. With chocolate, I never have any trouble knowing when someone's baking with my favorite flavor.

Now Jonathan's paragraph has plenty of examples, and they all support his topic sentence. Don't worry if you don't think of all your examples right away. As you read through your draft, just keep thinking about the best way to explain your ideas to your reader. Then add examples as they come to you.

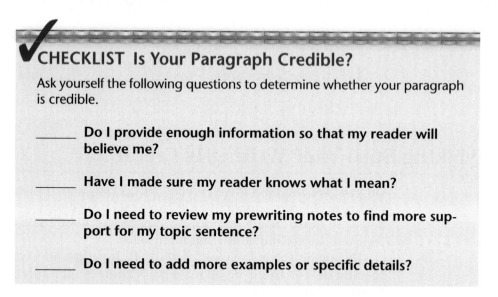

✔ CHECKLIST Is Your Paragraph Credible?

Ask yourself the following questions to determine whether your paragraph is credible.

_____   **Do I provide enough information so that my reader will believe me?**

_____   **Have I made sure my reader knows what I mean?**

_____   **Do I need to review my prewriting notes to find more support for my topic sentence?**

_____   **Do I need to add more examples or specific details?**

EXERCISE 2   REVISING TO MAKE A PARAGRAPH CREDIBLE

On the next page is the corrected version of the paragraph you revised in Exercise 1. In this exercise, you need to add specific details to make the paragraph more credible. Read Specific Details A and B, which follow the paragraph. Decide where in the paragraph each belongs. Then write the number of the sentence that each specific detail should follow. You may want to make other changes in the paragraph, but don't. *Pay attention only to adding more information for support.*

Nutritious Chocolate (Draft 2)

[1]Many myths surround chocolate. [2]The most significant myth is that chocolate makes you fat. [3]A myth surrounding chocolate is that it's unhealthy. [4]This isn't true. [5]One myth is that chocolate is made up only of fat. [6]Really, chocolate provides different types of calories. [7]In one ounce of milk chocolate, people get one gram of protein and fifteen grams of carbohydrates. [8]Of course, they also get nine grams of fat, but regular exercise will take care of that. [9]Overall, chocolate is healthier than people realize.

Specific Details

A. There are 140 calories in an ounce of semisweet chocolate and 150 calories in an ounce of milk chocolate. This might sound like a lot, but it's low compared with the number of calories in a bottle of sweetened iced tea. People get fat only if they eat too much chocolate.

This information belongs after sentence _____2_____ .

B. Chocolate contains zinc, iron, and other nutrients that make it a good part of people's diets. Milk chocolate also contains calcium, so it helps build strong bones.

This information belongs after sentence _____4_____ .

Making Sure Your Writing Is Clear

On your third pass through your paragraph, check that your support points are arranged in a logical, effective order. Decide where your support points should go, and then move them around, if necessary, to create a sense of progress and balance for your reader. Make sure, too, that you signal the order of your points by using transition words like *first, second,* and *finally* in your paragraph.

During his third pass through his paragraph, Jonathan added transitions. The transitions that Jonathan added are underlined.

Chocolate is my favorite flavor for many reasons. <u>First,</u> It's my dad's favorite flavor. Ever since I can remember, I've wanted to be like my dad, and loving chocolate was an easy way. <u>In fact,</u> I have great memories of the two of us licking dripping chocolate ice cream cones in summer and eating sticky chocolate candies right after Halloween. <u>Next,</u> I like chocolate because it offers variety in flavors. Depending on my mood, I can choose dark chocolate, milk chocolate, white chocolate, or even a combination. I love knowing that when I walk into an ice cream parlor, I can choose from at least five different ice cream flavors that have some kind of chocolate in them. Other flavors, like vanilla, come in only one boring flavor. <u>Finally,</u> chocolate is distinctive. No one could ever confuse it with another flavor like banana or strawberry, but some fruit flavors all blend together and taste the same. My mother loves to bake different kinds of fruit pies. <u>Even though</u> her pies taste great, they all taste the same, no matter what kind of fruit she uses. With chocolate, <u>however,</u> I never have any trouble knowing when someone's baking with my favorite flavor.

Although a reader might have been able to figure out which details illustrated certain support points before, the transitions that Jonathan added make the connections extremely clear. Now there is no doubt as to what his support points are, what order they take, or how they relate to each other.

As a result of his three passes, Jonathan's paragraph has become concise, credible, and clear.

✔ **CHECKLIST Is Your Paragraph Clear?**

Ask yourself the following questions to determine whether your paragraph is clear.

_____ **Do I have a logical organizational format that my reader can easily follow? What is it?**

_____ **Do I use transitional expressions to communicate what my points are and indicate which ones are most important?**

_____ **Do I need to explain any points more fully?**

_____ **Do I need to move or rearrange sentences to make my writing clearer?**

EXERCISE 3   REVISING TO MAKE A PARAGRAPH CLEAR

Below is the corrected version of the paragraph you revised in Exercise 2. You need to make sure the paragraph is clear. After reading the paragraph, answer the questions about clear writing that follow it.

Nutritious Chocolate (Draft 3)

^{1}Many myths surround chocolate. ^{2}One myth is that chocolate is made up only of fat. ^{3}Really, chocolate provides different types of calories. ^{4}In one ounce of milk chocolate, people get one gram of protein and fifteen grams of carbohydrates. ^{5}Of course, they also get nine grams of fat, but regular exercise will take care of that. ^{6}Another myth surrounding chocolate is that it's unhealthy. ^{7}This isn't true. ^{8}Chocolate contains zinc, iron, and other nutrients that make it a good part of people's diets. ^{9}Milk chocolate also contains calcium, so it helps build strong bones. ^{10}The most significant myth is that chocolate makes you fat. ^{11}There are 140 calories in an ounce of semisweet chocolate and 150 calories in an ounce of milk chocolate. ^{12}That might sound like a lot, but it's low compared with the number of calories in a bottle of sweetened iced tea. ^{13}People get fat only if they eat too much chocolate. ^{14}Overall, the myths are not true, and chocolate is healthier than people realize.

1. The paragraph gives support points in emphatic order (from least to most important). Write 1 before the least significant myth about chocolate, 2 before the next most important myth, and 3 before the most important myth.

   _____3_____ Chocolate makes you fat.

   _____2_____ Chocolate is unhealthy.

   _____1_____ Chocolate is made up only of fat.

2. Which support point would best be introduced by the word *Finally*?

   3—Chocolate makes you fat.

3. Which point would best be introduced by the phrase "Another myth surrounding chocolate"? 2—Chocolate is unhealthy.

4. Which term shows emphasis in sentence 10? <u>most significant</u>

_____

5. How many times does the writer repeat the words *myth* and *myths* in the paragraph? <u>⁵</u>

Using a Computer to Revise Your Draft

Revision is the part of the writing process where computers really help you.

- Computers are very useful for deleting information that doesn't help you develop your topic sentence. Since your draft on the word processor looks more finished than a handwritten one, it is easier to tell what information is off-topic or unnecessary.
- You can use the Cut and Paste functions to move examples from one part of your draft to another without having to retype your whole draft.
- Word processing programs let you easily insert transitional words and phrases, so your draft becomes much more finished without a lot of effort.
- Computers give you an early sense of how your finished product will look. Instead of a messy paper with scribbled-out passages and lines with arrows pointing every which way, your writing will automatically be lined up at the margin, equally spaced, and evenly printed.

A Revised Draft

The paragraph below has gone through all the necessary revisions and is now ready to be edited and handed in.

Nutritious Chocolate

Many myths surround chocolate. One myth is that chocolate is made up only of fat. Really, chocolate provides different types of calories. In one ounce of milk chocolate, people get one gram of protein and fifteen grams of carbohydrates. Of course, they also get nine grams of fat, but regular exercise will take care of that. Another myth surrounding chocolate is that it's unhealthy. This isn't true. Chocolate contains zinc, iron, and other nutrients that make it a good part of people's diets. Milk chocolate also contains calcium, so it helps build strong bones. The most significant myth is that chocolate makes you fat. There are 140 calories in an ounce of semisweet chocolate and 150 calories in an ounce of milk chocolate. That might sound like a lot, but it's low compared with the number of calories in a bottle of sweetened iced tea. People get fat only if they eat too much chocolate. Overall, the myths are not true, and chocolate is healthier than people realize.

Exchanging Help with Your Peers

Working with classmates, or **peer review,** is one of the best ways to improve your writing. Working with classmates allows you to do the following:

- Receive feedback without receiving a grade.
- Receive feedback from someone who shares your experiences, at least in the classroom.
- Gain ideas for your own work by seeing how your classmates have illustrated or organized their ideas in their writing.
- Ask questions about your writing in front of a few people, not the instructor or your whole class.
- Talk about strategies that can help you improve your writing before you try them out in your paper.

Remembering the Writer's Feelings

In general, working with classmates lets you give your paper a test run before your instructor sees it. Consider the following questions before beginning your peer review workshop.

- How do you feel when someone is reading something you've written?
- How much do you value another student's opinion about your writing? Would you rather have just the instructor's comments? Explain.
- If a friend asks you to read something he or she has written, what kind of feedback do you give your friend? Does your feedback change if the friend is a co-worker or classmate? Explain.

These questions should help you remember that writing is a form of personal expression. When we comment on other people's writing, we need to be polite and careful about their feelings.

Writing as a Response

Writing is such a personal experience that sometimes it's hard to open up and let other people read what you've written. However, allowing your classmates to help you to learn about gaps in support, weak connections, and overall strengths will ultimately help you write more effectively.

Peer Review Guidelines

Use the Peer Review Worksheet on the following page and the guidelines below to give constructive feedback to your classmates. Ideally, you will work in pairs or in small groups of three or four students. Each member of your group should have a copy of every group member's paragraph and a Peer Review Worksheet.

Since some classes last longer than others, focus only on the guidelines you have time to cover. Your instructor may tell you which ones to include or ignore for a particular assignment. Additionally, the Peer Review Worksheet includes specific space for comments on the topic sentence, support points, and details. Other comments should be written in the last section of the worksheet.

Follow these guidelines in evaluating your classmate's writing.

1. **Be kind.** Keep in mind that your classmates may feel nervous about letting you read their work, let alone comment on it. Therefore, do your best to be direct but kind in the comments you make to your peers. Criticism delivered with courtesy is much more likely to be helpful.

2. **Have the paragraph read aloud by someone other than the writer.** Reading along as the paragraph is read aloud forces everyone to slow down and read every word carefully. That way, people are not confused because they skipped a word or line by trying to read too quickly. Since the writers know what they mean to say, they might add emphasis or words that they think *should* be there but that end up being unclear. To best understand where the writer needs help, someone *not* familiar with the text should do the reading aloud.

3. **Tell the writer what you think the biggest strength of the paragraph is.** *Every* piece of writing has something positive about it, so work hard to find something nice to say to the writer, even if you're only complimenting

Peer Review Worksheet

Reviewer's name: _____ Date: _____

Writer's name: _____

Paragraph title: _____

1. One strength of this paragraph is _____

_____

_____

2. The topic sentence for this paragraph is _____

_____

_____

3. The support points for this paragraph are _____

_____

_____

4. Write down the specific details the writer uses to illustrate each support point.

   Details for support point 1: _____

   _____

   _____

   Details for support point 2: _____

   _____

   _____

   Details for support point 3: _____

   _____

   _____

5. Overall comments on this paragraph: _____

_____

_____

the writer on the topic of the paragraph. If you think the writer has some good examples or a solid title, mention that. You may think that the paragraph is well organized or even that it has the potential to be well organized. Try very hard to find something positive to say about the paragraph you're evaluating.

4. **Write down the topic sentence on the Peer Review Worksheet.** If you can identify the writer's topic sentence, then the writer is on the right track. If you write down another sentence, or if you're not sure which sentence is the topic sentence, talk to the writer about what his or her main idea is.

5. **If there is no clear topic sentence, help the writer revise or write one.** (If the writer does have a clear topic sentence, move on to the next guideline.) Discuss what the writer wants to say, and find the best way to say it. Talk, too, about the best way to incorporate the support points and specific details the writer has already written.

6. **Write down the support points for the topic sentence.** If you can identify the support points, the writer is probably on the right track. If you're not sure what the support points are, or if your idea of the support points differs from the writer's, talk about what the writer wants to communicate and how certain points will best help support the topic sentence.

7. **Make sure that the writer has specific details that illustrate every support point.** Tell the writer if he or she needs to offer more proof of the support points. You may suggest the kinds of examples, but the writer should come up with the specific details.

8. **Make sure the writer uses a strategy (such as chronological or emphatic order) to organize the ideas in the paragraph.** The paragraph may already be organized, or partly organized, according to one of the organizational strategies. In this case, help the writer put the support points into a logical order, discussing which points should go first or last and why.

9. **Make sure the writer uses transitions to signal the order of the support points and their level of importance.** Refer to the lists of transitions in Chapter 11 in order to make the connections between ideas clear.

10. **Offer any comments not covered by the earlier guidelines.** These comments may include discussion of details that seem off-topic, places where the writer needs more detail, or places where sentence-level errors make understanding the paragraph difficult.

The Peer Review Worksheet shown on the following page has been partly filled in by one of Jonathan's classmates.

Peer Review Worksheet

Reviewer's name: Ramona   **Date:** 10/6/05

Writer's name: Jonathan

Paragraph title: My Favorite Flavor

1. **One strength of this paragraph is** The topic choice (chocolate) is interesting.

2. **The topic sentence for this paragraph is**
   Chocolate is my favorite flavor for many reasons.

3. **The support points for this paragraph are** Chocolate is my dad's favorite flavor.
   Chocolate comes in a variety of flavors.
   Chocolate is distinctive.

4. **Write down the specific details the writer uses to illustrate each support point.**
   Details for support point 1: Memories of eating ice cream and Halloween chocolate with
   my dad.

   Details for support point 2: Can choose from at least five ice cream flavors with chocolate
   in them.

   Details for support point 3: All fruit pies taste alike, but chocolate is always distinctive.

5. **Overall comments on this paragraph:**
   Jonathan made his love for chocolate clear.

Making the Best Use of Other People's Feedback

Once we get someone's opinion of our writing, the trick becomes making good use of that opinion. The following guidelines are designed to help you make the most of other people's feedback.

Don't Expect People to Fix Everything.   No one knows everything. Getting good feedback on your writing doesn't guarantee that you will improve your writing enough, say, to raise your grade from a C to an A. The most you can expect from other people is their honest response. Then it's your job to revise your writing accordingly.

Don't Feel That You Have to Take Everyone's Advice.   Even though almost every piece of writing has room for improvement, don't make changes just because someone says you should. If the suggestions make sense to you—or if *everyone* in your group says the same thing—then you should probably consider revising your draft.

Ask People to Be Specific.   If you're not sure what people mean, ask them to explain further. The worst thing you can do in a peer review situation is to revise your draft when you're not sure how to go about it. If your group doesn't make its ideas clear, ask your instructor for further clarification.

Remember: People Are Trying to Help.   Even if you're disappointed that your classmates don't find your ideas as clear as you'd hoped, don't get mad. Accepting criticism from people is often difficult, so just do your best to listen and learn from your peers.

Setting Your Goals as a Writer

As you begin writing more frequently and for different assignments, you will discover your strengths as a writer. You may learn that you can write wonderful descriptions, that you're sharp at comparing and contrasting, or that you can make powerful argument. You will also learn what areas of your writing you need to focus your attention on.

One tool that can help you improve your writing one step at a time is a goal sheet. A goal sheet like the one on page 96 allows you to keep your topic sentence in mind at all times, emphasize what you're already doing well in your writing, and set specific goals for improvement. The goal sheet also allows you to tell your instructor and classmates—or peer reviewers—what you need from them.

The goal sheet works best if you use it right before you hand in your paper—when your ideas are fresh in your mind—and then review it when you begin another assignment. You may even want to attach it to your final draft so that your instructor can see what your goals for improvement are. Do your best to write well on your goal sheet, but don't worry if you have mistakes.

Look at the sample completed goal sheet on page 97. The student, Mario Biancini, has written a paragraph on a challenging job he recently held.

Notice that Mario isn't always looking for hard-and-fast answers. Sometimes he simply wants suggestions. Also, he isn't afraid to ask his instructor to look at something he feels good about, in this case his use of specific detail.

What You Know Now

Your writing can change over the course of an assignment. During Step 3 in the writing process, revising, you can change your writing to communicate your ideas more clearly. Revising involves rereading your paragraph several times. Each time, you focus on one aspect of your revising, asking yourself if your writing is concise, credible, and clear. You may benefit from peer review, which involves reading and commenting on other students' work. The last step in the writing process, editing, is covered in Chapter 7. During editing, you check to see if your paragraph is correct.

Goal Sheet

Name: _____

Class: _____

1. **My topic sentence for this assignment is** _____

_____

_____

2. **The skill I think I've improved in this assignment is** _____

_____

_____

The way I improved this skill is _____

_____

_____

3. **The skill I think I still need to work on is** _____

_____

_____

I plan to improve this skill by _____

_____

_____

4. **The aspect of my writing that my classmates told me to focus on is** _____

_____

_____

5. **What I want my instructor to notice or comment on in my writing is** _____

_____

_____

_____

Note: The goal sheet is a very effective tool for helping students implement the instructor's suggestions in their own writing. Additionally, its use encourages the student to choose what to work on first. Finally, the goal sheet is an effective way for instructors to keep in touch with students and learn whether students are understanding the course material well enough to apply it.

Goal Sheet

Name: Mario Biancini

Class: English 101, Section B

1. **My topic sentence for this assignment is** Working in a grocery store is a lot more difficult than people realize.

2. **The skill I think I've improved in this assignment is** the second C: credible writing. I think I've used details better in this paragraph than in my first ones.

   The way I improved this skill is I did two things. I talked to my instructor about what she meant by "specific details." I also tried to use examples that relate to people's five senses. I think these steps worked.

3. **The skill I think I still need to work on is** the third C: clear writing. I'm still not sure how to organize ideas. Sometimes time sequence order seems right, but then I think that emphatic order seems best. I don't know which one to use.

   I plan to improve this skill by I'll reread the section in the book on organization and go to the writing lab to get extra practice.

4. **The aspect of my writing that my classmates told me to focus on is** I want my classmates to pay attention to my organization. Maybe they can tell me if I'm organizing my ideas well or suggest ways to make my writing more clear.

5. **What I want my instructor to notice or comment on in my writing is** I want my instructor to notice two things. First, I want her to tell me if my examples are better, because I think they are. Second, I want her to pay attention to my organization, too, and help me decide how to organize my ideas.

The goal sheet is supposed to be completed right before students hand in their assignments. While their writing is fresh in their minds and they feel proud of themselves for having completed the assignment, students are more willing to be critical of themselves. Many times students merely repeat their instructor's suggestions about what to work on, so this sheet is more effective *before* the students get a grade. Also, since student assessments can be amazingly accurate, students' confidence gets a boost when they see that what they need to work on is also what their instructor thinks they need to work on.

WRITING PRACTICE Write and Revise Your Own Paragraph

In this chapter you learned something about one food—chocolate. Your assignment is this: *Write a paragraph about a food that is or is not very good for you.* Be sure to include reasons why the food is or is not good for you. Then give specific details from your life as proof of how good or bad the food is for you.

Follow these steps to write your paragraph.

1. Use at least two prewriting techniques to come up with ideas for your paragraph.
2. Use your notes from prewriting to write a rough draft of your paragraph.
3. Revise your paragraph, reading through it to check for the first three of the four Cs: *concise, credible,* and *clear* writing.

When you're finished, your paragraph should include the following:

- A clear topic sentence.
- Support points that relate to the topic sentence.
- Specific details that give proof of your support points.
- Transitions that connect your support points and specific details.

Lab Activity 6

For additional practice with revising, complete Lab Activity 6 in the Lab Manual at the back of this book.

7 Editing: Checking for Correctness

CULTURE NOTE *Winter Holidays*

Though most people in the United States are aware of Christmas and New Year's Day, many other holidays occur during the winter months. These other holidays have varied origins—some cultural, some religious, some societal—but they all include some sort of celebration. Two of these festivals are Boxing Day and Kwanzaa.

The Importance of Editing

You've moved around, filled in, and shored up different patches of your paragraph in Step 3 of the writing process (revising). Now you're ready to polish your work. **Editing**—changing your writing to make it more effective and to correct errors—is a painstaking, but very important, part of the writing process. So don't rush! It is during this stage that you address the fourth C—*correct* writing. Look at the "Writing Process" diagram on page 100 to see how editing fits into the writing process.

Think of editing as your last mirror-check before going to an important job interview. You wouldn't show up for an interview—after carefully preparing and dressing for success—with a big piece of spinach between your teeth. Similarly, you shouldn't forget to edit your work after you've spent much time and effort writing and revising it. A well-edited, error-free paragraph shows your reader you care about your work. It makes you look smart, professional, and prepared.

There are two parts to editing.

- Careful examination of your writing to see if you can make it smoother, more interesting, and more effective.
- Careful proofreading to catch and correct errors in grammar, punctuation, and spelling.

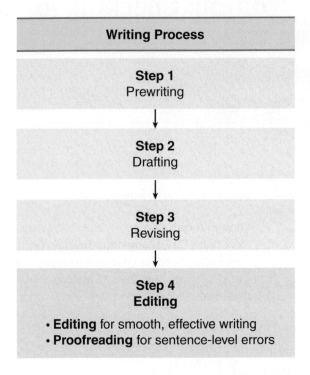

Writing Process
Step 1 Prewriting
↓
Step 2 Drafting
↓
Step 3 Revising
↓
Step 4 **Editing** • **Editing** for smooth, effective writing • **Proofreading** for sentence-level errors

Notice that both steps begin with the word *careful*. Taking care at this stage—to catch, eliminate, and correct errors—will go a long way toward making a good impression on your reader.

Editing for Smooth, Effective Writing

Once your paragraph is concise, credible, and clear, you need to make sure that your reader will enjoy your writing. You want your audience to read all the way to the end of the paragraph. That won't happen unless your writing is interesting and progresses smoothly. As you read your paragraph, answer the following questions.

- **Point of view.** Do I use the same pronoun throughout? Do I use the correct verb tenses throughout? (For more on using consistent verbs and pronouns, see Chapters 38 and 39.)
- **Appropriate language.** Do I use language that is appropriate for an academic assignment? Do I use unbiased, respectful language? (For more on sensitive language and word choice, see Chapters 12 and 13.)

A Kwanzaa Celebration

SURF THE NET A holiday based on African harvest festivals, Kwanzaa celebrates seven character traits emphasizing strength in community and responsibility. Search for "Kwanzaa" on the Internet, follow several links, and write a few sentences explaining what you learn.

- **Word use.** Have I chosen the best words I can? Is the writing too wordy? Are certain words repeated too often? (For more on using vivid examples and language, see Chapters 10 and 15.)
- **Sentence variety.** Have I used different kinds of sentences to keep my writing interesting? Do sentences flow logically and smoothly from one to the next? (For more on sentence variety and connecting sentences, see Chapter 55.)

You can be aware of these concerns during the drafting and revising process. However, once you reach the editing stage of the writing process, you should make sure your sentences are smooth, interesting, and effective. Look at the "Writing Process" diagram on the previous page to see how editing fits into the writing process.

Proofreading for Sentence-Level Errors

Proofreading means checking your writing for errors in grammar, punctuation, and spelling. **Proofreaders' marks,** shown on page 102, are a standard set of

Mark	Meaning	Example
∧	Insert	h∧ve
ℒ	Delete	some ~~some~~ cultural
⌣	Close up space	t⌣he
∽	Transpose	some⏋of⎿sort
#	Insert space	in#the
/ⓛⓒ	Make lowercase	Ørigins
≡ Ⓒⓐⓟ	Capitalize	New year's Day
—	Underline (or put in italics)	all
¶	Indent paragraph beginning	¶Though

Example

¶Though pretty much everyone in#the United States are is aware of Christmas and New year's Day, many other holidays occur during t⌣he winter months. Other holidays h∧ve many different Ørigins— some ~~some~~ cultural, some religious, some societal—but they all include some⏋of⎿sort celebration two of these festivals are Boxing Day and Kwanzaa.

symbols used by instructors, editors, and printers to show changes in written work. Become familiar with these symbols and use them as you proofread.

By now, however, you are so familiar with your paragraph that you probably skip right over some errors without noticing them. Use the following three proofreading techniques to force yourself to read slowly so you'll have a better chance of spotting mistakes.

Proofreading Sentence by Sentence

Reading your paragraph one sentence at a time allows you to identify grammar errors like run-on sentences, sentence fragments, and mistakes in subject-verb agreement and pronoun agreement. It also helps you identify awkward sentences or poor word choices.

During your first reading, check to be sure each sentence makes sense by itself. Then make sure that each sentence leads logically into the next. Use a piece of paper to cover all but one sentence so that you can focus on that sentence alone.

Proofreading Word by Word

Slowing down and reading your paragraph word by word will allow you to find other errors—such as apostrophe or capitalization errors—that you didn't notice when reading each sentence separately. Further, reading your paragraph aloud can help you determine whether you have repeated a word one too many times or have used too many long words when you could do with shorter ones. Use a pencil or your finger to point out each word as you read it.

Reading Your Paragraph Backwards

Reading your paragraph backwards helps you find spelling errors. Use a pencil or your finger to point to the words as you read. Because your paragraph won't make sense backwards, you won't be able to anticipate—and thus skip—the upcoming errors in a sentence. You won't be able to gloss over misspellings.

Using a Computer for Editing

Computers can help you edit your work, but use these tools with caution.

- The spelling checker will help you find spelling errors. It will not help you find **diction** errors (mistakes in word choice), however. For instance, the following sentence makes no sense: "Their are too daze left of the big sail." The computer won't catch any of the word-choice errors, though, since all the words are spelled correctly. The correct sentence should be "There are two days left of the big sale."

- Grammar checkers should be used carefully. Sometimes a computer's explanation will point out the error but not explain it. Other times the computer will be wrong. For instance, the following sentence is correct: "The engineer explained that that was the best method." The grammar checker marked the sentence wrong, indicating that the repetition of *that* was incorrect, but the sentence is not incorrect. To be safe, do your own proofreading when you've printed out your final draft.

To make the best use of your computer for editing, do the following:

1. Set the font on your computer to 12 point unless your instructor requests another size.
2. Set the margins to at least one inch unless your instructor recommends a different measurement.
3. Double-space your work.

4. Before you print out your draft, reread the entire piece, using the computer cursor (the blinking line that appears on the screen) to focus your attention on one line at a time. You can make changes as you go, and you will not feel overwhelmed by having to change everything at once.

EXERCISE 1 READING EACH SENTENCE SEPARATELY

The following paragraph contains several sentence-level errors. Read the paragraph and focus on finding errors in *sentence structure* and *punctuation*. Write the numbers of the sentences with these errors in the blanks at the end of the paragraph. Then make corrections in the paragraph. There are five sentence structure and punctuation errors in all.

Celebrate Boxing Day

¹Many smaller holidays have interesting origins, Boxing Day, for one, is a holiday in England that falls on December 26. ²In its early years, Boxing Day was a day for people to give money to church leaders/³In order for them to offer prayers for people's relatives at sea. ⁴The name "Boxing Day" come^s from the boxes that the church leaders ~~using~~ used to collect money. ⁵Later in England's history, Boxing Day served as the day that many servants received leftovers from their employers' Christmas feasts. ⁶Since at that time servants ~~are~~ were needed in large households to prepare elaborate holiday meals, the servants had to work on Christmas day. ⁷The next day, however, employers often gave their servants leftovers, which the servants could use for their own Christmas celebration. ⁸The leftovers were in boxes, so the name "Boxing Day" stuck. ⁹Eventually, Boxing Day ~~becomes~~ became a day for

employers to tip their servants. [10]Now, however, it's just a day that most people celebrate by not having to go to work.

The following sentences contain errors: __1__, __3__, __4__, __6__, __9__.

EXERCISE 2 READING EACH WORD SEPARATELY

In the following paragraph, look for errors in *capitalization*. Also look for unnecessary *repetition*. Then correct the errors you find, and answer the questions at the end of the paragraph. Errors appear in three sentences.

Celebrate Kwanzaa

[1]Kwanzaa, a holiday with contemporary origins, has its roots in African culture. [2]Founded in 1966 by Maulana Karenga, chairman of Black Studies at ~~c~~alifornia State University at Long Beach at the time, Kwanzaa is one African-American festival that has become known in mainstream America. [3]It's based on African harvest festivals, and it combines symbolism with ritual as a family and community festival. [4]The seven days of the festival emphasize the values of unity, self-determination, collective work and responsibility, cooperative economics, purpose, creativity, and faith. [5]Kwanzaa begins on ~~d~~ecember 26 and ends on New Year's Day, with a festival feast on December 31. [6]Some people celebrate the festival by exchanging gifts, while others emphasize its ~~a~~frican origins ~~of the festival~~ through traditional dress.

1. The following sentences contain errors: __2__, __5__, __6__.

2. How many times is the word *festival* used? _6, and *festivals* is used once_

3. What are some words or expressions the writer could use in place
Answers will vary. Possible response: Holiday, celebration,
of *festival?* _special day._

EXERCISE 3 READING A PARAGRAPH BACKWARDS

Read this paragraph backwards, and focus on looking for spelling errors.
Write the number of the sentences containing errors and the correct spellings
of the words in the blanks after the paragraph. There are five errors in all.

Celebrate St. Patrick's Day

¹One holday celebrated in the United States is St. Patrick's Day.
²Originating in Ireland, St. Patrick's Day honors St. Patrick, who
supposedly rid Ireland of snaks. ³On March 17, people are supposed
to whear green and pinch those who don't wear it. ⁴The wearing of
green is in honor of "The Emerald Isle," Ireland, and the pinching
represents the mouth of a snake. ⁵Some people go a step ferther
than just wearing green. ⁶The city of Chicago, for instance, dyes its
river green in honor of St. Patrick's Day. ⁷Other people celebrate by
marching in parades and lissening to Irish music. ⁸Last of all, some
people spend the day drinking green beer to toast "St. Paddy," as St.
Patrick is sometimes called.

1. The following sentences contain errors: _1_, _2_, _3_, _5_, _7_

2. The following words are mispelled: _holiday_, _snakes_,
wear, _further_, _listening_.

What You Know Now

The final step in the writing process is editing. During editing, you make sure your writing is smooth, interesting, and effective. Then you proofread for sentence-level errors in grammar, punctuation, and spelling. Proofreading three times—sentence by sentence, word by word, and backwards—helps you find and correct every error.

WRITING PRACTICE **Write Your Own Paragraph**

This chapter gave you some information on holidays that you might not celebrate or might not have known much about. Your assignment is this: *Write a paragraph about your most or least favorite holiday.*

Follow these steps to write your paragraph.

1. Use at least two prewriting techniques to come up with ideas for your paragraph.

2. Use your notes from prewriting to write a rough draft of your paragraph.

3. Revise your paragraph, reading through it to check for the first three of the four Cs: *concise, credible,* and *clear* writing.

4. Proofread your paragraph three times for grammar, punctuation, and spelling errors.

When you're finished, your paragraph should include the following:

- A clear topic sentence
- Support points that relate to the topic sentence
- Specific details that give proof of your support points
- Transitions that connect your support points and specific details

Lab Activity 7

For additional practice with editing, complete Lab Activity 7 in the Lab Manual at the back of the book.

8 Putting the Writing Process Steps Together

CULTURE NOTE *Running*

Though running has long been viewed as a punishing exercise, it has many psychological and physical benefits. As an athletic activity, running has its downside as well as its upside, from the pain of sore muscles to the runner's high.

The Writing Process in Action

Now that you have been through the writing process step by step, you'll find it helpful to see the process as a whole. This chapter will show you how a student, Sarah, worked through each stage of the writing process. Sarah's assignment was to write about an activity she *doesn't* enjoy. As she wrote her paragraph, Sarah referred to the "Writing Process Checklist" on the following page.

Step 1: Prewriting Activities

Sarah started her prewriting by doing some freewriting. Her sentence-level errors have been corrected for easier reading.

I hate to run. It makes me sweat, and it makes my muscles sore at first. It also gives me achy feet. Running makes me so hot and sweaty that sometimes I think I can't ever be cool and clean again. My soccer coach makes us run when we show up to practice, and if we're late, we have to run extra laps. Running is punishment on our team. We have to run a lot only if we're in trouble. Running never feels good. People tell me about "runner's high," but I never feel good running. Running is the worst type of exercise I can do.

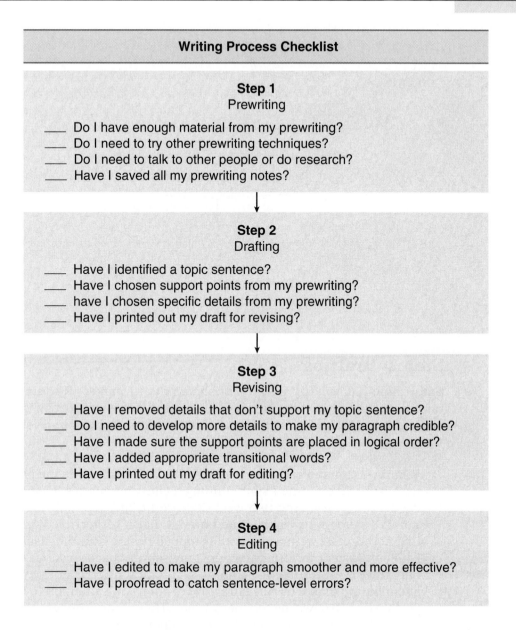

Writing Process Checklist

Step 1
Prewriting

____ Do I have enough material from my prewriting?
____ Do I need to try other prewriting techniques?
____ Do I need to talk to other people or do research?
____ Have I saved all my prewriting notes?

Step 2
Drafting

____ Have I identified a topic sentence?
____ Have I chosen support points from my prewriting?
____ have I chosen specific details from my prewriting?
____ Have I printed out my draft for revising?

Step 3
Revising

____ Have I removed details that don't support my topic sentence?
____ Do I need to develop more details to make my paragraph credible?
____ Have I made sure the support points are placed in logical order?
____ Have I added appropriate transitional words?
____ Have I printed out my draft for editing?

Step 4
Editing

____ Have I edited to make my paragraph smoother and more effective?
____ Have I proofread to catch sentence-level errors?

After this freewriting exercise, Sarah made a cluster diagram. She organized her ideas around the central concept of running as an unpleasant activity. Sarah's diagram includes ideas that will be her support points. She can add more specific details when she writes her rough draft.

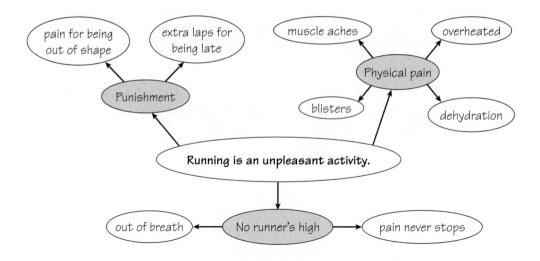

Step 2: Drafting

Sarah now has a basic point that she wants to make: "Running is an unpleasant activity." She has also developed some support points and details. Notice that Sarah's draft contains a number of sentence-level errors, which is acceptable at this stage.

> Running is an unpleasant activity. It's a painful and makes me phys-ically sore. Every time I start running, i get sore muscles. Last soc-cer season, it took me two weeks before I didn't feel that my leg muscles were on fire every time I moved. I also get terrible blisters that never really went away until I stopped runing. Running is pun-ishment. Except for our warm-ups, my soccer coach make us run only if we're in trouble for coming late to practice. Or not paying attention. He makes us run extra if we're not paying attention to him or if we do a drill wrong too many times. There is no "runner's high" for me. I've never had this feeling of "runner's high." I feel only pain when I run, and I feel only pain when I stop.

Step 3: Revising

Sarah's draft includes three support points: (1) running is painful, (2) running is punishment, and (3) there is no runner's high. It also has some good details. After taking a break, Sarah took out some unnecessary information, added extra information, and added transitional words. You'll notice that Sarah's revised draft still has some sentence-level errors.

Revised Draft

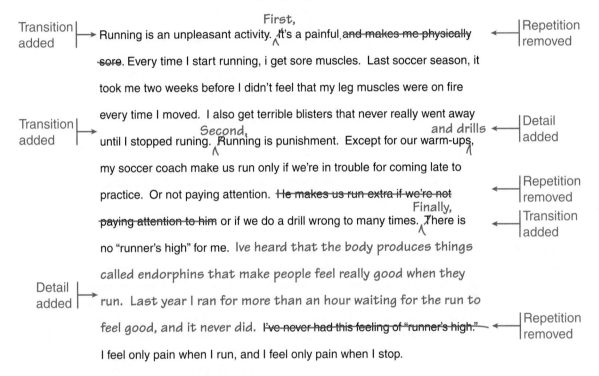

Step 4: Editing

Sarah's revised draft has a clear topic sentence, support points, specific details, and transitional words. All that remains is for Sarah to edit a portion of her paragraph for smooth writing and proofread for sentence-level errors. Sarah's edited draft shows the errors she corrected.

Edited Draft

¶ Running is an unpleasant activity. First, it's a painful. Every time I start running, i get sore muscles. Last soccer season, it took me two weeks before I didn't feel that my leg muscles were on fire every time I moved. I also get terrible blisters that never really went away until I stopped runing. Second, runing is punishment. Except for our warm-ups and drills, my soccer coach makes us run only if we're in trouble for coming late to practice, or not paying attention, or if we do a drill wrong too many times. Finally, there is no "runner's high" for me. I've heard that the body produces things called endorphins that make people feel really good when they run. Last year I ran for more than an hour waiting for the run to feel good, and it never did. I feel only pain when I run, and I feel only pain when I stop.

How to Tell What Comes Next

Sometimes your initial freewriting or clustering may produce enough information for your whole paragraph. When this happens, you should feel free to move steps around or spend more time on one step and less on another if that's what your writing demands. Don't worry if you don't have all the information you need right away. You may discover that you know more about your topic once you begin writing, or you may rediscover something you thought you couldn't use from your prewriting.

EXERCISE 1 IDENTIFYING THE NEXT WRITING PROCESS STEP

The writing samples below are at various stages of development. Choose the letter of the step that represents what the writer should do next.

1.   **Runner's High**

Running for exercise has many benefits. First of all, it allows me to be outside, not closed up in some gym or workout room. I get to see trees, flowers, and other people. Second, running gives me great results. I love how toned my legs get when I run regularly, and my stomach has even become more flat. People tell me that my skin seems to glow, too, maybe from improved circulation when I run. A third benefit of running is that I can eat anything I want and not gain weight. Running for just twenty-five minutes a day, four days a week, lets me eat until I'm full without worrying about whether my jeans will fit. It's great! Finally, runner's high makes running great all by itself. Even though sometimes I start my run feeling tired or achy, after a few minutes, I get the most wonderful rush. I've heard that the body releases endorphins, substances that take away physical pain and improve the mood. I believe it. When I feel the high, I don't feel any pain at all. I understand how people can get hooked on running!

The next step for the student is to

    a. Write a draft.　　　　　　**d.** Proofread and edit.

    b. Revise to add detail.　　　　(**e.**) Hand in the paragraph.

    c. Revise for organization and transitional words.

2.

Questions	Answers
What results does running give?	Toned legs, flat stomach, good skin
How does running affect eating	Eat whatever I want; clothes fit
How often should I run?	Twenty-five minutes, four days a week
What is runner's high?	Endorphin rush; pain leaves; mental lift

The next step for the student is to

    (**a.**) Write a draft.　　　　　　**d.** Proofread and edit.

    b. Revise to add detail.　　　　**e.** Hand in the paragraph.

    c. Revise for organization and transitional words.

3.　　Running for exercise has many benefits. It allows me to be outside. Running gives me great results. I love how toned my legs get when I run regularly, and my stomach has become flat! I can eat what I want and not gain weight. Runner's high makes running great.

The next step for the student is to

    a. Write a draft.　　　　　　**d.** Proofread and edit.

    (**b.**) Revise to add detail.　　　　Hand in the paragraph.

    c. Revise for organization and transitional words.

What You Know Now

The writing process involves four steps: prewriting, drafting, revising, and editing. Writers use these steps to come up with ideas, get them down on paper, and polish their writing. The steps are flexible. For example, you may wish to spend more time drafting and less time prewriting and editing. Knowing the four steps can help you develop your paragraph at every stage in writing.

WRITING PRACTICE Write Your Own Paragraph

People exercise in different ways. Some people, like the writers in this chapter, run to get in shape. Others, however, walk, swim, lift weights, play ball, ride bicycles, skate, or do any number of other activities. Your assignment is this: *Write a paragraph about an activity that you do to stay in shape.* If you don't do some type of formal exercise, then write about why you don't exercise.

Follow these steps to write your paragraph.

1. Use one or more prewriting techniques to come up with ideas.
2. Use your notes from prewriting to write a rough draft.
3. Revise your paragraph, reading through it to check for the first three of the four Cs: *concise, credible,* and *clear* writing.
4. Edit your paragraph for sentence effectiveness, word use, grammar, punctuation, and spelling.

When you're finished, your paragraph should include the following:

- A clear topic sentence
- Support points that relate to the topic sentence
- Specific details that give proof of your support points
- Transitions that connect your support points and specific details

Lab Activity 8

For additional practice with writing process steps, complete Lab Activity 8 in the Lab Manual at the back of the book.

PART THREE
The Elements of Good Writing

9   Writing an Effective Topic Sentence

  Science

Though studying physics or chemistry may seem to be of value only to people wishing to become scientists or astronauts, these subjects are an important part of our everyday lives. From the names of the planets in our solar system to the scientists who have shaped the way we think about our world, science helps us understand how and why the earth is, physically, as it is.

What Is a Good Topic Sentence?

We've seen that the most important part of any paragraph is the **topic sentence,** which expresses the main idea. If your topic sentence is strong, you will easily find support points and specific details that offer proof for it. The result will be a concise paragraph—unified and coherent. Remember: Everything you write in your paragraph should start with and return to the topic sentence.

Guidelines for Writing an Effective Topic Sentence

In academic writing, topic sentences can be long or short, and they can appear anywhere in a paragraph. This text, however, will encourage you to place your topic sentence first in your paragraph. The following simple guidelines will help you craft an effective topic sentence that will help make a paragraph concise. (See the "Paragraph Writing Skills" illustration on page 118 for questions to help you evaluate your own topic sentences.)

Paragraph Writing Skills

Skill 1
Writing an effective topic sentence
makes a paragraph *concise.*

- Is the topic sentence a complete sentence?
- Can the topic sentence be supported well in one paragraph?
- Does the topic sentence express my purpose?
- Does the topic sentence express my point of view about the topic?

↓

Skill 2
Using specific details for support makes a paragraph *credible.*

↓

Skill 3
Organizing and linking your ideas makes a paragraph *clear.*

↓

Skill 4
Writing correct sentences makes a paragraph *correct.*

Choose a Topic You Care About

Caring about your topic is the single most important rule you can follow in writing. If you choose a topic that does not interest you, you'll have a hard time coming up with enough support points and specific details to write a well-developed paragraph. Therefore, once your instructor has assigned a general topic, narrow it to something that interests you.

General Topic	Narrowed Topic
Frightening movies	*Psycho*
Contagious diseases	AIDS

EXERCISE 1 NARROWING YOUR TOPIC

Write a narrowed topic for each general topic below. An example is done for you. Answers will vary.

General topic: ___A person you admire_____

Narrowed topic: ___My father_____

1. General topic: Food you don't like

Narrowed topic: _Brussels sprouts_____

2. General topic: Do-it-yourself home repairs

Narrowed topic: _Fixing leaky toilet_____

3. General topic: Cooking

Narrowed topic: _Making meatloaf_____

4. General topic: Ways to relax

Narrowed topic: _Taking yoga_____

5. General topic: Public transportation

Narrowed topic: _Riding the subway_____

Let Your Topic Sentence Develop Slowly

Don't feel compelled to write a perfect topic sentence on the first try. Instead, do some prewriting and see what ideas seem dominant. Don't feel as if you have to include everything. Chances are, the ideas that you really want to explore will emerge as the strongest in your freewriting, listing, questioning, clustering, or outlining in your journal. Other details can be saved for later or simply discarded as you write your rough draft.

Theo's assignment was to write about a subject he would like to know more about. He began by freewriting.

There's so much I'd like to know more about. Where do I start? I guess I'd really like to understand science and space. I've always wanted to be a pilot, so maybe

Our Solar System

JOURNAL RESPONSE Our solar system—which includes our sun and the planets Mercury, Venus, Earth, Mars, Jupiter, Saturn, Uranus, Neptune, and Pluto—is one of many such systems in the vastness of space. Write a journal entry about what you imagine it would be like to travel in space. What might you find?

learning about these areas can help me get started. I probably need to know about weather and other things if I'm going to learn how to fly a plane. I've heard that flying a plane isn't too hard but that getting to be a pilot can be challenging. That's what I'd like to learn about, though.

In this freewriting sample, Theo begins by writing that he'd like to learn more about science and space. Very quickly, however, Theo discovers what he's really interested in: becoming a pilot. Right there, Theo has found the subject that his paragraph will address. The idea "getting to be a pilot can be challenging" could very well be the main idea that he puts in his topic sentence.

Make Sure Your Topic Sentence Is a Sentence

After you have an idea that interests you, make sure to state this idea in the form of a complete sentence, not just a phrase. A **sentence** communicates a complete thought. The phrase "having a job while I was in high school" doesn't tell your readers whether you enjoyed your job in high school or hated it. If you write "Having a job while I was in high school made my life stressful," your readers will know exactly what you're going to describe to them. The following examples show how phrases can be turned into sentences.

Phrases	Sentences
Learning to become a pilot	Learning to become a pilot is a difficult process.
Children having children	Having a child before you're an adult yourself can be a huge challenge.
Getting a college degree	Earning a college degree gave my dad options.

Make Sure Your Topic Sentence Is Not Too Broad

Sometimes, having too many possibilities for development can be a problem. In a single paragraph, you should use three or four support points with specific details. If you need more examples than that to develop your idea, you should narrow your topic sentence. The following topic sentence is too broad.

Too broad: Many scientists know many things.

While you could find numerous examples to support this topic sentence, you'd have a hard time covering even a fraction of the "many" scientists it mentions. A narrowed topic sentence would work better.

Effective: Sir Isaac Newton made important contributions to the study of gravity.

Too Broad	Effective
Employment is a huge problem.	Finding a job has been hard for me.
School is important.	An education gave me career choices.

EXERCISE 2 RECOGNIZING OVERLY BROAD TOPIC SENTENCES

In the space before each sentence write "Too broad" if the topic sentence is too broad, or write "Good" if the topic sentence is effective.

1. __Too broad__   Many scientists have contributed much to their fields of study.

2. _Good_ _____ The physicist Robert J. Oppenheimer made important contributions to atomic research.

3. _Too broad_ _____ Scientists understand a lot about the world.

4. _Too broad_ _____ Ancient Greek scientists were highly intelligent.

5. _Good_ _____ The Greek scientist Archimedes made great advances in his studies of buoyancy.

Make Sure Your Topic Sentence Is Not Too Narrow

One danger of writing about a subject you care about is focusing too closely on one aspect of that subject. For instance, if your topic is ways your sister used to annoy you, the topic sentence "My older sister used to put soap on my toothbrush" is too narrow. While the sentence might be used as a specific detail, as a topic sentence it doesn't give you much to talk about.

A topic sentence such as "My older sister was mean" raises the questions "How was she mean?" "How often was she mean?" "In what ways was she mean?" and "Why was she mean?" You won't answer all of these questions in one paragraph, but you get to choose which ones you want to answer. This topic gives you something to argue, and it also gives you room to offer examples of how your sister was mean.

In each example below, a topic sentence that is too narrow has been broadened to allow room for the writer to add support points and specific details to develop a paragraph.

Too Narrow	**Effective**
I didn't get hired at the medical center.	Getting a job at the medical center is difficult.
My parents got a divorce.	People get divorced for many reasons.
My uncle, a truck driver, had an accident.	Working as a long-distance trucker can be hazardous.

A different kind of narrow topic sentence is one that leads nowhere. Watch out for topic sentences that just state what the paragraph will be about, like this one: "This paragraph will be about the scientist Benjamin Banneker." The topic may interest you, but this topic sentence does not give a way to develop a whole paragraph. The following examples show how simple statements can become effective topic sentences.

Simple Statement	**Effective Topic Sentence**
The importance of Marie Curie is the subject of this paragraph.	Marie Curie made major contributions to science.
The contributions of the ancient Greek scientist Archimedes will be discussed in this paragraph.	The ancient Greek scientist Archimedes made important discoveries about water density and volume.

EXERCISE 3 RECOGNIZING OVERLY NARROW TOPIC SENTENCES

In the space before each sentence, write "Too narrow" if the topic sentence is too narrow, and write "Good" if the topic sentence is effective.

1. <u>Too narrow</u>   Marie Curie was the only scientist to win a Nobel Prize in both physics and chemistry.

2. <u>Good</u>   Marie Curie was an important scientist.

3. <u>Too narrow</u>   Benjamin Banneker taught himself to do calculus.

4. <u>Too narrow</u>   Robert J. Oppenheimer is known for his work on developing the atomic bomb.

5. <u>Too narrow</u>   Sir Isaac Newton was an English scientist.

Make Sure Your Topic Sentence Expresses Your Purpose

One of the purposes of writing is to inform, so you could write a paragraph informing the reader about *how* your sister sneakily put soap on your toothbrush. However, your usual purpose in writing an academic paragraph will be to persuade your audience. So in this book, we'll focus on writing topic sentences for persuasive paragraphs. Thus, your topic sentences needs to suggest that you intend to offer persuasive points—not just factual details—throughout your paragraph. Consider, for example, the following topic sentence.

Benjamin Banneker was an African-American scientist.

This topic sentence could work well as the topic sentence of an informative paragraph, but it doesn't allow for much development or discussion in a persuasive paragraph.

For an academic paragraph, a more effective topic sentence would be the following:

The African-American scientist Benjamin Banneker accomplished much in his life.

Now you not only have a topic for discussion—Benjamin Banneker—but you also have room to expand your ideas to include explanations of what his many accomplishments were.

A persuasive topic sentence (1) expresses an attitude or belief, (2) draws a conclusion, or (3) makes a recommendation. The following examples show how an informational topic sentence can be changed into a persuasive one.

Informational	**Persuasive**
Ice cream is one kind of dessert.	Ice cream <u>makes a great dessert</u>. (The phrase *makes a great dessert* expresses an attitude.)
Many high school students have jobs.	Having a part-time job in high school <u>can interfere with schoolwork</u>. (The phrase *can interfere with schoolwork* draws a conclusion for the paragraph to prove.)

EXERCISE 4 IDENTIFYING INFORMATIONAL AND PERSUASIVE TOPIC SENTENCES

In the blank before each sentence, write "Informational" if the topic sentence expresses the purpose of informing and write "Persuasive" if the topic sentence suggests that the paragraph's purpose is to persuade.

1. <u>Informational</u> Follow these steps to install your DVD player.

2. <u>Persuasive</u> Living in this city has been an exciting and educational experience.

3. <u>Persuasive</u> Undergraduates should be required to take two semesters of science to get a degree.

4. <u>Informational</u>   Traveling around Mexico this summer was fun.

5. <u>Persuasive</u>   Playing in a band has been a gratifying experience.

Make Sure Your Topic Sentence Is Complete

One way to make sure your topic sentence is neither too broad nor too narrow is to check for two components: your *topic* and your *point of view*. These two parts work together to create an effective topic sentence. Your subject for discussion is your topic, and what you think of that subject is your **point of view** about it.

For instance, this topic sentence lacks a point of view: "Science is not well known." The subject matter—science—is clear, but what the writer thinks about science is not. Does the writer want to write about the ways that people know little about science, why people know little about science, or even the effects of people knowing little about science? Doing even one of these is a huge task for a single paragraph, but doing all of them well is nearly impossible. The incomplete topic sentence leads, in this case, to too many choices.

An easy way to complete your topic sentence—and, thus, make it more manageable—is to include a word or phrase that says what's important or what you think about your narrowed topic. This word or phrase is easy to spot because it is the part of the topic sentence that communicates the writer's point of view about the narrowed topic.

The topic sentence "Science affects people's lives in many important ways" is complete. The reader can tell both what the *narrowed topic* is (science) and what the *writer's point of view* about the topic is (that science affects people's lives).

The topic sentences below are complete because they contain both a narrowed topic and the writer's point of view.

Narrowed Topic	Point of View
<u>Finding a job</u>	has been <u>hard</u> for me.
An <u>education</u>	<u>gave me options</u>.
My <u>friend Dolly</u>	has a <u>stressful job</u>.
<u>Getting a job at the medical center</u>	is <u>difficult</u>.
<u>Working as a long-distance trucker</u>	can be <u>hazardous</u>.

EXERCISE 5 IDENTIFYING PARTS OF THE TOPIC SENTENCE

In the topic sentences below, circle the topic and underline the word or phrase that gives the writer's point of view. An example is done for you.

If students underline an additional word (i.e., "many" in item 12), their answers can still be correct.

(Albert Einstein's studies) have had a <u>huge impact</u> on our lives.

1. The French scientist (Marie Curie) made <u>major contributions</u> to physics and chemistry.

2. The (scientific method) <u>helps scientists study</u> our world.

3. The physicist (Robert J. Oppenheimer) made <u>large advances</u> in atomic research.

4. The (calorie) is a measurement with <u>important</u> uses in both science and daily life.

5. The Greek scientist (Archimedes) made <u>great advances</u> in his studies of buoyancy.

6. The Italian scientist (Galileo Galilei) <u>suffered</u> as a result of his studies.

7. (Geometry,) the branch of math dealing with points and lines, <u>helps</u> us makes sense of our world.

8. The first (nuclear reactor) <u>would not exist</u> without the work of Italian-born scientist Enrico Fermi.

9. The (metric system) is more <u>logical</u> than the English system of measurement, which is still used in the United States.

10. (Memorizing) the periodic table of elements can have many <u>benefits</u>.

11. The (names) of the planets in our solar system have <u>interesting</u> origins.

12. (Studying science) can have many <u>benefits</u>.

13. (Learning about science) can <u>teach people about other subjects</u>.

14. (Science) is an <u>important part of history</u>.

15. (Scientists) have <u>suffered for their discoveries</u>.

Make Your Topic Sentence the First Sentence of Your Paragraph

Placing your topic sentence first in your paragraph helps you in two ways. First, it gives you a consistent reference point to make sure you're on target with your support points and specific details. Second, it gives your reader an immediate idea of what your paragraph will be about.

Once you've become a more experienced writer, you can put the topic sentence anywhere you like—even as the last sentence in your paragraph. While you're gaining confidence in your writing through your progress in this text, however, place your topic sentence first.

✓ CHECKLIST Does Your Topic Sentence Give Your Point of View?

- Does your topic sentence include words that express an attitude or a belief?

  Examples   Writing a paragraph is *hard* work.

  Cats are *easy* to care for as pets.

- Does your topic sentence include words that draw a conclusion?

  Example   My coach *helped* me make the most of my talent.

- Does your topic sentence include words that make a recommendation?

  Example   Marriage *should be* a short-term contract, not a lifetime commitment.

- Would the opposite of your topic sentence also make sense?

  Examples   Writing a paragraph is *not* hard work.

  Cats are *not* easy to care for as pets.

  My coach did *not* help me make the most of my talent.

  Marriage should *not* be a short-term contract, but a lifetime commitment.

EXERCISE 6 USING POINT-OF-VIEW WORDS OR PHRASES TO WRITE A TOPIC SENTENCE

Choose five narrowed topics from the list below. Then, write a word or phrase that offers your point of view about that narrowed topic.

Finally, write a topic sentence using both the narrowed topic and the point-of-view words that you chose. An example is done for you.

Narrowed Topics   Answers will vary.

Spicy food   Learning another language

Video games   Hip-hop music

The benefits of exercise   Taking dance lessons

Taking care of a puppy   Deciding to buy a car

Reality television shows   Doing good deeds

Topic: _Taking care of a puppy_____

Point-of-view words: _Exhausting_____

Topic sentence: _Taking care of a puppy is exhausting._____

1. Topic: _Answers will vary._____

   Point-of-view words: _____

   Topic sentence: _____

2. Topic: _____

   Point-of-view words: _____

   Topic sentence: _____

3. Topic: _____

   Point-of-view words: _____

   Topic sentence: _____

4. Topic: _____

   Point-of-view words: _____

   Topic sentence: _____

5. Topic: _____

Point-of-view words: _____

Topic sentence: _____

EXERCISE 7 IDENTIFYING THE TOPIC SENTENCE IN A PARAGRAPH

The following sentence groups contain the elements of a good paragraph: topic sentence, support points, and specific details. However, the topic sentence is not in the same place in both groups. Read each sentence group, and underline the topic sentence. Then fill in the blank that follows.

A.   **Suffering in Science**

[1]The scientist Antoine Lavoisier was beheaded during the French Revolution because the revolutionaries claimed France had "no need of scientists." [2]The American physicist Robert J. Oppenheimer lost his government security clearance because of his opposition to building of the hydrogen bomb. [3]<u>Many scientists suffered as a result of their scientific interests.</u> [4]The Roman Catholic Church forced Galileo Galilei to deny his belief that the earth revolved around the sun.

The topic sentence is sentence ____3____.

B.   **Helpful Inventions**

[1]In inventing the light bulb, Thomas Edison enabled us to have light at all hours, not just when the sun shines. [2]<u>Many inventions have made our lives easier and more enjoyable.</u> [3]Alexander Graham Bell invented the telephone, which lets us talk to people who are miles away. [4]The wireless telegraph, which was invented by Guglielmo Marconi, led to the creation of commercial radio.

The topic sentence is sentence ____2____.

Guglielmo Marconi and the Telegraph

WRITE A PARAGRAPH The invention of the wireless telegraph made immediate long-distance communication possible. What invention have you found helpful? Write a paragraph explaining how a certain invention—cell phone, computer, pager, stereo—has improved your life in some way.

C. **Smaller and Smaller**

[1]We can't see molecules with our bare eyes, but they are made up of smaller units of matter called atoms. [2]Atoms contain the smaller elements called protons, neutrons, and electrons. [3]Units of matter in science seem to get smaller and smaller, the closer you look. [4]Though protons and neutrons seem very tiny, even they are partially made of particles called quarks.

The topic sentence is sentence ____3____.

EXERCISE 8 WRITING TOPIC SENTENCES FROM DETAILS

Below are lists of specific details that can serve as the proof for a writer's topic sentence. Write a topic sentence that you think best includes all the details. Answers will vary.

1. Topic sentence: Many planets get their names from Roman mythology.

Specific details **a.** The Red Planet, Mars, is named for the Roman god of war because red is the color of the blood shed in war.

    b. Saturn, called the most beautiful of the planets, gets its name from the Roman god of agriculture.

    c. The fifth major planet from the sun is named Jupiter after the ruler of the Roman gods.

    d. Pluto, the smallest major planet and the one farthest from the sun, is named for the Roman god of the underworld.

2. Topic sentence: Three different scales are used to measure heat in science.

Specific details: **a.** The Celsius scale designates zero as the temperature at which water freezes and 100 degrees as the temperature at which water boils.

    b. The standard temperature scale in scientific work, called the Kelvin scale, measures heat starting at 273 degrees below zero on the Celsius scale.

    c. The Fahrenheit scale measures water freezing at 32 degrees and water boiling at 212 degrees, but its units of measurement are smaller than those of the Celsius and Kelvin scales.

3. Topic sentence: Many chemical elements are part of our everyday lives.

Specific details: **a.** The element chlorine is widely used for cleaning and sterilization.

    b. Gold, whose chemical symbol is Au, is an element that is highly valued for its beauty.

    c. The element of iron is used to make steel and has many other uses in our lives.

    d. Oxygen, one of the most important elements for humans, allows us to breathe.

What You Know Now

Writing a topic sentence involves combining a narrowed topic with words expressing your point of view. Writing a topic sentence that is neither too broad nor too narrow allows you to develop your ideas adequately in a single paragraph. Following the guidelines in this chapter can help you write an effective topic sentence.

WRITING PRACTICE Write Your Own Paragraph

This chapter has given you information on scientific topics. Besides science, many other subjects are important—and relevant—for people to study. Your assignment is this: *Write a paragraph about a subject that you would like to study or have enjoyed studying.* If no subject interests you, write about a subject that you would not like to study or have not enjoyed studying.

Follow these steps to write your paragraph.

1. Use one or more prewriting techniques to come up with ideas for your paragraph.

2. Write a topic sentence that includes a narrowed topic and point-of-view words.

3. Use your notes from prewriting to write a rough draft of your paragraph.

4. Revise your paragraph, reading through it to check for the first three of the four Cs: *concise, credible,* and *clear* writing.

5. Edit your paragraph for sentence effectiveness, word use, grammar, punctuation, and spelling.

When you're finished, your paragraph should include the following:

- A clear topic sentence
- Support points that relate to the topic sentence
- Specific details that give proof of your support points
- Transitions that connect your support points and specific details

Lab Activity 9

For additional practice with topic sentences, complete Lab Activity 9 in the Lab Manual at the back of the book.

10 Using Specific Details for Support and Illustration

CULTURE NOTE *Coffee*

Though long a staple at breakfast and in boardrooms, coffee has become increasingly popular in the United States over the past two decades. A large number of coffee drinks, ranging from plain black coffee to more complicated concoctions such as café lattes and white mochas, have become a regular part of seemingly everyone's day. Coffee has also become more than just a morning habit. Nearby coffeehouses and vendors make before-work, after-lunch, and late-night coffee consumption common.

Making Your Case

Even the most wonderful, clear topic sentences need help to be convincing. That's where specific details come in. Specific details make people believe you. If you offer proof to support your beliefs, your writing will be effective and professional. Using specific details in your writing helps you master the second of the four Cs: *credible* writing. The illustration "Paragraph Writing Skills" on page 134 shows how using specific details for support helps create an effective paragraph.

Three Types of Details

Evidence comes in many forms, and your specific details will come from many sources. Keep in mind that specific details should *add* information to support your points, not simply repeat the points. To find a broad range of information, use different types of proof. Three common types are described here.

Paragraph Writing Skills

Skill 1
Writing an effective topic sentence
makes a paragraph *concise.*

↓

Skill 2
Using specific details for support
makes a paragraph *credible.*

- Are my specific details directly related to my topic sentence?
- Do my details give information that will persuade my reader?
- Have I told the reader the sources for my specific details?
- Are my sources reliable?
- Have I given enough specific details to be convincing?
- Have I used vivid, specific language that appeals to the senses?

↓

Skill 3
Organizing and linking your ideas
makes a paragraph *clear.*

↓

Skill 4
Writing correct sentences
makes a paragraph *correct.*

Descriptions of Objects or Events in Your Life

You have a ready-made source of information available to you: your own life. Your own experiences can serve as proof of your ideas, particularly when your experiences directly support your point.

Coffee Field

WRITE A PARAGRAPH People view coffee differently, some praising its pick-me-up virtues as others denounce its taste and caffeine content. What do you think about coffee? Write a paragraph explaining your views on coffee or any other food or beverage you choose.

For instance, Marty sent his friend the following e-mail message about a new coffeehouse that he liked.

> I love the Java Joint. The coffee is really good, and after working in the Cuppa Joe café for all those years, I know coffee. Plus, I love their selection. At Cuppa Joe, I always felt a little guilty offering customers only three coffee choices. At the Java Joint, they offer more than ten.

Marty establishes credibility by mentioning that he used to work in a coffeehouse. Thus, he has the knowledge and experience to evaluate coffee.

Accounts of Events in Other People's Lives

Sometimes the best way to learn is to listen. Your friends, family, co-workers, and classmates have likely shared experiences with you, and these experiences may have a place in your writing. For instance, if your assignment is to write about the pros or cons of having a sibling and you are an only child, talking to a friend who has brothers or sisters can be a big help. Sandy, who is an only child, wrote this about siblings.

> Having brothers is a real bonus. Even though I'm an only child, I've seen the benefits of having brothers through my best friend, Margie. Margie has three older brothers, and she always knows all the current sports facts from listening to them. She gets teased a lot, but she's learned to dish it out so that she can take an insult from anyone—and give one back—without blushing the way I do.

Sandy uses her friend's experiences to support her ideas. Even though she doesn't have firsthand experience, she offers proof to support her point.

Facts That You've Heard About or Read in Trusted Sources

Just as your friends have had experiences that you haven't shared, so have other people. Watching the news or reading a newspaper provides you with information that you might need to support your topic sentence. For instance, suppose your instructor asks you to write about the effects of a natural disaster. You might have a hard time if you've never experienced a hurricane, earthquake, or flood. However, reading about a hurricane in the Caribbean could give you information you can use in your writing.

Harry, who had never experienced a natural disaster, discussed an earthquake like this:

> Earthquakes do an incredible amount of damage. I read in the *San Francisco Chronicle* that hundreds of people were injured during the 1989 earthquake. The newspaper also explained how thousands of people experienced damage to their homes or workplaces as a result of the quake and that traffic was backed up for months.

Possible Sources of Information

Documentary films	Reference books
Magazines	Television
Newspapers	Textbooks
Radio	Internet

When you're using information from experiences that are not your own, be sure to tell your reader where the information comes from. That way, your reader will not think you're trying to take credit for experiences you haven't had. Also, make sure that the source you use for support is credible. Stay away from unofficial documents that may not contain accurate information. See the box "Possible Sources of Information" above for a list of sources you can use.

Particularly on the Internet, make sure the sites you use as references are credible. Be especially careful of Web site addresses containing a tilde (~). This mark indicates that the site is operated by an individual, who could be anyone—including a child or a person playing online pranks. For more information on evaluating Internet sources, see Chapter 25. For more information on finding sources, see the chapter on Writing a Research Paper, which is online (www.ablongman.com/long).

Knowing What Details to Choose

One of the most important aspects of using specific details is knowing *which* details to use. For instance, if your assignment is to write about a childhood friend, you probably won't find many helpful details in a newspaper. Similarly, if your assignment is to write about a local news issue, your childhood experiences won't do you much good. In choosing your specific details, then, *let your topic determine what kinds of details to use.* Remember: You can always find information—you just have to know where to look.

EXERCISE 1 CHOOSING RELEVANT SOURCES FOR DETAILS

Below are possible topics for paragraphs. Decide what sources would be most helpful in finding details for a paragraph on that topic. Then write "My life," "Someone I know," or "Trusted sources" in the space after each topic. You may write more than one source for a topic. Two examples are done for you.   Answers will vary.

Benefits of owning a pet___My life_____

Hardships of homeless people _Trusted sources_____

1. Benefits of having strict parents _My life; someone I know_____

2. Downside to being a rebel _My life; someone I know_____

3. Hardships of moving around often _My life; someone I know_____

4. Success/failure of a professional athlete _Trusted sources_____

5. Benefits/downside to taking vitamins _Trusted sources; my life_____

EXERCISE 2 RECOGNIZING CREDIBILITY

The following two paragraphs address the topic of working in a coffeehouse. The writers of both paragraphs draw on their personal experiences to support their ideas. Which paragraph does a better job of credibly describing work in a coffeehouse?   "Coffee, Anyone?"

The Coffee Job

[1]Working in a coffeehouse is a lot of work. [2]One part of the job that is a lot of work is making the coffee. [3]There is a lot of it to make, and it always needs to be made. [4]Making the coffee is a lot of work, too. [5]Another way that a coffeehouse job is a lot of work is in cleaning up. [6]The coffeehouse sure could get messy, and I'd have to clean it up. [7]It seemed like the cleaning never stopped. [8]Last of all, dealing with people is a lot of work. [9]I could never get used to dealing with so many people and in so many ways. [10]Just thinking about that job makes me tired.

Coffee, Anyone?

[1]Working in a coffeehouse is much more difficult than people realize. [2]First, there's so much information to keep track of. [3]Not only do you have to know many types of coffees from Brazilian to French Roast, but you also have to know all the different drinks that can be made from those coffees. [4]In my five years at the Coffee Cup, I must have made a hundred kinds of coffee drinks: espresso, latte, cappuccino, mocha, not to mention all the iced coffee drinks. [5]Thinking about all of those coffee mixtures makes my head spin. [6]In addition to learning all that information, you have a lot of hard work to do. [7]Of course, you have to make the coffee. [8]Then, there are all the tables and chairs to wipe down after sticky hands have touched them. [9]Plus, there are always dishes to do. [10]At the end of a workday, my hands would be raw from all the cleaning. [11]Finally, dealing with people is a challenge. [12]Some people are really easy to serve and just want black coffee. [13]Other people, though, have to have their coffee drinks made a different way every time. [14]One person who came to the coffeehouse loved to order a nonfat decaffeinated mocha, but then he'd have me put double whipped cream on it. [15]I never did remember every single order, but I did get better. [16]For me, a coffee break meant there was no coffee in sight.

It's easy to believe that the second paragraph, "Coffee, Anyone?" was written by someone who worked in a coffeehouse. The writer uses support points that allow the reader to understand why the job was difficult, and he then uses specific examples to *show* the reader what he means. In the first paragraph, "The Coffee Job," the writer offers very few details that let the reader see how difficult his job was. Instead, the writer simply repeats his ideas over and over, which does little to prove his point.

EXERCISE 3 ANALYZING SPECIFIC DETAILS IN PARAGRAPHS

Reread "The Coffee Job" on the previous page and "Coffee, Anyone?" on this page. Then fill in the blanks.

1. In sentence 4 in "Coffee, Anyone?" the writer explains that he

worked for __5__ years at a coffeehouse called the Coffee Cup .

2. Does the writer of "The Coffee Job" mention any specific

experience working in a coffeehouse? <u>No</u>

3. Both paragraphs mention that cleaning is a big job in a coffee-house. Which paragraph offers more specific information about cleaning?

_____ "The Coffee Job"

___X___ "Coffee, Anyone?"

4. By reading sentences 1 to 5 of "Coffee, Anyone?" you can tell that the writer knows something about coffee. List three specific details that tell you this. Answers may vary.

a. He mentions different types of coffee.
_____

b. He mentions different coffee drinks.
_____

c. He mentions his five years of experience.
_____

5. In "The Coffee Job," the writer would be more convincing if he offered more details in sentence 6. Write down one type of cleaning job that you think the writer could have used for proof.

Answers will vary.
_____

_____

Writing Vivid Details

In addition to proving your point, specific details make your writing more interesting. After all, would you want to read about a car when you could read about a gleaming, candy-apple red convertible? Use your words to paint a picture for your reader, and your reader will want to read on.

Additionally, vivid descriptions lend credibility to your writing. If you're writing about your fear of bees, for instance, but all you can say is "I'm afraid of bees," your reader can't *see* how afraid you are. If, instead, you write about your sweaty palms, pounding heart, and dizziness at the sight of a bee, your reader will most likely acknowledge your fear.

Use Words That Appeal to the Five Senses

The best way to help someone understand what you've experienced is to make your writing as close to a physical experience as possible. Using words that appeal to the **senses**—that help your reader see, hear, smell, taste, and feel what you're describing—will make your points more vivid for readers. Saying that your sweater is soft is a good start, but saying that your sweater is as soft as a kitten's fur is better. Your reader will immediately know that the sweater feels soft *and* just how soft it is.

General	Specific
The risotto was flavorful.	The risotto tasted as though twelve cloves of garlic had exploded in my mouth.
The waterfall was pretty.	Millions of crystal drops cascaded through the air, reflecting sunlight before foaming into the current below.

EXERCISE 4   RECOGNIZING WRITING THAT APPEALS TO THE SENSES

One of the two paragraphs below has specific details that support its topic sentence, while the other does not. Which paragraph uses specific details more effectively? *"A Sense of Coffee"*

A Sense of Coffee

¹A well-brewed cup of coffee provides a wonderful experience for all my senses. ²First, before I even see the coffee, I can smell the aroma of specially blended Colombian coffee throughout the house. ³It smells a little like the first campfire of the morning on a cold camping trip and reminds me of my grandmother's baking. ⁴Then, still before I see the coffee, I can hear the "drip, sizzle, drip, sizzle, drip," sound that my brew makes as it drains from the water holder on my coffee machine into the coffeepot. ⁵It's music to my ears. ⁶The sight of fresh coffee, too, is glorious. ⁷The rich brown color reminds me of deep forests or newly plowed soil just waiting to be planted with seeds. ⁸Every image that comes to mind is of growing, living things, and the steam that floats up from the mug seems like a magic genie. ⁹Then comes the feel. ¹⁰I always pour it into my

favorite huge mug so I can use both hands to pick it up. [11]The mug is always very warm, and on cold mornings, the feel of the coffee mug is comforting. [12]Best of all is the taste. [13]Coffee tastes strong and gentle at the same time, like a chocolate cake made with butter. [14]Coffee also has a faint burned taste, maybe from the roasting of the coffee beans. [15]No matter how I come into contact with coffee, it's a treat.

The Coffee Experience

[1]Coffee really appeals to my senses. [2]The sight of coffee is unlike any other. [3]It just looks so inviting and delicious. [4]Then the smell of coffee is terrific, too. [5]Its smell always reminds me of so many things I like. [6]I never get tired of the smell! [7]Hearing coffee being brewed is great. [8]I can always imagine just what it sounds like, even if no coffee is being made right then. [9]Touching a coffee cup or mug makes me feel good. [10]Coffee makes me feel good even before I taste it, probably because I like the way it feels. [11]Finally, coffee tastes great. [12]It always tastes the same, but then it always tastes a little different, too. [13]I'll never forget my first cup of coffee. [14]It was great in every way.

The first paragraph, "A Sense of Coffee," uses vivid language to illustrate how coffee appeals to the writer's senses. As a result, a reader is more likely to enjoy the paragraph and also to believe that the writer knows what she's writing about. The second paragraph, "The Coffee Experience," has a clear topic sentence and is solidly organized, but it lacks detail. The reader is left wondering *what about* coffee is so "inviting and delicious," *why* it makes the writer "feel good," or *what about* coffee tastes "great."

EXERCISE 5 ANALYZING DETAILS THAT APPEAL TO THE SENSES

Reread the paragraph titled "A Sense of Coffee" on pages 141–142. Then fill in the blanks below.

1. In sentence 2, what is one type of coffee mentioned?   <u>Colombian</u>

2. In sentence 3, the writer compares coffee's aroma to _____
<u>the first campfire of the morning</u>   and   <u>grandmother's baking.</u>

3. From sentences 12, 13, and 14 choose at least one detail that appeals to the reader's sense of taste. Answers may vary.

Coffee tastes like a chocolate cake made with butter.

4. In sentence 7, the comparison of coffee's color to "newly plowed soil" appeals to the sense of sight _____ .

5. One other detail from the paragraph that is effective is _____ Answers will vary. , and it appeals to the sense of Answers will vary. .

Use Descriptive Modifiers

Place **modifiers**—descriptive words—before nouns. Writing about a crystal-clear lake gives your reader a much better idea of what you saw than simply referring to a lake. If you're describing an action, modifiers help, too. Rather than writing that your friend was in a hurry, write that he immediately sped away from muggers.

General	Specific
Jen's fat cat moves slowly.	Jen's obese Manx moves more slowly than a snail.
The cookies made me hungry.	The warm butter cookies made my stomach growl and my mouth water.

Use Proper Names and Specific Nouns and Verbs

Often the details we use to support a point in writing could be more convincing if they were more specific. For instance, if you're writing about how fast a car is, you'll probably make your point better if you use a **proper name,** writing that the car is a Porsche or a Lamborghini. Also, instead of simply mentioning a man, write about Tran Ngyuen. Or if you're writing about your childhood bike, refer to your Trek mountain bike. Using proper names narrows your description dramatically.

Another way to make your ideas clear to your reader is to use **specific nouns.** Specific nouns offer your reader a clear view of what you are describing. The following list shows the difference between general nouns on the left and proper names and specific nouns on the right.

General Nouns	Proper Names and Specific Nouns
hairstyle	pony-tail, up-do, braid
meal	feast, breakfast, lunch, dinner
cat	Siamese, tabby, calico
sport	hockey, football, basketball, hunting

Using words that appeal to the senses, descriptive modifiers, and specific nouns and verbs can make the meaning of a sentence clear and powerful.

General Sentence	Specific Sentence
I ate a large meal.	I feasted on an elegant supper of caviar and salmon.
The song was moving.	I found myself in tears by the end of the ballad.
I want to take a trip.	I want to soak up the sun on Maui, Hawaii.
The guy on the show is good.	Felicity Huffman on the TV program *Desperate Housewives* is my hero.

EXERCISE 6 WRITING PROPER NAMES AND SPECIFIC NOUNS

The following list contains nouns that could be more specific. After each general detail, write a more specific version using proper names and specific nouns. An example is done for you.   Answers will vary.

dessert   *Chocolate mousse*

1. street   Quiet, tree-lined boulevard

2. flower   Blood-red rose in full bloom

3. college class   Philosophy of Art

4. rain   Whipping, driving downpour

5. toy   Overpriced trinket

Use Specific Verbs

Another way to make your language more vivid is to use **specific verbs.** Rather than write that you sang a song, write that you belted out the melody. Or, instead of saying that you relaxed, write that you sank into the couch like a cherry sinking into whipped cream. The more specific you can make your verbs, the better your reader will understand your meaning. Here are some examples.

General Verbs	Specific Verbs
sit	recline, perch, roost, lounge
spoke	whispered, muttered, yelled, screamed
hit	thrashed, punched, pummeled

EXERCISE 7 WRITING SPECIFIC VERBS

The verbs in the following list could be more effective if they were more specific. In the space after each word, write a more specific verb (Example a) or the same verb with a modifier (Example b). The modifier can be either a word or a group of words. Answers will vary.

Examples

A. write   Scrawl

B. eat   Eat like a pig at a trough

1. hum   Hum like a refrigerator

2. walk   Stalk with clenched fists

3. drive   Creep along in the slow lane

4. watch   Peer from around a corner

5. knock   Tap lightly

EXERCISE 8 WRITING SPECIFIC SENTENCES

The sentences in the following list are not very specific. Rewrite them using specific words in order to make them clearer. An example is done for you.   Answers will vary.

It was a hot day.   The sun beat down, making the asphalt shimmer

in waves of heat.

1. The restaurant was dirty.

Le Cochon glistened with the grease of a thousand blue plate specials, and the fetid stench of yesterday's garbage permeated the room.

2. The instructor acted mean on the first day of class.

After snapping at the timid student and frowning at anyone who appeared to have a question, Mr. Snidely slammed the classroom door.

3. The movie had violent parts.

Between taking bullets and delivering punches and kicks, Neo hardly had time to think in *The Matrix*.

4. I hurt my hand.

I scalded my hand in the mangle at the dry cleaners.

_____

5. Her hair looked nice.

Her auburn locks fell in shimmering waves past her shoulders.

_____

6. The song sounded wonderful.

"O Canada" had the entire Montreal Stadium population on its feet.

_____

7. The cheese tasted terrible.

Her first bite of pepper jack scalded her tongue.

_____

8. Sam helped me at home.

Sam refinished my table, fixed my leaky faucet, and organized my pantry.

_____

9. Jonquil treated her friend nicely.

Jonquil never failed to offer her ear when Maggie felt blue.

_____

10. The refrigerator needed cleaning.

Green crud clogged the cracks in the shelves of my Frigidaire.

_____

What You Know Now

Using specific details helps your reader know that you are familiar with your topic. Specific details can come from several areas: descriptions of objects or events in your life, accounts of events in other people's lives, and facts that you've heard about or read in trusted sources. In addition, using vivid language can both build your credibility and make your language more appealing. To write vividly, use words that appeal to the five senses—descriptive words, proper names, and specific nouns and verbs.

WRITING PRACTICE Write Your Own Paragraph

This chapter has given you opportunities to practice writing specific sentences. Now, you can practice turning those details into a paragraph. Your assignment is this: _Choose a topic from the following list and write a fully developed paragraph._ Concentrate on making your details as specific as possible, and use language that _shows_ your reader what you mean.

Topics

Dirty restaurants	Car accidents	Exciting music
Sports injuries	Informative Internet sites	Wild clothing
Helpful friends	Relaxing weekend spots	Delicious meals

Follow these steps to write your paragraph.

1. Use one or more prewriting techniques to come up with ideas.

2. Use your notes from prewriting to write a rough draft.

3. Include details from your life, from other people's lives, or from trusted sources. Include language that appeals to the five senses.

4. Revise your paragraph, reading through it to check for the first three of the four Cs: *concise, credible*, and *clear* writing.

5. Edit your paragraph for sentence effectiveness, word choice, grammar, punctuation, and spelling.

When you're finished, your paragraph should include the following:

- A clear topic sentence
- Support points that relate to the topic sentence
- Specific details that give proof of your support points
- Transitions that connect your support points and specific details

Lab Activity 10

For additional practice with using specific details, complete Lab Activity 10 in the Lab Manual at the back of the book.

11 Organizing and Linking Ideas

CULTURE NOTE *Influential Musical Entertainers, 1930–1960*

Though many musicians and singers have made a difference in the way popular music has developed, some have had more influence than others. From 1930 to 1960, music in the United States changed considerably. Key musical entertainers from these years—including Benny Goodman, Ella Fitzgerald, Frank Sinatra, and Elvis Presley—had distinct styles, but each had a huge impact on popular music.

Arranging the Pieces

As you've been reading examples of effective writing in this book, you've seen that the way ideas are put together is important to make the writing clear. Additionally, you've seen how transition words link ideas together, creating connections between the topic sentence, support points, and specific details. The illustration "Paragraph Writing Skills" on page 150 shows how the skill of organizing and linking your ideas helps create an effective paragraph.

Organizing for Clarity

When we hear someone say, "You're really great, but . . . ," we immediately know that bad news is coming. How do we know? We know because *but* is one of those words that signals a change of direction. It's one of

Paragraph Writing Skills

Skill 1
Writing an effective topic sentence
makes a paragraph *concise*.

↓

Skill 2
Using specific details for support
makes a paragraph *credible*.

↓

Skill 3
**Organizing and linking your ideas
makes a paragraph *clear*.**

- Have I organized my ideas?
- Have I used time sequence for examples that have a specific period or for items that occur step by step?
- Have I used emphatic order to emphasize my most important point?
- Have I used transitional words and terms to link my ideas?
- Have I linked my ideas by repeating key words, using pronouns, and using synonyms?

↓

Skill 4
Writing correct sentences
makes a paragraph *correct*.

many transitional words that helps us show the direction we're going in our writing.

Coming up with a solid topic sentence and finding the details to support it are essential writing skills. Next, you need to practice organizing your ideas so that your reader will know just which ones are most important to you. You also need to link your ideas. Transitions help your reader understand when you're adding to a point, changing directions, or finishing up. Putting your ideas in a logical order and using transitional words to make your order clear will help you master the third of the four Cs: *clear* writing.

Two Types of Order

You can organize your ideas in two ways.

- Time sequence (chronological) order
- Emphatic order

Time Sequence Order

Using **time sequence (chronological) order** means organizing events in the order in which they happened. The time sequence method is especially helpful when you use examples that occur over a specific period. Time sequence is also useful for paragraphs explaining how something happened or for anything that must be explained in a series of steps. The following paragraph uses time sequence.

Ol' Blue Eyes

Known for his blue eyes and his smooth voice, the singer Frank Sinatra appealed to many audiences. In the big-band years of the 1940s, Sinatra appealed to bobby-soxers, or teenage girls, who at that time wore bobby socks. Young women screamed and fainted when he sang his hit song "This Love of Mine." In the 1950s Sinatra's career almost ended because of damage to his vocal cords, but he continued to be popular. Even when rock and roll started to dominate popular music, Sinatra's album *Songs for Swingin' Lovers* stayed on the music charts for more than a year. In the 1960s, his albums *Nice and Easy* and *Strangers in the Night* were number one hits, and he was successful singing in Las Vegas. These were the years when the "Rat Pack"—Sinatra's group of friends that included the stars Sammy Davis, Jr., and Dean Martin—was most famous. During the 1970s and 1980s, Sinatra's reputation still grew, but he performed less. In 1990, Sinatra celebrated his seventy-fifth birthday with a national tour even though his voice had faded somewhat. For all his accomplishments, Sinatra received the Legend Award at the 1994 Grammy Awards in New York. Even after his death in 1998, Frank Sinatra is loved all over the world.

EXERCISE 1 RECOGNIZING TIME SEQUENCE ORDER

Reread "Ol' Blue Eyes" and answer the following questions.

1. The writer of "Ol' Blue Eyes" uses time, as in "the 1940s," to indicate the start of new support points. Besides "the 1940s," what six other signals does the writer use to let you know that the examples in the paragraph are organized according to time sequence?

   a. 1950s   d. 1990

   b. 1960s   e. 1994

   c. 1970s and 1980s   f. 1998

2. Circle the letters of all of the following statements that are true.

   a. Time sequence order shows that Sinatra had a long career.

   b. Time sequence order shows some of the changes in Sinatra's audience over the years.

   c. Time sequence order tells the reader which is Sinatra's most important audience.

   d. Time sequence order emphasizes Sinatra's most famous songs.

Emphatic Order

Emphatic order means putting your ideas in order of *least* important to *most* important. Emphatic order allows for more flexibility than time sequence order because the writer gets to decide the importance of each point. That is, two people could organize the same subject matter differently—using emphatic order—because they see different points as being more or less important. The following paragraph is organized using emphatic order.

The King

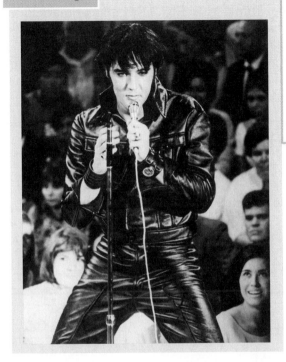

FOOD FOR THOUGHT The first music star to blend overt sexuality into his music, Elvis wowed crowds of swooning admirers. How important is sex appeal in making singers popular? Write a few sentences explaining the importance of sex appeal in singers' popularity.

Long Live the King!

Elvis Presley brought many changes to rock and roll music. First, his looks were different from those of traditional popular singers. He wore his black hair long and swept back off his face instead of short the way clean-cut young men did. He also wore tight pants and brightly colored shirts that were definitely not traditional. Second, Elvis's music had a sound all its own. Elvis combined parts of country music with rock and roll and blues. Some of his most popular songs were "Love Me Tender," "Hound Dog," and "Don't Be Cruel." Most important, Elvis made sex appeal part of his show. Instead of just standing behind his guitar and singing, Elvis moved his hips to his own rhythm. While girls in the audience swooned, other people were shocked. In fact, when Elvis first appeared on television in the 1950s, he was shown only from the waist up because his lower-body movements were considered too suggestive. With his looks, music, and sex appeal, the King changed rock and roll forever.

This writer organizes her ideas beginning with the point that is least important to her topic sentence and ending with the one that is most important. However, while *this* writer thinks that Elvis's sex appeal marked his greatest impact on rock and roll, another writer might think that Elvis's music or looks had the greatest impact.

As the writer, you rank the support points. Just be sure that your transition words and examples make clear why you've placed your support points in the order you have.

EXERCISE 2 RECOGNIZING EMPHATIC ORDER

Reread "Long Live the King!" Then answer the following questions.

1. What is the writer's topic sentence? _____

Elvis Presley brought many changes to rock and roll music.

2. What is the writer's first point? _____

Elvis's looks were different.

3. What is the second point the writer makes? _____

Elvis's music had a sound all its own.

4. What is the writer's most important point? _____

Elvis made sex appeal part of his show.

5. Do you agree with the writer's idea about which point is the most important? Why or why not? _____

Answers will vary.

Using Transitions

Transitions are words and expressions that organize and connect ideas. They can be placed at the beginning, middle, or end of a sentence. In the following examples, the transitions are in bold type.

To play piano well, you need to take lessons. Lessons alone, **however,** won't make you a great pianist. You have to have talent and perseverance, **too.**

To learn a new song, I read through the music **first,** humming the notes. **Next,** I pick out the notes and chords on my guitar. **Finally,** I practice playing the song over and over.

EXERCISE 3 RECOGNIZING TRANSITIONS IN CONTEXT

The paragraph below uses transitions to organize and connect ideas.

The Twist's Turn

The song called "The Twist" sung by Ernest Evans, popularly known as Chubby Checker, and the dance that went with it had a huge impact on American culture. First, the dance version of the twist revolutionized the way Americans danced. It allowed couples to break apart on the dance floor while still dancing together. Once Checker's song was played on *Dick Clark's American Bandstand* in 1961, both the song and the dance became enormously popular. Second, the song "The Twist" set a new standard for popularity in music. Once "The Twist" reached the number one spot on the *Billboard* chart in August 1961, it stayed there for eighteen straight weeks. In November of that year it reentered the charts for another twenty-one weeks. "The Twist" became the first single to appear in the number one spot in two different years. Finally, "The Twist" made its mark in advertising. In the early 1990s, for example, Nabisco borrowed the twist concept in its marketing of the Oreo cookie. Advertisements for Oreo cookies that featured Chubby Checker twisting a cookie resulted in one of the company's most successful advertising campaigns ever. Although many songs and dances have risen to popularity, few rival the twist in influence.

In "The Twist's Turn," what transitions introduced the three support points?

1. First

2. Second

3. Finally

Transitions can link ideas in several ways.

Time and time sequence:	**Later** he sang another song.
Emphatic order:	**Most important,** she was an exciting performer.
Addition:	They recorded the song **again.**
Space:	The recording studio is **nearby, opposite** the practice room.
Examples:	The bass is **one example of** a stringed instrument.
Change of direction:	That singer is good, **but I still** prefer Elvis.
Conclusion:	I practiced this song night and day. **As a result,** I can play it by heart.

The box on this page and the next gives lists of transition words and terms. Become familiar with these words, and use them in your own writing.

Transition Words and Terms

Words That Signal Time and Time Sequence Order

after	finally	shortly afterward
at last	first, second, third	soon
at the same time	immediately	subsequently
before	later	then
during	meanwhile	when
earlier	next	while

Words and Terms That Signal Emphatic Order

above all	first	most important
another	in the first place	most significantly
equally important	last	next
especially	least of all	
even more	most of all	

Transition Words and Terms (*cont.*)

Words and Terms That Signal Addition

additionally	for another thing	next
again	for one thing	second
also	furthermore	then
and	in addition	third
besides	last of all	too
first of all	moreover	

Words and Terms That Signal Space

above	here	opposite
across	in back of	there
before	in front of	to the east (north, etc.)
behind	nearby	to the left
below	next to	to the right
elsewhere	on the other side	

Words and Terms That Signal Examples

an illustration of	one example of	such as
for example	particularly	that is
for instance	specifically	

Words and Terms That Signal Change of Direction

although	in contrast	regardless
but	nevertheless	still
despite	on the contrary	though
even though	on the other hand	yet
however	otherwise	

Words and Terms That Signal Conclusion

as a result	in conclusion	then
consequently	in summary	therefore
finally	last	thus

EXERCISE 4 CHOOSING EFFECTIVE TRANSITIONS

For each underlined pair of terms, circle the correct transition for the sentences. An example is done for you.

Doris Day was a popular singer, (and)/in conclusion she was a popular actress as well.

1. The famous singer was born Doris Mary Anne von Kappelhoff, finally/(but) she changed her name to Doris Day.

2. (Although)/In addition Day first began training to be a professional dancer, a life-threatening accident prevented her from pursuing her dancing dreams.

3. Finally/(Instead) Day began singing during her recuperation from her accident.

4. Some of her most famous hit songs are "Sentimental Journey" (and)/last "Que Sera Sera."

5. As a film star, Day made her mark playing spunky, all-American characters; thus/(for instance), her character in *Pillow Talk* is a decorator who tries to fend off a womanizer.

6. The public believed that Day's charming, warm characters represented Day's own personality; (however)/therefore, Day's own life had its share of ups and downs.

7. (Alhough)/Additionally, Day was divorced twice early in her career, she seemed to find stability with Marty Melcher.

8. Consequently/(However) when Melcher died in 1968, Day learned that he had left her bankrupt, and she had no prospects of work.

9. Day was awarded $22.8 million in 1974 when she won a lawsuit against her former attorney for mismanaging her affairs, (but)/then she eventually accepted $6 million.

10. In retirement from the entertainment industry, Day is a prominent activist for animal rights; (in fact)/finally, she set up her own animal rights foundation.

Combining Organizing Strategies

Sometimes your topic sentence will allow you to use both organizational strategies at the same time. For example, you can use time sequence order in your paragraph but still save the most important reason for last. Read the following paragraph to see how the two strategies can work together. The support points, arranged in emphatic order, are introduced by transitional expressions in bold type. The specific details for each support point appear in time sequence order; the transitions that introduce these are underlined.

One Good Man

The big-band leader Benny Goodman had an important effect on the music world. **First,** Goodman provided Depression-era people with fast, upbeat dance music. Goodman combined jazz with more traditional big-band sounds to make a new music for young people called swing. Even though other bandleaders started playing the same kind of music, Goodman soon became known as the King of Swing. **Second,** Goodman set a new standard for the way people played big-band music. Goodman played the clarinet, and he had excellent musical skill and style. Whenever anyone wanted to play in Goodman's band, Goodman made sure the new player also had excellent musical skills. **Most significantly,** Goodman broke through racial barriers. <u>Before the mid-1930s</u>, black and white musicians were not allowed to play on the same stage together. Benny Goodman, who was white, hired the African-American musicians Teddy Wilson and Lionel Hampton to play with his musicians. <u>Later</u>, the trumpet star Cootie Williams and the guitarist Charlie Christian, who were also African-American, became part of Goodman's band. <u>Soon</u> musicians of different races were commonly seen on stage together. After Benny Goodman entered the music scene, it was never the same again.

In this paragraph, these support points are organized in emphatic order: Goodman started playing swing music, Goodman set a new standard for musical skills, and Goodman broke through racial barriers. The paragraph places Benny Goodman's most significant effect on music last, and the writer tells us that the last point is the most important by using the term *most significantly* to lead into it.

Take a look, however, at the specific details given for the last support point. These are organized in time sequence (chronological) order. The transitions that introduce the details—"Before the mid-1930s," "Later," and "Soon"—signal the time sequence.

Ella Fitzgerald (1917–1996)

SURF THE NET   Both as a singer with Chick Webb's band in the 1930s and as a soloist, Ella Fitzgerald distinguished herself as a great talent. Surf the Internet to learn about one musician mentioned in this chapter. Write a few sentences explaining what you learned about the musician you choose.

EXERCISE 5 PRACTICING PUTTING SENTENCES IN ORDER

The following groups of sentences make up short paragraphs. However, the sentences are out of order. Put the sentences in order by writing 1 in the space before the sentence that should come first (the topic sentence), 2 before the next sentence, and so forth.

1. a. ___3___ Next, she sang with Chick Webb's band.

    b. ___1___ The jazz singer Ella Fitzgerald accomplished much in her life.

    c. ___5___ Finally, she recorded many big hits, such as "A-Tisket, A-Tasket" and "Lady Be Good."

    d. ___2___ First, she won an amateur jazz singing contest at the Apollo theater in Harlem while she was still a teenager in 1934.

    e. ___4___ Eventually, Fitzgerald managed Webb's band after he died in 1939.

2. a. __4__ Most important, Bing Crosby was Frank Sinatra's inspiration. Sinatra heard Crosby sing in concert and decided to become a singer, too.

b. __1__ Perhaps no singer has had a greater influence on popular singing than Bing Crosby.

c. __3__ His biggest hit, "White Christmas," is still played often during the holidays.

d. __2__ Crosby was originally known for his crooning, or low, sentimental singing.

3. a. __3__ Calloway's orchestra also became famous when he broadcast its shows at the Cotton Club in Harlem over the radio during the 1930s and 1940s.

b. __2__ For one, his jazz orchestra was known for being very creative in its music.

c. __5__ Last, Calloway had many hit songs, including "Minnie the Moocher" and "Blues in the Night."

d. __1__ The jazz singer and bandleader Cab Calloway had many successes in his life.

e. __4__ Another success came when Calloway helped the jazz singers Pearl Bailey and Lena Horne become stars.

If students transpose answers a and e in order, their responses may still be correct.

Varying Transition Words and Terms

Often writers will use many transition words in one piece of writing. Keep in mind that transitions can come in the middle of a sentence and introduce details as well as support points. The following paragraph uses a variety of transition words and terms.

A Supreme Talent

[1]The singer and actress Diana Ross has had much success. [2]First, Ross was successful as part of a group. [3]For ten years, she was the lead singer with the Supremes, the most successful female trio of the 1960s. [4]With a total of twelve number-one

hits, including "Baby Love" (1964), "Stop! In the Name of Love" (1965), and "You Can't Hurry Love" (1966), the Supremes were second only to the Beatles in record sales during the 1960s. [5]Ross was also successful as a soloist. [6]In 1970 she left the Supremes and began a career on her own. [7]Her debut single, "Reach Out and Touch," became a major hit in 1970. [8]Additionally, her second single, a new version of the Marvin Gaye–Tammi Terrell song "Ain't No Mountain High Enough," made it to number one on the pop charts. [9]Finally, Ross was successful as an actress. [10]Right after her solo debut, Ross made her acting debut, playing the legendary singer Billie Holliday in the feature film *Lady Sings the Blues*. [11]The film met with critical and popular success, and Ross earned an Oscar nomination for Best Actress. [12]Ross spent the next two decades making many albums and starring in other films. [13]No matter what Diana Ross tried, she proved to be "supremely" talented.

EXERCISE 6 IDENTIFYING TRANSITION WORDS AND TERMS

Reread "A Supreme Talent." Then fill in the blanks.

1. What transition word does the writer use to begin sentence 2?

First

2. What transition word in sentence 5 shows addition?

also

3. Write the transition words in sentences 3, 6, and 10 that show time sequence. Note that the transition terms may give years, as in the phrase *In 1980*.

a. Sentence 3   For ten years

b. Sentence 6   In 1970

c. Sentence 10   Right after her solo debut

4. What signal word does the writer use in sentence 8 to show

addition? ___Additionally___

5. What transitions does the writer use to show that the support point

in sentence 9 is the last one? ___Finally___

Other Ways to Link Ideas

Aside from using transition, there are three other ways to link your ideas:

- Repeating key words
- Using pronouns
- Using synonyms

Repeating Key Words

When you repeat key words, you use important words related to your topic again and again throughout your paragraph. When not overdone, this technique can help your reader stay on track.

As you read the following paragraph, pay attention to the word *songs*. Circle it each of the eight times you find it. Notice how the repetition reinforces the use of the word in sentence 1, the topic sentence.

The Sounds of Music

[1]Singers play a large role in making songs famous. [2]In the musical drama *The Sound of Music*, the singer Julie Andrews makes many songs famous. [3]She sings "The Sound of Music," "My Favorite Things," and "Do-Re-Mi," among others. [4]Even though Andrews didn't write any of those songs, she is the one people think of when they hear those songs. [5]Another example comes from the musical *Oklahoma!* [6]In this musical play, Shirley Jones sings the songs "The Surrey with the Fringe on Top" and "People Will Say We're in Love."

⁷Richard Rodgers is the one who wrote the (songs,) but Jones is the one people remember. ⁸Finally, the (songs) in the movie *White Christmas* were written by Irving Berlin. ⁹However, when people hear the (songs)—for example, "White Christmas"—they think of Bing Crosby.

Using Pronouns

Another way to help your reader stay focused on your topic is to use pronouns. Pronouns remind the reader of the name they are replacing. Using pronouns keeps you from overusing repetition.

As you read the paragraph "A Meteoric Rise," pay attention to how the pronouns *he* and *his* take the place of *Haley* and *Haley's*. Circle each of the four times the pronoun *he* appears in the paragraph. Then underline the pronoun *his* each of the eight times it appears. Notice how the pronouns remind the reader of the name that appears in sentence 1, the topic sentence.

A Meteoric Rise

¹The singer and musician Bill Haley found his biggest success playing rock and roll. ²Early in his career, Haley played guitar and sang for country and western groups. ³Though (he) found work in bands such as the Downhomers, (he) became exhausted, disillusioned, and broke. ⁴At the next stage in his career, Haley formed his own country and western band, called Bill Haley and His Saddlemen. ⁵The group continued to play country music—they even wore white Stetson hats and cowboy boots—but they eventually adopted a new sound. ⁶With this new sound came Haley's greatest success. ⁷(He) decided to change the band's name to Bill Haley and His Comets, and with that, the group really took off. ⁸Starting with songs like "Rock the Joint," which sold 75,000 copies, Haley focused on the rock and roll world. ⁹In 1953 (he) wrote "Crazy Man Crazy," which became the first rock and roll record to make the *Billboard* pop chart Top 20. ¹⁰Haley gained lasting fame from the recording of "Rock Around the Clock," the song that introduced rock and roll to white America. ¹¹It became a huge hit as the title track of *The Blackboard Jungle*, a movie about juvenile delinquents. ¹²Haley's other big hit—"Shake, Rattle, and Roll"—was the first rock and roll record to sell a million copies. ¹³His next big hit— "See Ya Later, Alligator"—sold a million copies within a month. ¹⁴Though a talented country and western musician, Bill Haley's meteoric rise to success came with his Comets.

Using Synonyms

Using synonyms can help your reader follow your ideas while adding variety to your writing. A **synonym** is a word that has the same, or nearly the same, meaning as another word. For example, two synonyms for *singer* are *vocalist* and *diva*.

The following paragraph is a version of "The Sounds of Music" that appears on pages 163–164. In that version, the word *songs* appeared eight times. In this version, however, other words replace the word *songs* in some places.

The Sounds of Music

¹Singers play a large role in making songs famous. ²In the musical drama *The Sound of Music*, the singer Julie Andrews makes many numbers famous. ³She sings "The Sound of Music," "My Favorite Things," and "Do-Re-Mi," among others. ⁴Even though Andrews didn't write any of those hits, she is the one people think of when they hear those songs. ⁵Another example comes from the musical *Oklahoma!* ⁶In this musical play, Shirley Jones sings the melodies "The Surrey with the Fringe on Top" and "People Will Say We're in Love." ⁷Richard Rodgers is the one who wrote the numbers, but Jones is the one people remember. ⁸Finally, the songs in the movie *White Christmas* were written by Irving Berlin. ⁹However, when people hear the hits—for example, "White Christmas"—they think of Bing Crosby.

EXERCISE 7 USING SYNONYMS

Reread "The Sounds of Music." Then fill in the blanks.

1. What word does the writer use to replace *songs* in

sentence 2? <u>numbers   </u>

2. The same word for *songs* that the writer uses in sentence 2 also

appears in sentence <u> 7 </u>.

3. What word does the writer use to replace *songs* in

sentence 4? <u>hits   </u>

4. The same word that the writer uses in sentence 4 also appears in

sentence __9__.

5. How many times does the word *songs* appear in this version of the

paragraph? __3__

What You Know Now

Two ways to organize your ideas are by time sequence (chronological) order and emphatic order. These methods allow you to place your ideas in order of how they occurred and in order from least to most important. Transitional words and terms help your reader follow your ideas and connect them. Other methods—such as repeating key terms, using pronouns, and using synonyms—also help keep your reader on track.

WRITING PRACTICE Write Your Own Paragraph

You've had a chance to practice recognizing transitions during this chapter. Now it's time to practice using them in your own writing. Your assignment is this: *Write a paragraph describing your going-to-bed or getting-up-in-the-morning routine.* A possible topic sentence might be "Every night I go through the same steps before bed." Use specific times and activities that you usually follow. Use transitions to let your reader know which points come first, second, and last. After you've finished a draft, underline all the transitions you've used to link your ideas.

Use these techniques to write your paragraph.

1. Use one or more prewriting techniques to come up with ideas for your paragraph.
2. Write a clear topic sentence.
3. Use your notes from prewriting to write a rough draft of your paragraph.
4. Place your ideas in a logical order—either by time sequence order or emphatic order—and use transitions to connect them.
5. Revise your paragraph, reading through it to check for the first three of the four Cs: *concise, credible,* and *clear* writing.

6. Edit your paragraph for sentence effectiveness, word choice, grammar, punctuation, and spelling.

When you're finished, your paragraph should include the following:

- A clear topic sentence
- Support points that relate to the topic sentence
- Specific details that give proof of your support points
- Transitions that connect your support points and specific details

Lab Activity 11

For additional practice with organizing and linking ideas, complete Lab Activity 11 in the Lab Manual at the back of the book.

12. Sensitive Writing

The Underground Railroad was a network of houses and other safe places that slaves used as stops along their escape route. It was formed by abolitionists (people who felt that slavery should be abolished). The escapees traveled under cover of night from one "station" of the railroad to the next.

Harriet Tubman (1820–1913)

SURF THE NET One of the greatest conductors on the Underground Railroad, Harriet Tubman helped lead more than three hundred slaves to freedom. Search for information about Harriet Tubman or the Underground Railroad on the Internet. Summarize your findings in a few sentences.

What Is Sensitive Language?

You probably know that some language—such as profanity or slang—is inappropriate in certain situations. Using a four-letter word during a job interview, for instance, would not make a good impression on most employers. Similarly, using a derogatory or insulting term to refer to a woman when talking to a friend might offend him or her. By using **sensitive language** that is free from stereotypes and ethnic or gender slurs, you can make your point effectively while keeping your readers open to what you have to say.

Using Sensitive Language

Most people have heard stories about "ditzy blonds" or "dumb jocks." Generalizations like these can be very hurtful. Follow these guidelines in your writing.

- Don't exclude people.
- Don't make assumptions about groups of people.
- Don't call people by names they do not choose for themselves.
- Don't assume that all members of a group are the same.
- Don't mention a person's race, sex, age, sexual orientation, disability, or religion unnecessarily.

Don't Exclude People

In the past, the pronouns *he, his,* and *him* were used to mean "he or she," "his or her," and "him and her." Similarly, writers would write *man* and mean "all human beings." While most men had no trouble with these terms, many women came to feel excluded by them. In the past few decades, writers have become more sensitive to gender. Now, instead of writing "Man has made great progress," writers say, "People have made great progress." Thus, women are represented as well as men. You can use the following methods to include both genders in your writing.

1. Use *he or she* or *she or he* (and *his or her, her or his, him or her, her or him*).

Insensitive: Every member of the Underground Railroad jeopardized <u>his</u> safety. (Was it only men who participated in the Underground Railroad?)

Better: Every member of the Underground Railroad jeopardized his <u>or her</u> safety. (Both men and women are included.)

2. Use a plural noun, such as *people, persons,* or *humans.*

> Insensitive: Even a <u>person</u> with children had to risk <u>her</u> life while escaping or helping others to escape. (Is every person with children female?)

> Better: Even <u>people</u> with children had to risk <u>their</u> lives while escaping or helping others to escape.

Don't Make Assumptions About Groups of People

It's easy to make assumptions about groups or individuals—but it's insensitive and unfair to do so. For instance, assuming that only mothers are interested in a new playground leaves out the possibility that fathers are interested, too. To avoid making assumptions about groups of people, ask yourself the following questions.

■ Does my description apply to everyone in the group?

■ Could someone feel offended because he/she does not fit my description?

If you can answer *yes* to the first question and *no* to the second, your language is probably safe. Otherwise, think of ways to change your language.

> Insensitive: <u>Mothers</u> who take their children to the park are lobbying for a new playground.

> Better: <u>Parents</u> who take their children to the park are lobbying for a new playground.

Names of Groups

The following terms are generally considered acceptable by the groups they refer to. Keep in mind that the more specific the term, the better. For instance, referring to a group of Southeast Asian people as *Vietnamese, Hmong,* or *Laotian* is better than simply calling them *Asian.*

African-American or black	Indian (for people from India)
Asian	Latino/Latina
Caucasian or white	Native American (*not* Indian)
disabled (*not* handicapped)	

Don't Call People by Names They Do Not Choose for Themselves

The key to using sensitive language is to let people choose what they wish to be called. Letting people choose their own names applies to groups as well as individuals. For instance, *Oriental* is no longer the term of choice to identify people of Asian descent. Instead, the term *Asian* is generally considered to be respectful, but as noted earlier, more specific terms such as Laotian or Vietnamese may be even better. Follow these guidelines to avoid offending people.

- Find out what members of a group prefer to be called. If you're not sure whether to use *Hispanic* or *Latino,* for example, do some research or ask your instructor for the preferred term. Note that preferences can vary from group to group and from place to place. The point here is that some thought and research may be needed.

- Pay attention to how people are addressed. If everyone calls your supervisor Ms. Smith, for instance, you should call her that, too, unless she tells you otherwise.

- Sometimes members of a particular group will call themselves a name that they do not wish others to call them. For example, a man might talk about going to "boys' night out," but that doesn't mean he wants to be called "boy." Pay attention to what people *prefer* to be called even if that isn't what they call themselves.

Don't Assume That All Members of a Group Are the Same

It's unfair and inaccurate to assume that members of a group are all the same. To avoid stereotyping, do the following:

- Look for exceptions to the claim you want to make. If even one person doesn't fit the description you offer, don't use it.

  Insensitive: Teenagers are emotional and irritable.
  Better: Teenagers may sometimes express
                   volatile emotions.

- Avoid using absolute labels such as *all, none, always,* and *never.* A single exception renders them false.

- Avoid generalizations involving personal characteristics, attitudes, and achievements. Even something that seems complimentary, such as "Asian students are good at math," can offend a Vietnamese student who writes poetry or has no interest in math class.

Don't Mention a Person's Race, Sex, Age, Sexual Orientation, Disability, or Religion Unnecessarily

Being specific is important in writing because it helps your readers understand your ideas. However, describing someone in terms of race or gender can send an unspoken message of criticism.

If you're writing about someone who cut you off on the freeway, for instance, the only details you need to mention are those relevant to the other person's *driving*. Saying that "some jerk" cut you off isn't passing judgment on any particular group of people. Writing that the person who cut you off is a woman, for instance, implicitly states that all women are bad drivers. The driver's race, gender, age, disability, religion, and sexual orientation are irrelevant; talking about those factors only serves to communicate bad feelings about a particular group of people.

To avoid mentioning race, gender, or other characteristics unnecessarily, ask yourself the following questions.

■ In the same situation, would I want to be described in terms of my race, gender, or any other characteristic? If the answer is *no*, omit using such details.

■ Could my reader think that I am biased against a certain group of people because of the details I include? If the answer is *yes*, omit such details.

EXERCISE 1 IDENTIFYING INSENSITIVE LANGUAGE

Write OK by each sentence that isn't offensive and I by each sentence that contains insensitive language. Rewrite the sentences that contain insensitive language on a separate piece of paper. An example is done for you.

Answers will vary.

Insensitive: Since having children, Leigh doesn't work.

Better: Since having children, Leigh quit her job as a bank teller.

_____ I   **1.** Ronnie, the new Jewish student, is on my committee.

_____ I   **2.** The women at my church are more interested in socializing than anything else.

_____ OK   **3.** My ex-husband is a workaholic.

_____I_____ **4.** Of course Ted's clothing is fashionable; he's gay.

_____I_____ **5.** May I please speak to the man of the house?

_____I_____ **6.** When I learned that James was half African-American, I understood why he's so good at basketball.

_____OK____ **7.** When Tan forgot to shave, he looked like a shaggy bear.

_____I_____ **8.** Fahm, the deaf student, wrote an excellent essay.

_____I_____ **9.** I hope I don't have to dance with Andy; white guys don't have rhythm.

_____OK____ **10.** Koji Sukiyama has an incredible math mind.

EXERCISE 2 FINDING BIAS IN WRITING

The following paragraph contains five instances of insensitive language. In the spaces at the end of the paragraph, write the numbers of the sentences containing insensitive language. Then, briefly explain why that language is insensitive. The first item has been done for you. Answers will vary.

The Underground Railroad

[1]The Underground Railroad was neither underground nor a railroad. [2]The name was a secret code invented for the escape route used by slaves in the pre–Civil War days. [3]The slaves were aided by thousands of "conductors" who used covered wagons or carts with false bottoms to carry slaves from one "station" to another. [4]With the help of 3,000 conductors, more than 100,000 slaves escaped to freedom. [5]Harriet Tubman was the greatest single conductor in the history of the Underground Railroad, which is amazing considering she was just a woman. [6]An escaped slave herself, Tubman was a victim of brutality at an early age. [7]She received a fractured skull at age thirteen while defending another slave from a cruel master. [8]Since teenagers never think of anyone but themselves, Tubman's action was impressive. [9]Tubman earned the nickname "Moses" for her heroic exploits in leading slaves to the North, just as Moses led the Israelis out of Egypt to the

Promised Land. ¹⁰Returning nineteen times to the dangerous South, Tubman led more than three hundres slaves to freedom. ¹¹Some southern planters offered $40,000 for her capture, without success. ¹²Tubman carried a pistol on her freedom raids. ¹³If a wimpy slave had second thoughts about escaping, she pulled her gun and said, "You'll be free or die!" ¹⁴Harriet Tubman continued her courageous exploits during the Civil War. ¹⁵She became a nurse, which is a perfect job for a woman. ¹⁶She was also a scout and a spy for the Union army. ¹⁷In one campaign she personally led seven hundred fifty southern slaves to freedom. ¹⁸By being consistently brave and dedicated to her cause, Harriet Tubman proved to be the most important conductor on the Underground Railroad.

Sentence __5__	It's offensive to say that Tubman was "just" a woman.
Sentence __8__	It's insensitive to imply that all teens think only of themselves.
Sentence __9__	*Israelis* are citizens of current-day Israel. Use *Israelites, Hebrews, or Jews* for historical or biblical references.
Sentence __13__	It's insensitive to label a slave "wimpy."
Sentence __15__	It's insensitive to say that nursing is a perfect job for women.

EDITING PRACTICE

Rewrite the following sentences to make them free of insensitive language of the kind indicated before each sentence.   Answers will vary.

1. Don't exclude people: When man invented the wheel, he made his life

much easier.   When humans invented the wheel, they made their lives much

easier.

2. Don't make assumptions about groups of people: When Kyle and Jane

had their baby, of course Jane quit her job and stayed home.   When

Kyle and Jane had their baby, Jane quit her job and stayed home.

3. Don't call people names they don't choose for themselves: Those geeks made it impossible for the rest of us to get a good grade in the class.

Those students made it impossible for the rest of us to get a good grade in the

class.

4. Don't assume that all members of a group are the same: Heidi would

make a perfect cheerleader; she's a natural blonde, you know. Heidi

would make a perfect cheerleader.

5. Don't mention a person's race, sex, age, sexual orientation, disability, or religion unnecessarily: A rude Asian woman ran over my toe with a

shopping cart. A rude person ran over my toe with a shopping cart.

Lab Activity 12

For additional practice with sensitive writing, complete Lab Activity 12 in the Lab Manual at the back of the book.

13 Choosing the Best Words

Understanding Language Choices

Very few people speak the same way all the time. The words and tone of voice you use when talking to friends probably varies greatly from the language and tone you use with your instructors. We shape our language in many ways to make ourselves understood to different groups; the key is knowing when to use which type of language.

Choosing Language for Formal Writing Assignments

Using informal language with someone who knows you well can communicate your ideas every bit as effectively as using formal language—maybe even better. However, it's important to understand that when *speaking,* we have certain communication aids that are missing when we write: facial expressions, hand gestures, vocal inflection all help us communicate in person. Because these aids can't help us on paper, however, we must rely on standard forms of expression. Thus, we must make use of formal written English.

Abraham Lincoln (1809–1865)

SURF THE NET The sixteenth president of the United States, Abraham Lincoln reunited a country divided by social and financial differences. Search the Internet for information on Abraham Lincoln. Write a few sentences summarizing what you learn.

In academic writing, take care to avoid language that can interfere with, rather than assist, your communication.

- Slang
- Overly formal language
- Clichés (overused expressions)
- Wordiness

Slang

Slang is informal language, and it can be effective in spoken English. In writing, however, slang is unacceptable. In addition, slang can prevent you from communicating clearly. Though some slang expressions—such as "cool"—have stayed popular for decades, most slang words lose popularity quickly, or are known only to certain groups, so slang can leave your reader wondering what you mean. Further, slang can take the place of details necessary to communicate important ideas.

Slang: Lincoln thought the South was <u>dissing</u> the Union by seceding.

Standard: Lincoln thought the South showed disrespect for the Union by seceding.

Slang: Although Lincoln came from humble beginnings, he was <u>up for</u> being president.

Standard: Although Lincoln came from humble beginnings, he was ready to accept the challenge of being president.

Slang: Lincoln worked hard to become president; no one could call him a <u>slacker.</u>

Standard: Lincoln worked hard to become president; no one could call him lazy.

EXERCISE 1 CONVERTING SLANG TO STANDARD ENGLISH

In the following sentences, slang terms appear in italics. Rewrite each sentence using standard English expressions.   Answers will vary.

Slang: I worry that my little brother will get *caught in the crossfire* of my parents' divorce.

Standard: I worry that my little brother will suffer as a result of my parents' divorce.

1. Slang: Even after I *hit the books*, my instructor gave me a C–. *What's up with that?*

Standard: Even after I studied, my instructor gave me a C–. Why did she do that?

2. Slang: As a result of my *lame* grade, my financial aid chances went *down the tubes*.

Standard: As a result of my poor grade, my financial aid chances disappeared.

3. Slang: When I watch television, I end up *brain dead* and *stressed out*.

Standard: When I watch television, I end up tired and anxious.

4. Slang: After Dino *chewed out* his girlfriend, she *bailed on* him.

Standard: After Dino verbally attacked his girlfriend, she left him.

5. Slang: When my mother made fried chicken, I *scarfed it down.*

Standard: _When my mother made fried chicken, I ate it quickly and ethusiastically._

Clichés (Overused Expressions)

Clichés are overused expressions that are ineffective because of their overuse. Like slang, use of clichés often allows writers to omit key details. Read the following sentences to see how overused language weakens them. Some clichés must be rewritten to make their meaning more specific, and some can be omitted.

Cliché: <u>In this day and age</u>, Abraham Lincoln is considered an important political leader.

Better: Today, Abraham Lincoln is considered an important political leader.

Cliché: Lincoln hoped that the Union could be preserved without civil war. However, this was <u>easier said than done</u>.

Better: Lincoln hoped that the Union could be preserved without civil war. However, this goal could not be achieved.

Cliché: <u>Needless to say</u>, Lincoln was a great president.

Better: Lincoln was a great president.

Clichés

all work and no play	hustle and bustle
at a loss for words	in the nick of time
at this point in time	in this day and age
better late than never	it dawned on me
break the ice	it goes without saying
cold, cruel world	last but not least
cry your eyes out	living hand to mouth
drop in the bucket	make ends meet
easier said than done	one in a million
free as a bird	on top of the world
green with envy	out of this world
had a hard time of it	sad but true

(continued)

saw the light	too little, too late
short but sweet	took a turn for the worse
sigh of relief	tried and true
singing the blues	under the weather
taking a big chance	where he (she) is coming from
time and time again	word to the wise
too close for comfort	work like a dog

EXERCISE 2 REVISING OVERUSED EXPRESSIONS

In the following sentences, overused expressions are in italics. Rewrite each sentence, using a less common English expression. An example is done for you.   Answers will vary.

After my nap I felt *as fresh as a daisy.*

After my nap I felt refreshed.

1. I thought I wanted to be an engineer before I became one. I guess *the grass is always greener on the other side of the fence.*

I guess people often imagine that what they don't have is better than what they do have.

2. When my girlfriend moved to Iceland, I *cried my eyes out.*

When my girlfriend moved to Iceland, I was sad and lonely.

3. When finals week was over, Sam felt *as free as a bird.*

When finals week was over, Sam felt as though he'd been set free from prison.

4. The new restaurant on Broadway is *out of this world.*

The new restaurant on Broadway is outstanding.

5. When I was between jobs, I *lived hand-to-mouth.*

When I was between jobs, I barely managed to meet my expenses.

Overly Formal Language

Sometimes writers try to sound knowledgeable or intelligent by using big, impressive-sounding words. Using such words unnecessarily, however, makes the speaker or writer sound artificial or stuffy. The best writing is as clear and direct as possible.

Stuffy: While preparing himself for the undertaking to come, Lincoln read widely and consulted with his marital partner.

Better: While preparing for the challenge, Lincoln read widely and talked to his wife.

Stuffy: While the Union soldiers suffered unspeakable losses as a result of the tragedy known as the Civil War, their losses were but a fraction of those experienced by the downtrodden Confederate soldiers.

Better: While the Union soldiers suffered greatly from the Civil War, the Confederate soldiers suffered far more.

EXERCISE 3 OVERLY FORMAL LANGUAGE

In the following sentences, overly formal language appears in italics. Rewrite the sentences, using clear, direct language. An example is done for you.   Answers will vary.

Stuffy: Lincoln *acquired the skill of comprehending the written word* as a result of reading the Bible.

Better: Lincoln learned to read by reading the Bible.

1. I had an idea at work, but I was *terrified to communicate* it to my boss.

I had an idea at work, but I was afraid to tell it to my boss.

2. Tom thought Susanne wore an *overabundance of cosmetics.*

Tom thought Susanne wore too much makeup.

3. *Ron lost a battle to extreme exhaustion while attending a class.*

Ron fell asleep in class.

4. *As a result of the failure of my chronological device to hasten my departure from slumber,* I am late to class.

> Because my alarm clock didn't wake me up, I am late to class.

5. Whoever made these brownies is a *culinary expert of the first order.*

> Whoever made these brownies is a great cook.

Wordiness

Wordy writing contains unnecessary words or sentences. Getting to the point quickly will save you and your reader time and energy. The sentences below contain unnecessary words or phrases that add length but nothing else. You don't need to write all simple sentences that follow the same pattern, but you should always use the fewest words possible to get your ideas across.

Wordy: Lincoln was <u>of the opinion</u> that the secession of the South had many <u>negative drawbacks.</u> (*Of the opinion* is a longer way to say *thought;* a drawback is something negative, so writing *negative* is redundant.)

Better: Lincoln thought that the secession of the South had many drawbacks.

Wordy: It <u>seems to me</u> in my opinion that Lincoln <u>really and truly</u> worked hard <u>over the course of the many years that he served as president.</u> (The writer doesn't need to say "it seems to me" or "in my opinion." *Over the course of many years that he served as president* is a long way to say "during his presidency.")

Better: Lincoln worked hard during his presidency.

EXERCISE 4 ELIMINATING WORDINESS

Underline the wordy sections in the sentences below. Then, rewrite the sentences to eliminate wordiness. An example is done for you.   Answers will vary.

Wordy: Abraham Lincoln's accomplishments are his legacy <u>to the people who lived after him.</u>

Better: <u>Abraham Lincoln's accomplishments are his legacy.</u>

1. Wordy: Although Lincoln had <u>a great influence over many people,</u> he came from humble beginnings.

Better: <u>Although Lincoln greatly influenced many people, he came from humble beginnings.</u>

2. Wordy: His first home was a cabin <u>of just one room</u> in <u>an area with a sparse population of settlers</u>.

Better: His first home was a one-room cabin in a sparsely settled area.

3. Wordy: To attend school as a boy, Lincoln walked two miles to <u>his destination</u> of the schoolhouse each day.

Better: To attend school as a boy, Lincoln walked two miles to the schoolhouse each day.

4. Wordy: In school, Lincoln learned the <u>elementary basic rudiments</u> of reading, writing, and arithmetic.

Better: In school, Lincoln learned the rudiments of reading, writing, and arithmetic.

5. Wordy: When Lincoln was <u>only nine years of age</u>, his mother died.

Better: When Lincoln was nine, his mother died.

Alternatives to Wordy Expressions

Wordy Expression	Shorter Expression	Wordy Expession	Shorter Expression
a large number of	many	for the reason that	because
a period of a week	a week	four in number	four
arrive at an agreement	agree	in every instance	always
at all times	always	in my own opinion	I think
at an earlier point in time	before	in order to	to
at the present time	now	in the area of	around
at this point in time	now	in the nature of	like
because of the fact that	because	in the neighborhood of	around
big in size	big	in the event that	if
by means of	by	in the near future	soon
circle around	circle	in this day and age	today
connect together	connect	is able to	can
due to the fact that	because	large in size	large
during the time while	while	owing to the fact that	because
for the purpose of	for	past history	history

(continued)

Wordy Expression	Shorter Expression	Wordy Expession	Shorter Expression
plan ahead for the future	plan	true fact	fact
positive benefit	benefit	until such time as	until
postponed until later	postponed	white in color	white
return back	return		

EDITING PRACTICE

The following paragraph contains italicized examples of slang, overused expressions, and wordy and overly formal language. In the spaces following the paragraph, identify the poor language choices: S for "slang," C for "cliché," F for "formal language," or W for "wordy." On the lines provided, rewrite the section of the sentences containing poor word choices to make them more readable. The first item has been done for you. Answers will vary.

Lincoln's Legacy

[1]Although members of the Confederacy detested Abraham Lincoln, *he rocked.* [2]*First, he acquired his education from the informal sources provided him at home.* [3]*His mother kicked the bucket* when he was nine years old, so Lincoln didn't have the chance to learn from her. [4]Lincoln claimed that he wasn't sure how he learned to read and write, but *whether he had to beg, steal, or borrow his education, he got one.* [5]*Second, Lincoln worked like a dog.* [6]*He held many positions in a wide spectrum of workplaces:* he worked on a farm, split rails for fences, and managed a store in New Salem, Illinois. [7]He was also a captain in the Black Hawk War, so *people should have known not to mess with him.* [8]Lincoln also spent eight years in the Illinois legislature and worked in the courts *forever and a day.* [9]His *partner in law was said to say* of him, "His ambition was a little engine that knew no rest." [10]Finally, *Lincoln was of a charitable mindset.* [11]Although he did send troops to *take down* the Confederacy and bring the southern states back into the Union, he wanted the defeated Confederacy treated with "malice toward none and charity for all." [12]However, before his Reconstruction plans

were carried out, *the breath of life was snatched from him* at Ford's Theater in Washington. [13]*Thus ended the presidency of Abraham Lincoln and the life of Abraham Lincoln.*

Sentence 1: ____S____   Lincoln was a great president.

Sentence 2: ____F____   First, he was self-educated.

Sentence 3: ____S____   His mother died . . .

Sentence 4: ____C____   . . . he got an education in spite of all obstacles.

Sentence 5: ____C____   Second, Lincoln worked hard.

Sentence 6: ____F____   He held many jobs . . .

Sentence 7: ____S____   . . . people should have known he was an effective military leader.

Sentence 8: ____C____   . . . for a long time.

Sentence 9: ____W____   His law partner said of him . . .

Sentence 10: ____W____   . . . Lincoln was charitable.

Sentence 11: ____S____   . . . he did send troops to defeat the Confederacy . . .

Sentence 12: ____C____   . . . he was killed. . .

Sentence 13: ____W____   Thus ended the presidency and the life of Abraham Lincoln.

🔗 Lab Activity 13

For additional practice with word choice, complete Lab Activity 13 in the Lab Manual at the back of the book.

14 Improving Your Spelling

Understanding Your Spelling Habits

The key to spelling well is *paying attention to words* as you read and write. How do you figure out how to spell words? Do you guess? Do you ask someone? Do you use a dictionary? Paying attention to your spelling habits—what types of words you typically spell correctly and what types you have trouble with—can help you make fewer errors and correct the errors that do appear in your papers.

Improving Your Spelling

You may not think you're a "natural" speller, but you can improve your spelling if you take the initiative. Here are some methods that can help you.

- Reading
- Using a dictionary
- Creating your own spelling list
- Understanding basic spelling rules
- Memorizing words that look or sound alike
- Using a computer's spelling checker

Reading

The easiest way to improve your spelling is to read more. Reading from a variety of sources—newspapers and magazines, novels, self-improvement books, even cookbooks or music books—greatly increases your chances of seeing new words. Additionally, reading words in context—as opposed to studying a list or reading a dictionary—can help you learn the meanings of words, which will help you remember their spellings.

Using the Dictionary

Any time you read or write for college, keep a dictionary at your side. Looking up words in the dictionary takes very little time, but it can bring great rewards.

Creating Your Own Spelling List

Every time you misspell a word or read a word that is spelled differently from how you expected, add the correct spelling to your list. This list should include all the words you misspell now and in the future. Once you've identified the words that give you trouble, review your list regularly and practice using the words.

- **Say the words out loud.** Pronounce a word, spell it out loud to yourself, and say it again. Hearing the words and letters spoken may help you remember the correct spelling.
- **Give yourself hints.** Breaking a word into individual syllables can help you remember how to spell it. For instance, you might think of the word *together* as three short words: *to, get, her.* Similarly, *attendance* is made up of three short words: *at, ten, dance.*
- **Become an active reader.** When you're reading—for pleasure, for research, for class—keep your spelling list handy. Whenever you come across a word that's on your list, highlight it (unless it's in a borrowed book, of course). Seeing the word in context can help you remember its correct spelling.
- **Make flash cards.** Pull out your cards and read through them while you're waiting to see an instructor or at the bus stop; soon you'll master your list.

Understanding Basic Spelling Rules

Learn the three basic spelling rules about adding endings such as *-ed* or *-ing* to words ending with vowels versus consonants. (Vowels are the letters *a, e, i, o, u,* and sometimes *y.* Consonants are all other letters.)

- **Double the final consonant** if (1) the last three letters follow the pattern of consonant, vowel, consonant; (2) the word's accent or stress is on the last syllable or the word has only one syllable; and (3) the ending begins with a vowel.

begin + ing = begin<u>n</u>ing   occur + ing = occur<u>r</u>ing
brag + ed = brag<u>g</u>ed   omit + ing = omi<u>tt</u>ing
commit + ing = commi<u>tt</u>ing   slim + est = slim<u>m</u>est
drop + ed = drop<u>p</u>ed   stun + ing = stun<u>n</u>ing

■ **Change the final *y* to *i*** if the letter before the *y* is a consonant.

The *y* becomes *i*:   dr<u>y</u> + ed = dr<u>i</u>ed
                        heav<u>y</u> + er = heav<u>i</u>er

Keep the *y:*   dismay + ed = dismay<u>ed</u>
                obe<u>y</u> + ing = obe<u>y</u>ing

■ **Drop the final e** if the ending begins with a vowel.

Drop the *e:*   bit<u>e</u> + ing = biting
                car<u>e</u> + ing = caring

Keep the *e:*   hom<u>e</u> + less = hom<u>e</u>less
                car<u>e</u> + ful = car<u>e</u>ful

EXERCISE 1 ADDING WORD ENDINGS

Add the endings to each word shown. An example is done for you.

play + ed = <u>*played*</u>

1. sure + ly =   <u>surely</u>

2. marry + ed =   <u>married</u>

3. shop + ing =   <u>shopping</u>

4. love + able =   <u>lovable</u>

5. love + ly =   <u>lovely</u>

6. have + ing   <u>having</u>

7. try + es   <u>tries</u>

8. rip + ed   <u>ripped</u>

9. travel + ing   <u>traveling</u>

10. deny + es   <u>denies</u>

Memorizing the Meanings of Words That Look or Sound Alike

Recognizing homonyms and other words that look or sound alike is one more way to improve your spelling. (Review Chapter 54 for a solid understanding of homonyms.)

Using a Computer's Spelling Checker

The spelling checker on a computer can be a great help in locating and correcting typing and spelling errors. However, an electronic spelling checker will find only misspelled words, not misused words. For instance, in the sentence "Their is a knew dress on the stares," three words are used incorrectly—*their, knew,* and *stares*—but none is misspelled, so a spelling checker would miss the errors. The sentence should read "There is a new dress on the stairs."

For further assistance, ask someone (a friend, parent, or tutor) who spells better than you do to proofread your writing. *Do not* let that person make corrections, however. Instead, ask your proofreader to make a check mark in the margins of the lines that include spelling errors. Then you can locate the errors and correct them.

Frequently Misspelled Words

Study the list of commonly misspelled words below and memorize the words. For extra practice, add the words that give you the most trouble to your own spelling list or make flash cards for them.

ache	behavior	definite
address	brilliant	deposit
all right	business	describe
a lot	calendar	desperate
amateur	career	develop
among	careful	different
answer	cereal	disappoint
anxious	college	disapprove
argument	competition	disease
athlete	condition	doesn't
August	conscience	dozen
autumn	crowded	eighth
beginning	daughter	embarrass

(continued)

enough

environment

exaggerate

familiar

fascinate

February

finally

foreign

government

grammar

height

horse

illegal

immediately

important

integration

intelligent

interest

interfere

jewelry

knock

knowledge

library

maintain

mathematics

meant

minute

necessary

nervous

occasion

omit

opinion

opportunity

optimist

original

ounce

particular

people

perform

perhaps

personnel

possess

possible

potato

prefer

prejudice

prescription

privilege

probably

psychology

pursue

quarter

reference

rhyme

ridiculous

separate

similar

since

sincerely

soldier

speech

strength

studying

success

surprise

studying

taught

temperature

tenant

thorough

thought

tired

tongue

touch

Tuesday

until

unusual

variety

vegetable

villain

Wednesday

weight

window

writing

young

EXERCISE 2 IDENTIFYING CORRECTLY SPELLED WORDS

Circle the correctly spelled words in the sentences below. An example is done for you.

A few years ago, I planted my first (tomatoe, tommato, tomato) garden.

1. I had done careful research in (Febuary, (February,) Februrary).

2. In fact, I read all the gardening books at my local ((library,) libary, libbrary).

3. The first book (discribed, describbed, (described)) how to turn the soil in my garden after the long winter.

4. Another book told me how to place the (yung, (young,) yong) tomato plants into small holes in the dirt and then carefully cover the roots with more dirt.

5. I also learned that snail bait is (impotant, importent, (important)) when the tomato plants are small. Later, the plants grow small spikes that protect them from snails.

6. Throughout the summer, I ((maintained,) mantained, maintened) my garden by watering it every day, sometimes twice.

7. As the plant stalks grew taller, I tied them to wooden stakes, being (carful, (careful,) carefull) to prevent the tomato fruit from sitting on the ground where it could rot.

8. The result was tall, green stalks bearing ((brilliant,) briliant, brillient) red and orange tomatoes.

9. I felt so good every time I looked out my (wendow, windo, (window)) and saw my thriving garden.

10. Now, every fall I mark my (calender, (calendar,) callendar) to begin planting in the spring.

EDITING PRACTICE

The following paragraph contains twenty-two spelling errors. Cross out each misspelled word and write the correct spelling above it. Use a dictionary and the list of commonly misspelled words in this chapter if you need help. (All the health-related words, such as vitamin names, cancer-related terms, and *lycopene,* are spelled correctly.)

You Say Tomato

Though tomatoes were once ~~thoght~~ [thought] to be harmful to ~~peple's~~ [people's] health, they are ~~actualy~~ [actually] a healthy food. ~~Tomatos~~ [Tomatoes] contain large amounts of vitamin C. They also contain vitamin A, potassium, and iron. The red pigment ~~containd~~ [contained] in tomatoes is called lycopene. ~~Studys~~ [Studies] have shown that the lycopene in tomatoes is a ~~definit~~ [definite] health benefit and can reduce the risk of ~~develping~~ [developing] prostate cancer. New research is ~~begining~~ [beginning] to indicate that tomatoes may help prevent other types of cancer. When ~~choossing~~ [choosing] tomatoes, pick those with the most ~~briliant~~ [brilliant] shades of red. These have the ~~hiest~~ [highest] amounts of lycopene. ~~Altho~~ [Although] raw tomatoes are great, cooking them—~~especialy~~ [especially] in a ~~litle~~ [little] bit of olive oil—releases even ~~mor~~ ~~benifits~~ [more benefits]. Even better, tomatoes don't lose their ~~nutrishinal~~ [nutritional] value in high-heat ~~procesing~~ [processing], ~~makeing~~ ~~caned~~ [making canned] tomatoes and tomato ~~sause~~ [sauce] just as beneficial as fresh tomatoes.

⬭ Lab Activity 14

For additional practice with spelling, complete Lab Activity 14 in the Lab Manual at the back of the book.

15 Expanding Your Vocabulary

CULTURE NOTE *Florida*

The Sunshine State has long been known for beautiful beaches, wonderful weather, and fresh oranges. In the past few decades, however, Florida has gained prominence as a football power, a target for wild weather such as hurricanes, a safe haven for Cuban and Haitian refugees, and the state that tipped the 2000 presidential election.

Understanding the Value of a Wide Vocabulary

Being able to explain your ideas in different ways gives you options in your speech and writing. If one explanation doesn't convince your reader, another one, written using different expressions, just might. Give yourself every chance to succeed in your communication efforts by expanding your vocabulary.

Stretching Your Vocabularly

You can try four specific strategies to build a larger vocabulary.

- Reading for pleasure and education
- Using a dictionary
- Using a thesaurus
- Keeping a personal vocabulary journal

Everglades National Park

CRITICAL THINKING Famous for its wildlife and plant life, Everglades National Park is one of Florida's natural attractions. What does the photo above make you think of? In a few sentences, draw a conclusion about the Everglades, using specific details from the photo to support your ideas.

Study aids such as vocabulary workbooks can also help if you use them regularly. However, the tips listed in this chapter can help you build your vocabulary using the materials you already have: readings for class, paper to write on, and a writing instrument.

Tip: Visit **www.ablongman.com/vocabulary** or **www.vocabulary.com** for additional opportunities to build your vocabulary.

Reading for Pleasure and Education

Reading is the best way to build your vocabulary. Reading introduces you to new words and gives you the chance to learn their meanings from the context. The more you read, the more new words you'll learn. Ask your instructor or school librarian for suggestions of books you might enjoy, or read magazines (available free in most libraries) on topics that appeal to you.

Using a Dictionary

Perhaps the best way to learn the meanings of new words is to look them up in a dictionary as you encounter them. Keep a small dictionary with you when you're reading, and look up the meanings of any words that aren't familiar to you. That way, you'll know the meaning of that word for the sentence you're reading, and you'll also know the word's definition when you come across that word again.

Using a Thesaurus

A **thesaurus** is a book of **synonyms,** or words with similar meanings. When you're writing your college papers, keep a thesaurus handy. After you've used the same word two or three times, check the thesaurus for other words with similar meanings. Then, substitute a word from the thesaurus for the one you've been using.

For example, Nathan wrote the paragraph on the next page about Florida weather, but he noticed that he had used the word *weather* over and over. He looked up *weather* in a thesaurus and found many synonyms—*climate, the elements,* and *forces of nature,* among others. Nathan saw the word *wind* on the page opposite *weather* in the thesaurus, which also had synonyms he could use: *breeze, typhoon,* and *hurricane.* Although many other words were listed for *wind,* Nathan decided to use only the words that seemed familiar to him.

Popular Magazines That Can Help Build Your Vocabulary

Bon Appetit	*Muscle and Fitness*
Cooking Light	*Newsweek*
Essence	*People*
Family Fun	*Popular Mechanics*
Field and Stream	*Redbook*
GQ (Gentleman's Quarterly)	*Savoy*
Good Housekeeping	*Self*
In Style	*Sports Illustrated*
Marie Claire	*Time*

Electronic thesauruses can provide you with synonyms. However, use suggested words only if they are familiar to you; look up others in a dictionary first. Here's Nathan's paragraph, with synonyms inserted.

The weather in Florida is a constant source of interest and conversation because it can take so many forms. Because it is so far south, Florida's ~~weather~~ *climate* is often sunny and warm. However, along with ~~this weather~~ *these conditions* can come humidity, high concentrations of moisture in the air that can make people feel damp and sticky. Then there ~~is the weather~~ *are the elements* that can sometimes put people at their mercy, as during the ~~bad weather~~ *hurricane* season, for instance. Additionally, though Florida is known as the Sunshine State, weather often turns rainy when it seems least possible. Sleet, hail, and snow are not common types of weather in Florida, but the sun, rain, and combinations of those two make for interesting ~~weather~~ *conditions* all year long.

Nathan kept *weather* in three places, but he substituted the words *climate, conditions, the elements,* and *hurricane* in other places. This variety of words makes Nathan's writing more interesting to read.

EXERCISE 1 USING A THESAURUS

Look up each word in a thesaurus. Then, write down three possible synonyms for each word. An example is done for you. Answers will vary.

Word: house

Synonyms: ___home___ ___place___ ___abode___

1. Word: tree

Synonyms: ___sapling___ ___conifer___ ___evergreen___

2. Word: car

Synonyms: _____automobile_____   _____vehicle_____   _____station wagon_____

3. Word: music

Synonyms: _____melody_____   _____song_____   _____tune_____

4. Word: child

Synonyms: _____kid_____   _____toddler_____   _____teenager_____

5. Word: doctor

Synonyms: _____physician_____   _____specialist_____   _____internist_____

Keeping a Personal Vocabulary Journal

A personal vocabulary journal will help you improve your vocabulary. Every time you read something, highlight the words whose definitions you don't know. Then, either while you're reading or after you've finished, write those words in your personal vocabulary journal. Include the correct spelling of the word, its pronunciation, its parts of speech, and its most important meanings. For instance, if you added the word *labile* to your vocabulary journal, your entry might look like this. (See Chapter 16 for an explanation of the pronunciation symbols.)

Personal Vocabulary Journal

Word: labile   Pronunciation: `lā-bīl   Part of speech: adj.

Meanings: 1. Readily or continually undergoing chemical, physical, or biological change or breakdown. 2. Readily open to change.

Sentence: When Marcella turned thirteen, she became labile, changing from smiling to tearful in a few seconds.

EXERCISE 2 STARTING YOUR PERSONAL VOCABULARY JOURNAL

In a notebook, start a personal vocabulary journal. Look up five words that you would like to know better, and write their definitions in your list. Include the pronunciation and part of speech, and write a sentence that shows what the word means and how to use it. Follow the model given above.

EDITING PRACTICE

Read the following essay, which contains words you may not know. Choose five words that you would like to understand better, and add them to your personal vocabulary journal. Use the same format you followed in Exercise 2.   Answers will vary.

Fabulous Florida

Although Florida reinvented itself years ago as a fabulous retirement locale, it also has much to offer people at all stages of life. Every year from mid-February through March, Florida is host to thousands of college students enjoying spring break. Similarly, children and their families flock to DisneyWorld and Epcot Center throughout the year. Regardless of their rationale for visiting, tourists and residents alike enjoy the celebrated weather and desultory lifestyle that personify the Sunshine State. All in all, the state of Florida presents residents and visitors alike with a bevy of possibilities for entertainment and intellectual enhancement.

First is Florida's rich history. In 1513, the explorer Ponce de Leon, who gave Florida its name, arrived near the site of St. Augustine, where the Spanish would found the first true settlement in the North American continent about fifty years later. Spain laid a strong colonial claim but finally gave up Florida to the burgeoning United States in 1819. During its early history, many battles and skirmishes—between Spaniards and Native Americans, between the Spanish and Americans, and between the Union and the Confederacy, of which Florida was a part—contributed to the complexity of Florida's saga.

A second feature of Florida is Everglades National Park, spanning the southern tip of the Florida peninsula and most of Florida Bay. Everglades National Park is the only subtropical preserve in North America. It contains both temperate and tropical plant communities, including sawgrass prairies, mangrove and cypress swamps, pinelands, and hardwood hammocks, as well as marine and estuarine environments. The park is known for its rich bird life, particularly large wading birds such as the roseate spoonbill, wood stork, great blue heron, and various egrets. It is also the only place in the world where alligators and crocodiles exist side by side.

Finally, for people who want to learn about literary figures, there is the Key West residence of the American writer Ernest Hemingway. Hemingway's personal touches still abound throughout the house. The trophy mounts and skins were souvenirs of Hemingway's African safaris and numerous hunting expeditions out West. As visible and living links to the past, the descendants of Hemingway's cats inhabit the grounds. A story claims that Hemingway made the acquaintance of a sea captain who gave him an unusual six-toed tomcat. Today many of the Key West cats possess the unusual six toes.

Though "sun and fun" may be the quintessential Florida experience, the Sunshine State leaves no one out in its offerings for those at leisure. With its championship football teams, sunny days, and rich history, Florida offers relaxation, interest, and pleasure to almost everyone.

Lab Activity 15

For additional practice with vocabulary expansion, complete Lab Activity 15 in the Lab Manual at the back of the book.

16 Using the Dictionary

Diamonds have been given many definitions—"a girl's best friend" and "forever" among them—but they are a geological marvel as well. Although their romantic value is well known, diamonds are also essential for industrial tasks.

Benefits of Using the Dictionary

A good dictionary is one of the most valuable tools you can use in your writing. Specifically, the dictionary can help you with the following tasks.

- Improving your spelling
- Developing your vocabulary
- Discovering word histories

Here is the entry for the word *diamond* from *Merriam Webster's Collegiate Dictionary*.

di·a·mond \'dī(ə-)mund\ n, part of speech *often attrib* [ME *diamaunde*, fr. MF *diamant*, fr. OF, fr. LL *diamant-*, *diamas*, alter. of L *adamant-*, *adamas* hardest metal, diamond, fr. Gk] (14c) **1 a :** native crystalline carbon that is usu. nearly colorless, that when transparent and free from flaws is highly valued as a precious stone, and that is used industrially as an abrasive powder and in rock drills because of its great hardness; *also* : a piece of this substance **b :** crystallized carbon produced artificially **2 :** something that resembles a diamond (as in brilliance, value, or fine quality) **3 :** a square or rhombus-shaped figure usu. oriented with the long diagonal vertical **4 a :** a playing card marked with a stylized figure of a red diamond **b** *pl but sing or pl in* constr: the suit comprising cards marked with diamonds **5 :** a baseball infield; *also* : the entire playing field

In a dictionary entry, the first meaning given is the most commonly used definition of a word. It is followed by the less common meanings.

Diamond Mine in Africa

PLAN AN INTERVIEW In addition to having a rich mythical history and romantic associations, diamonds are valued in industry for their hardness. What do your friends or family think about diamonds? Interview two or three people about their attitudes toward diamonds. Summarize your findings in a few sentences.

Recommended Dictionaries

These are good dictionaries to use for your college classes.

The American Heritage College Dictionary

Merriam-Webster's Collegiate Dictionary

The Random House Webster's College Dictionary

Webster's New World Dictionary

Improving Your Spelling

The best place to check the correct spelling of a word is the dictionary. If you can't find the word immediately, look for other possible spellings. For instance, if you've spelled out the word *misteak* and can't find it in the dictionary, think about other ways to spell *steak*. Then, if you look for *mistake*, you'll find your word. Sometimes the beginning of a word may not be spelled the way you expect. The table below shows how the same sound can be spelled in different ways.

Tip: Many dictionaries are available on CD-ROM as well as in print. When using an electronic version of a dictionary, you can check the spellings of words as you write. Some word processing programs indicate a misspelled word as it appears in your writing, while others require you to press a key to use the spelling checker.

Tricky Word Beginnings

Beginning Sound	Possible Spellings	Examples
f	f	face
	ph	phase, phantasm
i	i	indirect
	e	eye, enlist
j	j	jelly
	g	gelatin, genius
k	k	keep
	c	cabin, captain, case
	ch	chasm, chemistry
	qu	quick, quarantine
n	n	no
	en	enemy, engine
	gn	gnaw, gnome
	kn	knight, knock, know
	pn	pneumatic
o	o	onset
	en	ensemble, envoy
r	r	righteous
	wr	wrap, wrinkle, write
s	s	silent
	c	celery, censor
	ps	psychology

EXERCISE 1 USING THE DICTIONARY TO IMPROVE YOUR SPELLING

Use a dictionary to look up the correct spelling of each misspelled word. Write the correct spellings.

1. amature	amateur	11. imediate	immediate
2. anser	answer	12. interfer	interfere
3. briliant	brilliant	13. minit	minute
4. carbin	carbon	14. nesessary	necessary
5. conciense	conscience	15. ommit	omit
6. concreet	concrete	16. oportunity	opportunity
7. daugter	daughter	17. personell	personnel
8. definet	definite	18. potatoe	potato
9. eigth	eighth	19. seperat	separate
10. enuf	enough	20. simular	similar

Developing Your Vocabulary

A word can have more than one common meaning—*diamond,* for instance, has several defintions. However, the diamond on a playing card and the diamond on a baseball field have little in common besides the shape. Use your judgment to decide which definition of a word is relevant.

EXERCISE 2 UNDERSTANDING MEANINGS FROM CONTEXT

Look up the underlined words in the paragraph below. Write at least two definitions for each word. Then, write the number of the definition that you think best fits. Answers will vary.

Known for their beauty, diamonds are also extremely <u>hard</u>. In fact, diamonds will cut through any <u>material</u>. Consequently, diamonds are used in cutting and grinding work. Industrial diamonds are embedded in steel drill bits and are also used for cutting metal machine parts. But diamonds have long been used outside industry, too. During World War II, only diamonds were hard enough to cut and shape the tools required for making airplane parts, vehicle <u>armor</u>, and other military hardware. At the time, U.S. industry was dependent on South African diamonds. Fearing the loss of this critical supply, the U.S. government developed an alternative, though it took another decade to find a substitute. However, diamonds remain the favored stone for cutting.

1. Word: hard

Meaning 1: Not easily dented, pierced, cut, or crushed

Meaning 2: Difficult

Most appropriate meaning: __1__

2. Word: material

Meaning 1: Matter or substance

Meaning 2: Cloth fabric

Most appropriate meaning: __1__

3. Word: armor

Meaning 1: Defensive covering for the body

Meaning 2: Quality or circumstance that gives protection

Most appropriate meaning: __1__

4. Word: dependent

Meaning 1: Hanging down

Meaning 2: Determined or conditioned by another

Most appropriate meaning: __2__

5. Word: critical

Meaning 1: To find fault

Meaning 2: Decisive, important

Most appropriate meaning: __2__

Meanings of Dictionary Usage Labels

Archaic	Outdated or no longer used
Colloquial	Conversational
Informal	Terms better used in casual or familiar expression
Nonstandard	Not conforming to usage characteristic of educated native speakers of a language
Obsolete	No longer in use or no longer useful
Rare	Seldom occurring or not often found
Vulgar	Coarse, crude, or undeveloped

Understanding Word Usage

In the dictionary, a word that is not standard English is given a **usage label** such as *archaic, colloquial, informal, nonstandard, obsolete, rare, slang,* or *vulgar.* For example, one way to describe an indiscreet or chatty person is to call him or her a *blabbermouth.* However, the dictionary labels this word *colloq.,* which means "colloquial," or conversational. Avoid nonstandard words in your college writing.

EXERCISE 3 RECOGNIZING USAGE LABELS

Look up the following words focusing on the definition given in paretheses. Write any labels your dictionary gives for the meaning shown.

1. crib ("cheat") _Informal_

2. drag ("no fun") _Slang_

3. snotty ("unpleasant") _Vulgar_

4. irregardless ("regardless") _Nonstandard_

5. drake ("a dragon") _Obsolete_

Discovering Word Histories

Understanding a word's history, or **etymology,** can help you remember its spelling and understand its meaning. Not all dictionaries contain word his-

Abbreviations of Root Languages

OE	Old English	Gr	Greek
ME	Middle English	Fr	French
L	Latin	OFr	Old French

tories; you're more likely to find this information in a hardbound dictionary than in a paperback one. Usually appearing in brackets before the definition, a word's history tells the languages and meanings from which the word is derived. For instance, *diamond* comes from the Greek root *adamas,* which meant a hard stone or substance.

EXERCISE 4 FINDING WORD HISTORIES

Look up the history of the following words in a dictionary and write what you find.

1. jungle _From Hindi; impenetrable thicket; tangled mass of tropical vegetation_

2. jukebox _Of West African origin; a coin-operated music player_

3. hamburger _From German; named for German town of Hamburg; beef patty sandwich_

4. judo _From Japanese; sport that emphasizes quick movement and use of leverage_

5. tuxedo _From Tuxedo Park, New York; single- or double-breasted jacket, usually black or dark blue_

Understanding the Dictionary

Understanding these parts of a dictionary definition will help you improve your spelling and pronunciation.

- Pronunciation key
- Irregular verb forms
- Parts of speech
- Irregular noun forms

Pronunciation Key

The dictionary's pronunciation key on page 208 tells you how a word should be pronounced.

- **Vowel sounds (a, e, i, o, u).** Symbols show how vowels should be pronounced. For instance, the sound of the vowel *a* as in *ate* is indicated like this: ā.
- **Schwa sound.** The schwa looks like an upside down *e* or ə. It stands for the sound *uh*, as in the slang expression "duh." The schwa sound is common in the English language.

  crocodile   'krä-kə-dīl

  happily   'ha-pə-lē
- **Accent symbols.** A word's syllables may receive different emphasis in pronunciation. For instance, the first syllable is stressed in the word *diamond*.

Tip: Dictionaries may use different pronunciation guides. Check the bottom of the dictionary page to find the guide.

EXERCISE 5 USING A PRONUNCIATION KEY

Using a dictionary, write pronunciation keys for each word on the blank lines. Include any accent marks. An example is done for you.

literary _____ 'lit-ə-'rer-ē _____

1. obsequious _____ ßb-'sé-kwé-əs _____

2. sententious _____ sen-'ten(t)-shəs _____

3. obstinate _____ 'äb-stə-nət _____

4. sanguine _____ 'saŋ-gwßn _____

5. telepathically _____ te-lə-'pa-thi-k(ß)lé _____

EXERCISE 6 TRANSLATING PRONUNCIATION SYMBOLS

Pronunciation keys for five words are written below. Write down the word that the pronunciation keys refer to, paying attention to spelling. Use a dictionary if necessary.

1. kō-ha-bə-'tā-shən _____ cohabitation _____

2. pər-'fəŋ(k)-t(ə)rē _____ perfunctory _____

3. 'de-səl-tȯr-ē _____ desultory _____

Pronunciation Symbols

For more information see the Guide to Pronunciation.

ə .... banana, collide, abut

ˈə, ˌə .... humdrum, abut

ə .... immediately preceding \l\, \n\, \m\, \ŋ\, as in battle, mitten, eaten, and sometimes open \ˈō-pᵊm\, lock and key \-ᵊŋ-\; immediately following \l\, \m\, \r\, as often in French table, prisme, titre

ər .... further, merger, bird

ˈər-
ˈə-r } .... as in two different pronunciations of hurry \ˈhər-ē, ˈhə-rē\

a .... mat, map, mad, gag, snap, patch

ā .... day, fade, date, aorta, drape, cape

ä .... bother, cot

är .... car, heart, bazaar, bizarre

aù .... now, loud, out

b .... baby, rib

ch .... chin, nature \ˈnā-chər\

d .... did, adder

e .... bet, bed, peck

er .... bare, fair, wear, millionaire

ˈē, ˌē .... beat, nosebleed, evenly, easy

ē .... easy, mealy

f .... fifty, cuff

g .... go, big, gift

h .... hat, ahead

hw .... whale as pronounced by those who do not have the same pronunciation for both *whale* and *wail*

i .... tip, banish, active

ir .... near, deer, mere, pier

ī .... site, side, buy, tripe

j .... job, gem, edge, join, judge

k .... kin, cook, ache

k̲ .... German ich, Buch; one pronunciation of loch

l .... lily, pool

m .... murmur, dim, nymph

n .... no, own

n .... indicates that a preceding vowel or diphthong is pronounced with the nasal passages open, as in French *un bon vin blanc* \œⁿ-bōⁿ-vaⁿ-blāⁿ\

ŋ .... sing \ˈsiŋ\, singer \ˈsiŋ-ər\, finger \ˈfiŋ-gər\, ink \ˈiŋk\

ō .... bone, know, beau

ȯ .... saw, all, gnaw, caught

œ .... French boeuf, feu, German Hölle, Höhle

ȯi .... coin, destroy

ȯr .... boar, port, door, shore

p .... pepper, lip

r .... red, rarity

s .... source, less

sh .... as in shy, mission, machine, special (actually, this is a single sound, not two); with a hyphen between, two sounds as in *grasshopper* \ˈgras-ˌhä-pər\

t .... tie, attack, late, later, latter

th .... as in thin, ether (actually, this is a single sound, not two); with a hyphen between, two sounds as in *knighthood* \ˈnīt-ˌhùd\

t̲h̲ .... then, either, this (actually, this is a single sound, not two)

ü .... rule, youth, union \ˈyün-yən\, few \ˈfyü\

ù .... pull, wood, book

ᵫ .... German füllen, hübsch, fühlen, French rue

ùr .... boor, tour, insure

v .... vivid, give

w .... we, away

y .... yard, young, cue \ˈkyü\, mute \ˈmyüt\, union \ˈyün-yən\

ʸ .... indicates that during the articulation of the sound represented by the preceding character, the front of the tongue has substantially the position it has for the articulation of the first sound of *yard*, as in French *digne* \dēnʸ\

z .... zone, raise

zh .... as in vision, azure \ˈa-zhər\ (actually, this is a single sound, not two); with hyphen between, two sounds as in *hogshead* \ˈhȯgz-ˌhed, ˈhägz-\

\ .... reversed virgule used in pairs to mark the beginning and end of a transcription: \ˈpen\

ˈ .... mark preceding a syllable with primary (strongest) stress: \ˈpen-mən-ˌship\

ˌ .... mark preceding a syllable with secondary (medium) stress: \ˈpen-mən-ˌship\

- .... mark of syllable division

( ) .... indicate that what is symbolized between is present in some utterances but not in others: *factory* \ˈfak-t(ə-)rē\

÷ .... indicates that many regard as unacceptable the pronunciation variant immediately following: *nuclear* \ˈnü-klē-ər, ˈnyü-, ÷-kyə-lər\

4. ə-'rī _____ awry _____

5. pri-züm _____ presume _____

Parts of Speech

A dictionary entry gives an abbreviation for a word's part of speech as indicated below. Some words can act as more than one part of speech.

adj.	adjective	n.	noun
adv.	adverb	prep.	preposition
conj.	conjunction	pron.	pronoun
interj.	interjection	v.	verb

EXERCISE 7   IDENTIFYING PARTS OF SPEECH USING THE DICTIONARY

Look up each word in a dictionary and write its part of speech. If more than one part of speech is listed, include them all.

1. rally _____ noun, verb _____

2. decency _____ noun _____

3. exacerbate _____ verb _____

4. quintessential _____ adjective _____

5. moreover _____ adverb _____

Irregular Verb Forms

The dictionary entry for an irregular verb gives all the main verb forms. For instance, for the verb *arise*, the dictionary lists *arose, arisen,* and *arising* as past tense, past participle, and present participle, in that order. (The verb forms for regular verbs are not given in the dictionary entry.)

EXERCISE 8 FINDING IRREGULAR VERB FORMS IN THE DICTIONARY

Look up the following verbs in a dictionary and write their forms. An example is done for you.

Word: drink

Past tense: _____ drank _____

Past participle: _____ drunk _____

Present participle: _____ drinking _____

1. Word: become

Past tense: _____ became _____

Past participle: _____ become _____

Present participle: _____ becoming _____

2. Word: draw

Past tense: _____ drew _____

Past participle: _____ drawn _____

Present participle: _____ drawing _____

3. Word: lie (as in "to lie down")

Past tense: _____ lay _____

Past participle: _____ lain _____

Present participle: _____ lying _____

4. Word: shake

Past tense: _____ shook _____

Past participle: _____ shaken _____

Present participle: _____ shaking _____

5. Word: write

Past tense: wrote
_____

Past participle: written
_____

Present participle: writing
_____

Irregular Noun Forms

Regular nouns are made plural by adding -s or -es. **Irregular nouns** do not follow these rules. For instance, if a word ends in *is*, such as *basis*, it has a special plural form: *bases*. The dictionary can help you learn the forms of irregular nouns.

Irregular Nouns

Singular	Plural
mouse	mice
child	children
leaf	leaves
thesis	theses
passerby	passersby

EXERCISE 9 FINDING THE PLURAL FORMS OF IRREGULAR NOUNS

Look up the following words and write their plural forms. If there is more than one possible plural form, list all of them.

1. hippopotamus _____ hippopotamuses, hippopotami _____

2. crisis _____ crises _____

3. formula _____ formulas, formulae _____

4. bacterium _____ bacteria _____

5. cactus _____ cactuses, cacti _____

EDITING PRACTICE

Look up the underlined words in the following paragraph. Write each word's pronunciation, part of speech, and first definition.

Diamonds were formerly believed to have special powers. First, their <u>physical</u> strength led to the idea that diamonds were powerful on the battlefield. Men once wore the gems into battle as good-luck charms. Diamonds were thought to protect their wearers from madness, violence, and fear. Another type of strength attributed to diamonds is the one most people are familiar with: the power of love. <u>Ancient</u> Greeks, believing that the fire of a diamond reflected the flame of love, thought that diamonds were teardrops from the gods. Ancient Romans also <u>endowed</u> diamonds with romantic powers, believing them to be splinters from falling stars that tipped the arrows of <u>Eros</u>, the god of love. In the Middle Ages, diamonds were credited with the power to reunite <u>estranged</u> marriage partners. Since the average diamond sold in a jewelry store is more than 100 million years old, the idea that "diamonds are forever" may hold more truth than we realize.

1. Word: physical

Pronunciation: fi-zi-kəl

Part of speech: Adjective

Definition: Of nature and all matter; natural; material

2. Word: ancient

Pronunciation: æán(t)-shßnt

Part of speech: Adjective

Definition: Of times in the past; of the world's early history

3. Word: endowed

Pronunciation: in-'daů(d)

Part of speech: Verb

Definition: Provided with some talent, quality, or value, etc.

4. Word: Eros

Pronunciation: 'er-äs

Part of speech: Noun

Definition: Greek god of erotic love

5. Word: estranged

Pronunciation: i-'strānj(d)

Part of speech: Verb

Definition: Removed, as from usual surroundings or associates; kept apart or away

Lab Activity 16

For additional practice using the dictionary, complete Lab Activity 16 in the Lab Manual at the back of the book.

PART FOUR
Strategies for Paragraph Development

17 Providing Illustrations and Examples

What Is an Illustration and Example Paragraph?

Suppose you want to set your friend up with your brother, but she remembers growing up with him and seeing him do things like make prank phone calls that didn't impress her. You think he has changed, and you offer the following examples to illustrate your brother's adult behavior.

- He gave your mother flowers just for being a great mom.
- He attends the community college while holding down a job.
- He has apologized for the way he acted when you were children.

Providing illustrations and examples is one of the simplest and most effective writing strategies. In an illustration and example paragraph, you offer specific details that fit logically into the larger picture.

Examples and illustrations can come from three sources.

- Descriptions of objects or events in your life
- Accounts of events in other people's lives
- Facts that you've heard about or read in trusted sources

217

New York City Skyline

FOOD FOR THOUGHT   Impressive for its landmark structures, New York City boasts such attractions as the Statue of Liberty, the Empire State Building, and the Chrysler Building. What impressions do you have of New York City? Write for ten minutes about what you know, think, or imagine about it.

Real-Life Writing

In real-life writing, writers use the strategy of providing illustrations and examples in a number of important settings.

For College

- Use illustrations and examples on placement or assessment tests.
- Use illustrations and examples on in-class essay exams—such as in history, English, or art courses—when you need to show your instructor that you know certain information.

In Your Personal Life

- Use specific examples in a letter to a friend to convince her that a new restaurant is worth trying.
- Use examples and illustrations in an e-mail to your friends to show them that an apartment is a good place to live.

At Work

- Cite examples of other stores to convince your boss to update your store's window displays.

- Give examples of the additional work you've done so that your boss might give you more responsibility and a raise.

A Model Paragraph: Illustration and Example

To use illustration and example, follow the basic format shown in the "Illustration and Example Paragraphs" diagram on page 220.

In the following paragraph, the writer has developed a topic sentence and provided illustrations and examples that prove the support points.

Big-City Life

Living in New York is exciting for many reasons. For instance, I have many different travel options. When I lived in other, smaller cities, I drove my car to work. I always took the same route and never saw much that was different. In New York, however, I can take the subway and see people from all over the city who ride in the same train car, or I can take a taxi (if I can afford it) and watch people out the windows. If the weather is nice, I can even walk. No matter which way I choose, I always see something new. Another illustration of New York's excitement is its architecture. Just walking down the street is like being in a museum. I can see the Chrysler Building, with its grimacing gargoyles, or the Empire State Building, rising up like a giant. I can also see the narrow, twisting streets of the Wall Street area, with famous buildings such as the New York Stock Exchange and Fraunces Tavern. Walking through New York is like taking secret passageways to new and wonderful places. A last example of New York's exciting life is the food. I can find pretty much any kind of food I'm in the mood for. Sometimes I want an Italian meal, so I head down to Little Italy. If I'm in the mood for Japanese food, there's always great sushi to be found. Sometimes, I just want a hot dog, and then I can find a vendor on a street corner who gives me my perfect lunch. Living in New York is never boring.

Illustration and Example Paragraphs
Topic sentence...*Stating the main idea*.............
↓
Support point 1.. ....Example or illustration........................ ....Example or illustration........................ Support point 2.. ....Example or illustration........................ ....Example or illustration........................ Support point 3.. ....Example or illustration........................ ....Example or illustration........................

The writer's topic sentence is "Living in New York is exciting for many reasons." The following support points show how living in New York is exciting.

1. Different travel options

2. Great architecture

3. Different foods

The writer uses these transitions to link the three support points: *for example, another illustration, a last example.* The transitions tell the reader to expect examples and illustrations.

EXERCISE 1 FINDING EXAMPLES IN A PARAGRAPH

Some of the details from "Big-City Life" on page 219 are filled in below. Write in the remaining details that the writer uses to illustrate her support points.

Support point 1:   Different travel options

Examples: *Subway ride*
_____

             Taxi ride
_____

             Walking
_____

Support point 2:   Great architecture

Examples: Chrysler Building

Empire State Building

Wall Street

Support point 3:   Different foods

Examples: Italian food in Little Italy

Japanese food

Hot dog from a vendor

Choosing a Good Topic for Development

Sometimes your instructor will give you a topic, but other times you'll choose your own. One way to find a topic that works well for using illustrations and examples is to do some prewriting. For instance, Luz wondered if she could write an effective paragraph about her neighborhood as a place to raise children. She made a cluster diagram to help her find examples. Nearly everything in the diagram supports the idea that her neighborhood is a good place to raise children.

Writing an Effective Topic Sentence

Luz organized her examples and illustrations according to the support points they illustrate.

Support point 1:   The neighborhood is convenient for raising children.

Support point 2:   Children can be safe and have fun in the neighborhood.

Support point 3:   There are many sources of support in the neighborhood for families.

After identifying support points from her cluster diagram, Luz wrote her topic sentence: "The Oak Grove neighborhood is a good place to raise

children." When she writes her rough draft, Luz can eliminate two examples—the absence of a gas station nearby and the lack of pets—since they don't illustrate any of her support points. Another point—about the neighborhood watch program—had potential for development, but since Luz found fewer details supporting that idea, she decided not to include it.

Developing Specific Details

When you have experience in the subject you're writing about, using examples from your own life will be most effective. However, if your topic is one that you know less about, you can use examples from other people's experiences or from trusted sources such as a magazine or newspaper. (See Chapter 10 for a list of sources to use.)

Some of the examples Luz developed during clustering came from her personal experience: "park is close" and "easy to find parking." Other examples came from Luz's discussion with others in the neighborhood: "many teenagers for baby-sitting" and "older women I can ask for advice." However, one illustration was a fact that Luz read in the local newspaper: "mall opening nearby."

For most of the assignments in this book, examples from your own life or from the lives of people you know will be adequate for support. When you write for more complicated assignments, however, you will need to use examples from additional sources. In many college courses, you'll need to read about a specific event or topic, learn about it, and then write what you've learned in an essay or report.

Read the paragraph that follows. Then read the outline that the writer used to develop the paragraph. How do you think the writer got his information for the examples in the paragraph? Do the examples come from his own life? Pay attention to the specific details that the writer chose.

On with the Show!

[1]Probably no other city has been a greater subject for artists and entertainers than New York, New York. [2]A case in point comes from the hundreds of songs about the city. [3]In the 1930s the songwriter Cole Porter wrote "I Happen to Like New York," and then Frank Sinatra made the song "New York, New York" famous by singing about "the city that never sleeps." [4]Further, in the 1980s, Billy Joel's "New York State of Mind" and Grand Master Flash and the Furious Five's song "New York, New York" became hits even though their messages about New York were less happy than the ones in earlier songs. [5]Movies are another example of how New York has influenced entertainment. [6]The movie *An Affair to Remember* featured the Empire State Building as a meeting place for lovers, and then both *Love Affair* and *Sleepless in Seattle* used the same romantic setting. [7]*King Kong* was an adventure movie set in New York, and *The Muppets Take Manhattan* showed the furry puppets all over the city. [8]Even movies like *Vanilla Sky* and *Phone Booth* were set in New York, too. [9]A final example of how New York is a subject for entertainment comes from television shows. [10]Many recent television programs, including *Will and Grace*, and *Law and Order*, are all set in New York. [11]In fact, it seems hard to find TV series that are *not* set in New York City. [12]All in all, New York is a big star!

Topic sentence: Probably no other city has been a greater subject for artists and entertainers than New York, New York.

a. Songs

1. Cole Porter, "I Happen to Like New York"
2. Frank Sinatra, "New York, New York"
3. Billy Joel, "A New York State of Mind"
4. Grand Master Flash, "New York, New York"

b. Movies

1. *An Affair to Remember*
2. *Love Affair*
3. *Sleepless in Seattle*
4. *King Kong*
5. *The Muppets Take Manhattan*
6. *Vanilla Sky*
7. *Phone Booth*

c. Television programs

1. *Will and Grace*
2. *Law and Order*

EXERCISE 2 PROVIDING SPECIFIC DETAILS

Each of the sentences below is a support point in a paragraph. Provide at least three examples that support each point. Answers will vary.

Support point: Many people are interested in buying a hybrid car.

Examples: Hybrids use a combination of gasoline and electric power.

Their motors efficiently provide plenty of power.

They usually get better than forty miles per gallon.

1. Support point: Reality TV shows are actually carefully staged.

Examples: _____

_____

_____

2. Support point: There are several ways to deal with a roommate who snores.

   Examples: _____

   _____

   _____

3. Support point: Computer blogs give everyone the ability to be "published."

   Examples: _____

   _____

   _____

4. Support point: Space exploration is (or is not) important to the future of our country.

   Examples: _____

   _____

   _____

5. Support point: History's most influential written works illustrate the saying "The pen is mightier than the sword."

   Examples: _____

   _____

   _____

Organizing and Linking Your Ideas

Once you've come up with a topic, written a topic sentence and support points, and supported those points with details, you're ready to organize your ideas using either time sequence (chronological) order or emphatic order. Writing an illustration and example paragraph gives you some freedom in organizing your ideas.

In "Big-City Life," on page 219, the writer loosely uses emphatic order. Even though she doesn't say she thinks that food is the most important aspect of living in New York City, her placement of "different foods" as the last support point makes that an important point. In "On with the Show!" on page 223, the writer uses a loose form of time sequence order. He doesn't say that his points occur in chronological order, but he begins with singers from the 1930s in his first support point, and he ends with television programs that still air today.

To introduce examples and link ideas, writers use **transitional expressions.** In the sentences that follow, the underlined transitional expression signals that an example or illustration is being introduced.

Another reason this is a good family neighborhood is that children can play safely. <u>For example</u>, there is a supervised playground nearby.

Transition Words and Terms That Signal Examples

an illustration of	particularly
for example	specifically
for instance	such as
one example of	that is

Changes After 9/11

[1]As a result of the terrorist attacks on September 11, 2001, New York City has changed considerably. [2]One example of how New York has changed is the security policies for travelers. [3]When I visited New York a year after the attacks, the other airplane passengers and I were not allowed to leave our seats for the last thirty minutes of the flight. [4]It's amazing how uncomfortable those airline seats are. [5]The pilot told us that this was a safety precaution that came about after the 9/11 attacks. [6]Another instance of how the Big Apple has changed is in what the souvenir shops advertise. [7]On my visit, I walked by a number of stores. [8]In the windows of many shops were messages like "We believe" and "Our hearts go out to the victims of the 9/11 tragedy and their families." [9]I had expected to see signs like "30% off" or "Come see our new fall clothes." [10]Instead—a year later—I was surprised to see so many stores sending messages of sympathy and hope. [11]We all need hope, especially if we have tough jobs. [12]A positive illustration of changes in New York City is that the

police officers and firefighters are considered heroes. [13]All over the city people are selling, and wearing, "NYPD" and "FDNY" T-shirts and hats. [14]Also, in front of fire stations all over the city are small shrines—little piles of flowers, pictures, and candles—in honor of the people who died trying to save others. [15]These people have always been heroes, but it seems that the September 11 attacks made everyone realize this.

EXERCISE 3 FOLLOWING THE FOUR Cs

Concise Writing

1. What two sentences in "Changes After 9/11" are off-target and should be removed? _____4, 11_____

2. What is the topic sentence of "Changes After 9/11"?

As a result of the terrorist attacks on September 11, 2001, New York City has

changed considerably.

Credible Writing

3. What are the three ways that New York has changed since the terrorist attacks, according to "Changes After 9/11"?

a. There are more safety precautions.

b. There are signs of sympathy and hope in store windows.

c. Police officers and firefighters are considered heroes.

4. What is one example that you think is particularly effective?

Answers will vary.

Clear Writing

5. What are the important transitional expressions that the writer uses to introduce support points in "Changes After 9/11"?

a. One example

b. Another instance _____

c. A positive illustration _____

6. a. What is the one positive change that the reader mentions in "Changes After 9/11"?

Police officers and firefighters are considered heroes. _____

b. Why do you think the writer put this point last?

Because this point is last and it is the only positive example, it's meant to

be taken as the most important. _____

Correct Writing

The sentences in this paragraph are all correct. To check for correctness in your own writing, go to Part 7, "Writing Correct Sentences."

What You Know Now

Using illustration and example to develop your ideas is an effective way to show your reader what you mean. Choose a topic that works well for illustration and example, and use your prewriting strategies to get started. Using examples from your own experiences, from other people's experiences, and from trusted sources can help you offer a range of support. Be sure to signal examples to your reader using relevant transition words and terms.

WRITING PRACTICE 1 Develop Details for a Topic Sentence

Below are five topic sentences that need support. For each topic sentence, provide one well-developed illustration. An example is done for you.

Answers will vary.

Topic sentence: Modern music includes many different sounds.

Support point: *Some songs even use sounds that aren't really musical.*

Example: *In the Bahamian song "Who Let the Dogs Out," for instance,*

the regular musical sounds of a melody and a beat are

highlighted by the barking of a dog throughout the song.

1. Topic sentence: Sharing a room with two siblings taught me how to get along with other people.

Support point: _____

Example: _____

_____

2. Topic sentence: Working as a pool cleaner for the summer was a hard job.

Support point: _____

Example: _____

_____

3. Topic sentence: Taking risks is necessary for success.

Support point: _____

Example: _____

_____

4. Topic sentence: Sometimes good things happen to you when you least expect them.

Support point: _____

Example: _____

_____

5. Topic sentence: Television shows rarely have stars that look like every-day people.

Support point: _____

Example: _____

_____

WRITING PRACTICE 2 Write an Illustration and Example Paragraph

Now write an illustration and example paragraph of your own.

Prewriting

1. Choose one of the following topics for your illustration and example paragraph.

   An exciting sport or activity

   A funny television show or movie

   A frustrating or satisfying job

   A funny person

   An irritating person

   A famous person

   A place from your childhood

2. Freewrite for five to ten minutes on the topic. Then, use at least one other prewriting technique—listing, questioning, keeping a journal, clustering, or outlining—to come up with more descriptive details.

If you need help coming up with a topic and doing prewriting, use the outline below. (Write your own topic sentence to reflect your ideas on a funny person you know.) Add your own specific details to complete the outline.

Topic sentence: _My uncle is very funny._____

  a. Always has a new joke.

      1. _____

      2. _____

      3. _____

  b. Performs a stand-up comedy routine at a local club.

      1. _____

      2. _____

      3. _____

  c. Helps lighten up family dinners.

      1. _____

      2. _____

      3. _____

Another helpful prewriting technique for writing an illustration and example paragraph is asking questions. To develop ideas about the topic "a place from my childhood," Henry used this technique.

Fourth-Grade Classroom

What was my teacher like?	Mrs. Smith was tough, strict, not always nice.
Who were my classmates?	Big kids picked on me.
What was the classroom like?	Too much chalk dust

Drafting

3. Write a topic sentence. Draw on your prewriting to find a point to develop through an entire paragraph. For instance, the answers to Henry's questions are all negative. Thus, a workable topic sentence could be "Thinking about my fourth-grade classroom can still make me nervous."

4. Choose support points and specific details. Henry wrote down the reasons thinking about his fourth-grade classroom makes him nervous.

   Mean teacher

   Big kids

   Chalk dust allergy

   Then, choose the details that you think best illustrate your support points and will make your paragraph believable. Henry chose the following details.

Support Point	Specific Details
Mean teacher	Mrs. Smith gave me detention for tapping my finger on the desk.
Big kids	Sam and Al picked on me during recess; Marc stole my lunch.
Chalk dust allergy	Constant sneezing, itchy skin

5. Arrange your support points using time sequence (chronological) or emphatic order. Decide which order works better by examining your details. If all of Henry's negative fourth-grade experiences occurred simultaneously throughout the school year, he should probably use emphatic order. However, if the negative events in fourth grade occurred one after another, Henry could use time sequence order. As you're organizing your ideas, be sure to eliminate details that don't fit.

6. Now write a draft of your paragraph using the topic sentence, your support points, and your specific details. Feel free to do more prewriting if you need additional specific details.

Revising

7. Check for the first three of the four Cs: *concise, credible,* and *clear* writing. Make any necessary changes to your draft.

Editing

8. Check your paragraph for the fourth C: *correct* writing. Proofread your paragraph to make sure you have used correct spelling, punctuation, and grammar.

WRITING PRACTICE 3 **Write a Paragraph About a Person**

Write about a person who has had an impact on your life. Choose Topic A or Topic B to write your paragraph. Remember to include a topic sentence, support points, and examples. If you need help, refer to Writing Practice 2 on pages 229–232.

Topic A

Write a paragraph about a person who has had a positive influence on you. This person can be someone you know well, or someone you've only seen on television. (A person does not need to be an active part of your life in order to have a positive influence on you.)

Possible Topics

Someone who encouraged you   Someone who taught you

Someone who disciplined you   Someone who rewarded you

Someone who set a good example for you   Someone who inspired you

Topic B

Write a paragraph about someone who has had a negative effect on your life. Again, this person does not need to be someone you know well. Use examples to show how the person influenced your life.

Possible Topics

Someone who embarrassed you   Someone who hurt your feelings

Someone who set a poor example   Someone who lied to you

Someone who discouraged you   Someone who cheated you

⌦ Lab Activity 17

For additional practice with providing illustrations and examples, complete Lab Activity 17 in the Lab Manual at the back of the book.

18 Narrating an Event or a Story

CULTURE NOTE *Fairy Tales*

As stories of good and evil, reward and punishment, fairy tales have been told for centuries. Though part of their appeal is entertainment, fairy tales were also used to show people the difference between right and wrong. In the twentieth century, fairy tales came under attack for emphasizing beauty and virtue above other qualities in women, but some tales have messages that everyone can appreciate.

What Is a Narrative Paragraph?

If you've ever sat down after a long day and explained to a friend just what happened to make that day rotten—your alarm clock didn't go off, your boss got mad at you, your car broke down, and your coffee spilled down the front of your white shirt—you've already practiced the art of narration, or of telling a story.

Narration is a paragraph development strategy that involves writing about events in the order in which they occur (time sequence order). Narration's purpose is to tell a story, so it works particularly well when you are writing about events that happen one after another.

Real-Life Writing

In real-life writing, we use narration frequently to provide "the whole story" or to give our readers a context for our arguments. Here are some situations in which you might use the strategy of narrating an event.

A Fairy Tale

JOURNAL RESPONSE Although many fairy tales end up happily, many tell grim stories designed to frighten children into obedience. What fairy tales are you familiar with? What do they mean to you? Write for ten minutes about the fairy tales you know or like best, explaining why a certain tale is meaningful to you.

For College

■ Use narration in history or political science exams or papers. Narrating events—especially those based on a timeline—can ensure that you include all the necessary details in the correct order.

■ Use narration for recounting events that occurred in your life.

In Your Personal Life

■ Use narration in a letter or in your own journal to describe an event or a series of events.

■ Use narration when writing a letter to a business to explain your experience with the customer service department.

At Work

■ In a memo, narrate your week-by-week interaction with a client during a project.

■ In a job application, offer a brief narrative that illustrates your qualifications for a job. For instance, tell step by step how you solved a particular problem.

A Model Paragraph: Narrative

To write a narrative paragraph, follow the basic paragraph format, shown in the "Narrative Paragraphs" diagram on page 236. The writer has developed a topic sentence and included details in time sequence order.

The Price for a Prince

[1]In the Hans Christian Andersen's tale "The Little Mermaid," the youngest daughter of the Sea King pays a great price for an attempt to win a prince. [2]The little mermaid loves a young human prince whom she has seen. [3]The prince has no idea of the little mermaid's existence, and even when she saves him from drowning, he believes another girl to be responsible. [4]The little mermaid decides to try to become human. [5]First, she approaches the sorceress of the sea and asks for her help. [6]Just finding the sorceress is unpleasant because the sorceress's captives try to grab and keep the little mermaid. [7]Next, the sorceress gives the little mermaid frightening news about the price she will have to pay. [8]Even after drinking the potion, the little mermaid can become human only if the prince marries her. [9]If the prince marries anyone else, the little mermaid must die. [10]Additionally, once the little mermaid becomes human, every time her feet touch the ground, she will feel as if she is walking on sharp knives. [11]The fee the sorceress requires is the little mermaid's lovely voice. [12]In exchange for a magic potion, the sorceress will cut out the little mermaid's tongue. [13]Eventually, the little mermaid drinks the potion, grows legs that feel piercing pain, and meets her prince. [14]He is enchanted with her, even allowing her to sleep on a cushion outside his bedroom door. [15]However, he marries neither princess. [16]The little mermaid has given everything for someone who will not return her love.

Narrative Paragraphs
Topic sentence..*Stating the event or story*..
↓
Event 1.. ....Details about the event......................... Event 2.. ....Details about the event......................... Event 3.. ....Details about the event......................... Event 4.. ....Details about the event......................... Event 5.. ....Details about the event.........................

EXERCISE 1 IDENTIFYING THE ELEMENTS OF A NARRATIVE PARAGRAPH

Reread "The Price for a Prince." Then, answer the questions and fill in the blanks that follow.

1. What is the starting point for the story? _____

The little mermaid loves a young human prince.

2. What is the ending point for the story?_____

The little mermaid has lost everything.

3. What steps does the little mermaid take to become human?

a. She visits the sorceress.

b. She has her tongue cut out.

c. She grows legs.

4. How does the prince react to the little mermaid? _____

He is enchanted by her but marries someone else.

5. What transitions does the writer use in the following sentences that help the reader move from one event to another?

Sentence 5: _First_____   Sentence 7: _Next_____

Sentence 8: _Even after_____   Sentence 10: _Additionally_____

Sentence 11: _last_____   Sentence 13: _Eventually_____

Choosing a Good Topic for Development

Sometimes your instructor will give you a topic, but when you have to choose your own, make sure your topic lends itself to telling a story. Many topics can be organized according to time sequence, but some are easier to write about than others.

Topics That Work Well for Narration	Topics That Don't Work Well for Narration
How you decided to try skydiving	The importance of preparing for skydiving
The first time you cried at a movie	Why movies make you cry

Topics that work well are limited to a certain event or time period. Topics that don't work have points that might not necessarily occur in chronological order. For instance, if movies make you cry because the screen images are large and because you are an emotional person, you might have a difficult time deciding which one of those points comes first according to time sequence order. Thus, explaining *why* you tend to cry is not the best choice for a narrative paragraph.

One way to tell if your topic will work well for narration is to *make a list of all the events that your paragraph will cover.* Listing will help you keep your facts in order and eliminate facts that are irrelevant.

For instance, in "The Price for a Prince" on page 235, the writer never mentions the other story line: that the little mermaid also wants to become human so that she can have an immortal soul. The writer also leaves out the details that the little mermaid has the chance—on the prince's wedding night—to kill him and become a mermaid again, but that she can't bring herself to harm him. While these details are interesting, they don't help the writer develop the idea in the topic sentence, that the little mermaid paid a great price for an attempt to win her prince. Notice, too, how the writer "hurries" through longer periods of time—for example, the little mermaid's whole life until she meets the sorceress—to focus on the events that matter most.

Dean's assignment below was to write a paragraph on a particularly good or bad event in his life. He began by making a list of events that occurred the day his high school soccer team won a championship.

> <u>Winning the big game</u>
>
> Lost to Seahall Spartans for past two years.
>
> They played dirty (we could, too).
>
> We knew we were better.
>
> Clear fall day.
>
> Good smell of newly mown grass.
>
> Won the coin toss at midfield.
>
> Coin glimmered as it fell.
>
> Coin seemed to fall in slow motion.
>
> Kicked off, passed to Andre, and scored in first five minutes.
>
> Other team scored in first half, too, but we dominated play.
>
> Coach was nervous.
>
> Ron, Steve, and Franco almost scored, but their goalie was awesome.
>
> Second half started badly (I slipped and missed a scoring chance).
>
> Shoe came untied.
>
> Got an assist for passing to Pablo for his header in.
>
> Thought we'd won for sure, but then Carlos fouled their striker in the penalty box.
>
> They shot a penalty kick and missed.
>
> Bobby and Jim controlled the ball for the last two minutes.
>
> We won.
>
> First time Grant High School won a soccer title.

Most of Dean's details show a progression from the start of the game through to the end. However, some details—the coach's nervousness and the fact that this was the high school's first soccer title—can be omitted from the paragraph because they don't lead to the winning moment of the game.

Writing an Effective Topic Sentence

After making his list, Dean realized that he mentioned the names of several teammates. This told him that their victory was a team effort. Thus, his topic sentence became "Winning the section title in varsity soccer was a complete team effort."

Developing Specific Details for Narration

To add information and interest to your narrative paragraphs, you can use three types of details.

- Background details
- Action details
- Sensory details

Background Details

Background details give information about other events that may have occured at the same time as the main event of your paragraph or earlier. The following background details come from Dean's prewriting list.

Lost to Seahall Spartans for past two years.

They played dirty (we could, too).

We knew we were better.

These details don't tell anything about the championship game. However, they help the reader understand why this game is so important to the writer.

Action Details

Action details move your story along from one point to the next. In a narrative paragraph, the writer doesn't use formal support points. Dean

referred to his prewriting list to find the action details that served as important place markers for his information. Thus, he knew he would write about
the following parts of the game.

> Early scoring by his team
>
> Missed shots and assists during the game
>
> Possible tie when Carlos was called for a foul

Dean decided that these were the pivotal action details he *had* to
include.

Sensory Details

Sensory details add information that makes your paragraph more vivid
and thus more interesting. For instance, Dean described the start of the soccer game using these details. He added sensory details to give the reader a
better feel for the day.

> Clear fall day.
>
> Good smell of newly mown grass.
>
> Coin glimmered as it fell.
>
> Coin seemed to fall in slow motion.

In Dean's paragraph, the phrase "smell of newly mown grass" and the
description of the coin as it "caught the sun and glimmered as it fell—as if
in slow motion" paint a picture for the reader. Even if the reader isn't a soccer fan, by including these sensory details, Dean hopes to make sure that
the reader will *want* to read his paragraph. Here is Dean's final draft.

A Team Effort

Winning the section title in varsity soccer was a complete team
effort. On the day of the big game—a bright, clear fall day—we all
felt nervous. We had come up against the Seahall High School Spartans for the last two years, and we'd lost both times. They played
dirty, but we knew we were the better team, so we were prepared to
take elbows to the head (and maybe give a few back) in order to win
the game. The smell of newly mown grass hit me as I stepped onto
the field for the coin toss. I called "heads," and as the coin fell, it
caught the sun and glimmered as it fell—as if in slow motion—to
land in the heads-up position. We chose to go with the wind first. As

Seahall kicked off, I stole the ball, sprinted up the side, and centered to Andre, who scored. We dominated play during the first half—Ron, Steve, and Franco came really close to scoring—but Seahall's goalie was awesome. By halftime, the Spartans had managed to score, too. The second half started badly because I slipped and missed what should have been an easy goal. Then my shoe came untied, and I almost missed trapping a key pass. We hit our stride, however, as I passed to Pablo. He had a great header in, and I got the assist. With a few minutes to go, we were starting to get excited, but then Carlos fouled their striker in the penalty box. Luckily, their kicker missed the penalty shot, and Bobby and Jim controlled the ball for the last two minutes. The only thing better than winning the game was knowing that we all had contributed.

Dean uses all three types of details—background, action, and sensory—to provide a context for his event, move the action along, and vividly illustrate the events leading up to the big win.

EXERCISE 2 ANALYZING A PARAGRAPH FOR GOOD NARRATION STRATEGY

Read the paragraph below. Then answer the questions that follow.

A Fairy Tale for Today

[1]The life and marriage of Lisa Halaby, an American, are a modern-day fairy tale. [2]Lisa Halaby was born in 1951 to an important Arab-American family that was involved in politics. [3]She grew up attending excellent private schools, and in 1969 she enrolled in Princeton University as part of the first coed class. [4]At Princeton, Halaby studied architecture and urban planning. [5]After she graduated, she took a job in the country of Jordan. [6]Since her father worked in politics in Jordan at that time, he introduced her to the King of Jordan, King Hussein I. [7]Halaby and King Hussein became friends, and later their friendship developed into a romance. [8]They were married in 1978, and Halaby became the first American-born queen of an Arab nation. [9]She took the name Noor al-Hussein, which means "Light of Hussein," and converted to the Islamic faith. [10]For the next twenty years, Queen Noor lived happily with King Hussein, and they had four children. [11]Even though she was a queen and did not need to work for a living, Queen Noor worked hard to improve the lives of women and children in Jordan. [12]In

particular, she worked to give women employment options without criticizing women who chose not to work for religious reasons. [13]King Hussein died in 1999, but Queen Noor continued to live in Jordan with her children. [14]Though many would say that Queen Noor is like a fairy-tale princess, she has done so much for others that she is also like a fairy godmother. Note: Be sure to explain to students that King Hussein I of Jordan was not the same person as Saddam Hussein.

1. Make a list of events in the paragraph. The first two items are done for you.

a. Lisa Halaby was born in 1951 to an important Arab-American family that was involved in politics.

b. She grew up attending excellent private schools.

c. In 1969 she enrolled in Princeton University as part of the first coed class.

d. At Princeton, Halaby studied architecture and urban planning.

e. After she graduated, she took a job in the country of Jordan.

f. Her father introduced her to the King of Jordan, King Hussein I.

g. Halaby and King Hussein became friends.

h. Their friendship developed into a romance.

i. King Hussein and Halaby were married in 1978, and Halaby became the first American-born queen of an Arab nation.

j. She took the name Noor al-Hussein, which means "Light of Hussein," and converted to the Islamic faith.

k. For the next twenty years, Queen Noor lived happily with King Hussein, and they had four children.

l. Queen Noor worked hard to improve the lives of women and children in Jordan.

m. King Hussein died in 1999.

n. Queen Noor continued to live in Jordan with her children.

2. The beginning of the paragraph contains many background details. Write down one background detail from the paragraph. Answers will vary.

Lisa Halaby was born in 1951 to an important Arab-American family that was involved in politics.

3. Write two action details from the paragraph.   Answers will vary.

a. At Princeton, Halaby studied architecture and urban planning.

b. Halaby became the first American-born queen of an Arab nation.

Organizing and Linking Your Ideas

One way to organize your ideas before writing them in a paragraph is to make a timeline. This horizontal list allows you to place events in the order in which they occurred, along with times or dates. That way, you can map out all the events you're writing about before you start drafting.

Unlike other kinds of paragraphs you've seen in this text so far, narrative paragraphs don't necessarily contain obvious individual support points. Also, they often don't use transitions such as *for one, another point,* or *finally* to introduce individual points. Still, you need to make sure that each event is clearly connected to the events before and after it.

But instead of writing *one example* or *another instance when,* you will use transitions that show time sequence order, such as the ones listed in "Transitions That Show Time Sequence" on page 247. These transitions will keep your reader on track.

EXERCISE 3 FOLLOWING THE FOUR Cs

Read the paragraph below. Then answer the questions that follow.

Lessons from Loss

[1]Until I "invested" my measly savings in a "can't miss" business opportunity, I thought Jack from "Jack and the Beanstalk" wasn't too smart when he traded the family cow for some beans. [2]However, after I made the mistake of listening to my sister's boyfriend Hank, I learned a number of lessons about money. [3]One lesson was to learn about what I put my money in. [4]Right when I started back to school after working to save money, Hank told me about a new computer company that would pay me triple whatever I put in. [5]Since I still needed money for school, I gave Hank my hard-earned cash even though I knew nothing about computers. [6]Like Jack's magic beans, my investment—I was sure—would bring me great profits. [7]I was wrong. [8]I never saw a penny of profit, or of my original money. [9]I also learned to be

persistent when I was expecting a payment. [10]After Hank missed the first three payment deadlines—offering flimsy excuses about how "complicated" the business was—I should have demanded my money back, but I didn't. [11]After six months I realized that my money—and my sister's—was gone for good, and by then so was Hank. [12]Because I'd lost my college money, I had to hustle around to get whatever loans I could from the school, the state, and my parents. [13]Luckily, I pieced together enough money to pay for school, and I read *Investing for Dummies* and learned how to make money grow. [14](Investing in my sister's boyfriend's "great opportunity" was not in the book.) [15]I still have some loans to pay back, but the lessons I learned from the experience were worth the price I paid. [16]Maybe Jack benefited from trusting someone for a few beans, but I wasn't so lucky.

Concise

1. What is the topic sentence of the paragraph "Lessons from Loss"?

However, after I made the mistake of listening to my sister's boyfriend Hank,

I learned a number of lessons about money.

2. What are some of the lessons that the writer learned about investing?

Learn about what you put money in.

Be persistent when expecting a payment.
Learn about how to make money grow.

Credible

3. What are some specific details the writer uses to show how his situation is similar to Jack's?

Both gave all they had for not much in return.

Both hoped to gain much for their trade/investment.

4. What are some specific details the writer uses to show how his life is different from Jack's?

The writer loses everything initially; the writer gains only through his own

actions, not through magic.

Clear

5. What transitions does the writer use in the following sentences to indicate when certain events occurred?

Sentence 2: <u>after I made the mistake of . . .</u>

Sentence 4: <u>Right when I started back to school . . .</u>

Sentence 11: <u>after six months</u>

6. What transitions does the writer use in sentences 2, 5, 10, 11, and 12 that show a change of direction in the writer's ideas? (Feel free to check the list of transitions in Chapter 11.) <u>however</u>, <u>since</u>, <u>after</u>, <u>after</u>, <u>because</u>.

EXERCISE 4 PROVIDING DETAILS FOR A NARRATIVE PARAGRAPH

The following sentences are possible topic sentences for narrative paragraphs. For each one, write four events that could help develop the topic sentence. An example is done for you.

Topic sentence: My sixteenth birthday proved to be one of the happiest days of my life.

Events: **a.** <u>I passed my driver's test.</u>

b. <u>I drove myself to best friend's house.</u>

c. <u>My best friend organized a "Sweet Sixteen/Happy Driving" party for me.</u>

d. <u>My workaholic dad took time off to come to the party.</u>

1. Topic sentence: My little brother learned an important lesson when he <u>Answers will vary.</u>.

Events: **a.** _____

b. _____

c. _____

d. _____

2. Topic sentence: Sometimes even a little gesture of kindness can go a long way.   *Answers will vary.*

Events: **a.** _____

   b. _____

   c. _____

   d. _____

3. Topic sentence: From the first moment I saw ____*Answers will vary.*____, I knew we would be good friends.

Events: **a.** _____

   b. _____

   c. _____

   d. _____

4. Topic sentence: My first day of college proved to be

_____*Answers will vary.*_____.

Events: **a.** _____

   b. _____

   c. _____

   d. _____

5. Topic sentence: On my first day at ____*Answers will vary.*____, I definitely got off on the wrong foot.

Events: **a.** _____

   b. _____

   c. _____

   d. _____

Transitions That Show Time Sequence

after	finally
as	later
as soon as	next
at last	now
at the same time	soon
before	then
during	upon
earlier	when
first	while

What You Know Now

Writing a narrative paragraph involves telling a story in time sequence order. While you may not have formal support points, every detail should help develop your topic sentence. An effective narrative paragraph includes three types of details: background details, action details, and sensory details.

WRITING PRACTICE 1   Write a Narrative Paragraph

Now write a narrative paragraph of your own.

Prewriting

1. Choose a topic for your narrative paragraph.

Possible Topics

Your first day at a new job or at college

Moving to a new home

An experience that made you sad

How a historical event affected you

A personal triumph or success

A family celebration

2. Freewrite for five to ten minutes on your topic. Then, use at least one other prewriting technique—listing, questioning, keeping a journal, clustering, or outlining—to see what information you have and where possible gaps are.

For narrative paragraphs, the prewriting technique of listing is very useful because it helps you keep important events in order. For example, here is a sample list on the topic "moving to a new home."

Moving Day

Woke up rested.

Called friends to make sure they could still help me.

Labeled boxes.

Loaded truck.

Steve broke my one good chair.

Sonya brought a great lunch (roast beef sandwiches).

Unloaded truck.

Started unpacking kitchen boxes.

Realized that boxes were labeled incorrectly.

Gave up for the day and just talked about old times.

Drafting

3. Write a topic sentence that includes a topic and point-of-view words. For example, here is a topic sentence for the listing done above.

Topic:	Moving to a new home
Point of view:	Friends can make a hard day good.
Possible topic sentence:	Moving to a new home showed me that friends can make even a hard day a good day.

4. Choose the support points (if your topic lends itself to using formal support points) and specific details. For instance, in the list above, the writer has already identified many details he wants to include in his paragraph. Some of these details address the moving process: "Labeled boxes," "Loaded truck." Other details emphasize the role his friends played in the moving process: "Steve broke my one good chair," "Sonya brought a great lunch."

5. Organize your details according to when they occurred, getting rid of irrelevant information. In other words, make sure all the details serve some purpose in your paragraph: background detail, action detail, or sensory detail. Remember to add transitions that express time sequence order.

6. Now write your draft. Do your best, but don't worry if your paragraph is not perfect the first time around.

Revising

7. Check for the first three of the four Cs: *concise, credible,* and *clear* writing. Make any necessary changes to your draft.

Editing

8. Check your paragraph for the fourth C: *correct* writing. Proofread your paragraph to make sure you have used correct spelling, punctuation, and grammar.

WRITING PRACTICE 2 **Write About an Important Day**

Choose either Topic A or Topic B. *Write a paragraph about a day that stands out in your mind, either for positive or negative reasons.* Think about the overall impression you have of that day, and then decide which events helped to make that day stand out.

Topic A

Write a paragraph about a day in your life that you would like to experience again. These are some days that may stand out in your mind.

A day when you proved you were right about something

A day when you tried something new and it worked

A day when you discovered that you were good at something new

A day when you solved a problem for someone else

Topic B

Write a paragraph about a time in your life that you are glad is over. Make sure that the time you write about is fairly short—a few hours, a day, or a week. Also, make sure that that period of time has a definite beginning and end. You might consider the following times in your life for this topic.

A time when you were sick or injured

A time when you had to admit that you were wrong

A time when you had to make a tough decision

A time when you were worried that you might fail

Once you have chosen a topic, listed some possible reasons for support, and written a possible topic sentence, try to think of details that will make your paragraph believable for your reader. For instance, if your topic sentence is "My high school graduation day was one of the best days of my life," write down all the events that made that day special. Use your list of events to help you write a draft of your paragraph. Make sure that you include only those details that support your topic sentence. Then, when you have a draft, revise for the four Cs: *concise, credible, clear,* and *correct* writing.

WRITING PRACTICE 3 Sell Yourself in Your Writing

Your assignment is this: *Write a paragraph in which you "sell yourself" to a coach, an instructor, or an employer.* Your purpose is to use narrative to persuade your reader to act: give you a starting position on the team, raise your grade in class, or give you a promotion at work. By narrating an event about yourself, your paragraph shows your reader that you have the necessary experience to succeed. However, you need to limit your paragraph to a short period in time: one practice, one day, or one specific period of time.

Lab Activity 18

For additional practice with writing a narrative paragraph, complete Lab Activity 18 in the Lab Manual at the back of the book.

19 Describing a Scene, a Person, or an Object

CULTURE NOTE *Influential Painters*

Though many significant international artists have made their mark in the United States, some have kept our interest more successfully than others. Different painters—including Pablo Picasso and Vincent van Gogh—have vividly captured different aspects of life, each using paint to communicate a unique view of the world.

What Is a Descriptive Paragraph?

If you've ever tried to tell someone what an incredible sunset over the ocean looked like, you know that description is important and challenging. Descriptions of the colors, the color changes, and the reflection of the sun on the water are all essential to helping someone else see what you saw.

Description is a paragraph development strategy in which you tell about a person, place, or object so clearly that your reader can form a mental picture from your words. Being able to describe something vividly comes in handy for any type of writing.

Real-Life Writing

In real-life writing, description helps us make our ideas clear and helps us communicate what we want.

Pablo Picasso, *Guernica*, 1937

CRITICAL THINKING Pablo Picasso's painting *Guernica* portrays the brutality of war. Can a painting like *Guernica* get people to change their minds about war? Can you think of a work of art, such as a song or photo, that has affected what you think about a subject? Explain in a few sentences.

For College
- Use descriptive writing in a history essay to show that you know how an important city looked or how people dressed.
- Use descriptive language in a science report to show that you understood the results of an experiment.

In Your Personal Life
- Use descriptions for romantic gestures, such as writing poetry about the one you love.
- Describe your apartment to a potential roommate, your car to a potential buyer, or a medical problem to your doctor.

At Work
- Use description on order forms and in reports to help make your requests clearly understood.

■ Describe a product—or the benefits of a product—to make that product more appealing and, thus, help you sell it.

A Model Paragraph: Description

Details in a descriptive paragraph may not be grouped into individual support points. Instead, every detail works to support the topic sentence. The key to writing a solid descriptive paragraph is to make your reader *see* whatever it is you're describing. Look at the "Descriptive Paragraphs" diagram below to see how one is organized. Then, read the following paragraph, paying attention to the way the writer describes the work of art.

Descriptive Paragraphs
Topic sentence....*Setting the scene*....................................
↓
Sensory detail 1 ....
Sensory detail 2 ....
Sensory detail 3 ....
Sensory detail 4 ....
Sensory detail 5 ....

Gory *Guernica*

In the painting *Guernica* by the Spanish painter Pablo Picasso, the many strange images portray the violence of war. My high school history teacher, Mr. Pazzoni, thought it would be a good idea for us to see some art that had political messages, so he brought in a photograph of Picasso's *Guernica*. I had to look at it for a few minutes to take it all in. Even though I saw just a photo of the painting, I could tell that the painting is huge, like a mural, and that it uses all kinds of shapes mixed up together. Then, I noticed all the weird body parts in the painting. Heads, feet, arms, and hands of both people and animals appear at odd angles throughout the painting. What's even stranger, though, is that the body parts are twisted and are not attached to full bodies. Even the animal heads seem to be screaming, and everyone in the painting seems to be in pain. Mr. Pazzoni explained that Guernica was a small town in Spain that Germany bombed during the Spanish Civil War and that Picasso was so upset by the bombing that he painted *Guernica* for the World's Fair in Paris in 1937. When I looked at the painting again, I could see the war signs. Flames and smoke seem to come out of nowhere, and broken knives, or swords, show up, too. The worst part, though, is the place where a howling woman is holding a dead baby. It's awful! The painting was a protest against the violence of war, and it definitely makes its point.

The writer's topic sentence is "In the painting *Guernica* by the Spanish painter Pablo Picasso, the many strange images portray the violence of war." The writer supports his topic sentence by identifying these main characteristics of the painting.

- Many kinds of shapes mixed together
- Images of twisted, unattached body parts
- Images that portray people and animals in pain
- Flames, smoke, and weapons emphasize the awfulness of the scene

The writer connects his points by using transitions such as *then, what's even stranger, when,* and *though*.

EXERCISE 1 IDENTIFYING DESCRIPTIVE DETAILS IN A PARAGRAPH

The writer of "Gory *Guernica*" describes the painting as being both violent and strange. Reread the paragraph to find details that illustrate each of the following ideas. Then, fill in the blanks below. Answers will vary.

1. Write three details that develop the idea of violence in the painting.

a. Screaming heads

   b. Flames _____

   c. Broken knives _____

2. Write three details that develop the idea that the painting is strange.

   a. Unattached body parts _____

   b. Twisted body parts _____

   c. Animal heads screaming _____

Choosing a Good Topic for Development

Sometimes your instructor will assign a topic, and other times you will choose your own. For a descriptive paragraph, choose something that you find interesting to look at or think about. You don't need to choose an artistic or complicated topic as long as you're interested in it. For instance, Leo is interested in construction, and he wants to see if he has enough information to write a descriptive paragraph. He begins by freewriting.

It's so cool to see a new building going up. I love the way the bulldozers have to make sure that the ground is level before anyone can start building. Watching the shiny (but sometimes dirty) machines push the dirt this way and that, smoothing out piles of soil, is hypnotizing. I could watch it all day. Then I love to see the foundation being poured, though my sister thinks I'm nuts. Something about all that heavy gray liquid concrete makes me want to press my hands into it. It always looks as if it'll feel cool, even on a hot day. I also love seeing the frame go up, with the wood boards and planks making the outline of a house begin to seem real.

Leo has plenty to say about construction, so he decides to use this topic for his paragraph.

Writing an Effective Topic Sentence

To write an effective topic sentence for a descriptive paragraph, think about how you want the reader to experience your topic. Leo needs to think about what he might say about construction, so he refers to his freewriting. He's particularly fascinated by the early stages of the building process; thus, his topic sentence is "The early stages of the building process are fascinating to watch." With that, he identifies three stages that he'll describe in his paragraph.

- Leveling the ground
- Pouring the foundation
- Erecting the frame

Developing Specific Details

Specific details are extremely important in descriptive paragraphs because they often make up the *entire* paragraph. Thus, it's essential to make every detail count. When choosing details for your paragraph, make sure to use the ones that most vividly bring your topic to life.

What Are Sensory Details?

To develop your descriptive paragraph, use **sensory details**—details that appeal to your reader's five senses.

- **Sight:** Use words that help your reader see colors, light, shadow, shapes, and textures: "The light in the old library streamed down the rows of books from large windows, making a checkerboard of light and shadow at the end of the aisles."
- **Smell:** Use words that let your reader associate what you're describing with specific, familiar scents: "The odors of gasoline, window cleaner, and bug spray reminded me of every family summer trip I ever took as a child."
- **Taste:** Words that remind your reader of powerful flavors are especially effective in describing taste: "Every ingredient Maria added to the bowl made my mouth water—potent cinnamon, moist brown sugar, creamy butter."
- **Touch:** Use words that help your reader feel the textures of what you're describing: "The grooves of the tree's bark felt like a cheese grater; they seemed as though they could scrape the skin off tender little fingers."
- **Hearing:** Use words that let your reader hear the sounds—and the quality of sounds—that you hear: "The screeching of birds before dawn—like a thousand poorly played violins—pierced my eardrums and woke me."

The Benefits of Sensory Details

Using sensory descriptions in your writing offers two main benefits. First, clear descriptions give you credibility. For instance, here are some details that could help your reader believe you have ridden in a hot-air balloon.

Sensory Details

The lurching sensation that you felt when the balloon began to rise

How much greener the ground looked when you could see the treetops instead of the dry grass

The whooshing sound the wind made as it blew past you in the balloon

Second, sensory details make your writing enjoyable to read. Think about a time when a friend has described dinner at a new restaurant: "It began with sharp cheese and fresh tomatoes on crispy crackers. Next followed a succulent steak surrounded by lightly browned potatoes and tender young vegetables. And the whole meal was topped off by a pie of sweet-tart blackberries in the flakiest pie crust ever." You can understand the restaurant's appeal because the sensory details are so vivid.

The paragraph that follows describes a room in a way that allows the reader to picture it.

The Studio of Secrets

My uncle Phil's art studio seems filled with secrets. Even before I'm actually inside the room, I feel a prickly sensation at the back of my neck because I'm never sure exactly what I'll find inside the special room. Just opening the heavy wooden door is a treat since my uncle almost always keeps it locked. Inside, the first thing I notice is the smell. The aromas of paint, paint thinner, and my uncle's day-old bologna sandwiches mingle together to create a scent that I've never smelled anywhere else. The smell is so strong that sometimes I feel as if I'm tasting the air, which is a strange sensation. Probably because it is so unusual, the combination of smells seems like a secret mixture of my uncle's. Next, the cloth-covered chairs, easels, and covered shapes always catch my attention. Uncle Phil never knows exactly what figure or scene he wants to paint next. Consequently, he keeps almost everything in the room covered with sheets so that nothing gets paint on it while he's deciding. When he has made up his mind about his next work, he unveils whatever figure or object he needs to work with and begins. Before he removes the sheet, though, the studio looks like a room filled with ghosts. Additionally, the sound of the room makes me think of secrets. The studio is so quiet that it seems as if the room must be hiding something. Really, though, I know that it's quiet because it's at the very top of the house, away from the noisy kitchen. I guess the part of the room that's the most mysterious is the feeling. Just standing in that quiet studio makes me feel creative, as if I could pick up my uncle's brushes and paint a masterpiece. Of course, he definitely would not like my touching his artist's tools, so I am content just to look around at Uncle Phil's mysterious studio.

EXERCISE 2 IDENTIFYING SENSORY DETAILS IN A PARAGRAPH

Below is a list of details from "The Studio of Secrets." Write down the sense that the detail appeals to: sight, hearing, smell, taste, or touch. An example is done for you.

1. Detail: "I feel a prickly sensation at the back of my neck . . ."

Sense: Touch

2. Detail: "The aromas of paint, paint thinner, and my uncle's day-old bologna sandwiches mingle together to create a scent . . ."

Sense: Smell

3. Detail: "I feel as if I'm tasting the air . . ."

Sense: Taste

4. Detail: ". . . cloth-covered chairs, easels, and covered shapes . . ."

Sense: Sight

5. Detail: "The studio is so quiet that it seems as if the room must be hiding something."

Sense: Hearing

EXERCISE 3 PRACTICE WRITING SENSORY DETAILS

Below is a list of support points from a variety of essays. For each one, write three descriptive details that appeal to the senses: sight, hearing, smell, taste, and touch. An example is done for you.   Answers will vary.

Support point: It's easy to tell when my mother is angry.

Details: **a.**   _Deep wrinkles in her forehead_

b.   _Mouth becomes puckered up_

c.   _Right index finger points menacingly_

1. Support point: Jake always looks happy when he watches a NASCAR event.

Details: **a.** _____

b. _____

c. _____

2. Support point: Samantha dressed as if she wanted to be a pop singer.

Details: **a.** _____

b. _____

c. _____

3. Support point: Tom always looks so healthy after a good workout.

Details: **a.** _____

b. _____

c. _____

4. Support point: Ray's house needs new plumbing.

Details: **a.** _____

b. _____

c. _____

5. Support point: Sondra built a snowman with her children.

Details: **a.** _____

b. _____

c. _____

Organizing and Linking Your Ideas

Once you have written a topic sentence, identified any support points, and come up with vivid, specific details to illustrate your ideas, you're ready to organize your paragraph. Emphatic order works well for descriptive paragraphs since many descriptions do not contain events that can be ordered chronologically. **Emphatic order** lets you organize your ideas from least to most important.

Words and Terms That Signal Emphatic Order

above all	last
another	least of all
equally important	most important
especially	most of all
even more	next
first	significantly
in the first place	

Words and Terms That Signal Space

above	near
across	next to
around	on a diagonal (catercorner)
before	on the other side
behind	opposite
below	outside
beyond	over
elsewhere	there
farther away	to the east (north, etc.)
here	to the left
inside	to the right
in back of	under
in front of	underneath
in the middle (center) of	

With descriptive paragraphs, you also have the option of using **spatial** organization—describing something in terms of its shape or layout. The writer of "The Studio of Secrets" on pages 257–258 for instance, moved randomly around the art studio as he developed the paragraph. The writer could, however, have started with details to the left of the door and worked his way around the room, ending with details to the right of the door. If you choose to use transitions that signal space, be sure you have a plan. Move through the place you're describing, from nearest to farthest, or from one side to the other.

EXERCISE 4 FOLLOWING THE FOUR Cs

Read the paragraph below, keeping in mind how good description includes details that appeal to the senses. Then, answer the questions that follow.

Unhappy Vincent van Gogh

[1]While he was alive, the Dutch painter Vincent van Gogh was the portrait of a tortured artist. [2]Because he suffered from mental illness, van Gogh's life contained few of the comforts that many people take for granted. [3]His appearance reflected his pain. [4]Upon meeting him, van Gogh's contemporaries noticed his tattered shoes and filthy clothing. [5]Though he had been raised by a loving family, van Gogh lived in a little hut near a sewer. [6]Consequently, his possessions—down to his undergarments—smelled as though they had never been clean. [7]In addition to his clothing, van Gogh's habits were very rough. [8]When he said prayers, he often knelt in mud or dirt, and he slept in straw. [9]His own parents, not understanding that their son was unwell, were a little afraid of him because they thought he lived like a beast. [10]Van Gogh's face showed pain and neglect, too, in its untrimmed beard and bloodshot eyes. [11]The rest of his head revealed the real shock. [12]One of his ears was missing because when he was very depressed after an argument with another artist, van Gogh had cut it off and given it to a prostitute. [13]Arguments or rejections affected van Gogh greatly because his illness caused him to react in irrational ways. [14]Above all, van Gogh felt tortured by what he viewed as his career failures—as an art dealer, in the ministry, and as an artist. [15]Even his artwork seems to reflect his personal misery, with its almost painfully intense colors against dismal backgrounds set down by short, stabbing brushstrokes. [16]Van Gogh's mental illness tortured him daily, making him very unhappy. [17]His unhappiness took the ultimate, final form of suicide when he shot himself at the age of thirty-seven. [18]In an

ironic twist, people today believe that van Gogh's personal torture may have contributed to his excellence as an artist. [19]If only van Gogh could have known how significant and beloved his work would become, perhaps he would not have suffered so greatly.

Concise Writing

1. What is the topic sentence for "Unhappy Vincent van Gogh"?

While he was alive, the Dutch painter Vincent van Gogh was the portrait of a tortured artist.

2. List three aspects of van Gogh's appearance that show that he was "tortured."

a. Clothing

b. Personal habits

c. Facial appearance

Credible Writing

3. What detail do you think is most effective in illustrating the topic sentence?

Answers will vary.

4. Write down two more details that develop the idea that van Gogh was a tortured artist. Be sure to identify the sense that the detail appeals to.

Answers will vary but may include these: filthy clothing (sight, smell); hut near a sewer (smell); knelt in mud or dirt to pray (sight, touch); cut off own ear (touch); used bright colors and stabbing strokes in paintings (sight)

Clear Writing

5. How many times does the writer use some form of the word *torture* in the paragraph? four

6. What transitions does the writer use in sentences 6, 7, and 14?

Sentence 6:   Consequently

Sentence 7:   In addition

Sentence 14: Above all

Correct Writing

The sentences in this paragraph are all correct. To check for correctness in your own writing, go to Part 7, "Writing Correct Sentences."

What You Know Now

Descriptive paragraphs seek to help a reader *see* the object of description. Using details that appeal to the five senses—sight, hearing, smell, taste, and touch—makes descriptions vivid. Descriptive paragraphs may contain formal support points, but they may also be a compilation of details that all work together to communicate a single idea. Descriptive paragraphs may be organized emphatically or spatially.

WRITING PRACTICE 1 Write a Descriptive Paragraph

Now write a descriptive paragraph of your own.

Prewriting

1. Choose a topic for a paragraph describing your favorite character from television, comic books, or the movies. Your character should *not* be a real person.

Fictional Characters

Godzilla	Wicked Witch of the West
Santa Claus	Shrek
Spider-Man	Lisa Simpson

2. After you've decided on a character, freewrite for five to ten minutes. Then, use at least one other prewriting technique—listing, questioning, keeping a journal, clustering, or outlining—to come up with more descriptive details. When you are writing a descriptive paragraph, two specific prewriting techniques can be especially helpful. Listing can help you see all your details together in one place, and outlining can help you group your details together logically. Here is a sample list on the topic "Wonder Woman."

Wonder Woman

Beautiful face	Strong
Intelligent	Perfect white teeth
Red, white, and blue outfit	~~Not sure what state she's from~~

Perfect hair and skin	Fast runner
Great figure	Golden lasso
Cool boots	~~Real identity is mild-mannered Diana Prince~~

Read over your prewriting and eliminate any details that do not seem to help describe your topic. In the list above, the writer has crossed out "Not sure what state she's from" and "Real identity is mild-mannered Diana Prince" because they don't directly describe Wonder Woman.

Drafting

3. Write a topic sentence if you haven't done so already. One possible topic sentence for the list above is "Wonder Woman seems to be the perfect female superhero."

4. Choose the support points and/or specific details for your paragraph, taking care to appeal to the reader's senses. Making an outline from your first list can help you plan your paragraph. A possible outline of the "Wonder Woman" paragraph follows.

Topic sentence: Wonder Woman seems to be the perfect female superhero.

   A. Beautiful appearance
      1. Perfect hair and skin
      2. Perfect white teeth
      3. Great figure

   B. Powerful
      1. Physically strong
      2. Fast runner
      3. Intelligent (brain power)

   C. Great accessories
      1. Red, white, and blue outfit
      2. Cool boots
      3. Golden lasso

5. Arrange your support points and details in a logical order. The outline above groups the details under three main support points, but you don't need to do that. Just make sure that your details have some logical connection to each other.

6. Now write a draft of your paragraph. Do your best to include important details and transitions, but don't worry if the paragraph is not perfect.

Revising

7. Check for three of the four Cs: *concise, credible,* and *clear* writing. Make any necessary changes to your draft.

Editing

8. Check your paragraph for the fourth C: *correct* writing. Proofread your paragraph to make sure you have used correct spelling, punctuation, and grammar.

WRITING PRACTICE 2   Describe a Place

Write a paragraph about a place on your campus. Make sure you choose a place that you are familiar with, and include details that appeal to the senses. Here are some suggestions.

Places on Campus

A classroom	The cafeteria
The library	An instructor's office
The gymnasium	The bookstore

Do some prewriting, as usual, to get your ideas on paper. Then think about your opinion of the place you want to focus on, and write your topic sentence. Remember that your topic sentence controls the direction of your paragraph. Possible topic sentences are these:

My math classroom is filled with tension.

The school cafeteria is a place that is bustling with activity.

The school library is a peaceful place.

My English instructor's office is cheerful.

The school gymnasium is a healthy place to spend time.

Consider *what about* the place you chose makes it special or distinctive to you. Does it have certain smells that you associate with it? Is there a particular feeling that you're aware of when you enter this place? Does the place have an unusual layout that stands out in your mind? These are the types of questions to ask yourself to find the details to support your topic sentence.

Once you have your topic sentence and some specific details, write your draft. In describing a place, use transitions that signal spatial order to direct your reader. (See "Words and Terms That Signal Space" on page 260.) These transitions direct your reader to mentally look around the place you're describing.

Revise your paragraph as necessary to make sure it's concise, credible, and clear. Proofread your paragraph for sentence-level errors.

WRITING PRACTICE 3 Describe an Object

Study any painting or photograph in this textbook.

How does it affect you?

Look at the painting for at least five minutes, paying attention to the people and the setting. Then, freewrite for five to ten minutes on what your overall impression of the painting is. Your topic sentence can be something like: "The photograph of tourists on the Great Wall of China (page 29) communicates a feeling of _____."

Some terms to fill in the blank are:

lasting strength	curiosity
timelesness	people connecting with nature

Write a paragraph describing the photograph according to your topic sentence. Be sure to list details that appeal to the senses:

- How do people or objects in the photograph look?
- How does the setting look?
- How do you think it feels to be in that photograph?
- What does the setting in the photograph smell like?
- What do you think it sounds like in the photograph?
- What tastes do you think you'd experience in the photograph?

For this assignment, not all the senses may be relevant.

Lab Activity 19

For additional practice with descriptive paragraphs, complete Lab Activity 19 in the Lab Manual at the back of the book.

20 Classifying and Dividing

CULTURE NOTE *Financial Habits*

The American Dream includes a home of our own, independence, and—of course—financial security. But how do we achieve this kind of security? Particularly in a time when corporate greed and an unstable stock market make the news daily, it's hard to know the best way to manage our financial futures. More than ever, now it's important to know about sound spending, saving, and investing practices.

What Are Classification and Division Paragraphs?

If you've ever shopped on the day before Thanksgiving, you know how important organization is. With so many people trying to get their groceries purchased, even the most organized market can seem like chaos. Some steps on the part of store management, however, make the shopping experience easier: having products classified into sections, having items grouped according to size and quantity, having sale items brightly marked. All these practices show an awareness of what the customer needs.

In your writing, too, organization is critical. Classification and division skills help you make your method of organization clear. **Classification** means grouping similar items together. On your shopping trip to the supermarket, suppose you visit the dairy section. In this section, you find milk, cheese, yogurt, butter, and cream—all dairy products. These foods have

New York Stock Exchange

JOURNAL RESPONSE The New York Stock Exchange serves as the hub of the world's financial center. How do you handle your finances? How did you form your financial habits? Write for ten minutes about the kind of spender or saver you are.

been grouped, or *classified*, as dairy products. **Division** means breaking down a single specific thing into its separate parts. The supermarket itself, for instance, has been *divided* into sections. Meat, produce, and frozen foods all have their sections. Similarly, areas like the checkout lanes, the storage area, the employees' area, and the offices represent other examples of the store's division.

For classification, ask "What idea can I use to group these items together? What do these items have in common?" For division, ask "What parts can I break this item into? What pieces is this item made up of?" Classification and division require similar skills, so you can think of them as a single strategy for developing a paragraph. To see how these paragraphs are organized, look at the "Classification and Division Paragraphs" diagram on page 269 and the example tables that follow.

Classification and Division Paragraphs

Topic sentence....*Stating the categories*...............................

....

↓

Category 1 ....

Category 2 ....

Category 3 ....

Classification

Pets	News Media	Music
Dogs	Newspapers	Classical
Cats	Television	Jazz
Birds	Internet	Rock and roll

Division

My Family	A Department Store	A Computer System
My mother	Women's clothing	Monitor
My father	Men's clothing	Keyboard
My brother Jon	Shoes	Mouse

Real-Life Writing

In real-life writing, classifying and dividing help us organize and keep track of our ideas.

For College

- Use division in a sociology paper to explain the structure of a society.
- Use classification in an anthropology essay to identify characteristics that groups have in common.

In Your Personal Life

- Divide your household chores and list them in categories: daily, weekly, monthly, seasonal.
- Make a list organizing your finances by classifying expenses in a budget.

At Work

- Make a list classifying supplies needed during your annual inventory.
- Make a list dividing your job into different tasks: working the cash register, helping customers, organizing store products.

A Model Paragraph: Classification and Division

Read the following paragraph to see classification and division at work.

So Many Spenders

^{1}Spenders can be divided into three types. ^{2}First are the "super spenders." ^{3}Super spenders spend money as soon as they get it. ^{4}Keeping money around, unspent, is impossible for super spenders, as is waiting for the big sale. ^{5}Unfortunately, super spenders also spend money they don't yet have. ^{6}They use credit cards to increase their spending power, which often leads them into trouble. ^{7}Super spenders definitely live on the edge, from paycheck to paycheck, waiting for the next thing to buy. ^{8}"Simple spenders" are the second type of spender. ^{9}Simple spenders are careful about the ways they part with their hard-earned cash. ^{10}They shop at outlets, wait for sales, and scan the sale racks at big stores in order to find the best deal. [11]Simple spenders always make sure they save a little bit of each paycheck so that they have a cash cushion to protect them from unexpected expenses such as a broken pipe or car repairs. [12]Simple spenders occasionally buy things simply for pleasure, but only if they can afford them. [13]The last group of spenders is "pretend spenders." [14]This group of spenders has little extra cash, so they just don't spend money unless they absolutely have to. [15]Rent, food, gas, and doctor bills all get paid, but a new stereo or dinner out has to wait until more money comes in. [16]However, even though pretend spenders don't spend much money, they do have a guilty secret: they love to shop. [17]Pretend spenders read mail-order catalogs and wander through the malls for hours, just looking at things. [18]Sometimes they even fill up shopping carts, but they never check out. [19]Pretend spenders who have access to the Internet also spend time "shopping" online, but they never push the last button to submit an order. [20]Thus, even though pretend spenders don't really buy much, they act as if they do.

EXERCISE 1 ANALYZING A CLASSIFICATION AND DIVISION PARAGRAPH

Reread "So Many Spenders." Then, answer the questions below.

1. What is the topic sentence of "So Many Spenders"? <u>Spenders can be</u>

<u>divided into three types.</u>

2. What are the three types of spenders that the writer describes?

a. <u>Super spenders</u>

b. <u>Simple spenders</u>

c. <u>Pretend spenders</u>

3. Give three specific details for super spenders.

a. <u>Super spenders</u>

Detail 1: <u>Spend money as soon as they get it.</u>

Detail 2: <u>Don't save.</u>

Detail 3: <u>Spend on credit.</u>

b. Simple spenders

Detail 1: Shop at outlets and sales.

Detail 2: Save money.

Detail 3: Spend only when they have money.

c. Pretend spenders

Detail 1: Don't have much cash.

Detail 2: Pay only necessary bills.

Detail 3: Shop but don't buy.

4. What kinds of transitions does the writer use to signal a change from one support point to another?

Sentence 2: First

Sentence 9: second

Sentence 13: last

Choosing a Good Topic for Development

Sometimes your instructor will give you a topic, but other times you'll choose your own. If you're asked to develop a classification or division paragraph, make sure you pick a topic that can be (1) broken down into smaller groups or (2) grouped according to a broader idea. One way to find a topic that works well for using classification or division is to prewrite.

Geraldine wondered if she could write an effective paragraph about the types of people who live in her neighborhood. She used listing to help her decide, making a general list first, and then making more specific lists for each category she identified. Her first list looked like this:

My neighbors

Families with young children   Invisible professionals   Elderly

After coming up with a general way to divide her neighbors, Geraldine began thinking of specific examples that illustrated each type of neighbor. She outlined her ideas.

A. Elderly neighbors

    1. Mrs. Platt is out walking or sitting in early morning and early evening.

    2. Mr. Tocterman sweeps constantly.

B. Families with young children

    1. Mrs. Taylor goes out walking with her kids late morning and late afternoon, between naps.

    2. The Hendricks family is always equipped with kid stuff (stroller, toys, snacks).

C. Invisible professionals

    1. Marla leaves before dawn and get home after dark.

    2. Todd has several people working for him (gardener, housekeeper, shoppers).

In this case, the connecting idea among all the people Geraldine writes about is that they are her neighbors. Within that category, three subcategories—elderly neighbors, families with young children, and invisible professionals—provide Geraldine with opportunities to develop her paragraph. Geraldine was happy that she had noticed so much about her neighbors, and she felt she had enough information to write an effective classification and division paragraph.

Writing an Effective Topic Sentence

Geraldine organized her categories according to how they came to her in her prewriting.

Category 1:	Elderly neighbors
Category 2:	Families with young children
Category 3:	Invisible professionals

After identifying these categories from her listing, Geraldine wrote her topic sentence: "Each of my neighbors in the Sierra Pines neighborhood seems to be one of three types." When she writes her rough draft, Geraldine can decide whether she has enough details for each type of neighbor or she needs to do more prewriting. Geraldine's key to writing a clear topic sentence was to identify her topic—her neighbors—and state how the topic will be discussed (categorizing by type). Thus, her reader knows exactly what to expect from the rest of Geraldine's paragraph.

EXERCISE 2 CLASSIFYING TOPICS FOR WRITING

Look at the topics given below. Then, decide what classification to use and what subcategories each topic should be divided into. Finally, write a topic sentence that best communicates your classification and division strategy for each topic. An example is done for you. Answers will vary.

Topic	Classified by	Subcategories
Friends	Neediness	Independent
		Need you sometimes
		Need you constantly

Topic sentence: Friends can be classified into three groups according to how much they need you.

1. Topic

	Classified by	Subcategories
Music	Volume	Easy listening, Hip-hop, Hard rock

Topic sentence: Music can be classified by how loudly it's best played.

2. Topic

	Classified by	Subcategories
Study habits	Student ambition	Students who want As, want to pass, or don't care

Topic sentence: Students can be grouped according to how driven they are to succeed.

3. Topic

	Classified by	Subcategories
Cooking	Culture	Mexican, Thai, Italian

Topic sentence: My friends fall into three categories, according to their culture.

Developing Specific Details

In some of your classes, you may write paragraphs or essays requiring you to research your topic using sources other than your own life. However, the classification and division paragraphs you'll write when using this book will ask you to draw on your own experiences for support.

For Geraldine to discover details about the types of neighbors on her block, she only had to think of the people she knew. Details like "Mr.

Tocterman sweeps constantly" or "equipped with kid stuff" came from Geraldine's observations. Only the information about the "invisible professionals" came from another source—her early-rising neighbors—since the professionals were almost always gone to work before Geraldine was up.

Here's some freewriting that another writer, Chuck, did in order to determine whether he had enough examples to write a full paragraph. His topic is "types of cooking."

How can I write about types of cooking? The only cooking I really like is my mom's, and she's a full-on American cook. She uses lots of beef in her stews and casseroles, and she loves to make creamy "hot dish" meals using can after can of cream of mushroom soup. She also makes great Jell-O treats: finger Jell-O, Jell-O parfaits—with whipped topping and canned fruit layered with the Jell-O—and Jell-O salads. I love Jell-O! Why do I have to write about other types of cooking? Mom's is good enough for me. She always has a lot of food, too, so if I want to bring a buddy (or three) home for dinner, that's no problem. Last week, she had so much meatloaf that half the football team came over after practice. Wait a second . . . I wonder if I can write about the types of Mom's cooking? Gotta ask my instructor about that.

Without realizing it at first, Chuck divides his mother's cooking into three categories: hot dishes, Jell-O dishes, and multi-serving dishes. Chuck discovers that he has enough information to write about the type of cooking he loves, his mom's.

Organizing and Linking Your Ideas

The key to classification and division paragraphs is to have a strong topic sentence. It should tell your reader how you will divide your topic into smaller parts, or subcategories, or classify all the subcategories through a connecting idea. **Emphatic order,** organizing your ideas from least to most important or interesting, is a good way to arrange your support points. Since you get to decide which points are most—or least—important when you're using emphatic order, pay attention to how much detail you derive from your prewriting. Chances are, the points that have the most detail will be the ones that matter the most to you, and those should be the ones you save for last.

Use transitional words and expressions to introduce specific details and link ideas. In the sentences that follow, the underlined transitional expressions signal that a specific detail is being introduced.

One more type of high-risk investment is international stocks.

Anxious bankers make up the second group of investors.

The last group of spenders is "pretend spenders."

Read the paragraph below, paying attention to how the topic sentence serves as a unifying concept for the entire paragraph.

The Ways We Save

People who save their money can be divided according to how much they trust others to handle it. First are easy investors, people who have great faith in financial institutions such as brokerage houses and financial consultants. These people have no problem writing out a check to a stockbroker every month and letting the broker invest their funds in stocks, bonds, or mutual funds. If the stock market goes down and these people lose money, they just figure that the market will go back up sometime. Anxious bankers make up the second group of investors. These people trust banks and credit unions and save their money in savings accounts and certificates of deposit (CDs). Anxious bankers don't move their money around as much as easy investors, and if interest rates on their savings go down, they become nervous. Last come the self-help savers. These people don't trust anyone else to handle their money. They don't trust stockbrokers, banks, or even each other. Consequently, self-help savers take care of their money themselves. They buy safes for their valuables, and some have been known to stuff large amounts of cash into their mattresses. People in this third group never worry about the stock market or about interest rates because all their cash is right at their fingertips.

EXERCISE 3 ANALYZING A PARAGRAPH FOR SUPPORT POINTS AND DETAILS

Fill in the outline for "The Ways We Save." The first item is done for you.

Answers will vary.

Types of Savers

A. _Easy investors_

　　1. _Trust others to manage their money._

2. Invest in stocks, bonds, and mutual funds.

3. Don't worry if they lose some money.

B. Anxious bankers

  1. Trust only banks and credit unions.

  2. Have savings accounts and CDs.

  3. Worry if interest rates go down.

C. Self-help savers

  1. Trust no one to handle their money.

  2. Buy safes and stuff money in mattresses.

  3. Don't worry about stock market since they don't invest.

"The Ways We Save" classifies people according to how much they trust others to handle their money. It could also have been organized, with some revision, by financial strategies or by the amounts of money that people invest. Often, information can be organized a number of ways. The writer's job is to choose the best idea to unify the paragraph. An alternative way of organizing the information from "The Ways We Save" follows.

Financial Strategies

    A. Investment markets
        1. Stocks
        2. Bonds
        3. Mutual funds

    B. Federally insured savings institutions
        1. Banks
        2. Credit unions

    C. Home security
        1. Safes for valuables
        2. Stuffing money into mattresses

If you want to write about a certain topic but are having a hard time classifying it in one way, there may be another way to organize your ideas.

EXERCISE 4 CLASSIFYING TOPICS DIFFERENT WAYS

Below are five groups. Write down two ways you can classify each group. An example is done for you. Answers will vary.

Topic		Classification
Instructors	a.	How much work they give
	b.	How nice they are
1. Students	a.	How hard they work
	b.	What kinds of classes they take
2. Cars	a.	What kind of gas mileage they get
	b.	What kind of image they project
3. Books	a.	How much they entertain
	b.	How much they inform
4. Diets	a.	How much they let you eat
	b.	What kinds of food they let you eat
5. Gardens	a.	How lovely they are
	b.	What kinds of food they provide

EXERCISE 5 FOLLOWING THE FOUR Cs

Read the following paragraph, noting that the writer classifies investments according to their level of risk. Then, answer the questions that follow.

Risky Business

Financial investments can be classified according to how risky they are, or how likely they are to cause the investor to lose money.

High-risk investments are the first category. Firms that are brand-new fall into this category because they're too new to guarantee success to their investors. Technology stocks are also considered high-risk since they, too, are new and their products often have no track record of success. One more type of high-risk investment is international stocks because foreign companies' success depends on factors that U.S. citizens can't control, such as foreign governments. People invest in these high-risk stocks because they offer the chance to make a lot of money. Medium-risk investments make up the second type of investments. Companies that have operated successfully for a long time are considered medium-risk. Companies such as General Electric and Boeing generate less money for investors than the high-risk stocks, but with less risk. These companies are sometimes called "blue chip" corporations, and they are considered fairly safe investments. The last type of investment is low-risk. Banks and bonds are low-risk investments. People can put their money into savings accounts or CDs at low interest rates and almost no risk because banks are insured by the federal government. People can also buy bonds from a company or a government, and the money they invest helps the company or government run. Bonds may not pay as much interest as stocks, but they're usually less risky. Government bonds are considered especially safe.

Concise Writing

1. What is the writer's topic sentence? Financial investments can be

classified according to how risky they are, or how likely they are to cause the investor to lose money.

2. What are the three categories of financial investments that the writer covers?

a. High-risk investments

b. Medium-risk investments

c. Low-risk investments

3. What concept are the categories classified by?

Risk

Credible Writing

4. What is one type of high-risk investment?   Answers will vary.

Brand-new companies; technology stocks; international stocks

5. What is a name for a safe investment in a traditionally successful

company? Blue chip stock

6. Name two types of investments that are considered low-risk.

Answers will vary.

a. Savings accounts

b. CDs or bonds

Clear Writing

7. How many times does the writer use some form of the word *risk* (including in the title)?   14

8. What are two other words that the writer uses frequently throughout the paragraph?

a. Investment

b. Money

9. What three transitions does the writer use to introduce each new type of investment?

a. first

b. second

c. last

Correct Writing

The sentences in this paragraph are all correct. To check for correctness in your own writing, go to Part 7, "Writing Correct Sentences."

What You Know Now

Classification and division paragraphs employ similar writing and thinking skills. Classification means grouping similar items together. Division means breaking down a single specific thing into its separate parts. Finding topics that can be easily divided or easily classified through a single concept is essential to writing effective classification and division paragraphs. Examples for these paragraphs can come from your own experiences or from other sources. Transitions let your reader know when you are moving from one classification group to another.

WRITING PRACTICE 1   Identify a Connecting Idea in Details

Below are short outlines of ideas. The general topic heads the list, followed by details that relate to that topic. Your job is to identify what the details have in common and write down the connecting idea that ties all the details together. An example is done for you.

General topic: Shoes

Details: Sandals, galoshes, snow boots

Connecting idea: *Seasonal shoes*

1. General topic: Desserts

Details: Frozen, baked, whipped

Connecting idea: How they're prepared

2. General topic: Cities

Details: Crime, traffic, pollution

Connecting idea: Negative aspects

3. General topic: Computers

Details: Help keep track of finances, help with schoolwork, help design party invitations and notes

Connecting idea: Ways they help

4. General topic: Books

Details: Have to read them for college, want to read them for pleasure, should read them for information

Connecting idea: Reasons to read them

5. General topic: Neighborhoods

Details: High crime rate, low crime rate, medium crime rate

Connecting idea: Crime rate

WRITING PRACTICE 2 Write a Classification and Division Paragraph

Now write a classification and division paragraph of your own.

Prewriting

1. From the list below, choose a topic that you think lends itself to being divided into separate parts or classified according to an overriding principle.

Topic

Parents	Cars	Travel
Doctors	Hobbies	School courses
People's manners	Entertaining	Movies

2. Freewrite on the topic of your choice for five to ten minutes. What are your initial ideas about classifying your topic? What details have you written that will work in a paragraph? One writer, Miranda, chose to freewrite on the topic "manners."

> My mother always wanted me to have good manners, but sometimes I think I'm the only one who cares. Everyone I know either pays so much attention to manners that they seem phony, or else they ignore manners completely. My friend Janey always wants her manners to be perfect, but then I worry when I'm around her that I'll say the wrong thing or use the wrong fork or something. But then Pete, my brother's buddy, says he doesn't care about manners at all, and he's always belching right when I'm about to start eating. I guess people just have to find manners that work well for them.

Miranda places people into at least two groups according to the kinds of manners they use. One group cares very much about manners, while the other group doesn't care at all. A third group could be people who care just enough about manners, and the connecting idea could be how much people care about manners.

After you've finished freewriting, use another prewriting technique—listing, questioning, keeping a journal, clustering, or outlining—to see other specific details you can develop. Outlining can be especially effective in planning classification and division paragraphs.

Drafting

3. Write a topic sentence that clearly divides or classifies your topic. For example, here is a topic sentence for Miranda's topic: "People can be

classified into three groups according to how much they care about good manners."

4. Choose the subcategories and specific details for your topic. In her outline Miranda identified three groups of people to discuss, and she offered some specific details for each group.

5. Arrange your support points—in this case, your subcategories—using a logical order, most likely emphatic order.

6. Write a rough draft of your paragraph, using details and transitions as best you can. Don't worry about making your paragraph perfect at this point; just get your ideas down in a basic order.

Revising

7. Check for the first three of the four Cs: *concise, credible,* and *clear* writing. Make any necessary charges to your draft.

Editing

8. Check your paragraph for the fourth C: *correct* writing. Proofread your paragraph to make sure you have used correct spelling, punctuation, and grammar.

WRITING PRACTICE 3 **Use Classification and Division in Real Life**

Classifying and dividing ideas can be helpful in everyday life. Choose either Topic A or Topic B below and write a paragraph.

Topic A

You have volunteered to be a student orientation counselor at your college, and you are telling a group of new students about the types of instructors on campus. *Write a paragraph dividing your college's instructors into types.* Your purpose is to prepare new students for a variety of experiences with instructors, so you must offer specific details about each type of instructor. Following are some possible ways to classify instructors.

How much work they give

How strict they are about attendance

How much they value in-class participation

How hard their tests are

How much out-of-class help they give

Topic B

You have volunteered to serve on a committee that helps instructors understand students. Your job is to tell the instructors how to recognize signs that students in their classes need help. *Write a paragraph classifying students who need help in their classes.* Make sure you use specific details about types of students to make your ideas clear. Following are some possible ways to classify students who need help.

How often they miss class

How often they do the homework

How well they perform on tests

How interested they seem in their test or class performance

How prepared they are for class (supplies, books, class handouts)

Lab Activity 20

For additional practice with classification and division paragraphs, complete Lab Activity 20 in the Lab Manual at the back of the book.

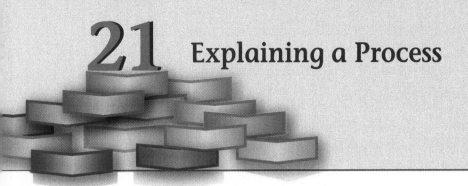

21 Explaining a Process

CULTURE NOTE *The U.S. Civil War and the Old South*

Although Americans have participated in many wars, battles, and conflicts around the world, none has resulted in the loss of as many American lives as our own Civil War. Fought for economic reasons as much as for ideological ones, the Civil War brought our country to the breaking point and back, causing the United States to ultimately become a single powerful nation.

What Is a Process Paragraph?

If you've ever tried to show someone how to do something, you know how important specific instructions are. **Explaining a process** means describing how to do something or how something works, step by step. This chapter will focus on two kinds of process paragraphs.

■ How-to paragraphs
■ Explanation paragraphs

How-To Paragraphs

How-to paragraphs tell a reader how to complete some action step by step. For instance, to tell a friend how to find your new apartment, you might write down instructions like this:

First, take I-5 South.

Second, take the Cabrillo Avenue exit.

Next, turn left onto Blossom Road.

Turn into the parking lot at 5226 Blossom Road.

Go left to apartment 3A.

In this process, the order is particularly important. The process determines the success of your friend's travel.

Explanation Paragraphs

The second kind of process paragraph is the explanation paragraph. **Explanation paragraphs** explain how something works, such as how a DVD player operates or how salmon swim upstream. Similarly, explanation paragraphs can explain historical events. In presenting an event such as a war or a political movement to your class, your instructor may talk in terms of a process, as though one step led to the next. However, often these "steps" became apparent only after the end result was achieved. For instance, in the paragraph on pages 287–288 in this chapter, you will read about how the Union defeated the Confederacy, primarily through economic measures. There were several stages in the Union's victory.

First, the North built its economic foundation on industry.

Second, the Union blockaded southern ports.

Then, the Union enrolled freed slaves as its army.

Finally, the Union cut off supplies by ruining train transportation for the South.

Real-Life Writing

In real-life writing, we explain processes all the time in order to teach people skills or explain how consequences came about.

For College

- Write about the process of meiosis in a biology class.
- In a history class, write about how women gained the vote or how the French Revolution came about.

In Your Personal Life

- Write notes to roommates or repair people about how you want something done.
- Write recipes or directions for a friend.

At Work

■ Write directions explaining how to use a piece of equipment.

■ Write notes to a new employee explaining office procedures.

A Model Paragraph: Explaining a Process

To explain a process, follow the basic paragraph format shown below in the illustration "Process Paragraphs." The writer of "A New Country from the Old?" has developed a topic sentence and then explained steps that make up the process of secession.

Process Paragraphs
Topic sentence.... Naming the process ....
↓
Step 1 ....Details about Step 1........................... Step 2 ....Details about Step 2........................... Step 3 ....Details about Step 3........................... Step 4 ....Details about Step 4........................... Step 5 ....Details about Step 5...........................

A New Country from the Old?

In the mid-nineteenth century, the southern states left the Union and formed the Confederate States of America, or the Confederacy. This process of forming the Confederacy involved many stages. First, after Abraham Lincoln was reelected president in 1860, the "fire-eaters"—pro-slavery extremists in the South—called a convention in South Carolina. The result of this convention was that South Carolina, considered the leader in many Deep South decisions, voted to leave the Union. The second stage took place when other states seceded. From December 1860 to February 1861, six other states left the Union: Mississippi, Florida, Alabama, Georgia, Louisiana, and Texas. In the third stage, the states that had seceded formed their own country. On February 4, 1861, these seven states sent delegates to Montgomery, Alabama, to form the Confederate States of America. The delegates elected their own president, Jefferson Davis of Mississippi, and drafted their own constitution. It was the formation of this new country that led to the Civil War.

EXERCISE 1 ANALYZING A PROCESS PARAGRAPH FOR STAGES AND DETAILS

Reread the paragraph "A New Country from the Old?" beginning on page 287. Then, fill in the blanks below.

1. Write down the topic sentence. In the mid-nineteenth century, the southern states left the Union and formed the Confederate States of America, or the Confederacy.

2. What stages are involved in the process above?

Stage 1: Fire-eaters called a convention.

Stage 2: Other states seceded.

Stage 3: Seceded states formed the Confederacy.

Choosing a Good Topic for Development

Sometimes your instructor will assign a topic, but often you will get to choose your own. When you choose your own topic for a process paragraph, make sure that it has distinct stages or steps that work together as part of a process. Many topics can seem as if they work well for explaining a process, but some are easier to write about than others.

Good Topics for Explaining a Process	Poor Topics for Explaining a Process
How to drive a car	The ways people learn to drive
How to use a computer program	Benefits of computers

Each of the "good" topics for a process paragraph deals with a skill or activity. The topics in the right-hand column do not offer the same opportunities for explaining step by step how to complete a process or how a process works. In fact, "benefits of computers" is not process-oriented at all.

One way to tell whether your topic will work well for process explanation is *to make a list of all the steps that your process involves.* For instance, in "A New Country from the Old?" the writer focuses on the stages through which the process of secession moved.

Yolanda was asked to write a paragraph explaining a process she had recently learned. She began by making a list of events that occurred the first time she made pancakes.

Making Breakfast on Mother's Day

Never made pancakes before but had watched Mom.

Turned on electric frying pan.

Put bacon strips in pan.

Bacon grease spattered on me.

Flipped bacon when it started to curl up.

Bacon smells so good.

Stirred pancake mix with milk and eggs.

Took bacon out of pan when crispy.

Poured out grease (left some to cook pancakes).

Poured batter into hot pan.

Flipped pancakes when bubbles appeared on top.

Took pancakes out when they were brown on bottom.

Served pancakes and bacon with butter, syrup, and milk.

These details show a progression from the start of the cooking process through the end. Some details—like Yolanda getting spattered with bacon grease and bacon smelling so good—can be omitted because they don't act as steps in the process.

Writing an Effective Topic Sentence

After looking over her list, Yolanda realized she had a complete account of how to make bacon and pancakes. She wrote the following topic sentence: "Making a bacon and pancake breakfast involves a number of simple steps."

Developing Specific Details

Sometimes the steps in a process include all the details necessary to communicate a point. For instance, as one step in making pancakes, Yolanda listed "Put bacon strips in pan." Some readers might want to know how many strips Yolanda put in, how far apart the strips were, and whether the strips were all the same size. If she had been writing for someone not familiar with cooking, she would have included more details to make the steps in the process clear.

Another important aspect of including specific details is choosing relevant steps in your process. Make sure, then, that *you include only those steps essential to the process you're explaining.* For instance, in almost any human process, breathing is necessary. When writing about a process, however, you ordinarily leave out breathing as a step since it's something we do without thinking. When writing your process paragraphs, make sure you focus on the steps most necessary to complete the task at hand.

EXERCISE 2 IDENTIFYING UNNECESSARY STEPS IN A PROCESS

Read the list of steps in the processes below. Cross out the unnecessary steps in each. An example is done for you.

Building a fire in the woods requires following a number of steps.

a. First, gather dry pine needles, small twigs and sticks, and some small logs.

b. Next, make a small pyramid of pine needles and twigs.

c. ~~Use your fingers to take a match out of the box.~~

d. Then, light the pyramid on fire.

e. As the flames grow, gradually add larger twigs and sticks until the fire is strong enough to burn logs.

1. Dressing to exercise requires some important steps.

a. First, put on comfortable clothing.

b. ~~Put your left foot through the left pant leg, followed by the right foot through the right pant leg.~~

c. Next, put on exercise shoes with good arch support.

d. Then, put sweatbands on your head and wrists.

2. Taking an engaging photograph involves a number of essential steps.

    a. Think ahead of time about how you want the final picture to look.

    b. Choose the main subject of the photo.

    c. Consider placing the main subject away from the center of the photo, for added visual interest.

    d. ~~Think about the best photos you have seen in books and museums.~~

    e. Focus carefully so the main subject will be sharp.

    f. Hold your hands rock steady as you press the shutter button.

3. There are several easy steps in making a delicious vinaigrette salad dressing.

    a. ~~Open the refrigerator and take out some garlic.~~

    b. Mince finely one or two cloves of garlic and put the garlic into a small bowl.

    c. Cut a fresh lemon in half, and squeeze the juice from one half into the bowl.

    d. Run the cold water and with your hand sprinkle in three quick bursts of water into the bowl, then triple the amount of liquid in the bowl by adding high-quality olive oil.

    e. Add salt and pepper to taste, and mix with a whisk.

4. You can prepare for most tests by following some important steps.

    a. First, take good notes in the days leading up to the test, and highlight the points your instructor emphasizes.

    b. Second, do any required reading early, so that you can give the text a second and third look before the test.

    c. Third, pretend you are the instructor, and ask yourself what you think would be challenging test questions; then, answer the questions.

    d. Fourth, review your answers and intensively study the areas in which you need to brush up.

    e. ~~Finally, have a good dinner the night before the test, making sure that it includes plenty of protein.~~

5. Changing the oil in a car is not difficult if you follow a few simple steps.

    a. Crawl under the car and locate the bolt on a fairly large tank; this is the discharge bolt.

    b. ~~Go to wherever you store your tools and find a wrench to remove the bolt.~~

    c. Place under the discharge bolt a shallow pan that is wide enough to hold four or five quarts.

    d. Remove the bolt with a wrench, let the oil drain into the pan, and then screw the bolt back in.

    e. Check your owner's manual for the proper amount of oil for your tank, normally four to five quarts, then pour the new oil into the proper spout in your engine.

Organizing and Linking Your Ideas

Process paragraphs, like narrative paragraphs, do not contain specific support points. Instead, the steps or stages in the process act as markers for your readers. Thus, one of the most important factors in writing a process paragraph is *keeping your steps in order.* Using time sequence order keeps you and your reader on track. For example, if you are explaining to someone how to make ice cream, you will most likely include the steps of getting the proper

Transition Words and Terms That Are Useful in Process Paragraphs

Transitions That Signal the Start of a Process

at first	first
begin by	initially

Transitions That Signal That the Process Is Still Going On

after	during	second, third, etc.
afterward	later	until
as soon as	meanwhile	when
before	next	while

Transitions That Signal the End of a Process

at last	finally
at the end	last

ingredients, mixing the ingredients, and freezing the liquid ice cream. Forgetting to tell someone, for instance, to mix all the ingredients before freezing them could result in a finished product that you're not happy with.

In a how-to process paragraph, transitions are particularly important. If you don't tell your readers when to perform certain steps, you run the risk of confusing them. Consult the box below for transitions that are useful in writing a process paragraph.

EXERCISE 3 PUTTING DETAILS IN ORDER

Below are short outlines for possible process paragraphs. The details listed are not in time sequence order. Put the details in order by writing the number 1 in front of the detail that should come first, 2 in front of the detail that should come second, and so on.

1. Topic sentence: Cultivating cotton by hand is an exhausting process.

_____3_____ **a.** Third, when the cotton is mature, it is picked.

_____2_____ **b.** Second, the cotton seeds are sown.

_____1_____ **c.** First, the soil must be prepared for planting.

_____4_____ **d.** Finally, the cotton lint, or fluffy cotton used to make clothing, is separated from the seeds.

2. Topic sentence: The Confederate army lost strength in stages.

_____2_____ **a.** The second stage came as more and more men were wounded, and the Confederate army shrank as a result of disease and injury.

_____3_____ **b.** Lack of food and poor preparation for a long, drawn-out battle led to the third stage, in which more men died.

_____4_____ **c.** Much later, toward the end of the Civil War, when the Confederacy began to lose hope, men deserted the army in what made up a final stage.

_____1_____ **d.** Initially, when men were eager to fight, the army lost men only when they died in battle.

3. Topic sentence: Making the perfect mint julep is an art.

_____1_____ **a.** First, gather three sprigs of fresh mint; tear the leaves off two of the mint sprigs, and place them in the bottom of a tall glass.

___2___ **b.** Second, add two teaspoons of cold water and one teaspoon of granulated sugar; then stir until the sugar dissolves and the mint leaves are bruised.

___4___ **c.** Stir and serve with the remaining mint leaves under a magnolia tree.

___3___ **d.** Third, fill the glass with finely crushed ice and pour two ounces of bourbon over the ice.

4. Topic sentence: General Ulysses S. Grant followed a pattern of courteous behavior that allowed the beaten Confederate soldiers to keep their dignity.

___4___ **a.** Finally, during the surrender of General Robert E. Lee at Appomatox Court House, Virginia, Grant did not gloat.

___2___ **b.** He gave orders allowing the Confederate soldiers to keep their firearms.

___3___ **c.** Third, Grant prevented Union forces from disturbing Confederate soliders on their return home.

___1___ **d.** First, Grant gave food to the hungry soldiers, believing that other courtesies would be lost on starved men.

5. Topic sentence: Reconstruction, the process of rebuilding the South after the Civil War, involved many stages.

___2___ **a.** The second stage in Reconstruction involved the federal government's division of the South into military-ruled districts.

___1___ **b.** First, Congress passed a series of Reconstruction Acts, designed to rebuild the southern states and readmit them to the Union.

___4___ **c.** Finally, Congress passed three key constitutional amendments designed to give former slaves full rights within the United States.

___3___ **d.** Third, former citizens of the Confederacy had to swear an oath of loyalty to be readmitted as United States citizens.

EXERCISE 4 ANALYZING A COMPLETED PROCESS

Read the following paragraph to see how the writer explains the process by which the Union defeated the Confederacy in the U.S. Civil War. Note how the writer uses transitions to link one step to the next. Then, answer the questions that follow.

Economically Conquered

[1]Before and during the U.S. Civil War, the Union followed a series of economic steps to defeat the Confederacy. [2]Before the war even started, the North took an important first step in ensuring its success, both economically and militarily. [3]The North built its economic foundation on industry rather than agriculture, so it contained the factories of the United States. [4]Thus, when war broke out, the Union was able to manufacture war supplies and tools. [5]Without having taken this first step toward economic power, the North would have had a much more difficult time supplying its own forces throughout the war. [6]A second step the Union took to defeat the Confederacy economically was establishing a naval blockade in 1862. [7]Since the southern states made their money from agriculture, primarily through growing cotton, they needed to sell their crops. [8]The blockade prevented the South from selling its goods to make money and from buying supplies. [9]Though the blockade didn't do much its first year in place, eventually it worked, and southern cities and troops couldn't get the funding or supplies they needed. [10]This step made southerners all the more dependent on their agricultural resources. [11]A third step the North took to defeat the South undermined the agricultural resources so necessary to the South's survival. [12]The Union passed the Emancipation Proclamation, which freed all slaves, in 1863. [13]Passing this proclamation gave the North a big advantage against the Confederacy, since the South's main labor force—African-American slaves—no longer had to work on southern plantations. [14]In fact, many African-Americans enlisted in the Union army and fought against the Confederates. [15]Eliminating the South's labor force and cutting off its naval suppliers left the South with one means of acquiring food and ammunition: the railroad. [16]Consequently, the fourth step in the process of economic defeat of the South was to ruin train transportation for the South. [17]General William Tecumseh Sherman, one of the North's most important military leaders, marched into Atlanta, Georgia, in November 1864 and burned it to the ground. [18]This act was devastating to

the Confederacy. [19]Since Atlanta was the railroad hub of the South, its destruction meant that the South's last main supply lines were cut. [20]By systematically destroying every means through which the South could make money and gain supplies, the Union forces ensured their victory in the Civil War.

1. What process is being explained in this paragraph? The process by which the Union economically defeated the Confederacy in the U.S. Civil War

2. List each of the four steps explained in "Economically Conquered."

   a. Establishing industry as the economic foundation of the North

   b. Imposing naval blockade

   c. Passing the Emancipation Proclamation

   d. Cutting off the railroad

3. What transition words signal the introduction of new steps in the process?

   Sentence 2: an important first step

   Sentence 6: second step

   Sentence 11: third step

   Sentence 16: fourth step

Developing a Process Paragraph

Prewriting

- Choose a topic that lends itself to time sequence (chronological) order and can be explained in individual steps.
- Use prewriting strategies to get your early ideas on paper.

Drafting

- Write a topic sentence that identifies your topic as one that can be explained through a series of steps or stages.
- Make a list of the steps or stages involved in the process you are explaining, considering which are most important to explaining your process.

- Organize your ideas, using transitions to connect your support points.
- Write a rough draft of your paragraph. (Feel free to do more prewriting to get more ideas down on paper.)

Revising

- Revise your work according to the first three of the four Cs: *concise, credible,* and *clear* writing.

Editing

- For the fourth C, *correct* writing, proofread your work for sentence-level errors.

EXERCISE 5 FOLLOWING THE FOUR Cs

Read the following paragraph, paying attention to the way the writer instructs the reader in how to learn about the U.S. Civil War. Then, answer the questions that follow.

How to Learn About the U.S. Civil War

Learning about the U.S. Civil War is possible in a number of simple steps. The first step is to ask yourself questions. Why is the war interesting to you? What do you already know about it? What do you want to learn? These questions will help you start your search for information, but this step is also one you will want to repeat periodically to renew your search. Next, see some movies. *Glory,* for example, focuses on the 54th Regiment of the Massachusetts Volunteer Infantry, an African-American regiment in the Union army. It's a serious movie based on history, but the excellent performances by Denzel Washington, Morgan Freeman, and Matthew Broderick make it entertaining as well. *The Civil War,* a multipart documentary by Ken Burns, is another cinematic way to learn about the Civil War. Seeing movies will help you determine whether you want to actively pursue your learning or whether you simply want to be entertained. If you decide to keep learning, a third step is to read about the Civil War. Reading takes more time and energy than seeing movies, so be prepared to invest yourself in your learning process. Civil War novels such as *Gone with the Wind* and *Cold Mountain* offer wonderful descriptions of the Old South without forgetting the painful details that accompanied the war. Books such as *They Fought Like Demons: Women Soldiers in the Civil War* offer factual accounts of a little-known aspect of the war. The last step in the process is to take classes. Since this step requires the greatest commitment on your part, make sure you've completed steps 1, 2, and 3 first. Taking classes will allow you to read about, write about, and discuss the U.S. Civil War with people who share your interest. By the time you've completed these steps, you may find someone asking *you* about the Civil War!

Concise Writing

1. What is the writer's topic sentence?

   Learning about the U.S. Civil War is possible in a number of simple steps.

2. What should you be able to do after you finish reading this

   paragraph? Learn about the Civil War

3. Write down the four steps involved in the process.

   a. Asking questions

   b. Seeing movies

   c. Reading books

   d. Taking classes

Credible Writing

4. What are some specific details that illustrate the second and third steps (support points) in the process of learning about the U.S. Civil War? Answers will vary.

   Support point 2: Seeing *Glory* or *The Civil War* documentary

   Support point 3: Reading *Gone with the Wind, Cold Mountain,* or *They Fought Like Demons*

Clear Writing

5. What words does the writer use to indicate each step in the process of learning about the Civil War?

   a. The first step

   b. Next

c. A third step _____

d. The last step _____

6. How many times does the writer use a form of the word *learn?*

7, including the title _____

Correct Writing

The sentences in this paragraph are all correct. To check for correctness in your own writing, go to Part 7, "Writing Correct Sentences."

What You Know Now

Process paragraphs can be either how-to or explanation paragraphs. They explain step by step how to do something, how something works, or how something happened. The steps or stages included should be only the most important ones necessary to communicate how the process works. Time sequence order and transitions are necessary in process paragraphs to keep a reader on track.

WRITING PRACTICE 1 Write Steps in a Process

Below are topic sentences for paragraphs that explain a process. Write down three to five steps that are involved in each process. Answers will vary.

1. By completing a number of steps, I improved my appearance.

a. _____

b. _____

c. _____

d. _____

e. _____

2. I plan to vote knowledgably in the next election.

a. _____

   b. _____

   c. _____

   d. _____

   e. _____

3. For me, writing a paragraph works the best if I follow this routine.

   a. _____

   b. _____

   c. _____

   d. _____

   e. _____

4. It's easy to get books from the library.

   a. _____

   b. _____

   c. _____

   d. _____

   e. _____

5. Learning how to _____ is a process involving many steps.

   a. _____

   b. _____

   c. _____

   d. _____

   e. _____

WRITING PRACTICE 2 Write a Paragraph Explaining a Process

Now write your own paragraph explaining a process.

Prewriting

1. Below is a list of topics for paragraphs that can be developed using the process strategy. Choose one topic that you have experience with, or select any other task you enjoy or do well.

Possible Topics

Losing weight

Studying for an exam

Learning to drive a car

Ironing a dress shirt

Getting your hair straightened or colored

Making a cup of tea

Taking a dog for a walk

Going fishing

Downloading files from the Internet

Stringing a guitar

2. Freewrite for five to ten minutes. In prewriting for a process paragraph, listing can be useful because a list helps you keep steps in order. Below is a sample list on the topic "ironing a dress shirt."

Ironing a Dress Shirt

Set up ironing board.

Fill iron with distilled water.

Plug in iron.

Spray starch onto collar, yoke, and cuffs of shirt.

Iron collar, yoke, and cuffs.

Spray sleeves with starch.

Iron sleeves.

Spray starch onto button side of shirt.

Iron button side of shirt.

Spray back of shirt with starch.

Iron back of shirt.

Spray buttonhole side of shirt with starch.

Iron buttonhole side of shirt.

Hang up shirt.

Drafting

3. Write a topic sentence if you haven't done so already. Don't worry if it's not exactly what you want for now. You can always revise it. A possible topic sentence for the topic above is "Ironing a dress shirt is one of the most repetitive processes I can think of."

4. Choose the steps in the process and the specific details relating to those steps that are the most important to explaining the process.

5. Organize your steps in time sequence order, using transitions to introduce new steps and link your ideas.

6. Write your draft. Include as many details and transitions as you can, but don't worry about making the draft perfect at this point.

Revising

7. Check for three of the four Cs: *concise, credible,* and *clear* writing. Make any necessary changes to your draft.

Editing

8. Check your paragraph for the fourth C: *correct* writing. Proofread your paragraph to make sure you have used correct spelling, punctuation, and grammar.

WRITING PRACTICE 3 Write to Teach Someone

Writing to explain a process can be useful when you are teaching someone how to do something or explaining a series of events. Choose Topic A, Topic B, or Topic C below and write a paragraph.

Topic A

You have volunteered to do community service to teach local youth how to do specific tasks connected with getting and keeping a job. Choose one topic from the list below. *Then, write a paragraph explaining how to perform the task you've chosen.*

How to prepare a résumé

How to write a cover letter

How to find the best organizations to which to apply

How to dress for the job interview

How to dress while on the job

How to negotiate your salary

How to act businesslike while on the job

How to make yourself valuable to your supervisor

Topic B

You have volunteered to talk to a group of high school students about the experiences that led you to go to college. Your purpose is to show these students that they, too, can attend college even if they're having trouble in high school. *Write a paragraph explaining the steps you follow to be a successful student.* You can include details about how you choose your classes, how you do or do not talk to a counselor, how you study, or how you budget your time.

Topic C

Because you have demonstrated excellent writing skills, you have been asked to teach your fellow students how to write a narrative paragraph. Your purpose is to show students that knowledge of certain methods and a little hard work can make the task go smoothly. *Write a paragraph explaining the steps you follow in writing a narrative paragraph.* You can include details about how you choose a good topic, prepare an effective topic sentence, develop specific details for your narration, or organize and connect your ideas. Feel free to consult Chapter 18 for information about narrative writing.

ᕫ Lab Activity 21

For additional practice with explaining a process, turn to Lab Activity 21 in the Lab Manual at the back of the book.

22 Comparing and Contrasting

What Is a Comparison or Contrast Paragraph?

It's easy to notice what a striking contrast, or difference, one red shirt makes in a crowd of black-clad dancers on a theater stage. Just as we admire the main dancer's skill, we also marvel at the dance group whose members are so similar, so "in step," that each seems hardly separate from the others. However, how much do people really pay attention to differences and similarities? How much should they?

The answers to these questions are important. Comparing and contrasting are skills that help us make well-informed, intelligent decisions. **Comparison** is the paragraph development strategy involving finding *similarities* between two things. The following sentences show comparison between two topics.

My brother and my father are two of the most stubborn men I know.

Although their areas of expertise are different, both Yo-Yo Ma and Wynton Marsalis are excellent musicians.

The Lotus Position

CONDUCT AN INTERVIEW Yoga has become increasingly popular over the past ten years. Interview two or three people you know about their attitudes toward yoga. What do they know about it? What experience do they have with it? What do they think about it? Write a few sentences summarizing what you learn.

Contrast is the paragraph development strategy focusing on the *differences* between two things. Below are examples showing contrast.

My friends Paula and Charlene couldn't be more different in their fashion styles if they tried.

History and science classes require very different skills for success.

Real-Life Writing

Comparison and contrast are part of our daily lives, even if we're not aware that they are. For example, writers often use comparison and contrast to persuade readers to agree with their point of view. Here are other instances where we use these strategies.

For College

- In literature class, compare or contrast two writers for their content or style.

- In science class, contrast the results of two experiments to learn about the hypothesis you are testing.

In Your Personal Life

- Write a note to a friend, contrasting two DVD players to decide which one is the better product.

- Write a note to your roomate comparing your new rental agreement with your previous agreement to make sure you will keep all your privileges in your apartment complex.

At Work

- Write a memo to your boss, contrasting your current performance with last year's performance to show your boss you deserve a raise.

- For a brochure, contrast your company's product with your competitor's to show how yours is superior.

A Model Paragraph: Contrast

Read the following paragraph. Pay attention to how the writer focuses on the differences between two types of gym members, yet clearly has a higher opinion of one than the other.

Working Out, or Working It?

[1]Although both fitness fakes and gym studs go to the gym regularly, their ideas of exercise differ greatly. [2]One of the first differences that jumps out is the way the two gym members are dressed. [3]From head to toe, everything about the fitness fake is brand-name and brand-new. [4]His headband sparkles white, and his gym shirt and shorts are pressed and tucked in. [5]In his hand, the fitness fake holds a bottle of the newest sports drink, and a iPod is attached to his waistband. [6]In contrast, the gym stud wears the same faded tank top and stretched-out shorts that he's worn every other day this week, and his one accessory is a plain plastic bottle filled with tap water. [7]The only part of the gym stud's outfit that looks as if it's been bought in the last six months is his footwear, because he knows that poor

arch support will result in injury. [8]The two members' workouts differ greatly, too. [9]The fitness fake may never get around to actually working out. [10]Instead, he adjusts his iPod, gets drinks of water, admires himself in the weight room mirrors, and chats with whoever is around. [11]If a machine that the fitness fake wants is being used, he just skips it. [12]Before calling it quits and getting a snack, the fitness fake puts in about ninety minutes at the gym, no more than fifteen minutes of which are spent exercising. [13]The gym stud, however, has a different type of workout. [14]After a warm-up jog on the treadmill, he stretches and then heads to one of the machines that will work his heart and lungs, such as the step mill or the rowing machine. [15]The gym stud steps—or runs, or cycles, or rows—for at least forty minutes, stopping only to check his pulse periodically. [16]After toweling off, he heads for the weight room. [17]He stretches a bit more and begins his lifting. [18]If a machine that the gym stud wants is in use, he stretches or uses something else until it is free. [19]After lifting weights, the gym stud stretches one last time and leaves. [20]All in all, the gym stud puts in ninety minutes at the gym, five times a week, and never wastes a minute. [21]The final difference between the two is the results they achieve. [22]The fitness fake never seems to get in shape; he spends hours at the gym, but he doesn't lose weight, can't run farther or lift more than he could six months before, and never gains additional flexibility. [23]The gym stud, however, stays fit and muscular, lengthens his cardio workouts regularly, increases the amount he lifts, and can place his palms to the floor while keeping his legs straight.

EXERCISE 1 ANALYZING A CONTRAST PARAGRAPH

Reread "Working Out, or Working It?" on pages 306–307. Then, answer the following questions.

1. What two types of people are being contrasted?

a. Fitness fakes _____

b. Gym studs _____

2. What is the writer's topic sentence? _____

Although both fitness fakes and gym studs go to the gym regularly, their

ideas of exercise differ greatly.

3. List the categories that are contrasted for the two groups (support points).

a. Attire

b. Workout

c. Results

4. What transitions show that the writer is switching from an example of one gym member to an example of another?

Sentence 6: In contrast

Sentence 13: however

Sentence 21: The final difference

5. Between the fitness fake and the gym stud, which gym member does the writer like more? Gym stud _____ How can you tell?

The gym stud isn't vain, works hard, actually uses the gym for its purpose, and gets results. The name *fitness fake* is negative.

A Model Paragraph: Comparison

Read the following paragraph to see how the writer uses comparison to draw a conclusion.

The Ideal Workout Spot

Although people may argue that exercising in a gym is the best way to stay fit, exercising on your own is every bit as beneficial. Working out at a gym allows you to stretch, run, lift weights, and participate in fitness classes all in one location. A gym lets you move from one fitness activity to the next, taking breaks or working harder as you decide. Many gyms also allow you to shower at the end of your workout. Working out on your own has many similar benefits. Without purchasing any more equipment that a gym member would, you can stretch in the comfort of your own home, run around your neighborhood, and perform exercises such as push-ups and sit-ups. Similar to a gym workout, a home workout allows you to move from one activity to the next. You can run around the block, stretch, do some sit-ups, and run more if you want to. Whatever you decide, you have options. After your workout, you may take a steamy shower. All the luxuries of a gym, without that monthly fee, are right in your own home.

EXERCISE 2 ANALYZING A COMPARISON PARAGRAPH

Reread "The Ideal Workout Spot" on pages 308–309. Then, answer the following questions.

1. What is the topic sentence for "The Ideal Workout Spot"? _____

Although people may argue that exercising in a gym is the best way to stay

fit, exercising on your own is every bit as beneficial.

2. What two types of workout places does the writer compare?

a. Gym _____

b. Home _____

3. What details does the writer use to show that the benefits of each workout place are the same?

a. Everything in one place _____

b. Easy movement from one exercise to the next _____

c. Post-workout shower _____

4. The writer concentrates on the similarities between gym and home workouts. What differences can you think of?   Answers will vary.

a. Less crowded at home/at gym _____

b. More camaraderie at a gym _____

c. Easier access at home; no driving or parking _____

Choosing a Good Topic for Development

To write an effective comparison or contrast paragraph, look for topics that have something important in common. For instance, if you choose a winter vacation and a sports car for a single comparison or contrast paragraph, you'll have a tough time finding common areas to discuss. Instead, comparing or contrasting a winter vacation and a summer vacation will offer you differences—the times of year of the vacations—but also enough similarities to write about.

Once you've decided on your two items for comparison or contrast, you need to decide *what aspects of the two items you wish to focus on*. If you're writing about two breeds of dogs, for example, what about them do you want to compare or contrast? You could mention their intelligence, friendliness, aggressiveness, cost, overall health, and indoor and outdoor habits. The point is to decide ahead of time, before writing a draft, just what areas you want to discuss.

Strong Topics for Comparison or Contrast	Weak Topics for Comparison or Contrast
Comparing Tim Duncan and Shaquille O'Neal	Comparing Tim Duncan and Hillary Clinton
Contrasting eating dinner at home with eating dinner out	Contrasting eating dinner at home with fasting
Contrasting Gloria Steinem with Susan B. Anthony	Contrasting Gloria Steinem with Lisa Simpson

Freewriting on possible comparison or contrast topics is a good way to determine whether you have enough information to develop a paragraph. Danielle thought about contrasting her life before she had a baby to her life after her son Josh arrived. Her freewriting ended up looking like this:

There are so many differences between my life before Josh was born and my life after Josh arrived that I'm not even sure where to start. For one thing, when I didn't have Josh, I was able to go anywhere I wanted whenever I wanted. Now, I have to do just about everything according to when Josh wants and needs it. And my life without Josh used to basically revolve around me. What do I feel like doing this weekend? How about going out to a movie tonight? But now I have to think about things like, If I take him to the playground now, will he have time for his nap this afternoon? What else? What else, what else? Oh, yeah. Another important difference is that I used to concentrate mostly on enjoying my life as much as possible. Now I focus on making sure I'm doing the right things for Josh.

In just a few minutes of freewriting, Danielle has identified three possible areas for development: ability to do whatever she pleases, who is most important in her life, and where her thoughts are focused.

EXERCISE 3 DEVELOPING TOPICS FOR A CONTRAST PARAGRAPH

Below each pair of topics for contrast, list three differences between the two. An example is done for you.   Answers will vary.

Topic: A children's movie and an R-rated movie

Differences: **a.** Amount of violence

b. Amount of profanity

c. Amount of nudity

1. Topic: Your friend's car and your father's car

Differences: **a.** _____

b. _____

c. _____

2. Topic: Your first haircut and your current haircut

Differences: **a.** _____

b. _____

c. _____

3. Topic: Your study habits in high school and your study habits now

Differences: **a.** _____

b. _____

c. _____

4. Topic: Your taste in music and your parents' taste in music

Differences: **a.** _____

b. _____

c. _____

5. Topic: A vacation in the snow and a vacation at the beach

Differences: **a.** _____

b. _____

c. _____

EXERCISE 4 DEVELOPING TOPICS FOR A COMPARISON PARAGRAPH

The following list contains topics for comparison. Below each topic, list three similarities between the two. An example is done for you.   Answers will vary.

Topic: Two friends, _Susanne_ and _Cindy_

Similarities: **a.** Both friendly _____

b. Both hard workers _____

c. Both interested in health careers _____

1. Topic: Two college teachers, _____ and _____

Similarities: **a.** _____

b. _____

c. _____

2. Topic: Two holiday celebrations, _____ and _____

Similarities: **a.** _____

b. _____

c. _____

3. Topic: Two sports, _____ and _____

Similarities: **a.** _____

b. _____

c. _____

Writing an Effective Topic Sentence

Once you've done some freewriting and identified possible areas for development, write your topic sentence. Ideally, your topic sentence will identify the two subjects that you are comparing or contrasting, and it will state whether you'll be discussing similarities or differences between these two subjects. For instance, Danielle wrote, "There are so many differences between my life before Josh was born and my life after Josh arrived. . . ." Right away, Danielle lets her reader know that she will concentrate on the differences between her life before Josh arrived and after. Here are some other effective topic sentences.

Copying music from the Internet without paying for it and robbing someone's house have aspects in common.

My history instructor and my English instructor have different teaching styles.

Developing Specific Details

Many comparison and contrast paragraphs require details from your own experience and observations. As you write longer, more involved assignments, you will need to consult other sources for information. An important characteristic of a comparison and contrast paragraph is _balance_. Make sure you include approximately the same information about both subjects being discussed.

Questions can help you make sure you include adequate details for both subjects being discussed. Danielle used questioning to see where she needed more information.

Question	Answer (Before Josh)	Answer (After Josh)
What did I do and when?	Whatever I wanted	Whatever Josh needs
Who is most important in my life?	Me	?
What did I concentrate on?	Enjoying my life	?

From this chart, Danielle can see that she needs more information about what life is like now that she has Josh. Once she fills in the blanks where the question marks are, she can begin another round of questioning to find specific details.

Question	Answer
What kinds of things do I do now?	Feed Josh, keep him clean, give him love, comfort him when he needs it
Who is most important to me?	Josh comes first now, but I can still go out to eat and see movies.
How do I feel about that?	Deprived, harassed, fulfilled, loving and loved
What do I focus on now?	Feeding and raising Josh well, not making a mistake

Organizing and Linking Your Ideas

Writers have two options for organizing the information in a comparison or contrast paragraph. These options are explained next.

Whole-to-Whole Approach

In the **whole-to-whole approach,** you first write down all the details about one subject in your paragraph; you then write down all the details about the other. The benefit of this organization is that the reader gets a full picture of one subject before going on to the next. Another plus is that transitions can be easier, since the paragraph doesn't jump back and forth. The challenge of this strategy, however, is keeping your reader from forgetting your first subject by the time you finish discussing the second one. The "Comparison and Contrast Paragraphs: Whole-to-Whole Approach" diagram on the next page shows how this approach is organized.

**Comparison and Contrast Paragraphs:
Whole-to-Whole Approach**

Topic sentence...*Stating the main idea*........................
....

↓

Subject A ....
............Support point 1 and specific details.............
............Support point 2 and specific details.............
............Support point 3 and specific details.............
Subject B ....
............Support point 1 and specific details.............
............Support point 2 and specific details.............
............Support point 3 and specific details.............

Danielle's outline uses the whole-to-whole approach. Notice that there are two subjects and each subject has three examples.

My life with Josh is very different from what it used to be without him.

   A. My life without Josh

      1. Went out to eat and went to movies whenever I wanted

      2. Didn't have to consider anyone else

      3. Did things I like, such as partying and dancing

   B. My life with Josh

      1. Feeding him, cleaning him, taking care of his needs first

      2. Always thinking about what he needs next

      3. I like different things, such as loving my baby

If Danielle had chosen to use the point-by-point method, her outline would have looked like this:

My life with Josh is very different from what it used to be without him.

   A. My priorities

      1. Before Josh, went out to eat and went to movies whenever I wanted

      2. With Josh, feeding, cleaning, taking care of his other needs come first

B. The person I care most about
  1. Before Josh, basically me
  2. With Josh, mostly him
C. What I like to do
  1. Before Josh, parties, dancing, movies, going out
  2. With Josh, loving my baby and spending time with him

In this form of Danielle's outline, she had to identify support points—the things and people she likes and cares most about. Some transitions that work very well in comparison and contrast writing are given in the box at the bottom of this page.

Comparison and Contrast Paragraphs:
Point-by-Point Approach

Topic sentence....*Stating the main idea*............
....

↓

Support point 1 ....
.........................Subject A.........................
.........................Subject B.........................
Support point 2 ....
.........................Subject A.........................
.........................Subject B.........................
Support point 3 ....
.........................Subject A.........................
.........................Subject B.........................

Transitions to Use in Comparison and Contrast Writing

Comparison		Contrast	
and	in the same way	although	in contrast
also	just as . . . so, too, is . . .	but	on the other hand
both	like	conversely	unlike
each of	neither	despite	whereas
in addition	similarly	however	while
	too		yet

EXERCISE 5 ANALYZING A PARAGRAPH FOR ELEMENTS OF CONTRAST

Read "Which Diet Is for Me?" below. Then, answer the questions that follow.

Which Diet Is for Me?

[1]Two diets—the high-protein, low-carb diet that my sister loves, and the balanced diet that my friend recommends—have many differences. [2]On the one hand, the high-protein diet lets me eat as much high-fat food—including bacon, butter, and sour cream—as I have room for. [3]It also lets me eat meat, which I love. [4]The theory behind this diet is that if I don't eat carbohydrates, the body's main source of energy, my body will burn fat for energy. [5]Since I need to lose fat, this sounds great. [6]The "catch" to the diet, however, is that I am not allowed to eat many breads or fruits. [7]The other downside to the high-protein diet is that I can't stay on it for too long, or it can cause health problems such as heart disease and colon cancer. [8]It's so hard to decide because everyone I know who has tried this diet loves it. [9]My sister, Jori, lost ten pounds in a month by using this diet, and she seems healthy. [10]On the other hand, a well-balanced diet seems like a smart, healthy choice. [11]With this option, I'm supposed to eat a lot of small servings of fruits and vegetables, fewer servings of meat and dairy, and just a bit of oil or fat. [12]Also, I should eat several small servings of breads and cereals. [13]The idea is that I should eat everything in moderation, which sounds good but which is hard for me. [14]The upside of this approach is that eating a well-balanced diet is not dangerous at all. [15]If I can find meals that include all the recommended food groups, I never have to stop this diet. [16]In addition, I can have dessert; I just have to be careful not to eat more than my share. [17]My friend, who is a dietician, recommends eating a balanced diet because she says that other diets—such as the high-protein one—are just gimmicky and unhealthy. [18]Maybe I'll just have to try both and see which one works for me.

1. Is the purpose of this paragraph to compare or contrast two

diets? <u>Contrast</u> _____

2. What is the topic sentence in "Which Diet Is for Me?" _____

<u>Two diets—the high-protein, low-carb diet that my sister loves, and the</u>

<u>balanced diet that my friend recommends—have many differences.</u>

3. The writer considers the foods in each diet. What other types of information does the writer use to evaluate the diets?

   a. Who recommends them

   b. How healthy they are

4. What specific foods can the writer eat on each of the diets?

   a. First diet: Bacon, butter, sour cream, meat

   b. Second diet: Everything in moderation

5. What strategy does the writer use to organize her ideas, whole-to-whole or point-by-point? Whole-to-whole strategy

6. What transition does the writer use to signal that she's starting a discussion of the balanced diet? On the other hand

7. The writer directly contrasts the diets in two sentences. What three sentences mention both diets? *Hint:* Look at the very beginning and very end of the paragraph.

   Sentence 1

   Sentence 17

EXERCISE 6 FOLLOWING THE FOUR Cs

Read the paragraph below. Then, answer the questions that follow. Pay close attention to the areas of comparison that the writer has chosen to write about.

Healthy Living

¹I recently moved back in with my father after he had a heart attack, and he's been driving me crazy ever since. ²I never dreamed that my father and I could become so much alike. ³I'm the health nut of the family, so my father has been copying my every move. ⁴For one thing, he has copied my diet. ⁵I always eat high-fiber cereals and

breads because fiber has been linked to weight loss and—some people think—to cancer prevention, and I eat five to nine servings of fruits and vegetables each day. 6At least two of those are "leafy greens" such as spinach or broccoli. 7Though my dad has always ignored the fat content in any food and rarely ate fresh fruits or vegetables, now he eats exactly what I eat at meals. 8His doctor told him that eating lean meats and staying away from high-fat dairy products and fried or processed foods can help lower his cholesterol from 232, which is too high, to under 200, which is considered healthy. 9I'm glad my dad is trying to be healthy, but I wish he would come up with his own ideas for meals! 10In addition to copying my diet, my dad is exercising the way I do. 11I compete in triathlons, so six days a week I swim, cycle, or run for at least an hour. 12Now my dad exercises like this, or tries to, too. 13Following his doctor's order, my dad walks, jogs, cycles, or swims at least twenty minutes four times a week. 14He's hoping to lower his resting heart rate from 96 beats a minute to 64, like mine, even though he's twenty-five years older than I am. 15A final way that my dad has become a "mini me" is in his social habits. 16I don't smoke or drink, because that would hurt me in competition. 17However, my dad smoked for more than twenty years and has had more than his share of beer. 18His doctor made him quit smoking while he was in the hospital, but my dad cut back on his drinking all by himself. 19Now he doesn't smoke, and he hardly drinks at all. 20He's really improving the way he takes care of himself, and I'm proud of him for that. 21I just hope he doesn't start wearing his hair like mine!

Concise Writing

1. Is the purpose of this paragraph to compare or contrast two

people? <u>Compare</u>

2. What is the topic sentence?

<u>I never dreamed that my father and I could become so much alike.</u>

3. What three areas of comparison, or support points, does the writer offer?

a. <u>Dad has copied diet.</u>

b. <u>Dad exercises.</u>

c. <u>Dad has improved social habits.</u>

Credible Writing

4. What specific details does the writer offer for each support point?

Details illustrating support point 1:

a. Dad eats fiber.

b. Dad eats fruits and vegetables.

c. Dad stays away from high-fat foods.

Details illustrating support point 2:

Dad exercises for twenty minutes a day, four times a week.

Details illustrating support point 3:

a. Dad quit smoking.

b. Dad drinks less.

5. What facts involving numbers show that the writer knows about health and fitness?

a. Cholesterol levels

b. Heart rates

c. Exercise frequency and duration

Clear Writing

6. What transitions does the writer use to signal the start of each support point?

Sentence 4: For one thing

Sentence 10: In addition to copying my diet

Sentence 15: A final way

7. How many times does the writer use some form of the word *health*? ____4____

Correct Writing

The sentences in this paragraph are all correct. To check for correctness in your own writing, go to Part 7, "Writing Correct Sentences."

What You Know Now

Comparing two topics involves finding similarities between them, while contrasting involves focusing on the differences. One key to writing an effective comparison or contrast paragraph is finding two subjects that have some common areas for comparison. Comparison and contrast paragraphs can be organized using the whole-to-whole approach or the point-by-point approach.

WRITING PRACTICE 1 **Write Topic Sentences for Comparison and Contrast Paragraphs**

On this and the following page are three topics that can be compared or contrasted. Write two topic sentences for each topic, one that shows a comparison relationship (similarities) and one that shows a contrast relationship (differences).

An example is done for you. Answers will vary.

Topic: Two books

Comparison: _Gone with the Wind_ and _The House of Mirth_ both explore how the main women characters are prepared for lives of wealth.

Contrast: _Gone with the Wind_ and _The House of Mirth_ show many differences in how women deal with adversity.

1. Topic: Two sports stars, Tiger Woods and Mia Hamm

   Comparison: Tiger Woods and Mia Hamm raised the bar for excellence in their sports.

   Contrast:
   Tiger Woods and Mia Hamm differ in their attitudes toward competition.

2. Topic: Two musical or fashion styles, hip-hop and blues

   Comparison:
   Hip-hop and blues music both rely on a solid underlying beat.

Contrast: _____

The lyrics for hip-hop and the blues cover different subject matters.

3. Topic: Being a student and being an employee

Comparison: Success as a student and as an employee depends on working

hard, following instructions, and trying my best.

Contrast: _____

Being a student is much harder than being an employee.

WRITING PRACTICE 2 Write a Comparison and Contrast Paragraph

Now write a comparison and contrast paragraph of your own.

Prewriting

1. Below is a list of topics for paragraphs that compare or contrast two items. Read the list, and think about whether you can find more similarities or more differences between the two subjects in each topic. Choose a topic and then decide whether to write a comparison or contrast.

Topics

Two family relationships

Two work relationships

Two entertainers

Two happy times in your life

Two friends

A shopping mall at different times of the year

Studying for an easy test and studying for a difficult test

A chore or task you love and a chore or task you hate

2. Do prewriting to develop your ideas. Questioning is a helpful type of prewriting for comparison and contrast paragraphs because it allows you to focus on the same areas for comparison or contrast with each subject in your paragraph. Look at the sample question-and-answer list below. This writer has chosen to contrast the shopping mall in two seasons, in July and December.

Question	Answer in July	Answer in December
Who is at the mall?	People looking for summer clothing: swimsuits, shorts	People looking for everything: clothing, holiday gifts, holiday decorations
What does the mall look like?	Decorations of sun, sand, beaches	Decorations of snow, Christmas, Hanukkah, New Year's Eve, Kwanzaa
How crowded is it?	Not crowded at all, especially in the morning	Extremely crowded all the time
How do store clerks act?	Bored but friendly	Hyper, stressed, too tired, not friendly

Drafting

3. Write a topic sentence. Make sure that the relationship you're writing about—comparison or contrast—is clear in your topic sentence. Here is a possible topic sentence: "It's amazing how different the mall can be depending on what time of year you go."

4. Choose your support points—the areas of comparison—and specific details.

5. Organize your ideas using the whole-to-whole or the point-by-point strategy. (See the diagrams on pages 315 and 316 if you need help remembering how these strategies work.)

6. Write your draft. Use freewriting to fill in the gaps with details, and keep checking to make sure your organization is consistent throughout your paragraph.

Revising

7. Check for the first three of the four Cs: *concise, credible,* and *clear* writing. Make any necessary changes to your draft.

Editing

8. Check your paragraph for the fourth C: *correct* writing. Proofread your paragraph to make sure you have used correct spelling, punctuation, and grammar.

WRITING PRACTICE 3 Use Comparison or Contrast in Real Life

Deciding between choices can be difficult, particularly when many choices exist. The situations in Topic A and Topic B below outline real-life situations requiring comparison or contrast as part of a decision-making process. Choose one of these topics and use your comparing or contrasting skills to help a friend make an important decision.

Topic A

Your friend is trying to decide which television programs to let her teenage daughter watch. You have volunteered to help with the decision-making process by viewing various programs you think might be suitable and reporting back to your friend. *Write a paragraph comparing or contrasting two television programs*. Be sure to focus on support points that let you consider both programs, such as characters, educational value, entertainment value, appropriateness for a teen, and music.

Topic B

Your friend is trying to decide between two instructors for a class he has to take, and you have had classes from both instructors. *Write a paragraph comparing or contrasting two instructors*. Think about what areas of comparison or contrast you want to focus on: how demanding the instructors are, how much work they give, how interesting they are, how approachable they are, or how much feedback they give. Then, include specific details from your own experiences and observations to make your points convincing.

Lab Activity 22

For additional practice with comparing and contrasting, complete Lab Activity 22 in the Lab Manual at the back of the book.

23 Explaining Cause-and-Effect Development

CULTURE NOTE ***The American Revolution***

The American Revolution had many causes and such far-reaching effects that pinpointing one cause or effect would be incomplete and inaccurate. However, three significant elements stand out: the American colonists' quest for freedom, the Boston Tea Party, and the Battle of Bunker Hill. Each was pivotal in deciding the outcome of the Revolutionary War, which ran from 1775 to 1781.

What Is a Cause-and-Effect Paragraph?

Every day we attempt to explain, predict, and control situations in our lives: why we were late, how we'll save enough money to buy holiday presents, how we can lose weight. These situations have one thing in common: the element of cause-and-effect reasoning.

In the **cause-and-effect** paragraph development strategy, you explain the reasons why something occurred (*causes*), the outcome of certain actions (*effects*), or both. In the following sentences, the causes are underlined.

> Moving back in with your parents as an adult can cause tension in the house.

> A number of happy surprises in his life have caused John to have a sunny outlook on life.

In the following sentences, the effects are underlined.

> Taking on additional responsibilities at work can greatly advance your career.

> Failing to study for final exams can affect a student's grades disastrously.

EXERCISE 1 FINDING CAUSES

Fill in the missing causes below. An example is done for you. Answers will vary.

Cause: <u>Eating too many candy bars before bed</u> Effect: Bad teeth

1. Cause: _____ Effect: Oversleeping

2. Cause: _____ Effect: Sunburn

3. Cause: _____ Effect: Car breakdown

EXERCISE 2 FINDING EFFECTS

Now, provide an effect for each of the following "causes." An example is done for you. Answers will vary.

Cause: Running a red light   Effect: <u>Crashing your car</u>

1. Cause: Not brushing your teeth Effect: _____

2. Cause: Doing your homework   Effect: _____

3. Cause: Taking on more   Effect: _____
responsibility at work

Real-Life Writing

Cause-and-effect reasoning plays a significant role in real-life activities.

For College

- In science classes, use cause and effect in writing about chemical reactions, environmental changes, and other subjects.
- In history class, use cause and effect in writing about social and political events.

In Your Personal Life

- Write a letter to a loan officer explaining the causes for some late payments noted on your credit rating.

- Write a letter to a friend or family member trying to convince him or her to stop smoking by explaining the effects of that habit on health.

At Work

- Write a memo to your boss showing how reorganizing an office routine will create greater efficiency.

- Write a memo to your boss explaining the causes for a shipment's being late.

A Model Paragraph: Cause and Effect

The sample paragraph below uses cause-and-effect reasoning to explain the role of the British in the Boston Tea Party.

The Boston Tea Party

[1]As one of the American colonists' first acts of defiance toward the British government, the Boston Tea Party took place when colonists dressed up as Native Americans, boarded a British merchant ship, and tossed hundreds of cases of tea leaves into Boston Harbor. [2]Though Americans took action and threw away the tea, in many ways the British caused the Boston Tea Party. [3]First, the British imposed high taxes on the colonies for tea and other imported products. [4]The colonists loved tea, but the tax on it was so high that they could barely afford it. [5]Second, Parliament passed the Tea Act of May 10, 1773. [6]This act adjusted import taxes so that English companies—such as the East India Company—could sell their tea for lower prices than American companies. [7]This act outraged the colonists, who recognized that the British government was favoring its own companies while putting American companies out of business. [8]Finally, England allowed only select Americans to sell tea. [9]Those Americans who were not chosen to sell tea feared the loss of their wealth and independence. [10]All these reasons combined to make the colonists rebel against England, board the British merchant ship, and throw away a small fortune in tea.

The Boston Tea Party

CRITICAL THINKING Colonists protested British taxation by tossing tea into Boston Harbor. People take political stands in various ways, even using violence to make their point. When do people go too far in expressing their views? Write a few sentences explaining how far people should go to make their views known.

EXERCISE 3 ANALYZING A CAUSE-AND-EFFECT PARAGRAPH

1. What is the topic sentence in "The Boston Tea Party"?

Though Americans took action and threw away the tea, in many ways the

British caused the Boston Tea Party.

2. What causes does the writer offer for the Boston Tea Party?

a. British imposed high taxes on tea.

b. British passed the Tea Act.

c. England let only a few Americans sell tea.

3. What three transitions does the writer list to introduce the support points?

Sentence 3: First

Sentence 5: Second

Sentence 8: Finally

Choosing a Good Topic for Development

Choose a topic that allows you to see how one event caused another. For instance, "how smoking causes lung disease" is a good topic, since there is a clear, medically supported link between these two. In contrast, writing about the causes of some types of cancer is tricky since even medical experts don't know this.

Second, make sure to narrow your topic so that you can cover it in a paragraph. Once you've narrowed your topic to an event that works well for cause-and-effect development, *decide whether the cause or the effect is more significant.* Many topics can be argued from either the cause or effect viewpoint, but usually one perspective—the cause or the effect—is stronger.

Martha wasn't sure what to write about, but she wanted to explore ways to prevent herself from getting sick so often. After looking through some health magazines, she did some freewriting on the subject.

> I am so sick of being sick! Every time I go to work or school, I feel as if I'm catching some new virus. I read that touching things like doorknobs, computer keyboards, and desktops is a sure way to become infected with a virus, and even shaking hands can spread illness. Since I work in a restaurant, I'm always touching things that other people have already touched. I know I don't wash my hands enough. I also learned that not getting enough sleep can affect my immune system and make it really easy for me to get sick. Whoever wrote that must not have been supporting herself through college! I only wish I could get more sleep.

Martha has identified two *causes* of getting sick: touching things that sick people have touched and not getting enough sleep. Martha decided that she had enough ideas to start writing.

Writing an Effective Topic Sentence

Make sure you clearly state in your topic sentence the element—cause or effect—you plan to write about. Try to put that element at the end of your topic sentence. For instance, the topic sentence "Many people who drink and drive end up with disastrous results" lets readers know that the writer plans to explain the effects of drinking and driving since "disastrous results" comes at the end of the sentence.

After Martha finished her freewriting, she identified two possible support points.

Support point 1:   Touching things that sick people have touched

Support point 2:   Not getting enough sleep

Noticing that both points deal with *causes* of sickness, Martha came up with her topic sentence: "Especially during cold and flu season, getting sick can be caused by several factors." From this topic sentence, a reader expects to learn *causes* of illness.

The right words can help your reader understand what you are focusing on. See the box below for words that mean "cause" and words that mean "effect."

Words That Signal Causes and Effects

Words for Cause	Words for Effect
basis	consequence
cause	effect
factor	outcome
motive	result
reason	

EXERCISE 4 IDENTIFYING CAUSES AND EFFECTS

In each of the sentences below, identify the cause and effect. An example is done for you.

Sentence: Sitting in the shade at the beach can cause sunburn as a result of the sun's glare off the sand.

Cause: _Sun's glare_____

Effect: _Sunburn_____

1. Sentence: Road construction led to a three-hour delay on the coastal highway.

Cause: Road construction

Effect: Three-hour delay

2. Sentence: Studying hard for finals paid off for Shauna when she earned three Bs and an A.

Cause: Studying hard for finals

Effect: Three Bs and an A

3. Sentence: A good vocabulary starts with reading.

Cause: Reading

Effect: Good vocabulary

4. Sentence: My headaches all seem to come from watching too much television.

Cause: Watching too much television

Effect: Headaches

5. Sentence: Knowing Carlos liked the color red, I bought a dress that color.

Cause: Carlos liked red

Effect: Buying a new dress

Developing Specific Details

Using prewriting techniques such as freewriting or clustering, you can discover support points and specific details for your topic. Be flexible. If you've decided to focus on causes but your prewriting yields many effects, think about rewriting your topic sentence with a new focus.

After freewriting, Martha knew she needed more information, so she used a cluster diagram to see where she could fill in details.

Martha remembered reading about poor diet being a cause of poor health, so she included that in her cluster diagram. Thus, she ended up with three solid points to develop in her paragraph. Sometimes specific details illustrating causes or effects will come from your own experiences, but if you have trouble thinking of enough detail to support your topic sentence, refer to other sources, such as talking to people or reading trusted publications.

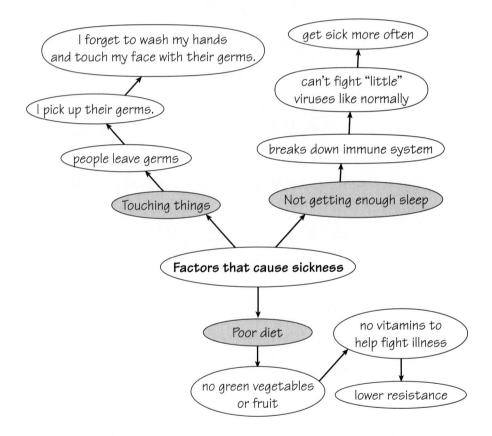

Organizing and Linking Your Ideas

Emphatic order—organizing your support points from least to most important—works well for cause-and-effect paragraphs. Remember that you as the writer get to decide which points are most—or least—important, and order them accordingly.

**Cause-and-Effect Paragraphs:
Proving Effects**

Topic sentence...*Giving the cause*.......................................
....

↓

Effect 1 ....
.............................Specific detail...................................
.............................Specific detail...................................
Effect 2 ....
.............................Specific detail...................................
.............................Specific detail...................................
Effect 3 ....
.............................Specific detail...................................
.............................Specific detail...................................

**Cause-and-Effect Paragraphs:
Proving Causes**

Topic sentence...*Giving the effect*.....................................
....

↓

Cause 1 ....
.............................Specific detail...................................
.............................Specific detail...................................
Cause 2 ....
.............................Specific detail...................................
.............................Specific detail...................................
Cause 3 ....
.............................Specific detail...................................
.............................Specific detail...................................

Even though Martha's first idea about illness was "touching things that sick people have touched," she decided to place that point last in her paragraph. For her, the idea that she could get sick just touching a doorknob that a sick person had touched was so unsettling that she wanted to make sure other people knew they should wash their hands frequently. This is the final order for Martha's support points.

Support point 1:   Not getting enough sleep

Support point 2:   Not eating well

Support point 3:   Touching things that sick people have touched

The "Cause-and-Effect Paragraphs: Proving Effects" and "Cause-and-Effect Paragraphs: Proving Causes" diagrams on the previous page show how a paragraph can be organized. For her paragraph, Martha followed the structure for proving causes. She also made sure to use transitions that signal empathic order, from the box on page 260.

EXERCISE 5 ANALYZING A PARAGRAPH FOR CAUSE AND EFFECT

Read the paragraph below and determine the causes and effects. Then answer the questions that follow.

The Battle of Bunker Hill

[1]The Battle of Bunker Hill, the first official battle of the American Revolutionary War, had far-reaching effects. [2]Actually fought on nearby Breed's Hill close to Boston, the Battle of Bunker Hill occurred in June 1775. [3]The first major effect was to show the American troops that they could inflict heavy losses on the British forces. [4]The battle took place only because the British charged up Breed's Hill, where the Americans were located, and attacked repeatedly. [5]General William Prescott, the American leader, would not let his troops fire until the Americans could "see the whites of their [the British soldiers'] eyes." [6]Thus, when the colonists fired, the British soldiers were close enough to be easy targets. [7]Though the British won the battle, many English soldiers died. [8]A second major effect of the Battle of Bunker Hill was that the English realized that defeating the Americans was not going to be easy. [9]Before this battle, the English tried to rule the Americans through laws passed in England. [10]However, because the Americans fought so hard against the English troops, England was forced to realize that the Americans meant business. [11]The war would not be over with one or two small battles. [12]The most significant effect of the Battle of Bunker Hill, though, was that it encouraged the colonists to continue to fight. [13]Since the war that followed led to the

freedom of the colonies from British rule, its beginning—at the Battle of Bunker Hill—was very important.

1. What is the topic sentence of "The Battle of Bunker Hill"? _____

The Battle of Bunker Hill, the first official battle of the American

Revolutionary War, had far-reaching effects.

2. From your reading of the topic sentence, do you think this paragraph will focus on the causes or the effects of the Battle of

Bunker Hill? Effects

3. List three important effects of this battle.

a. Showed Americans that they could hurt the British

b. Showed the British that the Americans wouldn't just go away easily

c. Encouraged the colonists to continue the fight

4. In the writer's view, what effect is the most important?

Encouraging the colonists to fight on.

5. How does the writer signal the start of support points?

Sentence 3: first

Sentence 8: second

Sentence 12: most significant effect

EXERCISE 6 FOLLOWING THE FOUR Cs

Read the paragraph below. Then, answer the questions that follow.

Why the Colonists Wanted Freedom

[1]A number of factors caused the thirteen American colonies to break away from England. [2]For one, the Americans wanted to make their own decisions about their daily lives. [3]For instance, the British

government passed the Stamp Act in 1765. [4]This act required the colonists to use special paper, acquired from stamp distributors, to print all their documents. [5]Because using this type of paper was inconvenient and expensive, the colonists wanted to use their own paper instead. [6]A second reason the Americans wanted independence was to have the power to do things the way they wanted. [7]As colonists, the Americans had to follow the laws that the British government passed, even though those laws were passed across the Atlantic Ocean in England. [8]So when England passed a law such as the Currency Act, which prohibited the Americans from printing their own money, the colonists had to obey. [9]The colonists wanted to be able to make decisions in their own cities and towns without being supervised by a country thousands of miles away. [10]Third, the colonists wanted independence from British rule. [11]England was ruled by King George, with help from Parliament, and kings were determined by birth. [12]The colonists wanted to be able to choose their own leaders through democratic election and, thus, have some say in who made their laws. [13]Most important, the colonists wanted independence because of money. [14]The English government caused the Americans to lose much money by making them pay taxes on such goods as tea, sugar, coffee, and textiles. [15]The British government also favored British companies over American companies to sell supplies to the colonies. [16]Thus, both American businesses and American consumers lost a lot of money through British interference. [17]The colonists wanted to be able to buy and sell their own goods and keep their profits for themselves or pay them to an American government, not an English king.

Concise Writing

1. What is the topic sentence for "Why the Colonists Wanted Freedom"?

A number of factors caused the thirteen American colonies to break away from England.

2. How many reasons does the writer of the paragraph give to support the main idea? Mark an X beside the correct answer.

a. _____ One

b. _____ Two

c. _____ Three

d. _X_ Four

3. What points does the writer offer in support of the topic sentence?

    a. Colonists wanted to make decisions in their daily lives.

    b. Colonists wanted power to do things their way.

    c. Colonists wanted independence from British rule.

    d. Colonists wanted freedom for financial reasons.

Credible Writing

4. What are some examples of how the British interfered (from the colonists' point of view) with the colonies? Answers will vary.

    a. Stamp Act

    b. Currency Act

    c. Import taxes

5. Write two other facts in the paragraph that lead you to believe that the writer knows why the colonists wanted freedom. Answers will vary.

    a. England was too far away to govern the colonies.

    b. Colonists didn't like paying someone they didn't choose, the King of England.

Clear Writing

6. What are four transitions the writer uses to direct the reader to notice the causes?

    Sentence 3: For instance

    Sentence 6: second

    Sentence 10: Third

    Sentence 13: Most important

7. What does the writer think is the most significant reason the American colonists wanted freedom? Money

8. Is this paragraph organized according to time sequence order or

emphatic order? <u>Emphatic order</u>

Correct Writing

The sentences in this paragraph are all correct. To check for correctness in your own writing, go to Part 7, "Writing Correct Sentences."

What You Know Now

Using cause-and-effect reasoning helps us explain, predict, and control various aspects of our lives. In choosing a topic for a cause-and-effect paragraph, look for a situation where one event caused another. Your topic sentence should make clear whether you're focusing on causes or effects. Organizing your ideas using emphatic order works well for cause-and-effect paragraphs.

WRITING PRACTICE 1 Provide Details for Effect Paragraphs

Below is a list of possible topic sentences for effect paragraphs. Choose a topic that appeals to you, and write one well-developed example that illustrates the cause of each underlined effect. An example is done for you. Answers will vary.

Topic sentence: Exercising regularly helps <u>improve my mood.</u>

Cause: <u>Whenever I go for a long run, for instance, I feel relaxed and ready for</u>

<u>the rest of the day. Even if I still have a lot of work to do, just getting to blow</u>

<u>off some steam through exercise helps me feel ready to meet the challenge.</u>

1. Topic sentence: Having an after-school job can cause <u>major stress</u> for teenagers.

Cause:_____

_____

_____

2. Topic sentence: <u>Students cheat in school</u> for many reasons.

Cause:_____

_____

_____

3. Topic sentence: You can try several techniques to earn a <u>promotion at work.</u>

Cause:_____

_____

_____

WRITING PRACTICE 2 **Provide Details for Cause Paragraphs**

Below are five topic sentences for cause paragraphs. Choose a topic and write on a separate sheet of paper one well-developed example that illustrates an effect of the cause given. The cause is underlined. An example is done for you.   Answers will vary.

Topic sentence: <u>Getting too much sun over long periods of time</u> can ruin your skin.

Effect: My friend Ron has skin like leather. It's so tough, dark, and wrinkled that it's hard to imagine he ever had soft, smooth skin. Ron has worked in construction for ten years, and even in that fairly short time, his face has aged to make him look ten years older than he actually is.

1. Topic sentence: <u>Spending more than you earn</u> can have serious consequences.

2. Topic sentence: <u>Volunteering to do community service</u> can be very rewarding.

3. Topic sentence: <u>Accepting dares from your friends</u> can be dangerous.

WRITING PRACTICE 3 Write a Paragraph Explaining Causes and Effects

Now write a cause-and-effect paragraph of your own.

Prewriting

1. Choose a topic for your paragraph from the lists below. The topics tell you whether to focus on causes or effects.

Causes	Effects
Overcrowding in schools	Alcohol or drug abuse
Taking the bus or subway	Taking steroids
Learning yoga	Treating people with respect
Road rage	Being a vegetarian

2. Freewrite for five to ten minutes to come up with details that will make your paragraph believable for your reader. For instance, if your topic is "treating people with respect," try listing times when being nice brought about beneficial changes in your life. A sample list follows.

Promotion at work (smiled at customers and thanked them for coming in)

Happy roommates (cooked dinner when it wasn't my turn)

Good friends (listened to them, offered advice when they wanted it)

Drafting

3. Write your topic sentence clearly emphasizing either causes or effects.

4. Choose the support points and specific details that best illustrate your topic sentence.

5. Organize your support points and details in emphatic order. If some details don't fit as well as others, leave them out. Be sure to use transitions.

6. Write a draft of your paragraph using the topic sentence, support points, and details that you've developed.

Revising

7. Check for the first three of the four Cs: *concise, credible,* and *clear* writing. Make any necessary changes to your draft.

Editing

8. Check your paragraph for the fourth C: *correct* writing. Proofread your paragraph to make sure you have used correct spelling, punctuation, and grammar.

WRITING PRACTICE 4   Explain the Causes or Effects of a Situation

Cause-and-effect reasoning often helps us to explain, predict, or control situations in our lives. Before beginning this assignment, think about how much influence you have over the lives of people you love. Choose either Topic A or Topic B below.

Topic A

You have received a letter from your child's teacher because he or she has missed a lot of school this semester. The reasons for your child's absence all relate to changes in your life: moving to another house, getting a new job, caring for a sick parent. *Write a letter to your child's teacher explaining the causes of your child's absence.* Be specific as to how the changes in your life have caused your child to miss school. Your topic sentence may be something like "Recent events in my life have caused my child to miss school." Be sure to use specific details to support your topic sentence.

Topic B

You have encouraged a shy friend to become involved in community activities, and your friend has blossomed into a more friendly, funny, confident person. *Write a letter to your friend telling him or her how proud you are of the changes in his or her personality.* Explain what you've noticed about your friend's behavior and attitude since he or she began the community involvement. Your topic sentence might read something like "Becoming involved in community activities has had many positive effects on you." Be sure to use specific details to support your topic sentence.

Lab Activity 23

For additional practice with cause and effect, complete Lab Activity 23 in the Lab Manual at the back of the book.

24 Defining Terms

What Is a Definition Paragraph?

We are constantly defining terms to better understand others and be understood ourselves. In the **definition** strategy of paragraph development, the writer explains one specific word or idea so that other people can understand it. Definition may be one of the most valuable skills a writer can master.

Real-Life Writing

Defining terms is important in everyday communication. Here are some real-life uses of definition.

For College

■ For a history exam, you are asked to define *imperialism* in terms of your country's growth.

■ In biology class, you are asked to define *pistil* on an exam.

In Your Personal Life

■ You and your partner continually redefine *discipline* in terms of raising your children.

- You and your friends define *honesty* and *trust* when you have conflicts.

At Work

- For a job application, you are asked to define yourself in one word.
- For an employee handbook, you define *responsibility*.

Types of Definitions and Model Paragraphs

You can define terms in a number of ways.

- Formal definition
- Definition by class the item belongs to
- Definition by negative example
- Definition by extended example

Formal Definition

A **formal definition** usually takes no more than two or three sentences. It's similar to what you might find in a dictionary. Here are three examples.

> A *bicycle* is a vehicle that has only two wheels.
> *Intelligence* is the ability to learn or understand from experience.
> *Vivacious* means "spirited and full of life."

Formal definitions quickly and accurately tell us what a word means. However, formal definitions are generally not the type of definition required for college writing.

EXERCISE 1 FINDING FORMAL DEFINITIONS

You may already know the formal definition of some of the words below; others may be unfamiliar to you. Write a formal definition for each word using a dictionary if you need to. Then, provide a sentence that illustrates the definition of the word. An example is done for you.   Answers will vary.

Word: Loneliness

Formal definition: ___Feeling of being alone when you don't really want___

___to be_____

Sentence: *Coming home to an empty house every day*

after my mom died filled me with loneliness.

1. Word: Friendly

Formal definition: _____

Sentence: _____

_____

2. Word: Boyfriend (or girlfriend)

Formal definition: _____

Sentence: _____

_____

3. Word: Escape

Formal definition: _____

Sentence: _____

_____

4. Word: Relaxation

Formal definition: _____

Sentence: _____

_____

5. Word: Exciting

Formal definition: _____

Sentence: _____

_____

Definition by Class

The type of definition that is more common in college writing is **definition by class.** Definition by class involves two main steps.

Step 1: Place the term you're defining into a general category, or class.

The following examples illustrate the first part of definition by class. The term being defined is in italics; the general category, or class, is in bold print.

> A *smooth talker* is a **person** . . .
>
> *Fear* is the **feeling** . . .
>
> A *hot rod* is a **car** . . .

In the above examples, *smooth talker* is placed into the general category *person,* while *fear* is labeled a *feeling. Hot rod,* finally, is put in the class *car.* In all cases, the definition places the term in a broad category before giving any other detail.

Step 2: Offer details to further clarify the term.

Begin a definition paragraph with a topic sentence that includes your general category or class, and then add details to make the meaning of your term clear. Your topic sentence will end up having two parts: the general category and some details.

Asking questions about the term you want to define can help you find examples for your definition. In the examples below, the term being defined is in italics, the general category is in bold print, and the defining details are underlined.

> For *smooth talker,* ask yourself *what kind* of person is a smooth talker? What makes such a person *different from* other people?
>
> A *smooth talker* is a **person** who can get out of any problem simply by using slick words, winks, and sly smiles.
>
> For *fear,* ask yourself *what kind* of feeling is fear? What about it is *different from* any other type of feeling?
>
> *Fear* is the **feeling** that something bad is about to happen.
>
> For *hot rod,* ask yourself *what kind* of car is a hot rod? How is it *special,* or *different from* other cars?
>
> A *hot rod* is a **car** that has been specially altered for power and speed.

Definition Paragraphs:
Definition by Class

Topic sentence giving defined term, general
category, and some specific details ....
....

↓

Specific detail 1 ....
....
Specific detail 2 ....
....
Specific detail 3 ....
....
Specific detail 4 ....
....
Specific detail 5 ....
....

The answers to the questions about the general terms provide details that complete the definition by class. The question "What kind?" is helpful in defining terms. Asking it throughout your writing process will help you find details to illustrate your term.

Definition-by-class paragraphs often contain support points and specific details to support their topic sentences. The model paragraph shown below, "An Ace," does just this. However, another way to write a definition-by-class paragraph is to list a series of details without any formal support points. The paragraph "Play Ball!" on page 353 offers a model of this kind of definition-by-class paragraph. See the "Definition Paragraphs: Definition by Class" diagram above for an idea of how to write this type of paragraph.

A Model Paragraph: Definition by Class

Read the paragraph below to see how definition by class works.

An Ace

¹In baseball, an *ace* is a pitcher who is extremely skilled. ²An ace is able to throw a range of pitches. ³Throwing "heat" means pitching fastballs that batters have a hard time hitting. ⁴An ace can also throw balls that don't just make a straight line from the pitcher's mound to

home plate. [5]Instead, a curve ball from a true ace can move any number of ways: breaking away from the batter, into the batter, or downward. [6]A knuckleball, thrown with the fingertips and a stiff wrist, moves very slowly, dancing around, making it unpredictable and very hard to hit. [7]Further, an ace can throw sliders, which are pitches that have speed like a fastball and movement like a curveball or knuckleball. [8]An ace also knows how to work with the catcher (the player who crouches behind home plate and catches the pitches) to mix up the pitches and the location of the pitches in order to confuse batters. [9]In addition to knowing how to throw different pitches, an ace knows when to let batters hit the ball. [10]An ace knows how to throw pitches that cause batters to pop the ball up into the air. [11]Those balls can be easier for a fielder to catch. [12]An ace also knows how to hurl pitches that batters hit downward—with luck, straight into the mitt of an infielder. [13]An ace is a valuable player for any team.

EXERCISE 2 ANALYZING A DEFINITION PARAGRAPH

Reread "An Ace" above. Then, answer the questions below.

1. What is the general class, or category, for *ace?* _Pitcher_____

2. In sentence 1, what information does the writer provide that shows that an ace is different from other pitchers?

_Extremely skilled_____

3. What are some skills the writer says an ace has?

a. _Throws a range of pitches._____

b. _Mixes up pitches and pitch locations._____

c. _Knows how to let batters hit the ball to make an out._____

4. What are some specific pitches that the writer names?

a. _Fastball_____

b. _Curve ball_____

c. _Knuckleball_____

d. _Slider_____

5. What transitions in sentences 4, 7, 8, 9, and 12 does the writer use to show addition, or more of the same type of information?

Sentence 4: ___also___

Sentence 7: ___Further___

Sentence 8: ___also___

Sentence 9: ___In addition___

Sentence 12: ___also___

6. What other word does the writer use in place of *ace?* ___Pitcher___

Definition by Negative Example

In **definition by negative example,** you state what a term is *not* and then state what the term *is.* An easy way to begin a paragraph that uses definition by negative example is to use a stereotype as the "negative" part of the definition and then add what the term *is* later in the sentence. In the following example, the negative part of the definition is in italics.

In baseball, a ace is *not simply a pitcher* but one who is extremely skilled.

Definition by Extended Example

In **definition by extended example,** a writer uses a single example throughout the entire paragraph. In this case, the paragraph begins with a one-sentence explanation of the term—the topic sentence. However, after the topic sentence comes one detailed example. This detailed example illustrates the term being defined. To get an idea of how to write this kind of paragraph, see the "Definition Paragraphs: Definition by Extended Example" diagram on page 349.

A Model Paragraph: Definition by Extended Example

Read the paragraph on the next page to see how the writer uses definition by extended example.

A Great Milestone

A milestone is a significant or important event in history. The inclusion of the baseball player Jackie Robinson in major league baseball is a milestone in baseball and American history. Right after the Civil War, black players were allowed to play on teams with white players. However, after Jim Crow laws restricting the rights of African-Americans were implemented in the late 1880s, black players were barred from professional baseball, so they formed their own teams. In 1920, the Negro National League was founded by Rube Foster, a talented African-American player. In 1945, when the general manager for the Brooklyn Dodgers saw Jackie Robinson play for a Negro league team, the Kansas City Monarchs, things started to change. In 1947 the Dodgers signed Robinson, who broke down the color barrier and became the first African-American player in the major leagues. Since then, major league baseball has included players of many backgrounds, including Latinos, Asians, African-Americans, and white players.

**Definition Paragraphs:
Definition by Extended Example**

Topic sentence giving defined term and example to be extended ....
....

↓

Specific detail 1 ....
....
Specific detail 2 ....
....
Specific detail 3 ....
....
Specific detail 4 ....
....
Specific detail 5 ....
....

EXERCISE 3 ANALYZING A DEFINITION BY EXTENDED EXAMPLE

Reread "A Great Milestone" on page 349. Then, fill in the blanks below.

1. What is the formal definition of *milestone* in "A Great Milestone"?

A milestone is a significant or important event in history.

2. What example does the writer use throughout the paragraph to define the word *milestone?*

Jackie Robinson's inclusion in major league baseball

3. What historical situation prevented black players from playing major league baseball? Jim Crow laws

4. What method of organization—time sequence (chronological) order or emphatic order—does the writer use? Time sequence

Jackie Robinson

FOOD FOR THOUGHT Jackie Robinson's talent and strength of character helped him break through the color barrier to play professional baseball. What barriers in sports still exist? Write a few sentences explaining how some groups may or may not still be left out in the professional sports world.

5. Aside from *baseball,* what three other words does the writer repeat throughout the paragraph?

a. Negro   **b.** league   **c.** players

Choosing a Topic for Development

Choosing a good topic for a definition paragraph will largely depend on what kind of definition paragraph you're writing. Most commonly, your instructor will assign you a definition-by-class paragraph and give you a topic to develop. In general, terms that mean different things to different people are suitable for development in a definition-by-class paragraph.

Emotions:	love, hate, happiness, loneliness, fear, sadness, joy, excitement
Family:	mother, father, sister, brother, grandmother, uncle, family, home
Stereotypes:	know-it-all, bad boy, Goody Two-shoes, nerd, jock, bully

Notice that all these terms allow for a range of explanations. Even terms such as *mother* or *father*—terms that most people understand—let you write about *what aspects* of motherhood or fatherhood mean the most to you.

In preparing to write a definition paragraph, do some prewriting to see what ideas come to mind on your topic. One student, Devon, decided to freewrite for ten minutes on the topic "know-it-all."

My sister Paula is a know-it-all. No matter what people are talking about, Paula is in on the conversation. Last week my buddies and I were talking about cars, and even though Paula is only fourteen and has never driven <u>anything</u>, she had an opinion about how to fix up an old Camaro. Besides that, she comes up with theories that no one else believes but that she swears are fact. One time she told me that if I put soap on my toothbrush before brushing my teeth, I'd get fewer cavities. She swore she'd heard it from the dentist, but he told me it was totally false information. Oh! Paula also is <u>never</u> wrong, even when she is.

Devon has identified three possible ways to define the term *know-it-all:* such a person is in on every conversation, has wacky theories, and is never wrong.

Writing an Effective Topic Sentence

As with choosing a topic, writing an effective topic sentence depends on the type of definition paragraph you're writing. When Devon analyzed the three points that surfaced in his freewriting, he realized that they all involved his sister claiming to know something that she didn't know. Thus, Devon's topic sentence was "A know-it-all is someone who claims to know things even if she doesn't know them."

If Devon were writing a definition-by-negative-example paragraph, his topic sentence might be "A know-it-all is not only someone who gets on your nerves but someone who claims to know things she doesn't know." For a paragraph using definition by extended example, Devon could use the same topic sentence that he used for his definition-by-class paragraph.

Developing Specific Details

The details you use will depend on the kind of definition paragraph you're writing. For instance, the paragraphs "An Ace" (page 346) and "Play Ball!" (page 353) are definitions by class. However, while the details in "An Ace" could all apply to a single type of player, the details in "Play Ball!" read more like a list of details than a single extended example. Whatever kind of details you use, draw from your own experiences, other people's experiences, and trusted sources as necessary in defining your term.

Organizing and Linking Your Ideas

Definition paragraphs can be organized in several ways. Generally, if your paragraph uses an extended example, time sequence (chronological) order—giving events in the order in which they happened—works well, since you'll be relating details of one occurrence. If you're writing a definition-by-class or definition-by-negative-example paragraph, your topic and examples will dictate the best order to use. For some paragraphs, emphatic order—from least to most important—might be most effective.

EXERCISE 4 **FOLLOWING THE FOUR Cs**

Read the paragraph below. Then, answer the questions that follow.

Play Ball!

Baseball is many experiences rolled into one. It is a day with your dad or your best friend under a blue sky. Baseball is the smell of hot dogs, popcorn, grass, and leather all mingled into one scent that surrounds you. It is the glory of seeing your team win the World Series, and it is the agony of watching as your favorite hitter strikes out with bases loaded. Baseball is having your own language, using expressions such as *RBI, K'd, double play, strike out, full count,* and *home run.* It is a feeling of pride, knowing that people like Jackie Robinson fought for racial equality while people like Lou Gehrig fought for their lives. Baseball is a feeling of history, knowing that the same number of games, the same number of players, and the same number of innings have been part of the game since the beginning. It is also a feeling of camaraderie as the faces of baseball become increasingly diverse: Japanese, Dominican, Cuban, and American. Baseball is the feeling of rage when the umpire calls a ball on what you knew was a strike, and it is jubilation when your team's shortstop makes an impossible catch to get your pitcher out of the inning. Baseball is sometimes confusion, when the announcer talks about a "six-to-four-to-three" double play and you're not sure what that means. Above all else, though, baseball is the sport that Americans claim as their own.

Concise Writing

1. What is the topic sentence for "Play Ball!"? _____

    Baseball is many experiences rolled into one.
    _____

2. What single idea do all of the examples in the paragraph relate to?

    Baseball
    _____

Credible Writing

3. Give three examples the writer uses to illustrate her topic sentence.
    Answers will vary.

   a. _____

b. _____

c. _____

4. List one example from the paragraph that you find particularly

interesting or effective. <u>Answers will vary.</u>_____

Clear Writing

5. How many times does the writer use the word *baseball* in this
paragraph? ___8___

6. What pronoun does the writer uses in place of *baseball?* ___It___

What You Know Now

Definition paragraphs develop the meaning of a word or expression. Definition-by-class paragraphs offer a one-sentence definition as the topic sentence and many examples to illustrate the concept. A definition by negative
example provides an example or examples of what the term is *not,* while a
definition by extended example uses a single example throughout the paragraph. Your topic sentence, examples, and organization will vary depending on the type of definition paragraph you write.

WRITING PRACTICE 1 Write a Definition Paragraph

Now write a definition paragraph of your own.

Prewriting

1. Choose a topic. Below is a list of topics for paragraphs that allow
you to use definition to develop your ideas. This list contains labels,
many of which are slang terms, for people with certain characteristics.
Read the list and think about the people you know who fit one of
these labels. Feel free to choose a term not on the list.

Topics

bookworm	sports fan	salesman
workaholic	procrastinator	hypochondriac

2. Freewrite for five to ten minutes on your topic. Below is an example of freewriting by a student, Brian, on the term *hypochondriac*. Brian has been assigned a definition-by-class paragraph.

> A hypochondriac is a person who thinks he's sick all the time. It's someone who's always looking for the smallest symptom of sickness and is actually disappointed if he doesn't find it. True hypochondriacs are excited to go to the doctor and seem sad if they're found to be totally healthy. Hypochondriacs seem to think that being ill makes them more interesting, which I think is bogus.

In writing a definition paragraph, the prewriting technique of questioning can be helpful. Look at the following question-and-answer list for the term *hypochondriac*.

Question	Answer
What is the formal definition of *hypochondriac?*	Extreme depression often centered on imaginary physical ailments
What is the general category for *hypochondriac?*	Person
What are some ways to recognize a hypochondriac?	Always has appointments with doctors; always brings up latest illness; subscribes to health-related magazines; takes herbal remedies

Drafting

3. Write your topic sentence. Your topic sentence should include a definition of your term, but this definition will vary depending on the kind of definition paragraph you're writing. Since Brian's paragraph is a definition-by-class assignment, his topic sentence places the term *hypochondriac* in a general category. Here's his topic sentence: "Hypochondriacs are people who think they are sick all the time."

4. Choose support points—if necessary—and specific details to develop your definition. If you want to use several short examples, do more freewriting to come up with them. If you want to use a single extended example, consider making a list or an outline to keep the points of your extended example in order.

5. Organize your ideas using emphatic order or time sequence (chronological) order. Keep in mind that time sequence order works very well for an extended-example paragraph.

6. Write your draft. Check to make sure your organization is consistent throughout your paragraph. Make sure all the details define your term. If any details do not, remove them.

Revision

7. Check your paragraph for the first three of the four Cs: *concise, credible,* and *clear* writing. Make any necessary changes to your draft.

Editing

8. Check your paragraph for the fourth C, *correct* writing. Proofread your paragraph to make sure you have used correct spelling, punctuation, and grammar.

WRITING PRACTICE 2 **Define an Emotion or a Quality**

Write a paragraph defining one of the terms below. If you need help getting started, follow the steps you used in Writing Practice 1 on pages 354–356.

kindness	sensitivity	strength	fear
power	confidence	anger	sorrow

WRITING PRACTICE 3 **Define Family**

Over the past ten years, the definition of the word *family* has caused politicians and religious leaders to debate each other and themselves, seeking to find one meaning for the term that everyone can agree on. Choose Topic A or Topic B and write a definition paragraph.

Topic A

In politics today, many leaders propose laws and bills that affect families. However, with changes in people's lifestyles, the definition of *family* has become unclear in many cases. *Write a paragraph defining the term* <u>family.</u> Use several examples to define your term, as opposed to a single extended example, in order to make the meaning of *family* clear.

Topic B

Using the same background information as in Topic A, *write a paragraph defining the term* <u>family</u> *but using a single extended definition.* You may use an example from your own family or friends, or you may use an example from television or the movies to illustrate your ideas.

Lab Activity 24

For additional practice with definition, complete Lab Activity 24 in the Lab Manual at the back of the book.

2.5 Arguing a Position

CULTURE NOTE • *Civility*

Civility is politeness; it means acting in ways that show consideration for others. Most of us know that it's courteous to say "please" and "thank you," and many of us are aware that in American culture, handshakes and eye contact are signs of respect. Many other areas of civility, however, such as cell phone etiquette, are still unclear.

What Is an Argument Paragraph?

The term *argument* usually implies something unpleasant: a combative discussion in which two people are tense and upset or a situation in which a group of people are yelling back and forth without listening to each other. For writers, however, to **argue** a position is simply to give reasons to back up your point of view. An **argument** is an exchange of ideas in which two sides attempt to persuade each other. The following sentences represent different sides of an argument. Each sentence also could be a topic sentence for a paragraph with support points and details.

Drunk driving penalties are unreasonably tough.

Drunk driving penalties need to be tougher.

The key to writing an argument paragraph is understanding that people do not necessarily start out agreeing with your point of view. Your job as a writer is to present enough information and explanation to persuade your reader of your main point. The illustration "Argument Paragraphs" on the next page gives you an idea of how to write this type of paragraph.

Argument Paragraphs
Topic sentence stating the argument ....
↓
Support point 1 ....Details from experience or ....facts from trusted sources................. Support point 2 ....Details from experience or ....facts from trusted sources................. Support point 3 ....Details from experience or ....facts from trusted sources................. Support point 4 ....Details from experience or ....facts from trusted sources.................

Real-Life Writing

Argument is relevant in many aspects of daily living. Read the examples below to see how argument skills are especially helpful in real-life situations.

For College

- Write a persuasive paper for a composition, rhetoric, or speech course.
- Write a letter to an instructor to persuade her that you deserve a higher grade.

In Your Personal Life

- Write an e-mail to a friend to dissuade him from making a poor choice.
- Write a letter to the city council, arguing that you need a stop sign on your corner.

At Work

- Write a memo to your boss to convince her to carry a new product. Offer factual reasons for its superiority.
- Write a memo to your boss to convince him to give you a raise. Clearly state your reasons for deserving it and your evidence for those claims.

A Model Paragraph: Argument

Read the following paragraph to see how offering support points and examples makes an argument.

No Need for Manners

[1]Manners are more trouble than they're worth. [2]Ever since I was a little girl, my mom has tried to teach me that manners are important. [3]I've said "please" and "thank you," I've written thank-you notes until doomsday, and I've stood up when people my parents' age enter the room. [4]No good has come from all my efforts. [5]First, manners are phony. [6]Last year I wrote thank-you notes to all of my friends when they gave me a surprise birthday party. [7]It took me hours to think of different ways to say thank you, and I used a lot of paper. [8]When my friends read my notes, they asked me if I was trying to be high-class. [9]They said they knew I wrote them only because I "had to." [10]My friends and I know each other well enough to tell whether we like each other's gifts; writing notes just puts pressure on the rest of us to do something we don't believe in. [11]Second, manners cause confusion. [12]My mom always taught me to be polite to people even if I didn't like them. [13]However, more than one boy has told me I've sent the wrong message to him because I was nice when I really wasn't interested. [14]If only I'd been honest and told the guys that I didn't want to go out with them, I'd have saved them—and myself—a lot of trouble. [15]Most important, manners are tricky. [16]My mother taught me never to eat with my hands, but using a fork, knife, and spoon isn't normal everywhere. [17]My friend Prassana is from Sri Lanka, and at dinner people in his family take food from a large bowl in the center of the table and eat it with their hands. [18]The first time I ate with Prassana's family, I asked for a fork. [19]I thought I was using good manners, but I felt so uncomfortable being the only one with silverware that I decided to eat with my hands, too. [20]Then I felt uncomfortable because I knew my mother would disapprove. [21]I couldn't win! [22]All in all, I think that if people just treat one another as adults, there's no need for manners.

EXERCISE 1 ANALYZING AN ARGUMENT PARAGRAPH

Reread "No Need for Manners" above. Then, answer the questions below.

1. What argument (or point) is the writer making?

Manners are more trouble than they're worth.

Fender Bender

CRITICAL THINKING According to civility expert P.M. Forni, anonymity—or feeling that no one knows who we are—contributes to incivility on the road. To what extent is this true? Write a few sentences explaining whether or not people are more likely to be rude if they don't know the people they're being rude to, or if they're unlikely to be caught.

2. In which sentence is the argument stated? _1 (topic sentence)_____

3. What three reasons does the writer give to support her topic sentence?

   a. _Manners are phony._____

   b. _Manners cause confusion._____

   c. _Manners are tricky._____

4. List three examples the writer gives to illustrate her support points.

   a. _Thank-you notes example_____

   b. _Confusing messages to boys_____

   c. _Custom of eating with hands in Sri Lanka_____

5. What three transitions does the writer use to signal the start of each support point?

Sentence 5: First

Sentence 11: Second

Sentence 15: Most important

6. How does the writer organize her ideas, in time sequence (chronological) order or emphatic order? Emphatic order

Choosing a Good Topic for Development

For the most part, arguments don't occur over topics that people agree on. If people are of one mind about an issue, there isn't much to say about it. Thus, in choosing a topic, follow these guidelines.

- Choose a topic you believe in.
- Choose a topic that has two sides.
- Choose a topic you know something about.

Choosing a Topic You Believe In

It's possible to write good paragraphs about issues you don't support, but it's much easier to write about topics that you believe in. Think about what's going on in your life right now—work, school, family responsibilities, relationships—and choose a topic that is relevant to your life. For instance, Guillermo was frustrated that his college provided so few student parking spots and that the spaces available were often dangerous after dark. Guillermo did some freewriting to see if he could write an argument in favor of expanding the student parking lot at his school.

I can't believe my stereo got stolen out of my car again! It's not right that I have to park off campus where there is no security and no lighting, and I bought a parking pass. If I buy a pass, I should be able to park on campus, but I can never find a spot even if I'm thirty minutes early to class. Also, there's room to park in the empty lot right next to the student parking area. The college president has been saying for two years that the lot is going to be paved over and made into *faculty parking spots, but I don't see my instructors parking off campus. Students should be able to use that lot for parking.*

Guillermo was happy to see that his frustrations could work as support points for an argument, so he decided to develop his topic further.

Writing an Effective Topic Sentence

In his freewriting, Guillermo identified these points for development.

Point 1:   Students who buy parking passes should get to park on campus.

Point 2:   Parking off campus is unsafe.

Point 3:   There's room to park on campus.

At first, Guillermo thought that each point should be developed into a paragraph of its own, but then he realized that a solid topic sentence could tie them all together. He wrote this topic sentence: "Hopkins College needs more on-campus student parking spaces." Guillermo can use his three points from freewriting as support points in his paragraph, adding details to develop his ideas.

Developing Specific Details

Just by making and supporting a point in other kinds of paragraphs, you've been sharpening your argument skills. Two additional techniques can help you make your argument paragraph even more effective.

- Making your side stronger
- Making the other side weaker

Making Your Side Stronger

You already know that once you find support points to back up your topic sentence, you need to use specific details to illustrate them. Specific details fall under the three categories listed below.

- Descriptions of objects or events in your life

- Accounts of events in other people's lives
- Facts that you've heard or read about from trusted sources

(For more information on types of specific details, see Chapter 10.)

Consulting Experts An **expert** is someone who has special skills or knowledge in a certain field. Organizations such as the American Medical Association and the Better Business Bureau, and the people who work there, are expert sources in their fields. Consulting and quoting experts can make your argument stronger. There are ways to get expert opinions even when you can't talk face-to-face with an authority.

- Read articles written by experts.
- Read articles that quote experts.
- Watch television interviews with experts.
- Listen to radio interviews with experts.

Seeing, hearing, or reading about experts' ideas can help you make your side of an argument stronger. For instance, since Guillermo is trying to convince his reader that Hopkins College needs more on-campus parking spaces, consulting the campus police reports helps him make his point.

Topic sentence:	Hopkins College needs more on-campus parking spaces.
Expert support:	According to Hopkins College campus police reports, 45 percent of students who park off campus suffer from some crime to themselves or their cars.

Reading Up on Your Subject Reading about your topic is a great way to expand your knowledge and make your argument stronger. Newspapers and magazines often carry general information on subjects of public interest. Books, although possibly useful, may contain more information than you need for a single paragraph.

Topic sentence:	Writing thank-you notes is important.
Expert support:	In her newspaper column *Miss Manners*, the etiquette expert Judith Martin writes that there is no excuse for failing to write a thank-you note.

Surfing the Net Credible Web sites, such as those operated by schools and respected organizations, can give you information to use in your argument. Online databases provide a huge amount of reliable information as well. With so many places to find information, however, you need to judge which sources are really helpful. For instance, if you wanted to know the health risks associated with smoking, you probably wouldn't want to read a report sponsored by a tobacco company. Make sure that the sources you use are ones you can trust. Talk to your school librarian about distinguishing reliable sources from unreliable ones.

If you're writing to convince a reader that smoking is unhealthy, for example, consulting the American Lung Association's Web site can help you make your point.

Topic sentence:	Smoking is harmful to your health.
Expert support:	According to the American Lung Association's Web site, smoking not only causes lung disease but also weakens your immune system.

Making the Opposing Side Weaker

As you've seen, every argument has an opposing one. To strengthen your own argument, you must understand the opposing one. That way, you can target the gaps in its information or logic.

Finding Incorrect Information in the Opposing Argument

One of Pamela's friends told her she should exercise every day, without taking a day off. Pamela researched the issue and learned that people should *not* exercise strenuously every day, and that the human body needs rest after a hard workout. Pamela's findings are easy to see in the list she wrote.

Other Side	My Side	Expert Opinion
Exercise daily.	You need some rest days.	The body needs rest days.
Only strenuous exercise promotes fitness.	Many kinds of exercise promote fitness.	Varying strenuous exercise with less strenuous exercise is best.

Looking for Unsupported Claims in the Opposing Argument

Even if an argument sounds logical or true, make sure the claims can be verified. For instance, if a friend says that a herbal remedy for a particular illness works because "everyone says so," you should ask who "everyone" is. Chances are, the number of supporters for the remedy is fewer than your friend claims.

Organizing and Linking Your Ideas

Once you have come up with a topic, written a topic sentence and support points, and supported those points with details, you're ready to organize your ideas. Using emphatic order—giving points from least to most important—works particularly well for argument paragraphs, since it lets you save your best argument for last.

Remember that Guillermo identified three support points (page 362).

- Students who buy parking passes should get to park on campus.
- Parking off campus is unsafe.
- There's room to park on campus.

Even though "Parking off campus is unsafe" was Guillermo's second point in his freewriting, he decided that it was the most important reason for needing more on-campus parking. Thus, he placed it last. Guillermo's final paragraph, with transitions in bold type, is below.

The Right to Park

Hopkins College needs more on-campus parking spaces. **First of all,** students pay for a parking permit. After spending $24 each semester, students should be able to find an on-campus parking space, even if it's way out by the stadium. If the college chooses to accept students' money for parking spaces, it should provide parking. **Second,** the college has additional, unused room for more parking spaces. According to the college facilities manager, Bob Reardon, the empty lot next to the main student parking lot is not being used. Even though the school president has been saying for two years that more faculty parking is going to be built on the empty lot, Mr. Reardon claims that he has heard nothing of this. Since I have never seen any of my instructors driving around off campus trying to find parking spaces, I assume that faculty already have sufficient parking. **Most important,** parking anywhere but on campus is unsafe. According to Hopkins College campus police reports, 45 percent of students who park off campus suffer from some crime to themselves or their cars. If almost half the students who park off campus are victims of crime, something needs to be done. Adding more parking spaces for students seems a logical solution.

Guillermo uses emphatic order to organize his ideas, using the transitions *first of all, second,* and *most important* to let his reader know which points are most significant.

EXERCISE 2 FOLLOWING THE FOUR Cs

Read the paragraph below. Then answer the questions that follow.

Benefits of Polite Behavior

[1]Treating people with respect has many benefits. [2]First, being polite can create employment opportunities. [3]Two years ago I worked as a receptionist at a doctor's office. [4]Because the office manager stressed being helpful and kind to the patients, I was polite to everyone. [5]One patient, Ms. Simmons, was always difficult. [6]She never remembered my name and always showed up late for her appointments. [7]It took quite an effort to be polite to her. [8]However, six months ago, I applied for a job at a large office with many doctors. [9]The big surprise was that Ms. Simmons worked there, and she was doing the hiring! [10]She told me in the interview that she remembered me and was always impressed with how courteous I was to everyone. [11]A second example of how manners can have benefits is in personal relationships. [12]According to the nationally known marriage counselors Judith Wallerstein and Sandra Blakeslee, married people who treat each other with respect often have a healthy relationship. [13]The marriage counselors claim that if people listen to each other and try to be considerate, everyone is happier. [14]Another area where being polite pays off is in business. [15]Sean Nguyen, a business owner in Minneapolis, Minnesota, claims that making his employees comfortable leads to a happier, better work force. [16]He pays them good wages, gives them health benefits, and has a policy of rewarding courteous and helpful behavior. [17]According to an article in *Money* magazine, his company became a multimillion-dollar company because of how hard its employees worked. [18]One last important area where manners can have benefits is at home. [19]To save money, my friend Jason lives with three other people in a small apartment. [20]They all go to school and have jobs, so they're often tired. [21]Because they want to get along, they have some unspoken rules. [22]No one drinks the last of the milk unless he can replace it, and no one plays loud music if someone else wants to sleep or study. [23]Even though the apartment still feels crowded, the roommates get along because they treat each other with respect. [24]Manners make life better in so many ways.

Concise Writing

1. What is the writer's argument? _Treating people with respect has_

many benefits.

2. What four areas does the writer identify for support?

   a. _Employment opportunities_

   b. _Personal relationships_

   c. _Business_

   d. _Home_

Credible Writing

3. Each sentence listed below marks the beginning of an example in "Benefits of Polite Behavior." Write down the four examples the writer offers to illustrate each area of support as well as the *type* of examples used (personal experience, friend's experience, reputable source, or expert opinion).

Example	**Type of Example**
Sentence 3: _New job_	_Personal experience_
Sentence 12: _Marriage_	_Expert opinion_
Sentence 15: _Business_	_Article in reputable magazine_
Sentence 19: _Roommate situation_	_Friend's experience_

Clear Writing

4. What transitions signal the beginning of new support points?

Sentence 2: _First_

Sentence 11: _second_

Sentence 14: _Another_

Sentence 18: _One last important area_

5. a. What organizational strategy—time sequence (chronological order or emphatic order—does the writer use? <u>Emphatic order</u>

b. Which point does the writer consider the most important?

<u>Benefits in the home</u>

c. How can you tell? <u>Use of "One last important area"</u>

Correct Writing

The sentences in this paragraph are all correct. To check for correctness in your own writing, go to Part 7, "Writing Correct Sentences."

What You Know Now

Writing an argument involves choosing a topic that you know something about and feel strongly about. Support for your argument can come from your own experiences, other people's experiences, trusted sources, and the Internet. Be careful, however, to avoid unreliable sources. You can develop your argument by making your side stronger or by making the opposing side weaker. Using emphatic order works well for argument paragraphs.

WRITING PRACTICE 1 Provide Support for Arguments

Each of the following sentences makes an argument. For each argument, write one well-developed sentence, backed up by a specific detail.
Answers will vary.

Argument: Health care insurance should be provided for everyone.

Support: <u>Not being able to afford health care isn't necessarily anyone's fault.</u>

<u>For instance, my neighbors have a little girl, Peggy, who has a rare illness. Peggy's medications are so expensive that my neighbors have hit the limit of their insurance coverage. They need help.</u>

1. Argument: Penalties for parking tickets should be stronger.

Support:_____

_____

2. Argument: Any professional athlete who breaks the law should be banned from the sport.

Support:_____

_____

3. Argument: Honesty is the best policy.

Support:_____

_____

4. Argument: Honesty is *not* the best policy.

Support:_____

_____

5. Argument: Attendance should count toward college students' grades.

Support:_____

_____

WRITING PRACTICE 2   Write an Argument Paragraph

Now write your own argument paragraph.

Prewriting

1. Choose a topic for development. Here is a list of possible topics for argument paragraphs.

Topics

Age as a factor in setting car insurance rates

Diamond rings as engagement gifts

Lighter sentences for criminals who have been abused by their parents

Prosecuting nursing home workers who abuse elderly residents

Allowing condom machines on campus

Automatically passing students with perfect attendance

Requiring military service for all eighteen-year-olds

Gay marriage

Affirmative action in college admissions

2. Freewrite on your topic for five to ten minutes. Outlining can be effective because it helps you keep track of both your supporting reasons and your specific details.

Below is a sample outline based on one of the topics from the list above, "diamond rings as engagement gifts."

Diamond rings as engagement gifts

    A. Couples just starting out need to save money.
        1. Expenses of getting married
        2. Expenses of moving into a home
        3. Expenses of starting a family, if they choose to

    B. Couples need to save time.
        1. Busy with wedding plans
        2. Ring shopping takes time
        3. Ordering and sizing ring takes time

    C. Diamonds put emphasis on things, not the relationship.
        1. Expensive ring may raise false expectations about lifestyle.
        2. Ring might put focus on wedding and money instead of love.

Drafting

3. Write a topic sentence. A possible topic sentence for the topic "diamond rings as engagement gifts" would be "Diamond rings can be a poor choice as engagement gifts."

4. Choose your support points and specific details. For this step, you may need to learn more about your topic. Notice that the outline in Step 2 above has many reasons that support the topic sentence, but it lacks specific details. In writing an argument paragraph, you may sometimes find details more easily after you've outlined your general points. Make sure all the details in your draft come from trusted sources. (See pages 83–84 for more on reliability of sources.)

5. Organize your points in a logical order, remembering that emphatic order works well for argument paragraphs. Add transitions that connect your ideas.

6. Now write your draft. Do your best, but don't worry if it's not perfect the first time around.

Revising

7. Check your paragraph for the first three of the four Cs: *concise, credible,* and *clear* writing. Make any necessary changes to your draft.

Editing

8. Check your paragraph for the fourth C: *correct* writing. Proofread your paragraph to make sure you have used correct spelling, punctuation, and grammar.

WRITING PRACTICE 3   Write to Effect Change

Having sharp argument skills can be a great benefit in life. Choose Topic A or Topic B below, and write an argument paragraph.

Topic A

Your neighbor has two dogs that bark loudly. Because the dogs sleep outside, they frequently keep you awake at night or wake you up early. You do not want to antagonize your neighbor, but you want her dogs to stop barking. *Write a paragraph persuading your neighbor to solve the barking-dog problem.* You might suggest that the neighbor train the dogs, let the dogs sleep inside, buy the dogs antibarking collars, get the dogs debarked through an operation, or move away from you. If you do not know how expensive or time-consuming one of the suggestions is, do some research to learn more about your topic. Keep in mind that your goal is to live without having to put up with the dogs' barking at inconvenient hours. A Web page that might prove helpful in learning about your topic is at http://www.sfspca.org/behavior/dog_library/barking.pdf.

Topic B

Because of all the crime stories broadcast on the news and written about in the newspaper daily, you want to organize a neighborhood watch program to protect your street from burglary and other crime. This program entails having all the neighbors on your street agree to post "Crime Watch" posters, exchange phone numbers, and look out for each other's property. *Write a letter to your neighbors convincing them to participate in a neighborhood watch program.* You may argue the benefits of participating in such a program, or you may argue the dangers of not having such a program in your neighborhood. Either way, learn about neighborhood watch programs in order to make your writing more convincing. Some possible places to find information are your local police department, neighborhoods with programs already in place, local community centers, and local schools. Your goal is to encourage as many of your neighbors as possible to join a program with you. A Web site that might prove helpful in learning about your topic is at http://www.ncpc.org/.

Lab Activity 25

For additional practice with argument, turn to Lab Activity 25 in the Lab Manual at the back of the book.

PART FIVE
Writing Essays

CHAPTER 26
The Essay and the Thesis Statement   375

CHAPTER 27
Prewriting for and Drafting Your Essay   399

CHAPTER 28
Revising and Editing Your Essay   417

26 The Essay and the Thesis Statement

CULTURE NOTE *Everyday Technology*

Though people claim to be frustrated with their computers and other people's cell phones, certain devices have made our lives much easier. From making immediate communication possible to storing our work—without paper, staples, or filing cabinets—technology smooths the edges of everyday work.

What Is an Essay?

Good news! Writing an effective essay involves the same skills that you've already practiced by writing effective paragraphs. In fact, you should make a point to keep using the same skills that you've been practicing throughout this text. Just as a paragraph is a group of sentences that work together to communicate an idea, an **essay** is a group of *paragraphs* working together to communicate an idea. An essay's purpose can be to persuade, to inform, or to entertain, and an essay's audience, at least when you're a student, will usually be your instructor.

Paragraphs and essays differ, however, in length and development. Whereas a paragraph might include only one or two specific details to support each point, an essay can devote a whole paragraph to developing a single support point. And where paragraphs can usually get by with a transition word to make connections clear, essays often use entire sentences to help keep the reader on track. While both paragraphs and essays concentrate on making a point, essays can contain many more subpoints, all of which need development. Finally, while a paragraph contains a topic sentence, an essay uses a **thesis statement** to give the essay's main idea, state the writer's purpose and point of view, and tell the reader what to expect.

Five-Paragraph Essays

Introduction
Opening: Gets reader's attention.
Thesis statement: Gives the writer's main idea, point of view, and purpose; tells the reader what to expect.

↓

Body Paragraphs
Body paragraph 1
Topic sentence
 Specific details

Body paragraph 2
Topic sentence
 Specific details

Body paragraph 3
Topic sentence
 Specific details

↓

Conclusion
Final thoughts: Adds something new that is closely related to the essay's main idea.
Summary: Repeats briefly the main idea and support points.

Essay Form

The five-paragraph essay is the most basic form. The "Five-Paragraph Essays" diagram above gives a visual representation of the essay. Notice how the body paragraphs follow the same format while the first and last paragraphs (the introduction and conclusion) are different.

A Model Essay

Read the following essay, paying attention to the way the writer, Andy, develops his body paragraphs. The thesis statement is in bold print, and the topic sentence for each body paragraph is in italics.

Helpful Technology

Introduction

    Almost every day, someone gripes about technology. My roommate, for instance, loves to complain about his computer, while my dad is constantly calling me with tension-filled questions about his VCR. If I hadn't had so many good experiences with modern technology, I might think that using anything invented after 1950 was a waste of time. **However, in my experience, cellular telephones, computers, and VCRs can make life much more pleasant.**

Body
paragraph 1

    First on my list of devices that improve my life come cell phones. In fact, cell phones saved my day yesterday. I overslept because we had a huge rainstorm that knocked out the power and kept my alarm from working. Our phone is a cordless model, so when the power went out, the phone did, too. However, I had recently charged my cell phone, and it worked even with the power off. I was able to call my boss and tell her that I'd be late because of the storm. She told me that so many people hadn't called in—and hadn't shown up—that she really appreciated my call. Once I was safely at work, my car was hit by a huge branch that had fallen as a result of the storm. My windshield was broken, and I couldn't get the branch off my car. Again my cell phone saved the day. I called my brother-in-law, who has a big truck. He came over, helped get the branch off, and towed my car to a garage. He also gave me a ride home. Since the storm was still going on, my car would have been in even worse shape if I'd had to leave it outside in all that rain. Finally, my cell phone kept me out of trouble with my girlfriend. Since I had to have my car towed, I was late for a date with her. However, I called her as I was riding with my brother-in-law, and I explained what happened. She was so relieved to hear from me that she wasn't even angry. Cell phones certainly saved the day!

Body
paragraph 2

    In addition to cell phones, computers are a constant source of assistance in my life. As a full-time student who works twenty-five hours a week, I have a lot of details to keep organized. Having a computer helps me keep my life in order. Just last week I had an essay due for my history class. I had printed the essay and was ready to hand it in, but my roommate got overly enthusiastic in his cleaning. He threw out my paper! If I hadn't saved my essay on the computer, all that work would have been for nothing. Additionally, I keep my calendar on my computer. Every Sunday night, I add everything I need to do that week and then print out that week's page. I carry my calendar with me wherever I go and add notes to it, which I put on my computer version each night. That way, I have saved records of what I've done, so if my boss needs to know how many hours I worked, I have my own version. I know I could carry around a little calendar booklet, but I like the professional way the computer-printed calendar looks. I'm not sure how I'd get along without my computer.

Body paragraph 3

Last but not least in making my life better is my VCR. Since I have to study and work so much, I don't get many chances to watch television. Especially when it's football season, I feel cheated if I can't root for the Buccaneers. The VCR keeps me from feeling that my life is all work and no play. My roommate helps me by taping the games I miss, so when I'm done with my homework—even if it's one in the morning!—I can sit down and watch my favorite team. Best of all, I can fast-forward through the commercials and the halftime reports, so I can watch a whole game in far less time than if I were watching it live. When it's not football season, I love to keep movies on hand so that I can unwind after a hard day. As a result of getting a little football or video reward, I'm more motivated to work hard the next day. My VCR is one source of entertainment that makes my life much better.

Conclusion

I suppose that if my cell phone, computer, and VCR ever break down, I'll be unhappy with them and maybe even throw them out the window as I've seen people on TV do. And since they seem to meet my current needs very well, I probably won't go out and buy any more soon. For now, I'm very happy with the comforts of modern technology, and I plan to use these three devices for a long time.

Writing an Effective Thesis Statement

The thesis statement is the most important part of an essay because it determines how you organize your ideas, what kind of specific details you use, and what kind of transitions you use. A thesis statement has the following characteristics.

- It usually comes in the first paragraph—the introduction—of an essay.
- It contains a narrowed topic and gives the writer's point of view on the topic.
- It must be at least one complete sentence, although it may be more than one sentence.
- It states the writer's purpose.
- It controls the direction of the essay.

See the Checklist for Writing a Thesis Statement below.

✔CHECKLIST Writing a Thesis Statement

- Does my thesis statement give the main idea of my essay?
- Does my thesis statement give my point of view?
- Does my thesis statement state my purpose?
- Does my thesis statement tell the reader what to expect?
- Is my thesis statement arguable?
- Is my thesis statement at least one complete sentence?

Don't feel compelled to write a perfect thesis statement immediately. Use prewriting activities, both for your essay and for your thesis statement, and see what ideas seem strongest. Chances are that you will want to explore the ideas that emerge as the strongest in your freewriting, outlining, or clustering. For example, the topic "drunk driving" could suggest several ideas: the damage it causes, the cost to taxpayers, and the danger to the driver, him- or herself.

Making Sure Your Thesis
Is a Complete Sentence

After you've come up with an idea that interests you, make sure to state it in a complete sentence. A thesis statement such as "Drunk driving penalties should be stiffer" gives you not only something to argue but also different ways to develop your ideas. Thesis statements can be more than one sentence, but for the essays you'll write using this text, it's a good idea to write thesis statements of a single sentence. Later, as you write longer, more complex essays, your thesis statement can take different forms. The examples below show how phrases fail to communicate the complete idea that you need from a thesis statement.

Not a sentence:	The need for longer school breaks
Sentence:	Full-time students need longer school breaks to perform their best.

Writing "The need for longer school breaks" will leave your reader wondering why you want to write about school breaks and what your position is on the subject. Instead, if you write "Full-time students need longer school breaks to perform their best," readers might disagree with you, but at least they will be clear as to what you're arguing.

Avoid starting your essay with comments such as "The purpose of this essay is to show that . . . " or "This essay will show the differences between. . . . " Introductory phrases such as these don't provide any essential information about your topic. A clear thesis statement will tell your readers all they need to know about what's to come in your essay.

Avoid:	In this essay, I will discuss how studying hard in college pays off.
Good:	Studying hard in college pays off.

The writer simply eliminated the "announcement" to end up with an effective thesis statement.

Making Sure Your Thesis Statement Is Broad Enough

The first thesis statement below would be hard to develop because it simply gives a fact. Restated, it is broad enough for an essay.

Not broad enough:	Top-of-the-line cell phones are expensive.
Broad enough:	Cell phones are not worth the money people pay for them.

If a thesis statement begins with "I think," the reader has a tough time arguing with *anything* the writer says.

Not broad enough:	I think that taxes are too high.

| Broad enough: | Payroll taxes are too high for people who earn minimum wage. |

People can believe or think whatever they choose. No one could reasonably argue that you *don't* think taxes are too high. Thus, avoid expressions such as *I think, In my opinion,* or *I believe* because these statements throw the focus of your writing onto *your* thoughts instead of the issue under discussion.

Making Sure Your Thesis Statement Is Narrow Enough

After you've crafted a thesis statement that can lead you in multiple directions, you face a new task: you must narrow your thesis statement to make it manageable. One way to narrow your thesis statement is to include a point-of-view phrase or clause, the way you use point-of-view words in a topic sentence. This lets your reader know the scope of your argument.

For instance, Andy, the writer of the technology essay on pages 377–378, began with a thesis statement that was too broad.

First try:	Modern technology is good.
Second try:	Cell phones, computers, and VCRs are helpful.
Third try:	In my experience, cellular telephones, computers, and VCRs can make life much more pleasant.

In Andy's first try, the terms "modern technology" and "good" led him in too many directions for his writing. His second try limits his topic to three specific devices and narrows "good" to the positive quality of "helpful." In his third try, Andy specifies that the three devices "can make life much more pleasant," and he adds the phrase "In my experience" to link his thesis to the rest of his introduction.

Making Sure Your Thesis Statement Is Arguable

Just as you take care to narrow the scope of your thesis, be sure that your thesis can be argued, that it is a topic people can have different opinions about. Having a definite opinion gives you momentum for writing a persuasive essay, and it lets your reader know where you stand. The following thesis statement is unclear; does the writer want tougher drunk driving laws or not?

Not arguable: We need tougher drunk driving laws, but we need to make sure they're not *that* tough.

Recognizing a problem with his thesis, the writer revised it to say that the laws need to be even tougher than they already are.

Better: Even though drunk driving laws are tough, we need them to be tougher.

Sometimes, as in an informative essay, your thesis statement may not appear to be arguable. For instance, the thesis statement "Coach Fowler's guidance taught me the value of hard work, teamwork, and perseverance" expresses an opinion based on the writer's experience. However, the writer's job is still to use details to illustrate the thesis, thus creating a convincing essay.

Making Sure You're Clear on the Purpose of Your Thesis Statement

Perhaps the most important part of your thesis statement is its purpose, the reason you're writing it, yet this is often unstated. Although your purpose can be to inform or entertain, most academic essays you write will be *persuasive;* they will try to convince your reader of your point of view. Your thesis statement needs to show that purpose.

Unclear purpose: I don't understand how movie stars can look the same year after year.

Here the writer's point is unclear. Is the writer arguing that movie stars look eternally young? Or is the writer critical of movie stars? The writer doesn't make a particular point, so the purpose of the thesis statement is unclear.

Better: Movie stars have to work too hard to stay young-looking.

Here the writer has a clear point: to convince readers that movie stars put in too much time and effort on their looks. Even if you disagree with the writer's claim, you know what the point of the essay is and that the writer cares about the topic.

Offering a "Map" of Your Essay

Some topics are easy to organize into general support points. For such topics, it is useful to mention your **map**—how you plan to organize your essay.

For instance, in his essay "Helpful Technology" on page 377–378, Andy mentions the three technological devices that he will discuss in his essay: cell phones, computers, and VCRs. Although his thesis statement would have been fine without this map, stating the specific items he'll discuss lets his readers know exactly what to expect. Additionally, a map gives him a plan to refer back to as he writes his essay.

EXERCISE 1 IDENTIFYING EFFECTIVE THESIS STATEMENTS

Read the sentence pairs below. Next, circle the letter of the sentence that is an effective thesis statement. Then, write a brief explanation of why the sentence you chose is the better thesis statement. An example is done for you.   Answers will vary.

a. My dog is a great pet for me.

b. Dogs make great pets.

The second sentence works better as a thesis statement because it gives the reader something to argue. It's hard to argue "Your dog is not a good pet for you" because the person making the claim will know the subject (her own dog) better than a reader.

1. **a.** Cooking is a helpful skill for students living on their own.

b. Cooking is good.

Sentence b is too broad. A reader will have a hard time arguing with it. Further, the statement is too innocuous; few people will argue "Cooking is *bad*."

2. a. In the next few pages, I will explain why joining the military is a good option for young adults.

b. Joining the military is a good option for young adults.

Sentence b avoids the announcement format that sentence a uses.

3. a. I am not sure why my job requires me to have a physical examination before starting work.

(b.) My job's physical examination requirement is a waste of time,
effort, and money.

Sentence b has a clear point—that physicals are a waste of time—and it

outlines the areas of development in the essay.

4. (a.) Tuition at my school is too high.

b. My school raised its tuition last semester.

Sentence b states a fact—that the school raised its tuition—and, thus, cannot

be developed into an essay or argued.

5. (a.) Living in a city is exciting for a single person.

b. I'm not sure why people can't enjoy living in a city.

Sentence b has no clear, arguable point or purpose. What is the writer

arguing? Why does the writer care about this topic?

Developing the Paragraphs in an Essay

Paragraphs can serve different functions. Some paragraphs grab your attention while others simply convey information. Still others condense or summarize the content of the whole essay. As you saw in the essay diagram on
page 376, an essay has three main types of paragraphs.

- Introductory paragraph   ■ Body paragraphs
- Concluding paragraph

Introductory Paragraph

Think about a time when you've given someone unexpected news. Did you just plunge in, or did you lead up to it in steps? An **introductory paragraph,** or **introduction,** provides background information and sets the tone for your essay. A good introduction has two components.

- An **opening** that catches the reader's attention.
- A **thesis statement,** which gives the main idea of the essay, states the writer's purpose and point of view, and tells the reader what to expect.

An introduction may also contain a **map** of your essay, a statement that shows your reader what your essay will cover or how it will be organized. In the thesis statement from his essay "Helpful Technology," Andy mentions the three areas he plans to develop—his map—at the end: "However, in my own experience, cellular telephones, computers, and VCRs can make life much more pleasant."

Writers can draw from a number of techniques to craft an effective opening.

Providing Background Information

One of the writer's most important jobs is making the essay relevant, or meaningful, to a reader. In the essay "Helpful Technology," Andy offers background details to prepare us for his discussion of technology: his roommate's frustration with his computer and his father's stress over using his VCR.

Andy's thesis, later in his introduction, makes the point that certain forms of technology can be helpful. In this case, he has prepared us for a discussion of technology by offering other people's attitudes toward it.

Using a Personal Anecdote

Telling a **personal anecdote,** a story from your personal experience, is another good way to catch your reader's attention.

> When I was a little girl, every room in our home felt cheerful and alive because of the living things my mother helped to grow. She had a gift for nurturing plants, and I vowed that my first home on my own would feel as cheerful as my childhood home had. Also, I wanted to show my mother that I had learned from her and that I, too, had a "green thumb" which would help me grow things. However, I was in for a horrible shock. **After making many mistakes, I learned that taking care of plants requires proper light, the right amount of water, and plant food.**

This writer begins her essay with a story that lets the reader know how she's connected to her topic. Explaining her mother's talent for gardening lets us see why the writer cares about gardening.

Beginning with a Quotation

Beginning your essay with a quotation is a good way to focus your reader's attention on a particular aspect of your topic.

> Gloria Steinem said, "A pedestal is as much a prison as any small, confined space." Arguing that women want to be taken seriously as equals, not simply dolled up to accessorize men, Steinem faced the challenge of being a young, attractive woman in a male-dominated world. However, she rose to this challenge admirably. **Because of her efforts, women now have many more options in their personal and professional lives.**

The quotation in this paragraph focuses the essay's topic (and the reader's attention) on women's roles. Arriving at the thesis statement (in bold print), the reader understands both the meaning of the quotation and the relationship between the quotation and the thesis statement.

Using Opposites

Using an example that contrasts with your thesis can be an effective and attention-grabbing way to begin your essay.

> "A friend is a present you give yourself." This quotation was printed on a pink coffee mug that my friend Pamela gave me in high school. At the time I received the mug, I was delighted with both the gift and my friendship. As time went on, however, I began to wish I could return the "gift." **Through Pamela's unkind put-downs, disloyal gossip, and unreliable behavior, I learned that not all friendships are positive.**

By opening with a quotation about friendship, the writer leads the reader to expect an essay on the virtues of the writer's friend Pamela. When the thesis statement (in bold print) switches perspective, the reader is intrigued by the contrast.

Asking Questions

Beginning your essay with a question forces the reader to think about responses.

> Have you ever thought about running away and joining the circus? Or have you thought that maybe your destiny in life is to

become famous? How do you find out the answers to these questions? And once you find out the answers, how do you decide
whether to act on them? **I learned in the eighth grade that running away to try to become famous is a hard way to live.**

The writer uses a number of questions to work his way to his thesis statement (in bold print), but the thesis statement itself is not a question.

EXERCISE 2 RECOGNIZING INTRODUCTION STRATEGIES

Read each of the following paragraphs, which use different introduction
strategies. Then, circle the letter that corresponds to the introduction
strategy used.

1.   "To thine own self be true." For as long as I can remember, my
father has told me this, explaining that if I'm not true to myself,
then I can't be true to anyone else, either. For years, I believed this
quotation, too. However, in my high school English class, my
teacher pointed out that Polonius—a crafty, sneaky character in
Shakespeare's *Hamlet*—said this. I figured that if someone who is
not entirely honest gives this advice, then it can't be all good. Since
then, I've changed my attitude. Though I try to be true to myself,
sometimes my ideas have to come second to other people's.

a. Background information   **b.** Personal anecdote

c. Quotation   **d.** Opposites

e. Questions   Students would also be correct to argue that this is a personal
anecdote or an opposite. Point out, however, that the
quotation at the start of the paragraph is a major element.

2.   I've often heard the saying "Nice guys finish last." For most of
my life, I've tried to be a good guy—being a team player in sports,
having a good attitude in school, respecting my girlfriends. You'd
think, from that saying, that I'd be a loser without any future or any
friends. Actually, being a nice guy has brought me rewards in my
athletic experiences, in my professional and academic experiences,
and in my personal life.

a. Background information   **b.** Personal anecdote

c. Quotation   **d.** Opposites

e. Questions   Students would also be correct to argue that this is a
personal anecdote. Point out, however, the "opposite"
nature of the opening sentence and the thesis statement.

3.   What inspires people to meet great challenges such as climbing
Mount Everest? What goes through the minds of the climbers as
they trudge, climb, and pull themselves through oxygen-poor air to
the summit? Are they trying to meet death head-on, or are they

simply bored with their lives? *Into Thin Air: A Personal Account of the Mount Everest Disaster,* by Jon Krakauer, reveals the challenges and consequences of climbing Mount Everest.

a. Background information   **b.** Personal anecdote

c. Quotation   **d.** Opposites

(**e.**) Questions

Body Paragraphs

The **body paragraphs** of an essay perform two main functions.

1. They make connections to the thesis statement.

2. They give support points and specific details that support the thesis statement.

Making Connections to the Thesis Statement

Each body paragraph must echo some part of the thesis statement. The easiest place to connect a body paragraph to the thesis is in the paragraph's topic sentence.

In his essay "Helpful Technology" on pages 377–378, Andy uses key terms from the thesis statement in each topic sentence to show the reader how the body paragraphs relate to the thesis statement.

Thesis statement:	However, in my experience, cellular telephones, computers, and VCRs can make life much more pleasant.
Topic sentence of first body paragraph:	First on my list of devices that improve my life come cell phones.

Giving Support Points and Specific Details That Support the Thesis Statement

All your evidence comes in the body paragraphs. In "Helpful Technology," Andy provides specific details to illustrate the benefits of modern technology. The topic sentence of each body paragraph, which gives its support point, echoes a section of the thesis statement, and each paragraph contains specific details that support the topic sentence of that paragraph.

In body paragraph 1 of the essay, Andy describes several instances in which using his cell phone saved him trouble.

Conclusion

A **concluding paragraph,** or **conclusion,** finishes your essay in one of these ways.

■ It ends with a question.   ■ It adds final thoughts.

Adding Final Thoughts

Though "Helpful Technology" could have ended with a summary, Andy chose instead to add a few final thoughts.

> I suppose that if my cell phone, computer, and VCR ever break down, I'll be unhappy with them and maybe even throw them out the window as I've seen people on TV do. And since they seem to meet my current needs very well, I probably won't go out and buy any more soon. For now, I'm very happy with the comforts of modern technology, and I plan to use these three devices for a long time.

This paragraph provides some new information about Andy's attitude toward modern technology. However, the information is closely related to the rest of the essay, so the reader stays on track.

Ending with a Question

Just as starting your essay with a question can be a great way to catch your reader's attention, ending with a question focuses your reader as well. Consider another version of the conclusion for "Helpful Technology."

> I rely on my cell phone, my computer, and my VCR every day. Without my cell phone, I would have trouble communicating in emergencies. Without my computer, my schoolwork and my job would not go as smoothly. And without my VCR, I would miss some of the

programs I enjoy. How could I enjoy my life as much if I didn't have all these helpful devices?

In this conclusion, Andy ends his essay by asking a question. But the reader already knows the "answer" because Andy has explained the benefits of these devices in his essay.

EXERCISE 3 WRITING A CONCLUSION

Read "A Gardener at Heart," below. This essay has no conclusion. Write a conclusion for the essay, using one of the development strategies outlined in this chapter. Answers will vary.

A Gardener at Heart

I grew up in an apartment, so whenever I'd see people mowing lawns or planting gardens on TV, it always looked like fun. Secretly, I wondered if I could be a good outdoor gardener. Last summer, I found out. I spent the summer with my grandparents, and they let me take care of their yard. I learned that even though gardening seems easy, it requires patience, consistency, and creativity.

My first lesson in yard work was a lesson in patience. I had always thought that I'd simply whip out a lawn mower, race up and down the yard a few times, and be done with it. I was so wrong. My grandfather showed me how to "edge" his front yard, pushing this spiky ball on the end of a stick along the border between the grass and the driveway. It was exhausting. Every time I'd seem to get going, I'd hit a big weed clump that would block the edging tool. I'd have to stop, pull the clump off the edger, and resume my work. Even though my grandparents' lawn is tiny, it took me an hour to do a satisfactory job.

My second lesson in lawn care—consistency—came in the area of spreading fertilizer. My grandfather explained that his lawn looked much nicer if he treated it with fertilizer every month during the growing season (spring and summer). He showed me how to pour fertilizer into the spreader and then walk up and down the lawn to distribute the fertilizer evenly. I did my best to walk in straight lines, up and down the grass, to make sure I didn't miss any spots. When I'd get hot, I'd take a break. Then I'd try to pick up where I'd left off. Unfortunately, I never remembered quite where that was, so I'd just start over at the beginning of the lawn. Within a week, I saw that being inconsistent had ruined my grandparents' yard. The place where I'd begun was "burned" dark brown from being overfertilized, while the other side of the lawn was the same weak green color it had always been. If I had spread the fertilizer in a consistent manner, the lawn wouldn't have looked so awful.

My only positive lesson in gardening—creativity—came when I decided to plant some flowers to surprise my grandmother. I had always thought that there were rules about what plants you could put in certain places. Well, the man at the garden store told me that as long as plants were planted in places where they could survive— with the right amount of light and water—then there was no rule against planting whatever I liked. I went crazy. My grandmother loves bright colors, so I planted bright red impatiens and yellow primroses in the shady places, orange pansies in the partial sun, and some wild-looking purple flowers (I never did learn their name) in the sun. I followed no rules, but I felt like an artist, adding splashes of color all over the place. Grandma loved the flowers.

Conclusion:

_____

_____

_____

_____

_____

The strategy I used in writing the conclusion to "A Gardener at Heart"

is <u>Answers will vary.</u>

What You Know Now

An essay differs from a paragraph in length and development. A crucial element to any essay is the thesis statement, the sentence that controls the direction of the essay. Having a clear, arguable thesis is important for good essay development.

Essays contain three main paragraph types: introductory paragraphs, body paragraphs, and concluding paragraphs. An effective introduction catches the reader's attention and leads into the thesis statement. Body paragraphs offer support points and specific details to support the thesis statement, and concluding paragraphs sum up or finish the writer's points.

WRITING PRACTICE 1 Turn a Paragraph into an Essay

For this assignment, choose a paragraph that you think you can develop further to write a complete essay. Then, follow the guidelines below.

Andy, the writer of "Helpful Technology" on pages 377–378, based his essay on a paragraph he had already written. Here is his original paragraph.

Super Cell Phones

Cellular phones saved my day yesterday. First, my cell phone helped me keep my job. I overslept because we had a huge rainstorm that knocked out the power that caused my alarm clock not to go off. Our phone is a cordless model, so when the power went off, the phone did, too. However, I had recently charged my cell phone, and it worked even with the power off. I was able to call my boss and tell her that I'd be late due to the storm. She told me that many people hadn't called in—and hadn't shown up—so she really appreciated my call. Second, my cell phone helped me save my car. While I was at work, my car was hit by a huge branch that had fallen as a result of the storm. My windshield was broken, and I couldn't get the branch off my car. Again my cell phone saved the day. I called my brother-in-law, who has a huge truck, and he came, helped me get the gravel off, and towed my car to a garage. He also gave me a ride home. Since the storm was still going on, my car would have been in even worse shape if I'd had to leave it outside in all that rain. Finally, my cell phone kept me out of trouble with my girlfriend. Since I had to have my car towed, I was late for a date with her. However, I called her as I was riding with my brother-in-law, and I explained what happened. She was so relieved to hear from me that she wasn't even angry. Cell phones certainly saved the day!

Prewriting

1. To make sure your paragraph can become an effective essay, ask your-self these questions.

   Will my topic sentence work as a thesis statement?

   How can I change my topic sentence, if necessary, into an effective thesis statement?

   Can I use my paragraph support points as essay support points?

Do I need more specific details for each support point, or do I need to develop the details I have?

What kinds of transitions do I need to make the connections to my thesis statement clear?

2. Freewrite for five to ten minutes. Pay attention to any new support points or specific details that arise during your freewriting.

Andy did some freewriting to see how he could come up with more information about his topic.

What else can I say about cell phones? I guess I could write about more times that cell phones have helped me out, but none of the other times seems as important as the ones in the paragraph. Also, I'm a little tired of writing about cell phones. Right now, I'm pretty excited about my computer. I don't know how I could survive without it—or my VCR, for that matter. Between saving all my work, keeping my calendar, and letting me tape stuff to watch later (the VCR, not the computer), my life is much better. Wait a minute. I might have something here!

Andy realized that he didn't have much more to say about cell phones but that he uses other forms of technology as well. He decided to expand his topic from cell phones to helpful devices.

Drafting

3. Modify your topic sentence into a thesis statement, using a map of support points. Andy changed his topic sentence into a broader thesis statement that includes the new material he uncovered during freewriting.

Topic sentence:	Cellular phones saved my day yesterday.
Thesis statement:	In my experience, cellular telephones, computers, and VCRs can make life much more pleasant.

4. Choose more specific details. With the broader thesis statement Andy developed two other support points that—along with the material on cell phones—showed how technology is helpful.

5. Organize your essay by making an outline to see how your ideas fit together and where you need more information. A completed outline of "Helpful Technology" appears below.

Helpful Technology

A. Introduction

   1. Roommate and my dad complain about computer and VCR.

2. I've had many good experiences with technology.

3. Thesis statement: In my experience, cellular telephones, computers, and VCRs can make life much more pleasant.

B. Body paragraph 1

1. Topic sentence: First on my list of devices that improve my life come cell phones.

2. Specific details illustrating topic sentence: Cell phones saved the day by letting me call work, get my car towed, and tell my girlfriend I'd be late.

C. Body paragraph 2

1. Topic sentence: In addition to cell phones, computers are a constant source of assistance in my life.

2. Specific details illustrating topic sentence: Computer let me print out papers again after roommate threw originals away; computer calendar helps keep me organized.

D. Body paragraph 3

1. Topic sentence: Last but not least in making my life better is my VCR.

2. Specific details illustrating topic sentence: Taping football games to watch after work or studying; watching movies to unwind

E. Conclusion

1. Summary: Remind reader of other people's frustration and my own satisfaction with devices.

2. Final thoughts: Mention that I'll use devices for a long time.

Andy's outline is complete, so he does not need to add information. Often, however, outlines are incomplete, thus revealing where additional details or topic sentences should be added. Although Andy has chosen topics, the outline helps Andy see how he will develop his ideas. He may need to do more prewriting to come up with specific details. Like Andy, you may need to do more freewriting to get enough material for your outline. Remember also to add transitions.

6. Write a draft of the essay, using your outline as a guide.

Revision

7. Check your essay for the first three of the four Cs: *concise, credible,* and *clear* writing. In particular, check to see that the topic sentence of each paragraph echoes the thesis statement in some way. Make any necessary changes to your draft.

Editing

8. Check your essay for the fourth C: *correct* writing. Proofread your essay to make sure you have used correct spelling, punctuation, and grammar.

WRITING PRACTICE 2 **Write an Introductory Paragraph**

Follow the guidelines below to write an introductory paragraph for an essay.

1. Choose one paragraph that you've already written for your English class, or select a topic from the list below.

Possible Topics

Compare two movies.

Contrast two people.

Explain the reasons that caused you to make a particular change in your life.

Explain the effects of a decision you made.

Argue for a change in your home, job, or school.

Reggie decided to write an introduction to an essay arguing that more phone lines should be available for students calling in to register for classes.

2. Freewrite for five to ten minutes to discover what comes to mind first about your topic. Here is Reggie's freewriting.

If I have to wait one more minute to get my classes, I'm going to explode! Don't these administrators know that people are busy? I've been patient and waited until it was my day to register, and now I can't get through on the phone. I've been trying for two hours—without ever getting through to the system—and now I have to go to work. I paid for my classes, so I should get to register!

3. Use one of the techniques mentioned in this chapter for writing an introduction.

- ■ Background information
- ■ Quotation
- ■ Questions
- ■ Personal anecdote
- ■ Opposites

Reggie used a question in his freewriting, so he decided to open his essay with questions.

> Do the administrators of Los Banos College know how long it takes to register for classes? Do they care? And if they do care, how will they solve the problem? These questions come up more and more as students try to use the automated phone registration system.

4. Write a clear thesis statement as the last sentence in your introductory paragraph. Make sure your thesis sentence includes a point-of-view word, and make sure it includes a map of your essay, if that seems appropriate. Reggie added his thesis statement (in bold print) to his introduction.

> Do the administrators of Los Banos College know how long it takes to register for classes? Do they care? And if they do care, how will they solve the problem? These questions come up more and more as students try to use the automated phone registration system. **College administrators need to solve the phone registration problem because it costs students more time, money, and energy than they can afford.**

Reggie not only makes a strong point—that college administrators need to solve the phone registration problem—but he outlines the three areas his essay will cover (time, money, energy) in a map.

WRITING PRACTICE 3 Write an Essay

Now it's your turn to write an essay. Follow the guidelines below.

Prewriting

1. Choose a topic for your essay. As a starting point for your essay, you may use the topic from a paragraph you've already written, or you may choose from the list below to write an essay from scratch.

Topics

A decision someone made that harmed your community

A decision someone made that helped your community

A place worth visiting

A candidate who should or should not be elected

Challenges of attending college

Benefits or drawbacks to buying a car

2. Freewrite for five to ten minutes on the topic of your choice. Then, use at least one other prewriting technique—listing, questioning, keeping a journal, clustering, or outlining.

If you need help coming up with a topic and doing prewriting, use the topic a "movie worth seeing" and fill in the scratch outline below. Add your own specific details to complete the outline, but don't feel that you have to fill in every space.

Topic: Strengths of *Master and Commander: The Far Side of the World*

A. Exciting action scenes

1. _____

2. _____

3. _____

B. Excellent acting

1. _____

2. _____

3. _____

C. Themes of camaraderie

1. _____

2. _____

3. _____

Drafting

3. Write a thesis statement. Draw on your prewriting to find a point that you can develop through an entire essay. For instance, in the scratch outline above, the details show why the writer thinks that *Master and Commander* is a movie worth seeing. Thus, a workable thesis statement could be "*Master and Commander: The Far Side of the World* is worth seeing for its exciting action scenes, excellent acting, and themes of camaraderie."

4. Choose support points and specific details. For instance, if your t hesis statement is "*Master and Commander: The Far Side of the World* is worth seeing for its exciting action scenes, excellent acting, and themes of camaraderie," write down all the examples of the three support points that come to mind. Choose the details that you think best illustrate your support points and will make your essay believable. For instance, for the support points listed above, you might choose the following details.

Support Point	Specific Details
Exciting action scenes	Realistic battles; vividly depicted storms
Excellent acting	Russell Crowe is great as the captain; Paul Bettany portrays the doctor well.
Themes of camaraderie	The captain and the doctor discuss a wide range of topics as friends; the captain guides the crew through danger and unrest.

Remember that in an essay, one support point will take up an entire paragraph, so think of enough details to develop each support point throughout a paragraph.

5. Organize your support points using time sequence (chronological) or emphatic order. Examine your details to decide which order works better. If all of the examples from *Master and Commander* occurred simultaneously in the movie, the writer should probably use emphatic order. However, if the examples occurred one after another, the writer could use chronological order. As you're organizing your ideas, eliminate details that don't fit. Use transitions that make your organization clear.

6. Now write a draft of your essay using the thesis statement, your support points, and your specific details. Remember that an essay includes an introductory paragraph with the thesis statement, body paragraphs with support points and specific details, and a concluding paragraph. Feel free to go back and do more prewriting if you need more information for specific details.

Revising

7. Make any necessary changes to your draft. Check for the first three of the four Cs: *concise, credible,* and *clear* writing.

Editing

8. Check your essay for the fourth C: *correct* writing. Proofread your essay to make sure you have used correct spelling, punctuation, and grammar.

Lab Activity 26

For additional practice with writing essay paragraphs, complete Lab Activity 26 in the Lab Manual at the back of the book.

27 Prewriting for and Drafting Your Essay

CULTURE NOTE *Running Revisited*

While running is widely recognized as good exercise, not everyone understands the excitement of seeing a competitive track race. Understanding both the everyday benefits of running and the special thrill that watching a race gives sports fans and couch potatoes alike a reason to appreciate this simple sport.

Using the Writing Process with Essays

A typical essay has five paragraphs: an introduction, three body paragraphs, and a conclusion. The opening and the thesis statement—which give the main idea of the essay, state the writer's purpose and point of view, and tell the reader what to expect—appear in the introduction. The body paragraphs contain support points and specific details. Finally, the conclusion gives a summary or adds final thoughts to the essay. For more information on the thesis statement and the parts of an essay, see Chapter 26.

The same writing process steps that helped you write an effective paragraph can help you write an effective essay.

Step 1: Prewriting—coming up with ideas
Step 2: Drafting—writing a rough draft
Step 3: Revising—making changes in your draft
Step 4: Editing—checking for correctness

In this chapter, you can practice using prewriting and drafting to start an essay. Chapter 28 shows you how to use revising and editing to finish your essay. The "Writing Process for Essays" diagram on page 400 will also help you see how the writing process can be used for essays.

399

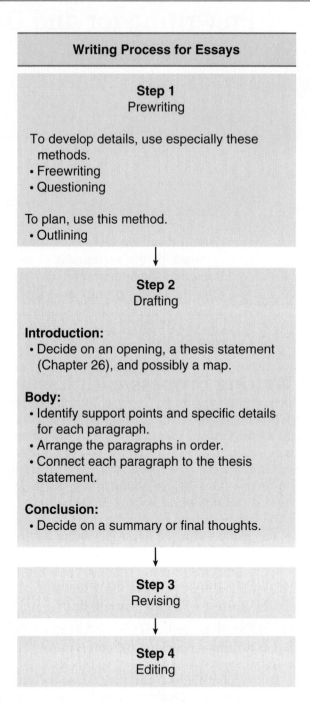

Writing Process for Essays

Step 1
Prewriting

To develop details, use especially these methods.
• Freewriting
• Questioning

To plan, use this method.
• Outlining

Step 2
Drafting

Introduction:
• Decide on an opening, a thesis statement (Chapter 26), and possibly a map.

Body:
• Identify support points and specific details for each paragraph.
• Arrange the paragraphs in order.
• Connect each paragraph to the thesis statement.

Conclusion:
• Decide on a summary or final thoughts.

Step 3
Revising

Step 4
Editing

A Model Essay

In the model essay that follows, the thesis statement is in bold print and the body paragraph topic sentences are in italics.

A Miler's Style

Introduction

I grew up watching the "classic" sports: football, basketball, and baseball. My whole family thought that individual sports didn't really count, and that competitive track runners—people who ran in circles for their races—were just crazy people who couldn't make the football team. Watching the state track and field finals, however, changed my mind about track. **Specifically, I discovered that competitive milers must use strategy, efficiency, and speed to win.**

Body paragraph 1

A miler's strategy is important right from the beginning. The fastest runners get to start closest to the inside of the track, so right from the beginning of the race, everyone is elbowing each other, trying to get in close to the middle. Watching people jostle each other as they try to pass—or fend passers off—makes the race seem like a fight. The first lap of the mile is fast because people want good positions on the track and because they're not yet tired. However, some runners deliberately hang back and wait to make their move. They hope that the "rabbits"—the runners who go out too fast—will burn out quickly so that the rest of the pack can set a more natural pace. Sometimes waiting like this works, but sometimes the patient runners get left behind and can't catch up. Knowing how fast to go—and when to go fast—is a huge part of a miler's success.

Body paragraph 2

Another part of a miler's success is efficiency. After the first lap (and often sooner), the runners start feeling tired. Some of them have run the first lap in under sixty seconds, a very fast pace, so they have to settle into a pace that they can maintain for the next three laps. The runners lengthen their strides, relax their shoulders, and pump their arms as fluidly as possible, trying to be efficient to save energy. At the start of the third lap, many runners are fading. The strongest, however, continue their mechanical motions in an effort to maintain speed without exerting themselves more. Because the racers slow down as they get tired, they must exert more energy just to maintain the same pace. Being efficient is the key here. If runners use extra energy to flail their arms or keep their shoulders hunched up, they won't be strong enough to keep up the pace. Many runners even try to "make a move" and pass people at the start of the third lap so that they can have a good position for the final turn around the track. Pushing to speed up or maintain a fast pace—when half of the race remains—requires ultimate efficiency. After seeing runners fight to maintain their pace, I figured they would be too exhausted for any kind of big finish.

Body paragraph 3

A big finish, however, is exactly what I saw. *One more quality that milers possess is speed.* Even though the mile is considered a distance race, its racers must be fast to win. As the racers approach the start of the last lap, also known as the bell lap or gun lap because a bell or gun is sounded at its start, some of them begin to accelerate. They shorten their strides, digging in around the turn, speeding up all the way. The fly down the backstretch, trying to catch others or not be caught themselves, and head into the final turn. The real speedsters make their moves here, starting a sprint at the top of the turn and barreling down the last straightaway. Sometimes the speedsters pass people and win. Often, however, the gutsy runners who started fast or sped up earlier will be too far away for them to catch. Either way, it's exciting to see long, lanky runners speeding toward the finish.

Conclusion   It took seeing a top-notch mile race to make me appreciate the excitement of track and field. Since that track meet, I've brought my father and my brothers to the track to see meets, and while they're not as impressed as I am, they don't consider runners "wanna-be" athletes any more. After all, anyone who can combine strategy, efficiency, and speed deserves a little respect.

Prewriting for Your Essay

While writing an essay may seem more intimidating than writing a paragraph, it's not really more difficult—just a bit more time-consuming. The trick is to plan your essay so that it includes the key support points and specific details it needs to be effective.

All the prewriting techniques covered in Chapter 4 can help you start your essay. Three are especially helpful: freewriting, questioning, and outlining.

- **Freewriting.** Freewriting is helpful in beginning an essay because it allows you to get ideas on paper without worrying about whether or not your writing is "right." Plan to freewrite frequently.

- **Questioning.** Asking questions can help you focus on the information you need to write a well-developed essay. For instance, in "A Miler's Style," Raoul had a pretty good initial idea why track meets didn't seem interesting. However, he needed information to support the idea that a mile race could require qualities he admired in other athletes. Asking questions helped him focus his writing on the areas that needed attention.

- **Outlining.** Raoul developed enough details from his freewriting and questioning to write a possible thesis statement. Then he started to plan his essay.

Writing an outline is often the single most helpful way to plan your essay. Begin with a simple outline—sometimes called a **scratch outline**—that contains few, if any, details. Look at the one below for "A Miler's Style."

A Miler's Style—Informal Outline

Possible thesis statement: Milers must use strategy, efficiency, and speed to win.

1. Milers must use strategy.
2. Milers need efficiency.
3. Milers need speed.

For an initial outline, this is enough. Raoul has added a possible thesis statement. Finally, he has put his support points in order. Raoul then wrote a second outline, after he did some thinking and research on the topic. This detailed outline helped him plan and organize his essay when he started drafting.

A Miler's Style

A. Introduction
   1. My family liked "classic" sports but not track.
   2. I saw state track and field finals and changed my mind about track.
   3. Thesis statement: Milers must use strategy, efficiency, and speed to win.
B. Milers use strategy.
   1. "Elbow" for good position.
   2. Go out fast.
   3. Hang back and wait.
C. Milers use efficiency.
   1. Milers are tired after a lap.
   2. Try to save energy in running style.
   3. Must try harder just to keep same pace.
D. Milers use speed.
   1. Some runners speed up during third lap.
   2. "Dig in" to speed up.
   3. Pass people on last lap.

E. Conclusion

    1. Seeing a track meet changed my mind about runners.

    2. My family watched meets and changed their minds, too.

Use the "Essay Planning Form" on page 406 to create an informal outline.

EXERCISE 1 OUTLINING TO PLAN AN ESSAY

Choose a thesis statement from the list below. Then, use the outline form that follows to plan an essay based on that thesis statement. You may substitute your own words for the underlined terms in the thesis statements, or you may write your own thesis statement.

1. In order to be successful in school, students must <u>study</u>, <u>ask for help</u>, and <u>go to class</u>.

2. <u>*Chicago*</u> is an excellent movie because of its <u>music</u>, <u>costumes</u>, and <u>story</u>.

3. The <u>Kings</u> are a great team because of their <u>talented players</u>, <u>good coaching</u>, and <u>generous owners</u>.

4. Getting fired from a job is easy if you <u>come late</u>, <u>don't do your work</u>, and <u>act rude to the boss</u>.

5. Using a computer is helpful for <u>completing schoolwork</u>, <u>staying organized</u>, and <u>tracking finances</u>.

Thesis statement: _____

A. Introduction

    1. _____

    2. _____

    3. _____

B. Body paragraph 1 support points _____

    1. _____

    2. _____

    3. _____

C. Body paragraph 2 support points _____

    1. _____

    2. _____

    3. _____

D. Body paragraph 3 support points _____

    1. _____

    2. _____

    3. _____

E. Conclusion

    1. _____

    2. _____

Drafting Your Essay

When you're ready to start drafting, gather your assignment, your prewriting results, your outline, and any other information you will need. You can draft by hand or on a computer (see Chapter 6 for tips on using a computer).

Writing a Strong Introduction

The thesis statement is the most important part of your introduction. It controls the direction of your entire essay and states the main idea that you want to communicate.

For "A Miler's Style" (pages 401–402), the writer modified his possible thesis statement to fit smoothly into his introduction and clarify his point of view.

Possible thesis statement:	Milers must use strategy, efficiency, and speed to win.
Final thesis statement:	Specifically, I discovered that competitive milers must use strategy, efficiency, and speed to win.

Essay Planning Form

Title: _____

Introduction

Opening: _____

_____

Thesis statement (with map, if needed): _____

_____

Body

Support point for paragraph 1: Topic sentence _____

_____

_____

    Specific details: _____

_____

_____

Support point for paragraph 2: Topic sentence _____

_____

_____

    Specific details: _____

_____

_____

Support point for paragraph 3: Topic sentence _____

_____

_____

    Specific details: _____

_____

_____

Conclusion

Summary or final thoughts: _____

_____

_____

Organizing and Connecting the Body Paragraphs Effectively

Use your outline to decide the order of your paragraphs. Think about whether time sequence order (chronological) or emphatic order (least to most important) is more effective for your purpose and reader. Pay particular attention to connecting your ideas. Four key strategies can help you connect your ideas effectively.

Repeating Key Words from the Thesis Statement In "A Miler's Style," Raoul uses the word *miler* in the topic sentence of all three body paragraphs, so the reader can easily see how the body paragraphs are connected to his thesis statement.

Repeating Key Words from the Preceding Paragraph At the end of body paragraph 1 in "A Miler's Style," Raoul states:

> Knowing how fast to go—and when to go fast—is a huge part of a <u>miler's success</u>.

He then begins body paragraph 2 with this statement:

> Another part of a <u>miler's success</u> is efficiency.

By repeating the words *miler's success,* Raoul connects the two paragraphs for the reader.

Using Transitional Terms to Signal Paragraphs In "A Miler's Style," Raoul begins each body paragraph with a transition that signals a new point. He begins body paragraph 1 by writing this:

> A miler's strategy is important right <u>from the beginning</u>.

In body paragraph 2, he writes

> <u>Another</u> part of a miler's success is efficiency.

He begins body paragraph 3 by stating

> <u>One more</u> quality that milers possess is speed.

By using the transitions *from the beginning, another,* and *one more,* Raoul lets the reader know that the essay is connected and moving along.

Using Transitional Sentences to Connect Paragraphs   In "A Miler's Style," Raoul ends body paragraph 2 by writing this:

> After seeing runners fight to maintain their pace, I figured they would be too exhausted for any kind of big finish.

Instead of jumping into his next support point—that milers have speed—Raoul uses a transitional sentence at the beginning of body paragraph 3 to continue the idea of a "big finish."

> A big finish, however, is exactly what I saw.

This sentence links the ideas in body paragraphs 2 and 3.

Writing a Sharp Conclusion

In your conclusion, you have the chance to reinforce your thesis. Using your outline, write a brief summary or add some final thoughts that will help convince your readers. For more on writing an effective conclusion, see Chapter 26.

EXERCISE 2 FOLLOWING THE FOUR Cs

Sarah based the following essay on a paragraph she wrote. Read "Runner's High," below, and answer the questions that follow.

Runner's High

[1]For years when my three older brothers would come back from football practice, I would hear about how awful running was. Their coaches made them run for punishment, for instance, if they showed up late to practice, and my brothers ran only if they absolutely had to. Before I tried it for myself, I had a horrible impression of running. However, since I wasn't any good at softball or soccer, I tried out for the high school cross-country team. Soon I discovered that many positive changes were occurring in my life. I was enjoying my time outside, my new fit body, my faster metabolism, and the "runner's high" that comes with exertion. In fact, through my experience as a runner, I've learned that running for exercise has many benefits.

²First of all, running allows me to be outside, not closed up in some gym or workout room. I get to see trees, flowers, and other people. I've read a lot of fitness magazines, and one article says that outdoor exercise gives people more of a mental lift than indoor exercise. I believe that. Even on days that are cold and rainy, when I don't want to run, within five minutes outside, I'm happy that I've started. There's just nothing like feeling cold air—or even cold rain—on my face as I run around the park. That's an experience I definitely can't get at a gym.

³Another benefit of running is the physical change my body undergoes. Within two weeks of regular running, my legs started looking more toned and my stomach became flatter. People tell me that my skin seems to glow, too, maybe from improved circulation when I run. I also notice that when I walk up a flight of stairs, I don't even get out of breath. When I don't run, however, I'm huffing and puffing by the tenth step. After a few weeks off, it takes me a while to get back in shape, but the benefits of running are always worth the effort.

⁴A third benefit of running is that I can eat anything I want and not gain weight. Just running for half an hour a day, four days a week allows me to eat until I'm full and not worry about whether or not my jeans will fit. I've learned from my coach that when I run, my metabolism speeds up, so I burn calories faster than when I'm not exercising. Even better, my metabolism *stays* faster for hours after my run, so my body keeps burning food even after my workout. I almost feel as if I'm cheating by getting the extra hours of additional calorie burning, but I love it.

⁵Finally, "runner's high" makes running great all by itself. Even though sometimes I start my run feeling tired or achy, after a few minutes, I loosen up and get the most wonderful rush. I've heard that the body releases endorphins, substances that take away physical pain and improve the mood. I've even heard that endorphins are actually addictive, so people can get physically hooked on them. It's true that when I feel the "high," I don't feel any pain at all, and I start feeling edgy if I can't run for a few days. I never thought I would be happy to be hooked on something, but I'm glad that running is my habit.

⁶All in all, though the sore muscles and sweat might turn people off, I understand how people can get hooked on running. Aside from the pounding my joints take from putting in miles each week, there is no downside to running for exercise. It's a habit that has so many benefits.

Concise Writing

1. Which of the following details does the writer use to introduce her topic? Circle all that apply.

   a. She ran with her dog.

   b. Her football-playing brothers hated running.

   c. She ran to win a bet with her brothers.

   d. She ran to lose weight after the holidays.

   e. She started running after finding she was not good at softball or soccer.

2. What is the thesis statement in paragraph 1 of "Runner's High"?

   In fact, through my experience as a runner, I've learned that running for

   exercise has many benefits.

3. What are the four support points the writer makes? *Hint:* Look at the map before the thesis statement, or look at the topic sentences in paragraphs 2 through 5.

   a. Being outside

   b. Physical benefits

   c. No weight gain

   d. Endorphin rush

Credible Writing

4. What details does Sarah use in paragraph 3 to show the physical benefits of running?

   a. Toned legs

   b. Flat stomach

   c. Glowing skin

   d. Don't get out of breath

5. What two experts (in paragraphs 2 and 4) does the writer cite to support her examples?

Paragraph 2: Fitness magazines

Paragraph 4: Coach

6. What details does Sarah use in paragraphs 1 and 6 to show that she understands that not everyone likes running?

a. Running as punishment for football-playing brothers

b. Sore muscles

c. Sweat

Clear Writing

7. What key word from the thesis statement does the writer repeat in her topic sentences for paragraphs 3 and 4? Benefit

8. What transitions does the writer use to introduce each support point?

Paragraph 2: First of all

Paragraph 3: Another benefit

Paragraph 4: A third benefit

Paragraph 5: Finally

How many times does the writer use a form of the word *run* (including in the title)?   27

Correct Writing

The sentences in this paragraph are all correct. To check for correctness in your own writing, go to Part 7, "Writing Correct Sentences."

What You Know Now

In writing essays, follow the first two steps in the writing process—prewriting and drafting—that you use for paragraphs. Be sure to include an introduction with your thesis statement, body paragraphs with support points and specific details, and a conclusion. When you organize your ideas, echo key words from the thesis, use transitional expressions, and use transitional sentences to connect your ideas.

WRITING PRACTICE 1 Write About a Personal Relationship

Write an essay about a relationship that has had a strong effect on you. The relationship may be positive or negative; it may be a current relationship or one in your past.

Prewriting

1. Choose a relationship for your essay topic. Some possibilities are:

   A parent   A sibling   A friend

   An instructor   A counselor   A coach

   An employer   A neighbor   A teammate

2. Begin by freewriting about the relationship for ten minutes.
3. Make an informal outline of your essay. Use more prewriting strategies to add specific details to your brief outline. Asking questions can help you get started.

Drafting

4. Write a thesis statement. Make sure it includes your main idea, your point of view, your purpose, and possibly a map of your essay to let readers know what to expect.
5. Choose support points and specific details that you think best illustrate your thesis and that will make your essay believable.
6. Organize your support points using time sequence (chronological) or emphatic order. You may create a detailed outline to help you or use the outline you developed during prewriting. Decide which order works better by examining your details. As you're organizing your ideas, eliminate details that don't fit.
7. Now write a draft of your essay. Remember that essays include an introductory paragraph with a thesis statement, body paragraphs with support points and specific details, and a concluding paragraph. Do more prewriting if you need more information for specific details.

Revising

8. Check your essay for the first three of the four Cs: *concise, credible,* and *clear* writing. Make any necessary changes to your draft.

Editing

9. Check your essay for the fourth C: *correct* writing. Proofread your essay to make sure you have used correct spelling, punctuation, and grammar.

WRITING PRACTICE 2 Write About a Personal Goal

Write an essay explaining how you have achieved, or will achieve, a personal goal. Your goal can be one that you have achieved already, or it can be one that you have set and are still working toward.

Prewriting

1. Choose a topic that interests you.

Possible Topics

College graduation	Getting in shape
Passing a class	Buying a car
Getting a job	Buying a house
Getting a promotion	Moving out on your own

2. Freewrite on your topic for ten minutes.

3. Make an informal outline using your topic or a possible thesis statement. A sample outline follows.

Thesis statement: Getting into shape involved more self-discipline than I ever thought I had.

A. Gave up sweets.

B. Made myself eat healthy foods.

C. Made myself exercise regularly.

Drafting

4. Write a thesis statement. Make sure your thesis includes your main idea, your point of view, your purpose, and possibly a map of your essay to let readers know what to expect.

5. Choose support points and specific details that you think best illustrate your thesis and will make your essay believable.

6. Organize your support points using chronological or emphatic order. Decide which order works better by examining your details. As you organize your ideas, omit unnecessary details. You may create a detailed outline to help you or use an outline you developed during prewriting.

7. Now write a draft of your essay. Remember that essays include an introductory paragraph that includes the thesis statement, body paragraphs that include support points and specific details, and a concluding paragraph. Feel free to do more prewriting if you need more information for specific details.

Revising

8. Check your essay for the first three of the four Cs: *concise, credible,* and *clear* writing. Make any necessary changes to your draft.

Editing

9. Check your essay for the fourth C: *correct* writing. Proofread your essay to make sure you have used correct spelling, punctuation, and grammar.

WRITING PRACTICE 3 Write About a Current Event

Every day the newspapers report local, statewide, nationwide, and international news. Often, the events they cover span several months. Spend a few weeks reading and clipping articles from the newspaper (or downloading them from a news Web site), and then write an essay about the event you've studied. Begin your writing process *after* you've read and learned something about your topic.

Prewriting

1. Choose an event from current news stories that interests you. Some possible topics follow.

    A war or conflict overseas

    An issue that affects the country (homelessness, taxes, immigration, drug testing at work)

    An issue that affects your state, county, or city (weather crises, education policies, crime)

    An election race

2. Freewrite for ten minutes about your topic. Focus your freewriting not only on what you know about your topic but also on what you'd like to know. An example of freewriting by one writer, Marty, follows.

    It really bothers me that this driver lost his temper and rammed his car into a family's van. The little girl in the family may never walk again, and the police aren't even sure if they arrested the right guy. I can't believe anyone would get so mad about not getting a parking space that he'd try to hurt someone, but that's what this guy did (or it looks like that anyway). Out-of-control driving can hurt people! What's worse is that then the guy drove away and didn't even see if he'd hurt anyone. It's lucky that a woman in the parking lot saw the whole thing and got part of his license plate; I hope the police found the right guy. I hope, too, that the little girl will be OK. People need to make sure they're under control when they drive.

Marty's freewriting reveals that he has been following the news story. Additionally, Marty identifies a possible thesis statement in his last sentence.

3. Make an informal outline of your essay. After rereading articles about his topic, Marty came up with support points that he could use for his essay. His outline looked like this:

Possible thesis statement: People need to make sure they're under control when they drive.

A. Introduction
   1. Comments about injuries from car accidents
   2. Comments about frustrations arising from driving
   3. Thesis statement
   4. Essay map: Accidents cost money; accidents cause stress; people get hurt.

B. Body paragraph 1: Accidents cost money.
   1. Example from articles about how much car damage costs
   2. Example from articles about how much injuries cost
   3. Get details on legal fees?

C. Body paragraph 2: Accidents cause stress.
   1. Example from articles about how the accident affected other drivers

D. Body paragraph 3: People get hurt.
   1. Example from articles on young girl's injuries
   2. Example from articles on both drivers' injuries

E. Conclusion
   1. Comments about the cost—money, stress, health—of losing control behind the wheel
   2. Comment about how public transportation is a good idea?

Drafting

4. Write a thesis statement. Make sure your thesis includes your main idea, your point of view, your purpose, and possibly a map of your essay to let readers know what to expect. Marty already had a possible thesis statement: "People need to make sure they're under control when they drive." But his outline showed him that he was focusing most specifically on the costs—or consequences—of driving while out of control. Thus, Marty revised his thesis statement: "Driving while out of control has serious consequences."

This new thesis statement accurately reflects the content of Marty's essay. Then Marty decided to include a map to keep himself and his reader on track. His thesis statement eventually read as follows:

Driving while out of control has serious consequences, including loss of money, increased stress, and injury.

From this thesis statement, a reader knows exactly what Marty is arguing and how he plans to develop his argument.

5. Choose support points and specific details that best illustrate your support points and will make your essay believable. Marty used the support points he had included in his outline. Then, from the articles he had read, he gathered specific details for his support points.

6. Organize your support points using time sequence (chronological) or emphatic order. Examine your details to decide which order works better. As you're organizing your ideas, eliminate details that don't fit.

7. Now write a rough draft of your essay. Remember that essays include an introductory paragraph with an attention-getting opening and a thesis statement; body paragraphs with support points and specific details; and a concluding paragraph with a summary or final thoughts. Feel free to do more prewriting if you need more information for specific details.

Revising

8. Check your essay for the first three of the four Cs: *concise, credible,* and *clear* writing. Make any necessary changes to your draft.

Editing

9. Check your essay for the fourth C: *correct* writing. Proofread your essay to make sure you have used correct spelling, punctuation, and grammar.

Lab Activity 27

For additional practice with essay planning, complete Lab Activity 27 in the Lab Manual at the back of the book.

28 Revising and Editing Your Essay

CULTURE NOTE *Processing Chocolate*

While people might think that chocolate is naturally delicious, chocolate actually must undergo many steps before becoming edible. From picking the cocoa bean through the roasting, grinding, and mixing process, chocolate changes greatly before taking the forms we recognize and appreciate.

Cocoa Bean Crop

WRITE A PARAGRAPH In its beginning as a cocoa bean, chocolate is unrecognizable as the treat people buy. Chocolate must change greatly before it is ready for the consumer. What else is changed in this way? Write a paragraph explaining how one thing—a potato, say—becomes something else, such as French fries.

417

Revising Your Essay

One of the greatest challenges in revising an essay is getting yourself to take apart, or adjust, something that already may look quite good. Essays, however, need even stronger connections than paragraphs, so revising for the four Cs is vital. Revising—making changes in your draft—is a creative process in which you unify your writing, add information, and strengthen connections between ideas, using all the skills you used in writing your rough draft. See the illustration "Writing Process for Essays" below to see where revising and editing fall in the writing process.

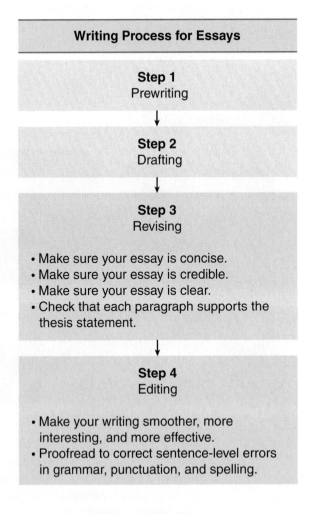

Writing Process for Essays

Step 1
Prewriting

↓

Step 2
Drafting

↓

Step 3
Revising

• Make sure your essay is concise.
• Make sure your essay is credible.
• Make sure your essay is clear.
• Check that each paragraph supports the thesis statement.

↓

Step 4
Editing

• Make your writing smoother, more interesting, and more effective.
• Proofread to correct sentence-level errors in grammar, punctuation, and spelling.

Making Sure Your Essay Is Concise

Sergei has chosen to write about the process by which cocoa beans become edible chocolate. He has already done some reading on the subject of processing chocolate and written a rough draft. Now he's ready for revision. As you read Sergei's essay, think of ways in which it can be made more concise.

The Process of Making Chocolate—Rough Draft

Introduction	[1]The cocoa bean must go through many steps to become the kind of chocolate we can buy in stores and eat.
Body paragraph 1	[2]The first step is harvesting the cocoa pods containing the beans and fermenting them for about six days. [3]Then, the cocoa beans are split from the pods and dried. [4]I never thought that a bean could end up being so delicious.
Body paragraph 2	[5]The next step in the process is to change the beans from plain, dried cocoa beans to two separate substances—cocoa powder and cocoa butter.
Body paragraph 3	[6]The third step is to make the cocoa powder into chocolate we can eat. [7]This process involves blending the cocoa powder back with the cocoa butter and chocolate liquor that was pressed out of the dried, ground beans. [8]This seems like a silly step since the powder and the cocoa butter were just separated from each other.
Body paragraph 4	[9]The next-to-last step is called conching, which is just a fancy name for blending and heating chocolate a special way. [10]A conch is a heated container filled with the blended, liquefied chocolate powder. [11]I'd always thought that a conch was a shell, but I guess there are different types of conches.
Body paragraph 5	[12]The final step involves tempering the chocolate. [13]All this means is that after the conching process, the chocolate is heated up and cooled down carefully to achieve the right texture and appearance.
Conclusion	[14]All in all, the chocolate we eat is very different from what nature starts out with.

After reading "The Process of Making Chocolate," ask yourself the following questions to determine whether Sergei's essay is concise.

Is the Thesis Statement Effective?   Sentence 1 is Sergei's thesis statement. It gives his main idea, point of view, and purpose, so Sergei does not need to revise it at this point.

Do All the Support Points Support the Thesis Statement? Sergei identifies steps in the process of making chocolate. These steps directly support the thesis statement.

Do All the Specific Details Support the Thesis Statement?
Sergei includes some good specific details that illustrate the process of making chocolate, but he also has some sentences that are off-topic.

Read his essay again, and cross out the sentences that do not support the thesis statement. (You should cross out sentences 4, 8, and 11.)

Make Sure Your Essay Is Credible

Now Sergei needs to provide more details to illustrate the ideas in his body paragraphs. Reread "The Process of Making Chocolate," keeping the following two questions in mind.

Is There Enough Information?   Body paragraphs 1 and 2 contain very little information other than their topic sentences. Body paragraphs 3 to 5 offer some details, but not enough for the reader to understand the entire process of making chocolate. Thus, all of the paragraphs need additional details.

Is More Support Needed?   Sergei already included everything he had from his prewriting, so he needs to gather more information for his essay. After reading an article about the drying process, Sergei revised body paragraph 1 as follows:

> The first step is harvesting the cocoa pods containing the beans and fermenting them for about six days. Then, the cocoa beans are split from the pods and dried. The best-quality chocolate is produced when the drying process is done by the sun for about seven days. Speeding up the drying process using artificial methods may be faster, but the chocolate doesn't end up nearly as good.

Going forward with his revision, Sergei adds details to support his thesis and make his essay credible. In addition, he does the following:

- Adds an attention-getting opening to his introduction
- Changes his thesis statement slightly to fit in the new introduction
- Adds some sentences and words to his body paragraphs
- Adds some final thoughts to his conclusion

These changes are underlined in his revised draft, which follows.

The Process of Making Chocolate—Revised Draft

Introduction

<u>I've always had a sweet tooth, and I've especially loved choco-</u><u>late. In fact, whenever I've ordered an ice cream cone, my only deci-</u><u>sion has been what kind of chocolate to get. I've always assumed</u> <u>that since chocolate was so easy to find, it must also be easy to</u> <u>make. However, according to my nutrition instructor, this isn't the</u> <u>case. From the time it's harvested until it appears in stores</u>, the cocoa bean must go through <u>a process of</u> many steps to become the kind of chocolate we <u>like to</u> eat.

Body paragraph 1

The first step <u>in the cocoa bean's journey to becoming chocolate</u> is harvesting the cocoa pods containing the beans and fermenting them for about six days. Then, the cocoa beans are split from the pods and dried. The best-quality chocolate is produced when the drying process is done by the sun for about seven days. Speeding up the drying process using artificial methods is faster, but the choco-late doesn't end up nearly as good.

Body paragraph 2

The next step in the <u>chocolate</u> process is to change the beans from plain, dried cocoa beans to two separate substances—cocoa powder and cocoa butter. <u>This process of separation involves roast-</u><u>ing the cocoa beans, grading them according to how good they are</u> <u>or what type of flavor they have, and grinding them up. This three-</u><u>step process results in a powder. The powder is then pressed to</u> <u>remove the cocoa butter, or the fat, which leaves cocoa powder.</u>

Body paragraph 3

The third step <u>in transforming the cocoa bean begins</u> to make the cocoa powder into chocolate we can eat. This process involves blending the cocoa powder back with the cocoa butter and choco-late liquor that was pressed out of the dried, ground beans. <u>Adding</u> <u>different amounts of cocoa butter, cocoa liquor, and other ingredi-</u><u>ents to the cocoa powder determines the type of chocolate you end</u> <u>up with. For instance, plain chocolate consists of cocoa powder,</u> <u>cocoa liquor, cocoa butter, and sugar. Milk chocolate, however, has</u> <u>milk or milk powder in it in addition to the cocoa powder, cocoa</u> <u>liquor, cocoa butter, and sugar. White chocolate is different, too. It</u> <u>contains cocoa liquor, cocoa butter, milk or milk powder, and sugar,</u> <u>but it has no cocoa powder. At this point, after all the ingredients</u> <u>have been added, the chocolate looks finished.</u>

Body paragraph 4

<u>However, to be truly finished, the chocolate still has two steps</u> <u>to go.</u> The next-to-last step is called conching, which is just a fancy name for blending and heating chocolate a special way. A conch is a container filled with the blended chocolate powder and kept heated to keep the blended chocolate in liquid form. <u>The length of</u>

time given to the conching process determines the final smoothness and quality of chocolate. The finest chocolate is conched for at least a week. After the process is completed, the chocolate is stored in heated tanks, ready for the final step.

Body paragraph 5

The final step involves tempering the chocolate. All this means is that after the conching process, the chocolate is heated up and cooled down carefully to achieve the right texture and appearance. Tempering the chocolate starts with cooling it in stages and then warming it up to liquid form again. Then the chocolate is cooled down one more time, so it ends up in a solid form.

Conclusion

All in all, the chocolate we eat is very different from what nature starts out with. From the bean to the bar, making chocolate involves far more effort than we make in just going to the candy section of the supermarket and choosing a brand. Even though I don't see myself making any chocolate from scratch, I really appreciate my candy bar a lot more now that I know how it's made.

Make Sure Your Essay Is Clear

Sergei's essay has an effective thesis statement, solid support points, and credible specific details. Now he needs to make sure that his connections are as strong as possible.

Are Key Words Repeated?   In his revised draft, Sergei's thesis statement says, in part, that "the *cocoa bean* must go through a process of many *steps* to become the kind of *chocolate* we like to eat." In the topic sentence of body paragraph 1, Sergei now repeats the words *step*, *cocoa bean*, and *chocolate*. Sergei passes the first test of clarity—repeating key words from the thesis statement—with flying colors.

Sergei states at the end of body paragraph 4 that the chocolate is ready for "the final step." He then begins body paragraph 5 with "The final step," connecting the two paragraphs for the reader. An added bonus is that the word *steps* appears in the thesis statement. Thus, Sergei makes connections between the two paragraphs *and* the thesis statement by repeating key words.

Do Transitional Expressions Signal the Support Points?
Sergei begins body paragraph 1 by writing "The *first* step in the cocoa bean's journey. . . . " In the next body paragraph, he begins with "The *next* step," and he uses similar terms to introduce each remaining support point. By using the transitions *first*, *next*, *third*, *next-to-last*, and *final*, Sergei makes the time sequence (chronological) order of the support points clear.

Are Transitional Sentences Used to Connect Paragraphs?

Sergei ends body paragraph 3 by writing that "the chocolate looks finished." But instead of jumping into his next support point—that chocolate needs to go through the conching process—Sergei uses a transitional sentence to move from the possibility of the chocolate being "finished" to the next step in processing chocolate. He writes, "However, to be truly *finished,* the chocolate still has two steps to go." This sentence links body paragraphs 3 and 4, successfully connecting the ideas of both paragraphs.

EXERCISE 1 ANALYZING AN ESSAY FOR ORGANIZATION AND SUPPORT

Reread Sergei's "The Process of Making Chocolate—Revised Draft" on pages 421–422. Then, answer the questions below.

1. What kinds of details does Sergei offer in his introduction to lead up to the thesis statement?

   a. Talks about his sweet tooth

   b. Likes only chocolate ice cream

   c. Always assumed that making chocolate was easy

2. What is the thesis statement? From the time it's harvested until it appears in stores, the cocoa bean must go through a process of many steps to become the kind of chocolate we like to eat.

3. Write down the steps explained in each of the body paragraphs.

   Body paragraph 1: Harvest, ferment, and dry the cocoa beans.

   Body paragraph 2: Separate cocoa powder from cocoa butter.

   Body paragraph 3: Blend cocoa butter and other ingredients back into the cocoa powder.

   Body paragraph 4: Conching

   Body paragraph 5: Tempering

4. Which step required the most specific detail as explanation of the process? Why? Step 3—blending ingredients; because there are many kinds of chocolate that can be made from the same ingredients.

5. What key words does Sergei echo throughout his essay?

Note: *Cocoa* is also a possible answer.

a. Chocolate

b. Process

c. Cocoa bean

d. Step

Checking Each Paragraph Individually for the Four Cs

Reading each paragraph in your essay one at a time lets you check the paragraphs individually for the first three of the four Cs. As you read each paragraph of your essay, look for the following components.

- A clear topic sentence that connects the paragraph to the thesis statement
- Clear support points, if appropriate, that support the topic sentence
- Relevant specific details that illustrate both the paragraph's topic sentence and the essay's thesis statement.

Editing Your Essay

Just as essays include more information than paragraphs, they can also—simply because they are longer—include more errors. Thus, **editing**—working on your writing to make it more effective and to correct errors—is essential. There are two parts to editing.

- Making your writing smoother, more interesting, and more effective
- Proofreading to correct sentence-level errors in grammar, punctuation, and spelling

Making Your Writing Smoother, More Interesting, and More Effective

After checking that your essay is concise, credible, and clear, you need to make sure that your reader will enjoy your writing. As you read your essay, answer the following questions.

- **Point of view.** Do you use the same pronoun throughout? Do you use the correct verb tenses? (For more on using consistent verbs and pronouns, see Chapters 41 and 42.)

- **Appropriate language.** Do you use language that is appropriate for an academic assignment? (For more on sensitive language and word choice, see Chapters 12 and 13.)

- **Word use.** Have you chosen the best words? Is the writing too wordy? Are certain words repeated too often? (For more on using vivid examples and language, see Chapters 10 and 15.)

- **Sentence variety.** Have you used a variety of sentences to keep your writing interesting? Have you made sure that one sentence flows logically and smoothly into the next? (For more on sentence variety and connecting sentences, see Chapter 55.)

These are points you will address first during drafting and again during revising. When you reach the editing stage of the writing process, you have another chance to make sure your writing is smooth, interesting, and effective.

Proofreading to Correct Sentence-Level Errors

During proofreading, you check your writing for errors in grammar, punctuation, and spelling. As you find errors, you might want to mark your corrections using **proofreaders' marks,** a standard set of symbols used by instructors, editors, and printers to show changes in written work. A chart of proofreaders' marks appears on page 102.

You can use three techniques to proofread your essay.

- Proofreading sentence by sentence. This step will help you find errors such as run-on sentences, sentence fragments, incorrect subject-verb agreement, and incorrect pronoun agreement.

- Proofreading word by word. This step will help you find apostrophe and capitalization errors and other errors that you might miss during the sentence-by-sentence proofreading.

■ Reading your essay backwards. This step can help you find spelling errors.

For each of these steps, read your essay over one more time, focusing on the task at hand. When you've finished editing your essay, read it again, just to be sure it is free of errors. For more help with editing, see pages 106–109.

What You Know Now

Revising an essay involves making sure the essay is *concise, credible,* and *clear,* as well as checking that each paragraph helps develop the thesis statement. Editing an essay consists of making the writing smoother, more interesting, and more effective. Use three proofreading techniques—proofreading sentence by sentence, proofreading word by word, and proofreading your essay backwards—to find spelling, punctuation, and grammar errors.

WRITING PRACTICE 1 Write About Giving Advice

We've all had successes and made mistakes in our lives, and sometimes we've benefited from what others have told or shown us. Write an essay in which you give advice to someone just entering high school.

Prewriting

1. Choose an advice topic based on your own experiences and observations.

Possible Topics

Be friendly to everyone.

Choose your friends carefully.

Work hard.

Don't work too hard.

Try hard to be well liked.

Don't worry about what people think of you.

Get a part-time job.

Focus only on school.

2. As always, freewrite for ten minutes about your topic, paying careful attention to the experiences that led you to hold your opinion on this kind of advice.

3. Make an informal outline to clarify your support points.

Possible thesis statement: Because it's impossible to please everyone, it's better to keep to yourself.

A. You're less likely to get put down by peers.

B. You're less likely to get called on in class.

C. You don't have to worry about being phony when you feel like being alone.

Remember that all prewriting strategies can be used effectively throughout the writing process. Even if you're almost finished with a draft of your essay, it's not too late to go back and ask questions or freewrite to come up with more details. For this essay, asking questions can help fill in the details to support the thesis.

Questions	Answers
How does keeping to yourself keep you from being put down?	People don't notice you, don't seek you out, don't make trouble for you.
How does keeping to yourself keep the instructor from calling on you?	Being quiet means you won't call attention to yourself; the instructor might not notice you if you're quiet.
How does keeping to yourself keep you from being phony?	Not as many people to talk to, so you can act naturally

Drafting

4. Write a thesis statement. Make sure your thesis includes your main idea, point of view, purpose, and possibly a map of your essay.

5. Choose support points and specific details that best illustrate your support points and that will make your essay believable.

6. Organize your support points using time sequence (chronological) or emphatic order. Examine your details to decide which order works better. As you're organizing your ideas, eliminate details that don't fit.

7. Now write a draft of your essay. Remember that essays include an introductory paragraph with the thesis statement, body paragraphs with support points and specific details, and a concluding paragraph. Feel free to do more prewriting if you need more information for specific details.

Revising

8. Check your essay for the first three of the four Cs: *concise, credible,* and *clear* writing. Make any necessary changes to your draft.

Editing

9. Check your essay for the fourth C: *correct* writing. Proofread your essay to make sure you have used correct spelling, punctuation, and grammar.

WRITING PRACTICE 2 Write About a Favorite Activity

Write an essay about an activity you enjoy. Begin by offering a brief overview of the activity, and use the body paragraphs to explain what you enjoy about the activity.

Prewriting

1. Choose a topic that interests you.

Possible Topics

Eating dinner at a favorite restaurant

Going to the movies

Hiking

Going to the beach

Participating in a sport

Relaxing at home

2. Freewrite on your topic for ten minutes to find details that will help you explain your enjoyment of this activity.

3. Make an informal outline or ask questions in order to organize your ideas. For her thesis statement, "My idea of heaven is eating dinner in a restaurant," the writer has written complete topic sentences for the outline below.

The Joy of Restaurant Eating

A. Introduction

    1. Story about disaster preparing dinner

    2. Comments about how I need a break

B. Body paragraph 1 topic sentence: First, I don't have to do anything to get ready for dinner.

    1. _____

    2. _____

    3. _____

C. Body paragraph 2 topic sentence: Second, I can look nice for dinner without worrying about ruining my clothes while cooking.

    1. _____

2. _____

3. _____

D. Body paragraph 3 topic sentence: Next, I can pay attention to conversation with my companion, not to the little details of a meal I've made.

    1. _____

    2. _____

    3. _____

E. Body paragraph 4 topic sentence: Finally, I can get up and leave, without lifting a finger to clean up.

    1. _____

    2. _____

    3. _____

F. Conclusion

    1. Eating out is a nice break.

    2. Eating out makes me appreciate cooking.

Notice that the writer has developed many important parts of her essay—including transition words at the start of her topic sentences—but still needs specific details.

Drafting

4. Write a thesis statement that includes your main idea, point of view, your purpose, and possibly a map of your essay.

5. Choose support points and specific details to illustrate your support points and make your essay believable.

6. Organize your support points using time sequence (chronological) or emphatic order. Examine your details to decide which order works better. As you're organizing your ideas, eliminate details that don't fit.

7. Now write a draft of your essay. Remember that essays include an introductory paragraph with the thesis statement, body paragraphs with support points and specific details, and a concluding paragraph. Feel free to do more prewriting if you need more information for specific details.

Revising

8. Check your essay for the first three of the four Cs: *concise, credible,* and *clear* writing. Make any necessary changes to your draft.

Editing

9. Check your essay for the fourth C: *correct* writing. Proofread your essay to make sure you have used correct spelling, punctuation, and grammar.

WRITING PRACTICE 3 Write About an Issue That Matters to You

Every day we encounter situations we wish we could change. We also encounter situations that—through other people's time and effort—have changed for the better. Think about what changes you have made or would like to make in your life. Choose either Topic A or Topic B below for your essay.

Topic A

Write an essay about a change that has occurred in your school, neighborhood, or city and that you feel good about. Your change may be as simple as adding speed bumps to a street where children play, or it may be as complex as the decision to elect a new mayor. Choose a topic that you can find information about in the newspaper or online, and *write about why the change you've noticed is positive.* Your thesis statement may be something like "Electing Mayor Johnson has proved to be beneficial to families, students, and the homeless." Then, follow the steps in Writing Practice 2 to develop your essay. Be sure to use specific details from written sources such as newspapers and from your own experiences and observations.

Topic B

Write an essay about a change in your school, neighborhood, or city that you think was a mistake. For instance, you can write about how making a two-way street into a one-way street has inconvenienced bicyclists and drivers. You can also write about how a new policy of keeping city parks open all night has led to more violence in your neighborhood. Your thesis statement may be something like "Making 21st Street into a one-way street has inconvenienced bicyclists and drivers alike." Then, follow the steps in Writing Practice 2 to develop your essay. Be sure to use specific details from written sources such as newspapers and from your own experiences and observations.

Lab Activity 28

For additional practice with revising an essay, complete Lab Activity 28 in the Lab Manual at the back of the book.

PART SIX
Writing for Different Purposes

Copyright © 2007 Pearson Education, Inc.

29 Essay Exams

Strife is nothing new in the United States. Even today, debates continue over whether or not requiring schoolchildren to refer to "one nation under God" in the Pledge of Allegiance violates the First Amendment. However, the Salem witch trials, in which twenty-seven people were convicted of practicing witchcraft and twenty were executed, stands out as a particularly bizarre moment in American history.

The Salem Witch Trials

CRITICAL THINKING

The Salem witch trials gained momentum as people accused others to avoid being accused themselves. Today, politicians run negative campaigns to show their opponents' flaws. Write a few sentences explaining why unkind or untrue comments are such powerful weapons.

What's Good About an Essay Exam?

No matter how well prepared students are, many still panic at the idea of the essay exam. Somehow, sitting down *in class* and facing a blank page seems to be a terrifying experience. Because essay exams become more common as you progress through college, knowing how to excel on them is crucial. A bright spot, however, is that **essay exams**—essays written in your classroom during an allotted amount of time—have many advantages.

- You can present information in a format you choose.
- You can use whatever details and information best address the exam questions.
- You can organize your information in the way you think is most effective.
- You can add a little style and spice to make your essay more interesting.

In short, writing an essay exam gives you power. If you have learned the material and are comfortable writing essays, you have an opportunity to show your instructor how much you know and how well you can express that information.

Before the Exam

The key to writing a strong essay for an exam is preparation. The following tips can help you prepare for the challenge of writing an in-class essay.

Knowing Your Subject Matter

The first step to writing a good in-class essay is studying your subject. Read everything the instructor has assigned, and memorize key people, places, and dates. The more information you know, and the better you know it, the better are your chances of writing a strong essay exam.

Predicting the Future

Wouldn't all tests be easier if you knew the text questions in advance? Paying attention can help you figure out what you need to know. Listen to what the instructor emphasizes, and notice what information your book develops most. Chances are, an essay question will be on a topic that your textbook or instructor has emphasized.

For instance, Mo Ling, a student in a U.S. history class, prepared for her essay exam by highlighting in her notes the topics that her instructor had spent the most time talking about. Mo Ling also made notes in her textbook on the topics that were covered the most thoroughly. After reviewing her notes, Mo Ling figured that the topic of the Salem witch trials—among others—had a very good chance of showing up on her test. To prepare for the test, she wrote out every question she could think of that related to the Salem witch trials. Here are some of her questions.

When and where did the trials take place?

What caused the trials?

Who was on trial? How were these people singled out?

What events made up the accusation, trial, and execution process?

What effects did the trials have on the Salem population?

What effects did the trials have on religious freedom?

Answering Your Questions About the Subject

After you identify possible questions for the exam, make sure you know the answers. Mo Ling thought about answers to every question she made up. A question such as "What were the causes of the Salem witch trials?" could end up as an essay topic. So understanding the subject, not just memorizing facts, is essential to preparing for an essay exam.

Making a Memory Plan

After you've identified possible test questions and answers, think of one- or two-word terms that help you remember the information. For instance, Mo Ling made the following list in response to this question: What were the causes of the Salem witch trials?

1. <u>Fear</u> of witchcraft brought from Europe
2. Unexplained <u>behavior</u> of young women in Salem
3. Ease of making <u>accusations</u>
4. Mass <u>hysteria</u>

Mo Ling could have decided to memorize the words *fear, behavior, accusations,* and *hysteria.* Those terms would then trigger her full responses to the exam question. However, she chose to simply remember the first letter of each word. She could even associate those letters with a saying that is easy to remember. For example the letters FBAH could be remembered as "Fierce Blows Always Hurt."

Fierce	**B**lows	**A**lways	**H**urt
Fear	**B**ehavior	**A**ccusations	**H**ysteria

The point is to find some technique that helps you remember the information you need for the exam.

During the Exam

There are several steps you can take during the exam to increase your chances of writing a good essay.

Reading the Instructions

Before you begin writing, *read the directions on the test*. The directions tell you *how* the instructor wants you to present the information. The box on the following page explains some key terms.

Here are some examples of essay questions.

Discipline has long been a part of child raising. Recently, however, certain types of discipline have come under scrutiny as instances of child abuse have become public. Is spanking an effective means of disciplining children, or is it cruel? <u>Write an essay arguing that spanking is or is not an effective means of disciplining children</u>.

In the example above, the key words to understand are *arguing, spanking,* and *effective*. The question asks the writer to *give reasons to support the idea* that spanking is (or isn't) an effective way to discipline children.

Often, we hear people of our parents' or grandparents' generation claim that life now isn't as good as it was when they were younger. Do you think the quality of your life has declined? <u>Write an essay comparing and contrasting some aspect of your life now to that aspect of your life as a child</u>.

The key terms to recognize in this essay question are *comparing, contrasting, your life now,* and *your life as a child*. This question asks students to *find similarities* and *differences* between some part of their lives now and some part of their lives in the past.

Key Essay Terms

Analyze means to break something into parts and then make connections between those parts. Analysis includes explaining why something happened or why you feel as you do. Other terms indicating analysis are *examine* and *explain*.

Argue means to take a stand on some aspect of a topic (see Chapter 25). Other words indicating that you take a stand are *defend* and *justify*.

Classify means to group items into subcategories (see Chapter 20).

Compare means to show similarities (see Chapter 22).

Contrast means to show differences (see Chapter 22).

Define means to state the meaning of a term clearly and completely (see Chapter 24).

Discuss means to carefully look at and present a subject through examples and illustrations.

Discuss causes means to talk about causes (see Chapter 23).

Discuss effects means to talk about effects or consequences (see Chapter 23).

Describe means to offer details (see Chapter 19).

Divide means to break something down into its parts (see Chapter 20).

Evaluate means to talk about advantages and disadvantages.

Illustrate means to give examples and illustrations (see Chapter 17).

Narrate means to tell how something has developed, step by step (see Chapter 18).

Summarize means to give a brief version of events or ideas (see Chapter 30).

Budgeting Your Time

Perhaps students' greatest fear in writing an essay exam is that they'll work hard to learn the material and prepare their ideas, only to run out of time during the test itself. Never fear! After you read the directions for your essay exam, you need to figure out how much time you have to plan, write, and proofread. Suppose you have 50 minutes for the exam. You could decide to spend your time like this:

10 minutes planning

35 minutes writing

5 minutes proofreading

If you're well prepared, you may spend less time planning, but it's better to have a good plan than to forge ahead writing a disorganized essay that may leave out key details. Allotting time for proofreading, even if you don't actually get to read over your essay, gives you options in terms of how much time you spend on each stage in writing an essay exam.

Making a Writing Plan

Making a list or an outline is an excellent way to plan your essay. Once you've read the instructions, write out the main concepts you want to include in your response. For instance, when Mo Ling read that she was to explain the causes of the Salem witch trials—a question she had anticipated and prepared for—she quickly wrote out her memory tool.

FBAH—*fear, behavior, accusation, and hysteria*

These terms triggered her memory of the trial's causes, and she was able to start planning her essay.

Next, Mo Ling made an outline. She wrote a possible thesis statement and jotted down details that supported the key terms she had remembered.

Possible thesis statement: Many factors caused the Salem witch trials to happen.

A. Fear of witchcraft brought from Europe

Puritan religion was rigid, left little room for actions that weren't strictly Christian; women had been recently executed in different parts of Europe for being witches.

B. Unexplained behavior of young women in Salem

Women murmured together, seeming to chant; women had uncanny ability to predict future.

C. Ease of making accusations

Young women, afraid of being accused of witchcraft, said they were under the "spell" of "witches" in Salem: women, mostly middle-aged, in their community.

D. Mass hysteria

People started pointing out each other as witches rather than run the risk of being accused themselves; trust eroded in the community; trials and executions happened because people were afraid for themselves; people were also afraid of appearing less than devout, so they went along with the actions of accusers.

This rough outline (which is really just an organized list) provided Mo Ling with the structure she needed to write her essay. Each lettered "cause" was a support point that could be a body paragraph in her essay; she needed only to add an introduction at the beginning and a conclusion at the end to have a complete essay. Mo Ling's completed essay begins below.

Write Neatly, on Every Other Line

Write neatly on every other line of your paper or exam booklet. Then, if necessary, you can go back and insert information or cross out a misspelled word and write the correction in the line above the mistake.

Write a Clear, Organized Essay

You've studied, planned, and relaxed. Now you're ready to write. Begin your essay exam just as you would begin any other essay.

- Write your introduction with a clear thesis statement.
- Connect your paragraphs to your thesis statement.
- Use the specific details you've learned from your studies to support your ideas.

Because of time limits, your work may not be as polished as an essay you would write outside class. Remember that the primary purpose of an essay exam is to show your knowledge. Therefore, don't worry about having an attention-getting opening or a dramatic conclusion. While these are important in an out-of-class essay, they are less important than including facts to show your instructor how much you know. Do your best to include transitions and details, but concentrate on following your plan and getting your information down in essay form as quickly as possible.

Here is Mo Ling's essay exam. The underlined sections indicate places where Mo Ling added information after she had written her initial draft.

Introduction   The United States has faced many conflicts over beliefs and lifestyles, but none was equal to the Salem witch trials in terms of frightening an entire population. Many factors caused the Salem witch trials to happen.

Body
paragraph 1

  The first factor in causing the witch trials was fear of witchcraft brought from Europe. The Puritan religion that caused many people to come to America was rigid, and it left little room for actions that were not strictly Christian. Women had been executed in different parts of Europe for being witches, and the beliefs that led to the executions followed people to the colonies.

Body
paragraph 2

  A second cause of the trials was the odd activity of the Salem community's girls. <u>Many young women began acting in ways that Salem residents could not understand</u>. The women, most of whom were in their teens, began meeting in dark forests and murmuring together. They also seemed to be saying incantations, <u>or spells</u>, and they appeared able to predict the future. These actions were thought to be signs of witchcraft.

Body
paragraph 3

  A third reason for the Salem witch ~~trails~~ ^{trials} was that it was easy for people to accuse others of witchcraft so they would not be accused themselves. For instance, the young women who met in the forest accused middle-aged women of Salem of putting them under "spells." That way, the young women were considered innocent victims, and the older women were the ones in trouble.

Body
paragraph 4

  Last of all, mass hysteria brought about the trials. People became so afraid of being accused themselves that they started accusing other people. Salem residents lived in fear that they would be accused of witchcraft even if they had never had anything to do with it. People went along with the accusers, too, so that they would not be accused. The trials and executions happened largely because people's fears got out of control.

Conclusion

  Today, if people say that politicians are leading a witch-hunt, they mean that others are being accused without evidence. The Salem witch trials were an example of a time when fear led people to do crazy things.

EXERCISE 1 ANALYZING AN ESSAY EXAM

Answer the following questions about Mo Ling's essay above.

1. What is the thesis statement in Mo Ling's essay? _____

  Many factors caused the Salem witch trials to happen.

2. What four areas does the writer identify as causes of the Salem witch trials?

 a. Fear _____

 b. Strange behavior _____

 c. Ease of making accusations _____

 d. Mass hysteria _____

3. What transitions does the writer use to signal the start of each new point in the body paragraphs?

a. first _____

b. second _____

c. third _____

d. Last of all _____

4. In the topic sentence for each body paragraph, the writer echoes key words from the thesis statement. What are these words?

a. Body paragraph 1: Witch trials _____

b. Body paragraph 2: Trials _____

c. Body paragraph 3: Salem witch trials _____

d. Body paragraph 4: Trials _____

5. What are the three sentence-level revisions the writer makes?

a. Paragraph 2: Added "Many young women began acting in ways that Salem residents could not understand."

b. Paragraph 2: Added "or spells" _____

c. Paragraph 3: Crossed out "trails" and spelled it correctly as "trials."

EXERCISE 2   ANALYZING ESSAY EXAM QUESTIONS FOR KEY TERMS

The groups of sentences below are possible essay exam questions. Underline the key words in each sentence. An example is done for you.

The Civil War had a huge effect on the entire U.S. economy. Write an essay discussing the most important economic effects of the Civil War.

1. Both Edith Wharton in *The House of Mirth* and Kate Chopin in *The Awakening* wrote about women's options in relationships and careers. Write an essay contrasting the main women characters in these two novels.

2. How are soccer and American football similar? Write an essay comparing the two sports.

3. How can a disorganized student make better use of his or her time? Write an essay <u>explaining</u> what <u>steps</u> a person can take to become more <u>organized</u>.

4. If it were passed, the Equal Rights Amendment would prohibit denial of rights on the basis of gender. Do you think the Equal Rights Amendment should be added to the Constitution? Write an essay <u>arguing</u> your position on this issue.

5. Many people debate whether illegal immigrants should be able to get driver's licenses. Write an essay <u>agreeing or disagreeing</u> with this concept.

What You Know Now

Writing an essay exam gives you an opportunity to show your instructor what you know, in a manner that works best for you. Studying the material, asking and answering sample test questions, and making a memory plan are keys to knowing your subject well. During the exam itself, concentrate on reading the instructions carefully, budgeting your time, and planning your essay according to the demands of the exam question.

WRITING PRACTICE 1 Prepare for an Essay Exam

Pretend you are taking an essay exam in one of your classes.

1. Make up three questions that your instructor could ask you to write an essay about.

   a. _____

   _____

   b. _____

   _____

   c. _____

2. Study the class material to find answers to your questions, and on another piece of paper write your answer.

3. Make an outline of your response to one of the questions, complete with a possible thesis statement.

Possible thesis statement: _____

    A. _____

        1. _____

        2. _____

        3. _____

    B. _____

        1. _____

        2. _____

        3. _____

    C. _____

        1. _____

        2. _____

        3. _____

WRITING PRACTICE 2 Write an Essay Exam in Response to a Reading

Follow the guidelines below to write an essay based on a reading.

1. Choose any article from a magazine or newspaper.

2. Read the article.

3. Follow the steps outlined in this chapter to prepare yourself to write an essay exam on that article. Be sure to include a list of possible essay questions on the article.

4. Write an essay in response to one of the essay questions you wrote, allowing yourself only 50 minutes to complete the assignment.

WRITING PRACTICE 3 Write an Essay Exam on a General-Interest Topic

Without realizing it, we are affected by situations and decisions that may seem to have no connection to us. Questions involving some everyday situations are listed below. Choose from Topics A, B, or C below, and write an essay exam in response to the question.

Topic A

Pet overpopulation is a problem that concerns many people. Though many domestic animals are well cared for, others are homeless. Should pet owners be forced to have their pets spayed or neutered in order to reduce the number of unwanted animals? *Write an essay discussing the benefits or drawbacks of forcing pet owners to spay or neuter their pets.*

Topic B

Many contemporary movies are remakes of movies made years ago. Many movies also explore the same material that earlier movies explored. *Write an essay comparing or contrasting two films focusing on the same time period, conflict, or person.* Some movie pairs to consider are the following:

Emma (with Gwyneth Paltrow) and *Clueless*

Gladiator and *Troy*

Dial "M" for Murder and *The Perfect Murder*

Romeo and Juliet (with Leonardo DiCaprio) and *Shakespeare in Love*

The Program and *Remember the Titans*

Gone with the Wind and *Glory*

Phone Booth and *Cellular*

*Psycho (*with Janet Leigh) and *Psycho* (with Ann Heche)

Topic C

As security measures and overcrowding make airline travel more stressful, travelers are faced with increasing incidents of rudeness from other travelers, such as people playing noisy video games or reclining their seats into other passengers' laps. What can be done? *Write an essay explaining how you think travelers should deal with rudeness from other passengers.*

Lab Activity 29

For additional practice with essay exams, complete Lab Activity 29 in the Lab Manual at the back of the book.

30 Writing Summaries

  ## *Malcolm X*

Hailed as the first true black revolutionary and the inspiration for the Black Power movement of the late 1960s, Malcolm X left a legacy that lingers more than forty years after his death. Born with the "slave" name Malcolm Little, which he ultimately abandoned, Malcolm X moved frequently and eventually drifted into crime. Malcolm X was in prison when he began his self-education process and became a follower of Black Muslim leader Elijah Muhammad. Initially espousing separatism and racial equality "by any means necessary," Malcolm X eventually turned away from Elijah Muhammad's guidance and adopted less extreme views toward race relations. He was shot by three men as he prepared to speak to his followers in Harlem's Audubon Ballroom on February 21, 1965.

Summaries Are Useful

A **summary** concisely restates a longer document—such as an essay, an article, or a book—emphasizing the key points and eliminating the less important details. When you write a summary, follow these guidelines.

- Use your own words, though you may want to borrow key phrases from the original.
- *Do not add your opinions or views of the material you're summarizing.*
- Present only what the original writer had to say.
- Give only the main points of the original but not the specific details unless one or more of them is unusually important.

Malcolm X (1925–1965)

FOOD FOR THOUGHT One of the civil rights movement's greatest advocates, Malcolm X preached ideas that did not initially include racial harmony. Malcolm X's message was not always heard favorably, but he was extremely influential. Who today speaks a message that people may not always want to hear?

Writing an Effective Summary

A good summary presents the main support points without misrepresenting the original text.

Step 1: Look Over the Document for Clues About What's Most Important   The most important ideas in a reading will stand out in some way: in the title, the thesis statement, the introductory paragraph, the topic sentences of body paragraphs, or the conclusion. Important ideas may also be identified through headings, italicized words, or words in bold print.

Step 2: Read the Entire Document   To summarize a reading accurately, you must understand it completely. Read the entire document to get a general idea of what the writer is saying.

Step 3: Reread the Document and Mark the Important Ideas
The more you work with the material you're summarizing, the better you

will understand and remember it. Rereading and underlining or highlighting key ideas is a good way to proceed. If you're not sure whether to underline an item, mark it and move on.

Step 4: Write a Rough Draft Using Your Own Words   Give the information in your summary in the same order that the writer uses in the original document. Do not use expressions such as "the author claims". or "the writer points out," which are unnecessary and make the summary longer than it has to be.

Step 5: Check Your Summary Against the Original   After you've drafted your summary, make sure that you have included the important details and omitted secondary or irrelevant details. Your summary should devote the same percentage of space to key points as the original does. Additionally, make certain that the information in your summary is accurate. Don't exaggerate or downplay details; simply restate the facts as they appear in the original.

Step 6: Revise Your Draft for Concise, Credible, and Clear Writing   Remember: The benefit of a summary is its brevity, so omit anything not absolutely essential to communicating the points of the original. Also, make sure that the connections between ideas are clear and logical.

Step 7: Proofread Your Summary   Correct any errors in spelling, punctuation, and grammar, following the editing tips from Chapter 7 for help with proofreading.

Step 8: Document Your Source   At the end of the summary, include information about the source—the author's name and the title and publication information the book, magazine, journal, newspaper, or online database or Web site where you found the original article.

A Model Summary

The following is a summary of an essay. The original article is approximately 900 words long, but the summary is about 150 words. Note how the writer includes some quotations from the article but few specific details.

In the essay "A Homemade Education," Malcolm X writes about how reading and copying the dictionary helped him discover the "freedom" of learning. Malcolm X writes that he started trying to improve his writing skills to communicate better with Elijah Muhammad. Malcolm X also explains how he wanted to build up his "stock of knowledge" to be able to contribute more to conversations. However, reading proved frustrating because he didn't understand many words. Malcolm X requested a dictionary from prison officials and began copying it to improve his penmanship as well as his reading and writing abilities. Malcolm X compares the dictionary to an encyclopedia, and he says that as his knowledge of words broadened, he was able "for the first time to pick up a book and read and now begin to understand what the book was saying." He became fascinated with books, which led to a feeling of freedom even while he was in prison.

> X, Malcolm. "A Homemade Education." *The Autobiography of Malcolm X.* By X and Alex Haley. Random, 1965.

EXERCISE 1 ANALYZING A SUMMARY

Reread the summary on page 447–448. Then, answer the questions below.
Answers will vary.

1. What is the thesis of the article being summarized? Malcolm X writes about how reading and copying the dictionary helped him to discover the "freedom" of learning.

2. What motivates Malcolm X to improve his reading and writing?

He wanted to communicate with Elijah Muhammad.

3. What does Malcolm X do to improve his reading and writing?

copies the dictionary

4. To what does Malcolm X compare the dictionary? an encyclopedia

5. What is one result of Malcolm X's copying the dictionary?

He was able to pick up a book and understand what it said.

What You Know Now

A summary is a brief restatement of someone else's work. In summaries, you include only the most relevant information.

WRITING PRACTICE 1   Write a Summary of a Chapter

Write a one-paragraph summary of a chapter from a book you are reading for another class. Concentrate on including those ideas that you think you'll need to remember for an exam. Follow the guidelines for writing a summary.

WRITING PRACTICE 2   Write a Summary of an Article

Read an article from a magazine or newspaper. Then, write a one-paragraph summary of it. Make sure you include only those details communicating the main point of the article. Include a copy of the article when you hand in your summary.

WRITING PRACTICE 3   Write a Summary of an Oral Presentation

Watch a television program, or listen to an interview on the radio. Then, write a one-paragraph summary of the program or interview. Begin your summary by stating the name and date of the program or interview you're summarizing. For instance, write "In the September 12, 2001, program *NBC Nightly News,* the news anchor Stone Phillips focused on the causes of terrorism in the United States."

Lab Activity 30

For additional practice with writing summaries, complete Lab Activity 30 in the Lab Manual at the back of the book.

31 Writing to Get a Job

Employers Value Good Writing Skills

For most people, writing is a necessary skill throughout life. Even people in careers that seem to require little writing—plumbers and mechanics, for instance—need to keep records, fill out order forms, track inventory, and apply for bank or credit accounts to keep their businesses running smoothly. Whatever career you want to pursue, learning to write well can give you an edge in the job market.

Crafting a Résumé

A **résumé** is a brief summary (usually one page) of your work qualifications. It is a record of your education, training, and job experience. The purpose of a résumé is to introduce you to a potential employer and get you an interview. The model below shows what one type of résumé looks like. The guidelines that follow it will help you create a résumé.

A Model Résumé

Your name, full address, and phone number

Items listed from most to least recent

Diploma, educational institution, and year graduated

Significant volunteer activities

Availability of references

Jane Michaels
1750 43rd Avenue Sacramento, CA 95823 (916) 555-2388

EXPERIENCE: **Sales Associate, Grand Department Store, 8/99–present**
I was trained to work in the Infants and Toddlers Department, but I have worked in many different areas when they needed help.

Sales Clerk, Monroe's Department Store, 7/97–99
I was primarily responsible for working in the Children's Department, but I also covered the teen and misses sections.

EDUCATION: **Bachelor of Arts, Fashion Merchandising, California State University, Stockton, 6/06**

Associate of Arts, English, Sacramento City College, Sacramento, 6/97

Diploma, Hiram Redding High School, Sacramento, 6/94

SPECIAL SKILLS: Through my work in retail clothing stores, I have developed organizational skillls. I have also become proficient at using both cash registers and adding machines.

ACTIVITIES: **Volunteer Story Reader for Children's Program, Belle Rivers Public Library, 8/99–present**
I spend two hours a month reading stories to visiting children.

REFERENCES: Available upon request.

Job title, employer, and dates employed

Brief description of job

Revelant skills

Making Your Résumé Look Professional

Print your résumé on good-quality paper, with a one-inch margin on all sides. Use an easy-to-read format, and always send a clean copy.

Emphasizing Your Good Points

While we're often taught not to brag about our accomplishments, a résumé is the place to emphasize your qualifications and skills. Mention any relevant extracurricular or volunteer activities you've been involved in. Don't, however, mention grades—unless they're Bs or better—or hobbies or personal interests. Always be honest on your résumé; exaggerating or fibbing about your accomplishments or responsibilities in previous jobs can have negative consequences.

Following a Logical Format

It's usual to start with your work experience. If you have no work experience, you can start with your education. Use a form of organization that's easy for an employer to follow. List experiences and educational activities in *reverse order,* starting with your most recent experience and working your way backward.

Be Brief

Chances are, an employer has limited time and many applications to read. Keep your résumé to a single page.

Omitting Unnecessary or Negative Details

Don't list your age, marital status, height, weight, health, or other personal details. Additionally, don't mention your previous salaries or reasons why you left your last job. These details say nothing about your qualifications for the job, and they may unfairly bias an employer against you.

Proofread, Proofread, Proofread!

A potential employer may interpret errors on your résumé as a sign that you are careless or sloppy. Ask a friend to read your résumé, too.

Mention That References Are Available

Do not write the names of your **references** (people who can vouch for you as a responsible employee) on your résumé. However, keep a list of names, addresses, and phone numbers that you can provide if the prospective employer asks for references. Make sure you've asked the people you're claiming as references for their permission to do so.

EXERCISE 1 PLANNING YOUR RÉSUMÉ

Use the form below to organize the information for your résumé. Be sure your information is accurate and clearly stated.

Résumé Outline Form

Name: _____

Address and phone number: _____

_____

E-mail address: _____

_____

_____

Experience: _____

_____

_____

Education: _____

_____

_____

Special skills: _____

_____

Activities: _____

_____

References: _____

_____

Writing a Letter to Apply for a Job

In addition to preparing a clear, error-free résumé, you must also write a **cover letter,** also called a **letter of application,** to a potential employer. The purpose of this letter is twofold: to introduce you to the employer and to highlight your skills.

When you write your cover letter, follow these guidelines.

■ Make your letter look professional.

■ Emphasize your good points.

■ Follow a logical format.

■ Be brief.

■ Omit unnecessary or negative details.

■ Proofread for accuracy.

Also follow these additional guidelines, illustrated in the model cover letter on page 455.

Give Your Address and the Date   Place your full return address and the date at the top of the letter.

Address the Letter Correctly   This step is very important. Make sure that the inside address (the address of the person you are writing to) appears *exactly* as it does in the advertisement for the job. Double-check the spelling of any contact names or addresses so that they are correct in your letter.

Begin with a Greeting   Part of making a good impression, even on paper, is being polite. If you know the name of the person who will read your application, use it. If not, you may open your letter with the greeting "Dear Sir or Madam."

A Model Cover Letter

<table>
<tr><td>

</td><td>

1750 43rd Avenue
Sacramento, CA 95823

</td><td>Your return
address</td></tr>
</table>

	1750 43rd Avenue Sacramento, CA 95823	Your return address
Inside address	Ms. Rachel Nguyen Manager Belle Femme Clothing Store 6601 Fourth Avenue Sacramento, CA 95864	November 15, 2005	Date

Greeting — Dear Ms. Nguyen,

Your purpose —   I am writing to apply for the job of assistant manager of the Fourth Avenue Belle Femme Clothing Store as advertised in the Sacramento Gazette.

Your qualifications —   In addition to completing my associate of arts degree from Sacramento City College, I am on my way to achieving a bachelor of arts degree in Fashion Merchandising from California State University in Stockton. I have learned about retail clothing stores both from my course work and from my two positions at Grand Department Store and Monroe's. As my résumé indicates, I am well qualified to work in your store.

Your availability for an interview —   I am very interested in working for you and would be more than willing to come for an interview. I am a high-energy employee who works hard and eagerly takes on responsibility. I have confidence that I can make a positive difference in your store.

Sincerely, — Closing

Jane Michaels

Jane Michaels — Your signature and typed name

Enclosure notation — enc.

Clearly State Your Purpose   In the first paragraph, tell the employer that you are writing to apply for a job, and explain how you heard about the job.

State Your Qualifications for the Job and Willingness to Be Interviewed   Briefly and clearly say why you are qualified for the job, and direct the reader to your résumé. Tell the employer that you are ready and willing to meet for an interview. Emphasize your enthusiasm for the job.

End Your Letter with a Closing Expression   Offering an appropriate closing will make a positive final impression on an employer. Be sure to sign your name in addition to typing it. A polite closing expression is "Sincerely" or "Sincerely yours."

Enclose Your Résumé   Put your résumé in the same envelope with your cover letter. Add the notation "enc." opposite your typed name to show that an item is enclosed.

Writing and Sending E-mail

Thanks to the Internet, people can be in touch quietly, easily, and immediately. E-mail also has the added benefit of not needing to be "answered" right away; you can send a message, and your recipient can read and respond when there's time. Be careful, however: just as there are rules for how to write business letters or how to properly address people on the telephone, there are also rules for email. Consider the following list.

Avoid Sending Potentially Offensive Messages. While you might get a chuckle from an off-color e-mail, someone else might not. Think twice before sending an e-mail message that could even remotely be considered offensive. Particularly at the office—where employers have a legal right to read your (even deleted) messages—what you think is a good joke might result in a bad ending. A good rule of thumb is never to send a message via e-mail that you wouldn't put on a postcard.

Avoid Sending Sensitive Messages. Even if you're dying to communicate something sensitive, don't do it through e-mail. While e-mail is extremely convenient, it does not give you an excuse to send inappropriate messages—such as notes of criticism, gossip, or personal news. For sensitive information, give people the courtesy of addressing them face-to-face, if possible; a phone call should be your next attempt. Sending e-mail, especially anonymous e-mail, to deliver a message that someone might not want to hear is unprofessional and impolite.

Avoid Sending Spam or Chain E-mail. There's little worse than opening an e-mail from a friend only to find that it contains a long, boring message or one that requires you to send copies of the e-mail to five people. While a few people might enjoy such messages, most do not. If you really think people will be interested in a forwarded message, do the following: make sure the message is legitimate, and ask potential recipients for permission before you send it.

Avoid Sending Unedited Messages. Even though e-mail is an informal way to communicate, sending a misspelled, error-ridden message is a sure way to confuse your reader and diminish your credibility. Most e-mail software can check grammar and spelling. If yours doesn't, cut and paste your message into a word processing program that has these functions, and then run a check.

Respond Quickly. Waiting too long to answer someone's e-mail sends a message of disrespect to that person. Even if you're too busy to answer an e-mail fully, sending a quick message—such as "I got your message and will get back to you by tomorrow"—will pay the sender the courtesy of a response. In general, you should answer e-mail messages within one day.

What You Know Now

Most jobs will require you to submit a résumé (a brief summary of your work qualifications) and a cover letter. The keys to both of these documents are accuracy, correctness, and brevity.

WRITING PRACTICE 1   Write a Cover Letter

Advertisements for three jobs appear below.

Dental—Registered Dental Assistant (RDA)

Seeking highly motivated RDA to join our practice. No experience necessary. Computer experience helpful. Many perks and great benefits. Send résumé and cover letter to Ruth Watkins, 72 Florence Boulevard, Fair Park, IL 60617.

Grocery—Section Manager

Now accepting applications for Bakery/Deli Plaza Manager. Great opportunity to work in our chain's nationally recognized flagship store in Northern Arizona. Send application, résumé, and cover letter to Aaron Greentree, 3315 Canyon Avenue, Flagstaff, AZ 43201.

Mechanic—Lawn Equipment

Established turf equipment company is seeking mechanics to work in our La Salle Island repair and new equipment preparation facility. The ideal candidate will have experience in electrical and hydraulic operations. Lawn equipment repairs experience a plus. This is an excellent career position. E-mail résumé and cover letter to Tomtruman@Elkke.com or send to Tom Truman, 4537 Lawn Lane, Atlanta, GA, 77089.

Pretend that you are applying for one of these jobs. Write a rough draft of a letter of application, following the guidelines in this chapter. Concentrate on writing a strong opening paragraph. If possible, ask your instructor or current employer for tips on how to make your opening paragraph more effective.

WRITING PRACTICE 2 Respond to a Help Wanted Ad

Read the advertisements for jobs in a local newspaper or magazine. Then, prepare your résumé as if you were applying for one of the jobs. Next, write a letter of application with clear opening and closing paragraphs, a detailed middle paragraph, and a polite greeting and closing expression. Take care to type the correct contact information in your letter.

Lab Activity 31

For additional practice with writing to get a job, complete Lab Activity 31 in the Lab Manual at the back of the book.

32 Proper Format

Called the City by the Bay, San Francisco, California, boasts an amazing diversity in its population, professions, and entertainment. From its competitive professional sports teams to its Golden Gate Bridge, San Francisco is one of America's most inspiring cities.

General Format Guidelines

Though content is the most important part of your paper, its appearance can affect how convincing you are. For the best results, follow the guidelines below.

- **Use a word processor or computer.** Printed pages look professional and are easier to read than handwritten ones. Computers also allow you to make formatting changes easily.

- **Use standard-sized typing paper, 8 1/2 by 11 inches.** This size paper is commonly used in copy machines and printers.

- **Double-space.** Leaving a blank line after every line of text makes a paper easier to read. Double spacing also gives your instructor or peers a place to write comments.

- **Leave a one-inch margin on all sides.** Leaving room around the edges makes your paper more readable and allows space for comments.

If you write a paper by hand, use blue or black ink, not a pencil. Write neatly on every other line. Make sure punctuation marks are clear and distinct, and leave space after each period.

A Model Student Essay

Raul wrote an essay using the style recommended by the Modern Language Association (MLA). For more information on MLA style, see the *MLA Handbook,* Sixth Edition.

Sierras 1

Raul Sierras

Professor Harris

English 50

12 September 2005

A Not-So-Perfect Day by the Bay

In the movies, San Francisco usually seems to be the perfect spot for a romantic trip. Lovers kiss at sunset on the Golden Gate Bridge, walk hand in hand on Fisherman's Wharf, and eat candlelit dinners on the Bay. My own experience in San Francisco was quite different. I had hoped to surprise my fiancée Cheryl with a day trip to the City by the Bay, and I planned every detail in advance, hoping to surprise her. However, when the big day arrived, I learned that even the best plans can fall apart. My day in San Francisco proved to be a day to forget.

Sierras 2

My first piece of bad news was the
traffic. Since we were going on a Saturday,
from just a hundred miles away, I thought
sure that we'd get an early start, park the
car, and have the rest of the day to explore
on foot. Boy, was I wrong! There was an
accident on the freeway leading into the
city, and even though it was 8 a.m. on a
weekend, the traffic was backed up for
miles. When we finally drove into the city,
we'd spent four hours in the car and were
already grouchy. Looking for a convenient
place to park to make up for the time lost
in traffic, I drove up to several parking
garages, only to learn that parking was $35
for the day! This was not in my budget, but
I decided to skip the fancy dinner and park
the car. The day was not off to a great
start. Our next frustration was the
weather. I'd checked the local weather and
had been assured of a "partially cloudy"
day. However, "partial" cloudiness in San
Francisco must be different from partial
cloudiness where I live because it was

Sierras 3

<u>completely</u> overcast all day long. Cheryl
and I were dressed in lightweight summer
clothes since it was August, but the
temperature never rose above 58 degrees, so
we were uncomfortably chilly all day long.
Our only relief came from staying in
motion, but after walking for three hours,
we were so tired that we had to stop to
rest, and then we froze. Additionally, when
we tried to watch the sunset from Coit
Tower, it was so foggy that we couldn't even
tell when the sun actually set. I guess I
could have used the weather to my advantage
and snuggled up to Cheryl for warmth, but
she was already so mad at me because of the
drive, the weather, and too much walking
that I decided to just stay cold.

The last irritation of the day came
from the one-way streets. We had parked
downtown in a parking garage that had been
very easy to find. Getting back to the
freeway, however, was not so easy. It was
dark when we left, and though Cheryl kept
looking at the map, she couldn't see much.

Sierras 4

Plus, every time she'd find a street that seemed to lead straight into the freeway, it would be a one-way street heading the wrong way. I think I must have circled the same two miles about six times before we finally saw a dirty sign (which we should have seen sooner) that pointed us in the right direction. I felt great relief as I entered the freeway, only to realize I was going in the wrong direction. This was not my day.

The only thing good that came from my day in San Francisco was that I learned what a trouper Cheryl is. She was mad at me early for the parking and weather, but once things began to get really frustrating, she just laughed. In fact, though it took forever finding the freeway, we were laughing so much at our poor sense of direction that we erased a lot of the day's earlier negative experiences. When I apologized to Cheryl for the day not being the perfect romantic experience, she smiled at me and said that as long as she's with me, things don't have to be perfect. We plan to visit San

```
                                    Sierras 5

Francisco again--in a different month, and

when we don't have to drive--and do it

justice. I just know that the City by the

Bay will be worth one more try.
```

The Golden Gate Bridge

JOURNAL ENTRY A combination of natural and manmade beauty, San Francisco, California, offers a range of culture, art, and activity. What do you know or imagine about San Francisco? Write for ten minutes about your impressions of San Francisco. (You do not need to have visited the city to write about it.)

Title and Heading

A clear, direct title and paper heading will make a good impression.

- **Write a brief descriptive title.** For instance, if the first sentence of your paper is "San Francisco is my favorite city for many reasons," your title could be "My Favorite City."
- **Center the title on the first line of the first page.** Do not use quotation marks, bold print, italics, or underlining, and do not add a period.
- **Capitalize the first, last, and main words in your title.** The following words usually do not require capitalization.

Articles:	a, an, the	*The Golden Gate Bridge and the Sea*
Prepositions:	in, of, to, etc.	"The City by the Bay"
Coordinating conjunctions:	for, and, nor, but, or, yet, so	*Alcatraz and the Long, Cold Swim*

- **Type your heading as instructed.** Include your name, your instructor's name, your course name or number, and the date. Some instructors prefer a separate cover sheet, while others ask for this information at the top of the first page or on the last page. If you are not sure where to place these details, ask your instructor.

Starting Your Paper

To start the text, skip a line after your title. Indent the first line five spaces from the left-hand margin. Additionally, indent each new paragraph.

Remember to number each page in the upper right-hand corner unless your instructor directs you to place the numbers elsewhere.

EXERCISE 1 CORRECTING MISTAKES IN FORMAT

Read the following passage. Then, write down the formatting errors you find. The first error has been identified for you.

<u>The city by the bay</u>

One of my favorite places to visit is San Francisco. One reason it is such a great city is the food.I love San Francisco sourdough bread, so I always get some when I go there.I also like saltwater taffy, which is easy to find down on the wharf.Another reason I like San Francisco is its football team.Even though my whole family likes the Oakland Raiders, I like

the Forty-Niners.

1. Title should be centered. _____

2. Title should not be underlined. _____

3. Main words in title should be capitalized. _____

4. First line should be indented. _____

5. There should be a space after each period. _____

EXERCISE 2 WRITING TITLES

Write a title for a paper based on each thesis sentence below. An example is done for you. Answers will vary.

Thesis: Riding a cable car in San Francisco is a crazy experience.

Title: A Crazy Ride or A Crazy Experience _____

1. Thesis: The former prison at Alcatraz is an interesting place to visit.

   Title: An Interesting Place _____

2. Thesis: The Forty-Niners are a great football team.

   Title: A Great Football Team _____

3. Thesis: San Francisco has been the inspiration for many songs.

   Title: An Inspiring City _____

4. Thesis: San Francisco has suffered from earthquakes.

   Title: A Shaky Place _____

5. Thesis: San Francisco has many impressive sights.

   Title: A City of Impressive Sights _____

EDITING PRACTICE

Mark any errors in format as you read the paragraph on the next page. Make corrections above the errors.

San Francisco Treats
"~~san francisco treats~~"

¶San Francisco has been the inspiration for many movies and songs#In the 1960s, Tony Bennett sang the hit song, "I Left My Heart^in San Francisco."#The band Journey also had a hit song, "Lights," which was popular in the 1980s and which featured San Francisco.¶Many movies have been set in San Francisco, too.#Disney made a number of movies in the late 1960s and 1970s about a Volkswagon Bug named Herbie.#More recently, Robin Williams starred in the movie *Mrs. Doubtfire.*#In this film he plays a San Francisco father who dresses up as^a woman and works as a nanny so he can visit his children.

Lab Activity 32

For additional practice with proper format, complete Lab Activity 32 in the Lab Manual at the back of the book.

PART SEVEN
Writing Correct Sentences

GRAMMAR AND PUNCTUATION DIAGNOSTICS

Grammar

The following exercises will help you recognize what you already know about grammar, punctuation, and mechanics and what areas you may need to learn more about. Do your best to answer the questions correctly, but don't worry about making mistakes. Your responses, even if they are not correct, will help your instructor see how best to help you improve your sentence-level writing skills.

Diagnostic Quiz

Take the following quiz to see how much you already know about grammar. The headings that appear throughout the quiz ("Fragments," "Run-On Sentences," and so forth) will help you identify which of your grammar skills need improvement. Read each item carefully. Then, determine whether or not an error is present in the underlined section. Place an X in the answer space if there is an error in the underlined section. Write a C in the answer space if the underlined section is correct.

Grammar Quiz

Fragments

___X___ **1.** <u>If I hadn't eaten so many Krispy Kreme doughnuts</u>. I might be able to fit into this size 6 dress.

___X___ **2.** I love doughnuts. <u>Because they are sweet and satisfying</u>.

___C___ **3.** <u>I have worked hard trying to find the perfect doughnut</u>.

___X___ **4.** I found Krispy Kreme doughnuts. <u>Which are the world's best.</u>

___C___ **5.** <u>However, whenever I eat a doughnut</u>, I immediately regret it.

___X___ **6.** I am unhappy with myself. <u>Even if I only eat one bite</u>.

Run-On Sentences

___X___ **7.** Chocolate can sometimes boost people's <u>moods it can</u> also cause people to get indigestion.

___C___ **8.** It's always hard to decide whether or not to eat chocolate. <u>Sometimes</u> eating it just isn't worth the stomachache.

___X___ **9.** However, I've become very good at preparing rich chocolate <u>desserts, the</u> secret is just not eating them.

___C___ **10.** People often wonder why I don't even taste my own chocolate <u>creations, but</u> it's too hard to stop eating once I start.

___C___ **11.** I've learned that using willpower early pays <u>off. I</u> don't get indigestion that way.

___X___ **12.** Every so often, though, I just have to have some <u>chocolate then</u> I have to put up with feeling queasy for a little while.

Regular Verbs

___X___ **13.** Annabelle <u>think</u> of others often.

___C___ **14.** Her mother <u>tells</u> her that it's good manners to consider other people.

___X___ **15.** However, Annabelle <u>live</u> her life to please herself.

___X___ **16.** She just <u>feel</u> happier if she's nice to other people.

Irregular Verbs

___X___ **17.** I have not <u>taked</u> a good math class all year.

___X___ **18.** Last year, Ms. Fontaine <u>teached</u> me a lot about algebra.

___X___ **19.** In fact, she <u>sweared</u> that I could learn trigonometry, too.

___C___ **20.** Unfortunately, she <u>left</u> our school in the spring.

Subject-Verb Agreement

___C___ **21.** Both of my parents <u>have</u> a few secrets.

___X___ **22.** One of my mother's secrets <u>are</u> that she likes *The Simpsons*.

___C___ **23.** My father's secrets <u>stay</u> in our family most of the time.

___X___ **24.** There <u>are</u> a rule in our family that we keep each other's secrets.

Verb Tense and Tense Consistency

___X___ **25.** Acting like a child was Andrew's best personality trait; he always <u>makes</u> me laugh.

___X___ **26.** One time, he spread food all over his face, and I <u>can't</u> stop myself from giggling.

___C___ **27.** Another time, he pretended that he <u>was</u> crying after he lost a toy.

___X___ **28.** Andrew's best act came when he <u>sucks</u> his thumb.

Pronoun Agreement

___C___ **29.** Every part of the country has <u>its</u> own special features.

___X___ **30.** For instance, people who visit New York love the tall buildings that amaze <u>you</u>.

___C___ **31.** If you should go to the American South, people will talk to <u>you</u> in charming voices.

___X___ **32.** Everyone in California seems to have <u>their</u> own special style.

___X___ **33.** I love Hawaii in the winter, but <u>they</u> have unpredictable weather.

___X___ **34.** Midwesterners have their own special habits, and I love <u>it</u>.

Pronoun Types

__X__ **35.** Between <u>he and I</u>, we have a lot to offer.

__C__ **36.** When I looked through the peephole, I saw that it was <u>he</u>.

Adjectives and Adverbs

__X__ **37.** Italian restaurants are the <u>most best</u> places for eating pasta.

__X__ **38.** I take my work <u>serious</u>.

Misplaced Modifiers

__X__ **39.** Lee loved eating ice cream sundaes in the huge bowl <u>with whipped cream on top</u>.

__X__ **40.** Marsha serves people ice cream in her own home <u>that she made with her new ice cream maker</u>.

__X__ **41.** I stopped eating the ice cream from the soda shop <u>that gave me a headache</u>.

__X__ **42.** I use only fresh cream in my ice cream maker <u>that comes from the neighbor's cow</u>.

Dangling Modifiers

__X__ **43.** <u>Sleeping with her head on my shoulder</u>, the blanket covered the baby.

__X__ **44.** <u>Drooling on my new sweater</u>, my lullaby put the infant to sleep.

__C__ **45.** <u>While she was sleeping</u>, her little face looked so sweet.

__X__ **46.** <u>Dreaming a happy dream</u>, smiling at the baby came easily.

Errors in Parallelism

__X__ **47.** I love getting my nails done, having my hair highlighted, and <u>to get facials</u>.

_____C_____ **48.** Taking care of myself makes me feel <u>confident, relaxed, and attractive</u>.

_____X_____ **49.** I've thought about attending beauty school; <u>or college is a possibility</u>.

_____X_____ **50.** Both beauty school and college would allow me to learn new skills, meet new people, and <u>to improve my life</u>.

Punctuation

Just as the grammar diagnostic test may have helped you see opportunities for improving your sentence skills, the punctuation test will help you see how much you already know about using commas and other punctuation. Additionally, this test will help you see areas that need improvement in using proper mechanics—capitalization and word choice, for instance—in your writing.

Diagnostic Quiz

The following quiz will help you determine your basic understanding of punctuation, mechanics, and word use. Read each sentence or group of sentences carefully. Then, decide whether errors are present in each underlined section. Write an X in the space if errors are present, or write a C if the underlined section is correct. The headings in the quiz ("Commas," "Apostrophes," and so forth) will help you determine your punctuation strengths or show you areas where you should improve your skills.

Commas

_____X_____ **1.** Some well-known Chicago figures include <u>Al Capone Richard Daley Harold Washington and Oprah Winfrey</u>.

_____C_____ **2.** <u>A few years ago</u>, Chicago decided to host an unusual art display.

_____X_____ **3.** Oprah Winfrey <u>one of Chicago's most famous residents</u> has done much to benefit other people.

_____C_____ **4.** <u>Chicago is run by aldermen</u>, but the Chicago mayor has influence as well.

_____C_____ **5.** <u>Frank Sinatra sang</u>, "Chicago is my kind of town."

_____X_____ **6.** Chicago is the home of <u>more than 2800000 people</u>.

_____X_____ **7.** I last visited Chicago on <u>May 5 2005</u>.

Apostrophes

_____C_____ **8.** <u>I've</u> had a cold for three <u>weeks</u>.

_____X_____ **9.** <u>Its</u> terrible, so I hope <u>youre</u> not going to get it.

_____X_____ **10.** At the <u>doctors</u> office, Ron has seen notices for flu shots.

_____C_____ **11.** However, <u>Ron's</u> never been very good at picking up hints.

Quotation Marks

_____C_____ **12.** My boyfriend always says, <u>"Gloria Steinem has hurt men."</u>

_____X_____ **13.** My mother told me, <u>You need to grow up to take care of a husband just as I did</u>.

_____X_____ **14.** A notable article that Gloria Steinem wrote was titled <u>The Moral Disarmament of Betty Coed</u>.

_____C_____ **15.** The term <u>"misogynist"</u> is never a compliment.

Capitalization

_____X_____ **16.** <u>my friend john and i</u> thought we'd try to see <u>victoria falls</u>.

_____C_____ **17.** We had packed our bags, loaded the <u>Honda Civic</u>, and filled the tank with <u>Chevron</u> gas before John said, "Maybe we should look at a map."

_____X_____ **18.** Judge Frawley presides over the court where <u>governor jones</u> is on trial.

_____C_____ **19.** Because I have always wanted to travel, I have taken <u>American Geography 101, French, and literature</u>.

33 Prepositional Phrases

CULTURE NOTE *Fables*

In a fable, a fictitious story meant to teach a lesson, the characters are usually talking animals whose behavior mirrors human behavior. Fables often combine entertainment with education and are an important part of folklore.

The Tortoise and the Hare

WRITE A PARAGRAPH Despite the fast-paced, high-tech lifestyle of many Americans, the lessons from Aesop's fables, such as "The Tortoise and the Hare," still hold meaning. What childhood lessons still hold meaning for you? Write a paragraph discussing which lessons learned in childhood are important to you.

Identifying Prepositional Phrases

A **phrase** is a group of related words lacking a subject and a verb. A **prepositional phrase** is a phrase beginning with a preposition. Many prepositional phrases show spatial and time relationships between ideas. Recognizing prepositional phrases can help you identify the subject and verb of a sentence, as you will see later in this chapter.

The easiest way to identify prepositional phrases is to look for prepositions (see the box below). A **preposition** shows the relationship between a noun or pronoun and the rest of a sentence. The prepositions are underlined in the following examples.

<u>in</u> the house   <u>with</u> her sister

<u>after</u> the game   <u>for</u> breakfast

Some of the words listed in the box below can also function as other parts of speech, such as conjunctions.

The words *to* and *through* are common prepositions. Here, *to* and *through* begin two prepositional phrases.

The way <u>to</u> a man's heart is <u>through</u> his stomach.

Common Prepositions

aboard	besides	on
about	between	onto
above	beyond	out
according to	by	outside
across	concerning	over
after	despite	through
against	during	throughout
along	except	to
along with	for	toward
among	from	under
around	in	underneath
at	inside	until
before	into	up
behind	like	upon
below	near	with
beneath	of	within
beside	off	without

To determine the end of a phrase, remember that *every preposition asks a question.* The noun that answers the question is the end of the prepositional phrase. When you see the word *to* in a sentence, ask yourself "To what?" When you see the word *through,* ask yourself "Through what?" In the example above, the nouns that answer those two questions—*heart* and *stomach*—mark the ends of the prepositional phrases.

There is no shortcut to learning the prepositions. You simply need to learn the list on page 478.

EXERCISE 1 WRITING PREPOSITIONAL PHRASES

Write two prepositional phrases using each of the prepositions below. Practice answering the question that the preposition asks. An example is done for you. Answers will vary.

Over   **a.** *Over the rainbow*   **b.** *Over the telephone*

1. After   **a.** _____   **b.** _____

2. Below   **a.** _____   **b.** _____

3. Toward   **a.** _____   **b.** _____

4. Until   **a.** _____   **b.** _____

5. Without   **a.** _____   **b.** _____

Using Prepositional Phrases to Identify the Subject and Verb of a Sentence

After you have identified the prepositional phrases in a sentence, cross them out.

Example: The way ~~to a man's heart~~ is ~~through his stomach~~.

You're left with *The way is.* These remaining words are the subject and verb of the sentence: *The way* is the subject, and *is* is the verb. By eliminating the prepositional phrases, you've made the job of identifying the subject and verb much easier.

Watching Out for Infinitives

An **infinitive** is a verb form that looks like a prepositional phrase but isn't. The infinitives underlined below are made up of the word *to* plus a verb—for example, *to run*.

Henry ran fast <u>to escape</u> the school bully.

<u>To get</u> good grades, Marian studied hard every night.

Before I could ask <u>to go</u> to the concert with Ben, he invited me.

Note that the infinitive in each sentence is *not* the verb.

EXERCISE 2 IDENTIFYING PREPOSITIONAL PHRASES

Identify the thirty-two prepositional phrases in the following sentences. Underline the prepositional phrases, and circle the prepositions. An example is done for you.

"The Grasshopper and the Ants" is a fable (by) Aesop.

1. One day (in) winter some ants were drying their supply (of) food.

2. The food was lying (in) a pool of water (after) a long rain.

3. A hungry grasshopper approached them and asked (for) a few grains (of) corn.

4. The grasshopper appeared to be weak (from) hunger.

5. The ants kept working (at) their drying (for) a long time (until) a few of them turned (to) the grasshopper.

6. The ants asked the grasshopper why she had no food (of) her own.

7. The grasshopper first turned away and then turned back (to) the ants (with) a tear (in) her eye.

8. The grasshopper complained that (during) summer she had had no time (for) gathering food.

9. "What," asked the ants, "kept you (from) finding food (until) winter?"

10. The grasshopper's tears flowed (to) the ground as she thought (about) her sad plight.

11. She said she was singing (underneath) a shady leaf and had no time left (for) work.

12. The ants went back (to) their hardworking sisters and discussed the matter (concerning) the hungry grasshopper.

13. Coming (to) an agreement (among) themselves, the ants all turned back (toward) the grasshopper.

14. "If you spent the days (of) summer singing, then you can spend the nights (of) winter dancing," said the ants, sending her away (without) a bite.

15. The moral (of) the story is "It is best to prepare today (for) the needs of tomorrow."

EDITING PRACTICE

Identify the eleven prepositional phrases in the following paragraph. Underline the prepositional phrases and circle the prepositions. There may not be a prepositional phrase in every sentence.

The North Wind and the Sun: A Fable

The North Wind and the Sun each claimed to be stronger than the other. Finally they agreed to test their powers (on) a traveler to see who could get him to remove his coat. The North Wind tried first, whirling furiously (around) the man, grabbing (at) his coat (in) a burst (of) power. But the harder the wind blew, the more closely the man wrapped his coat (around) himself. Next, it was the Sun's turn. First, the Sun beamed gently (upon) the traveler, who unbuttoned his coat and strolled (with) it loosely hanging open. Then the Sun shone brightly (in) full strength, and when the man had gone only a few steps, he was happy to take off his coat and continue (without) it. The moral of (the) story is this: Gentle persuasion works better than force.

Lab Activity 33

For additional practice with prepositions, complete Lab Activity 33 in the Lab Manual at the back of the book.

34 Subjects and Verbs

The Main Parts of a Sentence

Subjects and verbs are the basic units of sentences. In fact, a group of words can't be a sentence unless it includes both a subject and a verb. Some sentences also have **objects,** words that receive the action or direction of another word such as a verb or preposition.

Identifying Verbs

Verbs tell us what's going on in a sentence. They express any action or change in time and condition that takes place. **Main verbs** communicate the primary action or state of being in a sentence while **helping verbs** let us know when and under what conditions the action of the main verb took place. **Linking verbs** connect the subject to words that identify or modify it. Read the sentences below, and for each sentence, ask "What's going on?"

A rolling stone <u>gathers</u> no moss. (The stone is *gathering* no moss.)

Silence <u>is</u> golden. (Silence is identified as *being* golden.)

Still waters <u>run</u> deep. (Waters are *running* deep.)

Poor Richard's Almanack

FOOD FOR THOUGHT Known for its inventions and pithy sayings, Ben Franklin's book *Poor Richard's Almanack* contains expressions we still hear today, such as "haste makes waste." Write a few sentences explaining how certain expressions—heard from people you know—are meaningful for you.

Note that for the sentence containing *is,* the explanation of what's going on includes the word *being:* silence is *being* golden. Some verbs, such as the verb *to be,* do not show overt action so much as a state of being. Forms of the verb *to be* (*am, is, are, was, were, be, being, been*) can act as the main verb of a sentence.

Complete Verbs

Helping verbs work with main verbs to communicate *when* an action took place or the *conditions* under which it took place. The **complete verb** in a sentence includes helping verbs and main verbs. In order to fully understand the rules of grammar and punctuation, you need to be able to identify *all parts of the verb.*

The complete verbs are underlined in the following sentences. The helping verbs (in bold print) tell *when* the action of the main verb takes place.

A man **is** known by the company he keeps. (*Is* indicates when someone is known by his company: now, not in the past or future.)

The chickens **have** come home to roost. (*Have* indicates when the chickens came home: some time before now.)

In the following sentences, the helping verbs indicate *condition*. The helping verbs qualify whether or not the action of the main verb will actually take place.

I **would** try harder to memorize proverbs if I had help. (*Would* makes it clear that the writer will try harder only after receiving help.)

Julia **may** read the book you lent her. (*May* indicates a possibility that Julia will not read the book.)

Sometimes both types of helping verbs—those indicating time and those indicating condition—are used together in a sentence. The complete verbs in the following sentences are underlined.

She may have heard the news. (*May* casts doubt as to whether she has heard the news; *have* indicates that the news was received sometime before now.)

You should be going to work. (*Should* communicates a recommendation that someone go to work; *be* indicates that the action of *going* takes place now, not in the past.)

Linking Verbs

Linking verbs, which link the subject to words that identify or modify it, often indicate action that can't be seen.

Tom appears happy to be home.

Shaunte feels better about her decision to stay in school.

Think of linking verbs as equal signs when they are used as the main verb in a sentence. For instance, you could think of "Marina is my best friend" as "Marina = my best friend." Other linking verbs that act as equal signs are *appear, be* (*am, is, are, was, were*), *become, feel, look,* and *seem.*

Common Helping Verbs

is	can	might
do	shall	could
have	are	should
will	does	been
may	had	has
must	would	

EXERCISE 1 IDENTIFYING THE COMPLETE VERB

Underline the complete verb in each sentence below. *Hint:* Cross out any prepositional phrases first. The first one is done for you.

1. Certainly that new kid ~~at school~~ <u>will be</u> a thorn ~~in my side~~.

2. I <u>have learned</u> to take my grandmother's advice ~~with a grain of salt~~.

3. Nicola <u>is falling</u> ~~for the salesman's pitch~~ hook, line, and sinker.

4. I <u>would have gone</u> skiing if not ~~for my conscience~~.

5. Tonight ~~at seven o'clock~~ I <u>will be</u> off ~~to the land of Nod~~.

Identifying the Subject

The **subject** of a sentence says what the sentence is about. Once you've identified the verb, you can find the subject by asking yourself *who* or *what* is performing the action of the verb. The subject of a sentence is often a **noun**—the name of a person, place, thing, or idea. In the following sentences, the subjects are in bold print and the verbs are underlined.

Simple **conversation** <u>breaks</u> the ice at a party. (Who or what is doing the breaking? A *conversation* is.)

Frank <u>faced</u> the music after his conviction. (Who or what was doing the facing? *Frank* was.)

Time <u>is</u> money. (Who or what is money? *Time* is.)

Finding More Than One Subject or Verb

A sentence must have at least one subject and one verb, but some sentences may have more than one subject or verb. Subjects with more than one part are called **compound subjects.** Verbs with more than one part are called **compound verbs.** Finding subjects and verbs involves finding *all* subjects and verbs in a sentence.

John and Jane cut a rug at the dance. (*John* and *Jane* are the subjects of the sentence.)

John and Jane danced and sang until the cows came home. (*Danced* and *sang* are the verbs of the sentence.)

EXERCISE 2 IDENTIFYING SUBJECTS AND VERBS

Read the following sentences. Underline the subjects once and the complete verbs twice. Some sentences contain more than one subject or verb. *Hint:* Cross out any prepositional phrases first.

1. Tad and Rhea do things by the book.
2. When the cat is away, the mice will play.
3. You can never teach an old dog new tricks.
4. The grass is always greener on the other side of the fence.
5. Absence makes the heart grow fonder.
6. Jill does not judge a book by its cover.
7. Lightning never strikes twice in the same place.
8. Too many cooks spoil the broth.
9. You can't unscramble an egg.
10. One good turn deserves another.

What to Watch Out For

Finding subjects and verbs is often an easy process. However, some sentence elements can look like subjects and verbs and, thus, make the identification process more difficult. Some of the most common causes for confusion are explained below.

Nouns That Follow the Verb

Marco still <u>carries</u> a torch for Francine.

In the sentence above, you might have been tempted to choose *torch* as the subject of the underlined verb. This word isn't part of a prepositional phrase, and it is a noun. However, *torch* is not the subject of the sentence. Ask yourself who or what does the carrying. You can see that Marco, not the torch, is performing the action of the verb. Thus, *Marco* is the subject.

The subjects are underlined in the sentences below, and any nouns following the verb are in italics.

<u>Mom</u> baked a *cake* for my birthday. (*Mom,* not *cake,* is doing the baking.)

<u>Ana</u> found a gold *watch* near her *house.* (*Ana,* not *watch* or *house,* did the finding.)

Pronouns

A **pronoun** is a word that can take the place of a noun. Pronouns as well as nouns can be subjects. Watch for the following pronouns as the subjects of sentences.

I	it	you	we
he	they	she	

Treat pronoun subjects exactly the same way that you would treat any other subjects.

<u>I</u> went to the store.   <u>She</u> reads frequently.

Commands

Sometimes the subject of a sentence will be the pronoun *you,* but the word *you* will not appear in the sentence. For instance, in the saying "Don't burn your bridges behind you," the subject is actually *you.* Written out completely, the sentence is "(You) don't burn your bridges behind you." Because the sentence is a **command**—an order to do something—the writer doesn't need to include the subject specifically. Keep in mind that if a sentence appears to be giving an order, the subject is probably *you*. Each pair of sentences below contains one sentence where *you* is not written and one sentence where *you* is written in parentheses.

Wait for me after the game.   Don't go near the fire!

(You) wait for me after the game.   (You) don't go near the fire!

Understanding Objects

A **direct object** is a noun or pronoun that receives the action of the verb.

Ed drove his <u>car</u> too fast.

An **indirect object** is a noun or pronoun that receives the direct object.

I made <u>Alan</u> a sandwich.

The **object of a preposition** is the noun or pronoun introduced by a preposition.

The devil can cite scripture for his <u>purpose</u>.

No, not, and *always*

Watch out for words such as *no, not, never, always, still, very,* and *just*. These words are **adverbs,** words that describe verbs. They often sit right next to the verbs, but they are *not* part of the verb.

Marian <u>was</u> **always** <u>acting</u> like a prima donna. (*Was acting* is the verb; *always* is not part of the verb.)

Peter <u>would</u> **never** <u>steal</u> his sister's thunder. (*Would steal* is the verb; *never* is not part of the verb.)

Words Ending in *-ing*

Words ending in *-ing* are never the verb of a sentence all by themselves. (An *-ing* word can be part of the verb, but only if a helping verb is in front of it.)

Incorrect: Gary <u>driving</u> Maria crazy with his practical jokes. (*Driving* is not a complete verb. Thus, the group of words does not form a complete sentence.)

Correct: Gary <u>is driving</u> Maria crazy with his practical jokes. (*Is driving* is the whole verb, so the sentence is complete.)

Infinitives

Verbs with *to* in front of them are never the verb of the sentence.

Wilma <u>wanted</u> **to bury** the hatchet with Reni. (*Wanted,* not *bury,* is the verb.)

EXERCISE 3 FINDING COMPLETE SUBJECTS AND VERBS

In the following sentences, underline the subjects once and the verbs twice. Some sentences contain more than one subject or verb. Be sure to underline all parts of the verb. *Hint:* Cross out any prepositional phrases first.

1. Actions speak louder than words.

2. Beggars can't be choosers.

3. The early bird catches the worm.

4. Yolita can't hold a candle ~~to her mother~~.

5. After breaking up ~~with his girlfriend~~, Leon felt down ~~in the dumps~~.

6. A stitch ~~in time~~ saves nine.

7. It never rains but it pours.

8. A leopard can't change his spots.

9. (You) give him enough rope and he will hang himself.

10. Though he looked scruffy, my puppy proved to be a diamond ~~in the rough~~.

EDITING PRACTICE

In the italicized section of each sentence below, underline the subjects once and the verbs twice. *Hint:* Cross out any prepositional phrases first. An example is done for you.

When his sister totaled his car, *Joe hit the ceiling.*

1. *Hiro hoped that his hit album* would make him more than a flash ~~in the pan~~.

2. Coming home late from work five nights ~~in a row~~, *Suki was ~~in the dog-house with her husband~~.*

3. *Sarah figured that ~~after two weeks on the job~~,* she would know the ropes.

4. Juan wanted his promotion to be a secret, but *his boss let the cat ~~out of the bag~~.*

5. By the time the electricity came back on ~~at the end of the power black-out~~, *I was at the end of my rope.*

6. ~~After her job interview,~~ *Shawna waited ~~on pins and needles~~.*

7. When the scandal grew ~~out of proportion~~, *the company president passed the buck ~~to his vice president~~.*

8. After his boss hired a new assistant, *Robert believed himself to be a fifth wheel ~~at the office~~.*

9. *Plain old elbow grease* caused Terry to get the job done.

10. Though Tom had feet ~~of clay~~, *he seemed perfect ~~at first impression~~.*

Proverbs and Idioms Explained

These expressions appear in examples in this chapter.

"A rolling stone gathers no moss" means that (1) something or some-one on the move will pay the price of never putting down permanent roots; (2) people who are always on the move avoid responsibility; or (3) people who stay active will also stay vital.

"Silence is golden" means that silence is even better than speaking.

"Still waters run deep" means that a person who is quiet can have great depth of character.

"The chickens have come home to roost" indicates that the conse-quences of earlier actions or mistakes are being felt.

A "thorn in one's side" is something that gives constant irritation or pain.

To take advice "with a grain of salt" is to give it little credit.

To "fall for something hook, line, and sinker" means to believe it completely.

To go "off to the land of Nod" means to go to sleep.

To "break the ice" means to improve an awkward situation, often through conversation.

To "face the music" is to accept unpleasant consequences.

"Time is money" means that wasting time will lead to losing money.

(continued)

Proverbs and Idioms Explained *(continued)*

To "cut a rug" means to dance enthusiastically.

"Till the cows came home" means that something happened for a long time, usually all night.

To do something "by the book" is to follow established rules.

"When the cat is away, the mice will play" means that when the person usually in authority is gone, subordinates will act more freely.

"You can't teach an old dog new tricks" means that people who have done things the same way for a long time will not change.

"The grass is always greener on the other side of the fence" means that no matter what people have, they always want something different.

"Absence makes the heart grow fonder" means that we value things more when we are away from them.

"You can't judge a book by its cover" means that you can't always tell what something is like just by looking at it.

"Lightning never strikes twice in the same place" means that the same misfortune cannot happen to the same person twice. (In real life, however, lightning often strikes the same object again.)

"Too many cooks spoil the broth" means that when too many people work on the same thing, they ruin the results.

"You can't unscramble an egg" means that some processes are irreversible.

"One good turn deserves another" means that we should return favors people do for us.

To "carry a torch" for someone is to have romantic feelings toward that person.

"The devil can cite scripture for his purpose" means that even good things can be used for evil ends.

A "prima donna" is (1) the lead woman singer in an opera; (2) a demanding, hard-to-please person, usually a woman.

To "steal someone's thunder" means to take attention away from someone who has earned it.

To "drive someone crazy" means to irritate someone.

To "bury the hatchet" means to forgive and forget disagreements.

A "flash in the pan" is something that makes a brief but not lasting impression.

To be "in the doghouse" is to be in trouble.

To "know the ropes" is to be familiar with the way things are done.

Proverbs and Idioms Explained (*continued*)

To "let the cat out of the bag" is to tell a secret.

To be "at the end of one's rope" is to be out of patience.

To be "on pins and needles" is to be anxious about the outcome of something.

To "pass the buck" means to blame someone else instead of accepting responsibility.

To be a "fifth wheel" is to feel out of place.

"Elbow grease" means physical effort.

A person with "feet of clay" has character flaws that are not immediately obvious.

Lab Activity 34

For additional practice with writing correct sentences, complete Lab Activity 34 in the Lab Manual at the back of the book.

35 Clauses

CULTURE NOTE *Bread*

Although food varies from culture to culture, almost every type of cuisine includes some type of bread. From naan in India and tortillas in Mexico to croissants in France, bread plays a major role in many cultures' meals.

Clauses and Sentences

In almost every area of life, some elements of an object or a situation are more important than others. For instance, in a car, the fuel pump is more important than the audio components. Different sections of sentences are more important than others, too. One important aspect to writing well involves knowing how to emphasize the ideas that you think are the most important through their placement in a sentence.

What Is a Clause?

The basic unit of a sentence is the **clause,** which is a group of related words having a subject and a verb that work together to communicate an idea. The first two word groups below are examples of short clauses. Some examples of longer clauses follow.

Birds fly. (*Birds* is the subject; *fly* is the verb.)

Go! (*You* is understood to be the subject; *go* is the verb.)

Every season we bake a different type of bread to accompany our meals. (*We* is the subject; *bake* is the verb.)

If we ever had to give up eating bread, we would starve. (*We* is a subject, and *had* is a verb; *we* is a subject, and *would starve* is a verb.)

EXERCISE 1 IDENTIFYING CLAUSES AND PHRASES

Read the sentences below. Then, identify the italicized section of each sentence group as either a **phrase** (a group of related words that doesn't have a subject and a verb) or a clause. Write P for a phrase and C for a clause. *Note:* Crossing out the prepositional phrases and underlining the subjects and verbs may help you determine whether a group of words is a clause. An example is done for you.

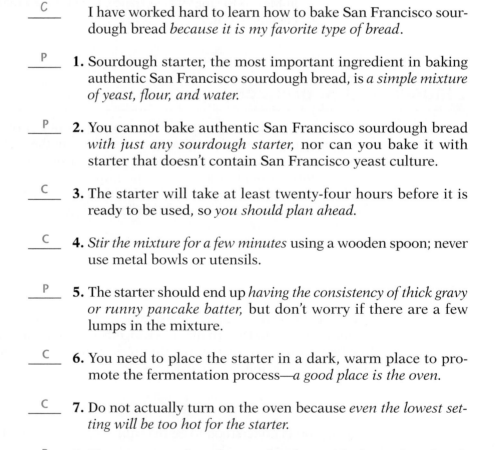

___C___ I have worked hard to learn how to bake San Francisco sourdough bread *because it is my favorite type of bread*.

___P___ **1.** Sourdough starter, the most important ingredient in baking authentic San Francisco sourdough bread, is *a simple mixture of yeast, flour, and water*.

___P___ **2.** You cannot bake authentic San Francisco sourdough bread *with just any sourdough starter,* nor can you bake it with starter that doesn't contain San Francisco yeast culture.

___C___ **3.** The starter will take at least twenty-four hours before it is ready to be used, so *you should plan ahead*.

___C___ **4.** *Stir the mixture for a few minutes* using a wooden spoon; never use metal bowls or utensils.

___P___ **5.** The starter should end up *having the consistency of thick gravy or runny pancake batter,* but don't worry if there are a few lumps in the mixture.

___C___ **6.** You need to place the starter in a dark, warm place to promote the fermentation process—*a good place is the oven*.

___C___ **7.** Do not actually turn on the oven because *even the lowest setting will be too hot for the starter*.

___P___ **8.** The starter needs *to ferment for about eight hours*, but there's no need to worry if you wait a little less or a little more time.

<u>P</u> **9.** *After eight hours or so*, add one cup of bread flour and one cup of water to the starter. You can also wait until the starter has reached its peak, when it becomes bubbly.

<u>C</u> **10.** Mix this additional flour and water into the starter. *Return the starter to the oven* and let it sit for another eight hours or so.

Independent Clauses

A clause that makes sense all by itself is an **independent clause.** An independent clause is a complete sentence. In the sentence "Birds fly," you may wonder why someone is giving you this piece of information, but you probably understand what the speaker is talking about without further explanation. The following sentences are examples of longer independent clauses.

Manuel retired from his job as a baker after forty-three years of service. (*Manuel* is the subject; *retired* is the verb.)

After returning home from the bakery, he decided to fix a snack. (*He* is the subject; *decided* is the verb.)

He piled meat, cheese, peppers, and tomatoes on some bread. (*He* is the subject; *piled* is the verb.)

Dependent Clauses

A group of words that has a subject and a verb but doesn't make sense all by itself is a **dependent clause.** When a dependent clause is not attached to an independent clause, it is a **fragment.** The dependent clauses are underlined in the sentences below.

<u>Because she was shy</u>, Mary never spoke up in class.

<u>Although I love music</u>, I prefer peace and quiet in the morning.

Each of the dependent clauses has a subject (*she, I*) and a verb (*was, love*). Remember that for a group of words to be a clause of any kind, it must have a subject and a verb. A dependent clause, however, has another element: a dependent word. Note that *a clause with a dependent word cannot be a sentence.* In the following clauses, dependent words are underlined. Cover the dependent words and read the clauses that remain.

<u>Because</u> she was shy

<u>Although</u> I love music

Dependent clauses are so named because they *depend* or *rely* on an independent clause to make sense. Without the dependent words, the clauses are *independent* and make sense all by themselves. With the dependent words, the clauses do not make sense on their own and are therefore *dependent* clauses. You'll need to memorize the list of dependent words in the box below.

Common Dependent Words

after	before	since	until
although	even though	though	when
because	if	unless	while

EXERCISE 2 IDENTIFYING CLAUSES

Read the clauses below. If a clause is independent, write IC in front of it, and if a clause is dependent, write DC. *Hint:* If you're not sure whether a clause is independent or dependent, read the clause aloud. If it sounds as if it needs more information to make sense, most likely it's a dependent clause.

_DC_ Because she was going to the store.

_DC_ **1.** When Christmas draws near.

_IC_ **2.** My grandmother always makes her famous stollen, a German Christmas bread.

_IC_ **3.** Stollen is a slightly sweet raised bread made with mashed potatoes.

<u>DC</u>   **4.** Because the bread is baked at festive times.

<u>IC</u>   **5.** It is decorated with raisins, candied fruits, and slivered almonds.

Sentences Built with Clauses

Independent clauses are important to recognize because they serve as the building blocks for longer, more complicated sentences.

Simple Sentences

A single independent clause is also called a **simple sentence.** The following independent clauses are simple sentences.

I love to eat bread for every meal. (*I* is the subject; *love* is the verb.)

Bread with jam remains my favorite food. (*Bread* is the subject; *remains* is the verb.)

Compound Sentences

A sentence containing two or more independent clauses joined together using a semicolon or a comma and a coordinating conjunction is called a **compound sentence.** Because every clause in a compound sentence is an independent clause, every part of the sentence is equally important. In the following compound sentences, brackets surround each independent clause. Notice that the comma and the conjunction are not part of either clause.

[I love to eat bread for every meal], and [I usually do].

[Without some kind of bread, a meal is incomplete], so [I always have rolls, whole loaves, and slices of bread on hand].

EXERCISE 3 IDENTIFYING CLAUSES IN A COMPOUND SENTENCE

Each of the following sentences is a compound sentence. Place brackets around the two independent clauses. *Hint:* Look for the comma and conjunction as a clue to where the clauses are separated. An example is done for you.

[Making yeast bread dough from scratch can be complicated] but [it's also very satisfying]

1. [First, you need to combine dry yeast with warm water] but [don't use hot water.]

2. [Hot water will kill the yeast] and [then your bread is doomed]

3. [Sift flour into a bowl] so [you can add it to the yeast mixture later]

4. [Mix together milk, butter, and maybe some sugar] or [heat these together on the stove]

5. [Mix everything together except the flour] and [then add the flour one cup at a time]

Complex Sentences

A sentence that combines at least one independent clause with at least one dependent clause is a **complex sentence.** Even though the word *complex* can make these sentences seem tricky, they're not difficult to write. Brackets surround each clause in the following complex sentences. Notice that when the dependent clause comes first, you must use a comma to separate the two clauses. However, if the independent clause comes first, you do not need a comma.

	dependent clause independent clause
Comma needed	[Before you go] [I want your keys]

dependent clause
[Whenever I feel blue about having to get out of bed

independent clause
in the morning] [I remember being unemployed]

independent clause   dependent clause
No comma   [I worry about you] [because I love you]

independent clause
[Thinking about those long, dull days makes me

dependent clause
appreciate having a job] [although I still wouldn't

mind sleeping in now and then]

The important part of recognizing and writing compound and complex sentences is being able to identify the clauses in each sentence. Remember to find the subjects and verbs in compound and complex sentences because they will help you identify each clause.

EXERCISE 4 IDENTIFYING CLAUSES IN COMPLEX SENTENCES

The following items are complex sentences. Place brackets around the two clauses in each sentence, and write DC above or below each dependent clause and IC above or below each independent clause. *Hint:* Look for the dependent word as a clue to the start of the dependent clauses. An example is done for you.

                              DC   IC
[Even though bread seems to be a basic food], [people find interesting ways to eat it.]

                                 IC   DC
1. [In Italy, stale bread becomes a delicious mush] [when people

              DC
dampen it with water]

             DC   IC
2. [When children eat bread], [they often tear off the crusts.]

                 IC   DC
3. [The "one-eye" is another tasty way to use bread] [although this dish

involves more than bread].

                 DC   IC
4. [If you tear out the center of a piece of bread], [a fried egg in the

bread's hole gives you a one-eye].

                       IC
5. [One of the most popular ways to eat bread is as turkey stuffing]
             DC
[when the holidays roll around].

EDITING PRACTICE

In the following sentences, identify each italicized word group: for a phrase, write P; for an independent clause, IC; and for an dependent clause, DC. *Hint:* Cross out prepositional phrases and underline subjects and verbs to help you determine whether or not a word group is a clause.

  P   **1.** *Making tortillas* is a difficult process.

Tortillas in the Making

WRITE A PARAGRAPH The process for making authentic tortillas can be quite difficult. The recipes or methods for making many foods have been handed down through generations. What foods does your family make? Write a paragraph explaining how to prepare one of your traditional family foods.

IC **2.** To make tortillas, first, *get some white corn grain* and boil it in a covered pot with some crumbled lime or wood ashes.

IC **3.** *This cooking process loosens the skins of the kernels,* which will be floating at the top of the liquid the next morning.

P **4.** Next, discard the skins and liquid *before washing the remaining kernels.*

IC **5.** *Then, start grinding the cooked corn with a grinding stone and pestle,* and remember that the dough dries out easily, so you need to keep a jug of water nearby.

<u> P </u>   **6.** Next, work the dough into small balls for *shaping tortillas;* the step that requires the greatest skill.

<u> P </u>   **7.** Try to create as thin and round a patty *of the dough as possible,* being careful not to lose too much moisture in this step.

<u> P </u>   **8.** Finally, fry both sides *of the tortilla for thirty to sixty seconds on a hot griddle* so that the resulting product is soft and pliable.

<u>DC</u>   **9.** *If the tortilla is either too dry or too wet* when you put it on the griddle, it will be ruined.

<u>IC</u>   **10.** Mexican women who make tortillas three times a day don't have to think about baking time or moisture content because *they simply know* when the dough is ready and how long they should fry it.

Lab Activity 35

For additional practice with clauses, complete Lab Activity 35 in the Lab Manual at the back of the book.

36 Run-On Sentences

CULTURE NOTE *William Shakespeare*

Perhaps the world's most famous writer, William Shakespeare is known for his range of works. From tragic plays such as *Romeo and Juliet* and *Hamlet* to comedies such as *A Midsummer Night's Dream* and *As You Like It,* Shakespeare continues to move audiences with his wit and sense of drama. His poems, too, stand as tributes to both love and heartache.

What Is a Run-On Sentence?

One of the most common mistakes in writing is the run-on sentence. Run-ons take two forms: the fused sentence and the comma splice. Both types of run-on sentences attempt to combine two independent clauses without proper conjunctions or punctuation. The result is a sentence that tries to do too much, thus confusing the reader.

Fused Sentences

A **fused sentence** is one in which the writer tries to join two independent clauses without any connecting words or punctuation.

Fused: William Shakespeare was an English playwright he is considered the greatest of writers in English.

Fused: Shakespeare's most famous works include plays he wrote many poems as well.

The writer has placed one independent clause after another without any connecting word or punctuation, thus creating a fused sentence.

Comma Splices

Comma splices are the most common type of run-on sentence. **Comma splices** join two independent clauses with a comma. A comma is not a strong enough punctuation mark to connect two independent clauses.

Comma splice: Many famous sayings have come from Shakespeare's plays, some sayings are so common that people don't even know they come from Shakespeare.

The writer has attempted to connect the two independent clauses with a comma. However, the connections need to be stronger and clearer.

EXERCISE 1 IDENTIFYING RUN-ON SENTENCES

Read the sentences below. Then, write F for a fused sentence, CS for a comma splice, or C for a correct sentence.

___F___ **1.** Many of Shakespeare's poems were sonnets the sonnet format is a fourteen-line verse.

___C___ **2.** Sonnets originated in Italy, and they often contain rhyming lines.

___CS___ **3.** Shakespeare's sonnets contained a couplet as the last two lines, a couplet is a pair of rhyming lines in a poem.

___CS___ **4.** In fact, Shakespeare's sonnets became famous, his type of sonnet is known as a Shakespearean sonnet.

___F___ **5.** Many of Shakespeare's sonnets are well loved one of his most famous sonnets is "Shall I Compare Thee to a Summer's Day?"

Fixing Run-On Sentences

There are four ways to correct run-on sentences.

- Make the run-on into two separate sentences.
- Use a comma and a coordinating conjunction.
- Use a semicolon.
- Create a dependent clause.

Making the Run-On into Two Separate Sentences

To change a run-on into two separate sentences, place a period at the end of the first independent clause and capitalize the first letter of the second independent clause. Here's how to use this method to fix the last fused sentence on page 502.

Correct: Shakespeare's most famous works include <u>plays. He</u> wrote many poems as well.

The trick to using this method effectively is determining where one clause (or complete idea) ends and the other begins. If you're not sure where to place the period and begin a new sentence, try reading the run-on out loud. Chances are, your voice will drop when you come to the end of the first clause.

Modern Rivals

CRITICAL THINKING *West Side Story* is one version of Shakespeare's play *Romeo and Juliet*. How realistic are television and cinema portrayals of family or gang conflicts that end in violence? Write a few sentences explaining how the entertainment industry is or is not realistic in showing conflict between families.

EXERCISE 2 CORRECTING RUN-ON SENTENCES

Each of the following sentences is a run-on. Some of the run-ons are fused sentences, and some are comma splices. Determine where the two clauses meet, and correct the run-ons using a period and a capital letter. Rewrite the sentences in the blanks. An example is done for you.

Run-on: One of Shakespeare's most famous plays is *Romeo and Juliet* it tells the story of two "star-crossed" lovers.

Correct: One of Shakespeare's most famous plays is *Romeo and Juliet*. It tells the story of two star-crossed lovers.

1. "Star-crossed" means unlucky, few people have luck as bad as Romeo and Juliet's. "Star-crossed" means unlucky. Few people have luck as bad as Romeo and Juliet's.

2. Romeo Montague and Juliet Capulet were the children of rival families the two families didn't get along. Romeo and Juliet were the children of rival families. The two families didn't get along.

3. Romeo meets Juliet at a Capulet party to which he was not invited, he and Juliet fall in love immediately. Romeo meets Juliet at a Capulet party to which he was not invited. He and Juliet fall in love immediately.

4. Romeo and Juliet decide very quickly to get married, they keep their marriage a secret. Romeo and Juliet decide very quickly to get married. They keep their marriage a secret.

5. Tybalt, Juliet's hotheaded cousin, doesn't like Romeo he picks a fight with Romeo. Tybalt, Juliet's hotheaded cousin, doesn't like Romeo. He picks a fight with Romeo.

6. During the fight, Romeo's friend Mercutio fights Tybalt, Romeo gets in the way, and Mercutio is killed. During the fight, Romeo's friend Mercutio fights Tybalt. Romeo gets in the way, and Mercutio is killed.

7. Tybalt tries to kill Romeo, he ends up getting killed by Romeo. ____

Tybalt tries to kill Romeo. He ends up getting killed by Romeo.

8. Tybalt's death leads to Romeo being banished from Verona, Juliet is

inconsolable over his departure. Tybalt's death leads to Romeo being

banished from Verona. Juliet is inconsolable over his departure.

9. Not knowing about the secret marriage, Juliet's mother arranges for Juliet to marry someone else, a friar and Juliet plan to reunite her

with Romeo outside the city. Not knowing about the secret marriage, Juliet's mother arranges for Juliet to marry someone else. A friar and Juliet plan to reunite her with Romeo outside the city.

10. Juliet plans to drink a sleeping potion to fake her own death, her

friend the friar writes a letter to Romeo telling him of the plan.

Juliet plans to drink a sleeping potion to fake her own death. Her friend the

friar writes a letter to Romeo telling him of the plan.

11. The letter does not reach Romeo, so he buys poison, he commits

suicide in Juliet's tomb. The letter does not reach Romeo, so he buys

poison. He commits suicide in Juliet's tomb.

12. Juliet's sleeping potion wears off, she wakes up to find Romeo dead

beside her. Juliet's sleeping potion wears off. She wakes up to find Romeo

dead beside her.

13. Juliet is devastated by finding Romeo dead, using Romeo's dagger,

she kills herself. Juliet is devastated by finding Romeo dead. Using Romeo's

dagger, she kills herself.

EXERCISE 3 CORRECTING RUN-ONS IN A PARAGRAPH

The following paragraph has five run-on sentences. Some of the run-ons are fused sentences, and others are comma splices. Find each run-on and correct it using a period and a capital letter.

Romeo's Everywhere

[1]*Romeo and Juliet,* the tragedy by William Shakespeare, has been performed in many modern ways. [2]The musical play and movie *West Side Story* may be the most famous version its main characters are from rival gangs—the Jets and the Sharks—rather than rival families. [3]In this story, the lovers, Maria and Tony, sing songs and dance as part of their tale their story ends as unhappily as Romeo and Juliet's does, however. [4]Another movie version of Shakespeare's play was directed by Baz Luhrmann in 1996 the stars are Leonardo DiCaprio and Claire Danes. [5]This movie uses loud, almost violent music and gaudy makeup and costumes to portray the two families only the characters of Romeo and Juliet seem innocent in any way. [6]Of course, they both die in this movie, too. [7]Finally, the movie *Shakespeare in Love,* directed by John Madden in 1998, contains yet another version of Shakespeare's "star-crossed lovers" theme. [8]In this movie, the lovers—played by Joseph Fiennes and Gwyneth Paltrow—are supposed to be the characters of Shakespeare himself and the lovely Viola. [9]Shakespeare is having trouble writing his latest play, and Viola inspires him. [10]Their love can never be the lovely Viola is pledged to marry wealthy Lord Wessex. However, at least no one dies in this version.

The sentences with errors are these: __2__, __3__, __4__, __5__, __10__.

Using a Comma and a Coordinating Conjunction

The second way to correct run-ons is by using a comma and a coordinating conjunction. **Coordinating conjunctions** are words that join elements of equal importance, such as two independent clauses. *Tip:* An easy way to remember the coordinating conjunctions is to think of FANBOYS, an acronym from the words *for, and, nor, but, or, yet,* and *so.*

Common Coordinating Conjunctions

Word	Meaning	Example
for	because	William Shakespeare is one of the world's famous playwrights, for he has written many well-known plays.
and	in addition	Shakespeare was an excellent playwright, and he was a talented poet, too.
nor	an addition of negative ideas	Not all of Shakespeare's works are easy to understand, nor are all of them enjoyable.
but	indicates opposition or change; means *however* or *except*	Shakespeare's tragedies are extremely sad, but they contain humor, too.
or	a choice	Many of Shakespeare's heroes face evil villains, or they face evil in themselves.
yet	same as *but*	Shakespeare's heroes usually have a major character flaw, yet playgoers still want them to succeed.
so	therefore; indicates a result	Shakespeare isn't always easy to read right away, so students need to practice reading his works.

Although all the coordinating conjunctions serve the same function, they mean different things, so choose your conjunction carefully. For instance, the fused sentence below can be corrected in a number of ways.

Fused: *Macbeth* is my favorite Shakespearean play the "tomorrow and tomorrow and tomorrow" speech is incredibly sad.

This sentence contains two independent clauses, but the reader cannot easily tell how the two ideas are related. Using a comma and a coordinating conjunction can help make this connection clear.

> Correct: *Macbeth* is my favorite Shakespearean play, and the "tomorrow and tomorrow and tomorrow" speech is incredibly sad. (This combination explains two things: first, *Macbeth* is the writer's favorite play; second, the speech is sad.)

> Correct: *Macbeth* is my favorite Shakespearean play, but the "tomorrow and tomorrow and tomorrow" speech is incredibly sad. (This combination explains that, although the speech is sad, *Macbeth* is still the writer's favorite play.)

Both corrected sentences make sense, and both are grammatically correct. However, the simple switch in coordinating conjunction—from *and* in the first sentence to *but* in the second—radically alters the meaning of the sentence.

EXERCISE 4 CORRECTING RUN-ONS USING COMMAS AND CONJUNCTIONS

Correct the following comma splices by inserting an appropriate coordinating conjunction. An example is done for you.

> People often think Shakespeare wrote only sad stories, ^*for* he did write many tragedies.

1. William Shakespeare wrote many tragedies, ^*but* he wrote many comedies as well.

2. *A Midsummer Night's Dream* is one of Shakespeare's most famous comedies, ^*and* many people think it is one of his funniest.

3. In *A Midsummer Night's Dream*, confusion is a huge cause of humor, ^*for* many characters have spells placed on them or wear disguises.

4. Love is another source of humor in *A Midsummer Night's Dream*, ^*or* at least love causes people to do silly things.

5. All the characters eventually end up as their normal selves and in

love with the "right" people, ^{so} this play has a happy ending.

EXERCISE 5 JOINING INDEPENDENT CLAUSES USING COORDINATING CONJUNCTIONS

Read the sentences below. Then, add an idea that logically follows from the first sentence. Use a comma and each of the coordinating conjunctions listed here to join the two ideas (*and, but, so, for*). An example is done for you.   Answers will vary.

I secretly want to learn to understand Shakespeare better,

but I'm afraid my friends will think I'm weird.
_____

1. I always look forward to the end of the school semester _____

_____

2. Tran seems to keep himself busy _____

_____

3. Latrice loves being a bartender_____

_____

4. I was tired after work _____

_____

5. Jesse wants to get a dog _____

_____

6. I want to sleep in on Saturday_____

_____

7. Maria loved being in school during the day_____

_____

8. I saw each *Star Wars* movie five times_____

_____

9. Pablo wanted to ask Rita out on a date_____

_____

10. My house was dirty after a party _____

_____

Using a Semicolon

A third way to fix run-ons is to link the two independent clauses with a semicolon. Essentially, if you can use a period to separate two clauses, you can use a semicolon instead; using semicolons as well as periods will give your sentences more variety.

Using a Semicolon to Separate Independent Clauses   If you discover a fused sentence or comma splice in your writing, simply place a semicolon between the two clauses.

Run-on:	The Shakespearean hero Macbeth thought he could escape destiny, he was wrong.
Correct:	The Shakespearean hero Macbeth thought he could escape destiny; he was wrong.
Run-on:	Not many parents choose the names of Shakespeare's heroines for their daughters few women today are named Desdemona or Ophelia.
Correct:	Not many parents choose the names of Shakespeare's heroines for their daughters; few women today are named Desdemona or Ophelia.

EXERCISE 6 USING A SEMICOLON TO CORRECT RUN-ONS

Insert a semicolon between the two clauses in each of the following run-on sentences. An example is done for you.

Watching plays in Shakespeare's day was physically uncomfort-

able people had to stand throughout the play.

1. Modern entertainment has been influenced by Shakespeare the

   singer Sting named one of his albums *Nothing Like the Sun,* after

   one of Shakespeare's sonnets.

2. The movie *Ten Things I Hate About You* is based on Shakespeare's

   The Taming of the Shrew both stories deal with the conflicts of love.

3. The actor Kenneth Branagh did some of his best acting in Shake-

   spearean plays he even starred in a movie version of *Henry V.*

4. The story of *Othello* was recently made into the movie *O* the main

   character in the movie is a high school basketball star.

5. Even one of *People* magazine's "sexiest men alive" starred in a

   Shakespearean movie Mel Gibson played the role of Hamlet on the

   big screen.

Using Semicolons with Transitions   Another way to use a semicolon is with a transitional word or phrase. These words can tell your reader
how the two ideas linked by the semicolon are related. The most common
transitions (also called **conjunctive adverbs**) that are used with semicolons
are listed in the box below.

Common Transitional Phrases (Conjunctive Adverbs)

Word/Phrase	Explanation
also	and
furthermore	and
in addition	and
moreover	and

however	but
nevertheless	but
on the other hand	but
in fact	indicates emphasis or gives an example
indeed	in fact
instead	indicates an alternative
meanwhile	during the time mentioned
otherwise	indicates a different outcome
as a result	indicates an effect
thus	indicates an effect
consequently	indicates an effect
therefore	indicates an effect

In the following examples, the corrected sentences use a transition with a semicolon to link two ideas.

Run-on: I read *Julius Caesar* twice, I did really well on my English exam.

Correct: I read *Julius Caesar* twice<u>; consequently,</u> I did really well on my English exam.

Run-on: I'm glad I had to read some Shakespeare for class I might never have done it.

Correct: I'm glad I had to read some Shakespeare for class<u>; otherwise,</u> I might never have done it.

Notice that you need to place a comma after the transition when it follows a semicolon.

EXERCISE 7 USING SEMICOLONS AND TRANSITIONS TO FIX RUN-ONS

Join the two clauses below using a semicolon and a transition from the list above. Be sure to choose a transition that makes sense in your sentence. Several different transitions may work equally well in a sentence. Remember to include a comma after the transition. An example is done for you. Answers will vary.

I'd like to be an English major ; therefore, I should read Shakespeare.

1. Many of Shakespeare's heroes have noble qualities ; however, they also have a

   tragic flaw.

2. A tragic flaw is a serious character weakness ; consequently, it is usually the cause

   of the hero's failure in the play.

3. For instance, Macbeth suffered from excessive ambition ; consequently, he died

   from trying to become too powerful.

4. One Shakespearean hero, Othello, was a great military leader ; on the other hand, he

   had a serious problem with jealousy.

5. Othello's jealousy caused him to lose his wife ; additionally, it caused him to lose

   his life.

6. If Othello had been able to see through Iago's lies, he could have

   had a happy marriage ; in fact, he loved Desdemona.

7. Hamlet is another hero with many positive qualities ; however, he possessed

   the flaw of indecision.

8. Because he couldn't make up his mind, Hamlet missed his chance

   for triumph ; instead, he and most of his friends and family died.

9. King Lear was a noble leader and loving father ; however, he suffered from

   vanity.

10. He gave his kingdom to his two lying, immoral daughters without

    considering the consequences ; therefore, even his loving, third daughter

    Cordelia was too late to save him.

Creating a Dependent Clause

The last way to fix a run-on sentence is to use a dependent word to make one of the clauses in a run-on subordinate to the other. **Subordination** means making one idea weaker, or less important, than the other one. That way, your reader can easily tell which one is the focus of the sentence. A list of common dependent words appears in the box below.

Common Dependent Words

after	before	since	until
although	even though	though	when
because	if	unless	while

Look at how the run-on sentences below have been rewritten so that one idea is less important than the other. Each new sentence contains a dependent clause and an independent clause. The dependent words are in bold print.

Run-on: I read Shakespeare, I was afraid I wouldn't understand him.

Correct: **Before** I read Shakespeare, I was afraid I wouldn't understand him.

Run-on: I read *Romeo and Juliet* I was surprised at how exciting it was.

Correct: **After** I read *Romeo and Juliet,* I was surprised at how exciting it was.

Run-on: Now I know to give plays a chance, I might like them.

Correct: Now I know to give plays a chance **because** I might like them.

Note: When the *dependent* clause comes first, a comma comes between the clauses. However, when the *independent* clause comes first, you don't need a comma.

EXERCISE 8 CORRECTING RUN-ONS USING DEPENDENT WORDS

Correct the run-on sentences on page 516 by using the dependent word given to make one of the ideas less important than the other. Remember to place a comma between the two clauses if the dependent clause comes first. An example is done for you.

> ~~even though~~   Shakespeare can be fun to read ^even though^ readers find him challenging.

1. ~~although~~   ^Although^ ~~M~~ost people read from left to right across the page,

poetry often requires a different reading strategy.

2. since   ^Since,^ ~~R~~eading one line at a time can be confusing, it is eas-

ier to read Shakespeare one sentence at a time.

3. because   Some lines contain the end of one sentence and the

beginning of another ^because^ Shakespeare wanted every line

to have the same number of syllables.

4. if   ^If^ ~~Y~~ou get confused, you can read aloud from the start

to the end of each sentence.

5. even though   Reading plays can be interesting ^even though^ they were meant to

be performed.

EXERCISE 9 USING DEPENDENT WORDS FOR SUBORDINATION

Fill in each blank with an appropriate dependent word from the box on page 515. Answers will vary.

1. _____If_____ you are interested, we can rent *Shakespeare in Love*.

2. We can order a pizza _____before_____ we start the movie.

3. _____Unless_____ you want to wait till the weekend, we can watch it tonight.

4. _____When_____ you see the movie, you'll recognize some of the lines from Shakespeare's works.

5. _____While_____ we watch the film, we can imagine Shakespeare writing his plays.

EDITING PRACTICE

Use one of the four methods of correcting run-ons to fix the fused sentences and comma splices below. Use each correction method at least twice. Rewrite the corrected sentences.   Answers will vary.

1. Women in Shakespeare's plays have many different roles almost every role is significant. Although women in Shakespeare's plays have many different roles, almost every role is significant. Women in Shakespeare's plays have many different roles. Almost every role is significant.

2. Some women are strong-willed and powerful, Lady Macbeth in *Macbeth* and Viola in *Twelfth Night* are two of these. Some women are strong-willed and powerful; Lady Macbeth in *Macbeth* and Viola in *Twelfth Night* are two of these. Some women are strong-willed and powerful. Lady Macbeth in *Macbeth* and Viola in *Twelfth Night* are two of these.

3. Lady Macbeth pushes her husband to commit murder her ambition causes her great unhappiness. Lady Macbeth pushes her husband to commit murder; however, her ambition causes her great unhappiness. Lady Macbeth pushes her husband to commit murder, but her ambition causes her great unhappiness.

4. Viola is a strong woman of action she gets what she wants in the end.

Viola is a strong woman of action, so she gets what she wants in the end. Viola

is a strong woman of action; thus, she gets what she wants in the end.

5. Other women, such as Ophelia in *Hamlet,* are unstable they are important

to the story. Even though other women, such as Ophelia in *Hamlet,* are

unstable, they are important to the story. Other women, such as Ophelia in

Hamlet, are unstable, but they are important to the story.

6. The witches in *Macbeth* possess magical powers, the ways they use their

powers bring tragedy to humans. The witches in *Macbeth* possess magical

powers, but the ways they use their powers bring tragedy to humans. The

witches in *Macbeth* possess magical powers; however, the ways they use their

powers bring tragedy to humans.

7. The witches use their power to tempt Macbeth their mysterious

language makes him believe he cannot be killed. The witches use their

power to tempt Macbeth, and their mysterious language makes him believe he

cannot be killed. The witches use their power to tempt Macbeth; their

mysterious language makes him believe he cannot be killed.

8. Titania, the queen of the fairies in *A Midsummer Night's Dream*, is

affected by magic she is placed under a spell. Titania, the queen of the

fairies in *A Midsummer Night's Dream,* is affected by magic; she is placed under a

spell. Titania, the queen of the fairies in *A Midsummer Night's Dream,* is affected

by magic, for she is placed under a spell.

9. Desdemona from *Othello* and Juliet from *Romeo and Juliet* are both

beautiful, they are both innocent as well. Desdemona from *Othello* and

Juliet from *Romeo and Juliet* are both beautiful, and they are both innocent as

well. Even though Desdemona from *Othello* and Juliet from *Romeo and Juliet* are

both beautiful, they are both innocent as well.

10. Shakespeare does not spare these innocent women they both suffer

and die. Shakespeare does not spare these innocent women; in fact, they both

suffer and die. Shakespeare does not spare these innocent women, so they both

suffer and die.

Lab Activity 36

For additional practice with clauses, complete Lab Activity 36 in the Lab
Manual at the end of the book.

37 Fragments

CULTURE NOTE *Marvels of Modern Construction*

From the Golden Gate Bridge in San Francisco to the Empire State Building in New York City, examples of amazing construction abound in the United States. Some structures are triumphs of function, while others enhance the beauty of their settings.

What Is a Fragment?

A sentence **fragment** is an incomplete idea that tries to stand alone as a sentence. Because fragments don't communicate a complete idea, they can be confusing. Even though we use sentence fragments all the time in speaking, fragments are unacceptable in standard written English. There are three major types of fragments.

- Dependent clause fragments
- Phrase fragments
- Missing-information fragments

Recognizing and Correcting Dependent Clause Fragments

A **dependent clause fragment** is a dependent clause that is not attached to an independent clause. These fragments are easy to recognize because they begin with a dependent word or term. A list of dependent words and terms follows on the next page.

Dependent Words and Terms

after	although	because
before	even though	how
if	in order that	since
so that	that	though
unless	until	what
whatever	when	whenever
wherever	whether	which
whichever	while	who
whoever	whose	

The dependent words are in bold print in the following dependent clause fragments.

Fragment: **Even though** people said the Brooklyn Bridge couldn't be built. The engineer J. A. Roebling knew he could do it.

Fragment: Building the Brooklyn Bridge involved a great commitment by the construction crews. **Because** the work was so dangerous.

Fragment: **After** many people gave their lives to the bridge. It was finally built.

The fragments above contain a subject and a verb, so at first glance, they look like sentences. However, the presence of a dependent term—*even though, because,* or *after*—turns each statement into a dependent clause. (Try reading each dependent clause by itself, and you'll hear that it seems incomplete.) Because each dependent clause lacks an independent clause, it is a fragment.

There are two primary strategies for eliminating dependent word fragments.

■ Attach the fragment to another sentence.

■ Turn the fragment into a complete sentence.

Attaching the Fragment to Another Sentence

The easiest way to correct a dependent word fragment is to attach it to another sentence. If a dependent clause comes before an independent clause, you must separate the two clauses with a comma.

Correct: **Even though** people said the Brooklyn Bridge couldn't be built, the engineer J. A. Roebling knew he could do it. (The fragment has been attached to the sentence that follows it.)

Correct: Building the Brooklyn Bridge involved a great commitment by the construction crews **because** the work was so dangerous. (The fragment has been attached to the sentence that precedes it.)

Correct: **After** many people gave their lives for the bridge, it was finally built. (The fragment has been attached to the sentence that follows it.)

Eliminating the Dependent Word

A second way to correct dependent clause fragments is this: eliminate the dependent word in the dependent clause and let the clause stand alone as a complete sentence.

~~Even though people~~ *People* said the Brooklyn Bridge couldn't be built. The

engineer J. A. Roebling knew he could do it.

Building the Brooklyn Bridge involved a great commitment by the

construction crews. ~~Because~~ *The work* ~~it~~ was so dangerous.

~~After~~ *Many* many people gave their lives for the bridge. It was finally built.

In each of these sentences, the fragment has been corrected by eliminating the dependent word. While eliminating the dependent word is an effective way to correct fragments, it can make your writing choppy. Use this technique sparingly.

The Brooklyn Bridge

JOURNAL RESPONSE At one time considered the eighth wonder of the world, the Brooklyn Bridge remains a construction marvel. What interesting buildings have you noticed in your neighborhood or city? Write for ten minutes about any buildings or structures in your area that you find interesting or unusual.

EXERCISE 1 ATTACHING DEPENDENT CLAUSES TO INDEPENDENT CLAUSES

Correct the following dependent clause fragments by attaching them to sentences that you write. Some require a sentence before the dependent clause and others require it after. Write your new sentence in the space provided. An example is done for you.   Answers will vary.

Because Amanda was wonderful with children *, she was in*

constant demand as a baby-sitter.

1. When the snow falls heavily_____

_____

2. Who is my best friend _____

_____

3. Before I can answer your question_____

_____

4. Where the deer and the antelope play_____

_____

5. Until we elect a new governor _____

_____

6. If the bus comes late one more time _____

_____

7. Whenever Tanya needed to do laundry_____

_____

8. As far as you can see _____

_____

9. The place where people come together to sing _____

_____

10. So that Tim could pay his bills _____

_____

EXERCISE 2 CORRECTING DEPENDENT CLAUSE FRAGMENTS IN A PARAGRAPH

The following paragraph contains five dependent clause fragments. Correct each fragment by using one of the techniques you learned in this chapter. Be sure to use each technique at least once.

Bridging the Gap

[1]The completion of the Brooklyn Bridge in 1883 was considered a miracle of modern construction. [2]It was built from 1869 to 1883 in New York City. [3]~~Where~~ *,where* buildings were no more than five stories tall and transportation was by horse and buggy. [4]Because it was the world's longest suspension bridge at the time of its completion. *,it* [5]~~It~~ was called the eighth wonder of the world. [6]The bridge was the first steel-wire suspension bridge in the world. [7]The bridge links lower Manhattan to Brooklyn and spans 1,595.5 feet (487 meters) across the East River. [8]The bridge is also a marvel of human commitment. [9]Engineer J. A. Roebling battled against the elements, corrupt politicians, and scientists. [10]~~Who~~ *who* claimed the massive bridge would collapse in the first strong wind. [11]Because he was so dedicated. [12]Roebling was involved in many aspects of construction, including diving to check the massive bases of the bridge. [13]These dives resulted in Roebling's death. [14]~~Before~~ *before* the bridge was completed. [15]Roebling's son had to finish the project.

The fragments are found in these word groups: __3__, __4__, __10__, __11__, __14__.

Recognizing and Correcting Phrase Fragments

Phrase fragments are the most common type of fragments. Phrase fragments come in three major forms.

■ *-ing* word fragments
■ *to* fragments
■ Extra-information fragments

Correcting *-ing* Verb Fragments

An *-ing* word fragment is a phrase that begins with the *-ing* form of a verb.

Fragment: Every year, thousands of tourists visit the Empire State Building. **Hoping** to see the stunning view.

Notice that the phrase containing the *-ing* word does not make sense all by itself. There are two ways to correct a fragment beginning with an *-ing* word.

■ Attach the *-ing* phrase to the sentence before or after it or build it into one of those sentences.
■ Turn the *-ing* phrase into a sentence.

Attaching the *-ing* Phrase to a Sentence   An easy way to correct a phrase fragment is to attach it or build it into a nearby sentence. For example, the fragment in the preceding example can be corrected as follows.

Correct: Every year, thousands of tourists visit the Empire State Building, **hoping** to see the stunning view. (The fragment has been attached to the sentence that precedes it.)

Correct: Every year, thousands of tourists hop**ing** to see the stunning view visit the Empire State Building. (The fragment has been built into the sentence that precedes it.)

Turning the *-ing* Phrase into a Sentence   Another way to correct an *-ing* word phrase fragment is to turn the phrase into a sentence. Do this by (1) adding a subject to the *-ing* phrase and (2) changing the *-ing* word to the correct verb form. In the examples that follow, the added subject is underlined once, and the new verb is underlined twice.

Fragment: The Empire State Building is the tallest building in New York City. **Having** regained that title because the World Trade Center was destroyed in 2001.

Correct: The Empire State Building is the tallest building in New York City. <u>It has regained</u> that title because the World Trade Center was destroyed in 2001. (*Having* has been changed to *It has regained*.)

Fragment: The Empire State Building has 102 floors and is 1,250 feet high. It **being** the workplace for 25,000 tenants.

Correct: The Empire State Building has 102 floors and is 1,250 feet high. <u>It is</u> the workplace for 25,000 tenants.

The two methods do not work equally well for all fragment corrections. In particular, it's often more effective to turn a fragment with the verb *being* into a sentence with *is* or *are*.

EXERCISE 3   CORRECTING *-ING* FRAGMENTS

The following passages contain *-ing* fragments. Rewrite each to eliminate the fragment.   Answers will vary.

1. Skyscrapers are buildings of great height. Being constructed on a steel skeleton. <u>Skyscrapers are buildings of great height. They are constructed on a steel skeleton.</u>

2. Originating in the United States in the late 1800s. The skyscraper soon became a common sight in large American cities. <u>Originating in the United States in the late 1800s, the skyscraper soon became a common sight in large American cities.</u>

3. Originally, the bottom floors of tall buildings had very thick walls. Holding up the higher floors. <u>Originally, the bottom floors of tall buildings had very thick walls holding up the higher floors.</u>

4. Builders soon found ways to strengthen the structure of tall buildings. Using cast iron along with masonry. <u>Builders soon found</u>

ways to strengthen the structure of tall buildings. They used cast iron along

with masonry.

5. Next came the invention of a metal framework to support the walls and the floors. Allowing buildings to use floor space efficiently.

Next came the invention of a metal framework that supported the walls and the floors. This invention allowed buildings to utilize floor space more efficiently.

Correcting *to* Fragments

To fragments, also called **infinitive fragments,** are easy to recognize. They begin with an infinitive—the word *to* followed by a verb. Correct such a fragment by attaching it to the sentence before or after it, just as you would do to correct an *-ing* fragment.

Fragment   A person must be very fit. To walk down the stairs of the Empire State Building.

Correct: A person must be very fit <u>to walk</u> down the stairs of the Empire State Building.

EXERCISE 4 CORRECTING *TO* FRAGMENTS

Rewrite each of the following passages, correcting the *to* fragments.
Answers will vary

1. The Golden Gate Bridge is a beautiful landmark. To see in California.

The Golden Gate Bridge is a beautiful landmark to see in California.

2. Not only is it lovely, but it is also an amazing construction work. It stretches 9,266 feet in length between San Francisco and Marin County. To make it the longest suspension bridge in the world.

Not only is it lovely, but it is also an amazing construction work. It stretches 9,266 feet in length between San Francisco and Marin County. It is the longest suspension bridge in the world.

3. Built from 1933 to 1937, the bridge seemed an impossible achievement. There were too many obstacles, such as the wide bay, steep banks, and turbulent tides. To allow the bridge to be built.

Built from 1933 to 1937, the bridge seemed an impossible achievement.

There were too many obstacles, such as the wide bay, steep banks, and

turbulent tides to allow the bridge to be built.

4. However, the plans of the engineer Joseph B. Strauss were a masterpiece. In four years, the longest, highest, most spectacular suspension bridge on earth was completed. To become one of the greatest symbols of American ingenuity.

However, the plans of the engineer Joseph B. Strauss were a masterpiece. In

four years, the longest, highest, most spectacular suspension bridge on

earth was completed to become one of the greatest symbols of American ingenuity.

5. The Golden Gate Bridge continues. To inspire people through its beauty and strength. It stands as a triumph in engineering.

The Golden Gate Bridge continues to inspire people through its beauty and

strength. It stands as a triumph in engineering.

Correcting Extra-Information Phrases

A third type of phrase sometimes ends up as a fragment. The **extra-information phrase** contains details that contribute meaning to a subject covered in another sentence, usually the previous sentence. See the following box for a list of words that often begin the extra-information phrases.

Words and Terms That Often Begin Extra-Information Phrases

also	for instance	like
especially	for one	such as
except	from	
for example	including	

A fragment that begins with the word *including* is an *-ing* fragment as well as an extra-information fragment. You can correct these two types of fragments in the same way, so don't worry about deciding which type of fragment an *including* fragment is.

The information provided in the fragment that follows is interesting and necessary for specific communication. However, because these details appear in a fragment, the reader will have difficulty understanding how they relate to the rest of the information provided.

Fragment: Many jobs are required to keep the Empire State Building in good shape. <u>Including</u> updating the elevators, cleaning, doing preventive maintenance, washing windows, and adding high-speed Internet connections.

Two main strategies can correct extra-information fragments.

- Attach the fragment to the sentence before or after it.
- Turn the fragment into a sentence by (1) adding a subject and verb or (2) revising it so that it makes sense on its own.

Attaching the Fragment to the Sentence Before or After It

When attaching an extra-information fragment (such as the one in the preceding example) to the previous sentence, remember to use a comma.

Correct: Many jobs are required to keep the Empire State Building in good shape, <u>including</u> updating the elevators, cleaning, doing preventive maintenance, window washing, and adding high-speed Internet connections. (The fragment is attached to the previous sentence.)

Turning the Fragment into a Sentence

You can correct an extra-information fragment by turning it into a sentence on its own. You can do this either by (1) adding a subject and a verb to the fragment or (2) revising the fragment to make it a sentence.

Fragment: Most people don't realize how much work is involved in maintaining the Empire State Building. <u>Especially</u> how long it takes to wash all the windows.

Correct: Most people don't realize how much work is involved in maintaining the Empire State Building. <u>Especially surprising is how long it takes to wash all the windows</u>.

Correct: Most people don't realize how much work is involved in maintaining the Empire State Building. <u>Washing the windows, for instance, takes a long time.</u>

EXERCISE 5 CORRECTING EXTRA-INFORMATION FRAGMENTS

Rewrite each of the following passages to correct the extra-information fragments. Answers will vary.

1. Many masterpieces of engineering and construction exist in the United States. Especially those built in the past century.

Many masterpieces of engineering and construction exist in the

United States, especially those built in the past century.

2. Some building masterpieces help preserve the environment. Such as the Alaska pipeline. _Some building masterpieces, such as the Alaska_

pipeline, help preserve the environment.

3. The Alaska pipeline allowed oil to be transported hundreds of miles. From Prudhoe Bay, Alaska, to the port of Valdez. _The Alaska_

pipeline allowed oil to be transported hundreds of miles from Prudhoe Bay,

Alaska, to the port of Valdez.

4. After oil was discovered in Prudhoe Bay in 1968, construction was delayed by environmentalists who feared negative effects from the pipeline. Especially the disruption of Alaskan ecosystems.

After oil was discovered in Prudhoe Bay in 1968, construction was delayed by
environmentalists who feared negative effects from the pipeline. They
especially feared the disruption of Alaskan ecosystems.

5. However, a benefit of the Alaska pipeline is that it prevents oil spills in the ocean. Such as the one by the _Exxon Valdez_ in 1989. _A benefit_

of the Alaska pipeline is that it prevents oil spills in the ocean, such as the

one by the Exxon Valdez in 1989.

Recognizing and Correcting Missing-Information Fragments

The last type of fragment is the **missing-information fragment.** This type of fragment leaves out an essential part of a sentence. The result is an incomplete idea. Missing-information fragments usually lack the subject of a sentence. Sometimes, however, missing-information fragments lack a verb.

> Fragment: Another marvel of construction is the Transcontinental Railroad, which linked both coasts in 1869. And made settlement of the West occur much more quickly. (The fragment contains no subject for the verb *made.*)

> Incorrect: The Union Pacific Railroad Company built from the east. And the Central Pacific Railroad Company from the west. (The fragment contains no verb for the subject *Central Pacific Railroad Company.*)

Missing-information fragments are easy to correct. Simply use the same techniques that you've used throughout this chapter to correct other types of fragments.

- Attach the fragment to the sentence before it.
- Add the missing information to the fragment and turn it into a complete sentence.

Attaching the Fragment to the Sentence Before It

Attaching the fragment to the preceding sentence brings about the following results.

> Correct: Another marvel of construction is the Transcontinental Railroad, which linked both coasts in 1869 <u>and made settlement of the West occur much more quickly</u>.

> Correct: The Union Pacific Railroad Company built from the east <u>and the Central Pacific Railroad Company from the west</u>.

Turning the Fragment into a Sentence

You can also provide the missing information to turn the fragment into a complete sentence.

> Correct: Another marvel of construction is the Transcontinental Railroad, which linked both coasts in 1869. <u>The railroad</u>

made settlement of the West occur much more quickly.
(The subject *the railroad* makes the sentence complete.)

Correct: The Union Pacific Railroad Company built from the east.
             The Central Pacific Railroad Company built from the west.
             (The verb *built* makes the fragment a complete sentence.)

Tip: While turning fragments into sentences can correct an error, it can also make your writing choppy or listlike, so be careful not to overuse this technique.

EXERCISE 6 CORRECTING MISSING-INFORMATION FRAGMENTS

Rewrite the following passages to correct the missing information fragments. Use each technique at least once.   Answers will vary.

1. One criticism of the transcontinental railroad construction concerns its employment practices. The Central Pacific Railroad employed Chinese immigrants. And let them do the hardest labor.

   One criticism of the transcontinental railroad construction concerns its

   employment practices. The Central Pacific Railroad employed Chinese

   immigrants and let them do the hardest labor.

2. The Union Pacific hired Irish immigrants to do the backbreaking work. And thus ensure that the railroad was completed.

   The Union Pacific hired Irish immigrants to do the backbreaking work and

   thus ensure that the railroad was completed.

3. These men were forced to work long hours under horrible conditions. And were not treated well. These men were forced to work long hours under horrible conditions and were not treated well.

4. Some historians have claimed that the Chinese workers were treated like slaves. And the Irish, too. Some historians have claimed

that the Chinese workers were treated like slaves. The Irish were treated

poorly, too.

5. The workers made the meeting of the two lines possible. And completed an important link across the United States.

The workers made the meeting of the two lines possible and completed an

important link across the United States.

EDITING PRACTICE 1

Each of the following passages contains at least one fragment. Underline each fragment. Then, rewrite the passage to correct it using one of the techniques from this chapter.   Answers will vary.

1. High-speed elevators have made indoor travel fast, but some people will climb the outside of a building. Even though that's <u>extremely dangerous.</u>

High-speed elevators make indoor travel fast, but some people will climb the

outside of a building even though that's extremely dangerous.

2. Recently, a French daredevil was caught. <u>Trying to scale a tall building in Singapore.</u> He had climbed several buildings before.

Recently, a French daredevil was caught trying to scale a tall building in

Singapore. He had climbed several buildings before.

3. Other daredevils enjoy the ride down. Some residents of Seattle, Washington, have parachuted from the Space Needle. <u>Which is sixty stories high.</u>

Other daredevils enjoy the ride down. Some residents of Seattle, Washington,

have parachuted from the Space Needle. It is sixty stories high.

4. Another building targeted by daredevils is the Sears Tower in Chicago, Illinois. <u>It being the second tallest building in the world at 1,454 feet.</u>

Another building targeted by daredevils is the Sears Tower in Chicago, Illinois. It

is the second tallest building in the world at 1,454 feet.

5. Finally, the Golden Gate Bridge is a favorite among a special group of daredevils. <u>People who scale the cables to the top.</u>

Finally, the Golden Gate Bridge is a favorite among a special group of

daredevils, people who scale the cables to the top.

EDITING PRACTICE 2

Read the paragraph below and identify the seven fragments. Then, correct the fragments using the techniques you learned in this chapter. Do not use the same technique for every correction. Answers will vary.

Sad Stories

[1]Though engineering masterpieces such as the Golden Gate Bridge and the Eiffel Tower fill us with awe. [2]~~They~~ , they also have many sad stories attached to them. [3]One type of sad story comes from the workers who die during construction of these wonderful structures. [4]Though often statistics are not kept on the people who die during construction, there are rough records for places like the Brooklyn Bridge. [5]Some twenty-seven people died during the construction of the Brooklyn Bridge. [6]~~Either by falling~~ They either fell from a great height or ~~meeting~~ met with some other misfortune. [7]Other structures have claimed the lives of workers. [8]Another type of sad story comes from attacks on tall buildings. [9]~~Such~~ , such as the attack on the World Trade Center on September 11, 2001. [10]Thousands of people died in the attacks. [11]~~Even~~ even though they were innocent and had nothing to do with the

cause of their own death. [12]Just the grandeur and height of the buildings made them targets. [13]Probably the saddest story comes from people who commit suicide from beautiful bridges or buildings. [14]Unfortunately, people often choose romantic places ~~to end their lives.~~ [15]~~Such~~ such as the Empire State Building in New York City or the Space Needle in Seattle. to end their lives [16]Authorities try their best to patrol these buildings/[17]~~In~~ in order to prevent more deaths. [18]However, those determined to end their lives can be difficult to stop. [19]More than a thousand lives have ended from the Golden Gate Bridge alone. [20]The beauty of magnificent buildings and bridges draws people there/[21]~~For~~ for their last view.

Fragments are found in these word groups: __1__, __6__, __9__, __11__ __15__, __17__, __21__.

Lab Activity 37

For additional practice with fragments, complete Lab Activity 37 in the Lab Manual at the back of the book.

38 Regular Verbs

CULTURE NOTE  *Psychology*

Psychology deals with mental processes. Psychologists study emotions, intelligence, consciousness, and perception as well as how these processes are connected. Though psychology experts agree on the importance of their field, they approach it with a wide variety of philosophies and practices.

The Principal Parts of Regular Verbs

Most verbs in English are **regular verbs,** which means they follow the same pattern in their principal parts. For instance, you form the past tense of regular verbs by adding *-d* or *-ed* to the present tense. All verbs have four **principal parts:** present, past, past participle, and present participle. These four parts help us create all the verb tenses—the **forms** of the verb—which tell us the time and condition under which the action of the verb takes place. For example, for the verb *to love,* the principal parts are *love, loved, loved,* and *loving.* The box below shows some examples of the four verb forms.

Principal Parts of Regular Verbs

Present	Past	Past Participle	Present Participle
search	searched	searched	searching
play	played	played	playing
travel	traveled	traveled	traveling

The Present Tense

The **present tense** of a verb is the form seen in the dictionary: *love, jump, pick*. The present tense allows us to communicate actions that occur *now*, that are ongoing, or that are generally true.

Action occurs now:	I <u>love</u> you.
Action is ongoing:	I <u>jump</u> to reach the high shelves in my closet.
Action is generally true:	Small children <u>pick</u> ladybugs from my rose bush.

The Past Tense

The **past tense** indicates actions that occurred before now. The past tense consists of the present plus *-d* or *-ed*: *loved, jumped, picked*.

Action occurred before now:	I <u>loved</u> you.
Action occurred before now:	In my old house, I <u>jumped</u> to reach the shelves in my closet.
Action occurred before now:	Small children <u>picked</u> ladybugs from my rose bush.

The Past Participle

The **past participle** is often the same as the past tense form, and indicates actions that occurred before now. It consists of the present plus *-d* or *-ed*: *loved, jumped, picked*. It works with forms of the helping verbs *have* or *be* or can be used alone as a modifier.

Past participle with form of *be:*	I <u>was loved</u> by my parents.
Past participle with form of *have:*	I <u>have jumped</u> to reach high shelves in my closet.
Past participle as modifier:	The <u>picked</u> roses soon began to droop.

The Present Participle

The **present participle** consists of the present tense plus *-ing: loving, jumping, picking*. It works with forms of *be* as a verb, works as a modifier, or works as a noun.

Present participle with form of *be:*	I <u>am loving</u> my time in New York.
Present participle as modifier:	The <u>jumping</u> lizards can be dangerous.
Present participle as noun:	<u>Picking</u> an outfit for school can take forever.

Forming the Tenses of Regular Verbs

Knowing when things happen is important. If you're explaining to your boss on Friday that you need a day off to study for an exam but then say, "My test was Thursday," your boss will wonder why you need time to study for a test that already occurred. The simple switch from *is* (present tense) to *was* (past tense) can radically alter your meaning. Thus, understanding the verb tenses—and knowing how to form them—is crucial to your success as a writer.

Present Tense

The **present tense** of a verb tells a reader that an action is going on right now, as opposed to sometime in the past or future. Form the present tense of regular verbs as follows:

■ Use the simple present form with *I, you, they,* and other plural subjects (*the man, the buildings*).

I **look** for a pot of gold at the end of every rainbow.

You **search** for your own treasure wherever you want.

They **discover** over and over again that fool's gold is worthless.

■ Add *-s* or *-es* to the present form if the subject is *he, she, it,* or any singular name. For instance, the following sentences contain verbs ending in *-s* or *-es*. Each action below is going on right now.

Mary **talks** constantly about her problems. (The subject is *Mary;* the present tense verb ends in *-s*.)

It **bothers** Mary to think of others. (The subject is *It;* the verb ends in *-s*.)

My counselor **preaches** to me about moving on with my life. (The subject is *counselor;* the verb ends in *-es*.)

My husband **tries** not to be bothered by my annoying laugh. (The subject is *husband;* the verb ends in *-es* after the *y* is changed to an *i*.)

EXERCISE 1 FORMING THE PRESENT TENSE OF REGULAR VERBS

Fill in the blanks with the correct present tense form of the verb in parentheses. There are fifteen verbs to change in all.

1. My brother (want) <u>wants</u> to change his personality.

2. My brother (seem) <u>seems</u> very angry whenever the things in his life don't work.

3. In fact, usually he (ruin) _ruins_____ things like his computer or his bicycle if they act strangely.

4. I (explain) _explain_____ to him that he should be more like me,

but this only (cause) _causes_____ him to get angry.

5. I also (recommend) _recommend_____ my school counselor to him,

but he (refuse) _refuses_____ to talk to her.

6. He (want) _wants_____ to solve his problems himself.

7. He (believe) _believes_____ that psychology (solve) _solves_____
all problems.

8. Thus, he (study) _studies_____ many books on the subject.

9. He also (watch) _watches_____ the television show *Frasier* even though the doctors on that show are psychiatrists, not psychologists.

10. My parents (hope) _hope_____ my brother (change) _changes_____

before he (wreck) _wrecks_____ something else!

EXERCISE 2 USING THE PRESENT TENSE OF REGULAR VERBS

Each of the sentences below contains an error in a standard present tense verb. In the italicized section of each sentence, cross out any incorrect present tense verbs and write in the correct verb form. An example is done for you.

seems
Psychology ~~seem~~ to have many different ways to explain behavior.

originates
1. *One popular theory of behavior ~~come~~ from the psychologist B. F. Skinner.*

emphasizes
2. *Skinner's theory ~~emphasize~~ the connections* between animal and

human behavior.

states
3. *The theory ~~state~~ that behavior* can be modified or conditioned.

pushes
4. Skinner is famous for developing a box where *an animal ~~push~~ a*

button to get food or water.

5. Supposedly, *the animal* ~~learn~~ *that* certain actions bring about certain results.
   [learns]

6. This process of associating the result with an action is a type of "conditioned response" experiment. *A conditioned response experiment* ~~try~~ to see if animals will act differently to get what they want.
   [tries]

7. The so-called *Skinner box*, ~~support~~ *Skinner's ideas* that animals can be conditioned to act a certain way.
   [supports]

8. *The box* ~~reveal~~ *effectively* that behavior can be modified.
   [reveals]

9. However, critics of Skinner's ideas claim that *not all behavior* ~~change~~ *with conditioning.*
   [changes]

10. *Some behavior* ~~starts~~ *from the way* people or animals are.
    [starts]

EXERCISE 3 CORRECTING PRESENT TENSE VERB ERRORS IN A PARAGRAPH

The following paragraph contains six errors in present tense verbs. Correct these errors.

Terms of Psychology

[1]In my introductory psychology course, I've learned many interesting terms. [2]For instance, a *compulsion* is an inner force that lead^s people to act against their will. [3]A compulsive gambler, for one, believe^s as though he or she must gamble. [4]I've also learned that *charisma* is a strong personal power that appeals to others. [5]A great leader benefit^s from charisma. [6]Many U.S. presidents have had charisma. [7]Another term I've learned is *brainwashing.* [8]Brainwashing force^s people to abandon their beliefs in favor of another set of beliefs. [9]My mother brainwash^es people into thinking they need to eat vegetables. [10]All in all, psychology offer^s me a lot!

Verb errors occur in these sentences: <u>2</u>, <u>3</u>, <u>5</u>, <u>8</u>, <u>9</u>, <u>10</u>.

Past Tense

The **past tense** of a verb indicates that an action occurred at some time in the past. For regular English verbs, the past tense form (in the principal parts) ends in -*d* or -*ed*. In the sentences below, each verb communicates that the action has already happened.

Last year, <u>I</u> **convinced** myself to overcome my fears.
My <u>friends</u> all **watched** me struggle.

To create the past tense verbs, the writer added -*d* or -*ed* to the present tense form.

EXERCISE 4 USING THE PAST TENSE FORM OF REGULAR VERBS

Fill in each blank with the past tense of the verb in parentheses.

1. I (start) _____started_____ working on my fear of heights.

2. I (climb) ___climbed_____ the fire escape to the top of my apartment building.

3. My mother (look) ___looked_____ up at me and (yell) ___yelled_____

for me to come down.

4. When I (reach) ___reached_____ the top, I (lift) ___lifted_____ my

hands over my head.

5. All my friends (applaud) ___applauded._____ .

6. Sigmund Freud, an Austrian doctor, (learn) ___learned_____ about medicine in the late 1800s and early 1900s.

7. He also (gain) ___gained_____ knowledge about the way the mind works.

8. Freud (develop) ___developed_____ a study of the mind (call)

___called_____ psychoanalysis.

9. According to Freud, psychoanalysis (provide) <u>provided</u>

patients with a way to understand their mental illnesses.

10. Freud (believe) <u>believed</u> that most mental illnesses (originate)

<u>originate</u> in childhood traumas.

Participles

Even though the term *participle* refers to a verb form, participles can be used as adjectives.

Past Participles as Adjectives The past participle verb form can serve as an adjective if it follows a linking verb or comes before a noun.

> The psychologist appeared <u>surprised</u> by my condition. (The adjective *surprised* describes the subject, *psychologist*.)

Sigmund Freud (1856–1939)

JOURNAL RESPONSE Although many psychologists today view Sigmund Freud's psychological theories as outdated or unsupported by scientific evidence, his ideas have had a profound impact on the study of behavior. What is your attitude toward therapy or counseling? Write for ten minutes, explaining your experiences and attitudes.

Words with Multiple Personalities

■ Sometimes a word that looks like a verb serves as a different part of speech. When a present participle acts as a noun, it is called a **gerund.**

<u>Running</u> is my favorite form of exercise. (The word *running* is a noun and is the subject of a sentence.)

■ A present participle that ends in *-ing* or *-ed* can be used as an adjective.

The <u>running</u> water felt icy cold. (The adjective *running* modifies the noun *water.*)

■ A present participle acts as a verb only if a helping verb accompanies it.

Angelo <u>was running</u> after the bus. (Here *running* is the action verb of the sentence. The word *was* is the helping verb.)

The <u>depressed</u> patient felt better after telling his story. (The adjective *depressed* describes the subject, *patient.*)

Remember that a participle acts as a verb only if it is accompanied by a helping verb.

My instructor <u>is pleased</u> when our class remembers his lessons. (The subject, *instructor,* performs the action *pleased,* which is accompanied by the helping verb *is.*)

Present Participles as Adjectives and Nouns   **Present participles**—verb forms ending in *-ing*—can also be used as adjectives.

My favorite <u>walking</u> stick is made from cherry wood. (The participle *walking* modifies the noun *stick.*)

EDITING PRACTICE 1

For each sentence, write the correct present or past tense form of the verb in the blank. The tense needed is given in parentheses after the sentence. You may need to add *-s, -es, -d,* or *-ed* to make the verb form correct.

1. Many people (suffer) *suffer* from the mental disorder depression.

Depression (express) <u>expresses</u> itself in many forms. (present tense)

2. My friend Randy (exhibit) _____exhibits_____ depression by feeling anxious.

He (act) _____acts_____ as if the world might end at any time; he (seem)

_____seems_____ worried. (present tense)

3. He (appear) _____appears_____ better when he (walk) _____walks_____

outside. The fresh air (help)_____helps_____ clear his mind. (present
tense)

4. Last semester, Randy (watch) _____watched_____ television twenty hours a
day. (past tense)

5. Last month he (learn) _____learned_____ to do yoga. He (stretch)

_____stretched_____ and (exhale) _____exhaled_____ his way back to feeling
better. (past tense)

EDITING PRACTICE 2 **Correcting Regular Verb Tense Errors**

Read the paragraph below. Then, edit any incorrect verbs by adding -*s* or
-*es* for the present tense or -*d* or -*ed* for the past tense. There are ten verb
errors in all.

Maniacs in Action

[1]A mania is abnormal or impulsive behavior. [2]When I was growing up, I often wonder^ed if the people in my family had certain
manias. [3]For instance, my aunt Margie certainly suffer^ed from klep-
tomania, or the impulse to steal. [4]She could never leave a shopping
mall without putting something she didn't buy into her pocket. [5]She
always said, "I have to have a little gift for myself," even if no one
want^ed to give her anything. [6]The mall security officers arrest^ed her
three times before she change^ed her behavior. [7]She still takes things

without paying for them, but only the free magazines by the
entrance to the stores. [8]My cousin Freddy had problems, too. [9]He
was a pyromaniac, or someone obsessed with fire. [10]He constantly
start^ed fires in inappropriate places, such as his parents' bedroom.
[11]The higher the flames rose, the more he celebrate^d. [12]One time he
even burned a hole in the kitchen table. [13]He had to go to counseling for a long time after that, but to this day he still <u>like</u>^s to light
matches. [14]Finally, my stepsister Clara showed signs of being a
megalomaniac, or someone who has delusions of grandeur. [15]She
stood in front of her stuffed animals for hours, bossing them around
and acting like a dictator. [16]She even try^ied to train her goldfish.
[17]Actually, she ended up being successful. [18]She manage^s a bank,
and everyone there is afraid of her. [19]They do anything she wants.
[20]Maybe being a maniac isn't always a bad thing.

Lab Activity 38

For additional practice with regular verbs, complete Lab Activity 38 in the
Lab Manual at the back of the book.

39 Irregular Verbs

Few places on earth remain unexplored. However, despite the fact that our maps are now crammed with names and symbols, there was a time when vast stretches of land and sea were undiscovered by any except those who lived there. Christopher Columbus, James Cook, and Sir Walter Raleigh are some of the explorers who mapped our world.

The Principal Parts of Irregular Verbs

Most English verbs are regular; those whose parts are always formed the same way. English also has many **irregular verbs,** which use unpredictable forms for the different tenses. For example, the past tense of *choose* is *chose,* and the past participle is *chosen.*

The list below shows the principal parts of the most common irregular verbs. If you're not sure what the past or past participle of a verb is, check this list below or look in a dictionary.

Principal Parts of Irregular Verbs

Present	Past	Past Participle	Present Participle
am (are, is)*	was (were, was)	been	being
arise	arose	arisen	arising
awake	awoke *or* awaked	awoke *or* awaked	awaking
become	became	become	becoming
begin	began	begun	beginning

(*continued*)

*The infinitive ("to" form) is *to be.*

Principal Parts of Irregular Verbs *(continued)*

Present	Past	Past Participle	Present Participle
bend	bent	bent	bending
bid	bid	bid	bidding
bite	bit	bitten	biting
blow	blew	blown	blowing
break	broke	broken	breaking
bring	brought	brought	bringing
build	built	built	building
burst	burst	burst	bursting
buy	bought	bought	buying
catch	caught	caught	catching
choose	chose	chosen	choosing
come	came	come	coming
cost	cost	cost	costing
cut	cut	cut	cutting
dive	dived *or* dove	dived	diving
do (does)	did	done	doing
draw	drew	drawn	drawing
drink	drank	drunk	drinking
drive	drove	driven	driving
eat	ate	eaten	eating
fall	fell	fallen	falling
feed	fed	fed	feeding
feel	felt	felt	feeling
fight	fought	fought	fighting
find	found	found	finding
flee	fled	fled	fleeing
fly	flew	flown	flying
forget	forgot	forgot *or* forgotten	forgetting
freeze	froze	frozen	freezing
get	got	got *or* gotten	getting
give	gave	given	giving
go (goes)	went	gone	going
grow	grew	grown	growing
hang (suspend)	hung	hung	hanging
have (has)	had	had	having

Principal Parts of Irregular Verbs *(continued)*

Present	Past	Past Participle	Present Participle
hear	heard	heard	hearing
hide	hid	hidden	hiding
hold	held	held	holding
hurt	hurt	hurt	hurting
keep	kept	kept	keeping
know	knew	known	knowing
lay	laid	laid	laying
lead	led	led	leading
leave	left	left	leaving
lend	lent	lent	lending
let	let	let	letting
lie	lay	lain	lying
lose	lost	lost	losing
make	made	made	making
meet	met	met	meeting
pay	paid	paid	paying
ride	rode	ridden	riding
ring	rang	rung	ringing
rise	rose	risen	rising
run	ran	run	running
say	said	said	saying
see	saw	seen	seeing
sell	sold	sold	selling
set	set	set	setting
send	sent	sent	sending
shake	shook	shaken	shaking
shrink	shrank	shrunk	shrinking
shut	shut	shut	shutting
sing	sang	sung	singing
sink	sank *or* sunk	sunk	sinking
sit	sat	sat	sitting
sleep	slept	slept	sleeping
slide	slid	slid	sliding
speak	spoke	spoken	speaking

(continued)

Principal Parts of Irregular Verbs *(continued)*

Present	Past	Past Participle	Present Participle
spend	spent	spent	spending
spring	sprang *or* sprung	sprung	springing
stand	stood	stood	standing
steal	stole	stolen	stealing
stick	stuck	stuck	sticking
sting	stung	stung	stinging
swear	swore	sworn	swearing
swim	swam	swum	swimming
swing	swung	swung	swinging
take	took	taken	taking
teach	taught	taught	teaching
tear	tore	torn	tearing
tell	told	told	telling
think	thought	thought	thinking
throw	threw	thrown	throwing
wake	woke *or* waked	woken *or* waked	waking
wear	wore	worn	wearing
win	won	won	winning
write	wrote	written	writing

EXERCISE 1 WRITING THE CORRECT FORM OF IRREGULAR VERBS

In each blank, write the correct past tense form of the irregular verb. If you're not sure of the correct verb form, check the list on pages 547–550. An example is done for you.

The Italian-born Christopher Columbus (be) __was__ a famous explorer in the 1400s.

1. Christopher Columbus tried to find new lands that (hold)

__held__ treasures.

2. If he (find) _found_ the right treasures, he could make a fortune selling them in Europe.

3. Columbus (swear) _swore_ that there were undiscovered lands across the ocean.

4. He (know) _knew_, however, that getting money for his journey would be hard.

5. King Ferdinand and Queen Isabella of Spain (lend) _lent_ him the money for his journey.

6. Columbus (buy) _bought_ three ships: the *Niña*, the *Pinta*, and the *Santa Maria*.

7. He (take) _took_ a new route toward China by sailing across the Atlantic Ocean.

8. Upon landing in the New World, Columbus (meet) _met_ the people we know as Native Americans.

9. He (think) _thought_ he was in India, so Columbus called the people of the New World Indians.

10. Columbus's discoveries (lead) _led_ to changes that affected people throughout the world.

EXERCISE 2 CHOOSING CORRECT IRREGULAR VERB FORMS

In each blank provided, write the correct form of the irregular verb shown. The tenses are indicated in parentheses. Check the list of irregular verbs on pages 547–550 if you need help. An example is done for you.

think   Many people (present) _think_ that being an explorer of new lands sounds exciting. At one time, I (past tense) _thought_ so, too. My friend Andy (present) _thinks_ that sailing around the world sounds great. However, he has never (past participle) _thought_ that dangers might be part of an explorer's job.

1. come   When a big storm (past) _came_ , sailors had to be ready. Foul weather was a sure sign that danger had (past participle) _come_ .

2. catch   Another danger came from pirates that were trying to catch explorers' ships. In many cases, pirates (past) _caught_ explorers' ships in the hopes of robbing them. If explorers were (past participle) _caught_ , they could lose everything: their cargo, their supplies, even their lives.

3. drink   Running out of fresh water to drink was a third danger. Sailors (past) _drunk_ water daily, so they had to carry fresh water in barrels on the ship. Once the sailors had (past participle) _drank_ the last of the water, they were in trouble unless they found a port quickly.

4. get   Yet another danger came if a sailor could not get enough vitamin C. Without vitamin C from fresh fruits and vegetables, sailors often (past) _got_ scurvy, a serious disease that caused people to feel weak and have spongy gums. Once a sailor had (past participle) _got or gotten_ scurvy, he could lose his teeth and get nosebleeds.

5. leave   A final danger of exploring came when the ship left port. When they (past) _left_ , sailors knew that they might never come back. They could get lost, get attacked, or die from hunger or thirst. Thus, once a sailor had (past participle) _left_ , his family knew he might never come home again.

The Big Three: *to be, to do,* and *to have*

The irregular verbs that routinely give writers the most trouble are three of the most common verbs: *to be, to do,* and *to have.* To avoid errors with these three verbs, memorize their correct forms.

Principal Parts

Once you've memorized the correct verb forms of *to be, to do,* and *to have,* you will be surprised at how often they appear in your writing.

Verb	Present	Past	Past Participle	Present Participle
to be	am, is, are	was, were	been	being
to do	do, does	did	done	doing
to have	have, has	had	had	having

Tenses

The verbs *to be, to do,* and *to have* are irregular: their tenses take unpredictable forms. For *to be,* the past tense changes depending on the subject.

To Be

Present Tense		Past Tense	
I	am	I	was
You	are	You	were
He, she, it	is	He, she, it	was
We	are	We	were
You (plural)	are	You (plural)	were
They	are	They	were

To Do

Present Tense		Past Tense	
I	do	I	did
You	do	You	did

He, she, it	does	He, she, it	did
We	do	We	did
You (plural)	do	You (plural)	did
They	do	They	did

To Have

Present Tense		**Past Tense**	
I	have	I	had
You	have	You	had
He, she, it	has	He, she, it	had
We	have	We	had
You (plural)	have	You (plural)	had
They	have	They	had

Avoiding Common Errors

People often use incorrect verb forms when speaking informally. Using the incorrect forms of the verbs *to be, to do,* and *to have* can hurt your credibility as a speaker and a writer, so be careful to avoid them.

Incorrect	**Correct**
~~I be.~~	I am.
~~He don't.~~	He doesn't.
~~She have.~~	She has.

EXERCISE 3 USING *TO BE, TO DO,* AND *TO HAVE* CORRECTLY

Circle the correct form of the verbs *be, do,* and *have* in each sentence.

1. Leif Ericson (was, were) a Norwegian explorer of about the year 1000.

2. He (is, be) known for his contributions to knowledge about North America.

3. Vinland (be, is) a place that Ericson supposedly discovered.

4. The location of Vinland (has, have) been in dispute since Ericson found it.

5. Some places said to be Vinland (are, is) the Canadian province of Newfoundland and the New England region of the United States.

6. Though Columbus is credited with being the first European to discover America, some people say Ericson (is, was).

7. Ericson's travels, however, (are, is) not documented as thoroughly as Columbus's.

8. Also, Ericson's exploration (did, done) not result in continuous colonization of America, as Columbus's did.

9. Ericson's discoveries (did, done), however, inspire others to explore.

10. If nothing else, Ericson's travels (was, were) the foundations for great tales of travel.

Viking Ships

CRITICAL THINKING The eldest son of Eric the Red, the Viking Leif Ericson was the first European to discover and settle Greenland. Explorers' travels have brought people from all parts of the world together. Do you think people are better off living near others of different backgrounds? Explain in a few sentences.

EXERCISE 4 USING THE PAST TENSE OF *TO BE, TO DO,* AND *TO HAVE*

Fill in each blank with the correct form of *be, do,* or *have.*

1. Captain James Cook _____was_____ an English explorer of the 1700s.

2. Few explorers accomplished as much as he _____did_____.

3. Australia _____had_____ its first European colony as a result of Cook's voyages.

4. Cook _____was_____ the first European to visit Hawaii.

5. Some people claim that the *Star Trek* character James T. Kirk _____was_____ meant to be a modern version of James Cook.

6. One reason for this _____is_____ the similarity of their names: James Cook and James Kirk.

7. Their ships _____had_____ similar names, too.

8. Cook's ship _____was_____ the *Endeavor,* and Kirk's ship was called the *Enterprise.*

9. Finally, Cook supposedly made the statement that he wanted to "go boldly" where no one had gone before. Kirk made almost the same statement that Cook _____did_____.

10. Kirk claimed he wanted to "boldly go" where no man had gone before. Though he lived centuries ago, James Cook _____had_____ a significant influence on the world.

EXERCISE 5 WRITING SENTENCES USING IRREGULAR VERBS

Write a sentence for the verb form given below using the tense shown in parentheses. See the list on pages 547–550 if you need help. An example is done for you. Answers will vary.

lie (past tense) Yesterday, I lay down for a nap after lunch.

1. *swim* (past)_____

2. *make* (past participle) _____

3. *bring* (past participle) _____

4. *wear* (past)_____

5. *hide* (past)_____

6. *draw* (past participle)_____

7. *freeze* (past)_____

8. *fly* (past) _____

9. *begin* (past participle) _____

10. *eat* (past) _____

EDITING PRACTICE

Circle the correct verb forms in the paragraph below.

A Gentleman and Explorer

Sir Walter Raleigh (was, were) an English explorer of the late 1500s and early 1600s. His expeditions (took, taking) him on voyages to the Americas, and he (made, making) great profits on his ventures. He (did, done) a great service to England by introducing two popular products from the New World: the potato and tobacco. His fame, however, (come, comes) largely from his good manners. Even today, Sir Walter Raleigh (be, is) an excellent example of a gentleman. People (think, thought) that he (went, going) to great lengths to treat others with courtesy. One well-known tale of his courtesy (tells, tell) of a time he (comes, came) across a mud puddle when the queen was near. Sir Walter Raleigh (lay, laid) his coat over the puddle so that Queen Elizabeth would not have to walk through the mud.

Lab Activity 39

For additional practice with irregular verbs, complete Activity 39 in the Lab Manual at the back of the book.

40 Subject-Verb Agreement

Understanding Subject-Verb Agreement

For sentences to make sense, subjects and verbs have to agree with each other. This means that if the subject is **singular,** then the verb should be singular. Also, if the subject is **plural,** then the verb must be plural. The subjects and verbs in the following sentences reflect the same numbers.

Brahms was a great conductor.

(Here the subject *Brahms* indicates a single person, while the verb *was* also indicates action by one person. If the subject were plural, the verb would be *were*.)

Classical music conductors often master many instruments.

(The plural subject *conductors* matches the plural verb form *master*. If the subject were *A conductor*, the verb would need to be *masters*.)

Subject-verb agreement—where the subject and verb reflect the same number—is one of the most important grammar skills you can master. The good news is that subject-verb agreement is usually simple to get right if the subject and verb are close to each other. However, errors in subject-verb agreement can happen in the following cases.

- Words come between the subject and the verb.
- The verb comes before the subject.
- The subject has two or more parts.
- The sentence contains an indefinite pronoun.

Agreement When Words Come Between Subject and the Verb

Sometimes when words come between the subject and verb, it's hard to decide what the subject of a sentence is. In the sentences below, a prepositional phrase comes between the subject (underlined once) and the verb (underlined twice). Remember that a prepositional phrase is *not* the subject.

> Musical compositions by Johann Sebastian Bach offer a music lover many choices.

(The subject *compositions* is plural, so the verb *offer* must also be plural.)

> One of Bach's most famous pieces is "Jesu, Joy of Man's Desiring."

(The subject *One* is singular, so the verb *is* must be singular too.)

The sentences are much easier to check for subject-verb agreement when the prepositional phrases are eliminated.

> Musical compositions ~~by Johann Sebastian Bach~~ offer a music lover many choices.

> One ~~of Bach's most famous pieces~~ is "Jesu, Joy of Man's Desiring."

EXERCISE 1 CHECKING FOR SUBJECT-VERB AGREEMENT WHEN THE SUBJECT IS SEPARATED FROM THE VERB

In the sentences below, circle the correct forms of the verbs in parentheses. *Hint:* Cross out the prepositional phrases to help you identify the subject and verb.

1. The career moves ~~in Johann Sebastian Bach's life~~ (was, (were)) many.

2. Even now, Bach's first opportunity ~~in his professional life~~ (seem, (seems)) exciting. Here's how things happened.

3. A church ~~in Arnstadt, Germany,~~ (offer, (offers)) him a job as organist and choirmaster.

4. The job in the church ((pays,) pay) well.

5. Bach's duties ~~at the church~~ ((demand,) demands) little time and energy.

6. One ~~of Bach's weaknesses~~ ((is,) are) the desire to attend concerts.

7. Music ~~in many forms~~ ((inspires,) inspire) Bach, so his superiors let him go ~~to some concerts.~~

8. Bach's enthusiasm ~~for concerts~~ (keep, (keeps)) him away ~~from the church~~ too much.

9. The leaders ~~in the church~~ ((scold,) scolds) Bach ~~for being away at concerts~~ too often.

10. The conflicts ~~between Bach and his superiors~~ ((drive,) drives) him away to look ~~for another job.~~

Agreement When the Verb Comes Before the Subject

Sometimes the verb in a sentence comes before the subject. In the following sentences, the subjects are underlined once and the verbs twice.

In Bach's collection of compositions are many fugues.

(The plural subject *fugues* comes after the verb *are*.)

What is a fugue?

(The singular subject *fugue* comes after the verb *is*.)

With the feelings of flight or escape come the different parts of the fugue.

(The plural subject *parts* agrees with the verb *come*.)

To find the subject, first eliminate prepositional phrases. Then ask yourself what the action of the sentence is and then *who* or *what* is performing that action. *Just because a word comes first does not mean it's the subject.*

EXERCISE 2 CHECKING FOR SUBJECT-VERB AGREEMENT WHEN THE VERB COMES BEFORE THE SUBJECT

In the sentences below, circle the correct form of each verb in parentheses.

1. Among Bach's works (exist, exists) many fugues.

2. From Latin (come, comes) the term *fugue*, which means "to chase" or "to escape."

3. All through a fugue (are, is) the sounds of three voices.

4. Expressed in the pattern of a fugue (are, is) the concept of three voices "chasing" each other.

5. At different points in the music (come, comes) the three voices.

6. In a later part of the fugue (come, comes) a second voice.

7. What (do, does) this second voice bring to the music?

8. Through the second voice (echoes, echo) the first voice's theme.

9. Into the music, but many notes higher, (sings, sing) a third voice.

10. What (is, are) the job of the third voice? It echoes the first theme yet again.

Agreement When the Subject Has Two or More Parts

Subjects with two or more parts are called **compound subjects.** Generally, these subjects are plural and require a plural verb.

Bach, Beethoven, and Brahms all come from Germany.

(The compound subject has three parts—*Bach, Beethoven,* and *Brahms*—so the verb *come* is plural.)

When the verb has both a helping verb and a main verb, the helping verb changes to agree with the subject.

People who study classical music have learned much about the music they love.

(The subject *People* is plural, so the helping verb *have* is plural.)

Beethoven's *Moonlight Sonata* is considered one of his finest works.

(The singular subject *Moonlight Sonata* agrees with the helping verb *is*.)

When subjects are joined by *either . . . or, neither . . . nor,* or *not only . . . but also*, the verb must agree with the subject that is closest to it.

Not only Beethoven and Brahms but also Bach was from Germany.

(Even though *Beethoven* and *Brahms* are part of the subject, *Bach* is the one the singular verb agrees with because it's closer.)

EXERCISE 3 MAKING VERBS AGREE WITH COMPOUND SUBJECTS

In the sentences below, circle the correct form of each verb in parentheses.

1. Many complicated terms and expressions in classical music (has, **have**) simple meanings.

2. A *virtuoso* and a person with great technical skill (is, **are**) the same.

3. Not only Bach and Beethoven but also Brahms (**was**, were) a virtuoso on several instruments.

4. The Italian terms *cantata* and *sonata* (**mean**, means) pieces to be performed, usually as solos accompanied by an orchestra.

5. Not only fugues but also the cantata (**is**, are) music meant to be sung.

6. On the other hand, the term *sonata* or *concerto* (indicate, **indicates**) music meant to be played on an instrument, not sung.

7. *Allegro* and *allant* (**mean**, means) that music should be played "bright" or "lively."

8. *Andante* and *lento* (**indicate**, indicates) a slower tempo.

9. Finally, the term *symphony* and the term *concerto* (**have**, has) similar original meanings.

10. Now, though, neither a symphony nor a concerto (**is**, are) the simple instrumental combination it once was.

Agreement When the Subject Is an Indefinite Pronoun

An **indefinite pronoun** does not refer to a specific person or thing. The indefinite pronouns listed below require singular verbs, even when they refer to more than one person.

anyone	anybody	anything	each
everyone	everybody	everything	either
no one	nobody	nothing	neither
someone	somebody	something	one

Tip: Make sure not to use the pronoun *they* to agree with *everyone* and *everybody*. Even though these words sometimes seem as if they should be plural, they are singular. For more on pronoun agreement, see Chapter 43.

Everyone listening to Bach was in a peaceful mood.

(The subject *everyone* takes the singular verb *is*.)

No one admits to taking my Brahms CD.

(The subject *no one* takes the singular verb *admits*.)

The indefinite pronouns listed below require plural verbs.

both	many
few	several

Both of my parents love hearing Beethoven.

(The subject *both* requires the plural verb *love*.)

EXERCISE 4   MAKING VERBS AGREE WITH INDEFINITE PRONOUNS

In the following sentences, circle the correct form of each verb in parentheses.

1. Anything related to classical music (is, are) intimidating to me.

2. Everything on classical CDs (sounds, sound) perfect.

3. Nevertheless, something (make, makes) me want to play in the school orchestra.

4. However, something (appears, appear) to be wrong with me when I try to understand or play classical music.

5. First, nothing about the sheet music (looks, look) as if it could ever sound pretty.

6. Second, classical music has different parts, and each (have, has) a tricky name such as *overture, coda,* or *air.*

7. In the orchestra, if people beside me (play, plays) off-key, no one seems to notice.

8. In fact, nobody else (admits, admit) to being out of tune or making mistakes.

9. Instead, everyone in the orchestra (blames, blame) me for making the music sound bad.

10. Neither of my parents (encourage, encourages) me to continue playing.

Ludwig van Beethoven (1770–1827)

FOOD FOR THOUGHT Despite being completely deaf by the end of his career, Beethoven composed pieces expressing the full range of human emotion. Should college students be required to learn about classical music? Write a few sentences explaining whether or not colleges should require this type of instruction.

EDITING PRACTICE 1

In the sentences below, circle the correct form of each verb in parentheses.

1. The mood swings and personality of Johannes Brahms (is, **are**) a contradiction.
2. Nobody (disagree, **disagrees**) that Brahms was full of bad humor and criticism.
3. People (**claim**, claims) that Brahms was prickly and kept to himself.
4. "The Outsider" (remain, **remains**) a name that Brahms even gave himself.
5. More than one person (tell, **tells**) of his sociable side.
6. The content of many letters (reveal, **reveals**) that Brahms had a large circle of friends and acquaintances.
7. Everyone who was an important part of his life (write, **writes**) of Brahms' wide range of interests.
8. Brahms' love interests or even his true love (remain, **remains**) a mystery.
9. From pages of letters and books (**speak**, speaks) colleagues and friends of Brahms about his love interests.
10. People claim that either his genius or his weaknesses (play, **plays**) a large role, even today, in understanding Johannes Brahms.

EDITING PRACTICE 2

The following paragraph contains ten errors in subject-verb agreement. Cross out the incorrect verbs, and write in the correct forms.

Lend an Ear to Beethoven

Many people ~~considers~~ [consider] Ludwig van Beethoven the greatest of all composers. First, Beethoven's music ~~cover~~ [covers] the range of human emotions. His Third Symphony, "Eroica," ~~express~~ [expresses] ideas of heroism while the *Moonlight Sonata* is sad. Another reason people ~~finds~~ [find] Beethoven so great is that his music ~~show~~ [shows] the talent of combining skills to write orchestral movements. For instance, Beethoven's famous Fifth Symphony ~~reveal~~ *reveals* his mastery of timing, writing chords, and mixing the sounds of different instruments. One more reason people find Beethoven such a powerful composer ~~are~~ *is* his effort to create flawless work that would last forever. Thousands of pages of drafts of his music ~~lets~~ *let* the world know how hard Beethoven tried to make his work perfect. His goal to be perfect ~~were~~ *was* even more difficult since he became totally deaf by the end of his career. From his first published composition at the age of twelve to his moving Ninth Symphony, Beethoven ~~stand~~ *stands* the test of time.

Lab Activity 40

For additional practice with subject-verb agreement, complete Lab Activity 40 in the Lab Manual at the back of the book.

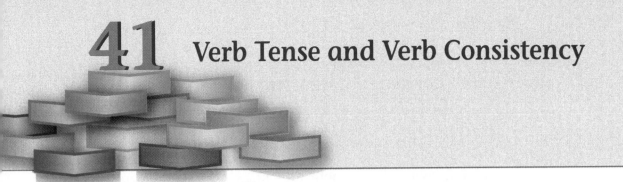

41 Verb Tense and Verb Consistency

CULTURE NOTE **American Legends**

Although the United States is young compared with many other countries, its history is rich in legends, which are stories handed down through generations and based in truth. Legends are similar to myths in that their central characters are usually larger than life.

Consistency in Verb Tense

Consistency in verb tense simply means using the same verb tense throughout your writing. If you start a story or example in the past tense, for instance, then you must write your entire paragraph or essay in the past tense. Otherwise, your *inconsistent* verb tenses will send a confusing message to your reader.

Sometimes longer works require the use of different verb tenses. In these cases, it is important to make sure your verbs are consistent through each section of your work rather than throughout the entire piece.

The following sentence sends an unclear message to the reader, who will not know whether the action is taking place now or has already taken place.

Incorrect: Paul Bunyan was a giant lumberjack who carries a huge axe. (The verb *was* is past tense, and the verb *carries* is present tense.)

The sentence can be revised in two ways.

■ Revise to put both verbs in the present tense.
   Correct: Paul Bunyan is a giant lumberjack who carries a huge axe.

■ Revise to put both verbs in the past tense.
   Correct: Paul Bunyan was a giant lumberjack who carried a huge axe.

EXERCISE 1 USING CONSISTENT VERB TENSE IN SENTENCES

The following sentences contain verb tense errors. Write the correct verb forms in the blanks. Use the underlined verb in the first part of each sentence as a clue to the correct verb tense. An example is done for you.

When I <u>was</u> a child, my mother (tuck) ____*tucked*____ me into bed every night. (The first verb of the sentence—*was*—is past tense, so the verb later in the sentence must also be past tense.)

1. She <u>sat</u> on my bed and (tell) __told_____ me stories about historical Americans.

2. Some of the stories <u>were</u> true, and some of them (be) __were_____ fiction.

3. I especially <u>loved</u> the story of Paul Bunyan, who (travel)

__traveled_____ around Minnesota with his blue ox, Babe.

4. I also <u>enjoyed</u> the story of Rip Van Winkel, who (love)

__loved_____ to sleep.

5. Now, however, I <u>am</u> an adult, so I rarely (listen) __listen_____ to bedtime stories.

6. Instead, I <u>tell</u> stories to my children, who (be) __are_____ very young.

7. They <u>like</u> to hear about Johnny Appleseed because they (love)

__love_____ to eat apples.

8. Although they never <u>get</u> to eat apples during the story, they still

(hope) __hope_____ that they might get to sometime.

9. My children <u>used</u> to like the story about John Henry because they

(want) __wanted_____ to hear about the race of man against machine.

10. Now, however, they <u>know</u> that story, so they (ask) __ask_____ to hear others.

Paul Bunyan and Babe the Blue Ox

G-9—Paul Bunyan and Babe, The Blue Ox

JOURNAL RESPONSE   Known for his huge appetite and gigantic stature, Paul Bunyan is a favorite American legend. Should stories like this be taught in school? Write for ten minutes discussing whether or not American legends such as Paul Bunyan or John Henry should be taught in schools.

EXERCISE 2 CHOOSING THE CORRECT VERB TENSE FOR CONSISTENCY

In the sentences below, circle the correct verbs in parentheses. An example is done for you.

Even when he was first born, Paul Bunyan (gives, (gave)) his parents a challenge.

1. Many stories tell about Paul Bunyan's adult life, and a few ((describe), described) his early years.

2. When Paul Bunyan was born, it (takes, took) five storks to deliver him to his parents.

3. At birth Paul weighed eighty pounds, and he (is, was) driven home in a lumber wagon.

4. In fact, the lumber wagon (becomes, became) his baby carriage.

5. Young Paul's appetite is incredible; he (eats, ate) forty bowls of oatmeal as the *start* to his breakfast.

6. Paul grows so fast that he (wears, wore) his father's clothes just one week after being born.

7. Paul's baby teeth were so big that he (has, had) to use a log as a teething toy.

8. Some people describe baby Paul's voice as a buzz saw, and others (say, said) it sounds like a bass drum.

9. In fact, his voice was so loud that he (empties, emptied) a pond of frogs with one yell.

10. Paul Bunyan is certainly tall, but the tales about him (are, were) taller.

Tip: Verb tense inconsistencies often creep into pieces of writing that are a paragraph or longer. When proofreading your work, pay close attention to verb tense in your paragraphs or essays.

Changing Verb Tense

Generally, you should keep your verb tense consistent throughout your sentence, paragraph, or essay. However, there are some instances when you may need to switch tenses.

When you want to indicate different times in one sentence, use different verb tenses.

Last fall I <u>panicked</u> during finals week, but this semester I <u>feel</u> more relaxed.

The verb *panicked* indicates an action that took place in the past, and the verb *feel* communicates another action that is taking place right now.

You may need to change verb tenses when you discuss the ongoing influence of people or events from the past. For example, the people who

Verb Tense in Stories

In writing about literature (poetry, stories, and novels), use the present tense to discuss the action and to talk about an author's writing style and technique. For instance, write, "William Shakespeare *explores* themes of love and revenge in his play *Othello*." Even though Shakespeare lived centuries ago, we still write about his works in the present tense.

the legends in this chapter are based on lived hundreds of years ago. To tell their stories straight through, we could use the past tense. However, even though the tales occurred in the past, their influence on us is ongoing. Thus, discussions of Paul Bunyan, John Henry, and Johnny Appleseed may begin in the present tense. For instance, the first two sentences in the paragraph "Man Versus Machine" below have different verb tenses.

One of the greatest legends in American history <u>is</u> the tale of John Henry.

John Henry <u>was</u> born a slave in the 1840s or 1850s in the American South.

The present tense verb *is* in the first sentence tells us that the influence of John Henry is still present, while the past tense verb *was* in the second sentence indicates an event that occured in the past: John Henry's birth.

EXERCISE 3 USING CONSISTENT VERB TENSE IN A PARAGRAPH

Circle the correct verbs in the paragraph below.

Man Versus Machine

One of the greatest legends in American history is the tale of John Henry. John Henry was born a slave in the 1840s or 1850s in the American South. After the Civil War, he (is, (was)) hired as a steel driver for the C&O Railroad. Steel drivers (spend, (spent)) their workdays driving steel drills or spikes into rock. John Henry (uses, (used)) a fourteen-pound hammer to drill ten to twenty feet in a twelve-hour day, the best of any man on the rails. The C&O's new line was moving along quickly until Big Bend Mountain (blocks, (blocked)) its path. The mountain was too vast to build around, so the men (have, (had)) to drive their drills through its belly. It (takes, (took)) a thousand men three years to finish the treacherous work. Visibility was poor, and the air inside the tunnel (is, (was)) thick with black smoke and dust. One day, a salesman (comes, (came)) to camp, boasting that his steam-powered machine could work faster than any man. A race was set: man against machine. Although John Henry (wins, (won)), he (dies, (died)) shortly after the contest, some say from exhaustion, some say from a stroke.

EDITING PRACTICE

Rewrite the following paragraph to use past tense verbs consistently. There are five errors in verb consistency in all.

Planting the Seeds of a Legend

Johnny Appleseed ~~is~~ **was** an American folk hero during the late 1700s and early 1800s. His real name was John Chapman, and he lived in New England. He ~~travels~~ **traveled** through Pennsylvania, Ohio, Indiana, and Illinois. At a time when frontier settlers ~~have~~ **had** little fruit to eat, he planted apple seeds. He also ~~starts~~ **started** an apple tree nursery in Pennsylvania and ~~encourage~~ **encouraged** settlers to plant orchards of their own. Johnny Appleseed became famous through the telling of his story. He is also the subject of a ballad by W. H. Venable and of many poems by Vachel Lindsay including one titled "In Praise of Johnny Appleseed."

Lab Activity 41

For additional practice with correct and consistent verb tense, complete Lab Activity 41 in the Lab Manual at the back of the book.

42 Pronoun Types

Copyright © 2007 Pearson Education, Inc.

 CULTURE NOTE — *The Olympic Games*

Even when world politics seem about to explode in violence or mistrust, the Olympic Games usually bring countries and cultures together in peace. Modeled after the games begun in ancient Greece, the modern Olympics consist primarily of athletic contests.

Recognizing Pronouns

Pronouns are words that take the place of nouns. They are essential to clear, concise communication because they allow us to substitute a short, easily recognizable word for another word or phrase.

The Olympic Games were held in honor of Zeus; the Olympic Games included athletic games and contests in dance and poetry.

In the preceding sentence, the subject *the Olympic Games* is written out twice. The sentence is shorter when it contains a pronoun instead. The pronoun *they* allows us to avoid repeating the subject *the Olympic Games*.

The Olympic Games were held in honor of Zeus; they included athletic games and contests in dance and poetry.

There are many types of pronouns. In this chapter, we focus on the five most common types.

- Subject pronouns
- Object pronouns
- Possessive pronouns
- Reflexive pronouns
- Demonstrative pronouns

Subject Pronouns

A **subject pronoun** is the subject of a sentence or clause.

Singular Subject Pronouns   **Plural Subject Pronouns**

I, you, he, she, it   we, you, they

The subject pronouns are underlined once in the sentences below; verbs are underlined twice.

They competed to honor the god Zeus, ruler of Olympus. (*They* is the subject of the verb *competed*.)

We have modeled our current Olympic games after those in ancient Greece. (*We* is the subject of the verb *have modeled*.)

Using a Subject Pronoun as Part of a Compound Subject

A **compound subject** is a subject with more than one part.

Incorrect:	Olympic athletes and me share an interest with my brother.
Correct:	Olympic athletes and I share an interest with my brother.
Incorrect:	Them and him are dedicated to sports.
Correct:	They and he are dedicated to sports.

If you're not sure which pronoun to use, try reading the sentence using the pronoun by itself as the subject. "Me share an interest" doesn't sound right, so you know to use the pronoun *I*.

Using a Subject Pronoun After Forms of *to be*

The forms of the verb *to be* are *am, is, are, was, were, has been*, and *have been*. Subject pronouns are used following any form of the verb *to be*.

Correct:	It was she who won the gold medal in 1964.
	It may have been they who boycotted the Olympics that year.

The sentences above may sound strange or artificial, but they are grammatically correct. Even though you can make your point in conversation by using expressions such as "It was her" or "It may have been them," these uses of pronouns are incorrect in standard written English. They should not appear in your writing. If you're not comfortable using subject pronouns after forms of the verb *to be*, revise your sentences.

Correct:	She won the gold medal in 1964.
	They boycotted the Olympics that year.

Using a Subject Pronoun After *than* and *as*

When a clause starts with *than* or *as*, use the subject pronoun.

Correct:	The Kenyans typically have faster distance runners *than* we.
	Although Florence Griffith Joyner set an Olympic record, the sprinter Marion Jones won more Olympic medals *than* she.

You can tell that the subject pronoun is correct by silently adding the verb that came earlier in the sentence.

The Kenyans have faster distance runners that we (have).

Although Florence Griffith Joyner set an Olympic record, the sprinter Marion Jones won more Olympic medals than she (won).

If your sentence doesn't make sense when you silently add the verb, you probably need to change your pronoun.

EXERCISE 1 CHOOSING THE CORRECT SUBJECT PRONOUN

In the following sentences, circle the correct subject pronouns in parentheses.

1. Though the Greek Olympic team is relatively small when compared with other teams, (it, he) is symbolically very important.

2. The ancient Greeks started the tradition of laying aside political and religious differences. (We, (They)) held the Olympic Games as a time of celebration.

3. It was ((they) them) who began the custom of holding the Olympics every four years.

4. The Greeks value the modern Olympics as much as (us, (we)).

5. Greece is still the source of the Olympic flame. (She, (It)) is lit by the sun's rays at Olympia, Greece, and then carried to the site of the Olympics.

6. Lighting the Olympic flame is no easy task. ((It) You) must be lit using only a parabolic mirror and the sun's rays.

7. Once the flame is lit, many hands carry the torch. (Them, (They)) ensure that the flame reaches the country of the Olympic Games safely.

8. In 1976, technology helped transport the flame to Canada. A satellite transmitted the flame from Athens, Greece, to Ottawa, Canada, where ((it) he) was carried to the Olympic site.

9. During the Montreal Olympic Games in 1976, an official relit the sacred Olympic flame with a cigarette lighter after it was drenched by a rainstorm, but ((he) him) was not supposed to do that.

10. The Olympic organizers had kept a reserve flame—originally lit at Olympia—on hand. (We, (They)) extinguished the "fake" flame and replaced it with an authentic Olympic one.

Object Pronouns

An **object pronoun** is used as the object of a verb or preposition. (**Prepositions** are words such as *about, for, behind*, and *to* that relate a noun or pronoun to the rest of a sentence. See page 478 for a list of prepositions.) An object pronoun can never be the subject of a sentence.

Singular Object Pronouns	**Plural Object Pronouns**
me, him, her, you	us, them, you

In the sentence below, the underlined object pronoun is the object of the preposition in italics.

After the American Rulon Gardner won his wrestling match, the Olympic official awarded a gold medal *to* him. (*Him* is the object of the preposition *to*.)

In the following sentence, the underlined pronoun is the object of the verb in italics.

My parents *told* me about the Olympics after their visit to the Sydney games. (*Me* is the object of the verb *told*.)

Sometimes writers aren't sure whether to use a subject pronoun or an object pronoun.

Incorrect:	*For* Rob and I, this Olympic event was the most meaningful.
Correct:	*For* Rob and me, this Olympic event was the most meaningful.
Incorrect:	The sports commentators *praised* he and she after their races.
Correct:	The sports commentators *praised* him and her after their races.

If you can't decide which pronoun to use, try saying the sentence aloud with each pronoun by itself. The pronoun that sounds correct will most likely be the right choice. For instance, "For *I* (drop the *Rob*), this Olympic event was the most meaningful" sounds awkward, but "For *me*, this Olympic event was the most meaningful" does not.

If a pronoun follows a preposition, it's likely to be an object of the preposition. If a pronoun follows a verb, it's likely to be an object of the verb.

EXERCISE 2 USING THE CORRECT OBJECT PRONOUNS

In the sentences below, circle the correct pronouns in parentheses.

1. The Olympic Games include many sports for (we, us) to view.

2. Running, jumping, and throwing are the first events my brother and (I, me) want to watch.

3. If the ancient Greeks didn't perform a feat for survival—like throwing a spear to get meat or defend a village—then it was not an Olympic sport for (they, them).

4. My brother and (I, me) love to watch the track and field competitions.

5. My sister tells (we, us) about her favorite event: synchronized swimming.

6. There's a pact between (she, her) and my mother to watch every synchronized swimming event they can find.

7. Those events give my mother and (she, her) great thrills.

8. My cousin Eugenia loves synchronized swimming even more than (they, them).

9. Synchronized swimming, however, with all the sequins and makeup and gelled hair, just doesn't seem like a sport to my brother or (I, me).

10. However, my brother is like (I, me). We try to appreciate the athleticism required for synchronized swimming.

Possessive Pronouns

A **possessive pronoun** shows that something belongs to someone or something. A list of possessive pronouns follows.

Possessive Pronouns

my, mine	our, ours
your, yours	your, yours
his, her, hers, its	their, theirs

The possessive pronouns are underlined in the sentences below.

Randy's television broke during the Olympics, so I let him watch my TV. (*My TV* means "The TV that belongs to me.")

Even though athletes win medals at the Olympics, the winners' countries claim the medals as theirs. (*Theirs* means "the medals that belong to the winners.")

Never use an apostrophe with a possessive pronoun. For more on apostrophes, see pages 638–639.

Incorrect:	The Olympic spirit will always have it's roots in Greece.
Correct:	The Olympic spirit will always have its roots in Greece.
Incorrect:	The five Olympic rings communicate a message that is uniquely their's.
Correct:	The five Olympic rings communicate a message that is uniquely theirs.

EXERCISE 3 USING POSSESSIVE PRONOUNS CORRECTLY

Correct the pronoun error in each sentence below. An example is done for you.

Of all the symbols associated with the Olympics, none is so widely
recognized as ~~it's~~ *its* flag.

1. On ~~it's~~ *its* white background, the Olympic flag has five different-

   colored rings.

2. The five continents each have a ring on the flag that is ~~their's~~ *theirs*.

3. This flag and the games it represents have helped build goodwill

   among nations, including ~~our's~~ *ours*.

4. Even when countries have boycotted Olympic competition, the flag

   has flown proudly over ~~it's~~ *its* events.

5. A symbol of hope for worldwide peace, the flag makes the state-

   ment "The games are everyone's, mine and ~~your's~~ *yours*."

Pronouns Ending in *-self* or *-selves*

Two kinds of pronouns end in *-self* or *-selves*.

- Reflexive pronouns
- Intensive pronouns

Reflexive Pronouns

A **reflexive pronoun** indicates that someone performed an action himself or herself. The reflexive pronouns are underlined in the following sentences.

In addition to the pride their countries feel for them, Olympic athletes feel proud <u>themselves</u>. (*Themselves* refers to *Olympic athletes*.)

The experienced athlete may train <u>himself</u>. (*Himself* refers to *experienced athlete*.)

Do not use a reflexive pronoun as the subject of a sentence.

Incorrect:	My mother and <u>myself</u> proudly watched the opening ceremonies of the Olympic Games.
Correct:	My mother and I proudly watched the opening ceremonies of the Olympic Games.

Tip: Think of a reflexive pronoun as a *reflection* of the subject. Thus, if the subject is *I*, the correct reflexive pronoun is *myself*. Since you can't have a reflection of an object without the object itself, you shouldn't use a reflexive pronoun—the *reflection* of the subject—unless the subject is present.

Intensive Pronouns

An **intensive pronoun** is used for emphasis. It always directly follows the word it refers to.

Marion Jones <u>herself</u> was pleased with her win in the hundred-meter dash. (*Herself* emphasizes that Marion Jones—in addition to others—was pleased with her win.)

EXERCISE 4 USING REFLEXIVE AND INTENSIVE PRONOUNS CORRECTLY

In the sentences below, write the correct reflexive or intensive pronoun in each blank.

1. Many Olympians <u>themselves</u> have reason to feel pride.

2. For instance, Ian Thorpe of Australia earned <u>himself</u> an Olympic gold medal in 2000.

3. The United States softball team played ___themselves___ into history by losing three games and then winning the gold medal.

4. Germany's Birgit Fischer distinguished ___herself___ by winning two gold medals in kayak events.

5. Australia ___itself___ felt pride at having hosted an excellent Olympic Games.

Demonstrative Pronouns

A **demonstrative pronoun** singles out a specific item or person.

Singular Demonstrative Pronouns	**Plural Demonstrative Pronouns**
this	these
that	those

In general, use *this* and *these* to indicate something or someone nearby, and use *that* and *those* to indicate something farther away. The demonstrative pronouns are underlined in the sentences below.

This is a great event.
These are some of the finest athletes I have ever seen.
An Olympic official would never overlook that.
His medals are those in the cabinet.

Demonstrative pronouns can be used as adjectives, too.

This year's Olympics included the triathlon as an event for the first time.
Men have competed in the hammer throw for decades, but the 2000 Olympic Games marked the first time women competed in that event.
These days, training for the Olympics is a full-time job.
About 11,000 athletes competed in those events in Australia.

Avoid using the expressions *this here* and *that there* in your writing. They are not acceptable in standard written English.

EXERCISE 5 USING DEMONSTRATIVE PRONOUNS CORRECTLY

In the following sentences, write the correct demonstrative pronouns in the blanks.

1. _These_____ days, people are interested in the money they can make from Olympic gold medals.

2. For _that or this_____ purpose, in 1994, the American figure skater Tonya Harding arranged to have another skater, Nancy Kerrigan, attacked.

3. In the national championships leading up to _those_____ Olympic Games, Harding thought she could win the gold medal if Kerrigan was out of the way.

4. However, while Harding did win _those_____ skating competitions, she did not win Olympic gold.

5. To _this_____ day, Harding is known for her dishonest plot.

EDITING PRACTICE

Circle the correct pronouns in the paragraph below.

Misleading Names

The summer Olympic Games contain many events with misleading names. For instance, the triple jump is a track and field event. The name implies that the event includes three jumps, but (it, they) is made up of a hop, a skip, and a jump. The athletes who compete in (this, these) event look as if (they, them) are doing a dance as (he or she, they) bounce down the runway. Not everyone is as coordinated as (them, they). Another event is the hammer throw. (These, This) event's name is misleading because the hammer looks nothing like a carpenter's tool. The hammer in the Olympic event is a metal ball that hangs from a wire handle. The athlete holds the handle with both of (his or her, their) hands, spins around to build momentum, and then releases the hammer into the air. Even though hammer throwers might not be as famous as other athletes, they earn (theirselves, themselves) pride through their

Mia Hamm in Action

JOURNAL ENTRY Retired star forward Mia Hamm led the U.S. women's soccer team to both World Cup and Olympic gold medals, as well as inspiring young women everywhere. What characteristics inspire you? Write a few sentences explaining why certain qualities—courage, strength, or perseverance, for instance—are particularly admirable to you, and give an example of someone who possesses each quality.

Olympic accomplishments. It is (they, them) who propel the weight over seventy meters. A favorite Olympic contest of (my, mine) is the butterfly stroke in swimming. Swimmers in (this, these) events must thrust (his or her, their) arms out at the sides at the same time and then bring (they, them) forward out of the water and down in a circular motion. Even though (that, those) stroke is called the butterfly, the swimmers look more like dolphins than butterflies. All in all, a sport can look very unlike what (its, it's) name suggests.

Lab Activity 42

For additional practice with pronoun types, complete Lab Activity 42 in the Lab Manual at the back of the book.

43 Pronoun Agreement

The second-largest state geographically (the largest is Alaska), Texas has a rich, rough history intertwined with the history of the entire United States. From its Lone Star State heritage to its variety of cultures, Texas has made its mark on many aspects of American life.

The Alamo

FOOD FOR THOUGHT Although Texans lost the battle of the Alamo, "Remember the Alamo!" became a rallying cry for Texans throughout the war they won against Mexico. What examples of positive results from negative situations can you think of? Write a few sentences about how a negative situation produced positive results.

Pronoun Agreement

Pronouns must be consistent in number with their **antecedents,** the word or words they replace. Singular antecedents require singular pronouns, just as plural antecedents require plural pronouns. In the examples that follow, the pronouns are underlined and their antecedents are in italics.

Correct: *Texans* swell their chests when talking about their state. (*Their* refers to *Texans* in both cases.)

Correct: The *flag* of Texas has undergone many changes throughout its life. (*Its* refers to *flag*.)

One *resident* of Texas claims he could never live anywhere else. (*He* refers to *resident*.)

Make sure that the pronouns you use in your writing always agree with their antecedents.

Incorrect: Texas is one place where a *person* can feel good about their life. (*Person* is singular, but the pronoun *their is* plural; the pronoun does not agree with its antecedent.)

Correct: In Texas, a *person* can feel good about his or her life.

In Texas, *people* can feel good about their lives.

Incorrect: *Each* of the three All-Pro Dallas Cowboys gave their autograph to the sick child. (*Each* is singular, but *their* is plural.)

Correct: *Each* of the three All-Pro Dallas Cowboys gave his autograph to the sick child.

Personal Pronouns

A **personal pronoun** refers to a specific person or thing.

Personal Pronouns

I, me, my, mine, myself	we, us, our, ours, ourselves
you, your, yours, yourself	they, them, their, theirs, themselves
he, him, his, himself	
she, her, hers, herself	
it, its, itself	

EXERCISE 1 PRACTICING PRONOUN AGREEMENT

Read the following paragraph, in which ten pronouns are underlined. Fill in the chart that follows with each pronoun's antecedent (the word the pronoun refers to). The first one has been filled in for you.

Six Flags over Texas

¹Though Texas has long been part of the United States, <u>it</u> has been a part of other countries, too. ²The expression "six flags over Texas" refers to the different countries that Texas has been part of. ³The first flag to fly over Texas was the Spanish flag. ⁴The Spanish claimed what is now Texas for <u>their</u> own from 1519 to 1685 and from 1690 to 1821. ⁵In 1685, under the Frenchman René-Robert Cavelier de La Salle, France claimed the eastern part of Texas near the Gulf Coast. ⁶La Salle called <u>his</u> claim Fort St. Louis. ⁷Though the fort was an important settlement for the French, <u>it</u> was doomed by bad luck. ⁸The French claim ended when La Salle was murdered by one of <u>his</u> own men. ⁹The third flag to fly over Texas was Mexican; <u>it</u> features an eagle, a snake, and a cactus on bars of red, green, and white. ¹⁰However, Texans revolted against Mexican rule and won <u>their</u> independence in 1836 when the Mexican general Antonio López de Santa Anna declared <u>himself</u> dictator. ¹¹From 1836 to 1845, Texas was <u>its</u> own republic, and during this time much of Texans' pride in <u>their</u> region developed. ¹²The Lone Star flag, the fourth to fly over Texas, still flies nearly everywhere in Texas today. ¹³The fifth flag to fly over Texas kept the red, white, and blue of the Lone Star flag, but <u>it</u> included a circle of stars for the Confederacy, which Texas joined from 1861 to 1865. ¹⁴Last but not least, Texas flew the flag of the United States from 1845 to 1861 and has flown <u>it</u> from 1865 to the present.

	Pronoun	Antecedent
Sentence 1	it	Texas
Sentence 4	their	Spanish
Sentence 6	his	La Salle
Sentence 7	it	fort
Sentence 8	his	La Salle
Sentence 9	it	flag
Sentence 10 (two pronouns)	their	Texans
	himself	Santa Anna
Sentence 11 (two pronouns)	its	Texas
	their	Texans'
Sentence 13	it	flag
Sentence 14	it	flag

Indefinite Pronouns

Indefinite pronouns are pronouns that do not refer to any specific person or thing. Make sure that when you use an indefinite pronoun as the subject of a sentence, the verb agrees with it.

The pronouns that agree with these must also be singular: *he, him, his, she,* or *her*. If you don't know the gender of *everyone* or *anyone* in a sentence, use the expressions he or she or him or her to include both sexes.

<u>Everyone</u> loves his football team in Texas.

Among Texan women, <u>no one</u> knows whether <u>she</u> will become a football widow in the fall.

However, since Texans are football fans, too, <u>somebody</u> usually has a party to watch the game in <u>his</u> or <u>her</u> home.

Pronoun Reference

Sometimes the antecedent to a pronoun is unclear. The following sentences contain unclear **pronoun references,** pronouns that do not seem to refer to anything in particular.

Unclear: When I called the University of Texas admissions office, they told me to send in an application. (The pronoun *they* doesn't refer to anyone specific; there is no plural word to act as an antecedent.)

To make the sentence clear, substitute a specific person for *they*.

Clear: When I called the University of Texas admissions office, the admissions clerk told me to send in an application.

Unclear: Kathy told Rhonda that her Texas accent was fading. (In this sentence, the reader wonders whose accent—Kathy's or Rhonda's—was fading.)

Clear: Kathy told Rhonda that Rhonda's accent was fading.

Clear: Kathy told Rhonda, "Your Texas accent is fading."

Unclear: I decided to move to Austin, which is great. (In this case, is the decision to move great? Or is Austin?)

Clear: I decided to move to the great city of Austin.

Clear: I made a great decision to move to Austin.

EXERCISE 2 MAKING CLEAR PRONOUN REFERENCES

Rewrite the following sentences to correct each unclear pronoun reference in italics. Answers will vary.

1. In *The History of Texas*, *it* says that few men are as important as Sam Houston. In *The History of Texas,* the authors say that few men are as important as Sam Houston.

2. Sam Houston led *them* in *their* struggle to win Texas's independence from Mexico. Sam Houston led Texans in their struggle to win independence from Mexico.

3. He served as president of the Republic of Texas and senator to the United States Senate. *It* required a lot of work. He served as president of the Republic of Texas and senator to the United States Senate, both of which required a lot of work.

4. He was elected governor of Texas just before the Civil War; *they* really wanted him to be their leader. He was elected governor of Texas just before the Civil War; Texans really wanted him to be their leader.

5. However, Houston opposed the Confederacy's president, so *he* was removed from office. However, Houston opposed the Confederacy's president, so Houston was removed from office.

Pronoun Consistency and Point of View

Good writing is clear and consistent in **point of view.** Point of view refers to the perspective of the writer: whether the writer is telling his or her own story (first person), giving directions or speaking directly to someone else (second person), or telling a story *about* someone else (third person).

First person: I was upset when my flight was canceled.
Second person: You should try to get another flight as soon as possible.
Third person: He decided to skip his trip completely.

Pronouns should be consistent throughout your writing. For instance, if you start a paragraph using *I*, don't suddenly switch to using *you*. Such shifts can be confusing to your reader.

| | Pronouns | |
Point of View	Singular	Plural
First person	I (me, my, mine, myself)	we (us, our, ourselves)
Second person	you (your, yours, yourself)	you (your, yours, yourselves)
Third person	he (him, his, himself)	they (them, their, theirs, themselves)
	she (her, hers, herself)	
	it (its, itself)	
	one (one's, oneself)	

The pronoun *one* is usually used to mean a single, unspecified person.

Walking though the Dallas–Fort Worth airport, <u>one</u> could get lost.

Shifting to *you* is an easy error to make because we use *you* to mean *one*.

Incorrect:	When <u>I</u> got off the plane in Dallas, <u>you</u> could feel the humidity.
Revised:	When <u>I</u> got off the plane in Dallas, <u>I</u> could feel the humidity.
Incorrect:	When <u>visitors</u> see the Alamo for the first time, <u>you</u> get goosebumps.
Revised:	When <u>visitors</u> see the Alamo for the first time, <u>they</u> get goosebumps.

A pronoun used as a subject must agree in number (singular or plural) with its verb in the sentence.

<u>He</u> <u>is</u> from Texas. (Both *he* and *is* are singular.)

<u>They</u> <u>know</u> their way around the city. (Both *they* and *know* are plural.)

Sometimes changing a pronoun requires you to change the verb in a sentence. When the subject of the sentence changes point of view, the verb must reflect that change.

<u>They</u> <u>want</u> to stay here in San Antonio. (The plural subject *They* requires a plural verb, *want*.)

<u>He</u> <u>wants</u> to move to Austin. (The singular subject *He* requires a singular verb, *wants*.)

EXERCISE 3 KEEPING POINT OF VIEW CONSISTENT

In the following sentences, correct any problems with inconsistent pronouns. Change the verb form if necessary. An example is done for you.

When visitors see the Alamo for the first time, ~~you~~ *they* get goosebumps.

1. When parents bring their families to the Alamo, ~~one~~ *they* must teach the

children to appreciate it.

2. For instance, when parents tell their six-year-olds about the men

who died defending the Alamo, ~~you~~ ^{they} often start by explaining who

Davey Crockett was.

3. If a parent wants to make seeing the Alamo a memorable experi-

ence, ~~they~~ ^{he or she} should tell the child about it ahead of time.

4. When children understand how "Remember the Alamo" became a

rallying cry for Texans, ~~one takes~~ ^{they take} pride even in the loss.

5. All in all, when parents prepare children to appreciate the Alamo,

~~you~~ ^{they} are giving the youngsters an unforgettable lesson.

EDITING PRACTICE 1

Circle the correct pronouns in parentheses below.

Texans: Rich in More Than History

¹Texans have gained prosperity from two main sources. ²After the Civil War, (he or she, *they*) profited from longhorn cattle. ³(*They,* he or she) not only provided food for the growing United States but also gave many people work. ⁴People had to raise, breed, and then herd the cattle. ⁵The American cowboy was born from the longhorn business, and (*his,* their) work on the range has been romanticized for decades. ⁶The legendary cattle drives that people read about in books and see in movies also received (his or her, *their*) start from cowboys' work on the range. ⁷Another natural source of wealth for Texas is (their, *its*) oil resources. ⁸Not far into the twentieth century, great oil gushers were discovered across Texas. ⁹Like the longhorns, oil brought prosperity not just to the people who discovered (*it,* them) but also to those who worked on drilling and processing (*it,* them). ¹⁰The oil business attracted additional businesses into oil communities to support the oil workers.

EDITING PRACTICE 2

In the sentences below, cross out the incorrect pronouns and write in the correct nouns. Then, circle the type of pronoun error made in each sentence. An example is done for you.

The image of the Texas cowboy has left ~~their~~ *its* mark on American culture.

a. Pronoun agreement *(circled)*   **b.** Pronoun reference   **c.** Point of view

1. When people see a cowboy in American movies, for instance, ~~you~~ *they* often also see scenes that resemble the plains of Texas.

a. Pronoun agreement   **b.** Pronoun reference *(circled)*   **c.** Point of view *(circled)*

2. A lone man on his trusty horse, Rusty shows ~~his~~ *his own or Rusty's* profile to the camera as the sun sets.

a. Pronoun agreement   **b.** Pronoun reference *(circled)*   **c.** Point of view

3. When the cowboy speaks, ~~their~~ *his* Texas accent comes through clearly in the greeting "Howdy, ma'am."

a. Pronoun agreement *(circled)*   **b.** Pronoun reference   **c.** Point of view

4. When a cowboy speaks to his partner, ~~his~~ *the cowboy's* expression and tone of voice are always serious.

a. Pronoun agreement   **b.** Pronoun reference *(circled)*   **c.** Point of view

5. When we see advertisements, too, ~~you~~ *we* often see cowboy images.

a. Pronoun agreement   **b.** Pronoun reference   **c.** Point of view *(circled)*

6. For years, one cigarette company has used a cowboy figure to promote ~~their~~ *its* products.

a. Pronoun agreement *(circled)*   **b.** Pronoun reference   **c.** Point of view

7. Every ad features a rugged, handsome cowboy smoking a cigarette or holding one in ~~their~~ *his* hands.

a. Pronoun agreement *(circled)*   **b.** Pronoun reference   **c.** Point of view

8. Certain clothing lines and car companies also show cowboys in ~~its~~ *their* ads.

   a. Pronoun agreement   **b.** Pronoun reference   **c.** Point of view

9. In fact, when you watch cowboys on television, ~~one~~ *you* can almost imagine being out on the range.

   a. Pronoun agreement   **b.** Pronoun reference   **c.** Point of view

10. Everyone who watches television must recall some time when ~~they~~ *he or she* saw a cowboy.

   a. Pronoun agreement   **b.** Pronoun reference   **c.** Point of view

Lab Activity 43

For additional practice with pronoun agreement, complete Lab Activity 43 in the Lab Manual at the back of the book.

44 Adjectives and Adverbs

What Is an Adjective?

An **adjective** describes a noun (person, place, or thing) or a pronoun. An adjective answers the question *which one, what kind,* or *how many.* Adjectives usually come before the word they describe, but they can come after forms of the verb *to be* (*am, is, are, was, were, have been*). Adjectives can also come after **linking verbs** such as *look, appear, become, feel, seem, smell, sound,* and *taste.* The adjectives are underlined in the following sentences, and the words they describe are in italics.

A dark *room* works best for sleeping. (The adjective *dark* describes *which* room the writer means.)

When my *room* feels cool, I always sleep well. (The adjective *cool* also describes *what kind* of room the writer means.)

Counting fifty *sheep* puts me to sleep. (The adjective *fifty* describes *how many* sheep the writer means.)

Types of Adjectives

People often think of adjectives as words that provide details appealing to the five senses—sight, sound, taste, touch, and smell—and often adjectives do just that. However, adjectives' primary job is to **modify,** or help identify, nouns or pronouns. Under that definition, several groups of words must be included as adjectives: articles, possessive and demonstrative pronouns, and numbers.

- **Articles**—the words *a, an*, and *the*—are adjectives that answer the questions *which one* and *how many*.

- **Possessive pronouns** show ownership or possession: *my, mine, your, yours, his, her, hers, its, our, ours, your, yours, their*, and *theirs*. These adjectives answer the question *which one*.

- **Demonstrative pronouns**—*this, that, these*, and *those*—introduce a specific person, place, or thing. These adjectives answer the question *which one*.

- **Numbers** answer the question *how many* and, thus, are adjectives.

EXERCISE 1 IDENTIFYING ADJECTIVES

Circle the adjectives in the following sentences. Remember to circle articles, possessive pronouns, demonstrative pronouns, and numbers.

1. Depriving (weary) people of sleep does not sound as though it would help people sleep better.

2. However, (the) process has had (excellent) results.

3. Rest therapy begins by having people keep (a) log of (their) (nightly) sleep.

4. After (a) (set) amount of time, (the) patients calculate (their) (average) amount of sleep.

5. (Some) people average (five) hours (a) night, and others sleep (seven) (glorious) hours.

6. Then, (these) (same) people allow themselves only (that) amount of sleep.

7. If (a) person must get up for work at 6:00 a.m. and (her) (average) (sleep) time is (six) hours, then she cannot go to bed until midnight.

8. (The) idea behind (the) program is that people will come to view (their) beds as places where they get to sleep rather than as places where they only try to sleep.

9. Although they are (skeptical,) people who have tried (this) program say it works to help them sleep without waking up.

10. (Their) bodies become so (tired) that they are (desperate) for (every) minute of slumber they can get.

Using Adjectives for Comparison

An important use for adjectives is making **comparisons,** the process of finding similarities or differences between two things. In the following examples, the adjectives are underlined and the words they describe are in italics.

My husband needs <u>less</u> *sleep* than I do.

In fact, I need the <u>most</u> *sleep* of anyone I know.

Comparative adjectives are used to compare *two* things. You can change most one-syllable adjectives and some two-syllable adjectives by adding *-er* to the end.

Sleeping in a tent is <u>harder</u> for me than for my brother.

The *pillow* on my bed is <u>softer</u> than the one in the guest room.

Superlative adjectives are used to compare three or more things. You can change most one- or two-syllable adjectives by adding *-est* to the end.

Of all my friends, Su has the <u>nicest</u> *bed.*

Kazuko and Margaret have warm comforters, but Su's is the <u>warmest</u> *comforter* of all.

Adjectives ending in *y*, however, must change the *y* to *i* before adding *-er* or *-est*.

I was <u>sleepier</u> after lunch than I was right before bed. (*Sleepy* becomes *sleepier*.)

For longer adjectives, add *more* when comparing two things or *most* when comparing three or more things.

The *mountains* are <u>more restful</u> than the city, but the *ocean* is the <u>most restful</u> place of all.

To make negative comparisons, use *less* when comparing two items and *least* when comparing three or more items.

Our *apartment* next to the rock band was <u>less restful</u> than our room at my parents' house.

Our apartment next to the fire station was the <u>least restful</u> *place* I ever lived.

Two points are important to keep in mind when using adjectives for comparison.

■ Use either *-er/-est* or *more/most* in making a comparison. Using both is incorrect.

Incorrect:	*I* was the <u>most</u> <u>sleepiest</u> I've ever been during my math class.
Correct:	*I* was the <u>sleepiest</u> I've ever been during my math class.
Incorrect:	*He* was <u>more</u> <u>happier</u> than I was after he took a nap.
Correct:	*He* was <u>happier</u> than I was after he took a nap.

■ Some adjectives have irregular comparative and superlative forms that you will have to memorize.

Adjective	Comparative	Superlative
bad	worse	worst
good	better	best
little (amount)	less	least
many	more	most
much	more	most
well	better	best

EXERCISE 2 USING THE CORRECT FORMS OF REGULAR ADJECTIVES

In each sentence, write the correct form of each adjective in parentheses in the blank. You may need to add *-er* or *-est*, *more*, or *most*. Two examples are done for you.

Of all the habits that can negatively affect sleeping, drinking alcohol is one of the ___most harmful___. (harmful)

I try to stay up ___later___ on Friday nights than on Monday nights. (late)

1. Last night, I felt ___sleepier___ than I usually do. (sleepy)

2. I wanted to go to bed ___earlier___ than usual, but I had work to do. (early)

3. In fact, the project I was working on is my ___most important___ task for my job. (important)

4. I made myself comfortable, hoping to feel ___more positive___ about working late than I usually do. (positive)

5. However, making myself comfortable was the <u>biggest</u> mistake I could have made. I fell asleep and accomplished nothing. (big)

EXERCISE 3 USING THE CORRECT FORMS OF IRREGULAR ADJECTIVES

In each sentence, write the correct form of each adjective in parentheses in the blank. You may need to add -er or -est, more, or most. An example is done for you.

I always sleep ___<u>better</u>___ on hard mattresses than on soft ones. (good)

1. Many tips can help people get a ___<u>better</u>___ night's sleep than they have gotten in the past. (good)

2. Getting of exercise makes people feel more ___<u>relaxed</u>___ than if they simply sit in a chair all day. (relaxed)

3. Exercising early in the day or just before sundown gives the

___<u>best</u>___ benefits. (good)

4. One of the ___<u>worst</u>___ mistakes people can make is using the bedroom to do work. (bad)

5. Working in the bedroom trains ___<u>many</u>___ people to think of their rooms as a place of business, not of rest; thus, getting to sleep is

___<u>harder</u>___ than if they only slept in their rooms. (many) (hard)

What Is an Adverb?

An **adverb** can describe a verb, an adjective, or another adverb. Many adverbs end in -ly. Adjectives answer the questions *how, when, where,* and *to what extent*. The adverbs in the following sentences are underlined and the words they describe are in italics.

After a lot of exercise, I *fall asleep* easily. (The adverb *easily* describes *how* the writer falls asleep.)

I *will get up* at the same time tomorrow as I do every day. (The adverb *tomorrow* describes *when* the writer will get up at the same time.)

My math teacher's lecture made me feel extremely *sleepy*. (The adverb *extremely* describes *to what extent* the writer felt sleepy.)

Tip: *Never, no, not,* and *very* are also adverbs.

EXERCISE 4 IDENTIFYING ADVERBS

Circle the adverbs in the sentences below.

1. Different strategies help me wake up easily each morning.

2. At night I set my clock radio to my favorite station and turn the volume up so that the music plays loudly the next day.

3. In the morning I brew a cup of very strong tea.

4. Before I take an extremely hot shower, I do my yoga exercises.

5. I've learned that doing things I enjoy when I wake up helps me not to dread getting out of bed.

Correcting Common Errors with Adjectives and Adverbs

Writers sometimes incorrectly use adjectives when they should use adverbs, especially after a verb. Adding *-ly* to the underlined adjectives makes them adverbs.

Incorrect: My roommate *sleeps* sound.

Correct: My roommate *sleeps* soundly.

Incorrect: To wake myself up, I *sing loud*.

Correct: To wake myself up, I *sing loudly*.

EXERCISE 5 CHOOSING BETWEEN ADJECTIVES AND ADVERBS

Circle the correct modifier in each sentence below. Remember that adjectives describe nouns and pronouns while adverbs describe verbs, adjectives, and other adverbs.

Important Sleep

People need to be (serious, seriously) about their sleep habits. When a person becomes (over, overly) tired, body and mind crave sleep (desperate, desperately). Rapid eye movement (REM) sleep is easy to recognize by the (quick, quickly) movements the sleeper's eyes make beneath the eyelids. Although it is (usual, usually) for REM sleep to come every ninety minutes or so during the night, REM sleep happens more (frequent, frequently) toward morning. A person who sleeps only a few hours misses the (real, really) important REM sleep periods when the brain restores itself most (efficient, efficiently). Brain connections can grow (noticeable, noticeably) during REM sleep, too. People should be (careful, carefully) in planning their sleep times so they can get enough rest.

Good and *Well*

The two words *good* and *well* are often confused. These words may seem to have the same meaning, but *good* is an adjective, which describes nouns and pronouns, while *well* is an adverb, which describes verbs, adjectives, and other adverbs. *Well* can also be used as an adjective to describe someone's health.

My new puppy is a good *sleeper.* (The adjective *good* modifies the noun *sleeper.*)

In fact, she has *slept* well from the moment I brought her home from the pound. (The adverb *well* modifies the verb *slept.*)

Aside from occasional indigestion, *she* is generally well. (The adjective *well* modifies the pronoun *she.*)

EXERCISE 6 USING *GOOD* AND *WELL* CORRECTLY

Circle the correct modifiers in parentheses below.

1. I suffer a lot if I don't sleep (good, well).

2. For instance, if my sleep isn't (good, well), I feel stiff in the morning.

3. The stiffness causes me to hunch over, which causes me not to drive (good, well).

4. Then, even if I wake up in a (good, well) mood, I always get a headache.

5. The headache ruins any chance I have of performing (good, well) at work.

EDITING PRACTICE

The following paragraph contains ten adjective and adverb errors in bold print. Cross out the incorrect word or words and write in the correct modifier.

How to Wreck Your Sleep

If you want to get a poor night's sleep, you can do that ~~easy~~ easily. First,

make sure you never go to bed or get up at the same time, and you

will keep your body ~~real~~ really confused. Another trick that works ~~good~~ well

is drinking caffeinated beverages. Coffee, tea, and soft drinks are

some of the ~~more good~~ better sleep wreckers. If that doesn't do the job,

drinking alcohol will ~~sure~~ surely get in the way of your slumber. Alcohol

makes people ~~more sleepier~~ sleepier than not drinking, but it also interferes with the sleep cycle. You might fall asleep **quick** after drinking alco- _(quickly)_

hol, but you're likely to wake up after a few hours. One more way to

make sure you don't sleep **good** is to think about your worries just _(well)_

as you're trying to drift off. This method is guaranteed to keep your

eyes open for the **most longest** time. Finally, sleeping in a hot room _(longest)_

is a sure way to make sleep come **slow**. _(slowly)_

Lab Activity 44

For additional practice with adjectives and adverbs, complete Lab Activity 44 in the Lab Manual at the back of the book.

4.5 Misplaced Modifiers

CULTURE NOTE *Tornadoes*

The subject of movies and a cause of great damage, tornadoes are formed from a combination of weather conditions. Some people make a career out of "chasing" tornadoes, but most residents of areas they affect find them more frightening than fascinating.

Tornado

JOURNAL RESPONSE Common in the midwestern United States, tornadoes are both powerful and terrifying. What is the most dramatic natural disaster or occurrence that you've experienced? Write for ten minutes about the most powerful storm, drought, earthquake, or other natural occurrence of your life.

What Is a Misplaced Modifier?

Modifiers (adjectives and adverbs) clarify our ideas and make them more vivid. However, just as a well-placed adverb or adjective can help us communicate our ideas, a misplaced modifier can confuse our readers. A **misplaced modifier** is a word or group of words in the wrong place. A misplaced modifier sends an incorrect message to the reader. In the sentences below, the misplaced modifiers are underlined and the words being modified are in italics.

Misplaced modifier: During the *rain* my brother stayed dry under his umbrella, <u>which was soaking</u> everyone.

(The modifier *which was soaking everyone* describes *rain*. However, the placement of the modifier makes it seem as if the modifier is describing *umbrella*.)

Misplaced modifier: *Jim* had always wanted to see a tornado <u>growing up in California</u>.

(Here *growing up in California* really modifies *Jim*, but the placement of the modifier makes it seem as if he wanted to see a *tornado* growing up in California.)

EXERCISE 1 INTERPRETING MISPLACED MODIFIERS

Underline the misplaced modifier in the following sentences. On the lines below, write (a) what the writer means and (b) what the sentence actually says. An example is done for you.

I saw the tornado blow over a huge tree <u>watching from the window</u>.

   a. I was watching from the window.

   b. The tree was watching from the window.

1. Tornadoes give me "bad hair" days <u>blowing through the sky</u>.

   a. Tornadoes are blowing through the sky.

   b. "Bad hair" days are blowing through the sky.

2. In fact, my permanent waves—that I <u>nearly</u> paid fifty dollars for—were blown right out!

    a. I paid nearly fifty dollars for the permanent waves.

    b. I nearly paid for the permanent waves.

3. I even prepared for tornadoes <u>wearing a hair net.</u>

    a. I was wearing a hair net.

    b. Tornadoes were wearing a hair net.

4. It didn't matter; the twister destroyed my "up-do" <u>with dangerous gusts.</u>

    a. The twister had dangerous gusts.

    b. My "up-do" had dangerous gusts.

5. I looked at my disheveled appearance in the mirror <u>with an angry expression.</u>

    a. I had an angry expression.

    b. The mirror had an angry expression.

6. My brother <u>almost</u> spent thirty dollars on his own twister problem.

    a. My brother almost spent thirty dollars, but he didn't.

    b. My brother spent (just under) thirty dollars.

7. He is addicted to watching tornado movies with <u>nacho cheese tortilla chips.</u>

    a. He eats nacho cheese tortilla chips while watching the movies.

    b. The movies have nacho cheese tortilla chips.

8. He's <u>nearly</u> seen *Twister* twenty times.

    a. He's seen the movie nearly (around) twenty times.

    b. He's avoided seeing the movie twenty times.

9. He also loves to watch the movie from the sofa <u>with the flying monkeys in it.</u>

    a. The movie has flying monkeys in it.

    b. The sofa has flying monkeys in it.

10. Last fall, he watched every movie, documentary, and news show <u>using a special setting on TiVo.</u>

    a. He used a special setting on TiVo.

    b. The news show used a special setting on TiVo.

Correcting Misplaced Modifiers

Most misplaced modifiers are simply too far away from what they're describing. Thus, the easiest way to fix a misplaced modifier error is to move the modifier as close as possible to what it's describing.

Misplaced modifier: During the rain my brother stayed dry under his umbrella, <u>which was soaking everyone.</u>

Correct: During the rain, <u>which was soaking everyone,</u> my brother stayed dry under his umbrella.

Incorrect: Jim had always wanted to see a tornado <u>growing up in California.</u>

Correct: <u>Growing up in California,</u> Jim had always wanted to see a tornado.

EXERCISE 2 IDENTIFYING AND CORRECTING MISPLACED MODIFIERS

Underline the misplaced modifiers below. Then, rewrite each sentence so that the modifier is placed correctly. An example is done for you.   Answers will vary.

Misplaced modifier: Many movies feature tornadoes <u>that are quite popular.</u>

Revised: Many movies that are quite popular feature tornadoes.

1. Misplaced modifier: In one film, a tornado picks up a house <u>called</u> *The Wizard of Oz*.

   Revised: In one film called *The Wizard of Oz*, a tornado picks up a house.

2. Misplaced modifier: The main character, Dorothy, was blown around by the tornado, <u>who was asleep in the house</u>.

   Revised: The main character, Dorothy, who was asleep in the house, was

   blown around by the tornado.

3. Misplaced modifier: Another movie features tornadoes <u>made in</u> <u>1996</u>.

   Revised: Another movie, made in 1996, features tornadoes.

4. Misplaced modifier: This film has many impressive special effects, <u>called *Twister*</u>.

   Revised: This film, called *Twister*, has many impressive special effects.

5. Misplaced modifier: The tornadoes in *Twister* make a house roll, a semi truck drop from the sky, and cows fly, <u>which are scary and</u> <u>dangerous</u>.

   Revised: The tornadoes in *Twister*, which are scary and dangerous, make a

   house roll, a semi truck drop from the sky, and cows fly.

🔗 Lab Activity 45

For additional practice with misplaced modifiers, complete Lab Activity 45 in the Lab Manual at the back of the book.

46 Dangling Modifiers

CULTURE NOTE *Milk*

Considered an excellent source of calcium, which is essential to a healthy diet, milk must pass through many steps before being sold in stores. From automated milking systems to proper temperature control, the milk-making process is more complicated than it may seem.

What Is a Dangling Modifier?

A **dangling modifier** is a group of words that opens a sentence but does not modify the noun following it. Most dangling modifiers contain a verb form, and often the words they are meant to modify do not actually appear in the sentence. In the following sentence, the underlined dangling modifier sends the wrong message.

Incorrect: <u>Packed with nine vitamins and minerals</u>, my teeth grow stronger from milk.

Read literally, this sentence says that someone's *teeth* are packed with vitamins and minerals. But the writer means to say that something else—*milk*—is packed with those nutrients.

Correcting Dangling Modifiers

The writer has three options for revision to correct a dangling modifier.

- Put the word being described right after the dangling modifier as the subject of the sentence.

    Correct: Packed with nine vitamins and minerals, *milk* makes my teeth grow stronger.

- Make the word being described part of the modifier.

    Correct: Because *milk* is packed with nine vitamins and minerals, my teeth grow stronger from it. (The reader now has no doubt that milk is what contains the nutrients.)

- Move the dangling modifier close to the word being described.

    Correct: My teeth grow stronger from *milk*, which is packed with nine vitamins and minerals. (The writer adds *which is* before the moved modifier in order to make the meaning clear.)

Cows Being Milked

PLAN AN INTERVIEW Having advanced beyond hand-milking for greater productivity, dairies use automated milking machines to milk cows. How much milk do your friends drink? Interview two friends to learn about their typical milk consumption. Write a few sentences summarizing your findings.

EXERCISE 1 INTERPRETING DANGLING MODIFIERS

Underline the misplaced modifiers in the following sentences. Then, on the following lines, explain (a) what the writer means and (b) what the sentence actually says. An example is done for you.

Taking twenty-four hours to be processed, cows provide milk.

    a. Writer's meaning: <u>The milk takes twenty-four hours to be</u>

    <u>processed.</u>

    b. Sentence meaning: <u>The cows take twenty-four hours to be</u>

    <u>processed.</u>

1. Milked with automated milking equipment, no human hands are used.

    a. Writer's meaning: <u>The cows are milked using automated milking</u>

    <u>equipment.</u>

    b. Sentence meaning: <u>Human hands are milked using automated milking</u>

    <u>equipment.</u>

2. Cleaned thoroughly before being attached to the milking machines, the milking process takes place on many cows at once.

    a. Writer's meaning: <u>The cows are cleaned thoroughly before being</u>

    <u>attached to the milking machines.</u>

    b. Sentence meaning: <u>The milking process is cleaned thoroughly before</u>

    <u>being attached to the milking machines.</u>

3. Stored in giant, chilled holding tanks, the cows give up to seven gallons of milk each.

    a. Writer's meaning: <u>The milk is stored in giant, chilled holding tanks.</u>

b. Sentence meaning: The cows are stored in giant, chilled holding tanks.

4. Delivered to a processing plant, special trucks arrive each day.

a. Writer's meaning: The milk is delivered to a processing plant.

b. Sentence meaning: Special trucks are delivered to a processing plant.

5. Flowing through stainless steel pipes into the processing plant, modern equipment helps make many dairy products.

a. Writer's meaning: Milk flows through stainless steel pipes.

b. Sentence meaning: Modern equipment flows through stainless steel pipes.

EXERCISE 2 IDENTIFYING AND CORRECTING DANGLING MODIFIERS

Underline the dangling modifiers below. Then, rewrite each sentence to correct the error. An example is done for you. Answers will vary.

Dangling modifier: Filled with bacteria, the French chemist Louis Pasteur discovered a way to "clean" raw milk. Answers will vary.

Revised: The French chemist Louis Pasteur discovered a way to

"clean" raw milk, which is filled with bacteria.

1. Dangling modifier: Heating milk at 161.5 degrees for fifteen seconds, the federal government requires raw milk to be pasteurized.

Revised: The federal government requires that raw milk be pasteurized, or

heated at 161.5 degrees for fifteen seconds.

2. Dangling modifier: <u>Coming straight out of the cow</u>, dairy farmers work hard to prevent germs and bacteria from growing.

Revised: Dairy farmers work hard to prevent germs and bacteria from

growing in milk that comes straight out of the cow.

3. Dangling modifier: <u>Making it safe to drink and fresh for long periods of time</u>, pasteurized milk is a healthy food.

Revised: Safe to drink and fresh for long periods of time, pasteurized milk is

a healthy food.

4. Dangling modifier: <u>A great favorite around the world</u>, dairies always use pasteurized milk for ice cream.

Revised: Dairies always use pasteurized milk for ice cream, which is a great

favorite around the world.

5. Dangling modifier: <u>Making sure it is safe to be turned into products such as yogurt and cottage cheese</u>, milk is tested by quality control labs.

Revised: Quality control labs test milk to make sure it is safe to be turned

into products such as yogurt and cottage cheese.

Lab Activity 46

For additional practice with dangling modifiers, complete Lab Activity 46 in the Lab Manual at the back of the book.

47 Errors in Parallelism

CULTURE NOTE *Cookies*

Invented by accident, cookies are one of the most popular finger foods in the United States. Cookies come in many varieties and serve as snacks, desserts, and gifts. Cookies are a great favorite among those who love sweets.

What Is Parallelism?

Clear, consistent writing requires parallel, or balanced, sentences. In **parallelism,** or **parallel structure,** two or more related words or groups of words have the same structure. The following sentences contain faulty parallel sentence structure.

Faulty parallelism: Cookies come in many shapes, sizes, and are of different flavors.

(The first two items in the series are nouns, but the third—*are of different flavors*—is not.)

Faulty parallelism: People enjoy eating cookies for snacks and when they want dessert.

(The first item in the series is a prepositional phrase, but the second is a clause.)

Read the corrected, parallel versions of the same sentences.

Revised: Cookies come in many <u>shapes</u>, <u>sizes</u>, and <u>flavors</u>.
           (The three items in the series are all plural nouns.)

Revised: People enjoy eating cookies <u>for snacks</u> and <u>for dessert</u>.
           (The two prepositional phrases *for snacks* and *for dessert* are parallel.)

Parallel structure gives your writing consistency and strength. The repetition of structures helps your reader anticipate points in your writing.

Recognizing Special Sentence Structures

Some sentence structures require parallelism. The following terms contain two parts that are used to link words or word groups. The words or word groups following each part must be parallel.

Terms Needing Parallel Structure

both . . . and   neither . . . nor
either . . . or   not only . . . but also

The underlined words or word groups in each sentence below are parallel.

Peanut butter cookies are *both* <u>tasty</u> *and* <u>filling</u>.
(*Tasty* and *filling* are both adjectives.)

People *either* <u>enjoy baking</u> *or* <u>dislike it</u>.
(*Enjoy baking* and *dislike it* are both verb phrases.)

I love *not only* <u>chocolate chip cookies</u> but also <u>brownies</u>.
(*Chocolate chip cookies* and *brownies* are both nouns.)

You can create parallel sentences using a variety of structures. Nouns, verbs, prepositional phrases, adjectives, and clauses can all help you make sentences parallel. The following example uses verbs to create parallel structure:

Rather than writing "measured ingredients," "creaming butter and sugar," and "roll dough," write, "My favorite cookies involve *measuring* the ingredients, *creaming* the butter and sugar, and *rolling* the dough."

All three verbs have *-ing* endings, which makes the sentence parallel.

EXERCISE 1 CORRECTING FAULTY PARALLELISM

The sentences below contain errors in parallelism. Rewrite each sentence using parallel structure. An example is done for you. Answers will vary.

Faulty parallelism: Cookies resulted first from a test, then from an experiment, and finally someone made a decision.

Revised: _Cookies resulted first from a test, then from an experiment, and finally from a decision._

1. Faulty parallelism: Originally, cooks wanted to test oven temperature, batter flavor, and that the consistency of the batter was good.

   Revised: _Originally, cooks wanted to test oven temperature, batter flavor, and batter consistency._

2. Faulty parallelism: Baking small amounts of batter not only told the cooks whether the temperature was correct but also it created a new treat.

   Revised: _Baking small amounts of batter not only told the cooks whether the temperature was correct but also created a new treat._

3. Faulty parallelism: Significant factors were color, shape, and how big the batter bits were.

   Revised: _Significant factors were the color, shape, and size of the batter bits._

4. Faulty parallelism: These features told the cooks both whether the oven was hot enough and the cooked batter's flavor.

   Revised: _These features told the cooks both whether the oven was hot enough and whether the cooked batter tasted right._

5. Faulty parallelism: The test cakes became known either as *koekje* in Dutch and *cookies* in English.

   Revised: _The test cakes became known as *koekje* in Dutch and *cookies* in English._

EXERCISE 2 WRITING PARALLEL SENTENCES

The sentences below are incomplete. Finish each sentence using parallel structure. An example is done for you. Answers will vary.

My favorite things about going to a Chinese restaurant are having great food, eating with chopsticks, and _getting fortune cookies_.

1. I like not only breaking the fortune cookies open _but also reading_.
my fortune.

2. Fortune cookies are usually light brown, crunchy, _and sweet_.

3. I find that the fortunes within the cookies are usually either educational _or complimentary._

4. After reading many, many fortunes from these cookies, I am convinced that they are neither wise _nor useful._

5. Nevertheless, the fortunes are often both clever _and funny._

Balanced Word Order

Sometimes using the same word order in two clauses creates a more effective sentence.

Unbalanced: One type of cookie is the drop cookie; molded cookies are another type.

(Although *type* is repeated, it has a different role in each clause.)

Balanced: One type of cookie is the drop cookie; another type is the molded cookie.

(Here, *type* is the subject of both clauses.)

A series of balanced sentences can make it easier for a reader to anticipate the writer's meaning.

Balanced: One type of cookie is the drop cookie. Another type is the molded cookie. A third type, my favorite, is the rolled cookie, which can be cut into shapes.

(Here, *type* is the subject of three sentences in a series.)

EXERCISE 3 WRITING BALANCED SENTENCES

Each of the following sentences will become the first of two balanced statements. Write your own second sentence with a structure that is parallel to, or balanced with, the first. *Hint:* You might find it helpful to start your sentence with a topic or situation that contrasts with the one given. An example is done for you.

Drop cookies are dropped onto a cookie sheet and then baked.

Answers will vary.

Bar cookies are baked in a pan and then cut into bars.

1. During vacation, I love to sleep in.

During the semester, I have to study.

2. My boyfriend thinks that women should work outside the home.

My father thinks that women should work inside the home.

3. When it's rainy, I feel like being lazy.

When it's sunny, I feel like being busy.

4. My study habits include drinking a lot of coffee.

My sleeping habits include using a lot of pillows.

5. The flower under the tree is lovely.

The shrub by the house is ugly.

EDITING PRACTICE

The following paragraph contains five errors in parallelism. Cross out the sections containing errors, and replace them with parallel constructions.

The Toll House Cookie: An American Treat

Not only was the invention of cookies an accident, ~~and~~ but the invention of the Toll House cookie was a surprise, too. In Massachusetts in the 1930s, Ruth Wakefield, an innkeeper, was baking cookies. Because she ran out of nuts, she needed a substitute. Either she could use nothing or ^she could^ use some chocolate. She read the recipe, looked around her kitchen, and ^cut up^ a bar of baking chocolate ~~ended up being cut~~ for her dough. The now-famous batter was made of flour, butter, and ~~it also had~~ a fair amount of brown sugar. Sure enough, the "accidental" cookies were a hit. They were named Toll House cookies after the inn. The cookies became famous, the Nestlé chocolate company heard about them, and ^Nestlé^ asked Ms. Wakefield for permission to print the recipe on its chocolate wrappers. Saying yes, Ms. Wakefield requested only a lifetime supply of chocolate in return.

Lab Activity 47

For additional practice with parallelism, complete Lab Activity 47 in the Lab Manual at the back of the book.

PART EIGHT
Punctuation and Mechanics

48 Commas

CULTURE NOTE *Chicago*

Third largest in the United States, behind New York and Los Angeles, Chicago is known as the Windy City both for its powerful gusts and its powerful politicians. Chicago's history includes the famous fire of 1871 and a rich athletic tradition that produced both basketball star Michael Jordan and the Bears football team.

Understanding Commas ,

Commas separate items in a sentence. It's easy to leave out commas by mistake or put them in where they don't belong, but a misplaced comma can radically alter the meaning of your sentence. Knowing how to use commas properly is essential to keeping your writing clear and easy to read. Commas have six main uses.

- Setting apart items in a series
- Setting off introductory material
- Setting off information that interrupts the main ideas in a sentence
- Joining two independent clauses also linked by a coordinating conjunction (*for, and, nor, but, or, yet,* or *so*)
- Setting off direct quotations from the rest of the sentence
- Clarifying everyday information such as dates, addresses, and numbers

You may have been taught that a comma signals a pause in a sentence, but this guideline can lead to mistakes. Commas actually direct the reader to *keep reading*. To signal a pause or break, writers use a semicolon, a colon, or a period.

Setting Items Apart in a Series

Use commas to set apart, or separate, items in a series. A **series** is two or more items—for example, two or more adjectives—in a row.

Chicago is known for its cold, gusty winds.

Also famous are its politics, the Sears Tower, and the Great Lakes.

Comma Before a Conjunction in a Series

In a series of three or more items joined by a conjunction, the final comma helps clarify meaning.

Confusing: I ordered three deli sandwiches: tuna salad, ham and cheese and pastrami on rye.

Clear: I ordered three deli sandwiches: tuna salad, ham and cheese, and pastrami on rye.

Commas in a Series of Adjectives

Use a comma between adjectives in a two-item series only if the word *and* can logically be substituted for the comma.

Chicago is known for its cold, gusty winds.

Chicago is known for its cold and gusty winds.

If the word *and* sounds strange between two adjectives, do not use a comma.

Chicago's mayor received a big fat raise.

(Saying "a big *and* fat raise" would sound strange, so omit the comma.)

EXERCISE 1 USING COMMAS IN A SERIES

Add commas where necessary in the following sentences.

1. Some well-known Chicago figures include Al Capone, Richard J. Daley, Harold Washington, and Oprah Winfrey.

2. All these people are known for their influence, intelligence, and success in their chosen areas.

3. Al Capone, however, chose to make his mark through illegal activities, such as gambling, prostitution, and bootlegging.

4. Richard J. Daley, on the other hand, was a charismatic, focused mayor who was known for his "machine" politics.

5. The first African-American mayor of Chicago, Harold Washington, was a decorated veteran of World War II, a member of the Illinois House and Senate, and a member of the U.S. House of Representatives.

Chicago Skyline

CRITICAL THINKING   As the third largest city in the United States, Chicago, Illinois, boasts an impressive skyline. After looking at the photo above, what do you think is the city's mood? Write a few sentences describing the mood of Chicago, using specific details from the photo to support your ideas.

Setting Off Introductory Material

Use commas to set off introductory material in a sentence.

Though famous for its sports and politics, Chicago is also famous for serving excellent steaks.

Different from steaks elsewhere in the country, Chicago steaks are sometimes served "blue."

In fact, the term "blue" for meat comes from the fact that the steak is so rare that it is still cool in the middle.

If the introductory phrase is very short and describes *when* or *where,* the comma is sometimes omitted.

In 1902 Richard J. Daley was born.

EXERCISE 2 USING COMMAS TO SET OFF INTRODUCTORY MATERIAL

Add commas where necessary in the following sentences.

1. A few years ago Chicago hosted an unusual art display.

2. Featuring life-sized cow sculptures all over the city, the display, entitled "Cows on Parade," met with mixed reactions.

3. Unlike their counterparts in the field, these cows were not simply black, brown, or spotted.

4. Instead, the Chicago cows were decorated in almost every way imaginable.

5. In designs from florals to plaids, the cows in Chicago made their own statement in the art world.

Setting Off Information That Interrupts the Main Ideas in a Sentence

One of the most important uses of the comma is to set off, or highlight, information that interrupts the main ideas in a sentence. Such information is often interesting and colorful, but it is usually not essential to understanding the main ideas.

Interruptions in the Middle of a Sentence

Use two commas to set off information that interrupts the middle of a sentence.

> Legend has it that the Great Fire, one of Chicago's most famous tragedies, had a humble beginning.

> Mrs. O'Leary's cow, not concerned with fire safety, kicked over a lantern in the barn.

> Thus, the Great Chicago Fire of 1871, which claimed thousands of lives, may have been started by a cow.

Essential and Unessential Information

Use commas to separate information from the rest of the sentence *only if that information is not essential to the sense of the sentence.* For instance, if you leave out the information between the commas, the sentences above about the Great Chicago Fire still make sense. Thus, the commas are necessary.

In the following sentence, the underlined information is necessary for the sentence to make sense. Therefore, no commas should be used.

> The cow <u>that supposedly started the Great Chicago Fire</u> belonged to Mrs. O'Leary.

Leaving out the information *that started the Great Chicago fire* would make the full meaning of the sentence unclear. Readers would not know *which* cow the writer is referring to. Similarly, the following sentence requires no commas.

> The barn <u>belonging to the O'Learys</u> was close to downtown Chicago.

The information *belonging to the O'Learys* is necessary to identify the barn. Without this information, the reader has no idea *which* barn the writer means.

Often you can tell whether commas are necessary by reading a sentence out loud. You can hear whether a piece of information is necessary to the meaning of the sentence. If the information is necessary, do not use commas. If the information is *not* needed for a full understanding of the sentence, use commas.

Additional Material at the End of a Sentence

Use commas to separate added material at the end of a sentence.

> Oprah Winfrey has made the most of her education and experience, becoming one of the most successful businesswomen in America.

In this case, *becoming one of the most successful businesswomen in America* could have come at the beginning or in the middle of the sentence instead of at the end.

> Becoming one of the most successful businesswomen in America, Oprah Winfrey has made the most of her education and experience.

> Oprah Winfrey, becoming one of the most successful businesswomen in America, has made of the most of her education.

Regardless of where it appears, the phrase provides extra information that is not essential to the meaning of the sentence. Thus, it must be set off from the rest of the sentence by a comma or commas.

Direct Address

When people are being **addressed**—spoken or written to—their names should be set off from the rest of the sentence.

> Jed, which way is Chicago?

> I know, Ronald, why you are doing this.

EXERCISE 3 USING COMMAS TO SET OFF EXTRA INFORMATION

Add commas where necessary in the following sentences.

1. Oprah Winfrey, one of Chicago's most famous residents, has done much to benefit other people.

2. Winfrey's proposal to require that convicted child abusers register in a national database, signed into law by President Clinton in 1994, shows her dedication to children's causes.

3. Reading another interest of Winfrey's is promoted by Oprah's Book Club.

4. Books that Winfrey presents on her show often become best-sellers. Thus, unknown writers who might not otherwise receive much public exposure are given an opportunity for success.

5. Finally, Oprah Winfrey has done much to promote women's issues. One of Winfrey's companies Oxygen Media, is dedicated to producing Internet and cable programming for women.

Joining Two Independent Clauses Linked by a Coordinating Conjunction

One of the most important comma uses is joining two independent clauses. When two independent clauses are joined *without* a comma, the result is a run-on sentence—a common error.

Keep in mind, too, that standard written English requires a coordinating conjunction (one of the FANBOYS: *for, and, nor, but, or, yet, so*) along with the comma.

The highs and lows of Chicago politics are famous**,** and many powerful Chicago politicians are Democrats.
independent clause

The aldermen of Chicago are one reason for Chicago's political fame**, for** aldermen are extremely powerful in the city's daily functions.

An alderman is like a city council member**, but** he or she is responsible for city regions known as wards.

The sentences contain two complete ideas in the form of two independent clauses. Thus, they also contain a conjunction and a comma.

Tip: Do not use a comma when a sentence has one subject but two verbs. In the following sentences, the nouns are underlined once and the verbs twice.

Aldermen address city issues and solve problems for their wards.

They listen to their ward residents and act according to the needs of the people.

EXERCISE 4 USING COMMAS TO JOIN INDEPENDENT CLAUSES

Add commas where necessary in the following sentences.

1. Unlike many other large cities, Chicago is run by aldermen‚but the mayor has influence as well.

2. Chicago aldermen are elected officials‚but the mayor may appoint an alderman if someone retires or resigns.

3. Chicago is divided up into fifty districts known as wards‚and an alderman is responsible for the issues of his or her ward.

4. Every ten years the wards are reorganized‚for some wards become more heavily populated than others.

5. Reorganization gives the wards equal population‚so they also have equal power.

6. Some wards are miles long‚but others are only one-half mile long.

7. Residents can seek help from city agencies‚or they can approach their alderman with their concerns.

8. Chicago aldermen have great power‚for Chicago has great resources in terms of people and money.

9. In Chicago, the aldermen are more important than state senators‚ for aldermen are the ones to whom most people turn.

10. Garbage collection is an important issue in urban areas‚but aldermen have to solve other problems as well.

Setting Off Direct Quotations

Use a comma to signal the start, and sometimes the end, of a quotation. In most cases, you should place periods and commas *inside* the quotation marks.

> The actor Gary Cole said‚ "I miss everything about Chicago except January and February." (The comma indicates the start of the quotation.)

> "Chicago will give you a chance‚" the writer Lincoln Steffens states. "The sporting spirit is the spirit of Chicago." (The comma indicates the end of a quoted sentence.)

"I set foot in this city," Oprah Winfrey claimed, "and just walking down the street, it was like roots, like the motherland. I knew I belonged here." (The paired commas signal an interruption in the quotation.)

EXERCISE 5 USING COMMAS TO SET OFF DIRECT QUOTATIONS

Add commas to set off the quotation in each sentence below.

1. As Frank Sinatra sang in a great song, "Chicago is my kind of town."

2. "I wrote about Chicago after looking the town over for years and years," said the poet Carl Sandburg.

3. Former Vice President Dan Quayle made a mistake when he said, "It is wonderful to be here in the great state of Chicago."

4. "Anywhere in the world you hear a Chicago bluesman play," said Congressman Ralph Metcalfe, "it's a Chicago sound born and bred."

5. "I give you Chicago," stated the writer H. L. Mencken. "It is not London and Harvard. It is not Paris and buttermilk. It is American in every chitling and sparerib. It is alive from snout to tail."

Clarifying Everyday Information

Commas help us make sense of and organize everyday information. Use commas in the following situations.

- **Dates**

  The Great Fire of Chicago, which began on October 8, 1871, was a catastrophe.

- **Addresses**

  My brother used to live at 9 Belden Avenue, Chicago, Illinois 60614.

- **Greetings and Closings of Letters**

  Dear Mom,

  Dear Professor Chen,

  Sincerely,

In business correspondence, use a colon (*Dear Sir:* or *Dear Madam:*) instead of a comma.

■ **Numbers**

When a Chicago millionaire made $2,500,368 in one year, he paid taxes in excess of $1,003,000.

EXERCISE 6 USING COMMAS TO ORGANIZE EVERYDAY INFORMATION

Add commas where necessary in the following sentences.

1. Chicago is the home of more than 2,800,000 people.

2. My favorite store is located at 450 Michigan Avenue, Chicago, Illinois.

3. September 4, 1983, was the day Oprah Winfrey came to Chicago.

4. Since that date, Oprah Winfrey has received praise from more than 100,000 fans.

5. I was sad to leave Chicago, but I love my beautiful house at 4500 J Street, Sacramento, California, where I live now.

EDITING PRACTICE 1

Add commas where necessary in the following paragraph. You will need to add twenty-two commas in all.

A Taste of Chicago

Because of its ethnic diversity, Chicago has much to offer in terms of food. From its Irish population, Chicago offers corned beef hash and green beer, especially on St. Patrick's Day. From its residents with a German heritage, Chicago gets wonderful beef sausage, called bratwurst, and sauerkraut. In fact, one of Chicago's most famous restaurants is the Berghoff Restaurant, located at 17 West Adams Street. This restaurant was the first to get a liquor license after Prohibition was repealed. People with Russian roots also have contributed to Chicago's food choices. At Russian Tea Time, also located on Adams Street, more than 10,000 people have been served vodka, beef stroganoff, and borscht. In the area of Chicago known as Greektown, one of the city's most famous restaurants is Pegasus Restaurant and Taverna. It is known for its fresh fish, authentic atmosphere, and flaming Greek cheese, called *Saganaki*. Perhaps the most famous Chicago food is the Chicago-style pizza. Deeper than regular pizzas, Chicago-style pizza has a thick crust. On top of the crust are piled layers of cheese, sauce, meat, and other assorted toppings. Two famous pizza restaurants in Chicago are Gino's East and Giordano's. These types of food and others are celebrated at the annual Taste of Chicago festival, which brings Chicago residents together to try wonderful food.

EDITING PRACTICE 2

Add commas as necessary to the following letter. You will need to add twenty commas in all.

Faye Johnson
53001 East Portola Avenue
Santa Ana, CA 92701

August 23, 2005

Dear Mom,

I'm having a great time here in Chicago! Every day Monte and I do something different. Yesterday we visited the Art Institute, took a skyline cruise on Lake Michigan, and saw a Cubs game. Even though the Cubs lost, the game was a lot of fun. I'm exhausted, but it's great to be here. Monte's family, his dad in particular, likes to eat as much as I do, so we've been trying new food every day. So far we've had pizza, hot dogs at the game, and steaks. I think I've gained 1,000 pounds. By the time I get home, I probably won't fit through the front door, so you should get the diet food ready for me. Actually, I'm not eating that much; it's so humid that I'm sweating off whatever I gain. Over the next few days, I plan to visit the Northwestern University campus (actually in Evanston, Illinois) along with the University of Chicago. Maybe that will get me motivated to fill out those college applications when I get home. Well, we're going to walk down Michigan Avenue to find souvenirs for you and Dad, so I need to end here.

Love,
Terrell

☞ Lab Activity 48

For additional practice with commas, complete Lab Activity 48 in the Lab Manual at the back of the book.

49 Apostrophes

CULTURE NOTE *Viruses*

Though almost everyone has suffered from the common cold, few people understand how colds come about or, more important, how they can be treated. From the sniffles to more dangerous strains, viruses affect us almost daily.

Understanding the Apostrophe'

One of the great time-savers in punctuation, the **apostrophe** allows us to omit letters and even whole words. The apostrophe has two main uses.

- Showing the omission of letters
- Showing possession or ownership

Showing the Omission of Letters

An apostrophe allows us to leave out letters in a **contraction,** one word that results from the combination of two words. Here are some common contractions.

can + not = can't	he + is = he's
I + am = I'm	she + is = she's
I + have = I've	who + is = who's
I + had = I'd	could + not = couldn't
I + will = I'll	did + not = didn't
I + would = I'd	do + not = don't

it + is = it's

it + has = it's

they + are = they're

you + are = you're

is + not = isn't

will + not = won't

would + not = wouldn't

Note that some contractions can be used for two different word combinations. For example, *I'd* can mean "I had" or "I would." You can tell the meaning of the contraction from its use in the sentence.

I'd thought the common cold was just one virus. (*I'd* means "I had.")

I'd go if you invited me. (*I'd* means "I would.")

EXERCISE 1 FORMING CONTRACTIONS

Combine the following words into contractions. An example is done for you.

here + is = ___here's___

1. he + would = ___he'd___

2. there + would = ___there'd___

3. we + will = ___we'll___

4. you + have = ___you've___

5. let + us = ___let's___

EXERCISE 2 CHANGING CONTRACTIONS INTO THEIR ORIGINAL WORD PAIRS

Change the following contractions into their original word pairs. If a contraction has two possible word pairs, write them both. An example is done for you.

you'd = ___you had___   ___you would___

1. we'll = ___we will___

2. he'd = ___he had___   ___he would___

3. she's = ____she is____   ____she has____

4. there's = ____there is____   ____there has____

5. they're = ____they are____

EXERCISE 3 FORMING CONTRACTIONS IN CONTEXT

Combine the words in parentheses into contractions.

1. (I have) ____I've____ had a cold for three weeks.

2. (You had) ____You'd____ better hope you (do not) ____don't____ get it.

3. The first symptom (you will) ____you'll____ notice is a tickle in your throat.

4. This might be all (you will) ____you'll____ get. If so, (you are) ____you're____ lucky!

5. (I am) ____I'm____ beginning to think (I will) ____I'll____ never recover.

6. (It is) ____It's____ no fun to have cold symptoms.

7. (I have) ____I've____ had all of these: runny or stuffy nose, sneezing, sore throat, cough, headache, mild fever, fatigue, muscle aches, and loss of appetite. Good health to you!

Showing Possession or Ownership

Many expressions can show ownership or possession—for example, *owned by, possessed by, belongs to,* and *of.*

the medicine <u>owned by</u> the drug store

the main entrance <u>of</u> the hospital

There is another, faster way to show the same thing: use an apostrophe, as explained in the following sections.

Singular Nouns

Add an apostrophe and -*s* ('*s*) to show possession or ownership if a noun is singular.

the drug store's medicine   the hospital's main entrance

If the noun is singular and already ends in -*s,* follow the same rule; add an apostrophe and -*s* to show possession.

Marcus's virus took a month to run its course.

EXERCISE 4 USING APOSTROPHES TO SHOW POSSESSION OR OWNERSHIP

Rewrite the underlined portion of each sentence to show possession or ownership. An example is done for you.

The health of Ron is a concern to us all. *Ron's health*

1. The sign owned by the pharmacy lists common illnesses.

The pharmacy's sign

2. Last year Ron had the telltale signs belonging to the flu.

the flu's telltale signs

3. The friends belonging to Ron noticed his low energy level.

Ron's friends

4. This year the concern of people for Ron has led them to drop hints.

People's concern

5. At the office of the doctor, Ron saw notices for flu shots.

the doctor's office

6. A bulletin from the office of the nurse urged people to get flu shots.

the nurse's office

7. Even the boss of Ron offered Ron time off to get a flu shot.

Ron's boss

8. However, these hints failed to sink into <u>the brain possessed by Ron</u>.

Ron's brain

9. He insists that <u>the office of the doctor</u> is too expensive and that the

school nurse just wants to bother people. doctor's office

10. I guess we'll all have to live with <u>the poor health of Ron</u>.

Ron's poor health

EXERCISE 5   SHOWING POSSESSION OR OWNERSHIP THROUGH APOSTROPHES

Rewrite the underlined portion of each sentence to show possession or ownership.

One Bad Virus

Zaire's river

The rare but deadly Ebola virus is named for <u>the river belong-</u>

virus's source

<u>ing to Zaire</u>. Although the <u>source of the virus</u> is unknown, monkeys

virus's carriers   the disease's symptoms

and humans may become the <u>carriers of the virus</u>. The <u>symptoms</u>

<u>of the disease</u> include fever, headache, and joint and muscle pain.

Ebola's symptoms

As the disease progresses, <u>the symptoms of Ebola</u> include vomiting,

diarrhea, abdominal pain, sore throat, rash, and chest pain. The dis-

blood's ability

ease may also affect internal organs and the <u>ability of blood</u> to clot.

patient's bleeding

When the blood fails to clot, the <u>bleeding of the patient</u> may extend

into internal organs and from body openings. In most of <u>the out-</u>

Ebola's outbreaks

<u>breaks belonging to Ebola</u>, the majority of cases occurred in hospi-

the facility's main problem

tal settings. In such cases, <u>the main problem of the facility</u> was inadequate medical supplies leading to poor infection control. <u>The</u>

<u>Ebola's presence</u>
<u>presence of Ebola</u> has not been confirmed in any humans in the

United States.

Plural Nouns

If a plural word already ends in -*s,* add an apostrophe to the word to show possession or ownership. Do not add another -*s.*

> My *doctors*' offices are large and cheerful. (The offices belong to more than one doctor.)

> My *friends*' flu bug has kept them sick for two weeks. (The illness affects more than one friend.)

> For plural nouns not ending in -*s,* add '*s* to show possession or ownership.

> the toys belonging to the children = the *children*'s toys

> the concern of the people = the *people*'s concern

EXERCISE 6 USING APOSTROPHES TO SHOW POSSESSION IN PLURAL NOUNS

In each blank, write the plural of the noun in parentheses. Then, rewrite the sentence to include the possessive plural form of the word. An example is done for you.

Sentence: The (drug) effects are still unknown.

Plural: drugs

Revised: The drugs' effects are still unknown.

1. Sentence: Several (disease) cures are derived from common sources.

Plural: diseases

Revised: Several diseases' cures are derived from common sources.

2. Sentence: (Medication) benefits are variable, but the benefit of rest is well-known.

Plural: Medications

Revised: Medications' benefits are variable, but the benefit of rest is well-known.

3. Sentence: Some (cold remedy) benefits can be the relief of symptoms.

Plural: cold remedies

Revised: Some cold remedies' benefits can be the relief of symptoms.

4. Sentence: However, some (medicine) side effects, such as drowsiness, make them poor choices.

Plural: medicines

Revised: However, some medicines' side effects, such as drowsiness, make them poor choices.

5. Sentence: (Nap) benefits, though, are undeniable.

Plural: Naps

Revised: Naps' benefits, though, are undeniable.

Unnecessary Apostrophes

Be careful not to misuse or overuse apostrophes. Avoid using apostrophes in two areas, in particular.

- No apostrophes with possessive pronouns
- No apostrophes with simple plurals

Do Not Use Apostrophes with Possessive Pronouns

Never use an apostrophe with a possessive pronoun (*his, hers, theirs, yours,* and so on).

Incorrect: Their's is the house next to the hospital.
Correct: Theirs is the house next to the hospital.

Incorrect:	~~Your~~'s is the face I love most.
Correct:	Yours is the face I love most.
Incorrect:	I am more worried about his health than about ~~her~~'s.
Correct:	I am more worried about his health than about hers.

Do Not Use Apostrophes with Simple Plurals

To make most nouns plural, add an -*s* to the end of the word. Plural nouns that end in -*s* are **simple plurals.** Never add an apostrophe to a simple plural. For instance, if you want to discuss more than one symptom, write *symptoms*. Do not write *symptoms'* or *symptom's* for the plural—both are incorrect. Keep in mind that the apostrophe shows possession or ownership.

Veronica**'**s watery eyes showed that she had a cold.

In this sentence, the only word requiring an apostrophe is *Veronica*. The -*'s* attached to *Veronica* shows that the eyes *belong to* Veronica. The -*s* on the word *eyes* simply shows that Veronica has more than one eye.

EXERCISE 7 USING APOSTROPHES CORRECTLY

In the following paragraph, rewrite the five words that require apostrophes. Then, make a list of all the simple plural nouns.

Be Clean, for Health's Sake

[1]Washing your hands can keep you from getting sick. [2]Because many people rub their eyes or touch their mouths with their hands, germs can spread to things they touch. [3]Never borrow a friends used
friend's
tissues. [4]Touching doorknobs or chairs can spread germs, as can handling a co-workers coffee mug. [5]If you use someone elses com-
co-worker's   *else's*
puter, you can pick up a virus left on the keyboard or mouse. [6]A desks surface is also packed with germs. [7]Wash your hands with
desk's

soap after using the restroom, and try to wash up after shaking

hands, too. [8]Soap<ins>Soap's</ins> action removes germs that can make people ill.

[9]Even though you might end up with dry skin from washing so

often, you'll also enjoy better health.

Simple plurals are found in the following sentences.

Sentence 1: <ins>hands</ins>

Sentence 2: <ins>eyes</ins>   <ins>mouths</ins>   <ins>hands</ins>   <ins>germs</ins>

<ins>things</ins>

Sentence 3: <ins>tissues</ins>

Sentence 4: <ins>doorknobs</ins>   <ins>chairs</ins>   <ins>germs</ins>

Sentence 6: <ins>germs</ins>

Sentence 7: <ins>hands</ins>   <ins>hands</ins>

Sentence 8: <ins>germs</ins>

EDITING PRACTICE 1

In the following paragraph, cross out the words that require apostrophes and write the correct form of each word above it. The first word has been done for you.

AIDS in Perspective

AIDS stands for acquired immune deficiency syndrome. ~~Its~~ <ins>It's</ins> one

of the worst illnesses a person can get. Though AIDS is a deadly

virus, ~~mens~~ <ins>men's</ins> and ~~womens~~ <ins>women's</ins> chances of catching it can be lowered.

First, though AIDS is contagious, it ~~isnt~~ isn't spread through casual con-

tact. No ~~ones~~ one's been known to catch AIDS from saliva or from tears.

However, contact with ~~someones~~ someone's bodily fluids—blood, semen, vagi-

nal fluids, or breast milk—can spread the disease. Without such

contact, the average ~~persons~~ person's chance of getting AIDS is small. Sec-

ond, though ~~its~~ it's fatal in many cases, AIDS does not kill its victims

instantly. In fact, some ~~individuals~~ individuals' lives hardly change for years. The

early symptoms of AIDS are much like flu symptoms: fever,

headache, sore muscles and joints, stomachache, swollen lymph

glands, or a skin rash. Even after ~~peoples~~ people's symptoms appear, some

patients live normally for years.

EDITING PRACTICE 2

In the blanks for each word, write the singular possessive, plural, and plural possessive forms. Then, on a separate piece of paper, write a paragraph using at least five of the words in the completed list. Your paragraph does not need to be serious.   Answers will vary.

	Singular Possessive	**Plural**	**Plural Possessive**
1. cold	cold's	colds	colds'
2. eye	eye's	eyes	eyes'
3. ear	ear's	ears	ears'
4. child	child's	children	children's
5. tummy	tummy's	tummies	tummies'
6. cough	cough's	coughs	coughs'

7. doctor	doctor's	doctors	doctors'
8. symptom	symptom's	symptoms	symptoms'
9. virus	virus's	viruses	viruses'
10. medicine	medicine's	medicines	medicines'
11. effect	effect's	effects	effects'
12. friend	friend's	friends	friends'

Lab Activity 49

For additional practice with apostrophes, complete Lab Activity 49 in the Lab Manual at the back of the book.

50 Quotation Marks

 CULTURE NOTE *Feminism and Gloria Steinem*

Although women still must push for equal pay and equal opportunities in the workplace, their abilities and contributions are taken far more seriously than they were in the 1960s. Much of the progress women have made can be attributed to the work of the feminist Gloria Steinem. Through her drive, perseverance, and charisma, Steinem made huge strides for women.

Understanding Quotation Marks " "

Quotation marks are used to set off specific words, expressions, or titles, signaling that what follows demands special attention. Quotation marks have three major functions.

- Setting off direct quotations
- Setting off titles of short works
- Setting off special words or expressions

Setting Off Direct Quotations

Use quotation marks to indicate that certain words are being spoken by a specific person.

> Gloria Steinem said, "A woman without a man is like a fish without a bicycle." (Quotation marks set off Steinem's exact words.)

643

Gloria Steinem

SURF THE NET With brains, beauty, and political brawn, Gloria Steinem paved the way for women in the workforce. Search the Internet for information about Gloria Steinem. Write a few sentences summarizing your findings.

"Most women," said Steinem, "are one man away from welfare." (The quotation is split up, so two pairs of quotation marks are needed to show exactly what Steinem said.)

One of my favorite quotations from Gloria Steinem says, "Without leaps of imagination, or dreaming, we lose the excitement of possibilities. Dreaming, after all, is a form of planning." (A quotation of more than one sentence needs only one set of quotation marks.)

Keep the following rules in mind when you use quotations.

■ Unless a quotation begins a sentence, it should usually be introduced by a comma.

■ A quotation begins with a capital letter.

■ Commas and periods at the end of a quotation go *inside* the quotation marks.

EXERCISE 1 USING QUOTATION MARKS CORRECTLY

In the following sentences, add quotation marks where necessary for the underlined quotations.

1. My boyfriend always says, "Gloria Steinem has hurt men."

2. I like to disagree with him, asserting, "She hasn't hurt men, but she has helped women."

3. When we disagree, we ask our teacher. He repeats, "Gloria Steinem is one of the most important women of the twentieth century."

4. My boyfriend usually claims, "I don't have anything against Gloria Steinem. I just don't know enough about her."

5. "Why don't you learn about her," I ask my boyfriend, "so that you can argue with me some more?"

6. The result of these debates is that my boyfriend has found a number of favorite Gloria Steinem quotations. One is, "It is more rewarding to watch money change the world than watch it accumulate."

7. Another of his favorite quotations deals with what's right. "Law and justice," Steinem wrote, "are not always the same."

8. As one Steinem quotation advises, "Power can be taken, but not given. The process of the taking is empowerment in itself."

9. I've taught my boyfriend one of my favorites. It reads, "We can tell our values by looking at our checkbook stubs."

10. "The truth will set you free," my boyfriend loves to quote, "but first it will piss you off."

EXERCISE 2 USING QUOTATION MARKS FOR CONVERSATION

Write down a short conversation using quotation marks to identify who is speaking. Include at least three quotations from each speaker. An example is done for you.   Answers will vary.

My boss said, "You have done a great job lately, so I'm thinking of promoting you."

I replied, "I'm happy that you appreciate my work, but I'm not sure I want to take on more responsibility."

"This is a good opportunity for you," she answered.

"Thanks for thinking of me," I responded, "but can I think about it for a few days?"

"Take your time and get back to me," she said.

"I will. Thank you again," I said.

Using Parts of Quotations

Sometimes you will want to quote only part of what someone said. In these cases, simply place the part that has actually been said in quotation marks.

Quotation:	Gloria Steinem said, "A pedestal is as much a prison as any small, confined space."
Part of quotation:	In Steinem's view, being on "a pedestal" is like being in "a prison." (Steinem used the specific words *a pedestal* and *a prison*, so the writer places them in quotation marks.)
Quotation:	Gloria Steinem says, "Without leaps of imagination, or dreaming, we lose the excitement of possibilities. Dreaming, after all, is a form of planning."
Part of quotation:	Gloria Steinem gives great value to dreaming, calling it "a form of planning." (Only the words said by Steinem are in quotation marks.)

Indirect Quotations

Often you may want to communicate what someone meant without setting off his or her exact words. Repeating other people's ideas without quoting them word for word is called **paraphrasing.** In these cases, you should not use quotation marks. Make sure, however, to tell who actually made the original statement.

Direct:	My history professor says, "Feminists have largely been misunderstood." (The writer is relating the exact words of a history professor.)
Indirect:	My history professor says that many people have not understood feminists. (The words of the indirect quotation differ from the words of the direct quotation; thus, the writer should not use quotation marks.)
Direct:	Rhonda's letter to her mother said, "I am going to be a writer like Gloria Steinem." (The writer is relating Rhonda's exact words.)

Indirect: Rhonda wrote a letter to her mother saying that she wants to be a writer like Gloria Steinem. (The writer does not use Rhonda's exact words, so no quotation marks are needed.) Answers will vary.

EXERCISE 3 USING INDIRECT QUOTATIONS

Revise the following sentences to change the direct quotations into indirect quotations. An example is done for you. Answers will vary.

Direct: My mother told me, "You need to grow up so you can take care of a family just as I did."

Indirect: *My mother told me that I need to grow up so I can take care of a family just as she did.*

1. Direct: However, I explained, "I want to do something else with my life."

Indirect: However, I explained that I want to do something else with my life.

2. Direct: She asked, "What could be more important than a family?"

Indirect: She asked what could be more important than a family.

3. Direct: I answered, "Making my own decisions is most important to me."

Indirect: I answered that making my own decisions is most important to me.

4. Direct: I explained, "I don't want to feel like a failure if I decide not to get married and have children."

Indirect: I explained that I don't want to feel like a failure if I don't get married and have children.

5. Direct: My mother finally agreed and said, "No, you should do what makes you happy."

Indirect: My mother finally agreed that I should do what makes me happy.

Setting Off Titles of Short Works

Use quotation marks to indicate the titles of short works such as the following:

■ Essays
■ Book chapters

- Newspaper and magazine articles

  Magazine article: "A Bunny's Tale" was one of Gloria Steinem's first published articles.

- Poems
- Songs

  Helen Reddy's hit "I Am Woman" could easily be interpreted as a feminist song.

The titles of longer works are indicated by underlining or italics.

- Newspapers

  New York Times, Christian Science Monitor

- Magazines

  Time, Newsweek, People

- Books

  The Fellowship of the Ring, Pride and Prejudice, Holes

- Albums and CDs

  Hotel California, Come Away with Me, Nice and Easy

- Movies

  Chicago; The Matrix; Star Wars: The Phantom Menace

Look at how quotation marks, italics, and underlining are used in the following sentences. *Note*: With a computer, you can use either italics or underlining for the titles of longer works. Ask your instructor for his or her preference.

The poem "For My Lover, Returning to His Wife" is in *The Collected Works of Ann Sexton*. (The poem title is set off by quotation marks while the book title is italicized.)

The article "Who Will Heed the Warnings of the Population Bomb?" from the *Los Angeles Times* deals with an important issue. (The article title is set off by quotation marks while the newspaper title is italicized.)

I love the song "Heart of Glass" from Blondie's *Parallel Lines*. (The song title is set off by quotation marks while the album title is italicized).

Did you see the episode "Guns, Not Butter" on the television show <u>The West Wing</u>? (The episode title is set off by quotation marks while the show title is underlined. The underlined title could also have been italicized, as in the preceding examples.)

EXERCISE 4 USING QUOTATION MARKS FOR TITLES

Add quotation marks or underlining as necessary in the following sentences.

1. Gloria Steinem wrote a number of books, one of which is titled <u>The Thousand Indias</u>.

2. Her article "A Bunny's Tale" came out the same year as her work <u>The Beach Book</u>.

3. Among her other accomplishments, Steinem co-founded <u>New York</u> magazine and <u>Ms.</u> magazine.

4. Recently, Gloria Steinem has been widely interviewed in newspapers such as the <u>Miami Herald</u> and magazines such as <u>Modern Maturity</u>.

5. She was also interviewed on CNN's online program <u>CNN Access</u>.

Setting Off Special Words or Expressions

Use quotation marks to set off words used in a specific sense or expressions of particular importance.

Some people think that the term "feminist" has a negative undertone.

Other people, however, claim that "feminist" actions can also include "feminine" women.

Single Quotation Marks '

Use single quotation marks to indicate a quotation within a quotation.

My friend Julie said yesterday, "I loved reading 'A Bunny's Tale' years after it was published."

This sentence contains an article title, which requires quotation marks. The regular quotation marks (" ") indicate that someone is speaking, and the single quotation marks (' ') surround the article title.

EXERCISE 5 USING QUOTATION MARKS IN YOUR WRITING

Read a paragraph in one of your textbooks. Then, write down a quotation from that book. Be sure to use quotation marks to set off the quotation, as in the following example.   Answers will vary.

Original: Some raps celebrate their sisters for "getting over" on men, rather than touting self-reliance and honesty.

—Tricia Rose, "Black Sistas," in *Black Noise: Rap Music and Black Culture in Contemporary America*

Quotation: In her essay "Bad Sistas" from her book <u>Black Noise: Rap Music and Black Culture in Contemporary America</u>, Tricia Rose writes, "Some raps celebrate their sisters for 'getting over' on men, rather than touting self-reliance and honesty."

EDITING PRACTICE

Add quotation marks and underlining where necessary in the following paragraph.

Gloria's Message for Me

Few people have had a greater influence on me than Gloria Steinem. My family comes from a country where men make all the decisions. Also, because my mother died when I was young, I was raised in a household with all men: four brothers, an uncle, and a father. They expected me to do all the household work, telling me, "A woman's place is in the home." I went to school even though my father constantly said, "School is a waste of time when all you'll do is find a man to marry." When I was a senior in high school, I learned about Gloria Steinem in my sociology class. My teacher told me that when Ms. Steinem applied for a job, the magazine editor told her, "We don't want a pretty girl. We want a writer." What impressed me most was that Ms. Steinem published all kinds of articles, for example, "After Black Power, Women's Liberation" and "The Disarmament of Betty Coed." She also helped found two magazines: <u>New York</u> magazine and <u>Ms.</u> magazine. She was engaged to her college boyfriend, so she could have gotten married, but she chose to fight for women. This made me think that I should fight for my life, too. I told my father that women can do more than take care of men. "I want to go to college," I said. At first, my father said, "No way." However, he came back later and said, "I'm very proud that you want to educate yourself. Go to college with my blessing." On top of that, he's helping me pay my tuition. Gloria Steinem helped me see that I have more options than I thought.

Lab Activity 50

For additional practice with quotation marks, complete Lab Activity 50 in the Lab Manual at the back of the book.

51 Other Punctuation Marks

CULTURE NOTE *Marilyn Monroe, an American Legend*

A sex symbol of the 1960s who became an American icon, Marilyn Monroe radiates a ditzy beauty. Partly because of her movie roles and partly because of her suicide at age thirty-six, Marilyn Monroe has had a great effect on America's ideas of femininity.

Marilyn Monroe

PLAN AN INTERVIEW Known for her platinum-haired appeal, Marilyn Monroe strove to be taken seriously as an actress. Interview two people about their reactions to Marilyn Monroe. Write a few sentences about what you learn.

Understanding Other Punctuation Marks

Commas, quotation marks, and apostrophes are very common punctuation marks. Some other forms of punctuation that are used less often also serve special functions.

- Semicolons
- Colons
- Hyphens
- Dashes
- Parentheses

Knowing how to use these forms of punctuation effectively can help you write a variety of sentences.

Semicolons ;

Use a **semicolon** to join two independent clauses.

> Marilyn Monroe played the role of a blond bombshell; she also played more serious roles.

> Marilyn Monroe experienced great success as a blond beauty; however, she wanted to be taken seriously as an actress in other roles.

A less common but still important use of the semicolon is to separate items in a series where the individual items contain commas. A **series** is two or more items in a row.

> Marilyn Monroe had several identities. She was Norma Jean, the small-town girl; Marilyn Monroe, the movie star; Marilyn, the sex symbol; and Marilyn, wife of three husbands.

> Some biographies of Marilyn Monroe are *Marilyn Monroe: The Biography,* by Donald Spoto; *Marilyn Monroe and the Camera,* by Jane Russell; and *The Ultimate Marilyn,* by Ernest W. Cunningham.

EXERCISE 1 USING SEMICOLONS CORRECTLY

Add semicolons where necessary.

1. Some of Marilyn Monroe's most famous movies are *All About Eve,* in which she first gained attention as a real star; *Some Like It Hot,* where she plays a woman named Sugar Kane;and *Niagara,* in which she plays an unfaithful wife who plots to kill her husband.

2. Marilyn Monroe had three husbands: James Dougherty, a man she met in an aircraft plant;Joe Dimaggio, the baseball star;and Arthur Miller, the playwright. ^

3. Marilyn Monroe is known for many things;her sex appeal is just one of them. ^

4. Marilyn Monroe has been paid tribute by many singers; Madonna, the American pop star, dressed like Marilyn Monroe in a music video.

5. Elton John, an English singer and composer, wrote the song "Candle in the Wind" as a tribute to Marilyn Monroe; its popularity was due in part to Marilyn Monroe's fame. ^

Colons :

Colons tell the reader to pay attention to what's coming. Use a colon for these purposes.

- To introduce a list
- To introduce a quotation of more than one sentence
- To call attention to words that follow
- To separate the hour and minutes in telling time

I've often heard that three of Marilyn Monroe's movies are her best: *Niagara, Bus Stop,* and *Some Like It Hot.* (The colon introduces the list of movies.)

Marilyn Monroe describes this experience in one of her biographies: "Sometimes I've been to a party where no one spoke to me for a whole evening. The . . . ladies would gang up in a corner and discuss my dangerous character." (The colon follows an independent clause and introduces a quotation longer than one sentence.)

Now that you've waited for her to come, here she is: Marilyn Monroe. (The colon calls attention to the name that follows.)

Marilyn Monroe has fans even at 5:00 a.m. on a Saturday. (The colon separates the hour from the minutes.)

EXERCISE 2 USING COLONS CORRECTLY

Use colons where necessary in the following sentences.

1. One statement of Marilyn Monroe's that I love is this:"All little girls should be told they're pretty, even if they're not."

2. Marilyn Monroe is one thing above all:a star.

3. At 7:30 p.m., my friends and I will watch *The River of No Return* starring Marilyn Monroe.

4. Marilyn Monroe is known for many traits:blond hair, voluptuous figure, soft voice, and pouty lips.

5. Another quotation of Marilyn Monroe's is as follows:"It's not true I had nothing on. I had the radio on."

Hyphens -

Use a **hyphen** to join two or more words working together to communicate one concept.

Marilyn Monroe was never considered one of the high- and-mighty actresses of her time.

One of the most talked-about movies that Marilyn Monroe made was *Some Like It Hot*.

Hyphens are also used to split a word at the end of a line. To divide a word at the end of a line, make the break between syllables. One-syllable words should never be hyphenated, and no word should be divided unless absolutely necessary. *Hint:* If you're not sure of syllable breaks, check the dictionary.

At the end of her career, Marilyn Monroe starred in a movie that her husband Arthur Miller wrote for her, *The Misfits*. (The hyphen indicates that the word *husband* continues on the next line.)

Tip: Many word processors and computers automatically keep whole words on one line; you will rarely need to use hyphens to divide single words.

EXERCISE 3 USING HYPHENS CORRECTLY

Add hyphens where necessary.

1. Starstudded casts of actors often accompanied Marilyn Monroe in her movies.

2. Though successful in her blond bombshell roles, she took acting classes purely for selfimprovement.

3. Monroe made a name for herself as a serious actress, but fans prefer her as a wideeyed, sexy airhead.

4. Although many people believe that Monroe's death was an accident, others think the star was strung out on drugs.

5. The early death of a wellknown entertainer always makes the news.

Dashes —

Use **dashes** to set off remarks that interrupt the flow of a sentence. The interruption signaled by a dash is longer and more pronounced than one set off by two commas. Sometimes the interruption is a complete clause. Dashes are made by typing two hyphens in a row. If you are writing dashes by hand, make them as long as two letters.

Marilyn Monroe's real name—Norma Jean Baker—became more familiar to the public with the popularity of Elton John's song "Candle in the Wind."

Because Marilyn Monroe wanted to be viewed as a serious actress—not just as the blond bombshell she played so well—she took acting lessons.

EXERCISE 4 USING DASHES CORRECTLY

Add dashes where necessary.

1. Marilyn memorabilia photos, books, calendars, for starters are available on eBay.

2. However, some stores these are usually vintage shops that carry unusual fashions also carry items with Marilyn's image.

3. I often dress up like Marilyn Monroe for Halloween and other parties, of course in a bubble-gum pink gown like the one she wore in *How to Marry a Millionaire.*

4. The woman who cuts my hair Sharrona Scissors, I call her covers the walls of her salon with Marilyn Monroe prints.

5. People often ask Sharrona if they can have her prints which seems rude to me but she always says no.

Parentheses

Parentheses also set off information that interrupts the flow of a sentence. Usually, however, the information in parentheses is interesting but not essential to understand the sentence. Common information set off in parentheses includes dates and page numbers.

In a biography of Marilyn Monroe's life **(**page 153**)**, the writer praises the actress for owning more than 200 books.

Marilyn Monroe **(**1926–1962**)** lived a very short life.

Tip: Any comma should go *after* parentheses, as illustrated in the first example above.

EXERCISE 5 USING PARENTHESES CORRECTLY

Add parentheses where necessary.

1. Did you know that Madonna (my favorite pop singer) dressed like Marilyn Monroe in one of her videos?

2. Though Madonna's image is very different from Marilyn Monroe's (Madonna is more independent) both women have made a mark in the world.

3. Some people even think that Madonna is smart not to imitate Marilyn Monroe too closely (who *could* impersonate Marilyn?) since no one could ever replace the real Marilyn.

4. In a collector's edition of a Hollywood magazine (page 32) Marilyn Monroe is featured.

5. Marilyn Monroe's second husband Joe Dimaggio (1914–1999) was a professional baseball player.

EDITING PRACTICE

Add the correct punctuation marks (colon, semicolon, hyphen, dash, or parentheses) where necessary in the following paragraph. You will need to add four hyphens, a pair of dashes, two colons, three semicolons, and one pair of parentheses.

Marvelous Marilyn

Marilyn Monroe (1926–1962) made her mark in many ways. First, she was a regular girl who "made it" as a movie star. She overcame hardship living with a mother who was mentally ill, living in foster homes, working as a child for horrible wages and became a symbol of how "average" people could rise to the top. Second, Marilyn Monroe made her mark as a beauty. Though today people value the skin-and-bones look as beautiful, Marilyn let herself look womanly with full curves. Even fans of the starved look appreciate Marilyn's feminine appearance. Marilyn Monroe was quoted as saying this: "I don't mind living in a man's world as long as I can be a woman in it." Finally, Marilyn Monroe made her mark as someone whose fame made her unhappy. She was loved on the screen for her performances: as a sexy, single upstairs neighbor in *The Seven Year Itch*; as a flask-wielding member of an all-girl band in *Some Like It Hot*; and as a faithless wife in *Niagara*. However, Marilyn Monroe still felt she needed to prove herself; she enrolled in acting classes. Even her attempts to improve herself left her feeling empty, she committed suicide in 1962.

⌛ Lab Activity 51

For additional practice with other punctuation marks, complete Lab Activity 51 in the Lab Manual at the back of the book.

52 Capitalization

CULTURE NOTE ***Natural Wonders of the World***

Though humans have learned how to dig long tunnels and erect massive skyscrapers, their work cannot rival what nature has created. From the Grand Canyon to Victoria Falls and the northern lights, the natural wonders of the world continue to amaze and delight us.

Main Uses of Capital Letters

Understanding the rules of capitalization can aid you greatly in your writing courses. Keep in mind that not all academic disciplines have the same conventions or rules for capitalization. For instance, some words may be capitalized in science classes but not in humanities courses. When in doubt about what should be capitalized, consult the dictionary. Capital letters are required for many common types of words.

- **Names of people and the pronoun *I*.**

  Yolanda, **F**rank, and **I** planned a big trip.

- **Names of specific places.** Capitalize the names of cities, states, countries, regions, lakes, parks, and mountains. Do not capitalize directions (north, west, etc.).

  I'm from **Y**akima, **W**ashington, in the **N**orthwest.

  We drove to **S**alt **L**ake **C**ity, **U**tah, where we saw the **G**reat **S**alt **L**ake.

- **Names of institutions.** Capitalize the names of government offices, businesses, and academic institutions.

  Department of the **T**reasury

  St. **J**ohn's **H**ospital

  University of **M**innesota

Victoria Falls

CRITICAL THINKING Forming the world's largest sheet of falling water, Victoria Falls churns the Zambezi river in Zimbabwe. The residents near Victoria Falls fear that increased tourism will spoil the environment. Write a few sentences discussing whether or not tourism should be limited to preserve the environment.

- **Names of holidays, months, and days of the week.** Capitalize the names of religious and secular holidays, the names of months, and the days of the week. Do not capitalize the names of the seasons of the year: spring, summer, fall, winter.

  I think that **V**alentine's **D**ay comes on a **F**riday this winter, but I know that it's **F**ebruary 14.

- **Brand names of products.** Capitalize the *name* of the product, but not the *type* of product.

Brand Name	**Product**
Goodyear	tires
Hershey's	chocolate
Nike	shoes
Perdue	chicken

  I donated my old **F**ord **T**aurus to a charity.

Names of Places to Be Capitalized

Cities: Paris, Tulsa, San Diego
States: West Virginia, Delaware, Montana
Countries: United Kingdom, Pakistan, People's Republic of China
Regions: New England, Old South

■ **Titles of written or performed works.** Capitalize the first, last, and main words in the titles of articles, books, magazines, newspapers, poems, stories, movies, songs, television shows, and your own papers. The following words usually do not require capitalization.

Articles	*a, an, the*	*Silence of the Lambs*
Prepositions	*in, of, to,* etc.	"Come Fly with Me"
Coordinating conjunctions	*for, and, nor, but, or, yet, so*	*Pride and Prejudice*

Aaron Copland's symphony *Appalachian Spring* is on my *Best American Composers* CD.

An article called "**T**he **W**onder of the **S**even **W**onders" in *National Geographic* told about the seven wonders of the natural world.

Then, I read a poem by John Barton called "**S**unrise, **G**rand **C**anyon," which made me really want to visit Arizona.

■ **First word in a sentence or direct quotation.**

Our trip to Mount Everest was a dream that we couldn't afford.

Devon exclaimed, "**L**et's go to Rio de Janeiro instead!"

EXERCISE 1 CORRECT CAPITALIZATION

Change small letters to capital letters where necessary. You will need to correct forty-four words in all. An example is done for you.

    I
i̶ saw a television special called "t̶h̶e̶ ̶s̶e̶v̶e̶n̶ ̶n̶a̶t̶u̶r̶a̶l̶ ̶w̶o̶n̶d̶e̶r̶s̶ <ins>The Seven Natural Wonders</ins> of the
w̶o̶r̶l̶d̶ <ins>World</ins>" and wanted to see at least one of them before going to
a̶m̶e̶r̶i̶c̶a̶n̶ ̶r̶i̶v̶e̶r̶ ̶c̶o̶l̶l̶e̶g̶e̶ <ins>American River College</ins> in the fall.

1. *Capitalize five words*: My my friend John ~~john~~ and I ~~i~~ want to see Victoria Falls ~~victoria falls~~.

2. *Capitalize six words*: After ~~after~~ all, it can't be that far to Victoria, British ~~victoria, british~~ Columbia ~~columbia~~, from where we're starting in Portland, Oregon ~~portland, oregon~~.

3. *Capitalize six words*: We had packed our bags from L. L. Bean ~~l. l. bean~~, loaded the Honda Civic, ~~honda civic~~, and filled the tank with Chevron ~~chevron~~ gas before John said, "Maybe ~~maybe~~ we should look at a Michelin ~~michelin~~ map."

4. *Capitalize eight words*: I ~~i~~ thought this was crazy since I ~~i~~ had seen a movie called *Victoria* ~~*Victoria*~~, read about Queen Victoria ~~queen victoria~~, and read an article in *Via* ~~*via*~~ magazine about Victoria Falls ~~victoria falls~~, so I was sure I knew everything about it already.

5. *Capitalize seven words*: John ~~john~~ insisted, saying, "We ~~we~~ can't be too careful." It's ~~it's~~ a good thing I ~~i~~ listened because Victoria Falls ~~victoria falls~~ turned out to be in Africa ~~africa~~.

Additional Uses of Capital Letters

Capital letters are necessary in other cases as well.

- **Titles before a person's name.** Capitalize titles that come directly before a name.

  My neighbor **Mr.** Curtis recommends his dentist, **Dr.** Chun.

  My neighbor recommends his dentist, Amanda Chun.

  Common Titles

Mr.	Dr.
Mrs.	Professor
Ms.	

- **Names showing family relationships.** Capitalize any name you might call a family member.

  I love **A**untie **R**ose, and **U**ncle **D**ave is a favorite, too.

  I asked **G**randma when she learned to ride horses.

If you place a possessive pronoun in front of a family name, do not capitalize the name.

I asked my grandma when she learned to ride horses. (The word *my* is a possessive pronoun, so *grandma* is not capitalized.)

■ **Names of groups.** Capitalize names of groups with specific affiliations, such as races and nationalities, religions, political groups, companies, unions, and clubs and other associations.

Buildings in our national parks are often modeled after **N**ative **A**merican themes. The **F**red **H**arvey **C**ompany hired the gifted architect Mary E. J. Colter to design buildings at the Grand Canyon.

Later, the company was sold to **A**mfac. (The word *company* is not capitalized when it is not part of a name.)

The most recent group of Grand Canyon tourists includes the **L**utheran **B**rotherhood management team, the **J**unior **L**eague of **T**allahassee, and leaders of the **A**merican **Y**outh **S**occer **O**rganization.

■ **Names of school courses.**

I took **C**hemistry 101, **B**iology 103, and **B**otany 203 last semester.

I have also taken many other **s**cience classes. (Do not capitalize the names of general subjects.)

■ **Historical periods, events, and documents.**

the **C**ivil **W**ar	the **R**enaissance
World **W**ar II	the **M**iddle **A**ges
the **V**ietnam **W**ar	the **G**reat **D**epression
the **T**reaty of **V**ersailles	the **C**onstitution

EXERCISE 2 USING CAPITAL LETTERS CORRECTLY

Change small letters to capital letters where necessary. Twenty-five words require capitalization.

Great Barrier Reef

The ~~great barrier reef~~ is another natural wonder I have always

Mr.   World War

wanted to visit. My neighbor, ~~mr.~~ Burns (a ~~world war~~ II veteran) has

Mother   Father

been there and says it is magnificent. However, ~~mother~~ and ~~father~~

Methodist

and everyone at the ~~methodist~~ Church worry that I will get into trou-

ble. Part of their worry is that the reef is so far away, along the

Punctuation and Mechanics

~~queensland~~ **Queensland** coast of ~~australia.~~ **Australia.** My parents also worry that I won't speak the language. They think that people speak ~~chinese~~ **Chinese** or ~~hindi~~ **Hindi** or some other language in ~~australia.~~ **Australia.** What they don't realize is that in ~~australia,~~ **Australia,** people speak ~~english!~~ **English!** I'll be fine, I tell them. Last semester I took ~~marine biology~~ **Marine Biology** 30 from ~~professor~~ **Professor** Diver in order to learn about the reef. Also, if I travel that far, I could see the ~~aborigines,~~ **Aborigines,** the original inhabitants of ~~australia.~~ **Australia.** The ~~great barrier reef~~ **Great Barrier Reef** has been designated a national marine park by the ~~australian~~ **Australian** government, so it's probably even educational. I would love to go snorkeling and see the reef's huge variety of plant and animal life.

Unnecessary Capitalization

Do not use capital letters where they are not needed.

Words that serve as general labels, like *city, river, artist, company, lawyer,* and *airport,* are not capitalized unless they are part of a name. Note that the underlined letters are not capitalized because they are general terms.

The <u>a</u>rtist Thomas Eakins painted grand American <u>l</u>andscapes of <u>r</u>ivers and <u>m</u>ountains.

Last <u>s</u>ummer we took an old-fashioned <u>p</u>addleboat, the *Sea Sprite,* down the Mississippi River. I was surprised by how interesting the river was. (The noun *river* is capitalized only when it is part of a name, *Mississippi River.*)

When we went hiking in the <u>m</u>ountains (the Rockies), I made sure to wear my trusty L. L. Bean <u>h</u>iking <u>b</u>oots. (The noun *mountains* is not capitalized because it is not part of a name; *hiking boots* is not capitalized even though it comes right after a brand name.)

EXERCISE 3 CORRECTING ERRORS IN CAPITALIZATION

Rewrite the incorrectly capitalized words below to begin with a small letter.

1. The ~~City~~ *city* of Rio de Janeiro sits on steep ~~Hillsides~~ *hillsides* that meet

   the sea.

2. Portugese ~~Explorers~~ *explorers* were the first Europeans to see the ~~Bay~~ *bay* in

   1502, when the ~~Area~~ *area* was occupied by Tupi Indians.

3. The explorers thought they had found a huge ~~River~~ *river*, so they called

   the bay Rio de Janeiro, meaning "River of January," in ~~Honor~~ *honor* of the

   ~~Month~~ *month* they arrived.

4. European ~~Settlement~~ *settlement* didn't take place on the bay until sixty years

   later when the Portuguese built a ~~Fort~~ *fort* to keep out French ~~Traders~~ *traders*.

5. Today, Rio's harbor and ~~Beaches~~ *beaches* are crowded, but the ~~Natural~~ *natural*

   ~~Beauty~~ *beauty* of Brazil's mountains by the ~~Bay~~ *bay* is unquestionable.

EDITING PRACTICE

Change small letters to capital letters where necessary. Twenty words require capitalization.

1. ~~one~~ *One* of the seven wonders of the natural world is the ~~aurora borealis~~ *Aurora Borealis*,

   also known as the northern lights.

2. According to ~~mother~~ [Mother] and ~~aunt~~ [Aunt] Parker, who used to live in ~~alaska~~ [Alaska], the

northern lights are caused by a reaction in the atmosphere near the

~~north pole.~~ [North Pole]

3. Our old ~~german~~ [German] friend in ~~new york, dr. frank,~~ [New York, Dr. Frank] used to be a scientist back

in ~~heidelberg, germany,~~ [Heidelberg, Germany] so he knows about the lights.

4. ~~he~~ [He] says that people have seen the lights as far south as the northern

~~united states,~~ [United States] and ~~alaska~~ [Alaska] residents see them often.

5. Our friend ~~dr. frank~~ [Dr. Frank] says, "~~though~~ [Though] the lights can be explained by science,

they are still amazing to see."

Lab Activity 52

For additional practice with capitalization, complete Lab Activity 52 in the Lab Manual at the back of the book.

53 Numbers and Abbreviations

Using Numbers

Depending on the nature or discipline of the paper you're writing, abbreviations may be acceptable. Rules also vary regarding spelling out numbers versus using numerals. For instance, in nontechnical writing—where the reader is not having to perform calculations while reading—numbers should be spelled out. For many math, science, and engineering courses, however, numerals and other abbreviations save time and space. While this chapter covers some rules for basic usage of abbreviations and numerals, always ask your course instructors what conventions they want you to follow.

Spelling Out Numbers

In nontechnical writing, spell out numbers that can be written in one or two words.

Spelled Out	Numerals
fifteen videos	106 children
twenty-five books	5,735 bonus points
two hundred years	25,697,005 entrants

Using Numerals for Everyday Information

Use numerals to express dates, times, page numbers, book sections, addresses, and percentages.

June 25, 1876

12:00 a.m.

page 5

chapter 1

1633 Broadway, New York, NY 10019

EXERCISE 1 USING NUMERALS CORRECTLY

Cross out the errors in numbers in the following sentences and write the correction above each one.

1. Crazy Horse (~~eighteen forty two~~ **1842** –1877) was a forceful Sioux leader

   in the Battle of the Little Big Horn.

2. He led warriors from ~~5~~ **five** different Native American tribes: Sioux,

   Cheyenne, Crow, Arikara, and Arapaho.

3. The Little Big Horn battlefield became a national monument on

   March 22, ~~nineteen forty six~~ **1946**.

4. After the Battle of the Little Big Horn, Chief Sitting Bull was

   arrested in Canada and held for ~~2~~ **two** years.

5. On his release, he hoped to influence his people ~~1~~ **one** last time through

   the Ghost Dance movement.

Using Abbreviations

In general, you should avoid using abbreviations in formal writing.

Incorrect:	I go to class on <u>Wed.</u> and <u>Fri.</u>
Correct:	I go to class on <u>Wednesday</u> and <u>Friday.</u>

Incorrect:	Alisha's mom is a <u>dr.</u>
Correct:	Alisha's mom is a <u>doctor.</u>

However, a few types of abbreviations are commonly used.

- **People's titles.** Abbreviate the following titles when they are used with proper names: *Mr., Ms., Mrs., Dr., Jr.,* and *Sr.* (Note that the title *Miss* is not an abbreviation.) Follow an initial in a person's name with a period.

  My history professor, *Dr.* Arrow, is an expert on the Battle of the Little Big Horn. (Do not abbreviate *professor* before a name: Professor Hector Romeis.)

  James T. Arrow, *Jr.,* my history professor's son, also knows a lot about the battle. (When commas are used with *Jr.,* place them before and after the title.)

- **Organizations and items known by their initials.** Many companies, government agencies, and other groups, as well as some common items, are known by their initials. Do not use periods with these abbreviations.

ATM	automatic teller machine	CIA	Central Intelligence Agency
CD	compact disc	NBC	National Broadcasting Corporation

- **References to time.** Use numerals when references to time are abbreviated. When using A.D., remember to write that designation *before* the year: A.D. 32.

a.m. *or* A.M.	350 B.C.
p.m. *or* P.M.	A.D. 100

  Tip: Spell out *noon* and *midnight* to avoid confusion between 12 P.M. and 12 A.M.

EXERCISE 2 ELIMINATING UNNECESSARY ABBREVIATIONS

Cross out the errors in abbreviations and write the correction above each one. There are fifteen words to correct in all.

1. At the ~~U. of Mont.~~, many ~~stud.~~ read about the Battle of the Little
   University of Montana   students
   Big Horn.

2. ~~Stats.~~ can give beginning ~~psych.~~ students a lot of ~~probs.~~
   Statistics   psychology   problems

3. Students in ~~poli. sci.~~ love to discuss ideas with their ~~profs.~~
   political science   *professors*

4. Next ~~Tues.~~, I will have to explain my ideas about Custer at the ~~mtg.~~
   Tuesday   *meeting*
   of ~~Am. Hist.~~ teachers.
   American History

5. The meeting is at the new library on Fourth ~~St.~~ in Charlotte,
   Street
   ~~NC.~~
   North Carolina

EDITING PRACTICE

Find the fourteen errors in numbers and abbreviations in the following paragraph. Cross out each mistake and write the correction above it.

A Last Stand for Many

To force the large Native American army back to the reservations, the army dispatched ~~3~~ columns to attack in coordinated fash-
three
ion, ~~1~~ of which contained Lieutenant Colonel ~~Geo.~~ Armstrong
one   *George*
Custer and the ~~7th~~ Cavalry. Spotting the Sioux village about ~~15~~ miles
Seventh   *fifteen*
away along the Rosebud River on June ~~twenty-fifth~~, Custer also
25
found a nearby group of about ~~40~~ warriors. Ignoring orders to wait,
forty
he decided to attack. He did not realize that the warriors in the village numbered ~~3~~ times his strength. Dividing his forces in ~~3rds~~,
three   *thirds*
Custer sent troops under Captain Frederick Benteen to prevent the
warriors' escape through the upper valley of the Little Bighorn River.
Major Marcus Reno's squadron of ~~one hundred seventy-five~~ soldiers
175
was to attack the northern end. However, Reno had to retreat, pur-

two
sued by 2 groups of Cheyenne and Sioux warriors. Just as they

finished driving Reno's men out, the Native Americans found

210
roughly ~~two hundred ten~~ of Custer's men coming toward the other

end of the village and forced the soldiers back. Meanwhile, a Sioux

force under Crazy Horse moved downstream and then doubled back

in a sweeping arc, closing in on Custer and his men in a pincer

move. The Sioux forces began pouring in gunfire and arrows. In less

one
than 1 hour, Custer and his men were killed in the worst U.S. mili-

260
tary disaster ever. Many of the ~~two hundred sixty~~ men under Custer's

command were scalped, but Custer was not.

Lab Activity 53

For additional practice with numbers and abbreviations, complete Lab
Activity 53 in the Lab Manual at the back of the book.

54 Words That Look and Sound Alike

CULTURE NOTE *Los Angeles*

The "City of Angels," Los Angeles, California, is known for its beaches, its glamorous lifestyle, and its proximity to Hollywood. Boasting beautiful weather and a diverse population, Los Angeles has been the setting for fame, fortune, and violence.

Understanding Homonyms

Many words sound like other words but have different spellings and different meanings. These words are called **homonyms.** Read the word groups that follow, paying attention to how the words differ from each other. Then, fill in each blank with a word from that group.

all ready   completely prepared
already   before; previously

I was _____all ready_____ to go to Los Angeles with my brother when he

called to say he had _____already_____ left.

brake   to stop; a device that stops a vehicle
break   to damage or cause to come apart; a pause or rest

If you're not prepared to _____brake_____ a lot in Los Angeles traffic,

you'd better take a long _____break_____ before getting into and out
of your car.

buy   to purchase
by   near; of; before

If you plan to ____buy____ something on Rodeo Drive, you had

better do it ____by____ finding something very, very small.

coarse rough
course school subject; a route; part of a meal

When I studied Los Angeles as part of my sociology ____course____,

I learned that people with ____coarse____ behavior live there in addition to people with nice manners.

hear   to experience sounds
here   in this place

If you live ____here____ in Los Angeles, you'd better be ready to

____hear____ all about the Lakers and the Dodgers.

hole   place where nothing is
whole complete; entire

Once I drove the ____whole____ way from my home to Los

Angeles with a ____hole____ in the door of my car.

its   belonging to *it*
it's   contraction of *it is* or *it has*

____It's____ easy to daydream about Los Angeles; ____its____
stars, stores, and beaches are fantastic.

knew past tense of *know*
new   fresh, unused; opposite of old

I ____knew____ that I should get a ____new____ swimsuit before
hitting the beaches.

know   to have knowledge about; to understand

no   a negative

What I didn't _____know_____ was that I had _____no_____ idea where to buy a cute swimsuit.

pair   set of two

pare   trim away excess

pear   type of fruit

When I found a suit with a _____pear_____ and apples design, I

bought a _____pair_____ of bikinis in the same fabric. Now I must

_____pare_____ down my figure to look good in it!

passed   past tense of *pass*

past   already happened

When I _____passed_____ the police car, I was afraid my clean driving

record would soon be a thing of the _____past_____.

peace   calmness; tranquillity

piece   part or section

The officer gave me a _____piece_____ of his mind about driving too

fast, but he didn't give me a ticket. He left me in _____peace_____.

plain   simple, unadorned

plane   aircraft

An impressive aircraft, the *Spruce Goose* is the biggest

_____plane_____ ever built. It is made of wood and covered in fabric,

but the _____plain_____ fact is that it's impressive because it's so big.

principal   the head administrator of a school; most important, consequential, or influential; a sum of money that gains interest

principle   a rule or law

A guiding ____principle____ of any high school ____principal____ in Los Angeles is that a diverse student population must be respected and appreciated.

right   opposite of left; correct; a privilege or power that someone has a just claim to

write   to print or mark words on paper

If you're facing south in California, the ocean will be to your

____right____. However, to avoid getting lost, you'd be wise to

____write____ down directions.

than   used to compare

then   at that time

Someday I want to shop on Rodeo Drive rather ____than____ at

flea markets. Until ____then____, I'm off to the sale racks.

their   belonging to *them*

there   at that place; word used with verbs like *is, are, was, were, had,* and *have*

they're   contraction of *they are*

Residents of Los Angeles are proud of ____their____ city's wide

range of entertainment. Living ____there____, these residents think

that ____they're____ the envy of people who don't live near the ocean.

threw   past tense of *throw*

through   passing from one side to another; all done

I ____threw____ the frisbee, hoping my dog would catch it.

However, he missed it, so the frisbee sailed ____through____ the air.

to   toward (They went *to* Los Angeles); part of an infinitive (*to go*)

| too | more than enough (There's *too* much to do in Los Angeles); in addition (I'm going to Los Angeles, *too*.) |
| two | the number 2 |

In ____two____ minutes, I am going ____to____ the beach.

Do you want to come, ____too____ ?

were	past tense of *be*
wear	to have on
where	in what place

____Where____ are you going in that outfit? Why would you

____wear____ that? I wouldn't if I ____were____ you.

| weather | atmospheric conditions |
| whether | if; in case |

____Whether____ it's January or June in Los Angeles, the

____weather____ is always lovely.

| whose | belonging to *whom* |
| who's | contraction of *who is* |

____Whose____ job is it to plan our next beach trip? I want to know

____who's____ in charge.

| your | belonging to *you* |
| you're | contraction of *you are* |

If ____you're____ ready, you can clean up ____your____ sandy footprints and go back to the beach.

EXERCISE 1 RECOGNIZING HOMONYMS

For each sentence below, write the correct word in the blank. Review the definitions on the previous pages if you need help.

1. its, it's   Los Angeles contains many famous landmarks. One

of ____its____ most famous sights is Olvera Street.

Olvera Street

WRITE A PARAGRAPH Revealing a different style from the beaches of Southern California, the Mexican market on Olvera Street offers an enticing selection of authentic goods. Los Angeles, California, offers great cultural diversity. What kind of diversity exists where you live? Write a paragraph describing the cultures in your home, neighborhood, or city. Note that diversity may include differences in race, religion, gender, age, sexual orientation, or interests.

2. right, write   Olvera Street is one of the oldest streets in Los

Angeles, running downtown _____right_____ through El Pueblo de Los Angeles.

3. know, no   _____No_____ other thoroughfare in Los Angeles boasts of more than thirty historic buildings or a Mexican marketplace that is full of food and craft stalls.

4. wear, where   Olvera Street is_____where_____ people can gain a sense of historic Los Angeles, before it became the second-largest city in the United States.

5. to, too, two   The Santa Monica Pier, _____too_____, is a wonderful place to visit.

6. passed, past   If you walk on the beach you'll be _____passed_____ by skaters, bicyclists, and joggers alike.

7. their, there, they're   Once _____there_____, on the pier itself, you can visit Pacific Park, an amusement park.

8. all ready, already   Best of all, your visit to the pier will seem as if it's _____already_____ paid for because it's free.

9. here, hear   If you ask about sights that are not free, you may _____hear_____ about Rodeo Drive shops.

10. weather, whether   _____Whether_____ you buy anything in the shops or not, strolling down Rodeo Drive will make you feel as if you're spending money.

Other Commonly Confused Words

Aside from homonyms, a number of other words look or sound enough alike to be confusing. As you did with homonyms, read the confusing word groups that follow, paying attention to how the words differ from each other. Then, fill in each blank with a word from that group.

a, an   Both *a* and *an* are generally used before other words to mean "one." Use *an* before words beginning with a vowel (*a, e, i, o, u*).

an ocean   **an** experience   **an** orange   **an** itch   **an** eyesore

Use *a* before words beginning with consonants (all other letters).

a beach   **a** visit   **a** yellow flower   **a** star   **a** great man

My friends and I had_____an_____urge to visit _____a_____ museum in Los Angeles.

accept   to receive; to agree to

except   but; to exclude

I have seen most of the museums___except___the Getty Center in

Brentwood. I may have to ____accept____the fact that a visit there must wait.

advice   noun meaning "opinion"
advise   verb meaning "to give advice" or "to counsel"

My mother would ____advise____ me to visit the Museum of

Contemporary Art (MOCA), but I rarely take her ____advice____.

affect   verb meaning "to influence" or "to change"
effect   noun meaning "result"; verb meaning "to cause"

My mother's views don't usually ____affect____ me, but I want to

see the ____effect____ of so much contemporary art in one place.

among   implies three or more
between   implies two

It was hard to choose ____among____ all the museums in Los Angeles.

____Between____ MOCA and the La Brea tar pits, I chose the tar pits.

beside   next to
besides   in addition to

Standing ____beside____ the tar pits, I noticed a strong smell.

____Besides____ that, I felt that I was too near the tar.

desert   stretch of dry land; to leave one's job or station
dessert   final course of a meal

The tar pits seemed as though they could still "eat" living creatures;

I felt that I could be____dessert____. Additionally, I kept feeling

warm, as if I were in the hot____desert____.

fewer   used to show smaller amount among things that can be counted

less   used to show smaller amount, degree, or value

I stayed at the tar pits _____less_____ than an hour and

saw _____fewer_____ than a dozen fossils in the museum.

lay   to put or place something (*Note:* The past tense of *lay* is *laid.*)

lie   to be prone (*Note:* the past tense of *lie* is *lay.*)

When I got home, I _____laid_____ my tar pits brochure on the

counter and decided to _____lie_____ down for a while.

loose   not tight; not restrained
lose   opposite of *win;* to misplace

I was afraid I might _____lose_____ my desire to see more museums,

but I wanted to rest in _____loose_____, comfortable sweats.

quiet   free from noise; peaceful
quite   very; completely

After a nice _____quiet_____ nap, I was _____quite_____ ready to visit
another museum.

raise   to lift an object; to grow or increase
rise   to get up by one's own power

I was now ready to _____raise_____ my standards and _____rise_____
to the challenge of visiting the Getty Center.

sight   something seen
site   location

The _____site_____ of the museum was quite a _____sight_____.

though   although; despite
thought   past tense of *think;* an idea

__Though__ going to important museums still makes me nervous,

the __thought__ of *not* going to them is scarier still.

EXERCISE 2 UNDERSTANDING COMMONLY CONFUSED WORDS

For each sentence below, write the correct word in the blank. Review the definitions on the previous pages if you need help.

1. among, between   __Among__ the Dodgers, the Lakers, and the Mighty Ducks, my favorite sports team is the Lakers.

2. beside, besides   Sitting __beside__ the basketball court at the Staples Center gives me chills.

3. quiet, quite   The entire arena is hushed and __quiet__ when the Lakers shoot a free throw.

4. loose, lose   Some players __lose__ their concentration in the silent arena and miss the shot.

5. though, thought   I never __thought__ I would like the basket ball team, originally started in Minneapolis–St. Paul. However, I guess everyone loves a winner!

6. buy, by   Before I __buy__ Lakers tickets, though, I check out the hockey schedule.

7. less, fewer   Although __fewer__ Californians than Minnesotans grow up playing hockey, it's still popular on the West Coast.

8. hole, whole   People used to expect the Mighty Ducks to lose

throughout the __whole__ season.

9. raise, rise   The players showed that they can __raise__ their level of play high enough to make the playoffs.

10. knew, new   While hockey may be a relatively _____ new _____ sport to California, it's gaining fans all the time.

EDITING PRACTICE

Correct the fifteen errors in word choice in the following paragraph.

The Magic Kingdom

Back in the early 1950s, when Anaheim was a small, ~~quite~~ *quiet* town surrounded by orange groves, Walt Disney, an illustrator and filmmaker, bought more ~~then~~ *than* 160 acres and began building his Magic Kingdom. No one ~~new weather~~ *knew whether* the park would be a success, but it certainly was expensive. ~~Threw~~ *Through* the building process, the cost rose to $17 million. It was 1955 before the park was ~~already~~ *all ready* to open. The original park consisted of five "lands": Main Street, Fantasyland, Adventureland, Frontierland, and Tomorrowland, ~~to~~ *too*. Many of the rides were not finished. Adventureland's only ride was the Jungle Cruise, and Tomorrowland had more exhibits ~~then~~ *than* rides. Of ~~coarse~~ *course*, many Disneyland ~~sites~~ *sights* did not exist in 1955; neither the Matterhorn nor the Monorail had been built yet. Some rides and exhibits that ~~where their~~ *were there* have long since been gone: the Aluminum Hall of Fame, Rocket to the Moon, a 20,000 Leagues Under the Sea exhibit, Space Station X-1 in Tomorrowland, and stagecoach rides in Frontierland. In

hear

fact, we rarely even ~~here~~ about those exhibits now. Fantasyland

had rides that are still open today: Snow White's Adventures,

Dumbo, and Mr. Toad's Wild Ride. The Autopia didn't arrive

until 1956, and "It's a Small World" came in 1966. Throughout

its   *effect*

~~it's~~ development, Disneyland has had a profound ~~affect~~ on

Southern California.

Lab Activity 54

For additional practice with words that look alike and sound alike, complete Lab Activity 54 in the Lab Manual at the back of the book.

55 Sentence Combining for Variety

Admired for his wacky wordplay and inventive characters, Theodore Geisel—better known by his pen name, Dr. Seuss—has made the use of rhythm and rhyme in children's books an art. His imaginative characters take outlandish risks and learn important lessons in the name of education and entertainment.

Recognizing Your Writing Style

The **style** of writing is what makes people like to read it. You may not realize it, but your writing has a style. It may be short, direct, and to the point, or it may be flowery, descriptive, and wandering. Whatever your style is, it's yours alone. If your words flow together seamlessly, and if your words and sentences are balanced between short and long ones, your writing will be more interesting to read.

Read the Culture Note about Dr. Seuss again, and then read the paragraph below. Which one is more enjoyable to read?

Theodore Geisel is admired for his wordplay. His wordplay is wacky. Theodore Geisel is also admired for his characters. The characters are inventive. Geisel is better known by his pen name, Dr. Seuss. Theodore Geisel uses rhythm and rhyme in children's books. He has made the use of rhythm and rhyme an art. Theodore Geisel's characters are imaginative. His characters take risks. The risks are outlandish. Theodore Geisel's characters learn lessons. The lessons are important. The lessons are in the name of education and entertainment.

No doubt, you noticed that the writing in the Culture Note is more interesting. Even though both paragraphs use the same words, the first version has greater **sentence variety,** mainly because it connects ideas with conjunctions and dependent words.

This chapter explores techniques you can use to make your writing more balanced and varied. Specifically, you can use three strategies to make your sentences more interesting.

- Adding equally important ideas (coordination)
- Adding less important ideas (subordination)
- Combining your sentences for brevity and variety

Coordination: Adding Equally Important Ideas

Coordination involves joining two complete, equally important ideas to form one sentence. If the sentences in a paragraph are all short, they begin to sound the same even though their content is different. For instance, read the following sentences, which are variations of lines in *Green Eggs and Ham,* a children's book by Dr. Seuss.

I am Sam.

I like green eggs and ham.

I like them in a house.

I like them with a mouse.

You probably have no trouble understanding these sentences. Each is a simple, correct sentence that communicates a single idea. Many developing writers write in simple sentences to avoid making errors. While this strategy makes sense, the result is boring for an adult audience. To make your writing more interesting, you can add a second simple sentence to the first. By doing so, you create a **compound sentence,** which joins two independent clauses. Remember that combining two complete ideas requires a comma and a coordinating conjunction (one of the FANBOYS: *for, and, nor, but, or, yet, so*). Here are two examples.

I am Sam, <u>and</u> I like green eggs and ham.

I like them in a house, <u>but</u> I never order them in a restaurant.

EXERCISE 1 COORDINATION—ADDING ANOTHER IDEA TO A SIMPLE SENTENCE

Add another complete idea to each simple sentence below, using a comma and a coordinating conjunction (*for, and, nor, but, or, yet, so*). An example is done for you.   Answers will vary.

Sentence: Today is your day.

Revised: ___Today is your day, and you deserve it!___

1. Sentence: You're off to great places.

Revised: ___You're off to great places, so you should pack.___

2. Sentence: You have many great ideas.

Revised: ___You have many great ideas, and you'll put them in motion.___

3. Sentence: You have many decisions to make.

Revised: ___You have many decisions to make, but you're ready for them.___

4. Sentence: You can steer yourself.

Revised: ___You can steer yourself, for you're well prepared.___

5. Sentence: You're on your own.

Revised: ___You're on your own, yet it's intimidating.___

6. Sentence: Some streets look good to visit.

Revised: ___Some streets look good to visit, for they are tree lined and cool.___

7. Sentence: A trip out of town can be exciting.

Revised: ___A trip out of town can be exciting, yet it can require preparation.___

8. Sentence: Some houses have lighted windows.

Revised: ___Some houses have lighted windows, but others are completely dark.___

9. Sentence: People are easily confused by maps.

Revised: ___People are easily confused by maps, so they should use guides.___

10. Sentence: People at the store are waiting in line.

Revised: People at the store are waiting in line, but they don't mind.

EXERCISE 2 COORDINATION—COMBINING TWO EQUALLY IMPORTANT IDEAS

Combine each pair of sentences into a single sentence, using a comma and a coordinating conjunction (*for, and, nor, but, or, yet, so*). An example is done for you.   Answers will vary.

Sentences: Dr. Seuss is known for his original stories. His books teach important lessons.

Combined: Dr. Seuss is known for his original stories, and his books

teach important lessons.

1. Sentences: In *Green Eggs and Ham,* one character does not want to try a new food. He puts up a great fight.

Combined: In *Green Eggs and Ham,* one character does not want to try a

new food, and he puts up a great fight.

2. Sentences: The character tries and likes the new food. The moral of that story is to keep an open mind.

Combined: The character tries and likes the new food, so the moral of that

story is to keep an open mind.

3. Sentences: Another story has a serious message. In this story, the main character is an elephant named Horton.

Combined: Another story has a serious message, but in this story the main

character is an elephant named Horton.

4. Sentences: Horton agrees to sit on an egg for Maizie, a lazy bird. He is "faithful, one hundred percent."

Combined: Horton agrees to sit on an egg for Maizie, a lazy bird, for he is

"faithful, one hundred percent."

5. Sentences: An elephant bird hatches out of the egg. Horton is rewarded for his efforts.

Combined: <u>An elephant bird hatches out of the egg, so Horton is rewarded</u>

<u>for his efforts.</u>

Subordination: Adding Less Important Ideas

Another technique to vary your sentences is **subordination,** which is the process of joining two ideas, but making one of them less important than the other. Specifically, subordination involves making one idea an independent clause and the other a **dependent clause** (a group of words having a subject, a verb, and a **dependent word** such as *although, because, since,* or *until.*) Though dependent clauses have a subject and a verb, they do not make sense all by themselves. Thus, they are less important than independent clauses in the same sentence.

See how subordination is used to vary some simple sentences.

I am Sam *even though I've always wanted to be named Harry.*

I like green eggs and ham *because my mother made them for me every day of my childhood.*

The writer has added a dependent clause—a group of words (written in italics, above) having a subject, a verb, and a dependent word—for variety. The writer could also have placed the dependent clause before the independent clause.

Even though I've always wanted to be named Harry, I am Sam.

Because my mother made them for me every day of my childhood, I like green eggs and ham.

Remember to add a comma after the dependent clause if you put it first.

Common Dependent Words

after	before	since	until
although	even though	though	when
because	if	unless	while

EXERCISE 3 SUBORDINATION—ADDING A LESS IMPORTANT IDEA TO A SIMPLE SENTENCE

Add a dependent clause to each of the following sentences. Remember to put a comma after the dependent clause if it comes first. An example is done for you.

Sentence: Tom went to the store.

Revised: Tom went to the store because he was out of milk.

1. Sentence: Karen's husband had an accident.

Revised: Karen's husband had an accident when he was skating.

2. Sentence: The girls fell asleep immediately.

Revised: Although they hadn't seemed sleepy, the girls fell asleep immediately.

3. Sentence: Tomatoes are a healthy food.

Revised: Tomatoes are a healthy food even if they are canned.

4. Sentence: Riding a bicycle can be a challenge.

Revised: After the training wheels come off, riding a bicycle can be a challenge.

5. Sentence: Telling someone the truth can be difficult.

Revised: Although it's the right thing to do, telling someone the truth can be difficult.

6. Sentence: Listening to classical music is a great way to relax.

Revised: Listening to classical music is a great way to relax unless you hate violins.

7. Sentence: Palm reading has become popular.

Revised: Because people are anxious about their future, palm reading has become popular.

8. Sentence: Exercising regularly has many benefits.

Revised: Exercising regularly has many benefits, though getting into a routine can take time.

9. Sentence: Moving into a new home can be stressful.

Revised: Although it's an exciting time, moving into a new home can be stressful.

10. Sentence: Volunteering for a nonprofit organization can be very rewarding.

Revised: Because people like to feel as though they're making a difference, volunteering for a nonprofit organization can be very rewarding.

EXERCISE 4 COMBINING TWO IDEAS USING SUBORDINATION

Add dependent words to one simple sentence in each pair to make it a dependent clause. Then combine the sentences into a single sentence. Be sure to use a comma between the clauses if you place the dependent clause first. An example is done for you. Answers will vary.

Sentences: One of Dr. Seuss's most beloved stories is *The Sneetches*. It sends a message of open-mindedness.

Revised: _Because it sends a message of open-mindedness, one of_

Dr. Seuss's most beloved stories is The Sneetches.

1. Sentences: The story successfully addresses the sensitive issue of prejudice. It uses humor to make its point.

   Combined: _Because it uses humor to make its point, the story successfully_

   addresses the sensitive issue of prejudice.

2. Sentences: The two kinds of Sneetches are almost exactly alike. The Sneetches with stars on their bellies think they are better than the Sneetches without stars.

   Combined: _The two kinds of Sneetches are almost exactly alike although the_

   Sneetches with stars on their bellies think they are better than the Sneetches
   without stars.

3. Sentences: The Sneetches without stars want to have stars. The star-bellied Sneetches are unkind to them.

   Combined: _The Sneetches without stars want to have stars because the star-_

   bellied Sneetches are unkind to them.

4. Sentences: A stranger named Sylvester McMonkey McBean offers hope to the Sneetches without stars. He has a star-adding machine.

   Combined: _A stranger named Sylvester McMonkey McBean offers hope to_

   the Sneetches without stars because he has a star-adding machine.

5. Sentences: The star machine is very expensive. The Sneetches without stars pay to get stars.

Combined: Even though the star machine is very expensive, the Sneetches

without stars pay to get stars.

6. Sentences: The original star-bellied Sneetches are unhappy. They see the new star-bellied Sneetches.

Combined: The original star-bellied Sneetches are unhappy when they see

the new star-bellied Sneetches.

7. Sentences: Sylvester McMonkey McBean offers to help the original star-bellied Sneetches. He also has a star-removal machine.

Combined: Since he also has a star-removal machine, Sylvester McMonkey

McBean offers to help the original star-bellied Sneetches.

8. Sentences: The original star-bellied Sneetches pay to have their stars removed. The star-removal machine is also expensive.

Combined: Even though the star-removal machine is also expensive, the

original star-bellied Sneetches pay to have their stars removed.

9. Sentences: All the Sneetches begin adding and removing stars constantly. They can't tell each other apart.

Combined: All the Sneetches begin adding and removing stars constantly

until they can't tell each other apart.

10. Sentences: The Sneetches discover that their stars make very little difference. Sylvester McMonkey McBean becomes very rich.

Combined: The Sneetches discover that their stars make very little

difference after Sylvester McMonkey McBean becomes very rich.

Combining Sentences for Brevity and Variety

In addition to simply making short sentences longer, sentence combining can alter the way your sentences flow together. Alternating your short sentences with longer ones or starting a longer sentence with a dependent clause can make your writing more interesting.

Combining Sentences to Avoid Repetition

Near the beginning of this chapter, you read a paragraph about Dr. Seuss that started like this:

Theodore Geisel is admired for his wordplay. His wordplay is wacky.

Look at the sentences again and notice which words are used in both. When you see a term repeated in consecutive sentences, you can often combine them. In this case, combining the two sentences results in a shorter sentence.

Theodore Geisel is admired for his wacky wordplay.

You have not changed the meaning, but you've omitted three words: *his, wordplay,* and *is.* If you can omit several words from every few sentences, your writing will be more compact.

Sometimes you can combine several sentences into a single sentence, as in the following example.

Original: Theodore Geisel's characters are imaginative. His characters take risks. The risks are outlandish.

Combined: Theodore Geisel's imaginative characters take outlandish risks.

Omitted words: *are, His characters, The risks are*

EXERCISE 5 COMBINING SENTENCES TO AVOID REPETITION

Combine each pair of sentences to form a single one. You may need to add or change some words to combine sentences logically. An example is done for you. Answers will vary.

Sentences: Dr. Seuss addresses adult themes in his stories. The themes are prejudice, war, and relationships.

Combined: *Dr. Seuss addresses the adult themes of prejudice, war, and relationships in his stories.*

1. Sentences: Dr. Seuss's stories combine elements. The elements are from classic tales and fables.

Combined: Dr. Seuss's stories combine elements from classic tales and fables.

2. Sentences: Fables usually contain animals. The animals are the main characters.

Combined: <u>Fables usually contain animals as the main characters.</u>

3. Sentences: Dr. Seuss's stories are like fables. Dr. Seuss's stories contain animals.

Combined: <u>Dr. Seuss's stories are like fables because they contain animals.</u>

4. Sentences: Fables often teach a lesson. The lesson is called a moral.

Combined: <u>Fables often teach a lesson called a moral.</u>

5. Sentences: Dr. Seuss's stories contain morals. The morals come from what the characters learn.

Combined: <u>Dr. Seuss's stories contain morals that come from what the characters learn.</u>

6. Sentences: The star-bellied Sneetches learn a lesson. The lesson is that appearances don't matter.

Combined: <u>The star-bellied Sneetches learn the lesson that appearances don't matter.</u>

7. Sentences: Classic tales often have tragic heroes. Tragic heroes have one fatal flaw.

Combined: <u>Classic tales often have tragic heroes who have one fatal flaw.</u>

8. Sentences: Dr. Seuss's animals often display one significant characteristic. The characteristic can be positive or negative.

Combined: <u>Dr. Seuss's animals often display one significant characteristic that can be positive or negative.</u>

9. Sentences: Horton the elephant, for instance, displays a characteristic. His characteristic is faithfulness.

Combined: <u>Horton the elephant, for instance, displays the characteristic of faithfulness.</u>

10. Sentences: Maizie the bird, however, displays a characteristic. Her characteristic is laziness.

Combined: <u>Maizie the bird, however, displays the characteristic of laziness.</u>

Combining Sentences for Variety

In addition to purging your sentences of unnecessary words, combining sentences can spice up your writing style. Read the following two paragraphs. Which one is more interesting? Why?

How Is Butter Better?

    The Butter Battle Book is written in classic Dr. Seuss fashion. It is a book about political tensions. The book examines the mentality of the arms race. The book also examines how minor differences between people can lead to misunderstanding and conflict. This story is of the Zooks and the Yooks. The story exposes the darker side of human nature. The story offers entertainment for children. Dr. Seuss started out as a political cartoonist. This book captures Dr. Seuss's views of the Cold War. The book makes people take sides based on their answer to the question "Do you eat your bread butter side up or down?"

The Butter Battle

    In classic Dr. Seuss fashion, *The Butter Battle Book*—a book about political tensions—examines the mentality of the arms race and how minor differences between people can lead to misunderstanding and conflict. This story of the Zooks and the Yooks exposes the darker side of human nature while still offering entertainment for children. Written by a man who started out as a political cartoonist, this book captures Dr. Seuss's views of the Cold War and makes people take sides based on their answer to the question "Do you eat your bread butter side up or down?"

    The second paragraph, "The Butter Battle," is more interesting because its sentences are more varied. The first paragraph is clear and informative, but every sentence begins the same way, with a subject followed closely by a verb. Writing similar sentences is not incorrect, but it does not make for entertaining reading.

    Look at the way sentences from the first paragraph are combined in "The Butter Battle."

Original:	This story is of the Zooks and the Yooks. The story exposes the darker side of human nature. The story offers entertainment for children.
Combined:	This story of the Zooks and the Yooks exposes the darker side of human nature while still offering entertainment for children.

The writer changed *offers* to *offering* and added the dependent word *while,* linking the sentences in the order in which they appeared in the first paragraph. You can add variety in many other ways as well, as these examples show.

Original: *The Butter Battle Book* is written in classic Dr. Seuss fashion. It is a book about political tensions.

Combined: *The Butter Battle Book*—a book about political tensions—is written in classic Dr. Seuss fashion. (The information from the second sentence is inserted into the middle of the first sentence and enclosed by dashes.)

Combined: A book about political tensions, *The Butter Battle Book* is written in classic Dr. Seuss fashion. (The information from the second sentence is placed at the beginning of the first sentence followed by a comma.)

EXERCISE 6 COMBINING SENTENCES FOR VARIETY

Combine the following pairs of sentences by moving the underlined information to the beginning or the middle of the resulting sentence. You may have to change the form of some words to combine the sentences logically. An example is done for you. Answers will vary.

Sentences: *How the Grinch Stole Christmas* tells the story of an unhappy creature. *How the Grinch Stole Christmas* is <u>one of Dr. Seuss's most popular tales</u>.

Combined: How the Grinch Stole Christmas, one of Dr. Seuss's

most popular tales, tells the story of an unhappy creature.

1. Sentences: The Grinch looks down from his cave and watches the Whos, who live below him. The Whos are <u>a happy group who fully enjoy the Christmas season</u>.

   Combined: The Grinch looks down from his cave and watches the Whos, a

   happy group who fully enjoy the Christmas season and live below him.

2. Sentences: The Whos' joy bothers the Grinch. The Whos' joy <u>is expressed in hand-holding and singing</u>.

   Combined: The Whos' joy, expressed in hand-holding and singing, bothers

   the Grinch.

3. Sentences: He decides to make them feel as bad as he does. He decides to <u>steal the Whos' Christmas</u>.

Combined: He decides to make them feel as bad as he does by stealing the

Whos' Christmas.

4. Sentences: The Grinch dresses up as Santa Claus and creeps into Whoville, where the Whos live. He goes <u>on Christmas Eve</u>.

Combined: The Grinch dresses up as Santa Claus and on Christmas Eve

creeps into Whoville, where the Whos live.

5. Sentences: The Grinch quietly takes down every sign of Christmas from every home in Whoville. The Grinch takes down <u>every ornament, tree, gift, and morsel of food</u>.

Combined: The Grinch quietly takes down every sign of Christmas—every

ornament, tree, gift, and morsel of food—from every home in Whoville.

6. Sentences: He even lies to a very little Who about taking her Christmas tree. He lies to <u>Cindy Lou Who</u>.

Combined: He even lies to a very little Who—Cindy Lou Who—about

taking her Christmas tree.

7. Sentences: The Grinch wakes up early expecting to hear the Whos sobbing with disappointment. The Grinch wakes up <u>the next morning</u>.

Combined: The Grinch wakes up early the next morning expecting to hear

the Whos sobbing with disappointment.

8. Sentences: The <u>Whos wake up</u>. However, they are simply happy to celebrate Christmas together.

Combined: When the Whos wake up, however, they are simply happy to

celebrate Christmas together.

9. Sentences: <u>He hears the Whos sing</u>. The Grinch feels his heart expand, and he reloads all the Whos' gifts and returns them to Whoville.

Combined: As he hears the Whos sing, the Grinch feels his heart expand,

and he reloads all the Whos' gifts and returns them to Whoville.

10. Sentences: The Whos are so pleased <u>with the Ginch</u>. The Whos invite him to stay and feast with them.

Combined: The Whos are so pleased with the Grinch that they invite him

to stay and feast with them.

EDITING PRACTICE

Rewrite the following paragraph on a separate piece of paper, combining sentences to avoid repetition and add variety. **Answers will vary.**

Dr. Seuss's last book was published in 1990. Dr. Seuss's last book is called *Oh, The Places You'll Go!* It is a wonderfully encouraging tale. It is a tale about life. Dr. Seuss encourages children. Dr. Seuss reminds children that they have brains. Dr. Seuss reminds children that they have the means to make changes. Dr. Seuss points out the various choices people make. He discusses these choices through zany, upbeat illustrations and rhyme. He talks about how hitting bottom is something that happens to everyone. Dr. Seuss says that people will certainly pull out of it. Dr. Seuss also discusses temptation. Dr.

Seuss discusses how temptation draws people and tries to lure them away from safety. Dr. Seuss discusses how temptation tries to lure people away from what they know. In the end, though, the story simply reinforces people's self-confidence. The story reminds people that taking a first step is progress.

Lab Activity 55

For additional practice with sentence combining, complete Lab Activity 55 in the Lab Manual at the back of the book.

Sample answers: Dr. Seuss's last book—*Oh, The Places You'll Go!*—was published in 1990. It is a wonderfully encouraging tale about life. Dr. Seuss encourages readers by reminding them that they have brains and the means to make change, and he discusses the various choices people make through zany, upbeat illustrations and rhyme. He talks about how hitting bottom is something that happens to everyone, but how people—as the readers of his book—will certainly pull out of it. Dr. Seuss also discusses temptation, how it draws people and tries to lure them away from safety and from what they know. In the end, though, the story simply reinforces people's own self-confidence by reminding them that taking a first step is progress.

56 Tips for Second-Language Writers

CULTURE NOTE *Football*

Considered by many to be the most "American" sport, football involves strength, speed, agility, and strategy. One of the few sports that includes separate teams for offense and defense, football teams include a range of players from highly specialized kickers to an assortment of "backs," or players who run and block other players.

Understanding ESL Needs

If you learned another language before you learned English, you have a tremendous advantage. Not only can you communicate in two languages, but you have the choice of using words and expressions from two languages in considering and developing your ideas. Writing English, however, presents certain challenges. English grammar is complex, and many rules have exceptions. **English as a second language (ESL)** students need to make sure they use the following elements correctly.

- Subjects
- Verbs
- Prepositions
- Articles
- Adjectives

Using Subjects Correctly

A group of words cannot be a sentence unless it has a subject. When writing English sentences, follow these rules.

- Include a subject in each clause.
- Make every noun a subject or an object.
- Avoid extra or unnecessary pronoun subjects.

699

Including a Subject in Each Clause

Every sentence must have a subject and a verb. Leaving out a subject results in a sentence fragment. In the examples that follow, the underlined word groups lack a subject.

Incorrect:	Football players get hurt often. <u>Get many injuries.</u> (The writer probably means "*They* get many injuries.")

The underlined phrase "Get many injuries." is labeled *fragment*.

Some sentences use a placeholder subject, such as *here, there,* or *it*.

Incorrect:	Are many fans in the stadium.
Correct:	<u>There</u> are many fans in the stadium.

The phrase "Are many fans in the stadium." is labeled *fragment*.

Incorrect:	Is the program for the football game.
Correct:	<u>Here</u> is the program for the football game.

The phrase "Is the program for the football game." is labeled *fragment*.

Incorrect:	Some football teams play in the snow. Is very cold.
Correct:	Some football teams play in the snow. <u>It</u> is very cold.

The phrase "Is very cold." is labeled *fragment*.

A sentence may require more than one subject. For instance, the following sentence has two **clauses** (groups of related words having a subject and a verb that work together to communicate an idea).

Football <u>fans</u> love to cheer even if <u>they</u> have never played the game.

"Football fans love to cheer" is labeled *main clause*; "fans" is labeled *subject*. "even if they have never played the game" is labeled *dependent clause*; "they" is labeled *subject*.

Because this sentence has two clauses, it requires two subjects: *fans* and *they*. Omitting one of the subjects would result in a sentence error.

Incorrect:	Although the football season is short, is intense.
Correct:	Although the football season is short, <u>it</u> is intense.
Incorrect:	Because football players are often injured, wear protective pads.
Correct:	Because football players are often injured, <u>they</u> wear protective pads.

Making Every Noun a Subject or an Object

In some languages, a word or phrase with no grammatical connection to the sentence announces what the sentence is about. This kind of structure is incorrect in English.

Incorrect:	Football dream I want to be a quarterback.

The term *football dream* has no grammatical connection to the rest of the sentence; it serves as neither a subject nor an object. Even though *football dream* appears early in the sentence—a typical place for the subject—it is not the subject because it does not go with the verb, *want*. The sentence subject is *I*. Furthermore, *football dream* is not an object of the verb *want* or of a preposition. You can revise this sentence in two ways.

■ Make the phrase a subject.

┌─── subject ───┐

Correct: My <u>football dream</u> is to be a quarterback.

■ Make the phrase an object.

┌prepositional phrase┐

Correct: In my <u>football dream</u>, I am a quarterback.

object

(*Football dream* is the object of a preposition. Notice that other words also had to be changed so that the sentence makes sense.)

Avoiding Extra or Unnecessary Pronoun Subjects

English does not permit a sentence to have repeated subjects for the same verb. Don't follow the subject with a pronoun that refers to that subject.

subject

Incorrect:	My <u>teacher</u> *she* loves to root for the Buffalo Bills.
Correct:	My <u>teacher</u> loves to root for the Buffalo Bills.
Correct:	<u>She</u> loves to root for the Buffalo Bills.

subject

Incorrect:	This <u>class</u> *it* does not discuss football often.
Correct:	This <u>class</u> does not discuss football often.
Correct:	<u>It</u> does not discuss football often.

Even if the subject is separated from the verb by several words, do not repeat the subject with a pronoun.

Incorrect:	The <u>players</u> who stand on the line of scrimmage *they* are called the linemen.
Correct:	The <u>players</u> who stand on the line of scrimmage are called the linemen.

EXERCISE 1 USING SUBJECTS CORRECTLY

Place a check mark in front of the correct sentence in each pair. An example is done for you.

✔ It was raining during the halftime show.

_____ Was raining during the halftime show.

_____ **1.** Football players need to take care of themselves because get hurt a lot.

✔   Football players need to take care of themselves because they get hurt a lot.

_____ **2.** Even when my brothers watch football, act as if they're playing it.

✔   Even when my brothers watch football, they act as if they're playing it.

✔ **3.** My favorite activity is watching professional football.

_____   My favorite activity I like to watch professional football.

_____ **4.** My goal it is to become a football coach.

✔   My goal is to become a football coach.

✔ **5.** My mother thinks football is too violent.

_____   My mother she thinks football is too violent.

Using Articles Correctly

Articles signal that a noun will follow. The **indefinite articles,** *a* and *an,* introduce a noun that cannot yet be specifically identified. Use *an* with a word that begins with a vowel (*a, e, i, o, u*) or a vowel sound.

<u>a</u> ball   <u>a</u> coach   <u>a</u> field   <u>a</u> sport   <u>a</u> player

<u>an</u> error   <u>an</u> injury   <u>an</u> ice pack   <u>an</u> elbow   <u>an</u> hour

These items could be *any* ball, coach, field, and so on. In using *a* or *an,* the writer does not identify any item in particular.

Tip: Even though *hour* begins with *h,* it takes *an* because the *h* is silent. The word *uniform* takes an *a* because it begins with a *y* sound.

The **definite article,** *the,* introduces a noun that refers to a specific, identifiable item.

<u>the</u> ball   <u>the</u> coach   <u>the</u> field   <u>the</u> error   <u>the</u> injury   <u>the</u> hour

In writing *<u>the</u> ball,* the writer has in mind a *particular* ball.

An article may come directly in front of a noun, or it can be separated from the noun by modifiers.

<u>a</u> new brown football

<u>an</u> exciting game

<u>the</u> experienced, overpaid coach

Using Articles with Nonspecific Nouns

A noun is **nonspecific** if the reader doesn't know its exact identity. Use *a* or *an* to introduce nonspecific nouns.

<u>A</u> football player is not allowed to bite his opponents. (The rule against biting refers to any football player, not one in particular.)

Using Articles with Specific Nouns

If a noun is **specific**—referring to something that can be identified in particular—use *the*. Here are some ways to identify a specific noun.

- From other information in the sentence.

    Watch me run into <u>the</u> middle of the football field during halftime. (*The* indicates that the "middle" is in the football field.)

- From other information in another sentence.

    I saw an exciting play on television. <u>The</u> play involved the quarterback and a wide receiver. (The play is the one mentioned in the previous sentence.)

- From general information.

    <u>The</u> force of gravity keeps us on <u>the</u> earth. (Here, *the* refers to "gravity" and "earth" because the reader can be expected to know what these are.)

- Before the superlative form of an adjective.

    <u>the</u> best day, <u>the</u> longest run

- Before numbers indicating sequence or order.

    <u>the</u> second step, <u>the</u> first time

Using Articles with Count and Noncount Nouns

Understanding count and noncount nouns helps you know when to use articles and what kind to use. **Count nouns** are nouns that identify people, places, things or ideas that can be numbered or counted and made plural.

five balls   three fields   two players

Determiners

Determiners are adjectives that *identify* rather than *modify* nouns.

Articles	a, an, the
Demonstrative pronouns	this, that, these, those
Possessive pronouns	my, our, your, his, her, its, their, mine, yours, hers, ours, theirs
Possessive nouns	Joe's, my mom's
Amounts	a few, a little, all, any, both, each, either, enough, every, few, little, many, much, neither, several, some, amount
Numerals	one, first, second, third, etc.

Noncount nouns refer to things that cannot be counted. For example, you cannot have *one* sunburn or *three* sweats.

sunburn   sweat   blood   fatigue

Noncount nouns cannot be given specific numbers to indicate amounts. However, their amounts can be described by using words that indicate non-specific amounts.

a bit   a little   a part of   a piece of   a section of   more   some

In the examples that follow, the modifiers are italicized, and the noncount nouns are underlined.

Tony felt *a bit of* <u>hunger</u> after playing football all day.

Examples of Noncount Nouns

Concepts and feelings	happiness, competition, ferocity, intelligence, athleticism
Activities	playing, cooking, watching, eating
Foods and drinks	meat, milk, chocolate, tea, water, lasagna
School courses	mathematics, English, French
Bulk materials	lumber, steel, concrete, grain, soil, wheat, flour
Weather	snow, sleet, hail, wind, thunder

During the winter, we received *more* <u>rain</u> than usual.

Only *a part of* the <u>class</u> wanted to study for the exam.

Some nouns can serve as both count and noncount nouns.

My mother uses different <u>flours</u> to make whole wheat bread. (*Flours* refers to individual types of flour, so it is a count noun).

<u>Flour</u> is an essential ingredient in my mother's bread. (*Flour* refers to a general concept; thus, it cannot be counted.)

Omitting Articles

Do not use articles with nonspecific plural nouns or nonspecific noncount nouns. (Plural nouns and noncount nouns are nonspecific when they indicate something in general.)

Nonspecific	**Specific**
<u>Plays</u> take place during the game.	*The* <u>plays</u> they made were tricky.
<u>Water</u> must be on hand for thirsty players.	*The* <u>water</u> is safe to drink.
<u>Coaches</u> in the NFL are fired and hired regularly.	*The* <u>coaches</u> for the Jaguars have experience.

Using Articles with Proper Nouns

Proper nouns—specific names of people, places, things, or ideas—are always capitalized. Most proper nouns do not require articles, but the following types use *the*.

- Plural proper nouns
  the Rockefellers   the Sawtooth Mountains
- Names of significant geographic areas
  the Sahara   the Southwest   the Pacific Ocean   the Seine River

Do not use *the* before the following types of nouns.

- Names of people and animals
  Joe Montana   Sparky
- Names of most places on land
  Europe   Florida   New York   Freeport Way   McKinley Park

■ Names of most countries

Canada   Vietnam   Mexico

Exception: the United States

■ Names of most bodies of water

Lake Norman   Niagara Falls   Folsom Lake

EXERCISE 2 CHOOSING THE CORRECT ARTICLE

Circle the correct answer from the words in parentheses.

1. The most necessary piece of equipment for the game of football is (the football, a football) itself.

2. (The pair of cleats, A pair of cleats) sat in my brother's closet for months until he bought a ball.

3. In colder parts of (the country, country), players must play in snow and freezing winds.

4. Playing in these conditions gives home teams in (the Wisconsin, Wisconsin) an advantage over warm-weather opponents.

5. Football players must have (the good attitude, a good attitude) no matter where they play.

Using Verbs Correctly

Every sentence must have a verb that is right for the sentence. In your writing, follow these guidelines.

■ Include verbs in all sentences.

■ Use the correct verb tense.

■ Use the progressive verb tense correctly.

Including Verbs in All Sentences

Every sentence must have a verb. Remember not to omit the *be* verbs (*am, is, are, was, were*).

| Incorrect: | Joe Montana's pass very good. | I a good wide receiver. |
| Correct: | Joe Montana's pass <u>was</u> very good. | I <u>am</u> a good wide receiver. |

Using the Correct Verb Tense

Verbs tell when the action of the sentence takes place. However, other words can also indicate time. Make sure that the verb tense makes sense with the rest of the sentence.

Incorrect:	Last week, I <u>see</u> a football game.
Correct:	Last week, I <u>saw</u> a football game. (The past tense verb *saw* is consistent with the time indicator *last week*.)
Incorrect:	Tomorrow I <u>played</u> catch with my brother. (The past tense verb *played* is inconsistent with the word *tomorrow*.)
Correct:	Tomorrow I <u>will play</u> catch with my brother.

Using the Progressive Verb Tense

The **progressive verb tense** consists of forms of the verb *be* and the *-ing* form (present participle) of the main verb. This tense indicates actions still occurring at a certain time.

Vinny Testaverde probably *will be* <u>playing</u> football in his fifties.

Verbs for the five senses, mental states, possession, and inclusion are not generally used in the progressive tense.

Incorrect:	I <u>am wishing</u> I could be a football player.
Correct:	I <u>wish</u> I could be a football player. (The word *wish* refers to a mental activity.)

Verbs Not Used in the Progressive Tense

Mental states	agree, believe, hate, imagine, know, like, love, prefer, think, understand, want, wish
Five senses	feel, hear, see, smell, taste, touch
Possession	belong, have, own, possess
Other verbs	be, contain, cost, have, include, mean, need, weigh

EXERCISE 3 USING CORRECT VERBS

Circle the correct verb form in each sentence.

1. Even after the game was over, I (hear, (heared)) the referee's whistle.

2. I (am seeing, (see)) football games on television every week.

3. The Super Bowl ((is my favorite), my favorite) of the year

4. Someday, my brother ((wants), is wanting) to play quarterback.

5. Yesterday, I ((watched,) watch) my favorite team lose a big game.

Using Adjectives Correctly

Adjectives—words that describe nouns or pronouns—and other modifiers usually come directly before or after nouns. Some modifiers need to be put in a specific order when they appear in a series.

■ **Articles and determiners** always come first in a series of adjectives.

the big strong football player

a brilliant coaching maneuver

an obvious mental error

■ **Nouns acting as adjectives** must come last in a series of adjectives.

the big strong <u>football</u> player (*Football* is an adjective describing *player.*)

a dark <u>coat</u> closet (*Coat* is an adjective describing *closet.*)

an enormous <u>shoe</u> size (*Shoe* is an adjective describing *size.*)

Other adjectives come between these two end points, typically in the following order.

1. Attitude, judgment, or opinion: lovely, difficult, kind, sweet, tough, beautiful, brutal

2. Size: big, small, gargantuan, Lilliputian, large, microscopic

3. Shape: oblong, cylindrical, rectangular, triangular, tall

4. Age: young, old, teenaged, preteen, adolescent, elderly

5. Color: red, white, blue, purple, pink

6. Nationality: German, Vietnamese, Russian, Cuban

7. Religion: Lutheran, Jewish, Buddhist, Catholic

Here are some examples of correctly ordered adjectives.

The <u>excellent young American football</u> *coach* was immediately successful.

He worked hard to recruit the <u>tough young high school</u> *players* for his team.

The coach wore <u>the striking orange nylon</u> *uniform* of his team.

EXERCISE 4 PLACING ADJECTIVES IN ORDER

Circle the correct choice in each sentence.

1. My family used to live behind (an old concrete football,) a concrete football old) stadium.

2. We could hear (the large noisy,) the noisy large) crowd cheering.

3. I appreciated the excitement that came from behind (the tall gray,) the gray tall) walls of the stadium.

4. I sneaked out my window—down (a wooden long, (a long wooden)) ladder—to go watch some games.

5. Though my ((stern Italian,) Italian stern) grandmother got mad at me, seeing the games was worth getting into trouble.

EXERCISE 5 WRITING ADJECTIVES IN CORRECT ORDER

In each sentence below, fill in the blank with three adjectives in the correct order. An example is done for you.   Answers will vary

The small young boy wanted to play on the high school football team.

1. He spent hours watching _the big tall_ players practicing their plays.

2. He finally worked up the courage to ask _a friendly football_ coach if he could try out for the team.

3. The coach gave the boy _an intense long_ look.

4. Then the coach muttered _an encouraging quick_ _____ answer.

5. _The eager new_ _____ member of the football team vowed to work as hard as he could to become a useful player.

Using Prepositions Correctly

From meaning alone, it can be hard to determine the correct preposition to use. Follow these guidelines for using the prepositions _at_, _in_, and _on_.

- _At_ can specify a certain point in time or space.

  The game begins <u>at</u> 6:00 p.m., so please be <u>at</u> the gate early.

- _In_ can specify stretches of time or space.

  I played football <u>in</u> high school <u>in</u> the 1990s.

- _On_ is used with names of streets (excluding precise addresses) and with days of the week or of the month. _On_ is also used to show an item's placement.

  When I lived <u>on</u> Mulberry Street, I placed a rocking chair <u>on</u> the front porch every year <u>on</u> July 4 to watch the fireworks.

EXERCISE 6 USING PREPOSITIONS

Circle the correct preposition in each sentence.

1. Whenever I watch football, I put my helmet (at, _on_) my head.

2. I did this a lot (_in_, at) the 1990s.

3. My brother said the game started (_at_, on) 7:00 p.m.

4. I watched the game (_at_, on) my friend's house.

5. My friend's house is (in, _on_) another street.

EDITING PRACTICE

Correct the underlined errors in the following paragraph.

American football

Many plays have made <u>football American</u> history. One of the

most famous plays is "the Catch." It took place at San Francisco's Candlestick Park ~~in~~ ^{on} January 10, 1982. The San Francisco Forty-Niners ~~trail~~ ^{trailed} the Dallas Cowboys 27 to 21 in a champi-onship game. Joe Montana, ~~medium-sized, wily~~ ^{wily, medium-sized} quarterback for the Forty-Niners, threw a pass that appeared to be heading for the stands. Wide receiver Dwight Clark, however, knew the ball was being thrown to him in the back of the end zone. The ~~experienced, tall~~ ^{tall, experienced,} Clark leaped as high as he could and, to his own amazement, made the catch. ~~Montana stunned~~ ^{Montana was stunned}, too. With the Catch, and the extra point, the Forty-Niners beat the Cowboys 28 to 27 and went on to beat the Cincinnati Bengals 26 to 21 in Super Bowl XVI. It was the first of four Super Bowl victories the Forty-Niners achieved ~~at~~ ⁱⁿ the 1980s. Historically, this game trans-formed the Forty-Niners into the great team who won five Super Bowl championships. ~~It where~~ ^{It was where} the legend really began. What few people consider is that the Forty-Niners ~~have~~ ^{had} good teams before 1981. It was just ~~that Cowboys~~ ^{that the Cowboys} denied them chances at Super Bowl glory. So "the Catch" not only symbolized the begin-ning of a great championship run but also marked the defeat of another great team, the Cowboys.

Lab Activity 56

For additional practice with tips for ESL writers, complete Lab Activity 56 in the Lab Manual at the back of the book.

PART NINE
Readings
for Informed Writing

HOW WE LEARN

WHAT WE VALUE

HOW WE LIVE

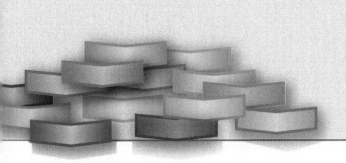

Tips for Reading Critically

Without realizing it, you have probably already engaged in critical reading. Every time you question a writer's credibility, you are reading critically. Critical reading is an essential skill that requires you to evaluate the information placed before you. The following suggestions can help you develop your critical reading skills.

1. **Read all titles, beginnings, and endings.** Such information gives you a preview of the upcoming section.

    - The title of a work gives a sense of the writer's tone and the scope of the information to follow.
    - Headings preview the main points and give a sense of the overall organization.
    - The first and last paragraphs often contain the main ideas.
    - Biographical or bibliographical material, which often appears at the end, reveals the context of the piece: when it was written, for whom it was written, why it was written.

2. **Prewrite.** Once you have a sense of where the writer is headed, spend a few minutes writing as quickly as you can about any ideas or questions that come to mind. What do you expect to learn from the material? What conclusions do you think the writer will reach? How relevant is the writer's message for you?

3. **Ask questions as you read.** After surveying the material, plunge in and read it from start to finish, keeping your prewriting ideas and questions in mind. What is the writer's primary argument? How is the writer developing his or her points? Is the writer fulfilling your expectations? How could the writer have been more persuasive?

4. **Ask how this reading relates to other material you've read.** Think about ideas that you have read or encountered before in your life, in other classes, and in other readings. Make notes in the margins so that

when you write a paragraph or essay based on a reading, you'll have clues about connections to outside material.

5. **Take notes as you read.** Use sticky notes, underline, or otherwise highlight key words, phrases, and ideas in the reading. Mark sentences that you think best reveal the writer's thesis, and identify examples that illustrate the main ideas. Make note of any questions that occur to you as you read. Identify words you are unfamiliar with and look them up in the dictionary later.

6. **Reread and rethink.** Just as you reread your own essays when you revise and clarify meaning, you should reread others' writings to make sure you fully understand the main ideas. A second reading can fill in any gaps in understanding.

7. **Write after you finish reading.** Summarize the main points, and ask yourself questions that will help you evaluate the content. Were your expectations fulfilled? Did the writer convince you of his or her point? What, if anything, made the writer's case most convincing? (Keep in mind that the strengths and weaknesses you note in others' writing can help you improve your own.)

8. **Talk it over.** Discuss the material with your classmates or friends. Talk about your impressions of the writer's argument. Share what you did or did not like or agree with in the piece, and then move on to how you formed those opinions. As you gather viewpoints, you may decide to revise or defend your own position.

How We Learn

One of the most important decisions we can make is how we plan to educate ourselves. Some people opt for formal education and spend years in school accumulating knowledge. The essays "Education," "Freedom," and "How I Started Writing Poetry" explore the realm of formal education. Other people choose to learn a hands-on trade, such as plumbing or carpentry. In these cases, people must learn to work with their hands, often forgoing the classroom for the shop or the workroom. " "A Homemade Education," and "All I Really Need to Know I Learned in Kindergarten" explain how lessons learned from "real life" are every bit as valuable as those learned in school. Finally, within education, several issues rear their heads as students attempt to sort out what they need to learn. "A Uniform Policy," "Education," "Hold Your Horsepower," "Grades and Self-Esteem," and "A Homemade Education" explore the relevance of outside influences such as school uniforms and car ownership on a student's academic performance and overall well-being.

Readings in This Section

1. "All I Really Need to Know I Learned in Kindergarten," *Robert Fulghum*
2. "A Homemade Education," *Malcolm X*
3. "How I Started Writing Poetry," *Reginald Lockett*
4. "Education," *E. B. White*
5. "Hold Your Horsepower," *Lyla Fox*
6. "Grades and Self-Esteem," *Randy Moore*

Robert Fulghum

From *All I Really Need to Know I Learned in Kindergarten*

Robert Fulghum describes himself as a philosopher. Over the course of his life he has held many jobs, ranging from cowboy to IBM salesman. He has also published essays and written for the theater. In this excerpt from *All I Really Need to Know I Learned in Kindergarten*, Fulghum distills his personal credo down into several simple rules that apply to all aspects of life.

BEFORE YOU READ

Think about the following questions. Write your responses on a separate sheet or in your journal.

- Make a list of any lessons or rules you learned as a young child that you think are still relevant today. Who taught you these rules?
- What about these rules made them relevant for you when you learned them?
- What makes them relevant for you now?

VOCABULARY DEVELOPMENT

Look up the following words in a dictionary. Write down their meanings on a separate sheet or in your journal.

credo (paragraph 1)   cynical (paragraph 2)

naïve (paragraph 2)   idealism (paragraph 2)

brevity (paragraph 3)   existential (paragraph 3)

extrapolate (paragraph 7)

"All I Really Need to Know I Learned in Kindergarten"

1   Each spring, for many years, I have set myself the task of writing a personal statement of belief: a Credo. When I was younger, the statement ran for many pages, trying to cover every base, with no loose ends. It sounded like a Supreme Court brief, as if words could resolve all conflicts about the meaning of existence.

2   The Credo has grown shorter in recent years—sometimes cynical, sometimes comical, sometimes bland—but I keep working at it. Recently I set out to get the statement of personal belief down to one page in simple terms, fully understanding the naïve idealism that implied.

3   The inspiration for brevity came to me at a gasoline station. I managed to fill an old car's tank with super-deluxe high-octane go-juice. My old hoopy couldn't handle it and got the willies—kept sputtering out at intersections and belching going downhill. I understood. My mind and my spirit get like that from time to time. Too much high-content information, and *I* get the existential willies—keep sputtering out at intersections where life choices must be made and I either know too much or not enough. The examined life is no picnic.

4   I realized then that I already know most of what's necessary to live a meaningful life—that it isn't all that complicated. *I know it*. And have known it for a long, long time. Living it—well, that's another matter, yes? Here's my Credo:

5   All I really need to know about how to live and what to do and how to be I learned in kindergarten. Wisdom was not at the top of the graduate-school mountain, but there in the sandpile at Sunday School. These are the things I learned:

Share everything.
Play fair.
Don't hit people.
Put things back where you found them.
Clean up your own mess.
Don't take things that aren't yours.
Say you're sorry when you hurt somebody.
Wash your hands before you eat.
Flush.
Warm cookies and cold milk are good for you.
Live a balanced life—learn some and think some and draw and paint and sing and dance and play and work every day some.
Take a nap every afternoon.
When you go out into the world, watch out for traffic, hold hands, and stick together.
Be aware of wonder. Remember the little seed in the Styrofoam cup: The roots go down and the plant goes up and nobody really knows how or why, but we are all like that.
Goldfish and hamsters and white mice and even the little seed in the Styrofoam cup—they all die. So do we.
And then remember the Dick-and-Jane books and the first word you learned—the biggest word of all—LOOK.

6   Everything you need to know is in there somewhere. The Golden Rule and love and basic sanitation. Ecology and politics and equality and sane living.

7   Take any one of those items and extrapolate it into sophisticated adult terms and apply it to your family life or your work or your government or your world and it holds true and clear and firm. Think what a better world it would be if we all—the whole world—had cookies and milk about three

o'clock every afternoon and then lay down with our blankies for a nap. Or if all governments had as a basic policy to always put things back where they found them and clean up their own mess.

8   And it is still true, no matter how old you are—when you go out into the world, it is best to hold hands and stick together.

AFTER YOU READ

Vocabulary Practice

1. Choose at least three words from the Vocabulary Development list on page 718 and write sentences using those words. You may write one sentence using all three words if you wish.   Answers will vary.

2. What word from the Vocabulary Development list means "believing that people are motivated in all their actions only by selfishness"? Use the word in a sentence that clearly shows its meaning.   Cynical. Answers will vary.

3. Fulghum claims that his kindergarten-learned lessons are important, yet his language reveals an audience of people who are not children. Choose at least three words or phrases from the essay and explain in a few sentences how these terms reveal Fulghum's intended audience.   Answers will vary.

Comprehension

Circle the correct answer.

1. Fulghum writes his credo every

    a. fall.   b. winter.

    c. spring.   d. summer.

2. Fulghum defines his credo as

    a. a personal statement of belief.

    b. a personal statement of goals.

    c. a personal list of complaints.

    d. a personal list of blessings.

3. The inspiration for Fulghum's latest credo came from his

    a. house.   b. office.

    c. bicycle.   d. car.

4. Which one of these rules is not part of Fulghum's credo?

    a. Play fair.

    b. Don't hit people.

      (c.) Feel proud of yourself for good deeds.

      d. Take a nap every afternoon.

5. What does Fulghum say is "the first word you learned—the biggest word of all"?

      a. Wait   b. Love

      c. Forgive   (d.) Look

Content

1. How often does Fulghum write his personal credo? *Every year*
2. What changes has his credo undergone over the years? *Shorter, longer, more and less cynical*
3. What are at least three lessons in Fulghum's credo? *Answers will vary.*

Style and Structure

1. To show how most important lessons are ones we already know
2. For adult readers who are interested in understanding their lives
3. Gas in his car; blankies and a nap. He wants to show that important lessons come from simple places.

1. What is Fulghum's purpose in writing this essay?

2. Whom is Fulghum writing his essay for? How can you tell?

3. Fulghum uses "the sandpile at Sunday School" to illustrate one of his ideas. What other specific details does Fulghum use? Why do you think he chooses such familiar images? Explain.

Writing Assignments

1. Fulghum claims that all he really needs to know he learned in kindergarten. Do you agree with him? *Write a paragraph agreeing or disagreeing with the idea that kindergarten has taught you the most important lessons of your life.* Be sure to use examples from your life to support your ideas.

2. What person or situation has taught you the most valuable lessons? *Write a paragraph explaining how a specific person or situation has taught you a valuable lesson.* Use details from your experience and observations to illustrate your ideas.

3. Although many lessons may be learned from teachers or parents, must some be learned through experience? What are these? *Write an essay explaining how some lessons must be learned through experience.* (If you believe that all lessons can be learned from teachers or parents, explain which lessons are easiest for teachers or parents to teach children.) Use specific details from your experience and observations to support your ideas.

Malcolm X

"A Homemade Education" from *The Autobiography of Malcolm X*

When Malcolm X was born in Omaha, Nebraska, in 1925, his name was Malcolm Little. His father was a minister, and he spent his early years in middle America. When his father died, Malcolm X became involved in street life and was sent to prison for burglary. His prison time, however, was a turning point in his life. Malcolm X began corresponding with Elijah Muhammad, leader of the Black Muslim movement. Eventually, he became a militant leader of the Black Revolution, rejecting the surname "Little" as his slave name and calling himself "Malcolm X." His assertion that African-Americans must gain their rights "by any means necessary" became one of his defining statements. Malcolm X was assassinated in 1965.

BEFORE YOU READ

Think about the following questions. Write your responses on a separate sheet or in your journal.

■ What kinds of educational experiences have you had? What have your parents, friends, or other acquaintances taught you? What kinds of formal schooling have you had?

■ What lessons have proved to be the most valuable to you? How did you learn them?

■ What type of education is more valuable to you: formal (in school) or informal (friends, family, and work, for instance)? Explain.

VOCABULARY DEVELOPMENT

Look up the following words in a dictionary. Write down their meanings on a separate sheet or in your journal.

stumble (paragraph 3)　　　　　　acquire (paragraph 4)

convey (paragraph 6)　　　　　　　emulate (paragraph 6)

immensely (paragraph 10)

"A Homemade Education"

1　　It was because of my letters that I happened to stumble upon starting to acquire some kind of homemade education.

2　　I became increasingly frustrated at not being able to express what I wanted to convey in letters that I wrote, especially those to Mr. Elijah

Muhammad. In the street, I had been the most articulate hustler out there—I had commanded attention when I said something. But now, trying to write simple English, I not only wasn't articulate, I wasn't even functional. How would I sound writing in slang, the way I would *say* it, something such as, "Look, daddy, let me pull your coat about a cat, Elijah Muhammad—"

3   Many who today hear me somewhere in person, or on television, or those who read something I've said, will think I went to school far beyond the eighth grade. This impression is due entirely to my prison studies.

4   It had really begun back in Charlestown Prison, when Bimbi first made me feel envy of his stock of knowledge. Bimbi had always taken charge of any conversation he was in, and I had tried to emulate him. But every book I picked up had few sentences which didn't contain anywhere from one to nearly all of the words that might as well have been in Chinese. When I just skipped those words, of course, I really ended up with little idea of what the book said. So I had come to the Norfolk Prison Colony still going through only book-reading motions. Pretty soon, I would have quit even these motions unless I had received the motivation that I did.

5   I saw that the best thing I could do was get hold of a dictionary—to study to learn some words. I was lucky enough to reason also that I should try to improve my penmanship. It was sad. I couldn't even write in a straight line. It was both ideas together that moved me to request a dictionary along with some tablets and pencils from the Norfolk Prison Colony school.

6   I spent two days just riffling uncertainly through the dictionary's pages. I'd never realized so many words existed! I didn't know *which* words I needed to learn. Finally, just to start some kind of action, I began copying.

7   In my slow, painstaking, ragged handwriting, I copied into my tablet everything printed on that first page, down to the punctuation marks.

8   I believe it took me a day. Then, aloud, I read back, to myself, everything I'd written on the tablet. Over and over, aloud, to myself, I read my own handwriting.

9   I woke up the next morning, thinking about those words—immensely proud to realize that not only had I written so much at one time, but I'd written words that I never knew were in the world. Moreover, with a little effort, I also could remember what many of these words meant. I reviewed the words whose meanings I didn't remember. Funny thing, from the dictionary's first page right now, that "aardvark" springs to my mind. The dictionary had a picture of it, a long-tailed, long-eared, burrowing African mammal, which lives off termites caught by sticking out its tongue as an anteater does for ants.

10   I was so fascinated that I went on—I copied the dictionary's next page. And the same experience came when I studied that. With every succeeding page, I also learned of people and places and events from history. Actually the dictionary is like a miniature encyclopedia. Finally the dictionary's A section had filled a whole tablet—and I went on into the B's. That was the

way I started copying what eventually became the entire dictionary. It went a lot faster after so much practice helped me to pick up handwriting speed. Between what I wrote in my tablet, and writing letters, during the rest of my time in prison I would guess I wrote a million words.

11   I suppose it was inevitable that as my word-base broadened, I could for the first time pick up a book and read and now begin to understand what the book was saying. Anyone who has read a great deal can imagine the new world that opened. Let me tell you something: from then until I left that prison, in every free moment I had, if I was not reading in the library, I was reading on my bunk. You couldn't have gotten me out of books with a wedge. Between Mr. Muhammad's teachings, my correspondence, my visitors—usually Ella and Reginald—and my reading of books, months passed without my even thinking about being imprisoned. In fact, up to then, I had never been so truly free in my life.

AFTER YOU READ

Vocabulary Practice

1. Choose at least three words from the Vocabulary Development list on page 722, and write sentences using those words. You may write one sentence using all three words if you wish.

2. Which word on the Vocabulary Development list means "to try to equal or surpass"? Use this word in a sentence that shows clearly what the word means.

3. What does the expression "Look, daddy, let me pull your coat about a cat, Elijah Muhammad—" indicate about Malcolm X's language? What kind of education does this expression reveal?   *Emulate*   He was fluent in slang, educated on the street.

Comprehension

Circle the correct answer.

1. Where was Malcolm X when he first decided to improve his reading and writing?
   a. In church   b. At home
   c. In prison   d. On the street

2. In order to improve his reading skills, Malcolm X began to read
   a. the Bible.   b. a dictionary.
   c. an encyclopedia.   d. letters from Bimbi.

3. Another skill Malcolm X practiced as he read was
   a. his penmanship.   b. his pronunciation.
   c. his facial expressions.   d. his posture.

4. Besides copying words, Malcolm X also wrote
   a. poetry.   b. songs.
   (c.) letters.   d. stories.

5. Malcolm X spent much of his free time
   a. praying.   b. speaking.
   c. singing.   (d.) reading.

Content

1. What were the initial problems that Malcolm X had with reading? How did these problems lead him to improve his vocabulary? He couldn't understand many words.

2. What steps did Malcolm X take to improve his vocabulary? What other improvements occurred as a result of his vocabulary improvement efforts? Requested paper, pencils, dictionary from prison and copied dictionary. He learned to read and write.

3. How did Malcolm X feel after he had copied the first full page of the dictionary? After reading extensively? Proud of himself; free

Style and Structure

1. What is the main idea of Malcolm X's essay? Restate his main idea in your own words. Taking responsibility for his education freed him from ignorance.

2. What transitions does Malcolm X use to lead the reader from step to step in his educational process? Look particularly closely in paragraphs 4, 9, and 10 for examples of specific transitions. Pretty soon, Moreover, Finally

3. What words or expressions does Malcolm X use that suggest that he is educated? What elements suggest that he is being informal, or conversational, in his writing? Answers will vary. Immensely, convey, use of first person, explanatory tone; "Look, daddy," "Funny thing"

Writing Assignments

1. Malcolm X writes that until he began understanding what he read, he "had never been so truly free" even though he was still in prison. *Write a paragraph in which you explain how reading, or any kind of intellectual activity, can make you "free."* Be sure to use examples from your own life in order to illustrate your points.

2. Think about the ways you have taken responsibility for your own education. *Then, write an essay explaining the steps you have taken to improve yourself as a student.* Consider your study habits, your writing habits, your social habits, your sleep habits, and any other habits that affect you as a student. Use details from your own experiences and observations to clearly present all the steps in your process.

3. Malcolm X writes that people who heard him speak often thought he had completed more formal education than he had. *Write a short essay in which*

you explain what qualities make a person seem "educated." Be sure to define what you mean by *educated* and then use your own experiences and observations in order to give proof for your ideas.

Reginald Lockett

"How I Started Writing Poetry"

A prolific writer with an urban heritage, Reginald Lockett's poetry, reviews, and prose have been widely published. Telling the stories of people who "don't make the news," Lockett uses rhythm and street language to make his works come alive. Currently, Lockett teaches at San Jose City College; his published books include *Good Time & No Bread, Where the Birds Sing Bass, and The Party Crashers of Paradise.* In this essay, Lockett examines the process by which he began writing poetry.

BEFORE YOU READ

- Explain how you became interested in a current activity or topic.
- To what extent, now or in the past, have you tried to project a particular image? Explain.
- What is your gut reaction to the word *poetry*?

VOCABULARY DEVELOPMENT

Look up the following words in a dictionary and write down their meanings:

cultivated (paragraph 1)	façade (paragraph 1)
prevalent (paragraph 1)	despicable (paragraph 1)
intriguing (paragraph 5)	continuous (paragraph 6)
delinquency (paragraph 6)	loathsome (paragraph 6)
tribute (paragraph 8)	roguish (paragraph 10)

"How I Started Writing Poetry"

1   At the age of fourteen I was what Richard Pryor over a decade later would call "going for bad" or what my southern-bred folks said was "smellin' your pee." That is, I had cultivated a facade of daring-do, hip, cool, con man bravado so prevalent among adolescent males in West Oakland. I "talked that talk and walked that walk" most parents found downright despicable. In their minds these were dress rehearsals of fantasies that were

Popsicles that would melt and evaporate under the heat of blazing hot real-
ities. And there I was doing the pimp limp and talking about nothing profound or sustaining. All I wanted to do was project that image of being
forever cool like Billy Boo, who used to wear three T-shirts, two slipover
sweaters and a thick Pendleton shirt tucked neatly in his khaki or black Ben
Davidsons to give everybody the impression that he was buffed (muscle
bound) and definitely not to be messed with. Cool. Real cool. Standing in
front of the liquor store on 35th and San Pablo sipping white port and
lemon juice, talking smack by the boat-loads until some *real* hoodlum from
Campbell Village (or was it Harbor Homes?) with the real biceps, the shonuff triceps and sledgehammer fists beat the shirt, both sweaters, the T-shirts
and pants right off of Billy Boo's weak, bony body.

2   Herbert Hoover Junior High, the school I attended, was considered one
of the toughest in Oakland at that time. It was a dirty, gray, forbidding-look-
ing place where several fights would break out every day. There was a joke
going around that a mother, new to the city, mistook it for the Juvenile
Detention Center that was further down in West Oakland on 18th and
Poplar, right across the street from DeFremery Park.

3   During my seventh-grade year there were constant referrals to the principal's office for any number of infractions committed either in Miss Oka-
mura's third-period music class or Mrs. George's sixth-period math class in
the basement, where those of us with behavioral problems and assumed
learning disabilities were sent. It was also around this time that Harvey Hen-
dricks, my main running buddy, took it upon himself to hip me to everything
he thought I needed to know about sex while we were doing a week's detention in Mrs. Balasco's art class for capping on "them steamer trunks" or "suit-
cases" under her eyes. As we sat there, supposedly writing "I will not insult
the teacher" one hundred times, Harvey would draw pictures of huge tits
and vaginas, while telling me how to rap, kiss, and jump off in some twanks
and stroke. Told me that the pimples on my face were "pussy bumps," and
that I'd better start getting some trim or end up just like Crater Face Jerome
with the big, nasty-looking quarter-size pus bumps all over his face.

4   Though my behavior left a lot to be desired, I managed to earn some
fairly decent grades. I loved history, art and English, and somehow managed to work my way up from special education classes to college prep
courses by the time I reached ninth grade, my last year at Hoover. But by
then I had become a full-fledged little thug, and had been suspended—and
damn near expelled—quite a few times for going to knuckle city at the drop
of a hat for any real or imagined reason. And what an efficient thief I'd
become. This was something I'd picked up from my cousins, R. C. and
Danny, when I started hanging out with them on weekends in San Francisco's Haight-Ashbury. We'd steal clothes, records, liquor, jewelry—anything for the sake of magnifying to the umpteenth degree that image of
death-defying manhood and to prove I was indeed a budding Slick Draw

McGraw. Luckily, I was never caught, arrested and hauled off to Juvenile Hall or the California Youth Authority like so many of the guys I ran with.

5   Probably through pressure from my parents and encouragement from my teachers and counselors, I forced myself to start thinking about pursuing a career after graduation from high school, which was three years away. Reaching into the grab bag of professional choices, I decided I wanted to become a physician, since doctors were held in such high esteem, particularly in an Afro-American community like West Oakland. I'd gotten it in my head that I wanted to be a plastic surgeon, no less, because I liked working with my hands and found science intriguing. Then something strange happened.

6   Maybe it was the continuous violence, delinquency and early pregnancies that made those Oakland Unified School District administrators (more than likely after some consultation with psychologists) decide to put a little Freudian theory to practical use. Just as I was grooving, really getting into this fantastic project in fourth-period art class, I was called up to the teacher's desk and handed a note and told to report to a classroom downstairs on the first floor. What had I done this time? Was it because I snatched Gregory Jones' milkshake during lunch a couple of days ago and gulped it down, savoring every drop like an old loathsome suck-egg dog, and feeling no pain as the chump, big as he was, stood there and cried? And Mr. Foltz, the principal, was known to hand out mass suspensions. Sometimes fifteen, twenty, twenty-five people at a time. But when I entered the classroom, there sat this tall, gangly, goofy-looking white woman who wore her hair unusually long for that time, had thick glasses and buckteeth like the beaver on the Ipana Toothpaste commercials. Some of the roughest, toughest kids that went to Hoover were in there. Especially big old mean, ugly Martha Dupree who was known to knock out boys, girls, and teachers when she got the urge. If Big Martha asked you for a last-day-of-school kiss, you'd better give it up or make an appointment with your dentist.

7   When Miss Nettelbeck finally got our attention, she announced that this was a creative writing class that would meet twice a week. Creative writing? What the hell is creative writing a couple of us asked. She explained that it was a way to express what was on your mind, and a better way of getting something off of your chest instead of beating up your fellow students. Then she read a few poems to us and passed out some of that coarse school-issue lined paper and told us to write about something we liked, disliked, or really wanted. What I wanted to know was, did it have to be one of "them pomes." "If that's how you want to express yourself, Reginald," she said. So I started racking my brain, trying to think about what I liked, didn't like and what I really wanted. Well, I liked football, track and Gayle Johnson, who would turn her cute little "high yella" nose up in total disgust every time I tried to say something to her. I couldn't stand the sight—not even the thought—of old monkey-face Martha. And what I really wanted was either a '57 Buick Roadmaster or a '56 Chevy with mag wheels and tuck 'n' roll

seats that was dropped in the front like the ones I'd seen older dudes like Mack's brother, Skippy, riding around in. Naw, I told myself, I couldn't get away with writing about things like that. I might get into some more trouble, and Big Martha would give me a thorough ass-kicking for writing something about mashing her face in some dough and baking me some gorilla cookies. Who'd ever heard of a poem about cars? One thing I really liked was the ocean. I guess that was in my blood because my father was then a master chief steward in the navy, and, when I was younger, would take me aboard ships docked at Hunter's Point and Alameda. I loved the sea so much that I would sometimes walk from my house on Market and West MacArthur all the way to the Berkeley Pier or take a bus to Ocean Beach in San Francisco whenever I wasn't up to no good. So I wrote:

> *I sit on a rock*
> *watching*
> *the evening tide*
> *come in.*
> *The green waves travel*
> *with the wind.*
> *They seem to carry*
> *a message of*
> *warning, of plea*
> *from the dimensions*
> *of time and distance.*

8   When I gave it to Miss Nettelbeck, she read it and told me it was good for a first attempt at writing poetry, and since there was still some time left in the period, I should go back to my seat and write something else. Damn! These teachers never gave you any kind of slack, no matter what you did and how well you did it. Now, what else could I think of to write about? How about a tribute to Miss Bobby, the neighborhood drag queen, who'd been found carved up like a Christmas turkey a week ago? Though me, Harvey and Mack used to crack jokes about, "her" giving up the boodie, we still liked and respected "her" because she would give you five or six dollars to run an errand to the cleaners or the store, never tried to hit on you, and would get any of the other "girls" straight real quick if they even said you were cute or something. So I wrote:

> *Bring on the hustle*
> *In Continental suits*
> *And alligator shoes*
> *Let fat ladies of the night*
> *In short, tight dresses*
> *And spiked heels enter.*
> *We are gathered here*

To pay tribute to
The Queen of Drag.

What colorful curtains
And rugs!
Look at the stereo set
And the clothes in the closet.
On the bed, entangled
In a bloody sheet,
Is that elegant one
Of ill repute
But good carriage
Oh yes! There
Was none like her.
The Queen of Drag.

9   When she read that one, I just knew Miss Nettelbeck would immediately write a referral and have me sent back upstairs. But she liked it and said I was precocious for someone at such an innocent age. Innocent! When was I ever innocent? I was guilty of just about everything I was accused of doing. Like, get your eyes checked, baby. And what was precocious? Was it something weird? Did it mean I was queer like Miss Bobby? Was I about to go to snap city like poor Donny Moore had a year ago when he suddenly got up and started jacking off in front of Mr. Lee's history class? What did this woman, who looked and dressed like one of them beatniks I'd seen one night on *East Side, West Side,* mean? My Aunt Audry's boyfriend, Joe, told me beatniks were smart and used a lot of big words like precocious so nobody could understand what they were talking about. Had to be something bad. This would mess with me for the rest of the week if I didn't ask her what she meant. So I did, and she told me it meant that I knew about things somebody my age didn't usually know about. Wow! That could only mean that I was "hip to the lip." But I already knew that.

10   For some reason I wasn't running up and down the streets with the fellas much anymore. Harvey would get bent out of shape every time I'd tell him I had something else to do. I had to, turning punkish or seeing some broad I was too chinchy to introduce him to. This also bothered my mother because she kept telling me I was going to ruin my eyes if I didn't stop reading so much; and what was that I spent all my spare time writing in a manila notebook? Was I keeping a diary or something? Only girls kept diaries, people may start thinking I was one of "them sissy mens" if I didn't stop. Even getting good grades in citizenship and making the honor roll didn't keep her off my case. But I kept right on reading and writing, looking forward to Miss Nettelbeck's class twice a week. I stopped fighting, too. But I was still roguish as ever. Instead of raiding Roger's Men's Shop. Smith's and Flagg Brothers' Shoes, I

was stealing books by just about every poet and writer Miss Nettelbeck read to the class. That's how I started writing poetry.

AFTER YOU READ

Vocabulary Practice

Answers will vary.

1. Choose at least three words from the list and write sentences using those words. You may write one sentence using all three words if you wish.

2. What word from the Vocabulary Development list means "to surpass in rank, dignity, or importance"? Use the word in a sentence to show clearly what it means.   Precede, answers will vary.

3. What are some terms that Lockett uses that show his "street" background? His intelligence? List five words to illustrate each quality.   Answers will vary. Shonuff triceps, Knuckle city, I was grooving, suck-egg dog, chump; despicable, bravado so prevalent, pursuing a career, continuous violence, delinquency and early pregnancies.

Comprehension

1. Which of the following is NOT an example of Lockett's "little thug" behavior?

   a. Fighting
   b. Stealing
   c. Using a gun
   d. Drinking someone else's milkshake

2. What reason does Lockett give for his early illegal acts?

   a. Trying to appear cool
   b. Trying to protect his territory
   c. Trying to protect his friends
   d. Trying to become a gang leader

3. Which topic below does Lockett consider write his first poem about?

   a. Big Martha Dupree
   b. Football and track
   c. '57 Buick Roadmaster
   d. The ocean

4. What word does Miss Nettleneck use to describe Lockett?

   a. perceptive
   b. precocious
   c. presumptuous
   d. pretentious

5. What were Lockett's parents' initial reactions to his new interest in school?

   a. They were enthusiastic.
   b. They were proud.
   c. They were worried.
   d. They were jealous.

Content

He was trying to be cool.

1. Why does Lockett say he "talked that talk and walked that walk" that most parents found "downright despicable"?

A creative writing course.

2. What changed Lockett's focus from street-related activities to writing?

3. How does Lockett's stealing change over the course of the essay? How is this significant of his personal changes?   At first he steals "anything" for the sake of proving he's cool—clothes, records, liquor, jewelry; later he steals poetry books. The change in stealing shows his change in interest.

Style and Structure

Many steps led to Lockett's starting to write poetry.

1. What is Lockett's main point? Rewrite it in your own words.

2. What steps, or stages, in his movement toward becoming a poet does Lockett develop?

3. Lockett uses slang in some places. How effective is it? Find some examples of Lockett's slang and discuss how effective they are.

> 2. At age 14 he tried to be cool and was often in trouble; he loved history, art, and English and earned good grades; starting thinking about a career; placed in creative writing course; wrote two poems; learned he was "precocious"; started stealing poetry books.
> 3. Answers will vary. "Smellin' your pee," "thug," "knuckle city," "suck-egg dog," "high yella," "ass-kicking," "snap city," "mess with me," "hip to the lip," turning punkish, "chinchy".

Writing Assignments

1. Lockett writes of how he projected an image to seem cool but eventually stopped "running up and down the stress with the fellas." *Write an essay explaining how you consciously changed your image at a certain point in your life. If you never changed your image, explain why you always maintained the same image.* Be sure to use examples from your own experiences and observations to illustrate your ideas.

2. By taking a creative writing course and reading, Lockett became a writer. *Write an essay explaining the process by which you learned, improved, or became something.* Be sure to use examples from your own experiences and observations to illustrate your ideas.

3. Lockett writes of various people—Billy Boo, his parents, Miss Nettleneck—who influenced him at various stages in his life. Who has influenced you? *Write an essay about the person or people who have been most influential to you and why.* Be sure to use examples from your own experiences and observations to illustrate your ideas.

E. B. White

"Education"

A well-known essayist and contributing editor to *The New Yorker*, E. B. White authored many works. Some of his best-known and most loved works are the children's tales *Stuart Little* and *Charlotte's Web*. He also revised William Strunk's work *The Elements of Style* and wrote the satire *Is Sex Necessary?* with James Thurber.

BEFORE YOU READ

Think about the following questions. Write your responses on a separate sheet or in your journal.

■ What does it mean to be educated? Who determines whether or not a person is educated?

■ What are some ways people can be educated?

■ What experience or situation was the most educational for you? Explain.

⬡ VOCABULARY DEVELOPMENT

Look up the following words in a dictionary. Write down their meanings on a separate sheet or in your journal.

Augean (paragraph 1)	bias (paragraph 2)
regimented (paragraph 2)	seminary (paragraph 3)
sallied (paragraph 3)	punctual (paragraph 3)
incubation (paragraph 3)	esoteric (paragraph 4)
apprehensive (paragraph 6)	laconic (paragraph 6)

"Education"

1   I have an increasing admiration for the teacher in the country school where we have a third-grade scholar in attendance. She not only undertakes to instruct her charges in all the subjects of the first three grades, but she manages to function quietly and effectively as a guardian of their health, their clothes, their habits, their mothers, and their snowball engagements. She has been doing this sort of Augean task for twenty years, and is both kind and wise. She cooks for the children on the stove that heats the room, and she can cool their passions or warm their soup with equal competence. She conceives their costumes, cleans up their messes, and shares their confidences. My boy already regards his teacher as his great friend, and I think tells her a great deal more than he tells us.

2   The shift from city school to country school was something we worried about quietly all last summer. I have always rather favored public school over private school, if only because in public school you meet a greater variety of children. This bias of mine, I suspect, is partly an attempt to justify my own past (I never knew anything but public schools) and partly an involuntary defense against getting kicked in the shins by a young ceramist on his way to the kiln. My wife was unacquainted with public schools, never having been exposed (in her early life) to anything more public than the washroom of Miss Winsor's. Regardless of our backgrounds, we both knew that the change in schools was something that concerned not us but the scholar himself. We hoped it would work out all right. In New York our son went to a medium-priced private institution with semi-progressive ideas of education, and modern plumbing. He learned fast, kept well, and we were satisfied. It was an electric, colorful, regimented existence with moments of pleasurable pause and giddy incident. The day the Christmas angel fainted and had to be carried out by one of the Wise Men was education in the highest sense of the

term. Our scholar gave imitations of it around the house for weeks afterward, and I doubt if it ever goes completely out of his mind.

3   His days were rich in formal experience. Wearing overalls and an old sweater (the accepted uniform of the private seminary), he sallied forth at morn accompanied by a nurse or a parent and walked (or was pulled) two blocks to a corner where the school bus made a flag stop. This flashy vehicle was as punctual as death: seeing us waiting at the cold curb, it would sweep to a halt, open its mouth, suck the boy in, and spring away with an angry growl. It was a good deal like a train picking up a bag of mail. At school the scholar was worked on for six or seven hours by half a dozen teachers and a nurse, and was revived on orange juice in mid-morning. In a cinder court he played games supervised by an athletic instructor, and in a cafeteria he ate lunch worked out by a dietitian. He soon learned to read with gratifying facility and discernment and to make Indian weapons of a semi-deadly nature. Whenever one of his classmates fell low of a fever the news was put on the wires and there were breathless phone calls to physicians, discussing periods of incubation and allied magic.

4   In the country all one can say is that the situation is different, and somehow more casual. Dressed in corduroys, sweatshirt, and short rubber boots, and carrying a tin dinner-pail, our scholar departs at the crack of dawn for the village school, two and a half miles down the road, next to the cemetery. When the road is open and the car will start, he makes the journey by motor, courtesy of his old man. When the snow is deep or the motor is dead or both, he makes it on the hoof. In the afternoons he walks or hitches all or part of the way home in fair weather, gets transported in foul. The schoolhouse is a two-room frame building, bungalow type, shingles stained a burnt brown with weather-resistant stain. It has a chemical toilet in the basement and two teachers above the stairs. One takes the first three grades, the other the fourth, fifth, and sixth. They have little or no time for individual instruction, and no time at all for the esoteric. They teach what they know themselves, just as fast and as hard as they can manage. The pupils sit still at their desks in class, and do their milling around outdoors during recess.

5   There is no supervised play. They play cops and robbers (only they call it "Jail") and throw things at one another—snowballs in winter, rose hips in fall. It seems to satisfy them. They also construct darts, pinwheels, and "pick-up sticks" (jackstraws), and the school itself does a brisk trade in penny candy, which is for sale right in the classroom and which contains "surprises." The most highly prized surprise is a fake cigarette, made of cardboard, fiendishly lifelike.

6   The memory of how apprehensive we were at the beginning is still strong. The boy was nervous about the change too. The tension, on that first fair morning in September when we drove him to school, almost blew the windows out of the sedan. And when later we picked him up on the road, wandering along with his little blue lunch-pail, and got his laconic report "All right" in answer to our inquiry about how the day had gone, our relief

was vast. Now, after almost a year of it, the only difference we can discover in the two school experiences is that in the country he sleeps better at night—and *that* probably is more the air than the education. When grilled on the subject of school-in-country vs. school-in-city, he replied that the chief difference is that the day seems to go so much quicker in the country. "Just like lightning," he reported.

◉ AFTER YOU READ

Vocabulary Practice

1. Choose at least three words from the Vocabulary Development list on page 733 and write sentences using those words. You may write one sentence using all three words if you wish.   Answers will vary.

2. Laconic. Answers will vary.

2. Which word on the Vocabulary Development list means "brief or terse in speech"? Use the word in a sentence that clearly shows its meaning.

3. White uses the terms "punctual as death," "with an angry growl," "picking up a bag of mail," and "the scholar was worked on" to describe aspects of his son's private school experience. On the basis of these terms, what do you think White's view of the school is?   Efficient but impersonal; adequate but not warm

Comprehension

Circle the correct answer.

1. White opens his essay with a description of
   - a. his son's teacher.
   - b. his own childhood teacher.
   - c. himself as a teacher.
   - d. his son.

2. What is White's attitude toward his son's teacher?
   - a. He thinks she is lazy.
   - b. He thinks she is unintelligent.
   - c. He admires her.
   - d. He thinks she is attractive.

3. Why does White say he favors public school?
   - a. His wife attended public school.
   - b. He was a teacher at a public school.
   - c. Students meet a greater variety of children in public school.
   - d. Students have more freedom at a public school.

4. Which one of the following aspects of city and country schools is not the subject of comparison in White's essay?
   - a. Plumbing
   - b. Mode of transportation to get to school
   - c. Cost
   - d. Formality of student attire

5. White's son claims that his day at the country public school goes
   - (a.) just like lightning.
   - b. just like molasses.
   - c. just like a cheetah.
   - d. just like mud.

Content

1. What change for his son is White worried about? Change from private city school to public country school

2. White claims his son's days at the private school are "rich in formal experience." Is this statement positive or negative? How can you tell?

   2. Negative. "punctual as death" bus; students "worked on" by teachers; no freedom to be a kid; everything supervised or directed

3. What details does White use to help the reader understand the differences between his son's schools? School bus vs. walking; dieticians and athletic instructors vs. unsupervised play with friends at lunch; many teachers "working on" son vs. one teacher for everyone

Style and Structure

1. What is the main idea of White's essay? Write his argument in your own words.

   1. The casual approach makes his son's country school better.

2. What is the topic sentence of paragraph 3? How does White support this topic sentence? His days were rich in formal experience. Details: school bus, teachers, supervised play

3. What transitions does White use to indicate the passing of time? Look particularly closely in paragraphs 3, 4, and 6 for examples.

   3. Paragraph 3: "At school," "for six or seven hours," "mid-morning." Paragraph 4: "at the crack of dawn," "when the road is open," "when the snow is deep," "in the afternoons." Paragraph 6: "still," "when later," "after almost a year"

Writing Assignments

1. White clearly favors one of his son's schools over the other. *Write a paragraph in which you compare or contrast two schools or classes that you have attended.* Use examples from your own experiences to illustrate your ideas.

2. Think about a time when you have changed schools, even moving from middle school to high school. *Write a paragraph describing yourself as a new student.* Use examples from your own experiences to illustrate your ideas.

3. White favors the public country school over the private city school. *Write an essay describing a class or school that you either liked or disliked very much.* Be sure to use examples from your own life for support.

Lyla Fox

"Hold Your Horsepower"

A concerned parent and teacher, Lyla Fox writes about the pressures teens face to both work and maintain superior academic achievement. Unfortunately, Fox concludes, the financial pressures override scholastic ones, and even the best students' schoolwork suffers as a result.

BEFORE YOU READ

Think about the following questions. Write your responses on a separate sheet or in your journal.

■ Did you have a job in high school? Why or why not?

■ What effect, if any, did your job have on your grades? If you never had a job, use the experience of someone you know who did.

■ Do you think having a job in high school is generally good for students or bad? Explain.

VOCABULARY DEVELOPMENT

Look up the following words in a dictionary. Write down their meanings on a separate sheet or in your journal.

revere (paragraph 1)

reconcile (paragraph 2)

forgo (paragraph 3)

lamenting (paragraph 5)

effigy (paragraph 11)

lauds (paragraph 1)

diligently (paragraph 3)

partake (paragraph 3)

sacrosanct (paragraph 6)

concede (paragraph 11)

"Hold Your Horsepower"

1   Folks in the small Michigan town where I grew up revere the work ethic. Our entire culture lauds those who are willing to work their tails off to get ahead. Though there's nothing wrong with hard work, I suggest that our youngsters may be starting too young—and for all the wrong reasons.

2   Increasingly I identified with Sisyphus trying to move that stone. There are more mornings than I would like to admit when many of my students sit with eyes glazed or heads slumped on their desks as I try to nurture a threatening-to-become-extinct interest in school. These are not lazy kids. Many are high-achieving 16- and 17-year-olds who find it tough to reconcile 7:30 a.m. classes with a job that winds down at 10:30 p.m. or later.

3   "What's wrong?" I asked a student who once diligently completed his homework assignments. He groggily grunted an answer. "I'm tired. I didn't get home until 11 p.m." Half the class nodded and joined in a discussion about how hard it is to try to balance schoolwork, sports and jobs. Since we end up working most of our adult life, my suggestion to the class was to forgo the job and partake of school—both intra- and extracurricular.

4   "Then how do I pay for my car?" the sleepy student, now more awake, asked. Click. The car. That's what all these bleary eyes and half-done papers are about. My students have a desperate need to drive their own vehicles

proudly into the school parking lot. The car is the teenager's symbolic club membership. I know because I've seen the embarrassed looks on the faces of teens who must answer "No" to the frequently asked "Do you have a car?" National Merit finalists pale in importance beside the student who drives his friends around in a shiny new Ford Probe.

5   My own son (a senior at the University of Michigan) spent a good part of his high school years lamenting our "no car in high school" dictate. When he needed to drive, we made sure he could always borrow our car. Our Oldsmobile 88, however, didn't convey the instant high school popularity of a sporty Nissan or Honda. Our son's only job was to do as well as he could in school. The other work, we told him, would come later. Today I see students working more than the legally permitted number of hours to pay for their cars. I also see once committed students becoming less dedicated to schoolwork. Their commitment is to their cars and the jobs that will help them make those monthly car payments.

6   Once cars and jobs enter the picture, it is virtually impossible to get students focused on school. "My parents are letting me get a car," one of my brightest students enthused a few months ago. "They say all I have to do is get a job to make the payments." All. I winced, saying nothing because parents' views are sacrosanct for me. I bit my cheeks to keep from saying how wrong I thought they were and how worried I was for her schoolwork. Predictably, during the next few months, her grades and attitude took a plunge.

7   I say attitude because when students go to work for a car, their positive attitude frequently disappears. Teachers and parents are on the receiving end of curved-lip responses to the suggestion that they should knuckle down and do some schoolwork. A job and car payments are often a disastrous combination.

8   These kids are selling their one and only chance at adolescence for a car. Adults in their world must help them see what their children's starry eyes cannot: that students will have the rest of their lives to own an automobile and pay expenses.

9   Some parents, I know, breathe a sigh of relief when their children can finally drive themselves to orthodontist appointments and basketball practice. This trade-off could mean teens' losing touch with family life. Having a car makes it easy for kids to cut loose and take part in activities far from home. Needing that ride from Mom and Dad helps to keep a family connection. Chauffeuring teens another year or two might be a bargain after all.

10   What a remarkable experience a school day might be if it were the center of teens' lives, instead of that much-resented time that keeps them from their friends and their jobs. Although we may not have meant to, parents may have laid the groundwork for that resentment. By giving kids permission to work, parents are not encouraging them to study. Parents have allowed students to miss classes because of exhaustion from the previous night's work. By providing a hefty down payment on a $12,000 car and

stressing the importance of keeping up the payments, they're sending a signal that schoolwork is secondary.

11   The kids I'm writing about are wonderful. But they are stressed and angry that their day has too few hours for too much work. Sound familiar? It should. It is the same description adults use to identify what's wrong with their lives. After reading this, my students may want to hang me in effigy. But perhaps some of them are secretly hoping that someone will stop their world and help them get off. They might also concede that it's time to get out of the car and get on mass transit. For students in large metropolitan areas, public transportation is the only way to get around.

12   Adults should take the reins and let teens off the hook. We must say "no" when we're implored to "Please let me get a job so I can have a car." Peer pressure makes it hard for kids to turn away from the temptation of that shiny four-wheeled popularity magnet. It's up to the grown-ups to let kids stay kids a little longer.

13   The subject of teens and cars comes up in my home as well as in my classroom. My 15-year-old daughter gave me some bone-chilling news yesterday. "The Springers got Suzi her own car!" she announced. "All she has to do is make the payments."

14   I smiled and went back to correcting the essays that would have been lovely had their authors had some time to put into constructing them. The payment, I told myself after my daughter went grudgingly to begin her homework, may be greater than anyone in the Springer family could possibly imagine.

AFTER YOU READ

Vocabulary Practice

1. Choose at least three words from the Vocabulary Development list on page 737 and write sentences using those words. You may write one sentence using all three words if you wish. Answers will vary.

2. Which word on the Vocabulary Development list means "an image or representation, especially of a person"? Use the word in a sentence that clearly shows its meaning. Effigy. Answers will vary.

3. What terms does Fox use to describe teen-owned cars in her essay? How do these terms help the reader understand the temptation of owning a car in high school? "Teenager's symbolic club membership," "shiny four-wheeled popularity magnet." Cars equal popularity for some students.

Comprehension

Circle the correct answer.

1. Lyla Fox thinks that high school students who have jobs are

    a. selling their one and only chance at adolescence for a car.

b. learning valuable life skills in a work setting.

c. training themselves to have the right priorities outside of school.

d. saving themselves the heartache of being poor.

2. Which of the following does Fox not list as a change in her students?

a. Plunging attitude

b. Fatigue

c. Increased absences

d. Resentment over having schoolwork

3. Why does Fox say her students want cars?

a. They want to prove they're adults.

b. They want to practice being responsible.

c. They want to be equals with their parents.

d. They want to be popular at school.

4. A benefit of students needing rides from their parents is

a. strengthened family connection.

b. strengthened resolve to be independent.

c. weakened desire to break parents' rules.

d. weakened connections with friends.

5. Fox sees high school students in her job as a

a. school nurse.   b. teacher.

c. counselor.   d. coach.

1. Fatigue; lessened interest in school; resentment over schoolwork
3. They're not receptive; they want to work so they can pay for their cars.

Content

1. What are some negative traits Fox notices in her students who have jobs?

2. What recommendation does Fox make to her students? That they quit their jobs and focus on school

3. How do her students react to Fox's suggestion?

1. Jobs and a car for high school students are a disastrous combination for academic achievement.
2. Sleepy students, falling grades, poor attitudes
3. Parents. They are the ones who can make the change because they are responsible for their children.

Style and Structure

1. What is Fox's focus in her essay? Write her main idea in your own words.

2. What examples does Fox use to show that her students do not benefit from car ownership? Cite the text to support your response.

3. For whom is Fox writing? Do you think her essay targets parents or students to a greater degree? Why?

Writing Assignments

1. Should high school students own—and pay for—their own cars? *Write a paragraph arguing that high school students should or should not own their own cars.* Give examples from Fox's essay and, if appropriate, from your own life to support your argument.

2. Fox writes a cause-and-effect essay, claiming that car ownership hurts students academically in high school. *Write a paragraph identifying other causes for lowered grades in high school, such as family trauma or peer pressure.* Use examples from your own life in order to illustrate your ideas.

3. Fox writes that car ownership can have negative effects on high school students' grades. What else can affect high school students' academic performance? *Write an essay explaining how factors other than car ownership can negatively—or positively—affect high school students' school performance.* Use specific details from your own experiences and observations to support your ideas.

Randy Moore

"Grades and Self-Esteem"

A teacher and concerned citizen, Randy Moore writes to raise people's consciousness about the causes and effects of academic failure. Citing the building of self-esteem, rather than the building of academic skills, as the primary goal for today's teachers, Moore argues that lowering standards and softening the blows of poor performance will ultimately hurt rather than help students.

BEFORE YOU READ

Think about the following questions. Write your responses on a separate sheet or in your journal.

■ How important are your grades to you? Explain.

■ How important is learning to you? Is it more, or less, important than getting good grades? Explain.

■ How has getting high—or low—grades made you feel?

VOCABULARY DEVELOPMENT

Look up the following words in a dictionary. Write down their meanings on a separate sheet or in your journal.

inevitably (paragraph 1)   firsthand (paragraph 1)
marginally (paragraph 2)   competent (paragraph 2)
dogma (paragraph 7)   precedes (paragraph 7)
dispense (paragraph 7)   crusaders (paragraph 8)
gurus (paragraph 8)   stigmatized (paragraph 8)

"Grades and Self-Esteem"

1   If you're around teachers long enough, the conversation will inevitably get around to "today's under-prepared students." We complain endlessly that students don't know anything, don't *want* to know anything, can't write well and can't think critically. Our complaints are supported by much evidence, including firsthand observations and declining scores on objective tests (e.g., SAT, ACT). Indeed,

- Only 11% of eighth-graders in California's public schools can solve seventh-grade math problems.
- More than 30% of U.S. 17-year-olds don't know that Abraham Lincoln wrote the Emancipation Proclamation. Almost half do not know who Josef Stalin was, and 30% can't locate Britain on a map of Europe.

2   Employers echo our complaints: 58% of Fortune 500 companies cannot find marginally competent workers, and the CEOs of major companies report that four of 10 entry-level workers cannot pass seventh-grade exams. Does all of this make a difference? Yes. For example, several major corporations now ship their paperwork to countries such as Ireland because U.S. workers "make too many mistakes."

3   We have many prepackaged excuses for our failures, some of which are partly valid and others that are self-delusion. I argue that a major reason for our failures is that the primary mission of many schools has shifted from education to "building self-esteem."

4   Disciples of the self-esteem mission for schools preach that we should take seriously—even praise—all self-expression by students, regardless of its content, context, accuracy or worth. This, the disciples claim, "humanizes" education and makes our courses "nonjudgmental." Everyone is right! Everyone's opinion has equal value! I'm OK, you're OK! Don't worry about learning, thinking or communicating; the important thing is to feel good about ourselves.

5   Of course, when we assign grades we become *very* judgmental. This upsets teachers who feel bad about holding students accountable to any kind of grading standards. To avoid feeling bad, these teachers lower their standards so that virtually all students meet them, regardless of the students' performance. There are many subtle examples of this: eliminating (or not recording) failing grades, allowing students to withdraw from courses when faced with making a poor grade, "dumbing down" our courses so that everyone "earns" an A or B, and renaming sub-remedial courses to make them appear to be academically viable. All of this produces grade inflation. Consider these facts:

- In 1966, high school teachers gave twice as many C's as A's. By 1978, the proportion of A's exceeded that of C's. In 1990, more than 20% of all students entering college had an A *average* for their entire high school career.

- In the 1980s, almost three-fourths of grades at Amherst, Duke, Hamilton, Haverford, Pomona, Michigan, North Carolina and Wisconsin were A or B. At Harvard, the average grade is now B+; at Princeton, 80% of undergraduates get *only* A's or B's.
- In some colleges, the *average* undergraduate is an "honors" student.

6   Many teachers have lowered their standards so far that most of their students—the same ones we claim cannot think critically and who employers know are unprepared for entry-level jobs—are A or B students. These teachers apparently think that our students, like the children at Lake Wobegon, are all above average.

7   The belief that self-esteem is a precondition to learning is now dogma that few teachers question. However, this confuses cause and effect. Granted, people who excel at what they do usually feel better about themselves than do frauds or convicted felons. But does high self-esteem *cause* success? To many educators, it apparently does: These people claim that self-esteem precedes performance, not vice-versa. I argue that self-esteem is *earned* and that schools, despite their good intentions, cannot dispense it as a prepackaged handout. We should avoid the "Wizard of Oz" syndrome in which we merely dispense substitutes for brains, bravery and hearts. We should insist on the real thing.

8   Despite having lowered our standards to new depths, many self-esteem crusaders claim that we've not lowered our standards far enough. For example, high school seniors in some states must pass a ninth-grade-level test before they can get their diploma. When some students failed the test repeatedly and were told they would not graduate, the self-esteem gurus immediately jumped to their defense. "Outrageous!" they claimed. "If students failed, the tests must be flawed!" One educator even proclaimed that the students "would be stigmatized the rest of their lives because they don't have a diploma." Of course, asking the students to work harder, repeat a grade or achieve a meaningful goal is out of the question because such requests could damage the students' self-esteem. The result? Students who could not pass the ninth-grade test "graduated" and received a "diploma of attendance" (ironically, the fact that many of the students *didn't* attend classes was the basis for their problem). I'm sure that employers—people who care less about "self-esteem" than integrity and productivity—will be *very* impressed by a "diploma of attendance."

9   The delusion that results from our current emphasis on self-esteem rather than education is best shown by the results of an international study of 13-year-olds that found that Koreans ranked first in math and Americans ranked last. Only 23% of Korean youngsters claimed that they were "good at mathematics," as compared to a whopping 68% of U.S. youngsters. Apparently, self-esteem has little to do with one's ability to do math.

10   The products of our current emphasis on "self-esteem"—that is, grade inflation, lowered standards, meaningless diplomas and an ignorance of important skills—greatly compromise our work: We cheat students out of a

quality education and give parents false hopes about their child's intellectual skills. Moreover, our teaching convinces students that achievement is an entitlement that is given, not earned. Luckily, life is not that way.

11   We cannot continue to equate higher self-esteem with lowered standards. If we do, we'll not only produce students who can't think, but also students who don't know what thinking *is*. At that point, self-esteem won't matter all that much.

12   We'll improve students' self-esteem most by helping and motivating our students to exceed *higher* standards. Only then will our students have accomplished something meaningful and will we have excelled at our work.

 **AFTER YOU READ**

Vocabulary Practice

1. Choose at least three words from the Vocabulary Development list on page 741 and write sentences using those words. You may write one sentence using all three words if you wish. Answers will vary.

2. What word from the Vocabulary Development list means "to surpass in rank, dignity, or importance"? Use the word in a sentence that clearly shows its meaning. Precede. Answers will vary.

3. What are some words or phrases that Moore uses to describe poor performance? Failure, underpreparedness, marginally competent, unprepared, lowered standards

Comprehension

Circle the correct answer.

1. Which of the following is not mentioned as an indication of poor student performance?
   a. Lowered standardized test scores
   b. Lack of basic knowledge about Abraham Lincoln
   c. Declining interest in literature
   d. Large corporations sending paperwork to Ireland

2. What does Moore claim is the cause of poor academic performance?
   a. Teachers' emphasis on sports in school
   b. Teachers' emphasis on students' self-esteem
   c. Parents' emphasis on students earning money
   d. Parents' emphasis on students becoming independent

3. How does Moore claim that educators treat students of varying ability?
   a. They take all answers seriously, regardless of accuracy or worth.
   b. They ridicule students who perform at low levels.

c. They praise students who earn high grades.

d. They encourage the good students to help the weak students.

4. According to Moore, what do self-esteem advocates say when students fail a test?

    a. It's the students' own fault.

    b. The students are not very smart.

    c. The teachers did a terrible job teaching.

    (d.) There must be something wrong with the test.

5. Why, according to Moore, do educators lower their standards?

    a. They're lazy.

    b. They're burned out from their jobs.

    (c.) They don't want to hurt students' feelings.

    d. They don't want students to be mad at them.

Content

1. Eliminating failing grades; allowing students to withdraw from courses instead of failing them; "dumbing down" courses; renaming subremedial courses

1. What are some ways Moore claims that educators lower their standards?

2. Employees are marginally competent; U.S. workers make too many mistakes.

2. What are employers saying about students' preparedness to work?

3. What does Moore say will be the result of equating self-esteem with lowered standards? *Students who can't think and who don't know what thinking is*

Style and Structure

1. Emphasizing self-esteem over academic accomplishment has dangerous consequences.

1. What is Moore's main point? Rewrite it in your own words.

2. For whom is Moore writing? Give some examples that best reveal his audience.

3. What examples does Moore use to illustrate his points?

Writing Assignments

1. Moore is critical of how teachers "dumb down" classes so that their students can achieve higher grades. Is he right? *Write a paragraph arguing whether or not teachers should make their classes easier for their students to pass.* Use examples from your own experiences and observations to illustrate your ideas.

2. Moore writes that today's students are unprepared for the workplace. Are you prepared? *Write a paragraph evaluating whether or not your education so far has prepared you for work.* Use examples from your experiences and observations to support your ideas.

3. Moore argues that self-esteem is earned. Through what experiences have you gained self-esteem? *Write an essay discussing experiences that have helped you build your self-esteem.* Use specific details from your life to support your ideas.

What We Value

Seemingly every day on television or in the newspaper, we learn about people whose "values" appear to have been compromised: people allow cameras into their personal lives for fame, sue one another over trivial injuries, and allow their children to watch or take part in overtly violent entertainment. The question arises: what is important to us, as a society? The essays "Money for Morality" and "The Ways We Lie" explore how we view honesty and responsibility, while "'Blaxicans' & Other Reinvented Americans," "Have You Heard? Gossip Turns Out to Serve a Purpose," and "Manners Matter" discuss how our actions can have far-reaching benefits or consequences. Finally, "Confessions of a Quit Addict" calls our attention to how abandoning values and responsibilities can result in great unhappiness, even as we think we are making ourselves content.

Readings in This Section

Richard Rodriguez

"'Blaxicans' and Other Reinvented Americans"

Raised in California, Richard Rodriguez is an editor at Pacific News Service and an essayist for PBS's *News Hour.* He is the author of *Brown: The Last Discovery of America,* the final book in his series about the intersection of his personal and public life. In this essay, Rodriguez examines race relations in a twenty-first century light, one which is no longer limited primarily to two groups.

BEFORE YOU READ

Think about the following questions. Write your response on a separate sheet or in your journal

■ What does the expression *race relations* mean to you? To what extent does it include specific races?

■ Do people from different ethnic groups live with or near you? How many groups? How do these groups get along?

■ To what extent is your life a mixture of cultures? What cultural influences other than your family's have you encountered? Explain.

VOCABULARY DEVELOPMENT

Look up the following words in a dictionary. Write down their meanings on a separate sheet or in your journal.

unsettling (paragraph 1)	ascendancy (paragraph 12)
peerless (paragraph 2)	denoting (paragraph 13)
dialectic (paragraph 5)	assimilation (paragraph 14)
surname (paragraph 6)	bombast (paragraph 17)
gringo (paragraph 10)	multiplicity (paragraph 19)

"'Blaxicans' and Other Reinvented Americans"

1   There is something unsettling about immigrants because . . . well, because they chatter incomprehensibly, and they get in everyone's way. Immigrants seem to be bent on undoing America. Just when Americans think we know who we are—we are Protestants, culled from Western Europe, are we not?—then new immigrants appear from Southern Europe or from Eastern Europe. We—we who are already here—we don't know exactly what the latest comers will mean to our community. How will they fit in with us? Thus we—we who were here first—we begin to question our own identity.

2   After a generation or two, the grandchildren or the great-grandchildren of immigrants to the United States and the grandchildren of those who tried to keep immigrants out of the United States will romanticize the immigrant, will begin to see the immigrant as the figure who teaches us most about what it means to be an American. The immigrant, in mythic terms, travels from the outermost rind of America to the very center of American mythology. None of this, of course, can we admit to the Vietnamese immigrant who served us our breakfast at the hotel this morning. In another 40 years, we will be prepared to say to the Vietnamese immigrant that he, with his breakfast tray, with his intuition for travel, with his memory of tragedy, with his recognition of peerless freedoms, he fulfills the meaning of America.

3   In 1997, Gallup conducted a survey on race relations in America, but the poll was concerned only with white and black Americans. No question was put to the aforementioned Vietnamese man. There was certainly no question for the Chinese grocer, none for the Guatemalan barber, none for the tribe of Mexican Indians who reroofed your neighbor's house.

4   The American conversation about race has always been a black-and-white conversation, but the conversation has become as bloodless as badminton.

5   I have listened to the black-and-white conversation for most of my life. I was supposed to attach myself to one side or the other, without asking the obvious questions: What is this perpetual dialectic between Europe and Africa? Why does it admit so little reference to anyone else?

6   I am speaking to you in American English that was taught me by Irish nuns—immigrant women. I wear an Indian face; I answer to a Spanish surname as well as this California first name, Richard. You might wonder about the complexity of historical factors, the collision of centuries, that creates Richard Rodriguez. My brownness is the illustration of that collision, or the bland memorial of it. I stand before you as an Impure-American, an Ambiguous-American.

· · ·

7   Race mixture has not been a point of pride in America. Americans speak more easily about "diversity" than we do about the fact that I might marry your daughter; you might become we; we might become us. America has so readily adopted the Canadian notion of multiculturalism because it preserves our preference for thinking ourselves separate—our elbows need not touch, thank you. I would prefer that table. I can remain Mexican, whatever that means, in the United States of America.

8   I would propose that instead of adopting the Canadian model of multiculturalism, America might begin to imagine the Mexican alternative—that of a mestizaje society.

9   Because of colonial Mexico, I am mestizo. But I was reinvented by President Richard Nixon. In the early 1970s, Nixon instructed the Office of Management and Budget to identify the major racial and ethnic groups in the

United States. OMB came up with five major ethnic or racial groups. The groups are white, black, Asian/Pacific Islander, American Indian/Eskimo, and Hispanic.

10   It's what I learned to do when I was in college: to call myself a Hispanic. At my university we even had separate cafeteria tables and "theme houses," where the children of Nixon could gather—of a feather. Native Americans united. African-Americans. Casa Hispanic.

11   The interesting thing about Hispanics is that you will never meet us in Latin America. You may meet Chileans and Peruvians and Mexicans. You will not meet Hispanics. If you inquire in Lima or Bogotá about Hispanics, you will be referred to Dallas. For "Hispanic" is a gringo contrivance, a definition of the world according to European patterns of colonization. Such a definition suggests I have more in common with Argentine-Italians than with American Indians; that there is an ineffable union between the white Cuban and the mulatto Puerto Rican because of Spain. Nixon's conclusion has become the basis for the way we now organize and understand American society.

12   The Census Bureau foretold that by the year 2003, Hispanics would outnumber blacks to become the largest minority in the United States. And, indeed, the year 2003 has arrived and the proclamation of Hispanic ascendancy has been published far and wide. While I admit a competition has existed—does exist—in America between Hispanic and black people, I insist that the comparison of Hispanics with blacks will lead, ultimately, to complete nonsense. For there is no such thing as a Hispanic race. In Latin America, one sees every race of the world. One sees white Hispanics, one sees black Hispanics, one sees brown Hispanics who are Indians, many of whom do not speak Spanish because they resist Spain. One sees Asian-Hispanics. To compare blacks and Hispanics, therefore, is to construct a fallacious equation.

13   Some Hispanics have accepted the fiction. Some Hispanics have too easily accustomed themselves to impersonating a third race, a great new third race in America. But Hispanic is an ethnic term. It is a term denoting culture. So when the Census Bureau says by the year 2060 one-third of all Americans will identify themselves as Hispanic, the Census Bureau is not speculating in pigment or quantifying according to actual historical narratives, but rather is predicting how by the year 2060 one-third of all Americans will identify themselves culturally. For a country that traditionally has taken its understandings of community from blood and color, the new circumstance of so large a group of Americans identifying themselves by virtue of language or fashion or cuisine or literature is an extraordinary change, and a revolutionary one.

. . .

14   I was on a British Broadcasting Corporation interview show, and a woman introduced me as being, "in favor" of assimilation. I am not in favor

of assimilation any more than I am in favor of the Pacific Ocean or clement weather. If I had a bumper sticker on the subject, it might read something like ASSIMILATION HAPPENS.

. . .

15   I am in favor of assimilation. I am not in favor of assimilation. I recognize assimilation. A few years ago, I was in Merced, California—a town of about 75,000 people in the Central Valley where the two largest immigrant groups at that time (California is so fluid, I believe this is no longer the case) were Laotian Hmong and Mexicans. Laotians have never in the history of the world, as far as I know, lived next to Mexicans. But there they were in Merced, and living next to Mexicans. They don't like each other. I was talking to the Laotian kids about why they don't like the Mexican kids. They were telling me that the Mexicans do this and the Mexicans don't do that, when I suddenly realized that they were speaking English with a Spanish accent.

16   On his interview show, Bill Moyers once asked me how I thought of myself. As an American? Or Hispanic? I answered that I am Chinese, and that is because I live in a Chinese city and because I want to be Chinese. Well, why not? Some Chinese-American people in the Richmond and Sunset districts of San Francisco sometimes paint their houses (so many qualifiers!) in colors I would once have described as garish: lime greens, rose reds, pumpkin. But I have lived in a Chinese city for so long that my eye has taken on that palette, has come to prefer lime greens and rose reds and all the inventions of this Chinese Mediterranean. I see photographs in magazines or documentary footage of China, especially rural China, and I see what I recognize as home. Isn't that odd?

17   I do think distinctions exist. I'm not talking about an America tomorrow in which we're going to find that black and white are no longer the distinguishing marks of separateness. But many young people I meet tell me they feel like Victorians when they identify themselves as black or white. They don't think of themselves in those terms. And they're already moving into a world in which tattoo or ornament or movement or commune or sexuality or drug or rave or electronic bombast are the organizing principles of their identity. The notion that they are white or black simply doesn't occur.

18   And increasingly, of course, one meets children who really don't know how to say what they are. They simply are too many things. I met a young girl in San Diego at a convention of mixed-race children, among whom the common habit is to define one parent over the other—black over white, for example. But this girl said that her mother was Mexican and her father was African. The girl said "Blaxican." By reinventing language, she is reinventing America.

19   America does not have a vocabulary like the vocabulary the Spanish empire evolved to describe the multiplicity of racial possibilities in the New

World. The conversation, the interior monologue of America cannot rely on the old vocabulary—black, white. We are no longer a black-white nation.

20   So, what myth do we tell ourselves? The person who got closest to it was Karl Marx. Marx predicted that the discovery of gold in California would be a more central event to the Americas than the discovery of the Americas by Columbus—which was only the meeting of two tribes, essentially, the European and the Indian. But when gold was discovered in California in the 1840s, the entire world met. For the first time in human history, all of the known world gathered. The Malaysian stood in the gold fields alongside the African, alongside the Chinese, alongside the Australian, alongside the Yankee.

21   That was an event without parallel in world history and the beginning of modern California—why California today provides the mythological structure for understanding how we might talk about the American experience: not as biracial, but as the re-creation of the known world in the New World.

22   Sometimes truly revolutionary things happen without regard. I mean, we may wake up one morning and there is no black race. There is no white race either. There are mythologies, and—as I am in the business, insofar as I am in any business at all, of demythologizing such identities as black and white—I come to you as a man of many cultures. I come to you as Chinese. Unless you understand that I am Chinese, then you have not understood anything I have said.

 **AFTER YOU READ**

Vocabulary Practice

1. Choose at least three words from the Vocabulary Development list on page 748 and write sentences using those words. You may write one sentence using all three words if you wish.   Answers will vary.

2. What word from the Vocabulary Development list means "the quality or state of being multiple or various"? Use the word in a sentence that clearly shows its meaning.   Multiplicity: Answers will vary.

3. Black, white, Hispanic, Asian-Hispanic, Laotian Hmong, Mexican, Chinese, African, Australian, Yankee; so much of America is blended that we're all "brown"; color has little to do with cultural identification.

3. What are some ethnic or racial groups Rodriguez identifies in his article? Why doesn't he just use *black, white,* and *brown* to describe these groups?

Comprehension

1. How does Rodriguez open his article?

   a. With a statement about foreigners

   b. With a statement about Americans

   c. With a statement about immigrants

   d. With a statement about illegal aliens

2. How does Rodriguez say the great-grandchildren of today's immigrants will view their great-grandparents?

   (a.) They will romanticize the great-grandparents.

   b. They will criticize the great-grandparents.

   c. They will idolize the great-grandparents.

   d. They will eulogize the great-grandparents.

3. What question does Rodriguez have about the black-and-white conversation?

   a. Why doesn't it solve any problems?

   (b.) Why doesn't it admit anyone else?

   c. Why doesn't it ever stop?

   d. Why doesn't it get to the point?

4. What does Rodriguez notice about Laotian Hmong children who dislike Mexican children?

   a. They eat, and enjoy, Mexican food.

   b. They participate in salsa dancing.

   c. They admire Latino baseball players.

   (d.) They speak English with a Spanish accent.

5. Based on where he lives, what ethnicity does Rodriguez claim he is?

   (a.) Chinese   b. Japanese

   c. Mexican   d. Spanish

Content

1. What does the term *Blaxican* mean? Who uses the term in Rodriguez's article?   Combination of *African* and *Mexican;* a girl with African and Mexican parents

2. In terms of ethnic and cultural mixing, why was the California Gold Rush so important?   When gold was discovered, the whole world met.

3. Why did Rodriguez identify himself as "Hispanic" when he was in college? It was the category on the census form he best fit into.

Style and Structure

People identify themselves ethnically according to their own definitions.

1. What is Rodriguez's point? Write his argument in your own words.

2. What kinds of examples does Rodriguez use to show how people are "reinventing" themselves? Laotian Hmong kids speaking with Spanish accent; "Blaxican" girl; Rodriguez describing himself as Chinese

3. Rodriguez uses questions throughout his essay (paragraphs 1, 5, 15, 19). What effect do his questions have on your reading of the article? Answers will vary. Questions focus attention on the point at hand, serve as transitions.

Writing Assignments

1. Rodriguez says that he identifies himself as Chinese because of the city he lives in. How do you identify yourself? *Write a paragraph in which you explain*

how you identify yourself. Some factors you might consider in identifying your-self: your parents' races or ethnicities, where you live, how you were raised. Use examples from your own experiences to illustrate your ideas.

2. Rodriguez mentions several ways that people identify themselves: through their parents, by means of made-up categories on a census form, through their cities. How do you think most people identify themselves? *Write a para-graph explaining how certain factors—such as where a person lives or who a per-son's parents are—determine a person's identity.* Use examples and illustrations from your own life to support your ideas.

3. Rodriguez writes of one girl who describes herself as "Blaxican" because her par-ents were African and Mexican. What is a term that identifies you? *Write an essay in which you "reinvent" yourself—giving yourself a new name, such as* Blaxican— *and describing yourself in terms of your culture.* Some aspects of your culture you may want to explain in your essay are language, food, entertainment, and reli-gion. Be sure to use examples from your own life for support.

Mary Arguelles

"Money for Morality"

Mary Arguelles is a freelance writer whose articles have appeared in *New Mother*, *Baby Talk*, and *Reader's Digest*. Ms. Arguelles has also produced and hosted *Twigs*, a local parenting education program in Reading, Pennsylvania. Her essay first appeared in the "My Turn" section of *Newsweek* in 1991.

BEFORE YOU READ

Think about the following questions. Write your responses on a separate sheet or in your journal.

■ How would you define a good deed?

■ What were the circumstances of your last good deed? Why did you do it? Did you expect a reward?

■ Do you think people should be rewarded for good deeds? Explain.

VOCABULARY DEVELOPMENT

Look up the following words in a dictionary. Write down their meanings on a sep-arate sheet or in your journal.

mandatory (paragraph 2)   sufficient (paragraph 2)

ubiquitous (paragraph 3)   collateral (paragraph 3)

mercenary (paragraph 3)   catapulted (paragraph 3)

elicit (paragraph 4)   kowtowing (paragraphs 5, 6)

"Money for Morality"

1   I recently read a newspaper article about an 8-year-old boy who found an envelope containing more than $600 and returned it to the bank whose name appeared on the envelope. The bank traced the money to its rightful owner and returned it to him. God's in his heaven and all's right with the world. Right? Wrong.

2   As a reward, the man who lost the money gave the boy $3. Not a lot, but a token of his appreciation nonetheless and not mandatory. After all, returning money should not be considered extraordinary. A simple "thank you" is adequate. But some of the teachers at the boy's school felt a reward was not only appropriate, but required. Outraged at the apparent stinginess of the person who lost the cash, these teachers took up a collection for the boy. About a week or so later, they presented the good Samaritan with $150 savings bond, explaining they felt his honesty should be recognized. Evidently the virtues of honesty and kindness have become commodities that, like everything else, have succumbed to inflation. I can't help but wonder what dollar amount these teachers would have deemed a sufficient reward. Certainly they didn't expect the individual who lost the money to give the child $150. Would $25 have been respectable? How about $10? Suppose that lost money had to cover mortgage, utilities and food for the week. In light of that, perhaps $3 was generous. A reward is a gift; any gift should at least be met with the presumption of genuine gratitude on the part of the giver.

3   What does this episode say about our society? It seems the role models our children look up to these days—in this case, teachers—are more confused and misguided about values than their young charges. A young boy, obviously well guided by his parents, finds money that does not belong to him and he returns it. He did the right thing. Yet doing the right thing seems to be insufficient motivation for action in our materialistic world. The legacy of the '80s has left us with the ubiquitous question: what's in it for me? The promise of the golden rule—that someone might do a good turn for you—has become worthless collateral for the social interactions of the mercenary and fast-paced '90s. It is in fact this fast pace that is, in part, a source of the problem. Modern communication has catapulted us into an instant world. Television makes history of events before any of us has even had a chance to absorb them in the first place. An ad for major-league baseball entices viewers with the reassurance that "the memories are waiting"; an event that has yet to occur has already been packaged as the past. With the world racing by us, we have no patience for a rain check on good deeds.

4   Misplaced virtues are rampant through our culture. I don't know how many times my 13-year-old son has told me about classmates who received $10 for each A they receive on their report cards—hinting that I should do the same for him should he ever receive an A (or maybe he was working on $5 for a B). Whenever he approaches me on this subject, I give him the same reply: "Doing well is its own reward. The A just confirms that." In other words, forget it! This is not to say that I would never praise my son for doing well in school. But my praise is not meant to reward or elicit future achievements, but rather to express my genuine delight in the satisfaction he feels at having done his best. Throwing $10 at that sends out the message that the feeling alone isn't good enough.

Kowtowing to Ice Cream

5   As a society, we seem to be losing a grip on our internal control—the ethical thermostat that guides our actions and feelings toward ourselves, others, and the world around us. Instead, we rely on external "stuff" as a measure of our worth. We pass this message to our children. We offer them money for honesty and good grades. Pizza is given as a reward for reading. In fact, in one national reading program, a pizza party awaits the entire class if each child reads a certain amount of books within a four-month period. We call these incentives, telling ourselves that if we can just reel them in and get them hooked, then the built-in rewards will follow. I recently saw a television program where unmarried, teenaged mothers were featured as the participants in a parenting program that offers a $10 a week "incentive" if these young women don't get pregnant again. Isn't the daily struggle of being a single, teenaged mother enough of a deterrent? No, it isn't, because we as a society won't allow it to be. Nothing is permitted to succeed or fail on its own merits anymore.

6   I remember when I was pregnant with my son I read countless child-care books that offered the same advice: don't bribe your child with ice cream to get him to eat spinach; it makes the spinach look bad. While some may say spinach doesn't need any help looking bad, I submit it's from years of kowtowing to ice cream. Similarly, our moral taste buds have been dulled by an endless onslaught of artificial sweeteners. A steady diet of candy bars and banana splits makes an ordinary apple or orange seem sour. So too does an endless parade of incentives make us incapable of feeling a genuine sense of inner peace (or inner turmoil).

7   The simple virtues of honesty, kindness and integrity suffer from an image problem and are in desperate need of a makeover. One way to do this is by example. If my son sees me feeling happy after I've helped out a friend, then he may do likewise. If my daughter sees me spending a rainy afternoon curled up with a book instead of spending money at the mall, she may get the message that there are some simple pleasures that don't require a purchase. I fear that in our so-called upwardly mobile world we are on a

downward spiral toward moral bankruptcy. Like pre–World War II Germany, where the basket holding the money was more valuable than the money itself, we too may render ourselves internally worthless while desperately clinging to a shell of appearances.

AFTER YOU READ

Vocabulary Practice

1. Choose at least three words from the Vocabulary Development list on page 754 and write sentences using those words. You may write one sentence using all three words if you wish. Answers will vary.

2. Which word on the Vocabulary Development list means "working or done for payment only; motivated by a desire for money or other gain"? Use the word in a sentence that clearly shows its meaning. Mercenary. Answers will vary.

3. All the terms refer to something monetary. Arguelles is using financial terms to underscore her argument that people expect monetary rewards even for what should be basic human kindness.

3. Arguelles uses terms such as *commodities, inflation*, and *savings bond*. What kinds of terms are these? What do they refer to? Why do you think Arguelles uses these terms?

Comprehension

Circle the correct answer.

1. What good deed does Arguelles use to open her essay?
   a. A boy returns a wallet to its owner.
   b. A boy returns money to a bank.
   c. A boy tackles a thief who has stolen a woman's purse.
   d. A boy returns an envelope that he has stolen.

2. How does the owner of the money reward the boy?
   a. By giving him $10
   b. By giving him a handshake
   c. By giving him a pat on the head
   d. By giving him $3

3. How do the boy's teachers respond to his good deed?
   a. They give him a cake.
   b. They give him a class party.
   c. They give him a savings bond.
   d. They give him a check.

4. Arguelles claims that the "legacy of the '80s" is
   a. "Why me?"   b. "What's in it for me?"
   c. "Why should I?"   d. "What if I don't?"

5. Arguelles claims that offering ice cream as a reward for eating spinach
   - (a.) makes spinach look bad.
   - b. makes children overeat.
   - c. makes ice cream taste bad.
   - d. makes children sick.

Content

3. It's a mistake; it's rewarding something that should be a reward in itself.

1. What situation first caused Arguelles to think about good deeds and rewards in our society? A boy who returned money is given a $150 savings bond by his teachers, who think that his $3 reward from the wallet isn't enough.
2. How does Arguelles feel about the role models in society—specifically, the boy's teachers? They are more confused than the children.
3. How does Arguelles feel about offering students money for good grades?

Style and Structure

2. Money for grades; paying single mothers to not get pregnant; bribing for spinach with ice cream

1. What is the main point of Arguelles's essay? Put her main idea into your own words. People should do good deeds for their own sake, not for rewards.
2. What examples does Arguelles use to support her main idea?
3. What words or expressions does Arguelles use to indicate that money has a strong influence on people's values? Commodities, inflation, reward, mortgage, collateral, mercenary

Writing Assignments

1. Arguelles is critical of people who reward scholarly performance with money. What do you think? *Write a paragraph in which you argue for or against the practice of rewarding scholarly performance.* Use details from the text and from your own experience to illustrate your ideas.
2. Arguelles argues, "Misplaced virtues are rampant through our culture." Is she right? *Write a paragraph either agreeing or disagreeing with the idea that society's values—as presented by Arguelles—are "misplaced."* Be sure to use experiences from your own life for support.
3. Think about why money is so important in society today. *Write an essay explaining the reasons money is a vital part of our lives.* Use clear support points and specific examples to make your ideas clear.

Stephanie Ericsson

"The Ways We Lie"

As the author of *Companion Through Darkness: Dialogues on Grief* and *Companion into Dawn: Inner Dialogues on Loving*, Stephanie Ericsson addresses the ways we attempt to fool ourselves and others with dishonesty as well as the consequences of such acts. Her essay was compiled from her notes for her book *Companion into Dawn* in 1997.

BEFORE YOU READ

Think about the following questions. Write your responses on a separate sheet or in your journal.

- What is your definition of a lie?
- What kinds of lies, if any, do you tell regularly? What are your usual reasons for telling lies?
- How harmful do you think society considers lying? How harmful do you consider lying?

VOCABULARY DEVELOPMENT

Look up the following words in a dictionary. Write down their meanings on a separate sheet or in your journal.

minimize (paragraph 3)	keels over (paragraph 4)
travails (paragraph 4)	penance (paragraph 6)
misdemeanors (paragraph 6)	facades (paragraph 10)
plethora (paragraph 11)	irreparable (paragraph 13)
indignantly (paragraph 16)	sleight of hand (paragraph 26)
methodical (paragraph 29)	reticent (paragraph 35)

"The Ways We Lie"

1   The bank called today and I told them my deposit was in the mail, even though I hadn't written a check yet. It'd been a rough day. The baby I'm pregnant with decided to do aerobics on my lungs for two hours, our three-year-old daughter painted the living-room couch with lipstick, the IRS put me on hold for an hour, and I was late to a business meeting because I was tired.

2   I told my client the traffic had been bad. When my partner came home, his haggard face told me his day hadn't gone any better than mine, so when he asked, "How was your day?" I said, "Oh, fine," knowing that one more straw might break his back. A friend called and wanted to take me to lunch. I said I was busy. Four lies in the course of a day, none of which I felt the least bit guilty about.

3   We lie. We all do. We exaggerate, we minimize, we avoid confrontation, we spare people's feelings, we conveniently forget, we keep secrets, we justify lying to the big-guy institutions. Like most people, I indulge myself in

small falsehoods and still think of myself as an honest person. Sure I lie, but it doesn't hurt anything. Or does it?

4   I once tried going a whole week without telling a lie, and it was para-lyzing. I discovered that telling the truth all the time is nearly impossible. It means living with some serious consequences: The bank charges me $60 in overdraft fees, my partner keels over when I tell him about my travails, my client fires me for telling her I didn't feel like being on time, and my friend takes it personally when I say I am not hungry. There must be some merit to lying.

5   But if I justify lying, what makes me different from slick politicians or the corporate robbers who raided the S & L industry?[1] Saying it's okay to lie one way and not the other is hedging. I cannot seem to escape the voice deep inside me that tells me: When someone lies, someone loses.

6   What far-reaching consequences will I, or others, pay as a result of my lie? Will someone's trust be destroyed? Will someone else pay *my* penance because I ducked out? We must consider the *meaning of our actions*. Deception, lies, capital crimes, and misdemeanors all carry meanings. *Webster's* definition of a *lie* is specific: *1: a false statement or action especially made with the intent to deceive; 2: anything that gives or is meant to give a false impression.*

7   A definition like this implies that there are many, many ways to tell a lie. Here are just a few.

8   **The White Lie:** The white lie assumes that the truth will cause more damage than a simple, harmless untruth. Telling a friend he looks great when he looks like hell can be based on a decision that the friend needs a compliment more than a frank opinion. But, in effect, it is the liar deciding what is best for the lied to. Ultimately, it is a vote of no confidence. It is an act of subtle arrogance for anyone to decide what is best for someone else.

9   Yet not all circumstances are quite so cut-and-dried. Take, for instance, the sergeant in Vietnam who knew one of his men was killed in action but listed him as missing so that the man's family would receive indefinite com-pensation instead of the lump-sum pittance the military gives widows and children. His intent was honorable. Yet for twenty years this family kept their hopes alive, unable to move on to a new life.

10   **Facades:** We all put up facades to one degree or another. When I put on a suit to go to see a client, I feel as though I am putting on another face, obeying the expectation that serious businesspeople wear suits rather than sweatpants. But I'm a writer. Normally, I get up, get the kid off to school, and sit at my com-puter in my pajamas until four in the afternoon. When I answer the phone, the caller thinks I'm wearing a suit (though the UPS man knows better).

11   But facades can be dangerous because they are used to seduce others into an illusion. For instance, I recently realized that a former friend was a

---

[1]In the 1980s, corrupt financiers who worked for savings and loan banks (S & Ls) defrauded thousands of people by selling them savings bonds of little or no value.

liar. He presented himself with all the right looks and right words and offered lots of new consciousness theories, fabulous books to read, and fascinating insights. Then I did some business with him, and the time came to pay me. He turned out to be all talk and no walk. I heard a plethora of reasonable excuses, including in-depth descriptions of the big break around the corner. In six months of work, I saw less than a hundred bucks. When I confronted him, he raised both eyebrows and tried to convince me that I'd heard him wrong, that he'd made no commitment to me. A simple investigation into his past revealed a crowded graveyard of disenchanted former friends.

12   **Ignoring the Plain Facts:** In the '60s, the Catholic Church in Massachusetts began hearing complaints that Father James Porter was sexually molesting children. Rather than relieving him of his duties, the ecclesiastical authorities simply moved him from one parish to another between 1960 and 1967, actually providing him with a fresh supply of unsuspecting families and innocent children to abuse. After treatment in 1967 for pedophilia, he went back to work, this time in Minnesota. The new diocese was aware of Father Porter's obsession with children, but they needed priests and recklessly believed treatment had cured him. More children were abused until he was relieved of his duties a year later. By his own admission, Porter may have abused as many as a hundred children.

13   Ignoring the facts may not in and of itself be a form of lying, but consider the context of the situation. If a lie is a false action done with the intent to deceive, then the Catholic Church's conscious covering for Porter created irreparable consequences. The church became a coperpetrator with Porter.

14   **Deflecting:** I've discovered that I can keep anyone from seeing the true me by being selectively blatant. I set a precedent of being up-front about intimate issues, but I never bring up the things I truly want to hide; I just let people assume I'm revealing everything. It's an effective way of hiding.

15   Any good liar knows that the way to perpetuate an untruth is to deflect attention from it. When Clarence Thomas[2] exploded with accusations that the Senate hearings were a "high-tech lynching," he simply switched the focus from a highly charged subject to a radioactive subject. Rather than defending himself, he took the offensive and accused the country of racism. It was a brilliant maneuver. Racism is now politically incorrect in official circles—unlike sexual harassment, which still rewards those who can get away with it.

16   Some of the most skillful deflectors are passive-aggressive[3] people who, when accused of inappropriate behavior, refuse to respond to the accusations. This you-don't-exist stance infuriates the accuser, who, understandably, screams something obscene out of frustration. The trap is sprung and the act of deflection successful, because now the passive-aggressive person can indignantly say, "Who can talk to someone as unreasonable as you?" The real issue is forgotten and the sins of the original victim become the

focus. Feeling guilty of name-calling, the victim is fully tamed and crawls into a hole, ashamed. I have watched this fighting technique work thousands of times in disputes between men and women, and what I've learned is that the real culprit is not necessarily the one who swears the loudest.

17   **Omission:** Omission involves telling most of the truth minus one or two key facts whose absence changes the story completely. You break a pair of glasses that are guaranteed under normal use and get a new pair, without mentioning that the first pair broke during a rowdy game of basketball. Who hasn't tried something like that? But what about the omission of information that could make a difference in how a person lives his or her life?

18   For instance, one day I found out that rabbinical legends tell of another woman in the Garden of Eden before Eve. I was stunned. The omission of the Sumerian goddess Lilith from Genesis—as well as her demonization by ancient misogynists as an embodiment of female evil—felt like spiritual robbery. I felt like I'd just found out my mother was really my stepmother. To take seriously the tradition that Adam was created out of the same mud as his equal counterpart, Lilith, redefines all of Judeo-Christian history.

19   Some renegade Catholic feminists introduced me to a view of Lilith that has been suppressed during the many centuries when this strong goddess was seen only as a spirit of evil. Lilith was a proud goddess who defied Adam's need to control her, attempted negotiations, and when this failed, said adios and left the Garden of Eden.

20   This omission of Lilith from the Bible was a patriarchal strategy to keep women weak. Omitting the strong-women archetype of Lilith from Western religions and starting the story with Eve the Rib helped keep Christian and Jewish women believing they were the lesser sex for thousands of years.

21   **Stereotypes and Clichés:** Stereotype and cliché serve a purpose as a form of shorthand. Our need for vast amounts of information in nanoseconds has made the stereotype vital to modern communication. Unfortunately, it often shuts down original thinking, giving those hungry for the truth a candy bar of misinformation instead of a balanced meal. The stereotype explains a situation with just enough truth to seem unquestionable. All the "isms"—racism, sexism, ageism, et al.—are founded on and fueled by the stereotype and the cliché, which are lies of exaggeration, omission, and ignorance. They are always dangerous. They take a single tree and make it a landscape. They destroy curiosity. They close minds and separate people. The single mother on welfare is assumed to be cheating. Any black male could tell you how much of his identity is obliterated daily by stereotypes. Fat people, ugly people, beautiful people, old people, large-breasted women, short men, the mentally ill, and the homeless all could tell you how much more they are like us than we want to think. I once admitted to a group of people that I had a mouth like a

---

[2]African-American judge accused of sexual harassment, nominatied by President George H. W. Bush to the U.S. Supreme Court in 1991.
[3]A psychological term applying to behavior that is hostile but not openly confrontational.

truck driver. Much to my surprise, a man stood up and said. "I'm a truck driver, and I never cuss." Needless to say, I was humbled.

22   **Groupthink:** Irving Janis, in *Victims of Group Think*, defines this sort of lie as a psychological phenomenon within decision-making groups in which loyalty to the group has become more important than any other value, with the result that dissent and the appraisal of alternatives are suppressed. If you've ever worked on a committee or in a corporation, you've encountered groupthink. It requires a combination of other forms of lying—ignorance of facts, selective memory, omission, and denial, to name a few.

23   The textbook example of groupthink came on December 7, 1941. From as early as the fall of 1941, the warnings came in, one after another, that Japan was preparing for a massive military operation. The Navy command in Hawaii assumed Pearl Harbor was invulnerable—the Japanese weren't stupid enough to attack the United States' most important base. On the other hand, racist stereotypes said the Japanese weren't smart enough to invent a torpedo effective in less than 60 feet of water (the fleet was docked in 30 feet); after all, U.S. technology hadn't been able to do it.

24   On Friday, December 5, normal weekend leave was granted to all the commanders at Pearl Harbor, even though the Japanese consulate in Hawaii was busy burning papers. Within the tight, good-ole-boy cohesiveness of the U.S. command in Hawaii, the myth of invulnerability stayed well entrenched. No one in the group considered the alternatives. The rest is history.

25   **Out-and-Out Lies:** Of all the ways to lie, I like this one the best, probably because I get tired of trying to figure out the real meanings behind things. At least I can trust the bald-faced lie. I once asked my five-year-old nephew, "Who broke the fence?" (I had seen him do it.) He answered, "The murderers." Who could argue?

26   At least when this sort of lie is told it can be easily confronted. As the person who is lied to, I know where I stand. The bald-faced lie doesn't toy with my perceptions—it argues with them. It doesn't try to refashion reality, it tries to refute it. *Read my lips* . . . No sleight of hand. No guessing. If this were the only form of lying, there would be no such thing as floating anxiety or the adult-children-of-alcoholics movement.

27   **Dismissal:** Dismissal is perhaps the slipperiest of all lies. Dismissing feelings, perceptions, or even the raw facts of a situation ranks as a kind of lie that can do as much damage to a person as any other kind of lie.

28   The roots of many mental disorders can be traced back to the dismissal of reality. Imagine that a person is told from the time she is a tot that her perceptions are inaccurate: *"Mommie, I'm scared."* "No you're not, darling." *"I don't like that man next door, he makes me feel icky."* "Johnny, that's a terrible thing to say, of course you like him. You go over there right now and be nice to him."

29   I've often mused over the idea that madness is actually a sane reaction to an insane world. Psychologist R. D. Laing supports this

hypothesis in *Sanity, Madness, and the Family*, an account of his investigation into the families of schizophrenics. The common thread that ran through all of the families he studied was a deliberate, staunch dismissal of the patient's perceptions from a very early age. Each of the patients started out with an accurate grasp of reality, which, through meticulous and methodical dismissal, was demolished until the only reality the patient could trust was catatonia.

30   Dismissal runs the gamut. Mild dismissal can be quite handy for forgiving the foibles of others in our day-to-day lives. Toddlers who have just learned to manipulate their parents' attention sometimes are dismissed out of necessity. Absolute attention from the parents would require so much energy that no one would get to eat dinner. But we must be careful and attentive about how far we take our "necessary" dismissals. Dismissal is a dangerous tool, because it's nothing less than a lie.

31   **Delusion:** I could write a book on this one. Delusion, a cousin of dismissal, is the tendency to see excuses as facts. It's a powerful lying tool because it filters out information that contradicts what we want to believe. Alcoholics who believe the problems in their lives are legitimate reasons for drinking rather than results of the drinking offer the classic example of deluded thinking. Delusion uses the mind's ability to see things in myriad ways to support what it wants to be the truth.

32   But delusion is also a survival mechanism we all use. If we were to fully contemplate the consequences of our stockpiles of nuclear weapons or global warming, we could hardly function on a day-to-day level. We don't want to incorporate that much reality into our lives because to do so would be paralyzing.

33   Delusion works as an adhesive to keep the status quo intact. It shamelessly employs dismissal, omission, and amnesia, among other sorts of lies. Its most cunning defense is that it cannot see itself.

34   These are only a few of the ways we lie. Or are lied to. As I said earlier, it's not easy to entirely eliminate lies in our daily lives. No matter how pious we may try to be, we will still embellish, hedge, and omit to lubricate the daily machinery of living. But there is a world of difference between telling functional lies and living a lie. Martin Buber[4] once said, "The lie is the spirit committing treason against itself." Our acceptance of lies becomes a cultural cancer that eventually shrouds and reorders reality until moral garbage becomes as invisible to us as water is to a fish.

35   How much do we tolerate before we become sick and tired of being sick and tired? When will we stand up and declare our *right* to trust? When do we stop accepting that the real truth is in the fine print? Whose lips do we read this year when we vote for president? When will we stop being so ret-

---

[4]Jewish theologian and philosopher.

icent about making judgments? When do we stop turning over our personal power and responsibility to liars?

36   Maybe if I don't tell the bank the check's in the mail, I'll be less tolerant of the lies told me every day. A country song I once heard said it all for me: "You've got to stand for something or you'll fall for anything."

 **AFTER YOU READ**

Vocabulary Practice

1. Choose at least three words from the Vocabulary Development list on page 759 and write sentences using those words. You may write one sentence using all three words if you wish. Answers will vary.

2. Travails.
Answers will vary.

2. What word from the Vocabulary Development list means "hard work; toil"? Use the word in a sentence that clearly shows its meaning.

3. What does the word *reticent* mean in the following sentence? "When do we stop accepting that the real truth is in the fine print? . . . When will we stop being so reticent about making judgments?"

   a. Silent   b. Obnoxious

   c. Funny   d. Immature

Comprehension

Circle the correct answer.

1. In her opening anecdote, to whom does Ericsson not tell a lie?

   a. The bank   b. Her client

   c. Her partner   d. Her daughter

2. How does Ericsson feel when she tries to go a whole week without lying?

   a. Paralyzed   b. Energyzed

   c. Proud   d. Defeated

3. The white lie assumes that the truth will

   a. make a bad situation worse.

   b. make the person telling the lie look bad.

   c. cause more damage than an untruth would.

   d. unburden whoever is telling the lie.

4. Omission involves telling

   a. none of the truth.   b. most of the truth.

   c. very little of the truth. d. all of the truth.

5. What kind of lie does Ericsson "like" the most?

    a. Delusion   b. Omission

    (c.) The out-and-out lie   d. Dismissal

Content

1. What does Ericsson mean when she says, "When someone lies, someone loses"? To what extent do you agree with her?

2. Why does Ericsson say we lie? What other reasons can you think of?

3. What lie does Ericsson say she likes best? Why?

Style and Structure

1. What is the main point of Ericsson's essay? Restate her main idea in your own words. Lying always has a price.

2. How well do Ericsson's examples illustrate her main idea? Do you agree with her main idea? Explain. Answers will vary.

3. What can you tell about Ericsson's audience? How do her vocabulary and examples target her audience? Her audience is adult and educated. Words such as *meticulously* are not often used for children. She targets people who lie; she implies, by her examples of common-place lies, that everyone lies. Thus, she targets everyone.

Writing Assignments

1. *Write a paragraph in which you assume the opposite stance from Ericsson and argue that lying is necessary, even beneficial.* You may use some of Ericsson's own examples to support your argument, but be sure to use your own experiences and observations, too.

2. At what point do you think children should be told the truth, regardless of its brutality or unpleasantness? *In a well-developed paragraph, explain when children should be told the truth,* offering examples from your life and from Ericsson's essay for support.

3. Think about your habits of telling the truth. Does lying really solve problems? *Write an essay arguing that telling a lie is or is not the easiest way to deal with a problem.* Use specific examples to illustrate your ideas..

Benedict Carey

"Have You Heard? Gossip Turns Out to Serve a Purpose"

Previously a writer for the *Los Angeles Times,* Benedict Carey wrote many articles on the subject of HIV and AIDS. As a health reporter, Carey began broadening his scope to include stories connected to the academic psychology community. In "Have You Heard?" Carey explores the reasons people "tell tales out of school" as well as the potential benefits of such storytelling.

BEFORE YOU READ

Think about the following questions. Write your responses on a separate sheet or in your journal.

- What is your attitude toward gossip, or talk about other people?
- To what extent do you participate in gossip of either a positive or negative type? Explain.
- What is one experience that you had in which gossip played a role in your life?

VOCABULARY DEVELOPMENT

Look up the following words in a dictionary. Write down their meanings on a separate sheet or in your journal.

peccadilloes (paragraph 2)	derogatory (paragraph 22)
sullies (paragraph 5)	gravitates (paragraph 28)
denigrate (paragraph 6)	factions (paragraph 28)
scuttlebutt (paragraph 18)	illicit (paragraph 18)
calibrated (paragraph 20)	shun (paragraph 26)

"Have You Heard? Gossip Turns Out to Serve a Purpose"

1   Juicy gossip moves so quickly—He did what? She has pictures?—that few people have time to cover their ears, even if they wanted to.

2   "I heard a lot in the hallway, on the way to class," said Mady Miraglia, 35, a high school history teacher in Los Gatos, Calif., speaking about a previous job, where she got a running commentary from fellow teachers on the sexual peccadilloes and classroom struggles of her colleagues.

3   "To be honest, it made me feel better as a teacher to hear others being put down," she said. "I was out there on my own, I had no sense of how I was doing in class, and the gossip gave me some connection. And I felt like it gave me status, knowing information, being on the inside."

4   Gossip has long been dismissed by researchers as little more than background noise, blather with no useful function. But some investigators now say that gossip should be central to any study of group interaction.

5   People find it irresistible for good reason: Gossip not only helps clarify and enforce the rules that keep people working well together, studies suggest, but it circulates crucial information about the behavior of others that

cannot be published in an office manual. As often as it sullies reputations, psychologists say, gossip offers a foothold for newcomers in a group and a safety net for group members who feel in danger of falling out.

6   "There has been a tendency to denigrate gossip as sloppy and unreliable" and unworthy of serious study, said David Sloan Wilson, a professor of biology and anthropology at the State University of New York at Binghamton and the author of *Darwin's Cathedral,* a book on evolution and group behavior. "But gossip appears to be a very sophisticated, multifunctional interaction which is important in policing behaviors in a group and defining group membership."

7   When two or more people huddle to share inside information about another person who is absent, they are often spreading important news, and enacting a mutually protective ritual that may have evolved from early grooming behaviors, some biologists argue.

8   Long-term studies of Pacific Islanders, American middle-school children and residents of rural Newfoundland and Mexico, among others, have confirmed that the content and frequency of gossip are universal: people devote anywhere from a fifth to two-thirds or more of their daily conversation to gossip, and men appear to be just as eager for the skinny as women.

9   Sneaking, lying and cheating among friends or acquaintances make for the most savory material, of course, and most people pass on their best nuggets to at least two other people, surveys find.

10   This grapevine branches out through almost every social group and it functions, in part, to keep people from straying too far outside the group's rules, written and unwritten, social scientists find.

11   In one recent experiment, Dr. Wilson led a team of researchers who asked a group of 195 men and women to rate their approval or disapproval of several situations in which people talked behind the back of a neighbor. In one, a rancher complained to other ranchers that his neighbor had neglected to fix a fence, allowing cattle to wander and freeload. The report was accurate, and the students did not disapprove of the gossip.

12   But men in particular, the researchers found, strongly objected if the rancher chose to keep mum about the fence incident.

13   "Plain and simple he should have told about the problem to warn other ranchers," wrote one study participant, expressing a common sentiment that, in this case, a failure to gossip put the group at risk.

14   "We're told we're not supposed to gossip, that our reputation plummets, but in this context there may be an expectation that you should gossip: you're obligated to tell, like an informal version of the honor code at military academies," Dr. Wilson said.

15   This rule-enforcing dynamic is hardly confined to the lab. For 18 months, Kevin Kniffin, an anthropologist at the University of Wisconsin, tracked the social interactions of a university crew team, about 50 men and women who rowed together in groups of four or eight.

16   Dr. Kniffin said he was still analyzing his research notes. But a preliminary finding, he said, was that gossip levels peaked when the team included

a slacker, a young man who regularly missed practices or showed up late. Fellow crew members joked about the slacker's sex life behind his back and made cruel cracks about his character and manhood, in part because the man's shortcoming reflected badly on the entire team.

17   "As soon as this guy left the team, the people were back to talking about radio, food, politics, weather, those sorts of things," Dr. Kniffin said. "There was very little negative gossip."

18   Given this protective group function, gossiping too little may be at least as risky as gossiping too much, some psychologists say. After all, scuttlebutt is the most highly valued social currency there is. While humor and story telling can warm any occasion, a good scoop spreads through a room like an illicit and irresistible drug, passed along in nods and crooked smiles, in discreet walks out to the balcony, the corridor, the powder room.

19   Knowing that your boss is cheating on his wife, or that a sister-in-law has a drinking problem or a rival has benefited from a secret trust fund may be enormously important, and in many cases change a person's behavior for the better.

20   "We all know people who are not calibrated to the social world at all, who if they participated in gossip sessions would learn a whole lot of stuff they need to know and can't learn anywhere else, like how reliable people are, how trustworthy," said Sarah Wert, a psychologist at Yale. "Not participating in gossip at some level can be unhealthy, and abnormal."

21   Talking out of school may also buffer against low-grade depressive moods. In one recent study, Dr. Wert had 84 college students write about a time in their lives when they felt particularly alienated socially, and also about a memory of being warmly accepted.

22   After finishing the task, Dr. Wert prompted the participants to gossip with a friend about a mutual acquaintance, as she filmed the exchanges. Those who rated their self-esteem highly showed a clear pattern: they spread good gossip when they felt accepted and a more derogatory brand when they felt marginalized.

23   The gossip may involve putting someone else down to feel better by comparison. Or it may simply be a way to connect with someone else and share insecurities. But the end result, she said, is often a healthy relief of social and professional anxiety.

24   Ms. Miraglia, the high school teacher, said that in her previous job she found it especially comforting to hear about more senior teachers' struggle to control difficult students. "It was my first job, and I felt overwhelmed, and to hear someone say, 'There's no control in that class' about another teacher, that helped build my confidence," she said.

25   She said she also heard about teachers who made inappropriate comments to students about sex, a clear violation of school policy and professional standards.

26   Adept gossipers usually sense which kinds of discreet talk are most likely to win acceptance from a particular group. For example, a closely knit

corporate team with clear values—working late hours, for instance—will tend to embrace a person who gripes in private about a colleague who leaves early and shun one who complains about the late nights.

27   By contrast, a widely dispersed sales force may lap up gossip about colleagues, but take it lightly, allowing members to work however they please, said Eric K. Foster, a scholar at the Institute for Survey Research at Temple University in Philadelphia, who recently published an analysis of gossip research.

28   It is harder to judge how gossip will move through groups that are split into factions, like companies with divisions that are entirely independent, Dr. Foster said. "In these situations, it is the person who gravitates into an intermediate position, making connections between the factions, who controls the gossip flow and holds a lot of power," he said.

29   Such people can mask devious intentions, spread false rumors and manipulate others for years, as anyone who has worked in an organization for a long time knows. But to the extent that healthy gossip has evolved to protect social groups, it will also ultimately expose many of those who cheat and betray. Any particularly nasty gossip has an author or authors, after all, and any functioning gossip network builds up a memory.

30   So do the people who are tuned in to the network. In one 2004 study, psychologists had college students in Ohio fill out questionnaires, asking about the best gossip they had heard in the last week, the last month and the last year. The students then explained in writing what they learned by hearing the stories. Among the life lessons:

31   "Infidelity will eventually catch up with you," "Cheerful people are not necessarily happy people" and "Just because someone says they have pictures of something doesn't mean they do."

32   None of which they had learned in class.

Benedict, Carey, "Have You Heard, Gossip Turns out to Serve a Purpose" from *The New York Times*, August 16, 2005. Copyright © 2005 The New York Times Co. Reprinted by permission.

AFTER YOU READ

Vocabulary Practice

3. Commentary, information, blather, inside information, important news, the skinny, best nuggets, the grapevine, scuttlebutt, talking out of school, discreet talk; so many names for *gossip* indicates that it's an entrenched, important part of our culture.

1. Choose at least three words from the Vocabulary Development list on page 767 and write sentences using those words. You may write one sentence using all three words if you wish.   Answers will vary

2. What word from the Vocabulary Development list means "to avoid deliberately and especially habitually"? Use the word in a sentence that clearly shows its meaning.   Shun. Answers will vary

3. What are some names Carey gives to gossip? What do these words—and the fact that there are so many—say about people's attitudes toward gossip?

Comprehension

1. How does Carey say that gossip moves?

   a. So unpredictably (b.) So quickly

   c. So hurtfully d. So slowly

2. How does heaving gossip make one high school history teacher feel?

   (a.) Better as a teacher, with some connection

   b. Worried as a teacher, with some caution

   c. Powerful as a teacher, with some influence

   d. Worse as a teacher, with some insecurities

3. What, according to experts in Carey's article, does gossip offer to newcomers?

   a. A code b. A guideline

   c. An "in" (d.) A foothold

4. Why did members of a crew team gossip about a particular team member?

   a. He was better than they were.

   b. He was the team captain.

   (c.) He was a slacker.

   d. He spread gossip about them.

5. According to Carey, what is one benefit of gossip?

   (a.) It buffers against low-grade depressive moods.

   b. It helps people vent their negative feelings.

   c. It helps people gather positive comments about themselves.

   d. It prevents people from committing suicide.

Content

1. Gossip helps clarify and enforce the rules that keep people working well together, circulates crucial information about the behavior of others, and offers a foothold for newcomers in a group and a safety net for group members who feel in danger of falling out.

2. When their news will help other people, as in the case of the ranchers.

3. Low-grade depressive moods, not feeling connected to the group

1. What are some reasons people find gossip "irresistible"?

2. Under what circumstances, according to the article, *should* people gossip?

3. What are some downsides of *not* gossiping, according to the article?

Style and Structure

1. What is Carey's point? Rewrite his main idea in your own words.   Gossip has a purpose.

2. New teacher is made to feel like part of the group; crew team defines and enforces team rules by gossiping about slacker rower; rancher tells people about his fence issue; prevents low-grade depressive moods

2. What kinds of examples does Carey use to show how gossip helps people?

3. What transitional words or expressions does Carey use at the start of paragraphs 17, 22, and 27?   As soon as, After, By contrast

Writing Assignments

1. Carey writes about a high school teacher who felt that gossip gave her "some connection" to others. Is gossip always positive? *Write a paragraph in which*

you explain how gossip has had a positive or negative effect on you or someone you know. Use examples from your own experiences to illustrate your ideas.

2. Carey writes about situations in which people feel they *should* be told some gossip. What situations, if any, require people to spread gossip? *Write a paragraph explaining how certain situations do or do not require people to spread gossip.* Use examples and illustrations from your own life to support your ideas.

3. Carey writes about different kinds of gossip: people who don't do their work, people who don't meet their responsibilities, and people who cheat, among others. What other kinds of gossip are there? *Write an essay in which you explain, using examples, at least three different kinds of gossip.* Be sure to use examples from your own life for support.

Judith Martin

"Manners Matter"

Widely known for her syndicated "Miss Manners" column, Judith Martin reigns as an expert on contemporary etiquette and has written several etiquette-oriented books, such as *Miss Manners Saves Civilization*. In "Manners Matter," Martin contrasts the law with etiquette, stating that each performs necessary functions in society, though etiquette often addresses conflicts before they escalate to the level where law must intercede.

BEFORE YOU READ

Think about the following questions. Write your responses on a separate sheet or in your journal.

■ Make a list of the manners you use daily. Your list may include such items as saying "please" or "thank you," and it may include more active forms of behavior such as letting a driver enter your lane ahead of you.

■ What kinds of people or situations cause you to use good manners?

■ How important do you think manners are?

VOCABULARY DEVELOPMENT

Look up the following words in a dictionary. Write down their meanings on a separate sheet or in your journal.

etiquette (paragraph 1)   repressive (paragraph 1) trivial (paragraph 2)   impulses (paragraph 5)

pillage (paragraph 5)   provocations (paragraph 6)

presiding (paragraph 8)   deduce (paragraph 2)

"Manners Matter"

1   Society's condemnation of etiquette for being artificial and repressive stems from an idealistic if hopelessly naive belief in what we might call Original Innocence—the idea that people are born naturally good but corrupted by civilization. This is a very sweet idea, but it bears no relation to human nature. Yes, we're born adorable, or our parents would strangle us in our cribs. But we are not born good; that has to be learned. And if it is not learned, when we grow up and are not quite so cuddly, even our parents can't stand us. . . .

2   Administering etiquette, like administering law, is more than just knowing a set of rules. Even the most apparently trivial etiquette rules are dictated by principles of manners which are related to, and sometimes overlap with, moral principles. Respect and dignity, for example, are two big principles of manners from which a lot of etiquette rules are derived. This does not mean that you can simply deduce your rules of behavior from first principles. There are things you just have to know, like whether a man is supposed to show respect by taking his hat off as in church, or putting a hat on, as in a synagogue.

3   Moral people who understand these principles still figure that civility is not a top-priority virtue. First, they're going to fix the world, and then on the seventh day they're going to introduce civility. Deep in their hearts, they think etiquette is best applied to activities that don't really matter much, like eating or getting married.

4   But the absence of manners is a cause of some of our most serious social problems. For instance, our school systems have broken down from what is called lack of discipline. What does that mean? It means that such etiquette rules as sitting still, listening to others, taking turns, and not hitting others have not been taught. A great deal of crime begins with the short tempers people develop from being treated rudely all the time, and from perceived forms of disrespect. Getting "dissed," as it's called in the streets, is one of today's leading motivations for murder.

5   Nor will the business of government be done well, or sometimes done at all, by people who can't work together in civil, statesman-like ways. That is why we have all those highly artificial forms of speech for use in legislatures and courtrooms. Even in a courtroom where freedom of speech is being defended, there is no freedom to speak rudely. In legislatures we have phrases like "my distinguished colleague seems to be sadly mistaken"—

because if we spoke freely and frankly, people would be punching each other out instead of airing arguments. We have a legal system that bars us from acting on natural human impulses to pillage, assault, and so forth. Whether we appreciate it or not, we also have an extra-legal system, called etiquette, that does many of the same things.

6   Law is supposed to address itself to the serious and dangerous impulses that endanger life, limb, and property. Etiquette addresses provocations that are minor but can grow serious if unchecked. Etiquette has some very handy conflict resolution systems—such as the apology, sending flowers in the morning, saying "I don't know what I was thinking"—that help settle things before they have to go through the legal system. But as we've seen in the past few decades, when people refuse to comply with etiquette the law has to step in. A classic example is smoking. We've had to use the law to explain such simple etiquette rules as: You don't blow smoke in other people's faces, and you don't blow insults into other people's faces pretending it's health advice. Sexual harassment is another example that had to be turned over to the law because those in a position of power refused to obey basic values as "Keep your hands to yourself."

7   It's a dangerous idea to keep asking the law to do etiquette's job. Not that I wouldn't love to have a squad of tough cops who would go around and roust people who don't answer invitations and write thank-you notes. But when we have to enlarge the scope of law to enforce manners, it really does threaten freedom. Even I think people should have a legal right to be obnoxious. I don't think they should exercise it. And I do think people should be prepared to take the consequences. If you stomp on the flag, some people will not want to listen to your opinions. If you disrupt and spoil activities for other people who want to participate, they're going to throw you out. Those are the mild little sanctions of etiquette, but they work.

8   Trying to live by law alone does not work. Every little nasty remark is labeled a slander and taken to court; meanness gets dressed up as "mental cruelty"; and everything else that's annoying is declared a public health hazard. That's why we need the little extra-legal system over which I have the honor of presiding.

 **AFTER YOU READ**

Vocabulary Practice

1. Choose at least three words from the Vocabulary Development list on pages 772–773 and write sentences using those words. You may write one sentence using all three words if you wish. Answers will vary.

3. Answers will vary; sets of rules, moral principles, virtue, problems, discipline, disrespect, pillage, assaults, impulses, provocations, conflicts, insults, sanctions, slander

2. What word from the Vocabulary Development list means "keeping down, or holding back"? Use the word in a sentence that clearly shows the meaning of the word. Repressive. Answers will vary.

3. Martin gives many examples of poor manners, from not taking a hat off in church to sexual harassment, some of which are not only poor manners, but also illegal acts. What kinds of words does Martin use to discuss various breaches in behavior? List at least three terms Martin uses and write sentences showing their meanings.

Comprehension

Circle the correct answer.

1. Martin opens her essay with a discussion of
   a. Original Sin.
   b. Original Innocence.
   c. Original Truth.
   d. Original Behavior.

2. Martin says that society condemns etiquette for being
   a. artificial and repressive.
   b. stale and old-fashioned.
   c. energized and in vogue.
   d. difficult and unnecessary.

3. Martin says that many forms of manners are related to
   a. lawful actions.
   b. kind behavior.
   c. moral principles.
   d. childlike innocence.

4. Which one of the following does Martin not specify as a problem stemming from poor manners?
   a. Sexual harassment
   b. Murder
   c. Slander
   d. Road rage

5. Besides etiquette, what other code of conduct does Martin say ensures that people do not treat each other horribly?
   a. The Ten Commandments
   b. The law
   c. The Koran
   d. People's natural instincts

Content

1. According to Martin, why are we "born adorable"? So our parents won't strangle us

2. What two things does Martin say, in paragraph 2, that people need to understand in order to practice good manners? Moral principles and specific knowledge

3. In what areas does Martin say people have developed "highly artificial forms of speech"? Why does she say we need them? Legislatures and courtrooms; so we don't punch each other out

Style and Structure

1. What is Martin's argument? State her main idea in your own words. Manners matter.

2. Smokers, sexual harassment, speaking in court.

2. What examples does Martin give to support her main idea?

3. Who is Martin's audience? How can you tell? Cite examples from the text to illustrate your ideas. Intelligent, informed people who are familiar with her examples such as legislature, synagogue, courtroom

Writing Assignments

1. Martin claims, "We are not born good; that has to be learned." What do you think? *Write a paragraph agreeing or disagreeing with the idea that people are not born good.* Give examples from the text and from your own life in order to illustrate your ideas.

2. Martin writes, "Etiquette addresses provocations that are minor but can grow serious if unchecked." *Using Martin's definition of "etiquette" as a starting point, write a paragraph illustrating that idea.* Use examples from different areas of life to clarify Martin's definition. Some possible examples to explore follow: using your car blinker to signal that you'd like to merge rather than simply forcing your way in; shouting only positive comments at a sports event rather than disparaging another team.

3. Think about the role that manners play in your life. *Then, write an essay arguing that manners are important in a specific area of life.* Some possible areas of your life to focus on are school, work, family relationships, nonfamily personal relationships, daily living, travel, politics, and entertainment (going to the movies or some type of performance or sports activity, for instance). Use specific details from your experience and observations to illustrate your ideas.

Barbara Graham

"Confessions of a Quit Addict"

A journalist, playwright, and author, Barbara Graham uses humor and irony to drive her points home. She has written *Women Who Run with the Poodles* in response to the more serious *Women Who Run with the Wolves* by Clarissa Pinkola Estes. In "Confessions of a Quit Addict," Graham explores her "addiction" to quitting from her first experience quitting to the beginning of her "recovery."

BEFORE YOU READ

Think about the following questions. Write your responses on a separate sheet or in your journal.

■ What do you think about quitting? What have you been told about quitting?

■ Have you ever quit something and felt good about it? Felt bad about it? Explain.

■ Are some reasons for quitting better than others? Explain.

VOCABULARY DEVELOPMENT

Look up the following words in a dictionary. Write down their meanings on a separate sheet or in your journal.

tenacious (paragraph 2)   disdainful (paragraph 2)

biochemical (paragraph 3)   mantra (paragraph 3)

collaborator (paragraph 4)   nirvana (paragraph 4)

lucrative (paragraph 4)   paradoxically (paragraph 8)

unbidden (paragraph 9)   conspicuous (paragraph 10)

"Confessions of a Quit Addict"

1   By the time I heard Timothy Leary chant "Turn on, tune in, drop out" from the stage of New York's Fillmore East, I had already quit college. The year was 1967, and Leary's battle cry was for me more a confirmation of what I already believed than a call to action.

2   I had never been much good at doing things that didn't arouse my passion. Even when I was a young girl, it was obvious that I had been born without the stick-to-it, nose-to-the-grindstone gene. I was stubborn, tenacious in my devotion to the people and things I loved, disdainful of everything else. There was no in-between. In high school I got straight A's in English and flunked math. When it came time for college, I enrolled at NYU because it was the only way I could think of to live in Greenwich Village and get my parents to pick up the tab. But I rarely made it to classes and dropped out one month into my sophomore year.

3   That was the first time I felt the rush of quitting, the instant high of cutting loose, the biochemical buzz of burning my bridges. The charge had to do not with leaving college for something else, but with leaving, period—the pure act of making the break. Suddenly it seemed possible to reinvent myself, to discard my old life like last year's outfit and step into a new one—free from the responsibilities and relationships that had dragged me down. I got an unlisted telephone number and warned my parents to stay away. "When one jumps over the edge, one is bound to land somewhere," wrote D. H. Lawrence, and for a long time this was my mantra.

4   It didn't take long for me to find a collaborator, a master of disappearing acts who made me look like a rookie. Brian was ready to morph one life into the next on the turn of a dime. I became his loyal apprentice, and during the summer of 1968, shortly after Bobby Kennedy and Martin Luther

King Jr. were gunned down, we sold everything we owned and quit our jobs, our friends, our apartment, the urban jungle, America and blight of Vietnam, and fled to Europe. But our new life didn't quite match our dreams: As winter neared, we found ourselves living in a rusty old van on the outskirts of Rome, hungry and cold and hard up for cash. From there, we boarded a freighter for Puerto Rico—which turned out not to be the nirvana we'd imagined, either—especially after the little episode with customs officials over a speck of hashish. Still, a pattern had been set: living in one place, dreaming of another, working at odd jobs (mine included secretary, salesgirl, cocktail waitress, draft counselor, nude model, warehouse clerk, candle maker), earning just enough money to get us to the next destination. We crisscrossed the United States, went north to British Columbia, and lived in every conceivable sort of dwelling from tenements and tents to farmhouses and plywood shacks. Sometimes I'd grow attached to a place and plant a garden, thinking that *this* time things would work out and we'd stay forever—or at least long enough to see the flowers bloom. But something always went wrong: It rained too much (British Columbia), the cost of living was too high (Colorado), the air wasn't pure enough (Southern California), or we couldn't find work that was meaningful, not to mention lucrative enough for us (everywhere).

5   For a long time it didn't matter that we weren't happy anywhere, because the rush of heading off into the unknown and starting over was more potent and trippy than anything we smoked, and we just kept going—even after our son, Clay, was born. But one day, in the mountains of Northern California, when our latest scheme for finding True Happiness—living close to nature, in a house we built, near another family—fell apart, I just snapped. In that moment I knew that I no longer had it in me to continue feeding on fantasies of a future that inevitably turned to dust. That night I made this entry in my journal: "I'm so sick of listening to ourselves talk about what's going to be—plans, plans, plans. I want to live in the present for once, not in the future. I mean *live*, settle down, make a home for my son." I had understood finally that the problem wasn't in the places we went or the people we found there but in ourselves. We could shed our surroundings but not our own skin. No matter who or what we left behind, our private demons followed, and our differences with one another erupted like a sleeping volcano the minute we stopped running. In the end, there was nowhere left to go, no place left to leave behind, no one left to say good-bye to except each other.

6   It had taken thousands of miles and one child for me to understand that the quitting I took for freedom was as much of a trap as the social conventions we were trying to escape. Together, Brian and I had been so busy saying no to everything that might limit our options that, except for Clay, we'd neglected to say yes to anything. We had no careers, few friends, and no place to call home. Moreover, what had begun as a journey to find our "true"

selves, independent of other people's expectations, had turned into an addictive cycle of fantasy and failure, followed by another stab at redemption. After seven years, I felt sad, spent, and more alienated than ever—from Brian, from the rest of the world, and, most frighteningly, from myself. More than anything, I longed to land *somewhere*.

7   Still, I don't consider myself a "recovering" quitter. That would put too negative a spin on an act that is sometimes the best, most honest, and most creative response to a life situation, as well as a tremendous source of energy and power. What's more, in the years since Brian and I went our separate ways, I've walked away from a marriage and a number of significant relationships, bailed out of college a second time (just a few credits shy of getting my degree), and moved back and forth across the country twice. As for my relationship to the workforce, it officially ended 15 years ago when I left a long-term (for me—it lasted all of eight months) position as the publicist for a hospital specializing in unusual diseases. I simply could not deal with a life in which I was expected to show up at the same place at the same time five days a week and not take frequent naps. So I did what any self-respecting jobaphobic would do: I became a writer.

8   But, paradoxically, knowing that I'll always have it in me to be a quit artist has in recent years made me want to hunker down, dig deeper, stick around long enough to watch the garden bloom. (I've even gone so far as to plant perennials.) This change has come gradually, on tiptoes, without the fanfare or splash of the Big Quit. Looking back at my current marriage of 12 years, I see that the constancy my husband and I have maintained despite our share of hard times would have, in the past, sent me scrambling in search of higher drama. For me, the act of staying put has required far more courage and humility than it once took to let go. This is somewhat ironic, considering that I used to believe that my capacity to turn my back and walk away from almost anyone or anything was a sure sign of bravery.

9   Over the years, I've also come to understand that even if I don't go chasing after change, it will do a perfectly good job of finding me. Upheavals, startling turns, and unpredictable shifts have all come unbidden—especially when I've been at my most settled. Besides, I've watched enough people I love die to know that no matter how hard we try to be the sole authors of our own stories, life itself will eventually have its way and quit *us*.

10   And though sometimes I miss the rush of cutting loose—and, God knows, the impulse still arises—I've learned that, for the most part, it's impossible to travel deep and wide at the same time. Now it's simply more interesting, more richly satisfying, to mine my life just as it is, with all of its wild imperfections and—superficially, at least—lack of conspicuous drama. My family, my home, close friendships, the natural world, and the worlds conjured in my work constantly surprise me with their nourishment—a thick and complex root system I might never have known if I hadn't stopped severing the ties that bind.

 **AFTER YOU READ**

Vocabulary Practice

2. Unbidden. Answers will vary.
3. Quit, dropped out, cutting loose, burning my bridges, making the break, reinvent myself, discard my old life, heading off, escape, Big Quit, chasing after change

1. Choose at least three words from the Vocabulary Development list on page 777 and write sentences using those words. You may write one sentence using all three words if you wish.   Answers will vary.

2. What word from the Vocabulary Development list means "not commanded or invited"? Use the word in a sentence to show clearly what it means.

3. Graham uses different terms for *quitting*. Make a list of these terms, and write a few sentences explaining which expressions for *quitting* you find most effective.

Comprehension

Circle the correct answer.

1. Graham describes herself as someone who lacked
   a. a love for life.
   b. a nose-to-the-grindstone gene.
   c. a positive self-image.
   d. supportive parents.

2. The first time Graham felt "the rush of quitting" came
   a. when she quit her job.
   b. when she moved out of her parents' home.
   c. when she dropped a class.
   d. when she quit college.

3. Who was Graham's "collaborator" in quitting?
   a. Ben   b. Barry
   c. Brian   d. Brad

4. In which of the following locations did Graham not live?
   a. Europe   b. Texas
   c. Puerto Rico   d. British Columbia

5. What did Graham do when she found a place she liked?
   a. Plant a garden   b. Paint the house
   c. Buy a bed   d. Make jam

Content

1. What does Timothy Leary's chant—"Turn on, tune in, drop out"—become for Graham?   A confirmation of what she already believed

2. How happy was Graham's life with Brian? Why?   Not very happy; tired, spent, alienated

3. Why does Graham become a writer?   Because she can't make herself hold down an eight-to-five job

1. Change can be good, but it won't solve problems all by itself.

3. Rusty van in Rome; problems in Puerto Rico; too much rain in British Columbia; too expensive in Colorado; dirty air in Southern California

Style and Structure

1. What is Graham's main idea? Rewrite her point in your own words.

2. Graham's essay is divided into two parts. What does Graham discuss in each part? The "glories" of quitting; the downside of quitting

3. What examples does Graham use to show that her life as a quitter wasn't everything she wanted it to be? Explain.

Writing Assignments

1. Graham writes about the "rush of quitting." How does quitting feel for you? *Write a paragraph describing how you felt when you quit something.* Use examples from your life to support your ideas.

2. Think about a time in your life when you felt forced to quit something. *Write a paragraph explaining the events that led you to make your decision—to quit or to continue.* Include illustrations from your life to make your ideas clear.

3. Graham writes that at one time she believed that turning her back "was a sure sign of bravery." How hard is quitting? *Write an essay in which you argue that quitting or staying put is the more difficult choice.* Include illustrations from your life to make your ideas clear.

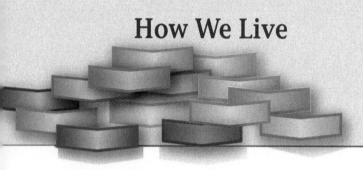

How We Live

Perhaps more significant than what we choose to learn or what we choose to believe is how we live on a daily basis. Do we retain the heritage we were born with, or do we forge ahead in an effort to "progress" to success? "Back, but Not Home" and "My Mother's English" explore the conflicts that affect people who are born into one culture and grow up in another. How we choose to vent our frustrations when life twists in ways we would not have chosen is another important theme. "The Plot Against People," "A Nonsmoker with a Smoker," and "What Is Poverty?" all seek to explore how we handle situations that have spun—in varying degrees—out of our control.

Readings in This Section

Maria Muniz

"Back, but Not Home"

A writer with Cuban roots, Maria Muniz examines the difficult choices that immigrants must make. Weighing the benefits of being American against the loss of her heritage, Muniz concludes that understanding one's background is essential to feeling at home in one's skin.

 BEFORE YOU READ

Think about the following questions. Write your responses on a separate sheet or in your journal.

■ What does *home* mean to you? Is it simply a place? Explain.

■ What city, state, or country do you consider your home now? How, if at all, has your definition of *home* changed over the course of your life?

■ How closely linked are your ideas of home to your cultural heritage?

VOCABULARY DEVELOPMENT

Look up the following words in a dictionary. Write down their meanings on a separate sheet or in your journal.

diplomatic (paragraph 1)   detachment (paragraph 4)

objectivity (paragraph 4)   transit (paragraph 5)

inability (paragraph 6)   relegated (paragraph 7)

fluent (paragraph 7)   incredulity (paragraph 7)

persistent (paragraph 9)   conviction (paragraph 9)

"Back, but Not Home"

1   With all the talk about resuming diplomatic relations with Cuba, and with the increasing number of Cuban exiles returning to visit friends and relatives, I am constantly being asked, "Would you ever go back?" In turn, I have asked myself, "Is there any reason for me to go?" I have had to think long and hard before finding my answer. Yes.

2   I came to the United States with my parents when I was almost five years old. We left behind grandparents, aunts, uncles, and several cousins. I grew up in a very middle-class neighborhood in Brooklyn. With one exception, all my friends were Americans. Outside of my family, I do not know many Cubans. I often feel awkward visiting relatives in Miami because it is such a different world. The way of life in Cuban Miami seems very strange to me, and I am accused of being "too Americanized." Yet, although I am now an American citizen, whenever anyone has asked my nationality, I have always and unhesitatingly replied, "Cuban."

3   Outside American, inside Cuban.

4   I recently had a conversation with a man who generally sympathizes with the Castro regime. We talked of Cuban politics, and although the discussion was very casual, I felt an old anger welling inside. After 16 years of

living an "American" life, I am still unable to view the revolution with detachment or objectivity. I cannot interpret its results in social, political, or economic terms. Too many memories stand in my way.

5   And as I listened to this man talk of the Cuban situation, I began to remember how as a little girl I would wake up crying because I had dreamed of my aunts and grandmothers and I missed them. I remembered my mother's trembling voice and the sad look on her face whenever she spoke to her mother over the phone. I thought of the many letters and photographs that somehow were always lost in transit. And as the conversation continued, I began to remember how difficult it often was to grow up Latina in an American world.

6   It meant going to kindergarten knowing little English. I'd been in this country only a few months, and although I understood a good deal of what was said to me, I could not express myself very well. On the first day of school I remember one little girl's saying to the teacher: "But how can we play with her? She's so stupid she can't even talk!" I felt so helpless because inside I was crying, "Don't you know I can understand everything you're saying?" But I did not have words for my thoughts, and my inability to communicate terrified me.

7   As I grew a little older, Latina meant being automatically relegated to the slowest reading classes in school. By now my English was fluent, but the teachers would always assume I was somewhat illiterate or slow. I recall one teacher's amazement at discovering I could read and write just as well as her American pupils. Her incredulity astounded me. As a child, I began to realize that Latina would always mean proving I was as good as the others. As I grew older, it became a matter of pride to prove I was better than the others.

8   As an adult I have come to terms with these memories and they don't hurt as much. I don't look or sound very Cuban. I don't speak with an accent, and my English is far better than my Spanish. I am beginning my career and look forward to the many possibilities ahead of me.

9   But a persistent little voice is constantly saying, "There's something missing. It's not enough." And this is why when I am now asked, "Do you want to go back?" I say "yes" with conviction.

10   I do not say to Cubans, "It is time to lay aside the hurt and forgive and forget." It is impossible to forget an event that has altered and scarred all our lives so profoundly. But I find I am beginning to care less and less about politics. And I am beginning to remember and care more about the child (and how many others like her) who left her grandma behind. I have to return to Cuba one day because I want to know that little girl better.

11   When I try to review my life during the past 16 years, I almost feel as if I've walked into a theater right in the middle of a movie. And I'm

afraid I won't fully understand or enjoy the rest of the movie unless I can see and understand the beginning. And for me, the beginning is Cuba. I don't want to go "home" again; the life and home we all left behind are long gone. My home is here, and I am happy. But I need to talk to my family still in Cuba.

12   Like all immigrants, my family and I have had to build a new life from almost nothing. It was often difficult, but I believe the struggle made us strong. Most of my memories are good ones.

13   But I want to preserve and renew my cultural heritage. I want to keep "la Cubana" within me alive. I want to return because the journey back will also mean a journey within. Only then will I see the missing piece.

 **AFTER YOU READ**

Vocabulary Practice

1. Choose at least three words from the Vocabulary Development list on page 783 and write sentences using those words. You may write one sentence using all three words if you wish.   Answers will vary.

2. Which word on the Vocabulary Development list means "flowing or moving smoothly and easily"? Use the word in a sentence that shows the word's meaning clearly.   Fluent. Answers will vary.

3. Cuban on the inside; American on the outside

3. Muniz uses terms like "exile," "Cuban," "American," and "Latina" to describe herself throughout her essay. Based on these terms, how do you think Muniz views herself in terms of her nationality? Explain.

Comprehension

Circle the correct answer.

1. How does Muniz describe herself?

    a. Inside American, outside Cuban

    (b.) Inside Cuban, outside American

    c. Inside Caucasian, outside Latina

    d. Inside Latina, outside Caucasian

2. What is Muniz's attitude toward the Castro regime in Cuba?

    a. She hates it.

    b. She loves it.

    c. She's confused about it.

    (d.) She can't be detached or objective about it.

3. How does Muniz say she feels when she visits relatives in Miami?

    (a.) Awkward   b. Cherished

    c. Loved   d. Resented

4. What assumptions did Muniz's elementary school teachers make about her?

    a. She was intelligent and articulate.

    b. She was lazy and bored.

    (c.) She was illiterate and unintelligent.

    d. She was lovely and talented.

5. Why does Muniz say she must return to Cuba?

    a. To see her husband

    (b.) To talk to her family there

    c. To support Castro

    d. To overthrow the government

Content

1. What does Muniz want to understand by going back to Cuba? *Her heritage; her family*

2. How does Muniz feel about her life in the United States? *It's her home, and she's happy here.*

3. What does Muniz say to help you understand the differences between her Cuban self and her American self? *She has American friends; she speaks good English; she feels that just being American "isn't enough"; she wants to see family.*

Style and Structure

1. What is the main idea of Muniz's essay? Write her argument in your own words. *You have to understand your past/your heritage to understand who you are now.*

2. What transitional words or phrases does Muniz use to indicate a change of direction? Look particularly closely at the beginnings of paragraphs for examples of transitions that signal change. *But, yet, although*

3. Is Muniz happy about her life now? List some details that indicate how she feels about her life. *She's happy, but something is missing; she misses her family; she has mostly American friends; she feels out of place among Miami Cubans.*

Writing Assignments

1. Muniz writes that she is "outside American, inside Cuban." *Write a paragraph in which you compare or contrast your "inside" with your "outside."* Use specific details from your own experiences to illustrate your ideas.

2. Maria Muniz writes that she feels awkward visiting relatives in Miami because they claim she's become "too Americanized." Have you ever changed in a way that made you no longer fit in with your old group? *Write a paragraph explaining how a change in you made you feel uncomfortable around a person or group of people.* Use examples from your experiences and observations to illustrate your ideas.

3. Maria Muniz writes that she realized as a child that because she was Latina, "teachers would always assume [she] was somewhat illiterate or slow" even though she proved to be a capable student. *Write an essay discussing a time when you felt your appearance or background prejudiced someone either for or against you.* Use specific details from the text and your experiences to illustrate your ideas.

Amy Tan

"My Mother's English"

Best known as the author of the novels *The Joy Luck Club*, *The Kitchen God's Wife*, and *The Bonesetter's Daughter*, Amy Tan received her master's degree in linguistics from San Jose State University before working as a language specialist with developmentally disabled children and then as a writer. In "My Mother's English," Tan explores the power or weakness that people possess as a result of their perceived language mastery, and she reveals how her mother's English-speaking skills often caused her to be treated with less respect than she deserved.

BEFORE YOU READ

Think about the following questions. Write your responses on a separate sheet or in your journal.

■ What kind of speaking skills do you possess? Make a list of the various groups you interact with, such as friends, family, co-workers, and teachers.

■ How does your speech differ from one group of your acquaintances, such as your friends, to others, such as those you listed in the previous question?

■ How do people's reactions to you change depending on your speech?

VOCABULARY DEVELOPMENT

Look up the following words in a dictionary. Write down their meanings on a separate sheet or in your journal.

aspect (paragraph 2)

nominalized (paragraph 2)

transcribed (paragraph 4)

fractured (paragraph 6)

regrettable (paragraph 9)

wrought (paragraph 2)

self-conscious (paragraph 3)

imagery (paragraph 6)

empirical (paragraph 7)

insular (paragraph 10)

"My Mother's English"

1   As you know, I am a writer and by that definition I am someone who has always loved language. I think that is first and foremost with almost every writer I know. I'm fascinated by language in daily life. I spend a great deal of time thinking about the power of language—the way it can evoke an emotion, a visual image, a complex idea or a simple truth. As a writer, language is the tool of my trade and I use them all, all the Englishes I grew up with.

2   A few months back, I was made keenly aware of the Englishes I do use. I was giving a talk to a large group of people, the same talk I had given many times before and also with notes. And the nature of the talk was about my writing, my life, and my book, *The Joy Luck Club*. The talk was going along well enough until I remembered one major difference that made the whole thing seem wrong. My mother was in the room, and it was perhaps the first time she had heard me give a lengthy speech, using a kind of English I had never used with her. I was saying things like "the intersection of memory and imagination," and "there is an aspect of my fiction that relates to this and thus." A speech filled with carefully wrought grammatical sentences, burdened to me it seemed with nominalized forms, past perfect tenses, conditional phrases, all the forms of standard English that I had learned in school and through books, a form of English I did not use at home or with my mother.

3   Shortly after that I was walking down the street with my mother and my husband and I became self-conscious of the English I was using, the English that I do use with her. We were talking about the price of new and used furniture and I heard myself saying to her, "Not waste money that way." My husband was with me as well, and he didn't notice any switch in my English. And then I realized why: because over the twenty years that we've been together he's often used that English with me and I've used that with him. It is sort of the English that is our language of intimacy, the English that relates to family talk, the English that I grew up with.

4   I'd like to give you some idea what my family talk sounds like and I'll do that by quoting what my mother said during a recent conversation which I videotaped and then transcribed. During this conversation, my mother was talking about a political gangster who had the same last name as her family, Du, and how the gangster in his early years wanted to be adopted by her family which was by comparison very rich. Later the gangster became more rich, more powerful than my mother's family and one day showed up at my mother's wedding to pay his respects. And here's what she said about that, in part, "Du You Sung having business like food stand, like off the street kind; he's Du like Du Zong but not Tsung-ming Island people. The local people call him Du, from the river east side. He belong to that side, local people. That man want to ask Du Zong father take him in become like own family. Du Zong father look down on him but don't take seriously until that man becoming big like, become a Mafia. Now important person, very hard

inviting him. Chinese way: come only to show respect, don't stay for dinner. Respect for making big celebration; he shows up. Means gives lots of respect, Chinese custom. Chinese social life that way—if too important, won't have to stay too long. He come to my wedding; I didn't see it I heard it. I gone to boy's side. They have YMCA dinner; Chinese age I was nineteen."

5   You should know that my mother's expressive command of English belies how much she actually understands. She reads the *Forbes Report*, listens to *Wall Street Week*, converses daily with her stockbroker, reads all of Shirley MacLaine's books with ease, all kinds of things I can't begin to understand. Yet some of my friends tell me that they understand 50 percent of what my mother says. Some say maybe they understand maybe 80 percent. Some say they understand almost nothing at all. As a case in point, a television station recently interviewed my mother and I didn't see this program when it was first aired, but my mother did. She was telling me what happened. She said that everything she said, which was in English, was subtitled in English, as if she had been speaking in pure Chinese. She was understandably puzzled and upset. Recently a friend gave me that tape and I saw that same interview and I watched. And sure enough—subtitles—and I was puzzled because listening to that tape it seemed to me that my mother's English sounded perfectly clear and perfectly natural. Of course, I realize that my mother's English is what I grew up with. It is literally my mother tongue, not Chinese, not standard English, but my mother's English which I later found out is almost a direct translation of Chinese.

6   Her language as I hear it is vivid and direct, full of observation and imagery. That was the language that helped shape the way that I saw things, expressed things, made sense of the world. Lately I've been giving more thought to the kind of English that my mother speaks. Like others I have described it to people as broken or fractured English, but I wince when I say that. It has always bothered me that I can think of no other way to describe it than broken, as it if were damaged or needed to be fixed, that it lacked a certain wholeness or soundness to it. I've heard other terms used, "Limited English" for example. But they seem just as bad, as if everything is limited including people's perceptions of the Limited English speaker.

7   I know this for a fact, because when I was growing up my mother's limited English limited my perception of her. I was ashamed of her English. I believed that her English reflected the quality of what she had to say. That is, because she expressed it imperfectly, her thoughts were imperfect as well. And I had plenty of empirical evidence to support me: The fact that people in department stores, at banks, at supermarkets, at restaurants did not take her as seriously, did not give her good service, pretended not to understand her, or even acted as if they did not hear her.

8   My mother has long realized the limitations of her English as well. When I was fifteen she used to have me call people on the phone to pretend I was she. In this guise, I was forced to ask for information or oftentimes

to complain and yell at people that had been rude to her. One time it was a call to her stockbroker in New York. She had cashed out her small portfolio and it just so happened that we were going to New York the next week, our very first trip outside of California. I had to get on the phone and say in my adolescent voice, which was not very convincing, "This is Mrs. Tan." And my mother was in the back whispering loudly, "Why don't he send me check already? Two weeks late. So mad he lie to me, losing me money." Then I said in perfect English, "Yes, I'm getting rather concerned. You had agreed to send the check two weeks ago, but it hasn't arrived." And she began to talk more loudly, "What you want—I come to New York, tell him front of his boss you cheating me?" And I was trying to calm her down, making her be quiet, while telling this stockbroker, "I can't tolerate any more excuses. If I don't receive the check immediately I'm going to have to speak to your manager when I arrive in New York." And sure enough the following week, there we were in front of this astonished stockbroker. And there I was, red-faced and quiet, and my mother the real Mrs. Tan was shouting at his boss in her impeccable broken English.

9   We used a similar routine a few months ago for a situation that was actually far less humorous. My mother had gone to the hospital for an appointment to find out about a benign brain tumor a CAT scan had revealed a month ago. And she had spoken very good English she said—her best English, no mistakes. Still she said the hospital had not apologized when they said they had lost the CAT scan and she had come for nothing. She said that they did not seem to have any sympathy when she told them she was anxious to know the exact diagnosis since her husband and son had both died of brain tumors. She said they would not give her any more information until the next time; she would have to make another appointment for that, so she said she would not leave until the doctor called her daughter. She wouldn't budge, and when the doctor finally called her daughter, me, who spoke in perfect English, lo-and-behold, we had assurances the CAT scan would be found, they promised a conference call on Monday, and apologies were given for any suffering my mother had gone through for a most regrettable mistake. By the way, apart from the distress of that episode, my mother is fine.

10   But it has continued to disturb me how much my mother's English still limits people's perceptions of her. I think my mother's English almost had an effect on limiting my possibilities as well. Sociologists and linguists will probably tell you that a person's developing language skills are more influenced by peers. But I do think the language spoken by the family, especially immigrant families, which are more insular, plays a large role in shaping the language of the child. . . . While this may be true, I always wanted to capture what language ability tests can never reveal—her intent, her passion, her imagery, the rhythms of her speech, and the nature of her thoughts. Apart from what any critic had to say about my writing, I knew I had succeeded where it counted when my mother finished reading my first book and gave me her verdict. "So easy to read."

⬡ AFTER YOU READ

Vocabulary Practice

1. Choose at least three words from the Vocabulary Development list on page 787 and write sentences using those words. You may write one sentence using all three words if you wish.   Answers will vary.

2. Wrought. Answers will vary.

2. Which word on the Vocabulary Development list means "formed or fashioned"? Use the word in a sentence that shows the word's meaning clearly.

3. Though Tan's mother makes herself understood, Tan described her mother's English as "broken" or "fractured." Why do you think nonstandard English is often given such negative descriptions? Explain.   Answers will vary.

Comprehension

Circle the correct answer.

1. Amy Tan says she speaks

   (a.) several distinct versions of the English language.

   b. several languages besides English.

   c. English only.

   d. Chinese only.

2. Which of the following is not mentioned as something Tan's mother understands?

   a. *Forbes*   b. *Wall Street Week*

   c. Amy Tan's books   (d.) The *San Francisco Chronicle*

3. Tan's mother's English has been described as

   a. poetic, pretty, and descriptive.

   b. childish, silly, and funny.

   (c.) broken, fractured, and limited.

   d. dirty, vulgar, and slimy.

4. With which of the following professionals has Tan served as translator for her mother?

   a. A dentist   (b.) A stockbroker

   c. An accountant   d. A lawyer

5. Tan's mother's English is

   a. a direct translation from Vietnamese.

   b. a direct translation from Japanese.

   c. a direct translation from Hmong.

   (d.) a direct translation from Chinese.

Content

1. Formal English; her mother's English; slang

1. What does Tan mean when she mentions "all the Englishes I grew up with"?

3. People ignore Tan's mother or don't take her seriously; Tan's mother gets extremely angry and has Tan translate for her.

2. Why doesn't Tan like the terms "broken English" or "Limited English"? What does she say they imply about the speaker? They imply that the speaker is broken or limited.

3. How is Tan's mother treated by the hospital staff? By her stockbroker? What is her mother's response to such treatment?

Style and Structure

1. People should-n't be judged on the basis of their spoken English.

1. What is Tan's main point? Write her main idea in your own words.

2. How does Tan show that other people have difficulty understanding her mother? Subtitles were used for her mother's interview; friends say they understand 50 or 80 percent, or nothing at all, of her mother's English.

3. For whom is Tan writing her essay? What assumptions can you make about her audience? Educated, interested people who care about language and its effect on humans

Writing Assignments

1. How powerful is spoken language? *Write a paragraph showing how your language—or the language of someone you know—has influenced others.* Give specific details from your life, or someone else's, to illustrate your ideas.

2. Have you ever had trouble being understood? *Write a paragraph explaining how you felt when you couldn't make yourself understood.* Use specific details from your life to support your ideas.

3. Tan writes about "all the Englishes" she grew up with. How does your language change when you're with different groups? *Write an essay illustrating how your language changes from one group, such as your family, to another, such as your friends or classmates.* Use your own experiences and observations to support your ideas.

Russell Baker

"The Plot Against People"

A two-time Pulitzer prize winner for his *New York Times* column and his autobiographical novel *Growing Up*, Russell Baker is known for his wit and humor in addressing topics familiar to many. In "The Plot Against People," Baker discusses the challenge humanity struggles daily to meet: dealing successfully with inanimate objects designed to help us.

BEFORE YOU READ

Think about the following questions. Write your responses on a separate sheet or in your journal.

■ Have you ever lost your temper with an inanimate object? What happened to make you lose your temper?

■ Why do you think people become angry with things that cannot move or think or speak?

■ What solutions, if any, can you offer to people who lose their temper with inanimate objects?

VOCABULARY DEVELOPMENT

Look up the following words in a dictionary. Write down their meanings on a separate sheet or in your journal.

cunning (paragraph 3)

locomotion (paragraph 6)

virtually (paragraph 8)

constitutes (paragraph 9)

baffled (paragraph 13)

plausible (paragraph 6)

burrow (paragraph 7)

invariably (paragraph 8)

conciliatory (paragraph 10)

aspire (paragraph 13)

"The Plot Against People"

1   Inanimate objects are classified scientifically into three major categories—those that break down, those that get lost, and those that don't work.

2   The goal of all inanimate objects is to resist man and ultimately to defeat him, and the three major classifications are based on the method each object uses to achieve its purpose. As a general rule, any object capable of breaking down at the moment when it is most needed will do so. The automobile is typical of the category.

3   With the cunning peculiar to its breed, the automobile never breaks down while entering a filling station which has a large staff of idle mechanics. It waits until it reaches a downtown intersection in the middle of the rush hour, or until it is fully loaded with family and luggage on the Ohio Turnpike. Thus it creates maximum inconvenience, frustration, and irritability, thereby reducing its owner's lifespan.

4   Washing machines, garbage disposals, lawn mowers, furnaces, TV sets, tape recorders, slide projectors—all are in league with the automobile to take their turn at breaking down whenever life threatens to flow smoothly for their enemies.

5   Many inanimate objects, of course, find it extremely difficult to break down. Pliers, for example, and gloves and keys are almost totally incapable of breaking down. Therefore, they have had to evolve a different technique for resisting man.

6   They get lost. Science has still not solved the mystery of how they do it, and no man has ever caught one of them in the act. The most plausible theory is that they have developed a secret method of locomotion which they are able to conceal from human eyes.

7   It is not uncommon for a pair of pliers to climb all the way from the cellar to the attic in its single-minded determination to raise its owner's blood pressure. Keys have been known to burrow three feet under mattresses. Women's purses, despite their great weight, frequently travel through six or seven rooms to find hiding space under a couch.

8   Scientists have been struck by the fact that things that break down virtually never get lost, while things that get lost hardly ever break down. A furnace, for example, will invariably break down at the depth of the first winter cold wave, but it will never get lost. A woman's purse hardly ever breaks down; it almost invariably chooses to get lost.

9   Some persons believe this constitutes evidence that inanimate objects are not entirely hostile to man. After all, they point out, a furnace could infuriate a man even more thoroughly by getting lost than by breaking down, just as a glove could upset him far more by breaking down than by getting lost.

10   Not everyone agrees, however, that this indicates a conciliatory attitude. Many say it merely proves that furnaces, gloves and pliers are incredibly stupid.

11   The third class of objects—those that don't work—is the most curious of all. These include such objects as barometers, car clocks, cigarette lighters, flashlights and toy-train locomotives. It is inaccurate, of course, to say that they *never* work. They work once, usually for the first few hours after being brought home, and then quit. Thereafter, they never work again.

12   In fact, it is widely assumed that they are built for the purpose of not working. Some people have reached advanced ages without ever seeing some of these objects—barometers, for example—in working order.

13   Science is utterly baffled by the entire category. There are many theories about it. The most interesting holds that the things that don't work have attained the highest state possible for an inanimate object, the state to which things that break down and things that get lost can still only aspire.

14   They have truly defeated man by conditioning him never to expect anything of them. When his cigarette lighter won't light or his flashlight fails to illuminate, it does not raise his blood pressure. Objects that don't work have given man the only peace he receives from inanimate society.

 AFTER YOU READ

Vocabulary Practice

1. Choose at least three words from the Vocabulary Development list on page 793 and write sentences using those words. You may write one sentence using all three words if you wish. Answers will vary.

3. "Goals," "cunning," "it waits," "all in league," "evolved a different way for resisting," "pliers to climb," "burrow," "purses. . . frequently travel." Using humor to give objects human qualities makes our frustration easier to understand since we imagine them to be working against us—as thinking beings would do.

2. What word from the Vocabulary Development list means "confused or puzzled"? Use the word in a sentence to show clearly what it means.   Baffled. Answers will vary.

3. Baker describes inanimate objects as having human feelings and thoughts. List at least three instances in which Baker endows objects with human characteristics. Then, write a few sentences explaining why you think he does this.

Comprehension

Circle the correct answer.

1. Which of the following is not a category that inanimate objects fall into?

   a. Things that break down
   b. Things that lose parts
   c. Things that get lost
   d. Things that don't work

2. What is the goal of all inanimate objects?

   a. To resist and ultimately defeat humans
   b. To torture and tease humans
   c. To thwart and confound humans
   d. To give pleasure to humans

3. Which one of the following is not given as an example of something that rarely breaks down?

   a. Pliers   b. Gloves
   c. Keys   d. Sunglasses

4. The fact that inanimate objects thwart humans in only one way each proves, according to some, that these objects are

   a. unimaginative.   b. lazy.
   c. stupid.   d. bored.

Content

2. To resist man and ultimately to defeat him

1. How does Baker classify inanimate objects?   Things that break down, things that get lost, things that don't work

2. What does Baker say is "the goal of all inanimate objects"?

2. Sophisticated readers; no mention of Internet, software, e-mail, cell phones, or pagers. These things can be very frustrating, but they came after Baker's time.

3. Cars break down only in the middle of nowhere; pliers "climb" to get lost; barometers work only when they're bought and then never again.

3. What proof does Baker offer for the idea that inanimate objects are "not entirely hostile to man"? Things stick to their roles. Furnaces break down but don't get lost while purses get lost but don't break down. Both objects could do something more frustrating than what they do; since they don't, they're not entirely hostile to man.

Style and Structure

1. Does Baker have a serious point? What is it?   Even though objects can't think for themselves, we blame objects for foiling us.

2. What audience is Baker addressing? What clues does he give you as to when this article was written, and for whom?

3. What examples does Baker give of the way inanimate objects thwart people?

Writing Assignments

1. Baker lists many objects that frustrate people. *Write one paragraph arguing that one object in particular is the most frustrating of all inanimate objects.* Be sure to use examples from your own experiences in order to illustrate your ideas. You do not need to choose an object that Baker uses in his essay.

2. Baker's essay was written before computers were widely used, so he has no examples associated with modern technology. *Write a paragraph classifying objects of one type—communications devices, for instance—according to how helpful or frustrating they are.* You may use humor if you like, but you do not have to. Be sure to use specific details from your own experience and observations in order to illustrate your ideas.

3. Think about machines or other inanimate objects that we rely on. *Write an essay classifying inanimate objects according to how much we need them.* For instance, you may classify them according to how often we use them or according to how important they are. A flashlight, for instance, is something you may not need very often, but it's very important when you do need it. Use examples from your own life and observations to illustrate your ideas.

Phillip Lopate

"A Nonsmoker with a Smoker"

A poet and essayist, Phillip Lopate has authored numerous works, among them *The Eyes Don't Always Want to Stay Open* and *Totally, Tenderly, and Tragically.* This essay, first published in *New Age Journal,* focuses on the differences—and conflicts—between people who smoke and those who don't.

BEFORE YOU READ

Think about the following questions. Write your responses on a separate sheet or in your journal.

■ If you are a smoker, what is your attitude toward nonsmokers? If you don't smoke, what is your attitude toward smokers?

■ What experiences have formed your attitudes toward people who approach smoking differently from the way you do? Explain.

■ What, if anything, do you admire or wish to emulate about someone who approaches smoking differently from the way you do? Explain. If there is nothing you admire, explain that.

⬡ VOCABULARY DEVELOPMENT

Look up the following words in a dictionary. Write down their meanings on a separate sheet or in your journal.

nicotine (paragraph 4)	winced (paragraph 12)
mutineers (paragraph 6)	complicitous (paragraph 15)
forbearance (paragraph 8)	impaled (paragraph 16)
maladroitly (paragraph 8)	evokes (paragraph 17)
docile (paragraph 11)	empathize (paragraph 13)

"A Nonsmoker with a Smoker"

1 Last Saturday night my girlfriend, Helen, and I went to a dinner party in the Houston suburbs. We did not know our hosts, but were invited on account of Helen's chum Barry, whose birthday party it was. We had barely stepped into the house and met the other guests, seated on a U-shaped couch under an A-framed ceiling, when Helen lit a cigarette. The hostess froze. "Uh, could you please not smoke in here? If you have to, we'd appreciate your using the terrace. We're both sort of allergic."

2 Helen smiled understandingly and moved toward the glass doors leading to the backyard in a typically ladylike way, as though merely wanting to get a better look at the garden. But I knew from that gracious "Southern" smile of hers that she was miffed.

3 As soon as Helen had stepped outside, the hostess explained that they had just moved into this house, and that it had taken weeks to air out because of the previous owner's tenacious cigar smoke. A paradigmatically awkward conversation about tobacco ensued: like testifying sinners, two people came forward with confessions about kicking the nasty weed; our scientist-host cited a recent study of indoor air pollution levels; a woman lawyer brought up the latest California legislation protecting nonsmokers; a roly-poly real estate agent admitted that, though he had given up smokes, he still sat in the smoking section of airplanes because "you meet a more interesting type of person there"—a remark his wife did not find amusing. Helen's friend Barry gallantly joined her outside. I did not, as I should have; I felt paralyzed.

4 For one thing, I wasn't sure which side I was on. I have never been a smoker. My parents both chain-smoked, so I grew up accustomed to cloudy interiors and ever since have been tolerant of other people's nicotine urges. To be perfectly honest, I'm not crazy about inhaling smoke, particularly when I've got a cold, but that irritating inconvenience pales beside the damage that would be done to my pluralistic worldview if I did not defend smokers' rights.

5 On the other hand, a part of me wished Helen *would* stop smoking. That part seemed to get a satisfaction out of the group's "banishing" her: they were doing the dirty work of expressing my disapproval.

6   As soon as I realized this, I joined her in the garden. Presently a second guest strolled out to share a forbidden toke, then a third. Our hostess ultimately had to collect the mutineers with an announcement that dinner was served.

7   At the table, Helen appeared to be having such a good time, joking with our hosts and everyone else, that I was unprepared for the change that came over her as soon as we were alone in the car afterward. "I will never go back to that house!" she declared. "Those people have no concept of manners or hospitality, humiliating me the moment I stepped in the door. And that phony line about 'sort of allergic'!"

8   Normally, Helen is forbearance personified. Say anything that touches her about smoking, however, and you touch the rawest of nerves. I remembered the last time I foolishly suggested that she "think seriously" about stopping. I had just read one of those newspaper articles about the increased possibility of heart attacks, lung cancer, and birth deformities among women smokers, and I was worried for her. My concern must have been maladroitly expressed, because she burst into tears.

9   "Can't we even talk about this without your getting so sensitive?" I had asked.

10   "You don't understand. Nonsmokers never understand that it is a real addiction. I've tried quitting, and it was hell. Do you want me to go around for months mean and cranky outside and angry inside? You're right, I'm sensitive, because I'm threatened with having taken away from me the thing that gives me the most pleasure in life, day in, day out," she said. I shot her a look: careful, now. "Well, practically the most pleasure. You know what I mean." I didn't. But I knew enough to drop it.

11   I love Helen, and if she wants to smoke, knowing the risks involved, that remains her choice. Besides, she wouldn't quit just because I wanted her to; she's not that docile, and that's part of what I love about her. Sometimes I wonder why I even keep thinking about her quitting. What's it to me personally? Certainly I feel protective of her health, but I also have selfish motives. I don't like the way her lips taste when she's smoked a lot. I associate her smoking with nervousness, and when she lights up several cigarettes in a row, I get jittery watching her. Crazy as this may sound, I also find myself becoming jealous of her cigarettes. Occasionally, when I go to her house and we're sitting on the couch together, if I see Helen eyeing the pack I make her kiss me first, so that my lips can engage hers (still fresh) before the competition's. It's almost as though there were another lover in the room—a lover who was around long before I entered the picture, and who pleases her in mysterious ways I cannot.

12   A lit cigarette puts a distance between us: it's like a weapon in her hand, awakening in me a primitive fear of being burnt. The memory is not so primitive, actually. My father used to smoke absentmindedly, letting the ash grow like a caterpillar eating every leaf in its path, until gravity finally top-

pled it. Once, when I was about nine, my father and I were standing in line at a bakery, and he accidentally dropped a lit ash down my back. Ever since, I've inwardly winced and been on guard around these little waving torches, which epitomize to me the dangers of intimacy.

13   I've worked hard to understand from the outside the satisfaction of smoking. I've even smoked "sympathetic" cigarettes, just to see what the other person was experiencing. But it's not the same as being hooked. How can I really empathize with the frightened but stubborn look Helen gets in her eyes when, despite the fact we're a little late going somewhere, she turns to me in the car and says, "I need to buy a pack of cigarettes first"? I feel a wave of pity for her. We are both embarrassed by this forced recognition of her frailty—the "indignity," as she herself puts it, of being controlled by something outside her will.

14   I try to imagine myself in that position, but a certain smugness keeps getting in the way (I don't have that problem and *am I glad)*. We pay a price for our smugness. So often it flip-flops into envy: the outsiders—wish to be included in the sufferings and highs of others, as if to say that only by relinquishing control and surrendering to some dangerous habit, some vice or dependency, would one be able to experience "real life."

15   Over the years I have become a sucker for cigarette romanticism. Few Hollywood gestures move me as much as the one in *Now Voyager,* when Paul Henreid lights two cigarettes, one for himself, the other for Bette Davis: these form a beautiful fatalistic bridge between them, a complicitous understanding like the realization that their love is based on the inevitability of separation. I am all the more admiring of this worldly cigarette gallantry because its experiential basis escapes me.

16   The same sort of fascination occurs when I come across a literary description of nicotine addiction, like this passage in Mailer's *Tough Guys Don't Dance:* "Over and over again I gave them up, a hundred times over the years, but I always went back. For in my dreams, sooner or later, I struck a match, brought flame to the tip, then took in all my hunger for existence with the first puff. I felt impaled on desire itself—those fiends trapped in my chest and screaming for one drag."

17   "Impaled on desire itself"! Such writing evokes a longing in me for the centering of self that tobacco seems to bestow on its faithful. Clearly, there is something attractive about having this umbilical relation to the universe—this curling pillar, this spiral staircase, this prayer of smoke that mediates between the smoker's inner substance and the alien ether. Inwardness of the nicotine trance, sad wisdom ("every pleasure has its price"), beauty of ritual, squandered health—all those romantic meanings we read into the famous photographic icons of fifties saints, Albert Camus or James Agee or James Dean or Carson McCullers puffing away, in a sense they're true. Like all people who return from a brush with death, smokers have gained a certain power. They know their "coffin nails." With Helen, each

cigarette is a measuring of the perishable, an enactment of her mortality, from filter to end-tip in fewer than five minutes. I could not stand to be reminded of my own death so often.

AFTER YOU READ

Vocabulary Practice

3. Nicotine urges, irritating inconvenience, forbidden toke, another lover, a weapon, little waving torches, frailty, nicotine trance, sad wisdom, beauty of ritual, squandered health. None of these terms is positive, so despite Lopate's attempt to understand smokers' rights, he's antismoking.

1. Choose at least three words from the Vocabulary Development list on page 797 and write sentences using those words. You may write one sentence using all three words if you wish.   Answers will vary.

2. What word from the Vocabulary Development list means "to have pierced with or as if with something pointed"? Use the word in a sentence that clearly shows its meaning.   Impaled. Answers will vary.

3. What are some ways Lopate describes smoking and cigarettes? What do these words—and the fact that there are so many—say about his feelings about the habit?

Comprehension

1. What reason does the hostess give Helen for asking her to smoke outside?

    a. She and her husband are "sort of addicted."

    b. She and her husband are "sort of protective."

    c. She and her husband are "sort of allergic."

    d. She and her husband are "sort of annoyed."

2. What is Lopate's attitude toward Helen's smoking?

    a. He constantly tries to get her to quit.

    b. He respects her smoking and has become a smoker.

    c. He wishes she'd smoke a pipe because it's more elegant.

    d. He'd like her to quit but won't push her.

3. How does Lopate characterize some of his motives for wanting Helen to quit?

    a. Unselfish   b. Selfish

    c. Biased   d. Objective

4. What happened to Lopate as a child that made him fear burns?

    a. His father dropped a lit cigarette ash down his back.

    b. His father handed him a red-hot frying pan.

    c. His father burned him with a cigarette lighter.

    d. His father never taught him to build a campfire.

5. What is Lopate a "sucker" for?
   a. Cigarette romanticism   b. Cigarette smoke
   c. Cigarette advertisements   d. Cigarette packaging

Content

1. How does Helen, Lopate's girlfriend, react when the hostess at a party asks her to smoke outside? *She is gracious as she leaves, but secretly she's furious.*
2. What is Lopate's attitude toward Helen's smoking? *He loves Helen and respects her choice to smoke, but he doesn't like it.*
3. In the last three paragraphs, what are Lopate's attitudes toward smoking in general? *Smug that he's not hooked, fascinated by the romantic gesture, attracted to the "umbilical to the universe," doesn't want to be reminded of his death so often as smoker's are.*

2. Story of separation of smokers and nonsmokers at a party; example of his relationship with Helen; his own comments about why he could never smoke.

Style and Structure

1. What is Lopate's point? Rewrite his main idea in your own words. *Smoking comes between people.*
2. What kinds of examples does Lopate use to support his main idea?
3. How does Lopate organize his essay? How can you tell? *Emphatic order. He gives his biggest reason for not liking smoking—death—at the end of the essay.*

Writing Assignments

1. Lopate writes, "A lit cigarette puts a distance between us." Is he right? *Write a paragraph in which you explain how lit cigarettes keep people farther apart, either physically or mentally.* Use examples from your own experiences to illustrate your ideas.

2. Lopate claims he wasn't sure "which side [he] was on." Are you sure of your own position? *Write a paragraph explaining whether or not smokers should be allowed to smoke in other people's homes.* Use examples and illustrations from your own life to support your ideas.

3. Lopate compares smoking to a "problem," a "dangerous habit, and a "vice or dependency." Compared with other potentially harmful habits—such as eating fatty foods or drinking in excess—how bad is smoking? *Write an essay in which you compare or contrast smoking to another habit.* Be sure to use examples from your own life for support. If you need more information about smoking to support your ideas, consult Web sites such as these: http://mens-health.health-cares.net/passive-smoking-hazards.php, http://philipmorrisusa.com/en/health_issues/surgeon_general_reports.asp

Jo Goodwin Parker

"What Is Poverty?"

This article was first published in *America's Other Children: Public Schools Outside Suburbia* in 1971. Ms. Parker preferred that her editor not include any biographical information about her when this article came out.

BEFORE YOU READ

Think about the following questions. Write your responses on a separate sheet or in your journal.

- How would you define the word *poverty?* On what is your definition based?
- How do you think people become poor?
- How does being around poor people make you feel? Explain.

VOCABULARY DEVELOPMENT

Look up the following words in a dictionary. Write down their meanings on a separate sheet or in your journal.

poverty (paragraph 1)	stench (paragraph 1)
anemia (paragraph 3)	devour (paragraph 5)
surplus (paragraph 11)	commodities (paragraph 11)
immoral (paragraph 12)	illegitimate (paragraph 12)
chisel (paragraph 13)	

"What Is Poverty?"

1   You ask me what is poverty? Listen to me. Here I am, dirty, smelly, and with no "proper" underwear on and with the stench of my rotting teeth near you. I will tell you. Listen to me. Listen without pity. I cannot use your pity. Listen with understanding. Put yourself in my dirty, worn out, ill-fitting shoes, and hear me.

2   Poverty is getting up every morning from a dirt- and illness-stained mattress. The sheets have long since been used for diapers. Poverty is living in a smell that never leaves. This is a smell of urine, sour milk, and spoiling food sometimes joined with the strong smell of long-cooked onions. Onions are cheap. If you have smelled this smell, you did not know how it came. It is the smell of the outdoor privy. It is the smell of young children who cannot walk the long dark way in the night. It is the smell of the mattress where years of "accidents" have happened. It is the smell of the milk which has gone sour because the refrigerator long has not worked, and it costs money to get it fixed. It is the smell of rotting garbage. I could bury it, but where is the shovel? Shovels costs money.

3   Poverty is being tired. I have always been tired. They told me at the hospital when the last baby came that I had chronic anemia caused from poor diet, a bad case of worms, and that I needed a corrective operation. I listened politely—the poor are always polite. The poor always listen. They don't say that there is no money for iron pills, or better food, or worm med-

icine. The idea of an operation is frightening and costs so much that, if I had dared, I would have laughed. Who takes care of my children? Recovery from an operation takes a long time. I have three children. When I left them with "Granny" the last time I had a job, I came home to find the baby covered with fly specks, and a diaper that had not been changed since I left. When the dried diaper came off, bits of my baby's flesh came with it. My other child was playing with a sharp bit of broken glass, and my oldest was playing alone at the edge of a lake. I made twenty-two dollars a week, and a good nursery school costs twenty dollars a week for three children. I quit my job.

4   Poverty is dirt. You can say in your clean clothes coming from your clean house, "Anybody can be clean." Let me explain about housekeeping with no money. For breakfast I give my children grits with no oleo or cornbread without eggs and oleo. This does not use up many dishes. What dishes there are, I wash in cold water and with no soap. Even the cheapest soap has to be saved for the baby's diapers. Look at my hands, so cracked and red. Once I saved for two months to buy a jar of Vaseline for my hands and the baby's diaper rash. When I had saved enough, I went to buy it and the price had gone up two cents. The baby and I suffered on. I have to decide every day if I can bear to put my cracked sore hands into the cold water and strong soap. But you ask, why not hot water? Fuel costs money. If you have a wood fire it costs money. If you burn electricity, it costs money. Hot water is a luxury. I do not have luxuries. I know you will be surprised when I tell you how young I am. I look so much older. My back has been bent over the wash tubs every day for so long. I cannot remember when I ever did anything else. Every night I wash every stitch my school age child has on and just hope her clothes will be dry by morning.

5   Poverty is staying up all night on cold nights to watch the fire knowing one spark on the newspaper covering the walls means your sleeping child dies in flames. In summer poverty is watching gnats and flies devour your baby's tears when he cries. The screens are torn and you pay so little rent you know they will never be fixed. Poverty means insects in your food, in your nose, in your eyes, and crawling over you when you sleep. Poverty is hoping it never rains because diapers won't dry when it rains and soon you are using newspapers. Poverty is seeing your children forever with runny noses. Paper handkerchiefs cost money and all your rags you need for other things. Even more costly are antihistamines. Poverty is cooking without food and cleaning without soap.

6   Poverty is asking for help. Have you ever had to ask for help, knowing your children will suffer unless you get it? Think about asking for a loan from a relative, if this is the only way you can imagine asking for help. I will tell you how it feels. You find out where the office is that you are supposed to visit. You circle that block four or five times. Thinking of your children, you go in. Everyone is very busy. Finally, someone comes out and you tell

her that you need help. That never is the person you need to see. You go see another person, and after spilling the whole shame of your poverty all over the desk between you, you find that this isn't the right office after all—you must repeat the whole process, and it never is any easier at the next place.

7   You have asked for help, and after all it has a cost. You are again told to wait. You are told why, but you don't really hear because of the red cloud of shame and the rising cloud of despair.

8   Poverty is remembering. It is remembering quitting school in junior high because "nice" children had been so cruel about my clothes and my smell. The attendance officer came. My mother told him I was pregnant. I wasn't, but she thought that I could get a job and help out. I had jobs off and on, but never long enough to learn anything. Mostly I remember being married. I was so young then. I am still young. For a time, we had all the things you have. There was a little house in another town, with hot water and everything. Then my husband lost his job. There was unemployment insurance for a while and what few jobs I could get. Soon, all our nice things were repossessed and we moved back here. I was pregnant then. This house didn't look so bad when we first moved in. Every week it gets worse. Nothing is ever fixed. We now had no money. There were a few odd jobs for my husband, but everything went for food then, as it does now. I don't know how we lived through three years and three babies, but we did. I'll tell you something, after the last baby I destroyed my marriage. It had been a good one, but could you keep on bringing children in this dirt? Did you ever think how much it costs for any kind of birth control? I knew my husband was leaving the day he left, but there were no good-byes between us. I hope he has been able to climb out of this mess somewhere. He never could hope with us to drag him down.

9   That's when I asked for help. When I got it, you know how much it was? It was, and is, seventy-eight dollars a month for the four of us; that is all I ever can get. Now you know why there is no soap, no needles and thread, no hot water, no aspirin, no worm medicine, no hand cream, no shampoo. None of these things forever and ever and ever. So that you can see clearly, I pay twenty dollars a month rent, and most of the rest goes for food. For grits and cornmeal, and rice and milk and beans. I try my best to use only the minimum electricity. If I use more, there is that much less for food.

10   Poverty is looking into a black future. Your children won't play with my boys. They will turn to other boys who steal to get what they want. I can already see them behind the bars of their prison instead of behind the bars of my poverty. Or they will turn to the freedom of alcohol or drugs, and find themselves enslaved. And my daughter? At best, there is for her a life like mine.

11   But you say to me, there are schools. Yes, there are schools. My children have no extra books, no magazines, no extra pencils, or crayons, or paper and most important of all, they do not have health. They have worms, they have infections, they have pink-eye all summer. They do not sleep well on the floor, or with me in my one bed. They do not suffer from hunger, my seventy-eight

dollars keep us alive, but they do suffer from malnutrition. Oh yes, I do remember what I was taught about health in school. It doesn't do much good. In some places there is a surplus commodities program. Not here. The country said it cost too much. There is a school lunch program. But I have two children who will already be damaged by the time they get to school.

12   But, you say to me, there are health clinics. Yes, there are health clinics and they are in the towns. I live out here eight miles from town. I can walk that far (even if it is sixteen miles both ways), but can my little children? My neighbor will take me when he goes; but he expects to get paid, *one way or another*. I bet you know my neighbor. He is that large man who spends his time at the gas station, the barbershop, and the corner store complaining about the government spending money on the immoral mothers of illegitimate children.

13   Poverty is an acid that drips on pride until all pride is worn away. Poverty is a chisel that chips on honor until honor is worn away. Some of you say that you would do *something* in my situation, and maybe you would, for the first week or the first month, but for year after year after year?

14   Even the poor can dream. A dream of a time when there is money. Money for the right kinds of food, for worm medicine, for iron pills, for toothbrushes, for hand cream, for a hammer and nails and a bit of screening, for a shovel, for a bit of paint, for some sheeting, for needles and thread. Money to pay in *money* for a trip to town. And, oh, money for hot water and money for soap. A dream of when asking for help does not eat away the last bit of pride. When the office you visit is as nice as the offices of other governmental agencies, when there are enough workers to help you quickly, when workers do not quit in defeat and despair. When you have to tell your story to only one person, and that person can send you for other help and you don't have to prove your poverty over and over and over again.

15   I have come out of my despair to tell you this. Remember I did not come from another place or another time. Others like me are all around you. Look at us with an angry heart, anger that will help you help me. Anger that will let you tell of me. The poor are always silent. Can you be silent too?

 **AFTER YOU READ**

Vocabulary Practice

1. Choose at least three words from the Vocabulary Development list on page 802 and write sentences using those words. You may write one sentence using all three words if you wish. Answers will vary.

3. Answers will vary. "Getting up every morning from a dirt- and illness-stained mattress"; "being tired"; "dirt"; "staying up all night on cold nights to watch the fire"; "asking for help"; "remembering"; "an acid that drips on pride"

2. What word from the Vocabulary Development list means "a quantity or amount over and above what is needed or used"? Use the word in a sentence that clearly shows the meaning of the word. Surplus. Answers will vary.

3. Parker defines poverty many different ways, each definition followed by examples. What terms does Parker use to define poverty? Of these, which terms are most powerful?

Comprehension

Circle the correct answer.

1. Parker opens her essay by asking the reader to
    a. give money to the poor.
    b. read without prejudice.
    c. listen to her.
    d. write a letter to the editor about the poor.

2. Which of the following is not one of the smells of poverty, according to Parker?
    a. Onions   b. Urine
    c. Smoke   d. Sour milk

3. Why does Parker say she doesn't bury her garbage?
    a. Shovels cost money.
    b. Her shovel is broken.
    c. She is too weak from fatigue.
    d. She cannot leave her children, even for a second.

4. Why does Parker say she and her children are not clean?
    a. She's lazy.
    b. She's too tired to clean.
    c. She thinks cleanliness isn't important.
    d. She has no money for hot water or enough soap.

5. Why does Parker have to stay up all night on cold nights?
    a. To make sure her children can breathe
    b. To make sure her house doesn't catch fire
    c. To make sure she can get her work done
    d. To make sure thieves don't steal her property

Content

1. List some ways Parker defines poverty.   Filth, fatigue, remembering, asking for help

2. Malnutrition, fatigue, filth, bleak future

2. What particular problems do Parker's children face because they live in poverty?

3. What effect do people's opinions of her and her children have on Parker?
They constantly beat her down and keep her from asking for help.

1. Poverty is a horrible, humiliating trap.
2. Descriptions of her home, her children's clothing, the smell, her experience trying to get help
3. People who probably think that poor people are wholly to blame for their problems. She seems to be "answering" people's criticisms.

Style and Structure

1. What is Parker's main point? Write her main idea in your own words.

2. What kind of specific details does Parker give to support her main idea?

3. Who is Parker's audience? How can you tell? Cite examples from the text to illustrate your ideas.

Writing Assignments

1. Parker's biggest challenge in life is living in poverty. She defines *poverty* several ways. *Write a paragraph defining a major challenge of your own: being a student, supporting yourself, being a parent, or being in a relationship, for instance.* Define that challenge in several ways, as Parker did, giving examples from your own life to illustrate your ideas.

2. Parker's problem is shared by millions of people. How can you help? *Write a paragraph explaining how you can or do help people living in poverty.* (If you do not help the poor, write about why you don't or can't.) Use specific details from your life to support your ideas.

3. Parker gives examples of how people's unkindness has affected her and her life choices. *Write an essay about a time when people's cruelty or kindness motivated you to change your situation or behavior.* Use specific details from your own life in order to illustrate your ideas.

Lab Manual

LAB ACTIVITY 1 Main Points, Support Points, and Specific Details

Objective To identify main points and develop support points and specific details.

Step 1: In the table below, Column A lists a topic for a paragraph. In Column B, write a topic sentence that clearly expresses the main point for a possible paragraph on the general topic given in Column A.

Column A: Topic	Column B: Topic Sentence (Main Idea)
Example: The scariest ride	Sudden drops, upside-down section, really high hills
1. My favorite activity	
2. My least favorite vegetable	
3. A popular place to eat	
4. A terrible place to eat	
5. A special day	

Now copy one of your topic sentences from Step 1 into Column C. In Column D, list the support points and specific details that would help you develop a paragraph using your topic sentence.

Column C: Your Topic Sentence (from Step 1)	Column D: Support Points and Specific Details
Example: The Ripper is worth riding twice.	• Exciting curves. • Terrifying plunges. • Nauseating "Loop the Loop" section. • Screeching halt.
Topic sentence:	Support point 1: _____ _____ Support point 2: _____ _____ Support point 3: _____ _____

Step 2: Now that you have practiced writing topic sentences and listing support points and specific details, go to **http://ablongman.com/long.** Click on **Resources for Writers,** and then click on **Activity 1** for practice choosing specific details to support topic sentences.

LAB ACTIVITY 2 Concise, Credible, and Clear Writing

Objective To choose appropriate support points and put them in a clear order.

Step 1: For each topic sentence below, list three support points that will help your reader believe the sentence. You may refer to the paragraphs about world geography in Chapter 2.

Example: Many Americans may not realize it, but world geography plays a big part in our lives.

Support point 1: _Many Americans eat Chinese food as often as_ _they can._

Support point 2: _Much of the clothing we wear was made in countries_ _other than the United States._

Support point 3: _Several of the invasive plants and animals now_ _threatening native North American species were imported from other regions._

1. Topic sentence: *Just about everyone I know had ancestors who came to America from other countries.*

Support point 1: _____

_____

Support point 2: _____

_____

Support point 3: _____

_____

2. Topic sentence: *The one place outside the United States that I would especially like to visit is _____ (fill in a place of your choice).*

Support point 1: _____

_____

Support point 2: _____

_____

Support point 3: _____

_____

3. Topic sentence: *I never want to travel outside the United States for several reasons.*

Support point 1: _____

_____

Support point 2: _____

_____

Support point 3: _____

_____

4. Topic sentence: *The United States depends on other countries and regions for many important things.*

Support point 1: _____

_____

Support point 2: _____

_____

Support point 3: _____

_____

5. Topic sentence: *The United States would be better off if it ended all dealings with other countries.*

Support point 1: _____

_____

Support point 2: _____

_____

Support point 3: _____

_____

Step 2: Now that you have practiced choosing support points to make your writing credible, go to **http://ablongman.com/long.** Click on **Resources for Writers,** and then click on **Activity 2** for practice writing a concise, credible, and clear paragraph.

LAB ACTIVITY 3 Audience and Purpose

Objective To write with a purpose for an audience.

Step 1: Suppose that you have to write a paragraph to your supervisor requesting a day off from work to go on a field trip for a class. Read the following list of details and put an X in front of the ones you could include in the paragraph. *Hint:* Five of the items listed could be included in the paragraph.

____X____ I have to go on a required school field trip for a class.

_____ I could make it back in time for my shift if I hurry, but I know I won't feel like working.

_____ I would rather go out with friends after the field trip instead of rushing back for work.

____X____ Because traffic is so unpredictable, the class may not get back on schedule.

____X____ The instructor is holding a study session after the field trip.

_____ I'll use any excuse to get out of work.

____X____ I have never requested a day off before.

____X____ I'm a good worker.

_____ I hate my boss.

Now write a paragraph to your supervisor requesting a day off from work to go on a required field trip. Remember to include details that will help you communicate with your reader.

_____

_____

_____

_____

_____

_____

_____

_____

_____

Step 2: Now suppose that you have to write a paragraph to your instructor explaining why your late paper should not lose points. Read the following list of details and put an X in front of the four details you could include in the paragraph.

_____ My friend had a huge party last weekend, so I didn't have time to work on the paper.

_____ I hate your class, so I just put off writing the paper until now.

___X___ I was on my way to school to turn in the paper when I got into a serious car accident.

___X___ I have a note from my doctor to prove that I was hospitalized overnight.

_____ I couldn't think of anything to write, and I didn't feel like asking you for help.

_____ I never pay attention to deadlines.

___X___ This is the first time I have ever turned in anything late to you.

___X___ I'm a serious student, and I want to do well in your class.

Now write a paragraph to your instructor explaining why your late paper should not lose points. Remember to include details that will help you communicate with your reader.

_____

_____

_____

_____

_____

_____

_____

_____

_____

_____

_____

Step 3: Now that you have practiced writing with a purpose for an audience, go to **http://ablongman.com/long.** Click on **Resources for Writers,** and then click on **Activity 3** for more practice with audience and purpose.

LAB ACTIVITY 4 Prewriting Practice

Objective To use different prewriting techniques.

Step 1: Here are some details that might be included in a paragraph about the Grammy Awards. Draw lines between the details that go together. You should end up with three groups. Some details do not belong in any group.

Now, put the details into outline form. Answers will vary.

A. Things people wear to the Grammy Awards

1. Fancy dresses

2. Expensive jewelry

3. Outrageous outfits

B. Things people say at the Grammy Awards

1. Introductions

2. Thank-you speeches

3. Jokes

C. Kinds of awards given at the Grammy Awards

1. Best pop vocalist—female

2. Best country vocalist—male

3. Best hip-hop/rap vocalist—male

Step 2: Now that you have begun to think about the Grammy Awards, list five questions that might help you come up with more details about the Grammy Awards. The first word of each question is provided for you.   Answers will vary.

Question 1: Who _____

_____?

Question 2: What _____

_____?

Question 3: When _____

_____?

Question 4: Where _____

_____?

Question 5: Why _____

_____?

Step 3: Now that you have tried clustering, outlining, and questioning, go to **http://ablongman.com/long.** Click on **Resources for Writers,** and then click on **Activity 4** for more prewriting practice.

LAB ACTIVITY 5 Writing a Rough Draft

Objective To write a rough draft.

Step 1: Think about what you like to do in your spare time. Use clustering to come up with some details on the topic. Some details have already been provided for you.

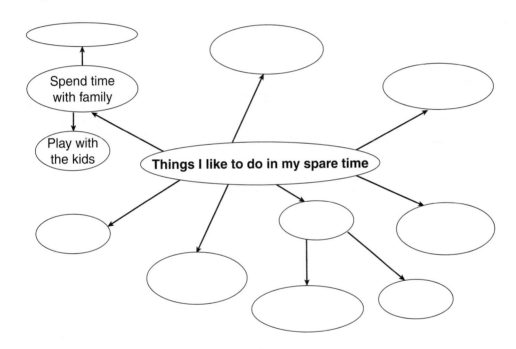

Now, write a rough draft of a paragraph using some of the details you came up with in your clustering diagram. The topic sentence has already been started for you.

Whenever I have spare time, my favorite thing to do is _____

_____

_____

_____

_____

_____
_____
_____
_____
_____
_____
_____
_____
_____
_____
_____
_____
_____
_____
_____
_____
_____
_____
_____
_____
_____
_____
_____
_____
_____
_____

Step 2: Now that you have written a rough draft by hand, go to **http:// ablongman.com/long.** Click on **Resources for Writers,** and then click on **Activity 5** for more practice with rough drafts.

LAB ACTIVITY 6 Revising a Draft

Objective To revise a draft.

Step 1: Read the following paragraph. Cross out any sentences that do not belong. Put a number in front of each sentence that belongs in the paragraph to indicate what order the sentences should follow. The first one has been done for you.

<u>1</u> My favorite dessert is tiramisu. <u>7</u> Besides the amazing taste, though, tiramisu is my favorite because it makes me think of Italy. <u>   </u> ~~Italy has the Vatican, the Leaning Tower of Pisa, and the Colosseum.~~ <u>12</u> Without a doubt, tiramisu will always be my favorite dessert. <u>3</u> Tiramisu is an Italian dessert made with grated chocolate, pieces of sponge cake called ladyfingers, and an Italian cream cheese called mascarpone. <u>4</u> The chocolate makes the dessert sweet but not sugary, and the ladyfingers are very delicate. <u>   </u> ~~Ladyfingers is an odd name for sponge cake, but I guess they're called that because they're shaped like a lady's fingers.~~ <u>10</u> Most of all, however, I love tiramisu because it is something that my great-aunt Bella introduced me to. <u>5</u> They are soaked in a combination of strong coffee and some kind of liqueur, which makes them very soft and extremely tasty. <u>6</u> The mascarpone is wonderfully creamy, and it helps hold the whole concoction together. <u>   </u> ~~I like lots of different cheeses, not just mascarpone.~~ <u>8</u> Although I've never been there, I've watched several travel shows about Italy, and I can just imagine sitting in a café, sipping espresso and eating tiramisu. <u>2</u> It's my favorite, first of all, because it is incredibly delicious. <u>9</u> To me, tiramisu is Italy. <u>11</u> She was the first to make it for me, and whenever I eat it now, I think fondly of her.

Step 2: The following paragraph is not credible because it is missing several specific details to support the topic sentence. (The topic sentence is underlined.) Revise the paragraph, adding specific details that support the topic sentence. Remember to make sure that the revised paragraph is clear and concise as well as credible.

<u>My friends are really great.</u> They are always supportive. They can make me laugh. Even when I think that I am too sad or upset to laugh, at least one of my friends finds a way to get me to smile. It's obvious that they care about me. I can tell.

Your revision:

My friends are really great.

_____

_____

_____

_____

_____

_____

_____

_____

_____

_____

_____

_____

_____

_____

_____

_____

_____

_____

_____

Step 3: Now that you have revised a paragraph, go to **http://ablongman.com/long.** Click on **Resources for Writers,** and then click on **Activity 6** for more practice revising.

LAB ACTIVITY 7 Editing and Proofreading

Objective To identify what to look for when editing and proofreading.

Step 1: Each of the following sentences contains one error. Rewrite the sentence to correct the error.

Example: Riding my bike to school.

Corrected: Riding my bike to school is good exercise.

1. He don't go to my school.

   Corrected: He doesn't go to my school.

2. Its very important to me.

   Corrected: It's very important to me.

3. My favorite fruits are apples bananas, and oranges.

   Corrected: My favorite fruits are apples, bananas, and oranges.

4. I think the books are her's.

   Corrected: I think the books are hers.

5. There dog is scary.

   Corrected: Their dog is scary.

6. He is the nicest person I have ever knowed.

   Corrected: He is the nicest person I have ever known.

7. Even though we were late. Answers will vary.

   Corrected: Even though we were late, we didn't miss the opening act.

8. He likes coffee, I like tea. Answers will vary.

   Corrected: He likes coffee; I like tea. He likes coffee, but I like tea.

9. One of the cats are missing.

   Corrected: One of the cats is missing.

10. The boxes are to heavy.

Corrected: The boxes are too heavy.

11. I had a lot of fun but I was also very tired later.

Corrected: I had a lot of fun, but I was also very tired later.

12. Rauls sister is here for a visit.

Corrected: Raul's sister is here for a visit.

13. Because we get along. Answers will vary

Corrected: Because we get along, we are usually partners in class.

14. I am going to chose the cheapest one.

Corrected: I am going to choose the cheapest one.

15. In the morning. Answers will vary

Corrected: In the morning, it began to rain.

Step 2: Now that you have practiced editing and proofreading, go to **http://ablongman.com/long.** Click on **Resources for Writers,** and then click on **Activity 7** for more help identifying problem areas.

LAB ACTIVITY 8 The Whole Writing Process

Objective To use the steps of the writing process.

Step 1: Examine this picture carefully, and make a list of specific details you notice.

Specific details:

_____   _____
_____   _____
_____   _____
_____   _____
_____   _____
_____   _____
_____   _____
_____   _____
_____   _____
_____   _____

Step 2: Now, using the details you listed, write a paragraph that begins with the topic sentence given. Remember to include only details that support the topic sentence and to organize your details in a logical order. Circle the transitional words or phrases you use to signal the order of your details.

Although its surroundings are beautiful, the house itself is not in the best shape.

_____

_____

_____

_____

_____

_____

_____

_____

_____

_____

_____

_____

_____

_____

_____

_____

_____

_____

_____

_____

_____

_____

_____

_____

_____

Step 3: Now that you have used the steps of the writing process, go to **http://ablongman.com/long.** Click on **Resources for Writers,** and then click on **Activity 8** for more practice with the whole writing process.

LAB ACTIVITY 9 The Topic Sentence

Objective To write topic sentences.

Step 1: For each general topic given, write a topic sentence that includes a narrowed topic and point-of-view words. Remember that a topic sentence expresses the main idea of a paragraph and can be supported with three or four support points and specific details.

1. General topic: *science*

   Topic sentence: _____

   _____

2. General topic: *math*

   Topic sentence: _____

   _____

3. General topic: *inventions*

   Topic sentence: _____

   _____

4. General topic: *space exploration*

   Topic sentence: _____

   _____

5. General topic: *medical discoveries*

   Topic sentence: _____

   _____

6. General topic: *technology*

   Topic sentence: _____

   _____

7. General topic: *engineering*

   Topic sentence: _____

   _____

8. General topic: *cloning*

   Topic sentence: _____

   _____

9. General topic: *organ transplants*

   Topic sentence: _____

   _____

10. General topic: *computers*

   Topic sentence: _____

   _____

Step 2: Now that you have practiced writing topic sentences with narrowed topics, go to **http://ablongman.com/long.** Click on **Resources for Writers,** and then click on **Activity 9** for practice with point-of-view words.

LAB ACTIVITY 10 Using Specific Details

Objective To use specific details to prove your point.

Step 1: For each of the following support points, write three sentences that use specific details to further describe the topic sentence. Remember that the details must help the support points contribute to the topic sentence.

Topic sentence: I love relaxing at the new coffeehouse in my neighborhood because it's kind of funky, the coffee is excellent, and the customers are interesting.

Example:
Support point: *The new coffeehouse in my neighborhood is very odd looking.*

Specific details:

The building is shaped like a giant pink coffeepot.

The walls and floor are a warm mocha color, and the counters are the color

of cream.

The tables and chairs resemble large black ceramic coffee mugs.

1. Support point: *This place makes my coffee just the way I like it.*

Specific details:

_____

_____

_____

_____

2. Support point: *Karla and Juan, who work the morning shift, are experts at their jobs.*

Specific details:

_____

_____

_____

_____

3. Support point: *Since I've been going there, I've noticed that some people give very detailed instructions about how to make their coffee.*

Specific details:

_____

_____

_____

_____

4. Support point: *Sometimes, I overhear the most interesting conversations.*

Specific details:

_____

_____

_____

_____

5. Support point: *My favorite part about going to the coffeehouse, though, is watching all of the funny-looking characters who come in for coffee.*

Specific details:

_____

_____

_____

_____

Step 2: Now that you have practiced writing sentences with specific details, go to **http://ablongman.com/long.** Click on **Resources for Writers,** and then click on **Activity 10** for more practice using specific details.

LAB ACTIVITY 11 Organizing and Linking Your Ideas

Objective To practice organizing and linking ideas.

Step 1: As you learned in Chapter 11, one way to link ideas is to use synonyms. In the table below, fill in at least one synonym for each of the given words or phrases.

Term	Synonym
Example: musical group	band
singer	vocalist, performer, crooner
song	tune, number, melody
concert	show, performance
audience	listeners, fans
songwriter	composer
famous person	celebrity, star, idol, icon
great	wonderful, excellent, terrific, super

Term	Synonym
loyal followers	fans, groupies, disciples
reviewer	critic
widely known	famous, renowned

Step 2: Now that you have practiced using synonyms, write a paragraph about your favorite musical group or singer, using at least five of the synonyms you listed in the above table. Circle the synonyms in your paragraph.

_____

_____

_____

_____

_____

_____

_____

_____

_____

_____

_____

_____

_____

_____

Step 3: Now that you have used synonyms, go to **http://ablongman.com/long.** Click on **Resources for Writers,** and then click on **Activity 11** for practice using synonyms.

LAB ACTIVITY 12 Sensitive Writing

Objective To use sensitive language.

Step 1: Decide whether each underlined word or phrase is a sensitive or insensitive use of language. Write OK above sensitive uses of language and X above insensitive uses of language.

Avoiding Insensitive Language

a. Don't exclude people.

b. Don't make assumptions about groups of people.

c. Don't call people by names they do not choose for themselves.

d. Don't assume that all members of a group are the same.

e. Don't mention a person's race, sex, age, sexual orientation, disability, or religion unnecessarily.

                  X   X

        All Californians are weird (1). The state is full of granolas (2)—

              X

those tree-huggers (3) who are always talking about cutting down

on pollution and protecting natural resources. A lot of granolas are

                 X   X

aging hippies or hippie wanna-bes (4). They're basically pot-heads

(5) anyway. Of course, California has a lot of racial and ethnic diver-

                              OK

sity; there are people whose ancestors came from all over the world

                                      X

(6) to settle in California. There are also computer geeks (7)—those

                         X

nerds who wear pocket protectors and talk about the latest *Star Trek*

                                             X

movie all the time (8). For instance, I met this African-American guy

(9) once who worked at some Web design firm in San Jose, and he

was totally into the whole *Star Trek* thing. I have to admit, though,

                              OK

that a lot of really bright men and women (10) work in Silicon Val-

ley. Another group of Californians consists of the Hollywood types

(11), who are so vain and superficial. I dated one of these Hollywood types once. She was a great-looking Mexican girl (12), but she used to be a rah-rah (13) in college, so she couldn't have been very bright—you know how dumb cheerleaders are (14). All in all, I'd say the state has a big mix of weird men and girls (15).

Step 2: For each insensitive section above, identify which "don't" applies. If the section was not insensitive, just write OK.

1. "All Californians are weird": _____d_____

2. "granolas": _____c_____

3. "tree-huggers": _____c_____

4. "aging hippies or hippie wanna-bes": _____c_____

5. "pot-heads": _____c_____

6. "people whose ancestors came from all over the world": _____OK_____

7. "computer geeks": _____c_____

8. "nerds who wear pocket protectors and talk about the latest *Star Trek* movie all the time": _____d_____

9. "African-American guy": _____e_____

10. "men and women": _____OK_____

11. "Hollywood types, who are so vain and superficial": _____b_____

12. "Mexican girl": _____e_____

13. "rah-rah": _____c_____

14. "you know how dumb cheerleaders are: _____d_____

15. "men and girls": _____c_____

Step 3: Now that you have practiced using sensitive language, go to **http://ablongman.com/long.** Click on **Resources for Writers,** and then click on **Activity 12** for more practice using sensitive language.

LAB ACTIVITY 13 Choosing the Best Words

Objective To avoid using slang, overused expressions, and overly formal language.

Step 1: Read the following paragraph, and label each underlined portion S for slang, O for overused expression, or F for overly formal language.

Learning about history is <u>easier said than done</u>[O]. Certainly, I am all for <u>the edification of the general populace</u>[F] when it comes to our nation's history, but I <u>don't get</u>[S] why we need to know so many dates, names, and events. <u>Needless to say</u>[O], I am not trying to <u>diss</u>[S] history instructors—<u>know what I'm saying</u>[S]? And I am certainly not <u>a slacker</u>[S]. However, is it <u>absolutely imperative</u>[F] that I <u>be cognizant of</u>[F] Paul Revere's birthdate or what <u>transpired</u>[F] during the Battle of Pea Ridge? <u>Endeavoring to retain historical minutiae</u>[F] simply <u>cramps my style</u>[S]. I don't want to sound as if I'm just <u>singing the blues</u>[O], but <u>in this day and age</u>[O] when life—and school—demand so much of us, I don't think it's unreasonable to focus on learning the meaning of history rather than on memorizing the details of it. Some may disagree with me or say that studying history is not a matter of doing one or the other, but at this point, I'm just <u>burned out on</u>[S] studying history.

Step 2: Rewrite the paragraph in the space provided, replacing the fifteen underlined words or phrases with more appropriate language. Answers will vary. A possible revision is given.

   Learning about history is not easy. Certainly, I am all for people learning about our nation's history, but I don't understand why we need to know so many dates, names, and events. I am not trying to be disrespectful of history teachers. And I am certainly not lazy. However, is it really crucial that I know Paul Revere's birthdate or what happened during the Battle of Pea Ridge? Trying to remember every historical detail simply annoys me. I don't want to sound as if I'm just complaining, but these days, when life—and school— demand so much of us, I don't think it's unreasonable to focus on learning the meaning of history rather than on memorizing the details of it. Some may disagree with me or say that studying history is not a matter of doing one or the other, but at this point, I'm just tired of studying history.

_____

_____

_____

_____

_____

_____

_____

_____

_____

_____

_____

_____

Step 3: Now that you have practiced using appropriate language, go to **http:// ablongman.com/long.** Click on **Resources for Writers,** and then click on **Activity 13** for more practice choosing the best words.

LAB ACTIVITY 14 Spelling Correctly

Objective To spell correctly.

Step 1: Read the following paragraph, and decide whether the underlined words are spelled correctly. Write C above the correctly spelled words. If an underlined word is misspelled, cross it out and write the correct spelling above it. The first one has been done for you.

> I love to eat ~~tomatos~~ *tomatoes*. It doesn't matter what kind they are—
>
> green, *plum* (C), roma, cherry, grape, heirloom, whatever—I love
>
> ~~eatting~~ *eating* them all. I like to eat them raw all by ~~themselfs~~ *themselves*, ~~choped~~ *chopped*
>
> up in a bowl of salsa, or even on a ~~peice~~ *piece* of crusty bread with fresh
>
> mozzarella and basil. I also like them cooked: baked, broiled,
>
> fried, grilled, or stewed. For example, I like them ~~backed~~ *baked* on top
>
> of a pizza, *stuffed* (C) with bread *crumbs* (C) and mushrooms, broiled
>
> with cheese and herbs, and layered in lasagna. Cherry tomatoes
>
> are ~~wonderfull~~ *wonderful* ~~griled~~ *grilled* on a skewer with beef or chicken; green
>
> tomatoes are great when *dipped* (C) in batter and fried; plum and
>
> roma tomatoes, *though* (C) delicious raw, are terrific in sauces and
>
> stews. I love tomato vinaigrette, sun-dried tomato pesto, and even
>
> tomato chow mein. *Although* (C) the grocery stores sell "vine-
>
> ~~rippened~~ *ripened*" tomatoes, nothing can beat a homegrown tomato. The
>
> smell of a ripe tomato is so *incredible* (C) it just cannot be ~~descrybed~~ *described*.
>
> And the taste is beyond ~~comparson~~ *comparison*. I can eat a ripe homegrown
>
> tomato like an apple because it's really sweet and juicy. Tomatoes,

especially
especialy the homegrown ones, are the best kind of food to eat,

            definitely   C
and they are definitly my favorite.

Step 2: In the space below, write a paragraph of at least six sentences about a fruit
or vegetable that you especially like or dislike. You may choose tomatoes, oranges,
cantaloupes, apples, kiwis, spinach, lima beans, broccoli, cauliflower, cabbage,
Brussels sprouts, grapefruit, or any other real or imaginary fruit or vegetable. Use
at least ten words from the list of frequently misspelled words in Chapter 14 (pages
189–190). When you're done, go back and look carefully for spelling errors in the
entire paragraph, and correct any that you find.

_____

_____

_____

_____

_____

_____

_____

_____

Step 3: Now that you have practiced spelling correctly, go to **http://
ablongman.com/long.** Click on **Resources for Writers,** and then click on **Activity
14** for more practice with correct spelling.

LAB ACTIVITY 15   Expanding Your Vocabulary

Objective To expand your vocabulary.

Step 1: Read the following paragraph. For each underlined word or phrase, substitute another word that means the same thing; write the new word above the underlined word. Try to find different synonyms for overused words. Use a dictionary or a thesaurus when you need help thinking of a new word. The first one has been done for you. Answers will vary. Sample answers are given.

There are basically three <u>places</u> *[sites]* I want to make sure to visit if I ever <u>go</u> *[travel]* to Florida: the Everglades, Disney World, and Epcot Center. I have heard a lot of interesting <u>things</u> *[facts]* about the Everglades from watching <u>different</u> *[various]* nature shows on the Discovery Channel and on public television. The fact that dangerous and exotic <u>animals</u> *[creatures]* live in the Everglades makes me eager to learn about the <u>place</u> *[locale]*. Of course, everyone knows about the seemingly prehistoric alligators living there, but did you know that some endangered species of birds and insects also make their home in this watery <u>place</u> *[location]*? The <u>different</u> *[assorted]* plant species are <u>interesting</u> *[fascinating]* to me as well; for instance, some <u>different</u> *[unusual]* plants grow in the Everglades that cannot be found anywhere else in the world. Although <u>going to</u> *[visiting]* Florida's natural environment is on my wish list, so is <u>going to</u> *[heading for]* some of Florida's other <u>places</u> *[destinations]*. Disney World and Epcot Center probably top the list for most children, but adults can find a lot of <u>things</u> *[activities]* to do there as well. Not many adults can resist the charm of Mickey Mouse and Donald Duck, but adults may also

terrific
find the <u>great</u> theater productions and music concerts put on at

entertaining
Disney World particularly <u>fun</u>. Some rides at Disney World are

certainly not for the timid, but thrill seekers and couch pota-

enjoyable
toes of any age should find something <u>fun</u> to do or see at this

amusement park   entertainment
<u>place</u>. The kind of <u>fun</u> offered at Epcot Center is a bit different,

appealing
but visitors of all ages find it <u>fun</u> nonetheless. The science exhibits

will attract the interest of future astronauts and scientists, but

they will definitely draw the attention of curious adults, too. Over-

wonderful
all, Florida seems like it would be a really <u>great</u> place to visit.

Step 2: Now that you have practiced expanding your vocabulary, go to **http://ablongman.com/long.** Click on **Resources for Writers,** and then click on **Activity 15** for more practice expanding your vocabulary.

LAB ACTIVITY 16 Using the Dictionary

Objective To use the dictionary to understand the meanings of words in context.

Step 1: Read the following paragraph. For each of the underlined words, write three dictionary definitions in the spaces provided. Circle the letter corresponding to the definition that best fits the word in the context of the paragraph. Then write your own sentence using the word appropriately. Answers will vary. Sample definitions have been given.

> It takes a lot of <u>hard</u> work to become a jeweler. Not only do you have to know all of the precious and semiprecious stones; you also have to know the <u>current</u> market value of precious metals such as silver, gold, and platinum. The prices of gold and silver have not been very <u>stable</u> lately, so it is difficult to keep up with all the changes. One of my friends who wants to be a jeweler told me that her favorite <u>part</u> of the jewelry business is designing the jewelry and her least favorite part is studying business strategies. She has been studying for a long time now, but she is almost at the <u>finish</u> line. Soon, the school will <u>present</u> her with her certificate.

Example: hard

a. *Stiff, firm, rigid*

(b.) *Difficult*

c. *Harsh, severe*

Your sentence:

My calculus test was really hard.

1. current

a. Appropriate definition: existing at the present time

b. Movement of water, as in flow of a river

c. A flow of electrical charge

Your sentence:

_____

2. stable

a. Appropriate definition: not changing

b. Sane, rational

c. A building in which domestic animals are sheltered

Your sentence:

_____

3. part

a. Appropriate definition: portion, section

b. Separate or divide

c. A role in a play

Your sentence:

_____

4. finish

a. Appropriate definition: the end

b. Bring to an end, complete

c. The final treatment or coating of a surface

Your sentence:

_____

5. present

a. Appropriate definition: give formally

b. Now

c. A gift

Your sentence:

_____

Step 2: Now that you have practiced using the dictionary to find meanings in context, go to **http://ablongman.com/long.** Click on **Resources for Writers,** and then click on **Activity 16** for more practice using the dictionary.

LAB ACTIVITY 17 Practice with Illustration and Examples

Objective To use examples in paragraphs.

Step 1: In the blanks below, give three specific examples for each of the topic sentence–support point pairs given.

Example:

Topic sentence: *I've heard that buildings can have personalities.*

Support point: *If that's so, then my bank is in a building with a formal, uptight personality.*

Specific example 1: The steel and glass facade seems to stare at me disapprovingly.

Specific example 2: Its height—more than thirty stories—feels intimidating.

Specific example 3: The entryway is guarded by a doorman and a security officer and decorated with thick carpets and antique tapestries.

1. Topic sentence: *A big city can sometimes be scary.*

   Support point: *There are a lot of people and cars everywhere.*

   Specific example 1: _____

   _____

   Specific example 2: _____

   _____

   Specific example 3: _____

   _____

2. Topic sentence: *There are a lot of fun things to do in a big city.*

   Support point: *Theater and dance clubs add a lot to the nightlife.*

   Specific example 1: _____

   _____

   Specific example 2: _____

_____

Specific example 3: _____

_____

3. Topic sentence: *Living on a farm sounds like hard work.*

Support point: *There are so many chores to do every day.*

Specific example 1: _____

_____

Specific example 2: _____

_____

Specific example 3: _____

_____

4. Topic sentence: *My hometown is a really interesting place.*

Support point: *The people who live here are real characters.*

Specific example 1: _____

_____

Specific example 2: _____

_____

Specific example 3: _____

_____

5. Topic sentence: *Las Vegas sounds like a pretty wild place.*

Support point: *Thousands of tourists visit each year and indulge all their desires.*

Specific example 1: _____

_____

Specific example 2: _____

_____

Specific example 3: _____

_____

Step 2: Now that you have practiced using specific examples, go to **http://ablongman.com/long.** Click on **Resources for Writers,** and then click on **Activity 17** for more practice using specific examples in paragraphs.

LAB ACTIVITY 18 Practice with Narration

Objective To use time sequence in paragraphs.

Step 1: Make a list of events that occurred on your first day of school. You may focus on your first day of kindergarten, your first day in a specific grade, or your first day at college.

_____   _____

_____   _____

_____   _____

_____   _____

_____   _____

Step 2: Write a topic sentence with a general topic and a point of view that gives your reader an overall idea of what your day was like. (For example, was it a happy, sad, frustrating, or busy day?)

Your topic sentence: _____

_____

Step 3: Look through your list of events, and cross out any that do not support your topic sentence. Then put a number in front of the remaining events indicating the order in which the events occurred. Write 1 in front of the first relevant thing that happened that day, 2 in front of the second thing, and so on.

Step 4: Write a paragraph about your first day of school, using your topic sentence and relevant events from your list. Remember to follow the time sequence you determined and include specific details to help tell the story of that day.

_____

_____

_____

_____

_____

_____

_____

_____

_____

_____

_____

_____

_____

_____

_____

_____

_____

_____

_____

_____

_____

_____

_____

_____

_____

_____

_____

_____

_____

_____

_____

_____

_____

_____

_____

Step 5: Now that you have practiced using time sequence, go to **http:// ablongman.com/long.** Click on **Resources for Writers,** and then click on **Activity 18** for more practice using time sequence in narrative paragraphs.

LAB ACTIVITY 19 Practice with Description

Objective To develop paragraphs using description.

Step 1: Three of the five senses (sight, smell, taste, touch, and hearing) are listed below each of the given topics. For each of the senses specified, write down three descriptive details.

Example: Your best friend

Sight: _Tall and slender like a fashion model_

_____ _Big brown eyes that always seem to be twinkling_

_____ _A smile as big and warm as her heart_

Touch: _Her fingers are calloused from playing the guitar._

_____ _The heels of her feet are rough and scratchy._

_____ _Her legs are smooth and soft, though rather dry._

Hearing: _Her voice is high and almost squeaky, like a cartoon character's._

_____ _When she laughs, she sometimes snorts._

_____ _Her big, clunky shoes make her sound like a horse when she walks._

1. Your favorite room in the house

Sight: _____

_____

_____

Touch: _____

_____

_____

Hearing: _____

_____

_____

2. Your favorite dessert

Sight: _____

_____

Smell: _____

_____

Taste: _____

_____

3. Your favorite animal

Sight: _____

_____

Touch: _____

_____

Hearing: _____

_____

Step 2: Write a draft of a descriptive paragraph about one of the topics above, incorporating the details you've listed. Remember to write a topic sentence that expresses the main idea of a paragraph and that can be supported with three or four support points and specific details.

_____

_____

_____

_____

_____

Step 3: Now that you have practiced developing a paragraph using description, go to **http://ablongman.com/long.** Click on **Resources for Writers,** and then click on **Activity 19** for more practice writing descriptive paragraphs.

LAB ACTIVITY 20 Practice with Classification and Division

Objective To use subcategories in classification and division paragraphs.

Step 1: List three specific details for each of the given subcategories.

Example: Restaurants classified by cost

Subcategory 1, inexpensive restaurants:

Dinners usually cost less than $10 per person.

Service is generally minimal.

Tablecloths are either nonexistent or plastic.

Subcategory 2, moderately priced restaurants:

Dinners usually cost between $10 and $15 per person.

Service is generally decent.

Tablecloths are a basic cotton.

Subcategory 3, expensive restaurants:

Dinners usually cost more than $20 per person.

Service is generally excellent.

Tablecloths are elegant.

1. Drivers classified by attitude

Subcategory 1, drivers who think they own the road:

_____

_____

_____

Subcategory 2, drivers who are responsible and considerate: _____

_____

_____

_____

Subcategory 3, drivers who are overly cautious:

_____

_____

_____

2. Schools classified by atmosphere

Subcategory 1, schools that are lively and sociable:

_____

_____

_____

Subcategory 2, schools that are quiet and serious:

_____

_____

_____

Subcategory 3, schools that are lively but focused:

_____

_____

_____

3. Movies classified by type

Subcategory 1, action movies:

_____

_____

_____

Subcategory 2, scary movies:

_____

_____

_____

Subcategory 3, romantic movies:

_____

_____

_____

Step 2: Now that you have practiced using subcategories, go to **http:// ablongman.com/long.** Click on **Resources for Writers,** and then click on **Activity 20** for more practice with using subcategories in classification and division paragraphs.

LAB ACTIVITY 21 Practice with Explaining a Process

Objective To explain a process, putting the steps in order.

Step 1: For each of the topics below, list the specific steps involved. *Hint:* You may not need all the lines, or you may need to add more.

Example: Typing a letter

a. Turn on the computer.

b. Start the word processing program.

c. Type the letter.

d. Proofread the letter and double-check the address.

e. Print the letter.

1. Registering for classes

a. _____

b. _____

c. _____

d. _____

e. _____

2. Deciding which classes to take

a. _____

b. _____

c. _____

d. _____

e. _____

3. Making a peanut butter and jelly sandwich

a. _____

b. _____

c. _____

d. _____

e. _____

4. Checking your e-mail

a. _____

b. _____

c. _____

d. _____

e. _____

5. Making a bed

a. _____

b. _____

c. _____

d. _____

e. _____

Step 2: Now that you have practiced putting the steps of a process in order, go to **http://ablongman.com/long.** Click on **Resources for Writers,** and then click on **Activity 21** for more practice putting the steps of a process in order.

LAB ACTIVITY 22 Practice with Comparison and Contrast

Objective To find and organize similarities and differences.

Step 1: For each of the given pairs, list three similarities and three differences.

	Similarities	*Differences*
Example: In-line skating/ ice-skating	Both provide aerobic exercise. Both develop leg muscles. Both can be done outdoors or indoors.	In-line skates have wheels; ice skates have blades. In-line skating can be done on almost any surface; ice-skating must be done on ice. In-line skating is a fairly new sport; ice-skating has been around for years.
1. Pet cats/ pet dogs		
2. High school students/ college students		

	Similarities	*Differences*
3. Professional athletes/ amateur athletes		
4. You ten years ago/ you now		

Step 2: Write a comparison topic sentence focusing on the similarities you came up with for one of the above topic pairs. Then write a contrast topic sentence focusing on the differences you came up with for one of the above topic pairs.

Comparison topic sentence: _____

_____

Contrast topic sentence: _____

_____

Step 3: Now that you have practiced finding similarities and differences, go to **http://ablongman.com/long.** Click on **Resources for Writers,** and then click on **Activity 22** for practice organizing similarities and differences.

LAB ACTIVITY 23 Practice with Explaining Cause and Effect

Objective To identify causes and effects.

Step 1: Make a list of three causes and three effects for each of the following topics.

1. Topic: *getting a cavity in a tooth*

Cause A: _____

Cause B: _____

Cause C: _____

Effect A: _____

Effect B: _____

Effect C: _____

2. Topic: *graduating from college*

Cause A: _____

Cause B: _____

Cause C: _____

Effect A: _____

Effect B: _____

Effect C: _____

3. Topic: *finishing a marathon*

Cause A: _____

Cause B: _____

Cause C: _____

Effect A: _____

Effect B: _____

Effect C: _____

4. Topic: *losing a lot of weight*

Cause A: _____

Cause B: _____

Cause C: _____

Effect A: _____

Effect B: _____

Effect C: _____

5. Topic: *getting lost*

Cause A: _____

Cause B: _____

Cause C: _____

Effect A: _____

Effect B: _____

Effect C: _____

Step 2: Choose one of the topics above and write one topic sentence emphasizing causes and one topic sentence emphasizing effects.

Causes topic sentence: _____

_____

_____

Effects topic sentence: _____

_____

_____

Step 3: Now that you have practiced identifying causes and effects, go to **http:// ablongman.com/long.** Click on **Resources for Writers,** and then click on **Activity 23** for more practice with causes and effects.

LAB ACTIVITY 24 Practice with Definition

Objective To identify general categories and use details to develop definitions.

Step 1: List three examples for each of the following terms.

Example: a kindhearted person

a. My friend Drew

b. My sister Sally

c. My mail carrier, Mr. Jones

1. a fun vacation spot

a. _____

b. _____

c. _____

2. a productive learning environment

a. _____

b. _____

c. _____

3. a responsible person

a. _____

b. _____

c. _____

4. a great place to live

a. _____

b. _____

c. _____

5. a real hero

a. _____

b. _____

c. _____

Step 2: Now, choose one of the examples from your lists above, and make a list of descriptive details for that example.

Example: my mail carrier, Mr. Jones

He collects canned goods for needy families four times a year.

He plays Santa at the local Salvation Army each Christmas.

He always takes time to chat with the elderly and young children on his route.

Your example: _____

Your descriptive details:

a. _____

_____

b. _____

_____

c. _____

_____

Step 3: Now that you have practiced using details to develop definitions, go to **http://ablongman.com/long.** Click on **Resources for Writers,** and then click on **Activity 24** for practice identifying general categories to develop definitions.

LAB ACTIVITY 25 Practice with Argument

Objective To identify reasons and write an argument paragraph.

Step 1: Write a topic sentence for an argument paragraph about each of the following topics. Then list three reasons supporting your argument.

Example:

Topic: *parking on campus*

Topic sentence: The parking problem on campus must be solved immediately.

Reason A: The school's neighbors resent the parking overflow on residential streets.

Reason B: It often makes students late for class.

Reason C: It creates an atmosphere of frustration and stress on campus.

1. Topic: *beer commercials*

Topic sentence: _____

_____

Reason A: _____

Reason B: _____

Reason C: _____

2. Topic: *college costs*

Topic sentence: _____

_____

Reason A: _____

Reason B: _____

Reason C: _____

3. Topic: *use of profanity*

Topic sentence: _____

_____

Reason A: _____

Reason B: _____

Reason C: _____

4. Topic: *gay marriage*

Topic sentence: _____

_____

Reason A: _____

Reason B: _____

Reason C: _____

5. Topic: *space exploration*

Topic sentence: _____

_____

Reason A: _____

Reason B: _____

Reason C: _____

Step 2: Choose one of the above topics and write an argument paragraph using the topic sentence and reasons you listed.

_____

_____

_____

_____

_____

_____

_____

_____

Step 3: Now that you have practiced identifying reasons and writing an argument paragraph, go to **http://ablongman.com/long.** Click on **Resources for Writers,** and then click on **Activity 25** for more practice identifying reasons supporting an argument.

LAB ACTIVITY 26 Writing Paragraphs for an Essay

Objective To develop an introductory paragraph and thesis statements.

Step 1: Choose one of the topics listed below and write an introductory paragraph on that topic using one of the methods listed. Then, rewrite the introductory paragraph using a different method. End the paragraph with your thesis statement on the line provided.

Topics:

- Sports
- Television
- Politics
- Careers

Methods:

- Give background information.
- Include a personal anecdote.
- Use a quotation.
- Use an example that shows the opposite of your main point.
- Ask questions.

Example:

Your topic: _Gardening_

Method: _Include a personal anecdote._

Your introduction: _Among my fondest memories of growing up with my grandmother are those mornings we spent working in the backyard garden. She was getting on in years by the time I, her youngest grandchild, had come along, but she was nonetheless a bundle of energy and strength in the garden. She taught me how to prepare the soil, when to water, where to plant marigolds so the worms wouldn't get to our tomatoes, and how to untangle the delicate tendrils and tissue-like petals of the sweet peas. Those mornings in the garden, I learned that food doesn't just come from the grocery store and that flowers don't just come from the florist. I learned that growing anything involves a lot of work and careful attention. I learned how to nurture._

Thesis statement: _Gardening isn't just a hobby; it's an education._

Your topic: _____

Method: _____

Your introduction: _____

_____

_____

_____

_____

_____

_____

_____

Thesis statement: _____

Step 2: Now, rewrite your introduction using the same topic but a different method.

New method: _____

Your new introduction: _____

_____

_____

_____

_____

_____

_____

_____

Thesis statement: _____

Step 3: Now that you have practiced an introductory paragraph, go to **http://ablongman.com/long.** Click on **Resources for Writers,** and then click on **Activity 26** for practice developing thesis statements.

LAB ACTIVITY 27 Planning an Essay

Objective To plan an essay.

Step 1: Make a brainstorming list and develop a plan for an essay using each of the following thesis statements.

Example:

Thesis statement: *Taking the bus to school is better than driving for a number of reasons.*

Brainstorming list: Taking the bus is cheaper.

I don't get stressed out hunting for a parking space.

I don't get stressed out on the highway.

Taking the bus helps the environment.

I meet interesting people on the bus.

I like my bus driver.

Topic sentence for body paragraph 1: Taking the bus helps me save money.

Topic sentence for body paragraph 2: I feel much less stress when I take the bus.

Topic sentence for body paragraph 3: I get to meet interesting people riding the bus.

1. Thesis statement: *My friend _____ (insert a friend's name) is a really interesting person.*

Brainstorming list: _____

_____

_____

_____

Topic sentence for body paragraph 1: _____

_____

Topic sentence for body paragraph 2: _____

_____

Topic sentence for body paragraph 3: _____

_____

2. Thesis statement: *One of my favorite television shows is* _____
(insert the show's name).

Brainstorming list: _____

_____

_____

_____

Topic sentence for body paragraph 1: _____

_____

Topic sentence for body paragraph 2: _____

_____

Topic sentence for body paragraph 3: _____

_____

3. Thesis statement: *It was absolutely the best day.*

Brainstorming list: _____

_____

_____

_____

Topic sentence for body paragraph 1: _____

_____

Topic sentence for body paragraph 2: _____

_____

Topic sentence for body paragraph 3: _____

_____

Step 2: Now that you have practiced developing a plan for an essay, go to **http://ablongman.com/long.** Click on **Resources for Writers,** and then click on **Activity 27** for more practice planning an essay.

LAB ACTIVITY 28 Evaluating Essay Support and Development

Objective To evaluate writing for adequate support and development.

Step 1: Read the following paragraph. Write down the numbers of the two sentences that should be omitted because they are repetitive or off the topic. Then write down the numbers of the three sentences that should be developed further.

Answers will vary.

(1)Planning a vacation can be a real challenge. (2)First, you have to decide what kind of vacation you want. (3)Then, you should think about where you want to go and what you can afford. (4)Some people gain weight while on vacation. (5)There's also the destination to consider. (6)Finally, you'll need to do some research and make reservations.

A. Which two sentences should be omitted? _4_ and _5_ .

B. Which three sentences need further development? _2_ , _3_ , and _6_ .

Make a list of details that could be added to improve the paragraph's development.

A. These details would help to develop the idea stated in sentence ____ better.

_____

_____

_____

_____

_____

B. These details would help develop the idea stated in sentence ____ better.

_____

_____

_____

_____

_____

C. These details would help develop the idea stated in sentence _____ better.

_____

_____

_____

_____

_____

Step 2: Now that you have practiced evaluating writing for adequate support and development, go to **http://ablongman.com/long.** Click on **Resources for Writers,** and then click on **Activity 28** for more practice evaluating support and development.

LAB ACTIVITY 29 Writing an Essay

Objective To interpret essay questions.

Step 1: Read each essay question and the outlines that follow it. Decide which outline best addresses the given question and put an X in front of it.

Essay question: Who was Virginia Woolf and why is she an important figure in English literature?

___X___ **Outline 1**

Thesis: *As an author, critic, and social commentator, Virginia Woolf is an important figure in English literature because of her artistry and her outspoken views on the position of women in society.*

    I. Who Virginia Woolf was

      A. Author

      B. Critic

   II. Her artistry

      A. Major novels—*To the Lighthouse, Mrs. Dalloway, Orlando*

      B. Artistic innovations—stream of consciousness, modernism

  III. Her outspoken views on women

      A. Feminism—*A Room of One's Own*

      B. Bloomsbury group

_____ **Outline 2**

Thesis: *Virginia Woolf was a woman writer in the early twentieth century who is important because she was well-known.*

    I. Woolf's life

      A. Daughter of Leslie Stephen

      B. Wife of Leonard Woolf

   II. Her fame

      A. Major novels—*To the Lighthouse, Mrs. Dalloway, Orlando*

      B. Literary circle—Bloomsbury group

  III. Early twentieth century

      A. Other famous writers of the time—James Joyce, D. H. Lawrence

      B. World War I

Essay question: What were two major causes of the French Revolution?

_____X_____ **Outline 1**

Thesis: *The French Revolution started with the fall of the Bastille and ended with the coronation of Napoleon.*

    I. Fall of the Bastille

        A. Bastille was a prison

        B. Peasants stormed it and released the prisoners

    II. Robespierre

        A. Leader of the Revolution

        B. Guillotine

    III. Napoleon

        A. General in the Revolution

        B. Josephine, his wife

_____ **Outline 2**

Thesis: *The growing gap between the aristocracy and the poor along with major agricultural setbacks led to the French Revolution.*

    I. Gap between aristocracy and poor

        A. Excesses of the wealthy classes

        B. Extreme poverty of the lower and working classes

        C. Indifference and abuse on the part of the aristocracy toward the poor

    II. Agricultural setbacks

        A. Drought and meager harvests

        B. Crippling legislation enforced against farmers

        C. Starvation among the poor and working classes

Step 2: Now that you have practiced interpreting essay questions, go to **http:// ablongman.com/long.** Click on **Resources for Writers,** and then click on **Activity 29** for more practice. Make sure that you will have thirty uninterrupted minutes to spend on the Web site; the online activity will be timed.

LAB ACTIVITY 30 Writing Summaries

Objective: To identify key points and ideas.

Step 1: Read the following paragraph, which summarizes the novel *Harry Potter and the Sorcerer's Stone*. Cross out any sentences that should be omitted from the summary. In the space below the paragraph, specify what kind of information should have been included but is missing.

Harry's parents have died, and he is being brought up by "muggles" Vernon and Petunia Dursley. ~~The Durselys are completely consumed by appearances and spend far too much time in their yard.~~ Harry has no ideas why the Dursleys force him to live in a tiny closet under the stairs, and treat him horribly. Dudley, the Dursley's obese son, mercilessly torments Harry. ~~Harry does get to go to the zoo on Dudley's birthday because there's no one who can stay with Harry on that day.~~ On his eleventh birthday, Harry Potter finally receives a letter, telling him that he is chosen as one of the future students of a special school. ~~In the process of trying to receive the letter, Harry is given a bigger room in the Dursley's home.~~ Hagrid finally introduces Harry into the real circumstances of his life. Harry still has a lightning-shaped scar on his forehead from events early in his life and is famous in the wizarding world. The Dursleys, terrified and disgusted by anything magical, never bothered to tell Harry anything about his past. Thus, Harry is delighted—and astounded—to begin his new education. At school, Harry meets his teachers, and becomes friends with Ron Weasley and Hermione Granger. ~~Harry also learns about chocolate frogs and other magical candy.~~ The three of them suspect that Severus Snape seems bent on stealing an object guarded by a three-headed dog, and they assume the responsibility themselves to find out what Snape's plan. ~~Snape is often described as having greasy black hair and a sneering expression.~~ Their quest for the truth leads across many obstacles, from keeping up the everyday school life, a bewitched Quidditch match, Fluffy, the three-headed monster dog, and some nearly deadly tasks they must overcome to learn the truth.

What kind of information needs to be included but is missing? You may want to review "Steps in Writing an Effective Summary" in Chapter 30 on pages 446–447.

What "muggles" are; why the Dursleys are keeping Harry; who Hagrid is; what sort of school

Harry will attend and what its name is; who Severus Snape is; what Quidditch is.

_____

_____

Read the following summary of *Fast Food Nation*, a book by Eric Schlosser. Cross out any sentences that should be omitted from the summary. In the space below the paragraph, specify what kind of information should have been included but is missing.

> (1)I read a book recently that goes into great detail about the fast-food industry in America. (2)It offers a history of the "founding fathers" of fast food, people like the McDonald brothers, Carl Karcher, and Ray Kroc. (3)After the historical background, however, the book quickly moves on to a discussion of almost every aspect of the fast-food industry, from its production of ingredients, to its advertising strategies, to its labor practices. (4)<u>There is a detailed description of how cattle are slaughtered and the risks that slaughterhouse workers have to deal with every day on the job.</u> (5)<u>Schlosser reveals some of the advertising tactics commonly used by the fast-food industry.</u> (6)<u>He talks about how the fast-food industry targets children, featuring playgrounds and free toys as a regular part of advertising campaigns.</u> (7)<u>He also points out that the fast-food industry has a very high turnover rate, partly because employees receive little salary and few benefits.</u> (8)He suggests that workers are often exploited to increase the company's profits. (9)<u>The book is very interesting, and I recommend that anyone who eats fast food should read it.</u>

What kind of information needs to be included but is missing? You may want to review "Steps in Writing a Good Summary" in Chapter 30.

Missing information:

_____

The name of the book, the publication information, and the full name of the author.
_____

_____

_____

Step 2: Now that you have practiced identifying key points and ideas, go to **http://ablongman.com/long.** Click on **Resources for Writers,** and then click on **Activity 30** for more practice identifying key point and ideas.

ACTIVITY 31 Writing to Get a Job

Objective To proofread cover letters and organize details in a résumé.

Step 1: Read the cover letter below. Cross out spelling and typing errors and write corrections above each error. There are eleven errors, including the one marked for you.

1700 Ledgewood Avenue
Cincinnati, OH 45206
July 15, 2005

Ms. Tanisha Curtis
Public Relations ~~Manger~~ *Manager*
Xavier University
3800 Victory Parkway
~~Cincinati~~, OH 45207 *Cincinnati*

Dear ~~Mr.~~ Curtis: *Ms.*

 I write to apply for the ~~postion~~ of administrative ~~asistant~~, as advertised *position* *assistant* in the *Cincinnati Enquirer*.

 I am one course away from ~~completin~~ my Associate of Arts degree at *completing* Raymond Walters Community College, where I majored in Business Communications. During the last six years, I have been a secretary in the Research and Development Office at Procter and Gamble. As you will see from the enclosed résumé, I am well qualified for the position you ~~advertized~~. *advertised*

 I am very ~~intrested~~ in working for you and would be happy to come in *interested* for ~~a~~ interview. I am a motivated and ~~responsibel~~ ~~employe~~ who works well *an* *responsible* *employee* with others in a professional setting. I am confident that I can make a positive contribution to your office.

Sincerely,

Drew Smith

Drew Smith

Step 2: The draft letter below needs improvement if it is to be effective. Imagine that you have strong qualifications for the job being offered, and rewrite the letter adding several specific and detailed qualifications you have. You may make up fictional qualifications, but be sure they are credible.

Dear Mr. Reo:

I write to apply for the position of computer sales representative in your store, as advertised in the *Ridgemont Gazette.*

I love computers and have worked with them a lot. I have also studied about them in school courses.

I would like to work at your company, and I think I can do the job well.

Sincerely,

Melissa Perez

Rewritten:

_____

_____

_____

_____

_____

_____

_____

_____

Step 3: Now that you have practiced proofreading a cover letter, go to **http://ablongman.com/long.** Click on **Resources for Writers,** and then click on **Activity 31** for practice organizing details in a résumé.

LAB ACTIVITY 32 Using Proper Format

Objective To use proper format for typed and handwritten papers.

Step 1: Mark the following paper, showing the writer what needs to be changed or added. One error has been marked for you. You should find ten more.

Add page number

Johanna Fong

English 100

Professor Klein   Move the professor's name above "English 100"

Add the date

San Francisco's Mission district Center title; capitalize "District"

Indent line

My favorite area in San Francisco is the Mission District.

It has a great mix of old and new: traditional Spanish-style

buildings dating

Needs one-inch right margin

Use the same font throughout

back a hundred years scattered in among the refurbished Art Deco

houses and contemporary office buildings. The people in the

neighborhood

also reflect a mix of old and new. Some have lived in the Mission District for

Maintain one-inch left margin

eighty years or more, and others are new arrivals still unpack-

ing boxes. All, however, may be found strolling through the

area, browsing in shop windows on Valencia Street, or stopping

in at the latest restaurant or taqueria on Guerrero. Sometimes

during the summer, crowds gather in Dolores Park to watch a

Double-space throughout

free play. No matter what the season, there is always something

interesting in the Mission.

Step 2: In the space below, write by hand a short paper for your English class using all the elements of the proper format. Your subject is what interests you most about San Francisco. You can write about the Forty-Niners, earthquakes, food choices, the Gold Rush, cable cars, anything you like. After you're done, reread your paper and correct any formatting errors.

_____

_____

_____

_____

_____

_____

_____

Step 3: Now that you have practiced using proper format, go to **http:// ablongman.com/long.** Click on **Resources for Writers,** and then click on **Activity 32** for more practice.

LAB ACTIVITY 33 Using Prepositional Phrases

Objective To use prepositional phrases.

Step 1: Write ten sentences about the picture below. Make sure that each sentence contains at least one prepositional phrase, and make sure to use at least ten different prepositions in total. Draw a line under each of your prepositional phrases.

Answers will vary.

Common Prepositions

aboard	at	concerning	near	to
about	before	despite	of	toward
above	behind	during	off	under
across	below	except	on	underneath
after	beneath	for	onto	until
against	beside	from	out	up
along	besides	in	outside	upon
along with	between	inside	over	with
among	beyond	into	through	within
around	by	like	throughout	without

Example: Above the pyramids, the sky is gray.

1. _____

_____

2. _____

_____

3. _____

_____

4. _____

_____

5. _____

_____

6. _____

_____

7. _____

_____

8. _____

_____

9. _____

_____

10. _____

_____

Step 2: Now that you have practiced using prepositional phrases, go to **http:// ablongman.com/long.** Click on **Resources for Writers,** and then click on **Activity 33** for more practice using prepositional phrases.

LAB ACTIVITY 34 Recognizing Subjects and Verbs

Objective To identify and use subjects and verbs.

Step 1: In each of the following sentences, insert an appropriate subject.

   Example: ___Skiing___ is my favorite winter sport.

1. ___Name will vary___ and I have been friends for a long time.

2. ___We___ have been through a lot of experiences together, both good and bad.

3. ___Answer will vary___ is one of the many things we have in common.

4. I would have to say that ___answer will vary___ is my friend's best quality.

5. ___We___ like to do many things together.

Step 2: In each of the following sentences, insert an appropriate verb. Some sentences require a main verb and a helping verb.

1. One thing that I ___like/enjoy___ doing in my free time is roller-blading or in-line skating.

2. In-line skating ___is___ a lot of fun and good exercise as well.

3. When I first tried to learn how to do it, I ___fell___ down a lot.

4. It ___was___ difficult to get my balance and to glide smoothly.

5. For a couple of hours, I thought that I ___would___ never ___get___ the hang of it.

6. Finally, though, I ___was___ able to move smoothly forward, backward, and even in circles.

7. I did ___have___ a few scrapes and bruises by the end of the day.

8. But I also ___had___ a wonderful time.

9. Now, I ___roller-blade or skate___ at least once a week if the weather is good.

10. The bonus is that I _____have lost_____ ten pounds so far.

Step 3: Select a proverb or idiom from the list "Proverbs and Idioms Explained" in Chapter 34 (pages 490–492). Then write a six-sentence paragraph about how your selected proverb or idiom relates to a real or imaginary experience you had. After you're done writing, go back and underline all of the subjects once, underline the verbs twice, and cross out the prepositional phrases.

_____

_____

_____

_____

_____

_____

_____

Step 4: Now that you have practiced using appropriate subjects and verbs, go to **http://ablongman.com/long.** Click on **Resources for Writers,** and then click on **Activity 34** for practice identifying subjects and verbs.

LAB ACTIVITY 35 Identifying and Using Clauses

Objective To distinguish and use independent and dependent clauses.

Step 1: For each of the following sentences, draw a single line under each independent clause and a double line under each dependent clause. Then draw a box around the dependent word or words.

Example: I never get tired of eating bread even though I have it almost every day.

1. Breads are interesting because they come in lots of shapes and sizes.

2. While most of us are familiar with the rectangular loaf shape, breads can also be round, braided, or even flat.

3. Sourdough breads and many rustic types of breads are often round or free-form in shape though they can also be found in loaf form.

4. Challah, a Jewish egg bread, is traditionally braided while brioche, a sweet French bread, is generally molded.

5. Tortillas, naan, and Armenian cracker breads, on the other hand, are flat although they sometimes puff up in the cooking process.

6. Even though breads can vary widely by shape, they can vary just as widely by size.

7. If you watch the Food Network, you may have seen at least one show featuring the largest bagel or hot dog bun ever made.

8. Similarly, you may have seen a cooking show featuring some of the smallest breads around—though technically they would be considered dumplings.

9. After I watch some of these bread shows, I feel inspired to try baking some odd-shaped or odd-sized breads of my own.

10. Luckily, I usually stop short of trying to bake a two-ton brioche unless, of course, I have a lot of flour!

Step 2: For each of the following items, use the clause given to write a complete sentence. An example has been done for you.

Clause: *because I can stuff meat, salad, and dressing inside them.*

Sentence: _I love pita bread pockets because I can stuff meat, salad, and dressing inside them._

1. Clause: *Whenever someone asks me what type of bread I want for my sandwich,*

   Sentence: _____

   _____

2. Clause: *so I usually buy that kind of bread when I am shopping.*

   Sentence: _____

   _____

3. Clause: *and I do not even like seeing that kind of bread in front of me on the table.*

   Sentence: _____

   _____

4. Clause: *When given a choice between corn bread, garlic bread, whole wheat bread, and plain white bread,*

   Sentence: _____

   _____

5. Clause: *but I like it best when it is toasted.*

   Sentence: _____

   _____

Step 3: Now that you have practiced distinguishing between independent and dependent clauses, go to **http://ablongman.com/long.** Click on **Resources for Writers,** and then click on **Activity 35** for more practice distinguishing clauses and phrases.

LAB ACTIVITY 36 Correcting Run-On Sentences

Objective To use coordinating conjunctions, dependent words, or transitions to correct run-on sentences.

Step 1: Correct the following run-on sentences by inserting the appropriate coordinating conjunction or the appropriate dependent word from the table below. Use a caret (^) to indicate where the insertion should be made. The clue in parentheses tells you whether to add a coordinating conjunction (cc) or a dependent word (dw).

Coordinating conjunctions	for	nor	or	yet	so
	and	but			
Dependent words	after	because	if	though	when
	although	even though	since	unless	

Example:

                                                        , but
I don't understand why William Shakespeare is such a big deal^ I guess a lot of people like him. (cc)

1. We always had to study him in school I didn't pay much attention. (cc)
We always had to study him in school, but I didn't pay much attention.

2. I couldn't understand the language it's English. (dw)
I couldn't understand the language even though/although/though it's English.

3. Reading Shakespeare aloud is very difficult many of the words are unfamiliar. (dw)
Reading Shakespeare aloud is very difficult because many of the words are unfamiliar.

4. Sometimes I could understand the plot I watched the movie version. (dw)
Sometimes I could understand the plot if/after I watched the movie version.

5. I have to admit that the stories are interesting there's often a lot of action. (cc)
I have to admit that the stories are interesting, and/for there's often a lot of action.

6. Either there's a funny twist in the plot there's a violent and dramatic climax. (cc)
Either there's a funny twist in the plot, or there's a violent and dramatic climax.

7. I really had to work hard to read Shakespeare's plays I felt proud of myself when I understood what was going on. (cc)   I really had to work hard to read Shakespeare's plays, so I felt proud of myself when I understood what was going on.

8. I still can't say that I'm a fan of Shakespeare I don't hate him either. (cc)
I still can't say that I'm a fan of Shakespeare, but I don't hate him either.

9. I became interested in Shakespeare's life I'm not crazy about his work. (dw)

I became interested in Shakespeare's life even though/although/though I'm not crazy about his work.

10. There is some controversy about whether he actually wrote the plays and sonnets attributed to him he came from humble beginnings. (dw) There is some controversy about whether he actually wrote the plays and sonnets attributed to him because he came from humble beginnings.

11. He wasn't from a wealthy family his parents didn't have high social status. (cc)

He wasn't from a wealthy family, and his parents didn't have high social status.

12. Some critics believe that he could not have had the education necessary to write what he supposedly wrote education was extremely expensive in Shakespeare's time. (dw) Some critics believe that he could not have had the education necessary to write what he supposedly wrote because/since education was extremely expensive in Shakespeare's time.

13. These critics have suggested that other writers of the period are more likely authors of Shakespeare's works the styles of these other writers are very different. (dw) These critics have suggested that other writers of the period are more likely authors of Shakespeare's works even though/although/though the styles of these other writers are very different.

14. Other critics point out that such arguments against Shakespeare's authorship are prejudiced they are based on Shakespeare's social status. (dw) Other critics point out that such arguments against Shakespeare's authorship are prejudiced since/because they are based on Shakespeare's social status.

15. Shakespeare seems a rather mysterious figure not a lot is known about his childhood or daily life. (cc) Shakespeare seems a rather mysterious figure, for not a lot is known about his childhood or daily life.

16. We know that he was born in Stratford-upon-Avon in 1564 we know that his birthday was in April. (cc) We know that he was born in Stratford-upon-Avon in 1564, and we know that his birthday was in April.

17. We know that he married Anne Hathaway we know that they had children. (cc)

We know that he married Anne Hathaway, and we know that they had children.

18. Basically, what we know comes from official records documenting births, marriages, and deaths it's hard to know anything about his personal life. (cc)

Basically, what we know comes from official records documenting births, marriages, and deaths, so it's hard to know anything about his personal life.

19. Today, people can find out all kinds of things about their favorite modern-day writers they want to. (dw) Today, people can find out all kinds of things about their favorite modern-day writers if they want to.

20. It is nearly impossible to learn anything new about long-dead authors a person is willing to do a lot of research. (dw) It is nearly impossible to learn anything new about long-dead authors unless a person is willing to do a lot of research.

Step 2: Now that you have practiced using dependent words and coordinating conjunctions to correct run-on sentences, go to **http://ablongman.com/long.** Click on **Resources for Writers,** and then click on **Activity 36** for more practice correcting run-on sentences.

LAB ACTIVITY 37 Correcting Fragments

Objective To identify fragments and change them into complete sentences.

Step 1: Make each of the following fragments into a complete sentence by adding your own independent clause. Answers will vary.

> **Example:** After thinking about it for a few hours, *I decided not to take his advice*.

1. Although there seem to be tall buildings everywhere, _____
   _____ .

2. When I look around my neighborhood, _____
   _____ .

3. After I get home from work in the evening, _____
   _____ .

4. _____
   even though I don't really care for it.

5. _____
   because I like to try new things.

6. When I take a day off, _____
   _____ .

7. In my hometown, _____
   _____ .

8. If I ever have a chance, _____
   _____ .

9. At the end of the day, _____
   _____ .

10. _____
    even though it's kind of scary.

11. Sometimes, when my friend laughs so hard that her stomach hurts, _____

_____ .

12. When the twins awoke from their nap, _____

_____ .

13. _____

because they loved it so much.

_____ .

14. In about ten years, _____

_____ .

15. _____

while we take a vacation.

Step 2: Now that you have practiced correcting fragments by adding an independent clause, go to **http://ablongman.com/long.** Click on **Resources for Writers,** and then click on **Activity 37** for more practice identifying fragments.

LAB ACTIVITY 38 Present and Past Tenses for Regular Verbs

Objective To use the present and past tenses of regular verbs.

Step 1: Fill in the following table with the proper form of the verb.

Subject	Verb	Present Tense	Past Tense
Example: I	like	I like	I liked
1. you	like	you like	you liked
2. they	like	they like	they liked
3. Ian	like	Ian likes	Ian liked
4. we	entertain	we entertain	we entertained
5. you	entertain	you entertain	you entertained
6. he	entertain	he entertains	he entertained
7. David and Maria	entertain	David and Maria entertain	David and Maria entertained
8. I	smile	I smile	I smiled
9. Ping	smile	Ping smiles	Ping smiled
10. you	smile	you smile	you smiled
11. we	smile	we smile	we smiled
12. it	bounce	it bounces	it bounced
13. both balls	bounce	both balls bounce	both balls bounced
14. we	bounce	we bounce	we bounced
15. they	bounce	they bounce	they bounced
16. Fido	bark	Fido barks	Fido barked
17. Rover and Spot	bark	Rover and Spot bark	Rover and Spot barked
18. I	enjoy	I enjoy	I enjoyed
19. Susan and Tim	enjoy	Susan and Tim enjoy	Susan and Tim enjoyed
20. Natalya and I	enjoy	Natalya and I enjoy	Natalya and I enjoyed

Step 2: Now, complete the following sentences using the proper verb tense.

Answers will vary; however, the proper verb tense is indicated.

Example: Yesterday, we (watch) _watched whales migrating offshore._

1. Last year, they (walk) _walked_ _____

_____

2. Now, I (enjoy) _enjoy_ _____

_____

3. We still (dislike) _dislike_ _____

_____

4. Last night, he (dream) _dreamed_ _____

_____

5. These days, we all (wish) _wish_ _____

_____

6. She still often (wonder) _wonders_ _____

_____

7. Even now, it (amaze) _amazes_ _____

_____

8. You always (ask) _ask_ _____

_____

9. When he was little, he (listen) _listened_ _____

_____

10. Until recently, they always (remember) _remembered_ _____

_____

Step 3: Now that you have practiced using present and past tenses of regular verbs, go to **http://ablongman.com/long.** Click on **Resources for Writers,** and then click on **Activity 38** for more practice with regular verbs.

LAB ACTIVITY 39 Present and Past Tenses for Irregular Verbs

Objective To use the present and past tenses of irregular verbs.

Step 1: Fill in the following table with the proper form of the verb.

Subject	Verb	Present Tense	Past Tense
Example: I	be	I am	I was
1. you	be	you are	you were
2. they	be	they are	they were
3. she	be	she is	she was
4. we	have	we have	we had
5. you	have	you have	you had
6. he	have	he has	he had
7. it	have	it has	it had
8. I	write	I write	I wrote
9. Jose and Cara	write	Jose and Cara write	Jose and Cara wrote
10. you	write	you write	you wrote
11. we	write	we write	we wrote
12. it	know	it knows	it knew
13. you	know	you know	you knew
14. we	know	we know	we knew
15. Suzy	know	Suzy knows	Suzy knew
16. I	eat	I eat	I ate
17. the neighbors	eat	the neighbors eat	the neighbors ate
18. Dave	eat	Dave eats	Dave ate
19. you	eat	you eat	you ate
20. we	eat	we eat	we ate

Step 2: Now, write the past participle of each of the following verbs in the blank.

Example: be ___*been*___

1. have ___*had*___

2. write ___*written*___

3. know ___*known*___

4. eat ___*eaten*___

5. fall ___*fallen*___

6. go ___*gone*___

7. sing ___*sung*___

8. forget ___*forgotten*___

9. think ___*thought*___

10. drive ___*driven*___

Step 3: Now that you have practiced using present and past tenses of irregular verbs, go to **http://ablongman.com/long.** Click on **Resources for Writers,** and then click on **Activity 39** for more practice with irregular verbs.

LAB ACTIVITY 40 Making Subjects and Verbs Agree

Objective To make subjects and verbs agree.

Step 1: Underline the subject and write the correct form of the given verb in the blank.

Example: He _____has_____ several classical CDs in his collection.
                          have

1. Bach, Beethoven, and Brahms _____are_____ widely known classical composers.
                                           be

2. Students of sacred music probably _____recognize_____ much of Bach's repertoire.
                                               recognize

3. Beethoven's best-known piece _____is_____ probably his Fifth Symphony.
                                          be

4. Brahms _____continues_____ to be well-known for his lullabies.
                   continue

5. References to any one of the "three Bs" _____appear_____ in some unexpected places.
                                                     appear

6. One popular rock-and-roll song of the fifties _____is_____ titled "Roll Over,
   Beethoven."   be

7. Fans of the *Peanuts* cartoon also _____know_____ Beethoven as Schroeder's
   favorite musician.   know

8. If one _____pays_____ close attention to the film *Psycho*, one will notice that
                  pay
   Norman listens to Beethoven's "Eroica" symphony.

9. Classical music _____plays_____ a key role in films such as *Mr. Holland's Opus*
   and *The Red Violin*.   play

10. Neither the symphony nor the sonata _____is_____ a popular musical form
    today.   be

11. However, many _____do_____ appreciate the classical forms.
                            do

12. Each of the "three Bs" _____does_____ continue to garner an audience.
           do

13. I _____have_____ so much to learn about their music and about them.
    have

14. Certainly, people _____find_____ their personal lives interesting.
         find

15. Several films _____have_____ been made about their lives.
        have

16. Most of these films, however, _____take_____ liberties with the truth.
           take

17. Fictionalizing the composers' lives _____seems_____ an odd thing to do since their actual lives are interesting enough.   seem

18. Brahms's mood swings, Bach's power struggles, and Beethoven's deafness
_____provide_____ plenty of material for filmmakers.
    provide

19. Yet filmmakers _____seem_____ to be most interested in each composer's love life.
       seem

20. At least the music always _____plays_____ a prominent role, even in the most far-fetched films.   play

Step 2: Now that you have practiced making subjects and verbs agree, go to **http://ablongman.com/long.** Click on **Resources for Writers,** and then click on **Activity 40** for more practice with subjects and verbs.

LAB ACTIVITY 41 Making Verb Tenses Correct and Consistent

Objective To use correct and consistent verb tenses.

Step 1: Cross out verbs as needed to make the verb tense in the paragraph consistent. Write the correct verb tense above each crossed-out verb. The first one is done for you. There are ten more errors in the paragraph.

When I was a child, I ~~use~~ *used* to hear my brothers talk about baseball legends. Babe Ruth, Cy Young, and Jackie Robinson ~~are~~ *were* mentioned on what seemed like a daily basis. I didn't really know who these men were or why they were considered legends in baseball. When I ~~start~~ *started* school and read "legends" about Johnny Appleseed, Paul Bunyan, and John Henry, I got even more ~~confuse.~~ *confused* Those legends ~~seem~~ *seemed* made-up or at least exaggerated. But the stories my brothers told about their baseball legends didn't seem made-up at all; they seemed to be about very real people. It wasn't until some time later that I ~~hear~~ *heard* the expression "a legend in one's own time." That saying is applied to someone who accomplished so much in a lifetime that he or she could be considered a legend. The expression ~~gets~~ *got* me thinking about those baseball players again. Babe Ruth ~~holds~~ *held* virtually every batting record that existed, and he seemed bigger than life to most of his fans. Cy Young was such a great pitcher that major league baseball ~~establishes~~ *established* an annual award in his name. Jackie Robinson's achievements were not restricted only to baseball because when

          broke
he ~~breaks~~ the color barrier, that signaled a major step forward not

only for professional sports but for the civil rights movement as

                    played
well. Even though these men ~~play~~ in different times, long before I

was born, their accomplishments were still talked about by people

old enough to remember seeing them play and by fans born long

after these legends had died. These players were not only legends

in their own time; they were legends for all time.

Step 2: Now that you have practiced correcting for verb consistency, go to **http://ablongman.com/long.** Click on **Resources for Writers,** and then click on **Activity 41** for more practice using correct tenses.

LAB ACTIVITY 42 Types of Pronouns

Objective To use the different types of pronouns.

Step 1: Replace the underlined words with the appropriate pronouns. Write your answer above the word you are replacing. The first one is done for you.

The winter Olympic Games include both widely popular winter sports and somewhat obscure events. For example, skiing is a sport that many amateur athletes participate in for fun, and <u>skiing</u>
[it]
is a major event in the winter Olympics. <u>Skiing</u>
[It]
takes a number of forms: cross-country, downhill racing, slalom, jumping, and freestyle. Ice-skating is another event that occupies much of the winter Olympics agenda. Speed skating, figure skating, and ice dancing are three types of skating; <u>the events</u>
[they]
have athletes competing individually, in pairs, or even in relay. Besides skiing and ice-skating, hockey is a hugely popular event at the winter Olympics. Spectators can watch some of <u>the spectators'</u>
[their]
favorite professional hockey players compete for <u>the players'</u>
[their]
native country. The event is the only one where everyone can see <u>everyone's</u>
[his or her]
favorite professionals compete with amateurs. The winter Olympic Games also feature more obscure events, however. While watching the last winter Olympics, for instance, my friend Stella and I discovered what <u>Stella and I</u>
[we]
thought was the strangest sport of all. <u>The sport</u>
[It]
is called curling. <u>Curling</u>
[It]
involves a team of three

contestants trying to move a heavy stone down an ice alley. One

person slides <u>the stone</u> down the alley like a bowling ball, and the

others run alongside the stone with brooms. Each of the

"sweepers" then sweeps the ice with the broom to try to steer the

stone toward a target painted on the ice. No one is allowed to

touch the stone once it begins to slide down the alley, so the only

way to control the stone is to sweep strategically. The team whose

stone is closest to the target when <u>the stone</u> stops sliding wins;

this team then moves on to the next round. It seems that the

winter Olympic Games have something for just about everyone.

Step 2: Now that you have practiced using different types of pronouns, go to **http://ablongman.com/long.** Click on **Resources for Writers,** and then click on **Activity 42** for more practice with pronouns.

LAB ACTIVITY 43 Pronoun Consistency

Objective To use consistent pronouns.

Step 1: In the paragraph below, underline all the pronouns and check for consistency. Look for pronoun agreement, clear pronoun reference, and consistent point of view. Cross out any incorrect pronouns (and verbs if necessary), and write in the appropriate changes above the crossed-out words. One correction is done for you. You should find nineteen pronouns to underline and six pronouns that need to be corrected.

Until recently, my sister and I thought that Texas was a huge,

                    were we
boring state; boy, ~~was I~~ wrong! We went to Austin and to San

Antonio to visit some old friends, and we found out that those two

                                  We
places are really interesting and fun. ~~You~~ would never have

guessed. Our friends in Austin showed us that the city has an

                            Its
incredible nightlife. ~~Their~~ music clubs and restaurants are first-

rate. There's even a television show about Austin's music scene

                                                        it
called *Austin City Limits*. We went to one of the shows, and ~~they~~

had my sister's favorite folksinger, Allison Kraus, on as the fea-

tured performer. After a few days in Austin, we went to San Anto-

nio and had a blast. We visited a bunch of cute shops that lined

the river, and we took a ride in a little boat on one of the canals.

San Antonio also has a lively music scene; the clubs and cafés are

                  they have
tiny, but ~~it has~~ incredible performers every night. Visitors to this

                              they'll
part of Texas always say that ~~you'll~~ come back, and the locals

them

seem to welcome us. My sister and I were wrong about Texas: it

may be huge, but it is definitely not boring!

Step 2: Imagine that you are a country western singer. Now write a paragraph of at least six sentences about your imaginary experience on tour. You can describe a typical day on tour, how you practiced with your band, what you will do with your pay at the end of the tour, whatever comes to your mind. In your paragraph, use at least five different pronouns. After you're done, reread your paragraph and correct any pronoun inconsistencies.

_____

_____

_____

_____

_____

Step 3: Now that you have practiced using consistent pronouns, go to **http://ablongman.com/long.** Click on **Resources for Writers,** and then click on **Activity 43** for more practice with pronouns.

LAB ACTIVITY 44 Using Adjectives and Adverbs

Objective To use adjectives and adverbs.

Step 1: In the table below, write in the correct form of the given adjective.

Basic Adjective	Comparative Adjective	Superlative Adjective
Example: hard	harder	hardest
1. good	better	best
2. strong	stronger	strongest
3. big	bigger	biggest
4. small	smaller	smallest
5. young	younger	youngest
6. old	older	oldest
7. hot	hotter	hottest
8. cold	colder	coldest
9. round	rounder	roundest
10. straight	straighter	straightest
11. silly	sillier	silliest
12. grumpy	grumpier	grumpiest
13. angry	angrier	angriest
14. happy	happier	happiest
15. hard	harder	hardest
16. easy	easier	easiest
17. soft	softer	softest
18. rough	rougher	roughest
19. nice	nicer	nicest
20. kind	kinder	kindest

Step 2: For each item, underline the adjective in the first sentence. Change the adjective into its adverb form, and write the adverb in the blank in the second sentence.

Example: Jose is a <u>calm</u> cook. He works methodically and ___calmly___ as he prepares meals.

1. Renee is a <u>careful</u> writer. She ___carefully___ researches each paragraph topic before writing.

2. My friend is a <u>good</u> swimmer. He swims equally ___well___ in a pool, a lake, or the ocean.

3. That movie's pace is too <u>slow.</u> It moved so ___slowly___ that I fell asleep halfway through it.

4. What <u>bad</u> brakes that bike has! They work especially ___badly___ in the rain.

5. Josh is a very <u>quick</u> eater. He ate so ___quickly___ once that he finished his lunch before I opened my lunch bag!

6. Anita has <u>strong</u> opinions about almost everything. She feels especially ___strongly___ about the proposed tax increase.

7. Our school choir has a <u>sweet</u> sound. When the choir performs, the songs float ___sweetly___ through the air.

8. Kyle can be <u>impulsive</u> sometimes. Once, he ___impulsively___ kissed a stranger as she walked by.

9. My homework was full of <u>incorrect</u> answers. Later, I found out that I had read the instructions ___incorrectly___ .

10. Anh likes to listen to <u>loud</u> music. She plays music so ___loudly___ that the neighbors often complain.

Step 3: Now that you have practiced using adjectives and adverbs, go to **http://ablongman.com/long.** Click on **Resources for Writers,** and then click on **Activity 44** for more practice with adjectives and adverbs.

LAB ACTIVITY 45 Correcting Misplaced Modifiers

Objective To correct misplaced modifiers.

Step 1: Rewrite each of the following sentences, placing the modifier in the correct place.

Example: A tornado watch can still frighten people, which is less severe than a tornado warning.

Rewritten: A tornado watch, which is less severe than a tornado warning, can still frighten people.

1. Kansas and Oklahoma which is the name given to an area where tornadoes are likely to form are considered part of Tornado Alley.

   Kansas and Oklahoma are considered part of Tornado Alley, which is the name given to

   an area where tornadoes are likely to form.

2. However, tornadoes sometimes appear outside of Tornado Alley; Roseville, California, was once struck by a tornado which is hundreds of miles from Tornado Alley.

   However, tornadoes sometimes appear outside of Tornado Alley; Roseville, California,

   which is hundreds of miles from Tornado Alley, was once struck by a tornado.

3. It lifted train cars from their tracks that weigh thousands of pounds.

   It lifted train cars that weigh thousands of pounds from their tracks.

4. People are generally accustomed to hearing television and radio announcers living in the Midwest issue tornado watches.

   People living in the Midwest are generally accustomed to hearing television and radio

   announcers issue tornado watches.

5. Often, a tornado watch won't get much attention which indicates that the conditions are favorable for tornado formation.

   Often, a tornado watch, which indicates that the conditions are favorable for tornado

   formation, won't get much attention.

6. A tornado warning, however, indicates that a tornado has already been spotted in the area and in a basement or a windowless room that people should take cover.

A tornado warning, however, indicates that a tornado has already been spotted in the

area and that people should take cover in a basement or a windowless room.

7. Some people are so fascinated by tornadoes called stormchasers that they will actually risk their lives to videotape a twister.

Some people called stormchasers are so fascinated by tornadoes that they will actually

risk their lives to videotape a twister.

8. Stormchasers are sometimes legitimate scientists and sometimes only curious amateurs featured in the Helen Hunt film *Twister* as well as in the IMAX film *Stormchasers*.

Stormchasers, featured in the Helen Hunt film *Twister* as well as in the IMAX film

Stormchasers, are sometimes legitimate scientists and sometimes only curious amateurs.

9. Because of some of the daring research done by professional stormchasers after they have formed, we have learned a great deal about how tornadoes behave.

Because of some of the daring research done by professional stormchasers, we have

learned a great deal about how tornadoes behave after they have formed.

10. Now warnings can be issued by meteorologists that are more timely and more accurate than ever.

Now warnings that are more timely and more accurate than ever can be issued by

meteorologists.

Step 2: Now that you have practiced correcting misplaced modifiers, go to **http://ablongman.com/long.** Click on **Resources for Writers,** and then click on **Activity 45** for more practice correcting misplaced modifiers.

LAB ACTIVITY 46 Correcting Dangling Modifiers

Objective To correct dangling modifiers.

Step 1: Rewrite each of the following sentences, placing the modifier in the correct place. Answers may vary; sample answers are given.

> **Example:** To avoid going to the dentist, milk became an important part of Marina's diet.
>
> Correct: Marina drank a lot of milk to avoid going to the dentist.

1. Handed down from my great-grandmother, I always use my favorite recipe.

   I always use my favorite recipe, which was handed down from my great-grandmother.

   _____

2. Built in 1927, Anya enjoys exploring the aisles of the main library.

   Anya enjoys exploring the aisles of the main library, which was built in 1927.

   _____

3. Served with a variety of treats from cookies to bananas, Reggie drank milk.

   Reggie drank milk with a variety of treats from cookies to bananas.

   _____

4. Containing only the freshest vegetables, Peter made a wonderful lasagna.

   Peter made a wonderful lasagna containing only the freshest vegetables.

   _____

5. Containing goat's milk, Allen's hands benefited from his "industrial strength" lotion.

   Allen's hands benefited from his "industrial strength" lotion, which contains goat's milk.

   _____

6. Digitally remastered, I bought Miles Davis's first album.

   I bought Miles Davis's first album, which was digitally remastered.

   _____

7. Painted a bright orange, Tisha loves her new car.

Tisha loves her new car painted a bright orange.

_____

8. Whipped up into a creamy mass, my brother detests evaporated milk as a substitute for cream.

My brother detests evaporated milk, whipped up into a creamy mass, as a substitute for

cream.

9. Ended predictably, they loved *The Matrix: Reloaded.*

_____

They loved *The Matrix: Reloaded,* which ended predictably.

10. Decorated with bright balloons, we walked into the room and were very surprised.

_____

We walked in the room decorated with bright balloons and were very surprised.

Step 2: Now that you have practiced correcting dangling modifiers, go to **http://ablongman.com/long.** Click on **Resources for Writers,** and then click on **Activity 46** for more practice correcting dangling modifiers.

LAB ACTIVITY 47 Correcting Faulty Parallelism

Objective To use parallel structure.

Step 1: Write a sentence for each of the following, and use parallel structure to include the given information. The hints tell you what kind of parallel structure to use.   Answers may vary.

> **Example:** to bake chocolate chip cookies, eating chocolate chip cookies, bought cookies (*Hint:* Use verbs.)
>
> I bake, eat, and buy chocolate chip cookies.

1. sugar cookies, lemon, cookies made with oatmeal (*Hint:* Use adjectives.)

   My favorites are sugar cookies, lemon cookies, and oatmeal cookies.

   _____

2. at the bakery, in the stores, my mother's house (*Hint:* Use prepositional phrases.)

   I can always get cookies at the bakery, in the stores, and at my mother's house.

   _____

3. I like chewy cookies, crispy cookies are my brother's favorite, crispy on the outside and chewy on the inside for my sister (*Hint:* Use independent clauses.)

   I like chewy cookies, my brother likes crispy cookies, and my sister loves cookies that are

   crispy on the outside and chewy on the inside.

4. in a jar, plastic containers, bags are good storage places (*Hint:* Use prepositional phrases.)

   You can store cookies in a jar, in plastic containers, or in bags.

   _____

5. for breakfast, as a snack, for dessert (*Hint:* Use prepositional phrases.)

   Sometimes, I have cookies for breakfast, for a snack, and, of course, for dessert.

   _____

6. gingerbread people, shapes of flowers, simple circles (*Hint:* Use nouns.)

Cookies come in all different shapes: people, flowers, even simple circles.

7. not only peanut butter, but also chocolate (*Hint:* Use adjectives.)

I love not only peanut butter cookies but also chocolate cookies.

8. smelling delicious, to taste scrumptious, brings back memories (*Hint:* Use verbs.)

Cookies smell delicious, taste scrumptious, and bring back memories.

9. dipped in chocolate, with colorful frosting, sprinkles with sugar (*Hint:* Use past participles.)

I have seen cookies dipped in chocolate, covered with colorful frosting, and sprinkled

with sugar.

10. what it looks like, smells good, its taste (*Hint:* Use verbs.)

I have a very simple way of judging a cookie: I look at it, smell it, and taste it.

Step 2: Now that you have practiced using parallelism, go to **http://ablongman.com/long.** Click on **Resources for Writers,** and then click on **Activity 47** for more practice with parallelism.

LAB ACTIVITY 48 Using Commas

Objective To use commas correctly.

Step 1: Insert commas where necessary. Identify the reason for inserting each comma.

Comma Uses

a. Setting apart items in a series

b. Setting off introductory material

c. Setting off information that interrupts the main ideas in a sentence

d. Joining two independent clauses also linked by a coordinating conjunction (one of the FANBOYS—*for, and, nor, but, or, yet, so*)

e. Setting off direct quotations from the rest of the sentence

f. Clarifying everyday information (such as dates, addresses, and numbers)

Example: I visited Chicago on July 12, 2005.
Reason: __f__

1. When I went to Chicago,I had a great time walking down the Miracle Mile.

   Reason: __b__

2. The Miracle Mile, believe it or not, is the name given to one of the city's main shopping districts.

   Reason: __c__

3. It is a mile-long stretch of shops and restaurants,and it includes the famed Art Institute of Chicago.

   Reason: __d__

4. The actual name of the street,however, is Michigan Avenue.

   Reason: __c__

5. I called home and told my brother,"This is a great city!"

   Reason: __e__

6. Chicago, like many great cities, is full of wonderful things to do and places to see.

   Reason: __c__

7. Besides the wonderful shops on the Miracle Mile, Chicago also has some of the best museums around.

   Reason: __b__

8. These include the Art Institute of Chicago, the Museum of Contemporary Art, and the Field Museum of Natural History.

   Reason: __a__

9. Several famous chefs have restaurants in the area; one example is Charlie Trotter's namesake restaurant at 816 West Armitage, Chicago, Illinois.

   Reason: __f__

10. When I got home from my Chicago visit, I told everyone, "I can't wait to return."

    Reason: __e__

Step 2: Now that you have practiced using commas, go to **http:// ablongman.com/long.** Click on **Resources for Writers,** and then click on **Activity 48** for more practice with commas.

LAB ACTIVITY 49 Using Apostrophes

Objective To use apostrophes correctly.

Step 1: In the appropriate box, rewrite each item using an apostrophe. Draw a line in the box that does not apply.

	Apostrophe Shows Possession	Apostrophe Shows Contraction
Example: the cold of my mother	my mother's cold	———
1. I have caught a virus.	———	I've caught a virus.
2. the germs of my brother	my brother's germs	———
3. the colds of the children	the children's colds	———
4. It is a virus.	———	It's a virus.
5. the illness of James	James's illness	———
6. the health advisory of the city	the city's health advisory	———
7. the ills of society	society's ills	———
8. Many do not get vaccinated.	———	Many don't get vaccinated.
9. His computer has got a virus.	———	His computer's got a virus.
10. health of Americans	Americans' health	———

	Apostrophe Shows Possession	Apostrophe Shows Contraction
11. I would get that checked.	———	I'd get that checked.
12. It is not too late.	———	It's not too late. It isn't too late.
13. diagnosis of both doctors	both doctors' diagnosis	———
14. welfare of citizens	citizens' welfare	———
15. They are doing well.	———	They're doing well.
16. You are looking well.	———	You're looking well.
17. assistance of nurses	nurses' assistance	———
18. treatment of Kara	Kara's treatment	———
19. friends of my family	my family's friends	———
20. resources of America	America's resources	———

Step 2: Now that you have practiced using apostrophes, go to **http:// ablongman.com/long.** Click on **Resources for Writers,** and then click on **Activity 49** for more practice with apostrophes.

LAB ACTIVITY 50 Using Quotation Marks

Objective To use quotation marks, single quotation marks, and underlining.

Step 1: Insert four sets of quotation marks. You will also need to underline four titles. The first insertion has been done for you.

Most people now understand that the term "feminist" describes anyone who supports equal rights and opportunity for men and women. In my women's studies class, for instance, we had an interesting discussion about changing attitudes toward feminism. Joaquin said, "My mother works hard at two jobs to support us; it's because of her that I'm a feminist." David admitted, "I thought I would never apply the word feminist to myself, but then I had two daughters who were offered lower salaries than their male colleagues." It seems that we all had a story to tell about the roots of our feminism. My story, however, had more to do with reading than with direct experience—although the time I was excluded from my brother's clubhouse at the age of ten probably had something to do with my feminist sensibilities, too. I told my classmates that my feminism was inspired by the pages of <u>Ms.</u> magazine. I initially assumed that the magazine contained articles bashing men. I discovered when I actually looked at it that it contains articles with titles like "Portable Health Insurance" and "A Daughter of Cambodia Remembers." It also publishes stories by writers like Alice Walker, whose most famous book is

<u>The Color Purple</u>, and Sandra Cisneros, whose novel <u>The House</u>

<u>on Mango Street</u> is a great read. The magazine also publishes

poetry by famous writers like Rita Dove, Lucille Clifton, and Adri-

enne Rich. I told my class that I learned about both women's

rights and human rights from reading <u>Ms.</u>

Step 2: Now that you have practiced using quotation marks, single quotation marks, and underlining, go to **http://ablongman.com/long.** Click on **Resources for Writers,** and then click on **Activity 50** for more practice.

LAB ACTIVITY 51 Using Other Punctuation Marks

Objective To use semicolons, colons, hyphens, dashes, and parentheses.

Step 1: Write your own sentences using the punctuation indicated. Answers will vary.

1. Use a semicolon to separate two complete ideas.

   Example: I like all flavors of ice cream; chocolate, however, is my favorite.

   Your sentence: _____

   _____

2. Use a pair of parentheses to enclose dates.

   Example: Her birthday (May 10) sometimes falls on Mother's Day.

   Your sentence: _____

   _____

3. Use a pair of dashes around additional information.

   Example: His only wall hanging—a colorful hand-stitched quilt—is truly a work of art.

   Your sentence: _____

   _____

4. Use a hyphen to join words communicating one concept.

   Example: I need an up-to-date map for my vacation.

   Your sentence: _____

   _____

5. Use a colon to introduce a list.

   Example: I got incredible bargains: a pair of shoes for $7.00, a dress for $2.50, and a hat for $1.00.

   Your sentence: _____

   _____

6. Use one dash to set off additional information at the end of the sentence.

Example: He ate ten large pizzas all by himself—in only ten minutes!

Your sentence: _____

_____

7. Use a semicolon to separate items in a series where the items contain commas.

Example: Sasha has visited several major cities: Frankfurt, Germany; Paris, France; Madrid, Spain; Vienna, Austria; Mexico City, Mexico.

Your sentence: _____

_____

8. Use parentheses to enclose page numbers.

Example: Near the end of the book (256–262), the author finally sums up his argument.

Your sentence: _____

_____

9. Use a colon to introduce a quotation.

Example: Elizabeth Barrett Browning is perhaps best known for a single line from one of her poems: "How do I love thee? Let me count the ways."

Your sentence: _____

_____

10. Use a hyphen to split a word at the end of the line.

Example: Spring is probably my favorite season because the flowers are begin-ning to bloom.

Your sentence: _____

_____

Step 2: Now that you have practiced using semicolons, colons, hyphens, dashes, and parentheses in your own sentences, go to **http://ablongman.com/long.** Click on **Resources for Writers,** and then click on **Activity 51** for more practice with these punctuation marks.

LAB ACTIVITY 52 Using Correct Capitalization

Objective To use capital letters correctly.

Step 1: Fill in the following table as directed. Answers will vary.

Reason to Use a Capital Letter	Your Example
A historical period or event	A historical period you studied: Example: Middle Ages A historical event you studied: Example: American Revolution
Names of people	Your full name: Your favorite celebrity's name:
Names of specific places	Your hometown (city, state, and country): A place you would like to visit:
Days of the week, months, holidays	Your birthday: The next holiday coming up:
Brand names of products	Your favorite cereal: Your favorite shampoo:
Titles of written or performed works	Your favorite song: A movie you like:

Reason to Use a Capital Letter	Your Example
People's titles	Your instructor's name, including title: Your doctor's name, including title:
Names of groups with specific affiliations	Your favorite sports team: A club at your school:
Names of school courses	Your toughest class: Your easiest class:
Names of languages	A language you want to learn: A language you know well:

Step 2: Now that you have practiced using capital letters correctly, go to **http://ablongman.com/long.** Click on **Resources for Writers,** and then click on **Activity 52** for more practice with capitalization.

LAB ACTIVITY 53 Using Numbers and Abbreviations

Objective To use numbers and abbreviations correctly.

Step 1: Find the errors in numbers and abbreviations in the following paragraph. Cross out each mistake and write the correction above it. There are thirty-three errors in all.

                                                               PBS

The director of the Public Broadcasting Service had decided to do a

                         Battle   Little   November

mini-series on the Batt. Of Litt. Big Horn last Nov. He had even hired

  Mr.   Mr.   program

Mister Brad Pitt and Mister Lou Diamond Phillips to star in the prog.

    Custer   Crazy Horse   hundreds

as Cust. And Craz. Hrse. However, after reviewing 100s of proposals for

                   Tuesday, Wednesday Thursday   Sunday

the series—to run Tues., Wed., and Thurs. after Super Bowl Sun. —the

director   criticism

dir. changed his mind due to criticism of the proposal. Some of the crit.

                            Montana   camera equipment

involved protests against spoiling the Mont. landscape with cam. equip.

     criticism money or financial   four times

Other crit. addressed $ issues since the cost was 4X larger than the bud-

                 people   summer

get. Finally, some peop. were concerned that the winter airing of a sum.

battle   9 p.m.

batt. at nine o'clock in the evening would confuse viewers who looked

     channel historical education   nothing

to the chan. for hist. ed. Thus, the whole thing came to Ø.

Step 2: Now that you have practiced using numbers and abbreviations, go to **http://ablongman.com/long.** Click on **Resources for Writers,** and then click on **Activity 53** for more practice with numbers and abbreviations.

LAB ACTIVITY 54 Using Words That Look and Sound Alike

Objective To use homonyms and commonly confused words correctly.

Step 1: Read the following paragraph, and write the correct word in each blank.

During our summer vacation last year, two friends and I decided to drive to Los Angeles and enjoy our ____break____ (brake, break) by having some new experiences. We didn't know it when we started out, but we were going to have many more adventures ____than____ (than, then) we had dreamed of. First of all, we ____thought____ (though, thought) that we were all ready for L.A. traffic because we brought along several CDs to listen to and a whole bunch of snacks. Boy, were we wrong! We were in bumper-to-bumper traffic for hours, and ____there____ (their, there, they're) seemed to be nothing but ____brake____ (brake, break) lights for miles. We listened to CDs for a little while, but very soon the honking horns were all that we could hear. Someone had been rear-ended in the next lane, and the drivers involved were out of ____their____ (their, there, they're) cars yelling at each other about who should ____accept____ (accept, except) responsibility for the accident. Of course, we didn't care ____whose____ (whose, who's) responsibility it was—we just wanted to get out of the traffic. Eventually, we were able to move to the right and get off the freeway. We found some ____peace____ (peace, piece) and ____quiet____ (quiet, quite) as we cruised down Melrose Avenue and stared at all the shops. We ____passed____ (passed, past) by some cute little boutiques, but we didn't stop because we didn't feel that we'd fit in ____among____ (among, between) all the wealthy-looking shoppers. ____Besides____ (Beside, Besides), we were only passing _____through_____ (threw, through) on our way to find a place to have lunch. As we turned off Melrose, however, we ran right into another "adventure." One of our tires ran over a big copper sculpture and got stuck in a huge hole in the road. We couldn't believe it. While we were examining our tire, a woman ran out of a shop and started yelling at us about ruining her sculpture. Why anyone would _____lay_____ (lay, lie) a sculpture in the road I'll never know, but this woman was convinced that she had every right to do so. Luckily, a police officer came along and made it clear _____to_____ (to, too, two) the woman that she would _____lose_____ (loose, lose) her argument in court, so she left us alone. The officer helped us push our car out of the hole and suggested we get the tire checked. We took his _____advice_____ (advice, advise) and went to the nearest tire shop, _____where_____ (wear, where) the mechanic checked our car for any damaging _____effects_____ (affects, effects) of our adventure. Fortunately he found none. Relieved, we decided to follow the _____principle_____ (principle, principal) of looking on the bright side, so we resumed our search for a good restaurant. The mechanic's _____advice_____ (advice, advise) was to try the famous Wolfgang Puck restaurant called Spago. _____It's_____ (Its, It's) a great place. We shared a pair of pizzas—we even got to watch the dough rising—and we sampled some excellent _____desserts_____ (deserts, desserts). We haven't decided _____whether_____ (weather, whether) the trip was worth all the adventures, but it certainly would have been less interesting with _____fewer_____ (fewer, less) adventures.

Step 2: Now that you have practiced using homonyms and other commonly confused words correctly, go to **http://ablongman.com/long.** Click on **Resources for Writers,** and then click on **Activity 54** for more practice with words that look alike and sound alike.

LAB ACTIVITY 55 Sentence Variety

Objective To vary your sentences.

Step 1: Extend the following sentences using the method and coordinating or subordinating terms indicated.   Answers will vary.

Example:
Coordination—but: *As a child, I loved to read stories.*
As a child, I loved to read stories, but I also liked to watch cartoons.

Subordination—when: *My favorite cartoons featured Bugs Bunny.*
When I was five, my favorite cartoons featured Bugs Bunny.

1. Coordination—but: *Books can be great teachers.*

_____

_____

2. Coordination—and: *Harry Potter books have been very popular.*

_____

_____

3. Subordination—when: *Many people lined up at bookstores to buy copies.*

_____

_____

4. Subordination—while: *Many adults like Harry Potter books as well.*

_____

_____

5. Subordination—although: *Many children still watch a lot of television.*

_____

_____

6. Coordination—so: *Parents are often glued to the TV set.*

_____

_____

7. Subordination—because: *Cartoons are not just for children anymore.*

_____

_____

8. Coordination—or: *For example, many adults watch* The Simpsons.

_____

_____

9. Coordination—but: *Animated films such as* Monsters, Inc. *are favorites with children.*

_____

_____

10. Subordination—even though: *I loved* A Bug's Life.

_____

_____

Step 2: Now that you have practiced varying your sentences, go to **http:// ablongman.com/long.** Click on **Resources for Writers,** and then click on **Activity 55** for more practice with sentence variety.

LAB ACTIVITY 56 Addressing ESL Issues

Objective To reduce typical ESL errors.

Step 1: Rewrite the following items, inserting an appropriate subject where necessary or omitting extra pronoun subjects. Remember that every independent or dependent clause must have a subject and that standard English does not permit a sentence to have repeated subjects for the same verb.

> **Example:** Because American restaurants serve large portions, am starting to get fat.
>
> *Because American restaurants serve large portions, I am starting to get fat.*

My favorite American restaurant it is McDonald's.
My favorite American restaurant is McDonald's.

1. Like many other fast-food restaurants, lets you "super-size" your order.

   Like many other fast-food restaurants, McDonald's lets you "super-size" your order.

2. A Big Mac, super-sized French fries, and a super-sized soda they have a total of more than a thousand calories.
   A Big Mac, super-sized French fries, and a super-sized soda have a total of more than a thousand calories.

3. Such a meal it also contains a high level of fat.

   Such a meal also contains a high level of fat.

4. Eat at McDonald's and other fast-food places often, so I am gaining weight.

   I eat at McDonald's and other fast-food places often, so I am gaining weight.

5. Is not like the food I used to eat in my home country.

   It is not like the food I used to eat in my home country.

6. Super-sizing food it was not an option unless I went to an American fast-food place in my old country.
   Super-sizing food was not an option unless I went to an American fast-food place in my old country.

7. Also, I get less exercise in the United States because drive everywhere.

Also, I get less exercise in the United States because I drive everywhere.

8. In my old country, walked or rode my bike all the time.

In my old country, I walked or rode my bike all the time.

9. Is no wonder I am gaining weight.

It is no wonder I am gaining weight.

10. I guess will have to cut down on my trips to McDonald's.

I guess I will have to cut down on my trips to McDonald's.

Step 2: Now that you have practiced using subjects correctly, go to **http:// ablongman.com/long.** Click on **Resources for Writers,** and then click on **Activity 56** for more practice reducing ESL errors.

Credits

Literary Credits

Mary Arguelles, "Money for Morality." First published in *Newsweek* (My Turn), 1991. Reprinted by permission of the author.

Russell Baker, "The Plot Against People." Originally published in *The New York Times*, June 18, 1968. Copyright © 1968 by The New York Times Co. Reprinted by permission.

Benedict, Carey, "Have You Heard, Gossip Turns Out to Serve a Purpose" from *The New York Times*, August 16, 2005. Copyright © 2005 The New York Times Co. Reprinted by permission

Stephanie Ericsson, "The Ways We Lie." Copyright © 1992 by Stephanie Ericsson. Originally published by *The Utne Reader*, November/December 1992. Reprinted by the permission of Dunham Literary as agents for the author.

Lyla Fox, "Hold Your Horsepower" from *Newsweek*, March 25, 1996. All rights reserved. Reprinted by permission of Newsweek.

Robert Fulghum, from *All I Really Need to Know I Learned in Kindergarten* by Robert L. Fulghum. Copyright © 1986, 1988 by Robert L. Fulghum. Used by permission of Random House, Inc.

Barbara Graham, "Confessions of a Quit Addict," originally published in *Utne Reader*, September/October 1996. Reprinted by permission of the author.

Reginald Lockett, "How I Started Writing Poetry" from *California Childhood* by Gary Soto. Reprinted by permission of Reginald Lockett.

Phillip Lopate, "A Nonsmoker with a Smoker" from *Against Joie de Vivre: Personal Essays*. Reprinted by permission of The Wendy Weil Agency, Inc. First published by Simon & Schuster. © 1989 by Phillip Lopate.

Malcolm X, "A Homemade Education." Copyright © 1964 by Alex Haley and Malcolm X. Copyright © 1965 by Alex Haley and Betty Shabazz. From *The Autobiography of Malcolm X* by Malcolm X and Alex Haley. Used by permission of Random House, Inc.

Judith Martin, "Manners Matter" from *The American Enterprise*, August 15, 1999. Reprinted with permission of The American Enterprise. On the web at www.TAEmag.com.

Randy Moore, "Grades and Self-Esteem," *The American Biology Teacher*, October 1993, Vol. 55, No. 7. Reprinted by permission of the National Association of Biology Teachers.

Maria Muniz, "Back, But Not Home." Originally published in *The New York Times* Op Ed, July 13, 1979, p. A25. Copyright © 1979 by The New York Times Co. Reprinted by permission.

Jo Goodwin Parker, from "What Is Poverty?" in *America's Other Children: Public Schools Outside Suburbia* by George Anderson. Copyright © 1971 by the University of Oklahoma Press, Norman. Reprinted by permission of the publisher. All rights reserved.

Richard Rodriguez, "'Blaxicans' and Other Reinvented Americans." Copyright © 2003 by Richard Rodriguez. Originally appeared in *The Chronicle of Higher Education*, excerpted from a speech before the University of Pennsylvania National Commission on Society. Reprinted by permission of Georges Borchardt, Inc., on behalf of the author.

Amy Tan, "My Mother's English." Copyright © 1990 by Amy Tan. Originally presented as a speech at the California Association of Teachers of English 1990 Conference. Reprinted by permission of the author and the Sandra Dijkstra Literary Agency.

E. B. White, "Education" from *One Man's Meat*. Text copyright © 1939 by E. B. White. Copyright renewed. Reprinted by permission of Tilbury House, Publishers, Gardiner, Maine.

Photo Credits

4: Photo courtesy of Silver Dollar City; **24**: Ace Stock/Alamy; **29**: Robert Harding Picture Library Ltd./Alamy; **46**: Getty Images; **55**: CORBIS; **68**: CORBIS; **76**: Ted Shreshinsky/CORBIS; **101**: Kwame Zikoma/SuperStock; **120**: NASA; **130**: Hulton-Deutsch/CORBIS; **135**: Caroline Penn/Corbis; **153**: CORBIS; **160**: CORBIS; **168**: Library of Congress; **177**: Library of Congress; **194**: Lew Wilson/Index Stock Imagery; **201**: Walter Bibikow/Index Stock Imagery; **218**: Steve McCurry/Magnum Photos; **234**: Blue Lantern Studio/CORBIS; **252**: © 2006 Estate of Pablo Picasso/Artists Rights Society (ARS), New York, Snark/Art Resource, NY; **268**: Mark Downey/Index Stock Imagery; **305**: Adam Rountree/AP; **328**: © PoodlesRock/CORBIS; **350**: Bettmann/CORBIS; **360**: Don Hammond/Agefotostock; **417**: Angelo Cavalli/SuperStock; **433**: Peabody Essex Museum; **446**: Bob Parent/Hulton Archive/Getty Images; **464**: Sime/eStock Photo; **477**: © 2006 Charles Walker/Topfoto/The Image Works; **483**: SuperStock; **500**: David McClain/Aurora Photos; **504**: Mirisch-7 Arts/United Artists/The Kobal Collection; **523**: Dan Herrick/KPA/Zuma Press; **543**: Bettmann/CORBIS; **555**: Christopher Wood Gallery, London, England/Bridgeman Art Library/SuperStock; **564**: Beethoven House, Vienna, Austria/ET Archive, London/Superstock; **569**: Lake County Museum/CORBIS; **583**: Giorgos Nissiotis/AP; **584**: D. Boone/CORBIS; **603**: Carol & Mike Werner/SuperStock; **609**: T. Vandersar/SuperStock; **623**: Bruce Leighty/Index Stock Imagery; **644**: Bettmann/CORBIS; **652**: John Springer Collection/CORBIS; **660**: Patrick Ward/CORBIS; **677**: Deborah Davis/PhotoEdit; **LM-17**: Dennis McDonald/PhotoEdit; **LM-67**: Keith Wood/Getty Images.

Index